FLORIDA
World History
ANCIENT CIVILIZATIONS

Houghton
Mifflin
Harcourt

correlated to the

Florida Next Generation Sunshine State Standards
for Social Studies

CONTENTS

LESSONS WITH EMBEDDED FLORIDA CONTENT EXPECTATIONS

Look for the Florida symbol throughout this book. It highlights specific content expectations to help you master the standards.

Printed in the U.S.A.

ISBN 978-0-544-82610-6

3 4 5 6 7 8 9 10   0868   25 24 23 22 21 20 19 18 17

4500654937   A B C D E F G

Educational Reviewers

Annette Boyd Pitts
Florida Law Education Association,
Executive Director
Project Citizen Florida, State Director
Tallahassee, Florida

Karen Chenoweth
University High School
Orange City, Florida

Alexander Gonzalez
King High School
Tampa, Florida

Kirk Murphy
West Shore Jr./Sr. High School
Melbourne, Florida

Sarah Armada
Tradewinds Middle School
Greenacres, Florida

WELLS'BUILT MUSEUM

A look into Orlando's African American heritage

Holt McDougal is proud to partner with Orlando's **Wells'Built Museum** and **Association to Preserve African American Society, History and Tradition Inc. (PAST).** Together, Wells'Built and PAST work to celebrate and preserve the rich African American history of Orlando and the central Florida region through research, museum exhibits, special events, and community outreach.

Dr. William Wells

William Monroe Wells was born in Ft. Gaines, Georgia, in 1889. He arrived in Orlando in 1917 after completing his medical training at Meharry Medical College. Since white physicians did not treat African American patients during segregation, Dr. Wells worked very hard to serve the growing African American population in the city. With the help of his assistant, Mrs. Josie Belle Jackson, Dr. Wells delivered more than 5,000 babies in Orlando. He treated patients who suffered from pneumonia, influenza, scarlet fever, and other serious illnesses before drugs like penicillin were introduced.

Many of Dr. Wells' patients were extremely poor. He treated them though they often could not afford to pay his fee. Although African Americans were taxpayers like other Orlando residents, they did not have access to recreational facilities, good schools, police protection, health care, and other services that were provided to white citizens. This situation led Dr. Wells to build a hotel and entertainment center for Orlando's African American community.

^ The reception hall to Wells' Built Museum

The Place to Be

In 1926 Dr. Wells began construction of the Wellsbilt Hotel to provide lodging to African Americans during segregation, when accommodations were not available to them in other areas of Central Florida. Next door Dr. Wells built the South Street Casino, a recreation center and performance hall. African Americans came from Sanford, Eatonville, and surrounding areas to Orlando to shop and take in performances of popular musicians at the South Street Casino. Dr. Wells booked big name entertainers such as Ray Charles, B.B. King, Louis Armstrong, Guitar Slim, and Bo Diddley, among others. After performing at the casino, the artists checked in at the historic Wellsbilt Hotel. In its heyday, the Wellsbilt provided lodging for clientele such as Peg Leg Bates, Ella Fitzgerald, Roy Campanella, Thurgood Marshall, and Jackie Robinson. The entertainers and athletes who frequented this establishment made it one of the most popular venues for African Americans in the South.

> For more information on the Wells' Built Museum, please visit www.pastinc.org/index.html

The Museum Today

After restoration, the name was changed to Wells' Built and today the Wells' Built Museum features over 6,000 square feet of display space. It retains the original hotel facade, a guestroom featuring authentic furniture, and bedding and decorations from the 1930s. It also reveals an original interior wall reflecting important architectural elements and designs unique to the period. Exhibition material on display includes official hotel documents, an original Negro League baseball jersey, photographs, artifacts, books, multimedia exhibits, slave records, and other items of historic significance.

^ South Street Casino and the Wellsbilt Hotel

Out of the Past—A Noble Witness
The Legacy of John Gilmore Riley

Holt McDougal has partnered with one of Florida's most influential authorities of African American history to bring you Out of the Past— A Noble Witness.

John Riley was born into slavery in September of 1857. During his 97-year lifetime, America suffered through the Civil War, the Spanish American War, two world wars, and the conflict in Korea. Riley witnessed the invention of the automobile, electric lights, and the telephone, and he was there when Tallahassee welcomed the first commercial air flight into town.

Riley was not just a passive observer; he was a catalyst for positive change. He secured an education at a time when few men of color were able to read or write. John seized every opportunity to acquire knowledge and was eager to pass his education on to others. He was still a young man when he was named principal of Leon County's Lincoln Academy. Riley became a successful businessman and participated in the modern day struggle for civil rights. He was deeply committed to his church and the Royal Arch Masons. His legacy continues in the work of the museum that bears his name today.

The museum is located near the heart of Tallahassee's historic downtown in the circa 1890 home that Riley built for his family. The restored, two-story structure sits at its original location in what was once a thriving, middle class, predominantly African American neighborhood. Today, the structure exemplifies the highest standards of historic preservation, and the Riley organization's influence has spread far beyond the tree-shaded house a former slave once called home.

Out of the Past is a 4-hour, 2-module, interactive presentation of the African American experience as seen through the eyes of Professor John G. Riley. Content was researched and developed by the Riley organization and promoted through the Florida African American Heritage Preservation Network. Technical services were donated by Learnsomething—an award-winning producer of distance learning products. Features include activities, quizzes, and material that **meets Florida Sunshine State Standards** in the classroom. An *Out of the Past Teachers' Guide* is available. Contact the John G. Riley House and Museum to secure a copy.

EDUCATION AND PUBLICATIONS

In 2009, Professor John G. Riley returned home in the form of an animatronic figure. Today, he greets visitors from the home office where he once conducted real estate transactions, prepared lesson plans, and carried out his duties as a Masonic, church, and community leader. Ever-changing exhibits fill the balance of the ground floor of Riley's restored home.

The Riley House and Museum also produces a wide array of print and multimedia projects. Riley's educational products are used in all of Florida's 67 school districts.

Products are also available under the FAAHPN 'brand'— including an information-packed *Guide to Core Competencies* for use by museum directors and staff. Of particular note is the *Florida Black Heritage Trail Magazine*, which was commissioned by VISIT FLORIDA and the Florida Department of State in 2002 and 2007 as a key marketing tool for tourism and economic development.

Many of these products can be purchased at an on-site gift shop or through the Riley Museum's online store. The Florida Network also has several traveling exhibits and can accommodate limited requests for technical assistance, speakers, and heritage tour guides.

These are just a few of the Riley House published projects.

For more information about exhibits and materials available through the John G. Riley House and Museum, visit their Web Site at www.rileymuseum.org

To learn more about Althemese Barnes and the Florida African American Heritage Preservation Network, go to www.faahpn.com/faaphn/

A NEW GENERATION OF NOBLE LEADERSHIP

When officials announced plans to demolish the Riley home in the 1970s, Althemese Barnes helped raise funds to purchase the property and support its initial restoration. In 1995, after 30 years, she retired from the Florida Department of Education. Barnes had also served 14 years as state secretary of the National Association for the Advancement of Colored People (NAACP) and was looking forward to a well-earned rest. Sadly, the Riley House was already in need of more repairs. Barnes stepped in and started the museum. This time—in her quest for more funding—Barnes attended historical and cultural preservation meetings, workshops, and grant hearings. She was surprised to see so few people of color in attendance. Clearly, Black Heritage institutions were operating outside the mainstream of existing preservation initiatives.

Barnes' leadership paved the way for change. In 1997, she organized a state-wide historic preservation conference. Over 125 museum directors, government officials, and preservation advocates attended. Directors of small heritage museums were finally connected to mainstream industry professionals. Barnes saw this as a first step to providing professional development and skill training through workshops, peer assistance programs, and ongoing technical assistance. The Florida African American Heritage Preservation Network was formalized in 2001 under the auspices of the Riley organization. FAAHPN's primary goal is "to promote the preservation of African American landmarks and legacies and assist statewide museums in discovering, archiving, and illuminating the blended interrelationships of African American, Native American, and European peoples through tourism and education."

Barnes' enthusiasm and persistence have won over a devoted group of public officials, corporate sponsors, community activists, and volunteers. She has proven herself to be a master at leveraging limited resources—often serving without pay to further FAAHPN's mission. Barnes secured a start-up grant from the Elizabeth Ordway Dunn Foundation, obtained financial support from the Florida Legislature, and has successfully competed for corporate funding and federal grants. Officials from the State Office of Historic Preservation recently acknowledged FAAHPN as the catalyst for an astronomical increase in African American historic properties being listed in the National Register of Historic Places. State heritage tourism revenue is rising. Barnes' work has been recognized by the Smithsonian Institute, the Association for African American Museums, and IMLS. Her efforts have also been acknowledged by the United Nations.

Althemese Barnes has motivated both students and adults to preserve America's blended heritage. Like Professor Riley, she has inspired everyone she meets to make learning a lifelong adventure.

©All photos courtesy of the John G. Riley House and Museum

Beyond the Walls
Programs and Partnerships of the Riley Initiatives

- **Riley's Kids** receive academic support and are encouraged to explore careers in history, museum management, and historical preservation.

- **Blended Lives** is produced annually in partnership with Tallahassee's Goodwood Museum and Gardens. Activities focus on the parallel lives of black and white citizens prior to desegregation.

- The **Student Intern Program** pairs post-grads with experienced museum directors. Students receive hands-on field training; directors learn new collection management techniques.

- The **Riley Archives at Tallahassee Community College** houses research material, documents, and photographs relating to the broad spectrum of the African American experience.

- The **Florida African American Museum Exchange** program helps participants secure training, digitize documents, and photograph other collectibles—many of which have been placed online.

- The **Smithsonian National Museum of African American History and Culture** will open in 2015. Riley and Florida Network partners have helped collect materials—earning Florida a presence on the National Mall.

- The **Mississippi Blues Trail** honors Mississippi-born blues performers. In 2010, the Network sponsored a historical marker at Florida's Bradfordville Blues Club—one of only seven sites outside Mississippi.

- The Riley Musuem formed—and continues to sponsor—an **African American Civil War Reenactment Unit.** The museum also promotes an annual **Emancipation Proclamation** and other historical re-creation events.

Other significant Riley partners:

- **City of Tallahassee**
- **Florida State Legislature & Department of State**
- **History Department of Florida A&M University**
- **Institute of Museum and Library Services**
- **Leon County School Board**
- **Leon County Board of County Commissioners & Office of Tourist Development**
- **Tallahassee Downtown Improvement Authority**
- **Frenchtown Historic Neighborhood**
- **Florida and National Black Chambers of Commerce**
- **Tallahassee Trust for Historic Preservation**

Florida

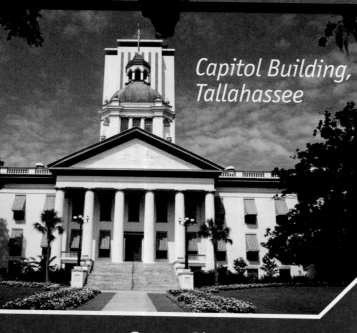

Capitol Building, Tallahassee

Space Shuttle, Cape Canaveral

South Beach, Miami

As you read the following pages and work through the unpacking of the Florida Next Generation Sunshine State Standards for Grade 6 Social Studies, you will discover the big ideas and key concepts that your teacher expects you to learn and understand.

You will see two things:

1 what the standard actually says

2 **What does it mean?**
an explanation to help you understand the big ideas within the standard

Florida Next Generation Sunshine State Standards for Social Studies

ENGLISH LANGUAGE DEVELOPMENT

>ELD.K12.ELL.SI.1

English language learners communicate for social and instructional purposes within the school setting.

What does it mean?
English language learners speak and listen in everyday and educational situations at school. Go to the Focus on Writing and Focus on Speaking activities in the Chapter Reviews for help.

>ELD.K12.ELL.SS.1

English language learners communicate information, ideas and concepts necessary for academic success in the content area of Social Studies.

Mockingbird

Orange blossom

What does it mean?

English language learners communicate social studies content to achieve academic success. Go to the Unit Writing Workshops and the Focus on Writing and Focus on Speaking activities in the Chapter Reviews for help.

HEALTH EDUCATION

>HE.6.C.2.4

Investigate school and public health policies that influence health promotion and disease prevention. Examples: Fitness reports for students, school zone speeding laws, school district wellness policies, and helmet laws.

What does it mean?

Investigate how school and government policies can effect health promotion and disease prevention. Examples include fitness reports, school zone speeding laws, wellness policies, and helmet laws. Go to page 97 in the Teacher's Edition for help.

LANGUAGE ARTS

LAFS.6.SL.1.1 **Engage effectively in a range of collaborative discussions (one-on-one, in groups, and teacher-led) with diverse partners on grade 6 topics, texts, and issues, building on others' ideas and expressing their own clearly.**

a. Come to discussions prepared, having read or studied required material; explicitly draw on that preparation by referring to evidence on the topic, text, or issue to probe and reflect on ideas under discussion.

b. Follow rules for collegial discussions, set specific goals and deadlines, and define individual roles as needed.

c. Pose and respond to specific questions with elaboration and detail by making comments that contribute to the topic, text, or issue under discussion.

d. Review the key ideas expressed and demonstrate understanding of multiple perspectives through reflection and paraphrasing.

What does it mean?

Actively participate in a variety of discussions.

a. Read any required material beforehand in order to come to the discussions prepared.

b. Work with others to set goals and processes for the discussions.

c. Ask and respond to questions that relate to the topic.

d. Review and restate different points of view.

Go to the Unit Writing Workshops for help.

LAFS.6.SL.1.2 **Interpret information presented in diverse media and formats (e.g., visually, quantitatively, orally) and explain how it contributes to a topic, text, or issue under study.**

What does it mean?

Analyze main ideas and details presented on various media and relate them to the topic under study. Go to the Focus on Writing activities in the Chapter Reviews for help.

LAFS.6.SL.1.3 **Delineate a speaker's argument and specific claims, distinguishing claims that are supported by reasons and evidence from claims that are not.**

What does it mean?

Evaluate a speaker's argument and identify any false reasoning or evidence. Go to the Primary Source feature on page 38 for help.

(tl)© Randolph Femmer/National Biological Information Infrastructure (tr)©Jeremy Woodhouse/Photodisc/Getty Images

>LAFS.6.SL.2.4

Present claims and findings, sequencing ideas logically and using pertinent descriptions, facts, and details to accentuate main ideas or themes; use appropriate eye contact, adequate volume, and clear pronunciation.

What does it mean?

Organize and present information in a logical sequence and style that is appropriate to the task and audience. Go to the Focus on Speaking activities in the Chapter Reviews for help.

LAFS.68.RH.1.1 Cite specific textual evidence to support analysis of primary and secondary sources.

What does it mean?

Use ideas and details from primary and secondary sources, such as the date the source was created and who wrote the source and why, to analyze the main idea and significance of the source. Go to Social Studies Skills on page 114 for help.

LAFS.68.RH.1.2 Determine the central ideas or information of a primary or secondary source; provide an accurate summary of the source distinct from prior knowledge or opinions.

What does it mean?

Analyze the main ideas of both primary and secondary sources. Understand how main ideas and key events progress throughout the text in order to summarize these concepts. Go to Reading Social Studies on page 52 for help.

LAFS.68.RH.1.3 Identify key steps in a texts description of a process related to history/social studies (e.g., how a bill becomes law, how interest rates are raised or lowered).

What does it mean?

Identify the key steps in a process related to history or other social studies disciplines such as how a bill becomes or law or how interest rates change over time. Go to Unit 3 Writing Workshop on page 195 WW1 for help.

LAFS.68.RH.2.4 Determine the meaning of words and phrases as they are used in a text, including vocabulary specific to domains related to history/social studies.

What does it mean?

Analyze specific words and phrases in a text, including key social studies vocabulary terms, to understand what they mean. Go to Reading Social Studies on page 4 for help.

LAFS.68.RH.2.5 Describe how a text presents information (e.g., sequentially, comparatively, causally).

What does it mean?

Tell how a text uses a particular structure—such as sequence, compare and contrast, or cause and effect—to organize and present information. Go to Reading Social Studies on pages 26, 84, and 292 for help.

LAFS.68.RH.2.6 Identify aspects of a text that reveal an author's point of view or purpose (e.g., loaded language, inclusion or avoidance of particular facts).

What does it mean?

Distinguish features of a text that communicate an author's purpose and point of view, such as the use of loaded language and the selection of particular facts and information. Go to Reading Social Studies on pages 200 and 522 for help.

LAFS.68.RH.3.7 Integrate visual information (e.g., in charts, graphs, photographs, videos, or maps) with other information in print and digital texts.

What does it mean?

Combine text and a range of visual tools—charts, graphs, photographs, videos, maps—to communicate information in print and digital formats. Go to Social Studies Skills on pages 78, 152, and 284 for help.

LAFS.68.RH.3.8 Distinguish among fact, opinion, and reasoned judgment in a text.

What does it mean?

Identify the differences between facts, opinions, and reasoned judgment in a primary or secondary source. Go to Reading Social Studies on pages 200, 258, and 466 for help.

LAFS.68.RH.3.9 Analyze the relationship between a primary and secondary source on the same topic.

What does it mean?

Choose a topic and consult a primary and secondary source about that topic. Compare and contrast the ways that these sources address your chosen topic. Go to Social Studies Skills on page 114 for help.

LAFS.68.WHST.1.1 Write arguments focused on discipline-specific content.

a. Introduce claim(s) about a topic or issue, acknowledge and distinguish the claim(s) from alternate or opposing claims, and organize the reasons and evidence logically.

b. Support claim(s) with logical reasoning and relevant, accurate data and evidence that demonstrate an understanding of the topic or text, using credible sources.

c. Use words, phrases, and clauses to create cohesion and clarify the relationships among claim(s), counterclaims, reasons, and evidence.

d. Establish and maintain a formal style.

e. Provide a concluding statement or section that follows from and supports the argument presented.

What does it mean?

Develop written arguments focused on topics related to history, geography, economics, or government that include:

a. a clear introduction and organization of topics, claims, and counterclaims

b. strong accurate support for claims

c. words, phrases, and clauses that improve flow and connect claims with supporting reasons and evidence

d. a formal style

e. a strong concluding statement that summarizes the argument

Go to the Unit Writing Workshops for help.

LAFS.68.WHST.1.2 Write informative/explanatory texts, including the narration of historical events, scientific procedures/experiments, or technical processes.

a. Introduce a topic clearly, previewing what is to follow; organize ideas, concepts, and information into broader categories as appropriate to achieving purpose; include formatting (e.g., headings), graphics (e.g., charts, tables), and multimedia when useful to aiding comprehension.

b. Develop the topic with relevant, well-chosen facts, definitions, concrete details, quotations, or other information and examples.

c. Use appropriate and varied transitions to create cohesion and clarify the relationships among ideas and concepts.

d. Use precise language and domain-specific vocabulary to inform about or explain the topic.

e. Establish and maintain a formal style and objective tone.

f. Provide a concluding statement or section that follows from and supports the information or explanation presented.

What does it mean?

Write informative and explanatory texts to describe historical events, scientific procedures/experiments, or technical processes that include:

a. a clear introduction and organization, including headings and graphic organizers (when appropriate)

b. sufficient supporting details and background information

c. cohesive transitions to link ideas

d. precise language and relevant vocabulary

e. a formal style

f. a strong conclusion that restates the importance or relevance of the topic

Go to the Unit Writing Workshops for help.

LAFS.68.WHST.2.4   Produce clear and coherent writing in which the development, organization, and style are appropriate to task, purpose, and audience.

What does it mean?

Produce texts that are appropriate to the task, purpose, and audience for whom you are writing. Go to the Unit Writing Workshops for help.

LAFS.68.WHST.2.5   With some guidance and support from peers and adults, develop and strengthen writing as needed by planning, revising, editing, rewriting, or trying a new approach, focusing on how well purpose and audience have been addressed.

What does it mean?

With help form other students and adults, plan, revise, and refine your writing to address what is most important for your purpose and audience. Go to the Unit Writing Workshops for help.

LAFS.68.WHST.2.6   Use technology, including the Internet, to produce and publish writing and present the relationships between information and ideas clearly and efficiently.

What does it mean?

Use technology to share your writing and to provide links to other relevant information. Go to Using the Internet activities in Chapter Reviews for help.

LAFS.68.WHST.3.7   Conduct short research projects to answer a question (including a self-generated question), drawing on several sources and generating additional related, focused questions that allow for multiple avenues of exploration.

What does it mean?

Engage in short and more complex research tasks that include answering a question or solving a problem by using multiple sources. The product of your research should demonstrate your understanding of the subject. Go to Unit 4 Writing Workshop for help.

LAFS.68.WHST.3.8   Gather relevant information from multiple print and digital sources, using search terms effectively; assess the credibility and accuracy of each source; and quote or paraphrase the data and conclusions of others while avoiding plagiarism and following a standard format for citation.

What does it mean?

Conduct effective searches and carefully analyze the relevance of sources in order to gather useful information from a variety of sources, while following a standard citation format to avoid plagiarism. Go to Unit 4 Writing Workshop for help.

LAFS.68.WHST.3.9   Draw evidence from informational texts to support analysis reflection, and research.

What does it mean?

Paraphrase, summarize, quote, and cite primary and secondary sources to support your analysis, reflection, and research. Go to the Unit Writing Workshops for help.

LAFS.68.WHST.4.10   Write routinely over extended time frames (time for reflection and revision) and shorter time frames (a single sitting or a day or two) for a range of discipline-specific tasks, purposes, and audiences.

What does it mean?

Write for many different purposes and audiences both over short and extended periods of time. Go to the Focus on Writing activities in the Chapter Reviews for help.

MATHEMATICS

>MAFS.K12.MP.1.1

Make sense of problems and persevere in solving them.

Mathematically proficient students start by explaining to themselves the meaning of a problem and looking for entry points to its solution. They analyze givens, constraints, relationships, and goals. They make conjectures about the form and meaning of the solution and plan a solution pathway rather than simply jumping into a solution attempt. They consider analogous problems, and try special cases and simpler forms of the original problem in order to gain insight into its solution. They monitor and evaluate their progress and change course if necessary. Older students might, depending on the context of the problem, transform algebraic expressions or change the viewing window on their graphing calculator to get the information they need. Mathematically proficient students can explain correspondences between equations, verbal descriptions, tables, and graphs or draw diagrams of important features and relationships, graph data, and search for regularity or trends. Younger students might rely on using concrete objects or pictures to help conceptualize and solve a problem. Mathematically proficient students check their answers to problems using a different method, and they continually ask themselves, Does this make sense? They can understand the approaches of others to solving complex problems and identify correspondences between different approaches.

What does it mean?
Understand the problems put in front of you and work through them until a solution is found. Applying math skills in social studies course work often takes the form of analyzing data in tables, graphs, and models. Go to the Focus on Mathematics activity on page 116 for help.

>MAFS.K12.MP.3.1

Construct viable arguments and critique the reasoning of others.

Mathematically proficient students understand and use stated assumptions, definitions, and previously established results in constructing arguments. They make conjectures and build a logical progression of statements to explore the truth of their conjectures. They are able to analyze situations by breaking them into cases, and can recognize and use counterexamples. They justify their conclusions, communicate them to others, and respond to the arguments of others. They reason inductively about data, making plausible arguments that take into account the context from which the data arose. Mathematically proficient students are also able to compare the effectiveness of two plausible arguments, distinguish correct logic or reasoning from that which is flawed, and if there is a flaw in an argument, explain what it is. Elementary students can construct arguments using concrete referents such as objects, drawings, diagrams, and actions. Such arguments can make sense and be correct, even though they are not generalized or made formal until later grades. Later, students learn to determine domains to which an argument applies. Students at all grades can listen or read the arguments of others, decide whether they make sense, and ask useful questions to clarify or improve the arguments.

What does it mean?
Use logic and evidence to construct reasoned arguments and analyze the arguments of others using those same skills. Application of this skill in social studies course work most often comes in the form of written essays. However, direct application of math skills can be used when determining the story behind the numbers on a graph or critiquing someone else's conclusions about a set of data. Go to Social Studies Skills on page 20 for help.

>MAFS.K12.MP.5.1

Use appropriate tools strategically.

Mathematically proficient students consider the available tools when solving a mathematical problem. These tools might include pencil and paper, concrete models, a ruler, a protractor, a calculator, a spreadsheet, a computer algebra system, a statistical package, or dynamic geometry software. Proficient students are sufficiently familiar with tools appropriate for their grade or course to make sound decisions about when each of these tools might be helpful, recognizing both the insight to be gained and their limitations. For example, mathematically proficient high school students analyze graphs of functions and solutions generated using a graphing calculator. They detect possible errors by strategically using estimation and other mathematical knowledge. When making mathematical models, they know that technology can enable them to visualize the results of varying assumptions, explore consequences, and compare predictions with data. Mathematically proficient students at various grade levels are able to identify relevant external mathematical resources, such as digital content located on a website, and use them to pose or solve problems. They are able to use technological tools to explore and deepen their understanding of concepts.

What does it mean?

When approaching a problem, use the tools best suited to the job. In social studies course work, some of those tools are written essays, maps, graphs, and models. For example, a graph is often a better tool for visualizing the historical trends of a nation's economy than trying to describe those trends in an essay. Go to Social Studies Skills on page 152 for help.

>MAFS.K12.MP.6.1

Attend to precision.

Mathematically proficient students try to communicate precisely to others. They try to use clear definitions in discussion with others and in their own reasoning. They state the meaning of the symbols they choose, including using the equal sign consistently and appropriately. They are careful about specifying units of measure, and labeling axes to clarify the correspondence with quantities in a problem. They calculate accurately and efficiently, express numerical answers with a degree of precision appropriate for the problem context. In the elementary grades, students give carefully formulated explanations to each other. By the time they reach high school they have learned to examine claims and make explicit use of definitions.

What does it mean?

Be precise when communicating ideas and answers to others. In social studies as in math, precision avoids uncertainty and ensures the meaning and intent of arguments and solutions is understood. Go to the Calculate question on page 194 for help.

CIVICS AND GOVERNMENT

>SS.6.C.1

Demonstrate an understanding of the origins and purposes of government, law, and the American political system.

What does it mean?

Understand the sources of the democratic concepts that form the basis for government, law, and the American political system. Go to Chapter 8, *Ancient Greece,* for help.

SS.6.C.1.1 Identify democratic concepts developed in ancient Greece that served as a foundation for American constitutional democracy. Examples are polis, civic participation and voting rights, legislative bodies, written constitutions, rule of law.

What does it mean?

Describe the democratic ideas that developed in ancient Greece and how those ideas came to serve as the basis for constitutional democracy in the United States. Go to Chapter 8, *Ancient Greece,* for help.

SS.6.C.1.2 **Identify how the government of the Roman Republic contributed to the development of democratic principles (separation of powers, rule of law, representative government, civic duty).**

What does it mean?

Explain how a number of key principles developed by the Roman Republic contributed to the development of modern democracy. Go to Chapter 10, *The Roman Republic,* for help.

>SS.6.C.2

Evaluate the roles, rights, and responsibilities of United States citizens, and determine methods of active participation in society, government, and the political system.

What does it mean?

List the major rights that citizens of the United States enjoy, and describe the responsibilities that those citizens have. Identify how citizens can participate in American society, government, and politics. Go to the Democracy Then and Now feature in Chapter 8, *Ancient Greece,* for help.

SS.6.C.2.1 **Identify principles (civic participation, role of government) from ancient Greek and Roman civilizations which are reflected in the American political process today, and discuss their effect on the American political process.**

What does it mean?

Describe the democratic principles developed in ancient Greece and Rome that can be seen in the American political process today. Explain how these principles continue to affect politics and government in the United States. Go to Chapter 8, *Ancient Greece,* for help.

ECONOMICS

>SS.6.E.1

Understand the fundamental concepts relevant to the development of a market economy.

What does it mean?

Identify and explain the key concepts that must be in place before a market economy can develop. Go to *Spotlight on Economics* for help.

SS.6.E.1.1 **Identify the factors (new resources, increased productivity, education, technology, slave economy, territorial expansion) that increase economic growth.**

What does it mean?

List the economic factors that are critical to increasing economic growth. Go to the History and Geography feature on pages 384–385 for help.

SS.6.E.1.2 **Describe and identify traditional and command economies as they appear in different civilizations.**

What does it mean?

Compare the characteristics of traditional and command economies that have appeared over time in various civilizations. Go to *Spotlight on Economics* for help.

SS.6.E.1.3 **Describe the following economic concepts as they relate to early civilization: scarcity, opportunity cost, supply and demand, barter, trade, productive resources (land, labor, capital, entrepreneurship).**

What does it mean?

Explore how fundamental economic concepts such as scarcity and barter were handled by people living in early civilizations around the world. Go to *Spotlight on Economics* for help.

Lake Eola, Orlando

>SS.6.E.2

Understand the fundamental concepts relevant to the institutions, structure, and functions of a national economy.

What does it mean?

Explore how fundamental economic ideas apply across a nationwide economy. Go to "Rome's Growing Empire," pages 325-326, and "Ghana Controls Trade," pages 386-387, for help.

SS.6.E.2.1 **Evaluate how civilizations through clans, leaders, and family groups make economic decisions for that civilization providing a framework for future city-state or nation development.**

What does it mean?

Analyze how economic decisions made by clans, leaders, and family groups in early civilizations paved the way for later city-states and nations to arise. Go to the margin feature on page 383 for help.

>SS.6.E.3

Understand the fundamental concepts and interrelationships of the United States economy in the international marketplace.

What does it mean?

Examine the concepts and relationships that define the United States' place as a member of a world-wide economy. Go to Chapter 11, *Rome and Christianity*, and Chapter 13, *Early African Civilizations*, for help.

SS.6.E.3.1 **Identify examples of mediums of exchange (currencies) used for trade (barter) for each civilization, and explain why international trade requires a system for a medium of exchange between trading both inside and among various regions.**

What does it mean?

Describe the currencies that different civilizations used for trade. Understand why currencies are essential to international trade and how countries exchange their currencies in order to trade with one another. Go to the History and Geography feature on pages 384–385, and the text discussion that follows on pages 386–387, for help.

SS.6.E.3.2 **Categorize products that were traded among civilizations, and give examples of barriers to trade of those products.**

What does it mean?

Identify the primary trade goods produced by various civilizations, and describe the barriers that existed to the trade of these goods. Go to the History and Geography feature on pages 384–385, and the text discussion that follows on pages 386–387, for help.

SS.6.E.3.3 **Describe traditional economies (Egypt, Greece, Rome, Kush) and elements of those economies that led to the rise of a merchant class and trading partners.**

What does it mean?

Explore the characteristics of traditional economies, and identify what led to the development of a more advanced economic system that created a merchant class and trading partners. Go to the discussion of Egypt and Kush on pages 109–111 for help.

SS.6.E.3.4 **Describe the relationship among civilizations that engage in trade, including the benefits and drawbacks of voluntary trade.**

What does it mean?

Explore how various civilizations traded with one another, and describe the possible benefits and drawbacks they experienced in trading with one another. Go to the discussion of Egypt and Kush on pages 109–111 for help.

GEOGRAPHY

>SS.6.G.1

Understand how to use maps and other geographic representations, tools and technology to report information.

What does it mean?

Analyze maps and use other tools and technologies to learn about geography. Go to Chapter 1, *Uncovering the Past,* for help.

SS.6.G.1.1 **Use latitude and longitude coordinates to understand the relationship between people and places on the Earth.**

What does it mean?

Understand how latitude and longitude is used to pinpoint locations on Earth and shed light on relationships between people and places. Go to *Spotlight on Geography* for help.

SS.6.G.1.2 **Analyze the purposes of map projections (political, physical, special purpose) and explain the applications of various types of maps.**

What does it mean?

Understand that historians use several types of maps, and identify the types of information that these maps offer. Go to *Spotlight on Geography* for help.

SS.6.G.1.3 Identify natural wonders of the ancient world. Examples are Seven Natural Wonders of Africa, Himalayas, Gobi Desert.

What does it mean?

List and describe some of the natural wonders of the ancient world, including the Himalayas, the Gobi Desert, and the Seven Wonders of Africa. Go to the maps on pages 125, 161, and 381 for help.

SS.6.G.1.4 Utilize tools geographers use to study the world. Examples are maps, globes, graphs, charts and geo-spatial tools such as GPS (global positioning system), GIS (Geographic Information Systems), satellite imagery, aerial photography, online mapping resources.

What does it mean?

Use maps and other geographical tools to better understand the world. Go to the History and Geography feature on pages 234–235 for help.

SS.6.G.1.5 Use scale, cardinal, and intermediate directions, and estimation of distances between places on current and ancient maps of the world.

What does it mean?

Analyze map elements such as scale and a compass rose to understand cardinal directions from and to particular locations, and distances between locations. Go to *Spotlight on Geography* for help.

SS.6.G.1.6 Use a map to identify major bodies of water of the world, and explain ways they have impacted the development of civilizations. Examples are major rivers, seas, oceans.

What does it mean?

Identify on a map the world's major bodies of water, and describe how these bodies of water have affected the development of various civilizations. Go to the discussion of Phoenician trade on pages 76–77 for help.

SS.6.G.1.7 Use maps to identify characteristics and boundaries of ancient civilizations that have shaped the world today. Examples are Phoenicia, Carthage, Crete, Egypt, Greece, Rome, Kush.

What does it mean?

Work with maps to learn the characteristics and boundaries of the world's major ancient civilizations and to see how the influence of these characteristics and boundaries can be seen today. Go to the History and Geography feature on pages 190–191 for help.

>SS.6.G.2

Understand physical and cultural characteristics of places.

What does it mean?

Describe various locations by their major physical and cultural characteristics. Go to the History and Geography feature on pages 384–385 for help.

SS.6.G.2.1 Explain how major physical characteristics, natural resources, climate, and absolute and relative locations have influenced settlement, interactions, and the economies of ancient civilizations of the world.

What does it mean?

Describe how ancient civilizations were affected by geographical factors such as terrain, availability of natural resources, climate, and location. Explain how these factors affected settlement, how civilizations interacted, and whether they thrived economically. Go to the History and Geography feature on pages 384–385 for help.

SS.6.G.2.2 Differentiate between continents, regions, countries, and cities in order to understand the complexities of regions created by civilizations. Examples are city-states, provinces, kingdoms, empires.

What does it mean?

Use geographic factors to understand how a given area can be characterized by its size. Go to the discussion of regions on page 15 for help.

SS.6.G.2.3 Analyze the relationship of physical geography to the development of ancient river valley civilizations. Examples are Tigris and Euphrates [Mesopotamia], Nile [Egypt], Indus and Ganges [Ancient India], and Huang He [Ancient China].

What does it mean?

Explain why physical geography so strongly affected the way that ancient river valley civilizations developed. Go to the History and Geography feature on pages 58–59 for help.

SS.6.G.2.4 Explain how the geographical location of ancient civilizations contributed to the culture and politics of those societies. Examples are Egypt, Rome, Greece, China, Kush.

What does it mean?

Identify the ways in which geography shaped the cultures and governments of ancient civilizations. Go to the History and Geography feature on pages 58–59 for help.

SS.6.G.2.5 Interpret how geographic boundaries invite or limit interaction with other regions and cultures. Examples are China limits and Greece invites.

What does it mean?

Explore how the interaction between regions and cultures has been encouraged or hindered by geographic boundaries. Go to the History and Geography feature on pages 190–191 for help.

SS.6.G.2.6 Explain the concept of cultural diffusion, and identify the influences of different ancient cultures on one another. Examples are Phoenicia on Greece and Greece on Rome.

Gusman Center for the Performing Arts

What does it mean?

Define *cultural diffusion,* and explore how different ancient civilizations influenced one another. Go to the discussion of Christianity in ancient Rome on pages 337–338 for help.

SS.6.G.2.7 **Interpret choropleths or dot-density maps to explain the distribution of population in the ancient world.**

What does it mean?

Understand that a choropleth map is one that is shaded or colored to highlight a certain type of information. Use a choropleth map to identify how populations were distributed in the ancient world. Go to *Spotlight on Geography* for help.

>SS.6.G.3

Understand the relationships between the Earth's ecosystems and the populations that dwell within them.

What does it mean?

Explain how people around the world are affected by Earth's ecosystems. Go to the discussion of geography and ancient Egypt on pages 86–89 for help.

SS.6.G.3.1 **Explain how the physical landscape has affected the development of agriculture and industry in the ancient world. Examples are terracing, seasonal crop rotations, resource development.**

What does it mean?

Analyze how farming and industry in ancient civilizations were affected by physical geography. Go to the discussion of geography and ancient Egypt on pages 86–89 for help.

SS.6.G.3.2 **Analyze the impact of human populations on the ancient world's ecosystems. Examples are desertification, deforestation, abuse of resources, erosion.**

What does it mean?

Explore how people living in ancient times affected Earth's ecosystems. Go to the discussion of China during the Han dynasty on pages 186–187 for help.

>SS.6.G.4

Understand the characteristics, distribution, and migration of human populations.

What does it mean?

Describe the cultures of ancient civilizations, and explore how they moved and where they settled. Go to the discussion of the people of West Africa on pages 382–383 for help.

SS.6.G.4.1 **Explain how family and ethnic relationships influenced ancient cultures.**

What does it mean?

Describe the ways that the relationships between families and between ethnic groups affected the cultures of ancient civilizations. Go to the discussion of the people of West Africa on pages 382–383 for help.

SS.6.G.4.2 **Use maps to trace significant migrations, and analyze their results. Examples are prehistoric Asians to the Americas, Aryans in Asia, Germanic tribes throughout Europe.**

What does it mean?

Locate on maps the large-scale movements of people from one region to another, and describe the cultural and political results of these movements. Go to page 203 for help.

SS.6.G.4.3 **Locate sites in Africa and Asia where archaeologists have found evidence of early human societies, and trace their migration patterns to other parts of the world.**

Florida oranges

What does it mean?
Identify the earliest known sites of human habitation in Africa and Asia, and describe migration patterns that flowed from these locations. Go to page 29 for help.

SS.6.G.4.4 Map and analyze the impact of the spread of various belief systems in the ancient world. Examples are Buddhism, Christianity, Judaism.

What does it mean?
Trace on a map the spread of various ancient belief systems, and describe how cultures were affected as these belief systems spread. Go to the discussion of the Aryan migration on pages 128–129 for help.

>SS.6.G.5

Understand how human actions can impact the environment.

What does it mean?
Describe how ancient peoples affected the environment. Go to pages 40–43 for help.

SS.6.G.5.1 Identify the methods used to compensate for the scarcity of resources in the ancient world. Examples are water in the Middle East, fertile soil, fuel.

What does it mean?
Understand how ancient cultures thrived while living in environments that offered only scarce resources. Go to pages 40–43 for help.

SS.6.G.5.2 Use geographic terms and tools to explain why ancient civilizations developed networks of highways, waterways, and other transportation linkages.

What does it mean?
Review maps and other geographic tools to explore why ancient civilizations developed

Florida

Naples Beach

highways and other means of transportation. Go to the History and Geography feature on pages 330–331 for help.

SS.6.G.5.3 Use geographic tools and terms to analyze how famine, drought, and natural disasters plagued many ancient civilizations. Examples are flooding of the Nile, drought in Africa, volcanoes in the Mediterranean region, famine in Asia.

What does it mean?
Understand how geographic tools and terms can help you learn how ancient civilizations were affected by famine, drought, and natural disasters. Go to the History and Geography feature on pages 234–235 for help.

>SS.6.G.6
Understand how to apply geography to interpret the past and present and plan for the future.

What does it mean?
Understand the tools that geographers use to learn about the past and plan for the future. Go to *Spotlight on Geography* for help.

SS.6.G.6.1 Describe the Six Essential Elements of Geography (The World in Spatial Terms, Places and Regions, **Physical Systems, Human Systems, Environment, The Uses of Geography) as the organizing framework for understanding the world and its people.**

What does it mean?
Explain how the Six Essential Elements of Geography provide a framework for understanding the world. Go to *Spotlight on Geography* for help.

SS.6.G.6.2 Compare maps of the world in ancient times with current political maps.

What does it mean?
Understand the ways in which ancient world maps differ significantly from modern political maps. Go to the Interpreting Maps questions on pages 74, 179, 275, and 365 for help.

WORLD HISTORY

>SS.6.W.1
Utilize historical inquiry skills and analytical processes.

What does it mean?
Use the skills and processes that historians rely on to understand the past. Go to the Social Studies Skills lessons that appear at the end of each chapter for help.

SS.6.W.1.1 Use timelines to identify chronological order of historical events.

What does it mean?

Know that timelines are a useful tool in understanding the order in which historical events have occurred. Go to the timelines that appear at the end or beginning of each chapter, and the Social Studies Skills lesson that appears at the end of Chapter 11 for help.

SS.6.W.1.2 Identify terms (decade, century, epoch, era, millennium, BC/BCE, AD/CE) and designations of time periods.

What does it mean?

Understand the different terms (such as *decade*, *century*, and *era*) that denote periods of time. Go to the Reading Social Studies lesson on pages 4–5 for help.

SS.6.W.1.3 Interpret primary and secondary sources. Examples are artifacts, images, auditory sources, written sources.

What does it mean?

Understand the important role that primary and secondary sources play in researching and analyzing world history. Go to the Social Studies Skills lesson that appears at the end of Chapter 4 for help.

SS.6.W.1.4 Describe the methods of historical inquiry and how history relates to the other social sciences. Examples are archaeology, geography, political science, economics.

What does it mean?

Identify how historical research can be effectively carried out, and explain how history relates to other social sciences (such as geography and economics). Go to the Social Studies Skills lessons that appear at the end of Chapters 6 and 12 for help.

SS.6.W.1.5 Describe the roles of historians and recognize varying historical interpretations (historiography).

What does it mean?

Analyze how historians work to increase knowledge of the past, and understand that historians sometimes differ in their interpretations of historical events. Go to Chapter 1, *Uncovering the Past,* for help.

SS.6.W.1.6 Describe how history transmits culture and heritage and provides models of human character.

What does it mean?

Explain how culture and heritage are transferred by history, and understand how this process offers models of human character. Go to pages 7–9, and the Biography on page 207, for help.

Jacksonville skyline

>SS.6.W.2

Describe the emergence of early civilizations (Nile, Tigris-Euphrates, Indus, and Yellow Rivers, Meso and South American).

What does it mean?

Detail how ancient civilizations arose in river valleys and in Central and South America. Go to Chapter 3, *Mesopotamia and the Fertile Crescent,* Chapter 4, *Ancient Egypt and Kush,* Chapter 5, *Ancient India,* Chapter 6, *Ancient China,* and Chapter 16, *The Early Americas,* for help.

SS.6.W.2.1 Compare the lifestyles of hunter-gatherers with those of settlers of early agricultural communities.

What does it mean?

Explain how the hunter-gatherer way of life differed from the lifestyle of cultures that depended on farming. Go to Chapter 2, *The Stone Ages and Early Cultures,* for help.

SS.6.W.2.2 Describe how the developments of agriculture and metallurgy related to settlement, population growth, and the emergence of civilization.

What does it mean?

Understand the cause-and-effect relationship between farming and improved metal-working, and the beginning of civilization. Go to Chapter 2, *The Stone Ages and Early Cultures,* for help.

SS.6.W.2.3 Identify the characteristics of civilization. Examples are urbanization, specialized labor, advanced technology, government and religious institutions, social classes.

What does it mean?

Explain the features that distinguish civilizations from other forms of social organization (such as a hunter-gatherer society). Go to Chapter 3, *Mesopotamia and the Fertile Crescent,* for help.

SS.6.W.2.4 Compare the economic, political, social, and religious institutions of ancient river civilizations. Examples are Nile, Tigris-Euphrates, Indus, Huang He.

What does it mean?

Identify and compare the major characteristics of the ancient river civilizations. Go to Chapter 3, *Mesopotamia and the Fertile Crescent,* for help.

SS.6.W.2.5 Summarize important achievements of Egyptian civilization. Examples are agriculture, calendar, pyramids, art and architecture, hieroglyphic writing and record-keeping, literature such as The Book of the Dead, mummification.

What does it mean?

Identify the key achievements of the ancient Egyptian civilization. Go to Chapter 4, *Ancient Egypt and Kush,* for help.

SS.6.W.2.6 Determine the contributions of key figures from ancient Egypt. Examples are Narmer, Imhotep, Hatshepsut, Ramses the Great, Akhenaten, Tutankhamun.

What does it mean?

Explore how leading figures in ancient Egypt contributed to their society. Go to Chapter 4, *Ancient Egypt and Kush,* for help.

SS.6.W.2.7 Summarize the important achievements of Mesopotamian civilization. Examples are cuneiform writing, epic literature such as Gilgamesh, art and architecture, technology such as the wheel, sail, and plow.

What does it mean?

Describe the major achievements of Mesopotamian civilization. Go to Chapter 3, *Mesopotamia and the Fertile Crescent,* for help.

SS.6.W.2.8 Determine the impact of key figures from ancient Mesopotamian civilizations. Examples are Abraham, Hammurabi, Nebuchadnezzar, Cyrus, Zoroaster.

What does it mean?

Understand how leading individuals from Mesopotamian civilizations contributed to their societies. Go to Chapter 3, *Mesopotamia and the Fertile Crescent,* for help.

SS.6.W.2.9 Identify key figures and basic beliefs of the Israelites and determine how these beliefs compared with those of others in the geographic area. Examples are Abraham, Moses, monotheism, law, emphasis on individual worth and responsibility.

Ringling Brothers Museum, Sarasota

© Ilene MacDonald/Alamy

What does it mean?

Name leading ancient Israelites and explain their significance. Know the fundamental beliefs of the ancient Israelites and compare these beliefs to those of other nearby peoples. Go to Chapter 7, *The Hebrews and Judaism,* for help.

SS.6.W.2.10 Compare the emergence of advanced civilizations in Meso and South America with the four early river valley civilizations. Examples are Olmec, Zapotec, Chavin.

What does it mean?

Explain how the civilizations of Meso and South America were similar to and different from the four early river valley civilizations. Go to Chapter 3, *Mesopotamia and the Fertile Crescent,* and Chapter 16, *The Early Americas,* for help.

>SS.6.W.3

Recognize significant events, figures, and contributions of classical civilizations (Phoenicia, Greece, Rome, Axum).

What does it mean?

Identify important individuals, events, and ideas of ancient Phoenicia, Greece, Rome, and Axum. Go to Chapter 4, *Ancient Egypt and Kush,* Chapter 8, *Ancient Greece,* Chapter 9, *The Greek World,* and Chapter 10, *The Roman Republic,* for help.

SS.6.W.3.1 Analyze the cultural impact the ancient Phoenicians had on the Mediterranean world with regard to colonization (Carthage), exploration, maritime commerce (purple dye, tin), and written communication (alphabet).

What does it mean?

Explore how the ancient Phoenicians affected the Mediterranean world. Describe their efforts at colonization, exploration, trade, and written communication. Go to Chapter 3, *Mesopotamia and the Fertile Crescent,* for help.

SS.6.W.3.2 Explain the democratic concepts (polis, civic participation and voting rights, legislative bodies, written constitutions, rule of law) developed in ancient Greece.

What does it mean?

Describe the key democratic principles developed by the ancient Greeks. Go to Chapter 8, *Ancient Greece,* and Chapter 9, *The Greek World,* for help.

SS.6.W.3.3 Compare life in Athens and Sparta (government and the status of citizens, women and children, foreigners, helots).

What does it mean?

Compare and contrast the governments and cultures of the Greek city-states of Athens and Sparta. Go to Chapter 8, *Ancient Greece,* and Chapter 9, *The Greek World,* for help.

SS.6.W.3.4 Explain the causes and effects of the Persian and Peloponnesian Wars.

What does it mean?

Trace the events leading to the Persian and Peloponnesian Wars, and describe the effects of these conflicts. Go to Chapter 9, *The Greek World,* for help.

SS.6.W.3.5 Summarize the important achievements and contributions of ancient Greek civilization. Examples are art and architecture, athletic competitions, the birth of democracy and civic responsibility, drama, history, literature, mathematics, medicine, philosophy, science, warfare.

What does it mean?

Identify the major accomplishments and contributions of Greek civilization. Go to Chapter 8, *Ancient Greece,* and Chapter 9, *The Greek World,* for help.

SS.6.W.3.6 Determine the impact of key figures from ancient Greece. Examples are Aristophanes, Aristotle, Hippocrates, Herodotus, Homer, Pericles, Plato, Pythagoras, Socrates, Solon, Sophocles, Thales, Themistocles, Thucydides.

What does it mean?

Describe how leading individuals in Greece affected their societies and influenced later cultures. Go to Chapter 8, *Ancient Greece,* and Chapter 9, *The Greek World,* for help.

SS.6.W.3.7 Summarize the key achievements, contributions, and figures associated with The Hellenistic Period. Examples are Alexander the Great, Library of Alexandria, Archimedes, Euclid, Plutarch, The Septuagint, Stoicism, Ptolemy I.

What does it mean?

Identify the leading individuals and major achievements of the Hellenistic period. Describe the influence that this period has had on later civilizations. Go to Chapter 9, *The Greek World,* for help.

SS.6.W.3.8 Determine the impact of significant figures associated with ancient Rome. Examples are Augustus, Cicero, Cincinnatus, Cleopatra, Constantine the Great, Diocletian, Tiberius and Gaius Gracchus, Hadrian, Hannibal, Horace, Julius Caesar, Ovid, Romulus and Remus, Marcus Aurelius, Scipio Africanus, Virgil, Theodosius, Attila the Hun.

What does it mean?

Identify leading Romans and describe how they affected their society. Go to Chapter 10, *The Roman Republic,* and Chapter 11, *Rome and Christianity,* for help.

SS.6.W.3.9 Explain the impact of the Punic Wars on the development of the Roman Empire.

What does it mean?

Understand that the Punic Wars led to the removal of a major obstacle to the growth of the Roman Empire. Go to Chapter 10, *The Roman Republic,* for help.

State marine mammal

© Steven Trainoff Ph.D./Flickr/Getty Images

SS.6.W.3.10 Describe the government of the Roman Republic and its contribution to the development of democratic principles (separation of powers, rule of law, representative government, civic duty).

What does it mean?

Analyze the principles underlying the Roman Republic's government and identify key contributions that the Romans made to democratic government. Go to Chapter 10, *The Roman Republic,* for help.

SS.6.W.3.11 Explain the transition from Roman Republic to empire and Imperial Rome, and compare Roman life and culture under each one.

What does it mean?

Understand the issues and events that caused Rome to change from a republic to an empire led by an emperor. Describe how Roman life and society changed after Augustus became Rome's first emperor. Go to Chapter 10, *The Roman Republic,* and Chapter 11, *Rome and Christianity,* for help.

SS.6.W.3.12 Explain the causes for the growth and longevity of the Roman Empire. Examples are centralized and efficient government, religious toleration, expansion of citizenship, the legion, the extension of road networks.

What does it mean?

Analyze why the Roman Empire was able to extend its territorial control and why the empire maintained its power for so long. Go to Chapter 10, *The Roman Republic,* and Chapter 11, *Rome and Christianity,* for help.

SS.6.W.3.13 Identify key figures and the basic beliefs of early Christianity and how these beliefs impacted the Roman Empire. Examples are Christian monotheism, Jesus as the son of God, Peter, Paul.

What does it mean?

Describe the fundamental beliefs of early Christians, and explain how Christianity came to affect the Roman Empire. Go to Chapter 11, *Rome and Christianity,* for help.

SS.6.W.3.14 Describe the key achievements and contributions of Roman civilization. Examples are art and architecture, engineering, law, literature, technology.

What does it mean?

Name and describe the major achievements of the Roman Republic and the Roman Empire. Go to Chapter 10, *The Roman Republic,* and Chapter 11, *Rome and Christianity,* for help.

Tampa Bay harbor

SS.6.W.3.15   Explain the reasons for the gradual decline of the Western Roman Empire after the Pax Romana. Examples are internal power struggles, constant Germanic pressure on the frontiers, economic policies, over dependence on slavery and mercenary soldiers.

What does it mean?

Analyze why the Western Roman Empire gradually fell into decline. Go to Chapter 11, *Rome and Christianity,* for help.

SS.6.W.3.16   Compare life in the Roman Republic for patricians, plebeians, women, children, and slaves.

What does it mean?

Understand how the lives of patricians, plebeians, women, children, and slaves differed from one another during the Roman Republic. Go to Chapter 10, *The Roman Republic,* for help.

SS.6.W.3.17   Explain the spread and influence of the Latin language on Western Civilization. Examples are education, law, medicine, religion, science.

What does it mean?

Trace how the language of the Romans, Latin, continued to influence Western civilization centuries after the fall of the Western Roman Empire. Go to Chapter 11, *Rome and Christianity,* for help.

SS.6.W.3.18   Describe the rise and fall of the ancient east African kingdoms of Kush and Axum and Christianity's development in Ethiopia.

What does it mean?

Analyze the rise of Kush and Axum to power, and explain why these kingdoms eventually collapsed. Trace how and why Christianity became a major religion in Ethiopia. Go to Chapter 4, *Ancient Egypt and Kush,* for help.

>SS.6.W.4

Recognize significant events, figures, and contributions of classical Asian civilizations (China, India).

What does it mean?

Understand the major individuals and events that contributed to the development of ancient India and ancient China. Go to Chapter 5, *Ancient India,* and Chapter 6, *Ancient China,* for help.

SS.6.W.4.1   Discuss the significance of Aryan and other tribal migrations on Indian civilization.

South Beach, Miami

What does it mean?

Describe the tribal migrations that affected ancient India. Explain why the Aryan migration was particularly significant. Go to Chapter 5, *Ancient India,* for help.

SS.6.W.4.2 Explain the major beliefs and practices associated with Hinduism and the social structure of the caste system in ancient India. Examples are Brahman, reincarnation, dharma, karma, ahimsa, moksha.

What does it mean?

Understand the key aspects of Hinduism and analyze how Hinduism affected the development of ancient India. Describe the caste system that developed in India. Go to Chapter 5, *Ancient India,* for help.

SS.6.W.4.3 Recognize the political and cultural achievements of the Mauryan and Gupta empires.

What does it mean?

Trace the rise of the Mauryan and Gupta empires, and describe the major political and cultural achievements of each. Go to Chapter 5, *Ancient India,* for help.

SS.6.W.4.4 Explain the teachings of Buddha, the importance of Asoka, and how Buddhism spread in India, Ceylon, and other parts of Asia. Examples are The Four Noble Truths, Three Qualities, Eightfold Path.

What does it mean?

Outline the major teachings of Buddha, and identify why the Mauryan ruler Asoka is a significant figure in Indian history. Trace the spread of Buddhism across India, Ceylon, and other parts of Asia. Go to Chapter 5, *Ancient India,* and Chapter 6, *Ancient China,* for help.

SS.6.W.4.5 Summarize the important achievements and contributions of ancient Indian civilization. Examples are Sanskrit, Bhagavad Gita, medicine, metallurgy, and mathematics including Hindu-Arabic numerals and the concept of zero.

What does it mean?

Name and describe the leading achievements of ancient Indian civilization. Go to Chapter 5, *Ancient India,* for help.

SS.6.W.4.6 **Describe the concept of the Mandate of Heaven and its connection to the Zhou and later dynasties.**

What does it mean?

Explain what is meant by "Mandate of Heaven," and describe its relationship to the Zhou and later dynasties of China. Go to Chapter 6, *Ancient China,* for help.

SS.6.W.4.7 **Explain the basic teachings of Laozi, Confucius, and Han Fei Zi. Examples are filial piety, the role of kinship in maintaining order, hierarchy in Chinese society.**

What does it mean?

Describe the fundamental principles taught by Laozi, Confucius, and Han Fei Zi. Go to Chapter 6, *Ancient China,* and Chapter 14, *China,* for help.

SS.6.W.4.8 **Describe the contributions of classical and post classical China. Examples are Great Wall, Silk Road, bronze casting, silk-making, movable type, gunpowder, paper-making, magnetic compass, horse collar, stirrup, civil service system, The Analects.**

What does it mean?

Identify the leading achievements of classical and post classical China. Go to Chapter 6, *Ancient China,* and Chapter 14, *China,* for help.

SS.6.W.4.9 **Identify key figures from classical and post classical China. Examples are Shi Huangdi, Wu-ti, Empress Wu, Chengho.**

What does it mean?

List leading individuals of classical and post classical China, and explain why their contributions are significant. Go to Chapter 6, *Ancient China,* and Chapter 14, *China,* for help.

SS.6.W.4.10 **Explain the significance of the silk roads and maritime routes across the Indian Ocean to the movement of goods and ideas among Asia, East Africa, and the Mediterranean Basin.**

What does it mean?

Analyze how the major east-west silk roads and sea routes led to the exchange not only of goods, but also ideas between eastern and western civilizations. Go to Chapter 6, *Ancient China,* for help.

SS.6.W.4.11 **Explain the rise and expansion of the Mongol empire and its effects on peoples of Asia and Europe including the achievements of Ghengis and Kublai Khan.**

What does it mean?

Trace the rise of the Mongol empire and describe how the spread of Mongol control affected peoples across Asia and Europe. Identify the key achievements of Ghengis and Kublai Khan. Go to Chapter 14, *China,* for help.

SS.6.W.4.12 **Identify the causes and effects of Chinese isolation and the decision to limit foreign trade in the 15th century.**

What does it mean?

Explain why China entered into a period of isolation beginning in the 15th century, and describe the major effects of that decision. Go to Chapter 14, *China,* for help.

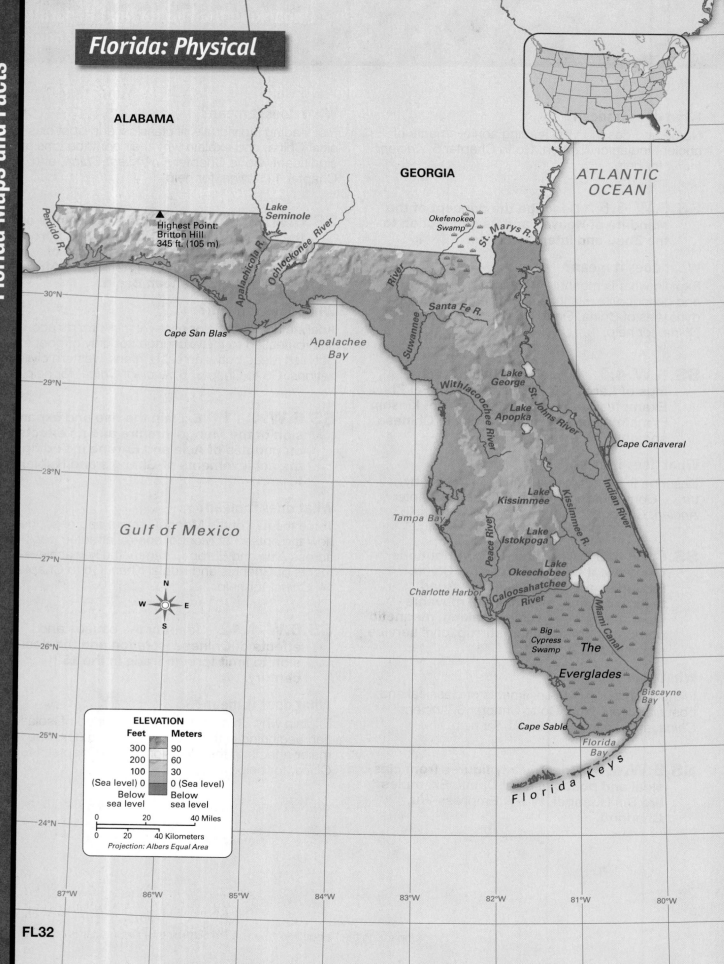

Florida: Physical

ALABAMA

GEORGIA

ATLANTIC OCEAN

Perdido R.

Lake Seminole

▲ Highest Point: Britton Hill 345 ft. (105 m)

Okefenokee Swamp

St. Marys R.

Apalachicola R.

Ochlockonee River

Cape San Blas

River

Suwannee

Santa Fe R.

30°N

Apalachee Bay

Withlacoochee River

Lake George

St. Johns River

29°N

Lake Apopka

Cape Canaveral

28°N

Gulf of Mexico

Lake Kissimmee

Kissimmee R.

Indian River

Tampa Bay

Lake Istokpoga

27°N

Peace River

Lake Okeechobee

N
W   E
S

Charlotte Harbor

Caloosahatchee River

Miami Canal

26°N

Big Cypress Swamp

The

Everglades

Biscayne Bay

Cape Sable

25°N

Florida Bay

ELEVATION

Feet	Meters
300	90
200	60
100	30
(Sea level) 0	0 (Sea level)
Below sea level	Below sea level

0   20   40 Miles

0   20   40 Kilometers

Projection: Albers Equal Area

Florida Keys

24°N

87°W   86°W   85°W   84°W   83°W   82°W   81°W   80°W

Florida: Political

ALABAMA

GEORGIA

ATLANTIC OCEAN

Lake Seminole

Perdido R.

De Funiak Springs

Gonzalez

Marianna

Navarre

Pensacola

Panama City

Apalachicola R.

Ochlockonee River

★ Tallahassee

Crawfordville

Perry

River

Live Oak

Santa Fe R.

Starke

Suwannee

Gainesville

Chiefland

Ocala

Withlacoochee River

Lake George

Apalachicola

Apalachee Bay

St. Marys R.

Fernandina Beach
Timucuan Ecological and Historic Preserve

Jacksonville

St. Augustine

Palatka

Palm Coast

Daytona Beach

Lake Apopka

St. Johns River

Deltona

Canaveral National Seashore

Homosassa Springs

Titusville

Spring Hill

Orlando

Cocoa Beach

Tarpon Springs

Winter Haven

Melbourne

Clearwater

Tampa

Lake Kissimmee

Sebastian

St. Petersburg

Indian River

Vero Beach

Tampa Bay

Wauchula

Kissimmee R.

Bradenton

Lake Istokpoga

Port St. Lucie

Sarasota

Peace River

Okeechobee

Jupiter

Lake Okeechobee

Port Charlotte

West Palm Beach

Charlotte Harbor

Caloosahatchee River

Cape Coral

Ft. Myers

Miami Canal

Bonita Springs

Deerfield Beach
Ft. Lauderdale

Naples

Big Cypress National Preserve

Hollywood

Hialeah

Marco Island

Miami

Biscayne Bay

Everglades National Park

Homestead

Florida Bay

Key West

Marathon

Gulf of Mexico

N W E S

★ State capital
• Other cities

0   20   40 Miles
0 20 40 Kilometers
Projection: Albers Equal Area

30°N
29°N
28°N
27°N
26°N
25°N
24°N

87°W 86°W 85°W 84°W 83°W 82°W 81°W 80°W

Governors of the State of Florida

Military Governor

Andrew Jackson
(March 10–November 12, 1821)

Territorial Governors

William DuVal (1822–1834)
John Henry Eaton (1834–1836)
Richard Keith Call (1836–1839)
Robert Raymond Reid (1839–1841)
Richard Keith Call (1841–1844)
John Branch (1844–1845)

State Governors

William Dunn Moseley (1845–1849)
Thomas Brown (1849–1853)
James E. Broome (1853–1857)
Madison Starke Perry
(1857–1861)
John Milton (1861–1865)
Abraham Kurkindolle Allison
(April 1–May 19, 1865)
William Marvin
(July 13–December 20, 1865)
David Shelby Walker (1865–1868)

Harrison Reed (1868–1873)
Ossian B. Hart (1873–1874)
Marcellus L. Stearns (1874–1877)
George Franklin Drew (1877–1881)
William D. Bloxham (1881–1885)
Edward A. Perry (1885–1889)
Francis P. Fleming (1889–1893)
Henry L. Mitchell (1893–1897)
William D. Bloxham (1897–1901)
William S. Jennings (1901–1905)
Napoleon Bonaparte
Broward (1905–1909)
Albert Gilchrist (1909–1913)
Park Trammell (1913–1917)
Sidney Catts (1917–1921)
Cary Hardee (1921–1925)
John Martin (1925–1929)
Doyle Carlton (1929–1933)
Dave Sholtz (1933–1937)
Fred Cone (1937–1941)
Spessard Holland (1941–1945)
Millard Caldwell (1945–1949)
Fuller Warren (1949–1953)

State flag

Dan McCarty
(January 6– September 28, 1953)
Charley Johns (1953–1955)
LeRoy Collins (1955–1961)
Farris Bryant (1961–1965)
Haydon Burns (1965–1967)
Claude Kirk (1967–1971)
Reubin Askew (1971–1979)
Bob Graham (1979–1987)
Wayne Mixson (January 3–6, 1987)
Bob Martinez (1987–1991)
Lawton Chiles (1991–1998)
Buddy MacKay (1998–1999)
Jeb Bush (1999–2007)
Charlie Crist (2007–2011)
Rick Scott (January 4, 2011–)

Florida Government

Executive Branch	Legislative Branch	Judicial Branch
Carries out the laws and policies of state government	Makes state laws	Interprets state laws

Executive Branch — Governor
- Elected by voters to a four-year term
- May serve two consecutive terms
- Signs bills into laws and has veto power

Lieutenant Governor
- Elected along with the governor to a four-year term
- Would become governor should the office become vacant due to death, impeachment trial, or incapacity

Florida Cabinet
- Consists of the Attorney General, the Commissioner of Agriculture, and the Chief Financial Officer
- Independently elected to four-year terms
- Serve as chief advisors to the governor

Legislative Branch — Bicameral System
- Legislature made up of two houses, the Senate and the House of Representatives
- Both houses take part in drafting and passing laws

State Senate
- 40 members
- Elected to four-year terms
- No term limits

House of Representatives
- 120 members
- Elected to two-year terms
- No term limits

Judicial Branch — County Courts
- At least one judge per county
- Elected to six-year terms

Circuit Courts
- State's highest trial courts
- Judges elected to six-year terms
- Have most general jurisdiction

District Courts of Appeal
- More than 50 judges serve in 5 appellate districts
- Judges appointed by the governor, then retained or rejected by voters
- Six-year term if retained

Supreme Court
- Highest state court
- Consists of 7 justices
- Justices appointed by the governor, then retained or rejected by voters
- Six-year term if retained

Florida State Facts

State animal	Florida panther
State anthem	"Florida (Where the Sawgrass Meets the Sky)"
State beverage	Orange juice
State bird	Mockingbird
State butterfly	Zebra Longwing
State flower	Orange blossom
State freshwater fish	Largemouth bass
State marine mammal	Manatee
State reptile	Alligator
State saltwater fish	Sailfish
State saltwater mammal	Porpoise
State shell	Horse conch
State tree	Sabal palm
State wildflower	Coreoposis
Capital	Tallahassee
Song	"Old Folks at Home (Swanee River)"
Motto	In God We Trust
Nickname	The Sunshine State
Year of statehood	1845
Highest natural point	345 feet
Total area	58,560 square miles
National rank in total area	22
Total coastline	1,197 miles
Population	19,893,297 (2014 estimate)
National rank in population	3
Most populous city	Jacksonville
Most populous metropolitan area	Miami-Ft. Lauderdale
Largest lake	Lake Okeechobee, 700 square miles
Number of counties	67
Bordering states	Alabama, Georgia

Florida oranges

State reptile

Florida manatee

Florida Maps and Facts

Florida

SS.6.E.1.3 Describe the following economic concepts as they relate to early civilization: scarcity, opportunity cost, supply and demand, barter, trade, productive resources (land, labor, capital, entrepreneurship).

SPOTLIGHT ON
Economics

What Is Economics?

Economics may sound dull, but it touches almost every part of the human experience, past and present. Here are some examples of the kinds of economic choices you may have made yourself:

- Which pair of shoes to buy—the ones on sale or the ones you really like, which cost much more
- Whether to continue saving your money for the DVD player you want or use some of it now to go to a movie
- Whether to give some money to a fundraiser for a new park or to housing for the homeless

As these examples show, we can think of economics as a study of choices. These choices are the ones people make to satisfy their needs or their desires.

Governments make similar choices about the needs of their countries. What goods should be made? How should they be made? What services should be offered? Who should be able to buy these goods and services?

Studying economics will help you understand the choices made by other people. Learning from their experiences—and their mistakes—will help you better understand history and the world in which we live. It will also help you make better economic choices.

How Economies Work

People, businesses, and countries obtain the items they need and want through economic activities such as producing, selling, and buying goods or services. Countries differ in the amount of economic activity that they have and in the strength of their economies. The basics of every economy, however, remain the same.

Every economy is based on the exchange of goods and services. A **good** is an object or material that humans can purchase to satisfy their wants and needs. Goods can be anything from a flower seed to a ten-bedroom house. A **service** is any activity that is performed for a fee. The gardener who plants the seed and the housekeeper who cleans the house each provide a service. Teachers, doctors, and lawyers also provide services.

Every good or service has a price. Changes in prices usually result from the operation of the laws of supply and demand. **Supply** is the amount of goods and services that are made available by producers willing to sell them. The **law of supply** states that businesses will produce more products when they can sell them at

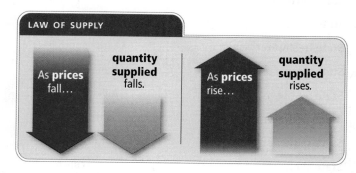

higher prices. They will produce fewer products when prices are low.

Demand is people's desire for a good (or service) and their ability to pay for it. The **law of demand** states that buyers will demand, or want, a greater quantity of a good when its price is low. Likewise, as prices rise, the quantity demanded falls. In other words, when the price of a good goes up, people buy less of that good.

The sale and purchase of goods and services are influenced by many factors. These factors include how many people want the good or service and the availability of a good or service. Opportunity cost also affects the exchange of goods and services. **Opportunity cost** is the value of what is given up when another good or service is chosen. Suppose you are a metal worker in the ancient Nubian city of Meroë. You use a piece of iron to create a farming tool. Because you used the iron to make a tool, you cannot use that same piece of iron to make a weapon. The opportunity cost of the farming tool is the value of the weapon that you did *not* make.

How Resources Are Used

The availability of goods and services also depends on the availability of the resources needed for those goods and services. A **resource** is a supply of something that is useful. There are three major kinds of resources: natural, human, and capital. A **natural resource** is any material in nature that people use and value. Like our civilization today, ancient civilizations needed natural resources such as water to survive. Ancient farmers, like farmers today, also needed land to farm. Human resources are the people needed to make a product or provide a service. These resources provide the **labor**, or work, that goes into a product or service. **Capital** is the wealth needed to provide a good or service. Capital resources can also include the technology needed to produce a good or provide a service.

Most goods and services use a combination of resources. For centuries, farmers in China have grown rice. Growing rice requires natural resources (land, water, rice seeds), human resources (farmers), and capital resources (money, tools). The ancient Greeks became skilled shipbuilders. They used natural resources (wood), human resources (ship builders), and capital resources (tools) to build the ships. The ships themselves became capital resources when they were used to help the Greeks trade.

Sometimes supply of a resource runs low. This is called **scarcity**. Scarcity can result from natural disasters, such as droughts. Ancient Egypt, for example, faced scarcity in the years when the Nile

Early farmers built irrigation systems to bring water to their fields.

River did not flood. The Black Death created a scarcity of labor during the Middle Ages. Scarcity can also result from overuse of a resource. In ancient Kush, for example, ironmakers used up the forests near Meroë. This overuse caused a scarcity of wood.

No matter the cause, scarcity can create serious problems for a civilization. Lack of water kills crops. Lack of crops means lack of food. Lack of food means people and animals go hungry. Going hungry can cause people and animals to die or to move their society somewhere new. Scarcity can weaken a civilization, as it did in ancient Kush. However, some civilizations had plans to deal with scarcity. For example, in ancient Egypt during prosperous years, the pharaoh and his officials made sure food was saved for years of scarcity.

Sometimes, scarcity occurs because a good or resource is difficult to find or acquire. Silks and spices from Asia, for example, were once scarce in Europe because of the time and effort it took to move the goods between continents. In these instances, scarcity adds to a product's value. High demand for scarce products can cause the prices of these goods to rise. Higher prices can cause buyers to look elsewhere for the products or to buy different products.

Surplus, the opposite of scarcity, occurs when a society has more of a resource or good than it can use. Ancient Egypt saved its surplus to use during years of scarcity. The Inca did the same. Other civilizations traded their surplus resources. In ancient Mesopotamia, farming techniques created a food surplus. This surplus meant fewer farmers were needed. As a consequence, ancient Mesopotamia became the first society to develop a division of labor.

Today farmers still build irrigation systems to bring water to their fields.

SS.6.E.1.2 Describe and identify traditional and command economies as they appear in different civilizations.

SS.6.E.3.2 Categorize products that were traded among civilizations, and give examples of barriers to trade of those products.

SS.6.E.3.3 Describe traditional economies (Egypt, Greece, Rome, Kush) and elements of those economies that led to the rise of a merchant class and trading partners.

Economic Systems

Civilizations throughout history have developed different systems to help them make economic choices about goods, resources, scarcity, and surplus. These systems help societies decide how resources are used, what goods and services to produce, how to produce them, and for whom to produce them. In ancient Athens, for example, all economic choices were once made by a small group of rich landowners, or aristocrats. In other cultures, economic choices were made by a king. All economic systems can be categorized as one of four types: traditional, command, market, or mixed.

In a **traditional economy**, production is based on customs and tradition. People grow their own food, make their own goods, and use barter to trade. This type of economy was common among early hunter-gatherer societies.

In a **command economy**, the government makes all economic decisions. Ancient Egypt had a command economy. The pharaoh controlled all the land and other resources. Pharaohs used some of these resources for large building projects, such as canals and pyramids.

The Inca also used a command economy. Government officials told each household what work to do and handed out resources to Inca households. Today the countries of Cuba and North Korea have command economies.

In a **market economy**, the government has little say about what, how, or for whom goods are produced. These economic choices are made by individuals instead. **Entrepreneurship**, the act of setting up a business, is a common feature of a market economy. An entrepreneur is an individual who takes on the risk of starting a business in order to make a profit. Entrepreneurship is more common in modern times than it was in ancient times. In fact, entrepreneurs played an important role in the Industrial Revolution of the nineteenth and twentieth centuries. Today Germany and the United States have market economies.

A **mixed economy** blends features of command, market, and traditional economies. The manor system used in medieval Europe was a mixed economy. The feudal lord assigned land to his subjects (command economy). Serfs grew their own food, made their own goods, and traded with each other for what they needed (traditional economy). The serfs also gave the lord a portion of their crops and goods (command economy). Today, most countries have a mixed economy.

How Goods and Resources Are Exchanged

All economic systems need ways to acquire goods and resources. People and businesses obtain the items they need by buying or trading goods and services. Countries trade with each other to obtain the resources, goods, and services they need. Very often, a country will have multiple trade partners. Some early civilizations, such as the Phoenicians and the Arabs, built large empires based on the trade of goods.

To trade successfully, ancient civilizations began to use money. **Money** is anything that people accept as payment for goods or services. At different times and places, money has taken a variety of forms. For example, in Africa, salt from the Sahara was once traded for gold from West Africa; and in southern Mexico, the ancient lowland Maya traded cacao and cotton for the jade and obsidian found in the Mayan highlands.

Traders from the north of Africa used camel caravans to carry huge slabs of salt to the south.

SS.6.E.3.1 Identify examples of mediums of exchange (currencies) used for trade (barter) for each civilization, and explain why international trade requires a system for a medium of exchange between trading both inside and among various regions.

SS.6.E.3.4 Describe the relationship among civilizations that engage in trade, including the benefits and drawbacks of voluntary trade.

Spotlight on Economics ···∨

Indian coin

Chinese paper money

Roman coin

Before the use of money, trade happened through **barter**—the direct exchange of goods or services for other goods or services. Today, most trade involves **currency,** or the paper money and coins used as a medium of exchange. The use of currency is rooted in the ancient world. Ancient India and Rome used coins. The ancient Chinese used both coins and paper money. Currency made trade easier within and among various regions. It had a standard value and was lighter to carry than bags of goods.

Trade between countries has not always been easy. Barriers can prevent or limit the amount of trade with a society. Sometimes barriers are geographic features, such as an ocean, a mountain range, or a desert. For example, the Atlantic Ocean prevented trade between Europe and the Americas until ships that could safely cross the ocean were built. In other cases, governments have created their own barriers to trade. In the 1600s, for example, Japanese leaders chose to cut off contact—and trade—with the rest of the world.

Despite the barriers, however, trade has always created ties between distant countries and cultures. Trade across the Silk Road, for example, established a connection between Europe and China. Because of this connection, the Black Death was carried from Asia to Europe by traders. Trade routes also helped in the spread of Islam and Christianity. Christianity traveled along the roads of the Roman Empire. Islam traveled along the caravan routes of the Arabian Peninsula and the international routes used by Arab merchants.

Over time, trade and technology have brought countries even closer together. This process is called **globalization**. Economic events in one country can affect other countries around the world. In the 1930s, for example, the United States suffered a Great Depression. The U.S. economy suffered a severe decline. Many businesses closed and many U.S. workers lost their jobs. Because of the economic ties between the United States and the rest of the world, the economic decline spread to Europe, Japan, and other parts of the world. In 2007, the United States again suffered an economic decline. Like the Great Depression, the effects of this decline also spread around the world. As these events show, the economic choices made by one country can have far-reaching consequences.

SPOTLIGHT ON
Geography

Maps

Latitude and Longitude   A **globe** is a scale model of the Earth. It is useful for showing the entire Earth or studying large areas of Earth's surface.

To study the world, geographers use a pattern of imaginary lines that circles the globe in east-west and north-south directions. It is called a **grid**. The intersection of these imaginary lines helps us find places on Earth.

The east-west lines in the grid are lines of **latitude**, which you can see on the diagram. Lines of latitude are called **parallels** because they are always parallel to each other. These imaginary lines measure distance north and south of the **equator**. The equator is an imaginary line that circles the globe halfway between the North and South Poles. Parallels measure distance from the equator in **degrees**. The symbol for degrees is °. Degrees are further divided into **minutes**. The symbol for minutes is ´. There are 60 minutes in a degree. Parallels north of the equator are labeled with an N. Those south of the equator are labeled with an S.

The north-south imaginary lines are lines of **longitude**. Lines of longitude are called **meridians**. These imaginary lines pass through the poles. They measure distance east and west of the **prime meridian**. The prime meridian is an imaginary line that runs through Greenwich, England. It represents 0° longitude.

Lines of latitude range from 0°, for locations on the equator, to 90°N or 90°S, for locations at the poles. Lines of longitude range from 0° on the prime meridian to 180° on a meridian in the mid-Pacific Ocean. Meridians west of the prime meridian to 180° are labeled with a W. Those east of the prime meridian to 180° are labeled with an E. Using latitude and longitude, geographers can identify the exact location of any place on Earth.

Your Spot in the World Use a globe to find the approximate latitude and longitude of where you live. Next find a major city that is located on about the same line of latitude. You can use a globe to identify approximate locations using latitude and longitude; however, you can use a GPS (global positioning system) to identify specific locations using latitude and longitude. Use a GPS, if one is available, to find the specific location of your school and your home.

Lines of Latitude

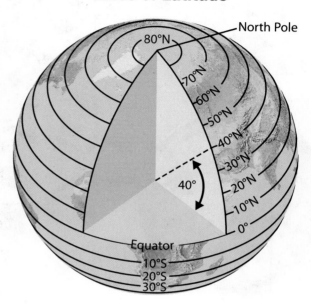

Lines of Longitude

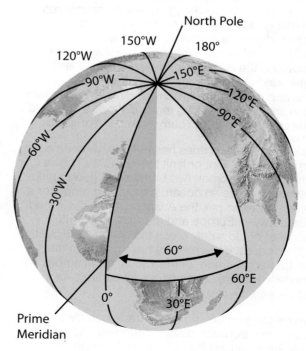

The equator divides the globe into two halves, called **hemispheres**. The half north of the equator is the Northern Hemisphere. The southern half is the Southern Hemisphere. The Roman and Aztec Empires were located in the Northern Hemisphere. The Inca Empire was in the Southern Hemisphere. The prime meridian and the 180° meridian divide the world into the Eastern Hemisphere and the Western Hemisphere. The Aztec, Inca, and Maya lived in the Western Hemisphere. The Egyptian and Persian Empires were in the Eastern Hemisphere. Look at the diagrams on this page. They show each of these four hemispheres.

Land and Water   Earth's land surface is divided into seven large landmasses, called **continents**. Landmasses smaller than continents and completely surrounded by water are called **islands**.

Geographers organize Earth's water surface into major regions too. The largest is the world ocean. Geographers divide the world ocean into the Pacific Ocean, the Atlantic Ocean, the Indian Ocean, and the Arctic Ocean. Lakes and seas are smaller bodies of water. Many early civilizations developed along bodies of water. The Roman Empire, for example, was centered on the Mediterranean Sea.

Northern Hemisphere

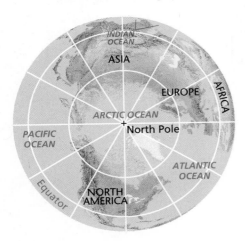

Southern Hemisphere

Western Hemisphere

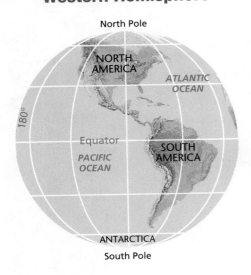

Eastern Hemisphere

Map Projections

A **map** is a flat diagram of all or part of Earth's surface. Mapmakers have created different ways of showing our round planet on flat maps. These different ways are called **map projections**. Because Earth is round, there is no way to show it accurately on a flat map. All flat maps are distorted in some way. Mapmakers must choose the type of map projection that is best for their purposes. Many map projections are one of three kinds: cylindrical, conic, or flat-plane.

Cylindrical projections are based on a cylinder wrapped around the globe. The cylinder touches the globe only at the equator. The meridians are pulled apart and are parallel to each other instead of meeting at the poles. This causes landmasses near the poles to appear larger than they really are. The map below is a Mercator projection, one type of cylindrical projection. The Mercator projection is useful for navigators because it shows true direction and shape. However, it distorts the size of land areas near the poles.

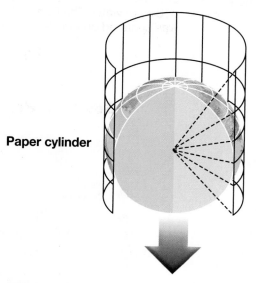

Paper cylinder

Mercator projection

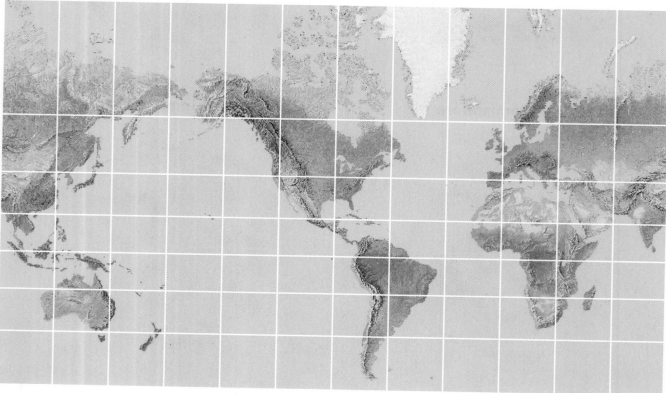

Conic projections are based on a cone placed over the globe. A conic projection is most accurate along the lines of latitude where it touches the globe. It retains almost true shape and size. Conic projections are most useful for showing areas that have long east-west dimensions, such as the United States.

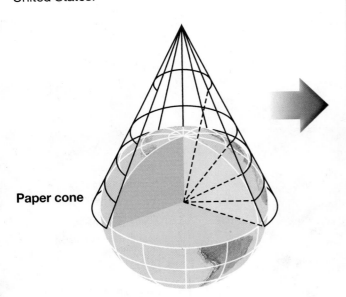

Paper cone

Conic projection

Flat-plane projections are based on a plane touching the globe at one point, such as at the North Pole or South Pole. A flat-plane projection is useful for showing true direction for airplane pilots and ship navigators. It also shows true area. However, it distorts the true shapes of landmasses.

Flat-plane projection

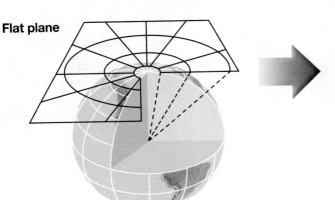

Flat plane

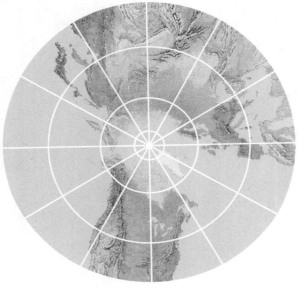

Reading a Map   Maps are like messages sent out in code. To help us translate the code, mapmakers provide certain features. These features help us understand the message they are presenting about a particular part of the world. Of these features, almost all maps have a title, a compass rose, a scale, and a legend. The map below has these four features, plus a fifth—a locator map.

❶ Title

A map's **title** shows what the subject of the map is. The map title is usually the first thing you should look at when studying a map, because it tells you what the map is trying to show.

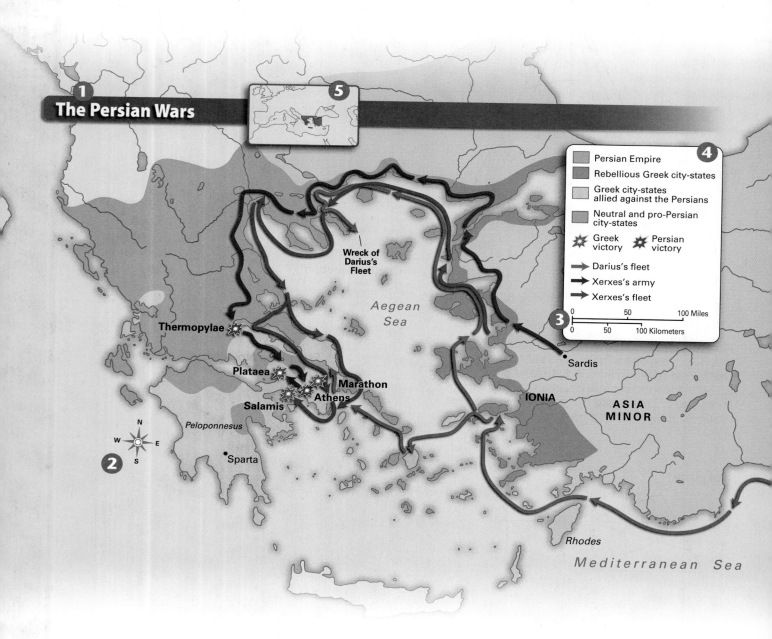

The Persian Wars

Legend:
- Persian Empire
- Rebellious Greek city-states
- Greek city-states allied against the Persians
- Neutral and pro-Persian city-states
- ✦ Greek victory
- ✦ Persian victory
- → Darius's fleet
- → Xerxes's army
- → Xerxes's fleet

Scale: 0 — 50 — 100 Miles
0 — 50 — 100 Kilometers

Labels on map: Wreck of Darius's Fleet, Aegean Sea, Thermopylae, Plataea, Marathon, Athens, Salamis, Peloponnesus, Sparta, Sardis, IONIA, ASIA MINOR, Rhodes, Mediterranean Sea

N W E S (compass rose)

❷ Compass Rose

A directional indicator shows which way north, south, east, and west lie on the map. North, south, east, and west are **cardinal directions**. Some mapmakers use a "north arrow," which points toward the North Pole. Remember, "north" is not always at the top of a map. The way a map is drawn and the location of directions on that map depend on the perspective of the mapmaker. Most maps in this textbook indicate direction by using a compass rose. A **compass rose** has arrows that point to all four principal directions. Sometimes a compass rose will also have arrows that point to intermediate directions. Northeast, northwest, southeast, and southwest are **intermediate directions**.

❸ Scale

Mapmakers use scales to represent the distances between points on a map. Scales may appear on maps in several different forms. The maps in this textbook provide a **bar scale**. Scales give distances in miles and kilometers.

To find the distance between two points on the map, place a piece of paper so that the edge connects the two points. Mark the location of each point on the paper with a line or dot. Then, compare the distance between the two dots with the map's bar scale. The number on the top of the scale gives the distance in miles. The number on the bottom gives the distance in kilometers. Because the distances are given in large intervals, you may have to approximate the actual distance on the scale.

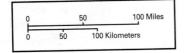

❹ Legend

The **legend**, or key, explains what the symbols on the map represent. Point symbols are used to specify the location of things, such as cities, that do not take up much space on the map. Some legends show colors that represent certain features like empires or other regions. Other maps might have legends with symbols or colors that represent features such as roads. Legends can also show economic resources, land use, population density, and climate.

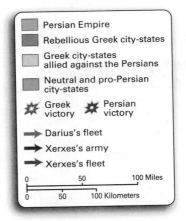

❺ Locator Map

A **locator map** shows where in the world the area on the map is located. The area shown on the main map is shown in red on the locator map. The locator map also shows surrounding areas so the map reader can see how the information on the map relates to neighboring lands.

Different Kinds of Maps   As you study the world's regions and countries, you will use a variety of maps. Political maps and physical maps are two of the most common types of maps you will study. In addition, you will use special-purpose maps. These maps might show climate, population, resources, ancient empires, or other topics.

Political maps show the major political features of a region. These features include country borders, capital cities, and other places. Political maps use different colors to represent countries, and capital cities are often shown with a special star symbol.

The Aztec Empire

SIERRA MADRE ORIENTAL

Lerma River

Tula

Lake Texcoco

Tenochtitlán

Texcoco

Tlacopán

Tlaxcala

Balsas River

SIERRA MADRE DEL SUR

PACIFIC OCEAN

Gulf of Mexico

Cempoala

Teotitlán

Bay of Campeche

Mitla

Isthmus of Tehuantepec

Xoconocho

The Aztecs' magnificent capital, Tenochtitlán, was built on an island in Lake Texcoco.

Aztec Empire

0   50   100 Miles

0   50   100 Kilometers

Spotlight on Geography ....∨

Physical maps show the major physical features of a region. These features may include mountain ranges, rivers, oceans, islands, deserts, and plains. Often, these maps use different colors to represent different elevations of land. As a result, the map reader can easily see which areas are high elevations, like mountains, and which areas are lower.

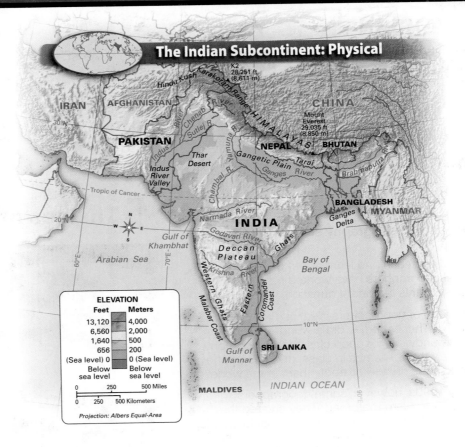

The Indian Subcontinent: Physical

K2 28,251 ft (8,611 m)
Mount Everest 29,035 ft (8,850 m)

IRAN
AFGHANISTAN
CHINA
Hindu Kush
Karakoram Range
HIMALAYAS
Chenab R.
Sutlej R.
Indus River
PAKISTAN
NEPAL
BHUTAN
Thar Desert
Gangetic Plain
Tarai
Yamuna R.
Ganges River
Brahmaputra River
Indus River Valley
Tropic of Cancer
Chambal R.
BANGLADESH
MYANMAR
30°N
Narmada River
Ganges Delta
INDIA
20°N
Godavari River
Gulf of Khambhat
Deccan Plateau
Ghats
Bay of Bengal
Arabian Sea
Krishna River
Western Ghats
Eastern Ghats
60°E
70°E
Malabar Coast
Coromandel Coast
10°N
Gulf of Mannar
SRI LANKA
MALDIVES
INDIAN OCEAN
80°E
90°E

ELEVATION

Feet	Meters
13,120	4,000
6,560	2,000
1,640	500
656	200
(Sea level) 0	0 (Sea level)
Below sea level	Below sea level

0   250   500 Miles
0   250   500 Kilometers

Projection: Albers Equal-Area

Special-purpose maps focus on one special topic, such as climate, resources, or population. These maps present information on the topic that is particularly important in the region. Depending on the type of special-purpose map, the information may be shown with different colors, arrows, dots, or other symbols. For example, the dot-density, or choropleth, map (at right) shows the distribution of the population of ancient Egypt. Each dot represents 500 people. The dots are clustered around the Nile River with no dots in the desert area away from the river.

Using Maps in Geography
The different kinds of maps in this textbook will help you study and understand geography. By working with these maps, you will see what the physical geography of places is like, where people live, and how the world has changed over time.

Different Views As you work with the maps in your textbook, get a different view by comparing the map to satellite images and aerial photographs of the same area. You can find these, along with online mapping resources, by doing some research on the Internet.

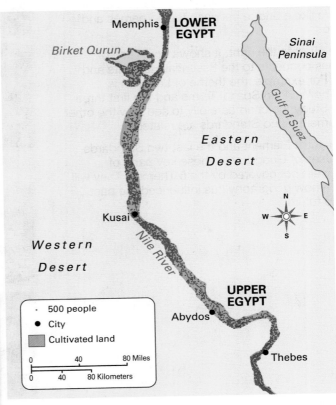

Memphis
LOWER EGYPT
Birket Qurun
Sinai Peninsula
Gulf of Suez
Eastern Desert
Kusai
Western Desert
Nile River
UPPER EGYPT
Abydos
Thebes

• 500 people
● City
Cultivated land

0   40   80 Miles
0   40   80 Kilometers

SPOTLIGHT ON
Geography

Themes and Essential Elements of Geography

To study the world, geographers have identified 5 key themes, 6 essential elements, and 18 geography standards.

"How should we teach and learn about geography?" Professional geographers have worked hard over the years to answer this important question.

In 1984 a group of geographers identified the 5 Themes of Geography. These themes did a wonderful job of laying the groundwork for good classroom geography. Teachers used the 5 Themes in class, and geographers taught workshops on how to apply them in the world.

By the early 1990s, however, some geographers felt the 5 Themes were too broad. They created the 18 Geography Standards and the 6 Essential Elements. The 18 Geography Standards include more detailed information about what geography is, and the 6 Essential Elements are like a bridge between the 5 Themes and 18 Standards.

Look at the chart to the right. It shows how each of the 5 Themes connects to the Essential Elements and Standards. For example, the theme of Location is related to The World in Spatial Terms and the first three Standards. Study the chart carefully to see how the other themes, elements, and Standards are related.

The last Essential Element and the last two Standards cover The Uses of Geography. These key parts of geography were not covered by the 5 Themes. They will help you see how geography has influenced the past, present, and future.

5 Themes of Geography

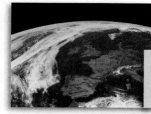

Location The theme of location describes where something is.

Place Place describes the features that make a site unique.

Regions Regions are areas that share common characteristics.

Movement This theme looks at how and why people and things move.

Human-Environment Interaction People interact with their environment in many ways.

SS.6.G.6.1 Describe the Six Essential Elements of Geography (The World in Spatial Terms, Places and Regions, Physical Systems, Human Systems, Environment, The Uses of Geography) as the organizing framework for understanding the world and its people.

6 Essential Elements

18 Geography Standards

1. How to use maps and other tools
2. How to use mental maps to organize information
3. How to analyze the spatial organization of people, places, and environments

I. The World in Spatial Terms

4. The physical and human characteristics of places
5. How people create regions to interpret Earth
6. How culture and experience influence people's perceptions of places and regions

II. Places and Regions

7. The physical processes that shape Earth's surface
8. The distribution of ecosystems on Earth

9. The characteristics, distribution, and migration of human populations
10. The complexity of Earth's cultural mosaics
11. The patterns and networks of economic interdependence on Earth

III. Physical Systems

12. The patterns of human settlement
13. The forces of cooperation and conflict

IV. Human Systems

14. How human actions modify the physical environment
15. How physical systems affect human systems
16. The distribution and meaning of resources

V. Environment and Society

17. How to apply geography to interpret the past
18. How to apply geography to interpret the present and plan for the future

VI. The Uses of Geography

World History

ANCIENT CIVILIZATIONS

Houghton
Mifflin
Harcourt

HISTORY

Program Consultants

Contributing Author

Kylene Beers
Senior Reading Researcher
School Development Program
Yale University
New Haven, Connecticut

A former middle school teacher, Dr. Beers has turned her commitment to helping struggling readers into the major focus of her research, writing, speaking, and teaching. She is the former editor of the National Council of Teachers of English literacy journal *Voices from the Middle* and has also served as NCTE president. Her published works include *When Kids Can't Read: What Teachers Can Do* (Heinemann, 2002).

General Editor

Frances Marie Gipson
Secondary Literacy
Los Angeles Unified School District
Los Angeles, California

In her current position, Frances Gipson guides reform work for secondary instruction and supports its implementation. She has designed curriculum at the district, state, and national levels. Her leadership of a coaching collaborative with UCLA's Subject Matter Projects evolved from her commitment to rigorous instruction and to meeting the needs of diverse learners.

Senior Literature and Writing Specialist

Carol Jago
English Department Chairperson
Santa Monica High School
Santa Monica, California

An English teacher at the middle and high school levels for 26 years, Carol Jago also directs the Reading and Literature Project at UCLA. She has been published in numerous professional journals and has authored several books, including *Cohesive Writing: Why Concept Is Not Enough* (Boynton/Cook, 2002). She became president of the National Council of Teachers of English (NCTE) in 2010.

Consultants

John Ferguson, M.T.S., J.D.
Senior Religion Consultant
Assistant Professor
Political Science/Criminal Justice
Howard Payne University
Brownwood, Texas

Rabbi Gary M. Bretton-Granatoor
Religion Consultant
Director of Interfaith Affairs
Anti-Defamation League
New York, New York

J. Frank Malaret
Senior Consultant
Dean, Downtown and West Sacramento Outreach Centers
Sacramento City College
Sacramento, California

Kimberly A. Plummer, M.A.
Senior Consultant
History-Social Science Educator/ Advisor
Holt McDougal

Andrés Reséndez, Ph.D.
Senior Consultant
Assistant Professor
Department of History
University of California at Davis
Davis, California

Reviewers

Contents

↗ Online Resources
• Reading Like a Historian
• Geography and Map Skills Handbook
• Economics Handbook

HISTORY
MADE EVERY DAY.

HISTORY® is the leading destination for revealing, award-winning, original non-fiction series and event-driven specials that connect history with viewers in an informative, immersive and entertaining manner across multiple platforms. HISTORY is part of A+E Networks, a global entertainment media company that includes, among others, A&E®, HISTORY®, Lifetime®, H2®, FYI™, and LMN®.

HISTORY programming greatly appeals to educators and young people who are drawn into the visual stories our documentaries tell. Our Education Department has a long-standing record in providing teachers and students with curriculum resources that bring the past to life in the classroom. Our content covers a diverse variety of subjects, including American and world history, government, economics, the natural and applied sciences, arts, literature and the humanities, health and guidance, and even pop culture.

The HISTORY website, located at **www.history.com**, is the definitive historical online source that delivers entertaining and informative content featuring broadband video, interactive timelines, maps, games, podcasts and more.

"We strive to engage, inspire and encourage the love of learning..."

Since its founding in 1995, HISTORY has demonstrated a commitment to providing the highest quality resources for educators. We develop multimedia resources for K–12 schools, two- and four-year colleges, government agencies, and other organizations by drawing on the award-winning documentary programming of A&E Television Networks. We strive to engage, inspire and encourage the love of learning by connecting with students in an informative and compelling manner. To help achieve this goal, we have formed a partnership with Houghton Mifflin Harcourt.

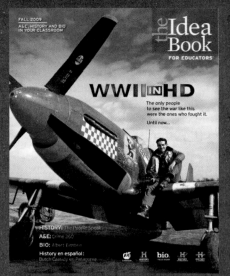
The Idea Book for Educators

Classroom resources that bring the past to life

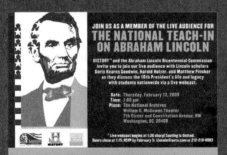
Live webcasts

HISTORY Take a Veteran to School Day

In addition to premium video-based resources, **HISTORY** has extensive offerings for teachers, parents, and students to use in the classroom and in their in-home educational activities, including:

▶ *The Idea Book for Educators* is a biannual teacher's magazine, featuring guides and info on the latest happenings in history education to help keep teachers on the cutting edge.

▶ **HISTORY Classroom (www.history.com/classroom)** is an interactive website that serves as a portal for history educators nationwide. Streaming videos on topics ranging from the Roman aqueducts to the civil rights movement connect with classroom curricula.

▶ **HISTORY email newsletters** feature updates and supplements to our award-winning programming relevant to the classroom with links to teaching guides and video clips on a variety of topics, special offers, and more.

▶ **Live webcasts** are featured each year as schools tune in via streaming video.

▶ **HISTORY Take a Veteran to School Day** connects veterans with young people in our schools and communities nationwide.

In addition to **HOUGHTON MIFFLIN HARCOURT**, our partners include the *Library of Congress*, the *Smithsonian Institution, National History Day, The Gilder Lehrman Institute of American History,* the *Organization of American Historians*, and many more. HISTORY video is also featured in museums throughout America and in over 70 other historic sites worldwide.

Become an Active Reader

Did you ever think you would begin reading your social studies book by reading about reading? Actually, it makes better sense than you might think. You would probably make sure you learned some soccer skills and strategies before playing in a game. Similarly, you need to learn some reading skills and strategies before reading your social studies book. In other words, you need to make sure you know whatever you need to know in order to read this book successfully.

Tip #1

Use the Reading Social Studies Pages

Take advantage of the two pages on reading at the beginning of every chapter. Those pages introduce the chapter themes; explain a reading skill or strategy; and identify key terms, people, and academic vocabulary.

Themes

Why are themes important? They help our minds organize facts and information. For example, when we talk about baseball, we may talk about types of pitches. When we talk about movies, we may discuss animation.

Historians are no different. When they discuss history or social studies, they tend to think about some common themes: Economics, Geography, Religion, Politics, Society and Culture, and Science and Technology.

Reading Skill or Strategy

Good readers use a number of skills and strategies to make sure they understand what they are reading. These lessons will give you the tools you need to read and understand social studies.

Key Terms, People, and Academic Vocabulary

Before you read the chapter, review these words and think about them. Have you heard the word before? What do you already know about the people? Then watch for these words and their meanings as you read the chapter.

Gives you practice in the reading skill or strategy.

Tells which theme or themes are important in the chapter

Explains a skill or strategy good readers use

Identifies the important words in the chapter.

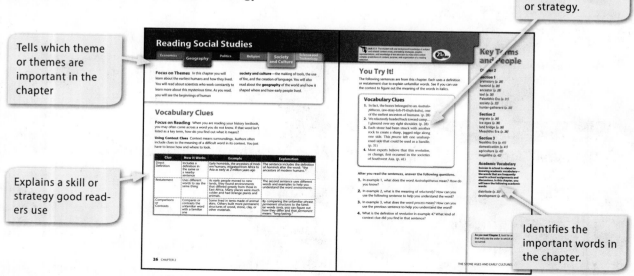

Tip #2
Read like a Skilled Reader

You will never get better at reading your social studies book—or any book for that matter—unless you spend some time thinking about how to be a better reader.

Skilled readers do the following:

- They use prereading strategies: that is, they preview what they are supposed to read before they actually begin reading. They look for vocabulary words, titles of sections, information in the margin, or maps or charts they should study.

- They divide notebook paper into two columns titled "Notes from the Chapter" and "Questions or Comments I Have." They take notes in both columns.

- They make graphic representations, such as charts and diagrams.

- They read like **active readers**. The Active Reading list below shows you what that means.

- They use clues in the text to help them figure out where the text is going. The best clues are called signal words.

Chronological Order Signal Words: *first, second, third, before, after, later, next, following that, earlier, finally*

Cause and Effect Signal Words: *because of, due to, as a result of, the reason for, therefore, consequently*

Comparison/Contrast Signal Words: *likewise, also, as well as, similarly, on the other hand*

Active Reading

Successful readers are **active readers**. These readers know that it is up to them to figure out what the text means. Here are some steps you can take to become an active, and successful, reader.

Predict what will happen next based on what has already happened. When your predictions don't match what happens in the text, re-read the confusing parts.

Question what is happening as you read. Constantly ask yourself why things have happened, what things mean, and what caused certain events.

Summarize what you are reading frequently. Do not try to summarize the entire chapter! Read a bit and then summarize it. Then read on.

Connect what is happening in the part you're reading to what you have already read, your existing background

knowledge, and your knowledge of related content areas.

Clarify your understanding. Stop occasionally to ask yourself whether you are confused by anything. You may need to re-read to clarify, or you may need to read further and collect more information before you can understand.

Visualize what is happening in the text. Try to see the events or places in your mind by drawing maps, making charts, or jotting down notes about what you are reading.

Tip #3

Pay Attention to Vocabulary

It is no fun to read something when you don't know what the words mean, but you can't learn new words if you only use or read the words you already know. In this book, we know we have probably used some words you don't know. But, we have followed a pattern as we have used more difficult words.

Key Terms and People

At the beginning of each section you will find a list of key terms or people that you will need to know. Be on the lookout for those words as you read through the section.

Much of Egyptian religion **afterlife**, or life after death. T believed that the afterlife

Religion and Egyptian Life

The ancient Egyptians had strong religious beliefs. Worshipping the gods was a part of their everyday lives. Many Egyptian religious customs focused on what happened after people died.

The Gods of Egypt

Like Mesopotamians, Egyptians practiced polytheism. Before the First Dynasty, each village worshipped its own gods. During the Old Kingdom, however, Egyptian officials tried to give some sort of structure to religious beliefs. Everyone was expected to worship the same gods, though how they worshipped the gods might differ from one region of Egypt to another.

The Egyptians built temples to the gods all over the kingdom. The temples collected payments from both the government and worshippers. These payments allowed the temples to grow more influential.

Over time, certain cities became centers for the worship of certain gods. In Memphis, for example, people prayed to Ptah, the creator of the world.

The Egyptians had gods for nearly everything, including the sun, the sky, and the earth. Many gods mixed human and animal forms. For example, Anubis, the god of the dead, had a human body but a jackal's head. Other major gods included
- Re, or Amon-Re, the sun god
- Osiris, the god of the underworld
- Isis, the goddess of magic, and
- Horus, a sky god, god of the pharaohs

Emphasis on the Afterlife

Much of Egyptian religion focused on the **afterlife**, or life after death. The Egyptians believed that the afterlife was a happy place. Paintings from Egyptian tombs show the afterlife as an ideal world where all the people are young and healthy.

The Egyptian belief in the afterlife stemmed from their idea of *ka* (KAH), or a person's life force. When a person died, his or her *ka* left the body and became a spirit. The *ka*, however, remained linked to the

CHAPTER 4

The griots' stories were both entertaining and informative. They told of important past events and of the accomplishments of distant ancestors. For example, some stories explained the rise and fall of the West African empires. Other stories described the actions of powerful kings and warriors. Some griots made their stories more lively by acting out the events like scenes in a play.

In addition to stories, the griots recited **proverbs**, or short sayings of wisdom or truth. They used proverbs to teach lessons to the people. For example, one West African proverb warns, "Talking doesn't fill the basket in the farm." This proverb reminds people that they must work to accomplish things. It is not enough for people just to talk about what they want to do.

In order to tell their stories and proverbs, the griots memorized hundreds of names and events. Through this memorization **process** the griots passed on West African history from generation to generation. However, some griots confused names and

events in their heads. When this happened, the facts of some historical events became distorted. Still, the griots' stories tell us a great deal about life in the West African empires.

West African Epics

Some of the griot poems are epics—long poems about kingdoms and heroes. Many of these epic poems are collected in the *Dausi* (DAW-zee) and the *Sundiata*.

The *Dausi* tells the history of Ghana. Intertwined with historical events, though, are myths and legends. One story is about a seven-headed snake god named Bida. This god promised that Ghana would prosper if the people sacrificed a young woman to him every year. One year a mighty warrior killed Bida. As the god died, he cursed Ghana. The griots say that this curse caused the empire of Ghana to fall.

The *Sundiata* is about Mali's great ruler. According to the epic, when Sundiata was still a boy, a conqueror captured Mali and killed Sundiata's father and 11 brothers

ACADEMIC
VOCABULARY
process a series
of steps by which
a task is
accomplished

Oral Traditions
West African storytellers called griots had the job of remembering and passing on their people's history. Here, people gather to perform traditional dances and to listen to the stories of a griot.

397

r.
as
d

ACADEMIC VOCABULARY

process a series of steps by which a task is accomplished

Academic Vocabulary

When we use a word that is important in all classes, not just social studies, we define it in the margin under the heading Academic Vocabulary. You will run into these academic words in other textbooks, so you should learn what they mean while reading this book.

Words to Know

As you read this social studies textbook, you will be more successful if you know or learn the meanings of the words on this page. There are two types of words listed here. The first list contains academic words, the words we pointed out at the bottom of the previous page. These words are important in all classes, not just social studies. The second list contains words that are special to this particular topic of social studies, world history.

Academic Words

acquire	to get
affect	to change or influence
agreement	a decision reached by two or more people in a group
aspect	part
authority	power or influence; right to rule
classical	referring to the cultures of ancient Greece and Rome
competition	a contest between two rivals
conflict	an open clash between two opposing groups
consequences	effects of a particular event or events
contracts	binding legal agreements
defend	to keep secure from danger
development	creation; the process of growing or improving
distribute	to divide among a group of people
efficient	productive and not wasteful
establish	to set up or create
features	characteristics
function	work or perform
ideals	ideas or goals that people try to live up to
influence	change, or have an effect on
innovation	a new idea, method, or device
logical	reasoned, or well thought out
method	a way of doing something
motive	reason for doing something
neutral	not engaged in either side
opposition	the act of opposing or resisting
policy	rule, course of action
primary	main, most important
principles	basic beliefs, rules, or laws
procedure	the way a task is accomplished
process	a series of steps by which a task is accomplished
purpose	the reason something is done
rebel	to fight against authority
role	a part or function; assigned behavior
strategy	a plan for fighting a battle or war
structure	the way something is set up or organized
values	ideas that people hold dear and try to live by
vary	to be different

Social Studies Words

AD	also CE, refers to dates after Jesus's birth
BC	also BCE, refers to dates before the birth of Jesus of Nazareth
BCE	refers to "Before Common Era," dates before the birth of Jesus of Nazareth
CE	refers to "Common Era," dates after Jesus's birth
century	a period of 100 years
civilization	the culture characteristic of a particular time or place
climate	the weather conditions in a certain area over a long period of time
culture	the knowledge, beliefs, customs, and values of a group of people
custom	a repeated practice; tradition
economy	the system in which people make and exchange goods and services
era	a period of time
geography	the study of the earth's physical and cultural features
physical features	the features on the land's surface, such as mountains and rivers
politics	government
region	an area with one or more features that make it different from surrounding areas
resources	materials found on the earth that people need and value
society	a group of people who share common traditions
trade	the exchange of goods or services

How to Make This Book Work for You

Studying history will be easy for you using this textbook. Take a few minutes to become familiar with the easy-to-use structure and special features of this history book. See how this textbook will make history come alive for you!

Unit

Each chapter of this textbook is part of a Unit of study focusing on a particular time period. Each unit opener provides an illustration, usually showing a young person of the period, and gives you an overview of the exciting topics that you will study in the unit.

Chapter

Each Chapter includes a chapter-opener introduction with a time line of important events, a Social Studies Skills activity, Chapter Review pages, and a Standardized Test Practice page.

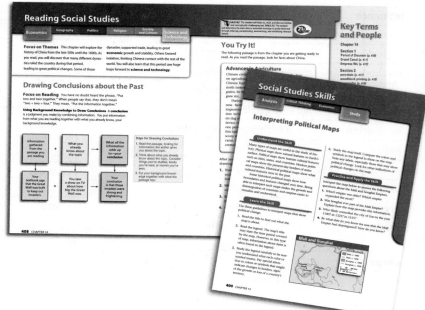

Reading Social Studies These chapter level reading lessons give you skills and practice that you can use to help you read the textbook. Within each chapter there is a Focus on Reading note in the margin on the page where the reading skill is covered. There are also questions in the Chapter Review activity to make sure that you understand the reading skill.

Social Studies Skills The Social Studies Skills lessons give you an opportunity to learn and use a skill that you will most likely use again. You will also be given a chance to make sure that you understand each skill by answering related questions in the Chapter Review activity.

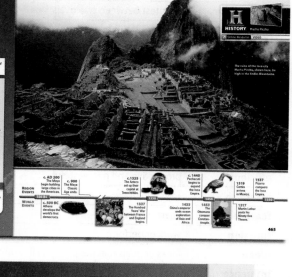

Section

The Section opener pages include Main Idea statements, an overarching big idea statement, and Key Terms and People. In addition, each section includes the following special features.

If You Were There . . . introductions begin each section with a situation for you to respond to, placing you in the time period and in a situation related to the content that you will be studying in the section.

Building Background sections connect what will be covered in this section with what you studied in the previous section.

Short sections of content organize the information in each section into small chunks of text that you shouldn't find too overwhelming.

Taking Notes suggestions and online graphic organizers help you read and take notes on the important ideas in the section.

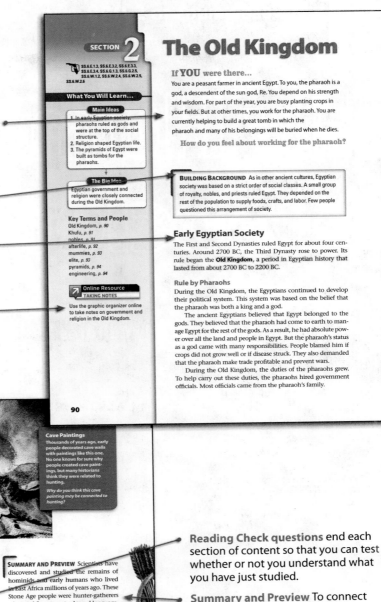

SECTION 2

SS.6.E.1.3, SS.6.E.3.2, SS.6.E.3.3, SS.6.E.3.4, SS.6.G.1.3, SS.6.G.2.5, SS.6.W.1.2, SS.6.W.2.4, SS.6.W.2.5, SS.6.W.2.6

What You Will Learn...

Main Ideas
1. In early Egyptian society, pharaohs ruled as gods and were at the top of the social structure.
2. Religion shaped Egyptian life.
3. The pyramids of Egypt were built as tombs for the pharaohs.

The Big Idea
Egyptian government and religion were closely connected during the Old Kingdom.

Key Terms and People
Old Kingdom, p. 90
Khufu, p. 91
nobles, p. 91
afterlife, p. 92
mummies, p. 93
elite, p. 93
pyramids, p. 94
engineering, p. 94

Online Resource
TAKING NOTES
Use the graphic organizer online to take notes on government and religion in the Old Kingdom.

The Old Kingdom

If YOU were there...

You are a peasant farmer in ancient Egypt. To you, the pharaoh is a god, a descendent of the sun god, Re. You depend on his strength and wisdom. For part of the year, you are busy planting crops in your fields. But at other times, you work for the pharaoh. You are currently helping to build a great tomb in which the pharaoh and many of his belongings will be buried when he dies.

How do you feel about working for the pharaoh?

BUILDING BACKGROUND As in other ancient cultures, Egyptian society was based on a strict order of social classes. A small group of royalty, nobles, and priests ruled Egypt. They depended on the rest of the population to supply foods, crafts, and labor. Few people questioned this arrangement of society.

Early Egyptian Society

The First and Second Dynasties ruled Egypt for about four centuries. Around 2700 BC, the Third Dynasty rose to power. Its rule began the **Old Kingdom**, a period in Egyptian history that lasted from about 2700 BC to 2200 BC.

Rule by Pharaohs

During the Old Kingdom, the Egyptians continued to develop their political system. This system was based on the belief that the pharaoh was both a king and a god.

The ancient Egyptians believed that Egypt belonged to the gods. They believed that the pharaoh had come to earth to manage Egypt for the rest of the gods. As a result, he had absolute power over all the land and people in Egypt. But the pharaoh's status as a god came with many responsibilities. People blamed him if crops did not grow well or if disease struck. They also demanded that the pharaoh make trade profitable and prevent wars.

During the Old Kingdom, the duties of the pharaohs grew. To help carry out these duties, the pharaohs hired government officials. Most officials came from the pharaoh's family.

90

Cave Paintings
Thousands of years ago, early people decorated cave walls with paintings like this one. No one knows for sure why people created cave paintings, but many historians think they were related to hunting.

Why do you think this cave painting may be connected to hunting?

Scholars know little about the religious beliefs of early people. Archaeologists have found graves that included food and artifacts. Many scientists think these discoveries are proof that the first human religions developed during the Stone Age.

READING CHECK Analyzing What was one possible reason for the development of language?

SUMMARY AND PREVIEW Scientists have discovered and studied the remains of hominids and early humans who lived in East Africa millions of years ago. These Stone Age people were hunter-gatherers who used fire, stone tools, and language. In the next section you will learn how early humans moved out of Africa and populated the world.

Section 1 Assessment

Reviewing Ideas, Terms, and People
1. **a. Identify** Who found the bones of Lucy?
   b. Explain Why do historians need archaeologists and anthropologists to study **prehistory**?
2. **a. Recall** What is the scientific name for modern humans?
   b. Make Inferences What might have been one advantage of walking completely upright?
3. **a. Recall** What kind of **tools** did people use during the **Paleolithic Era**?
   b. Design Design a stone and wood tool you could use to help you with your chores. Describe your tool in a sentence or two.
4. **a. Define** What is a **hunter-gatherer**?
   b. Rank In your opinion, what was the most important change brought by the development of language?

Critical Thinking
5. **Evaluate** Review the notes in your chart on the advances made by prehistoric humans. Using a graphic organizer like the one here, rank the three advances you think are most important. Next to your organizer, write a sentence explaining why you ranked the advances in that order.

| 1. | 2. | 3. |

FOCUS ON WRITING
6. **Listing Stone Age Achievements** Look back through this section and make a list of important Stone Age achievements. Which of these will you include on your storyboard? How will you illustrate them?

34 CHAPTER 2

Reading Check questions end each section of content so that you can test whether or not you understand what you have just studied.

Summary and Preview To connect what you have just studied in the section to what you will study in the next section, we include the Summary and Preview.

Section Assessments The section assessment boxes provide an opportunity for you to make sure that you understand the main ideas of the section. We also provide assessment practice online!

Early Humans and Societies

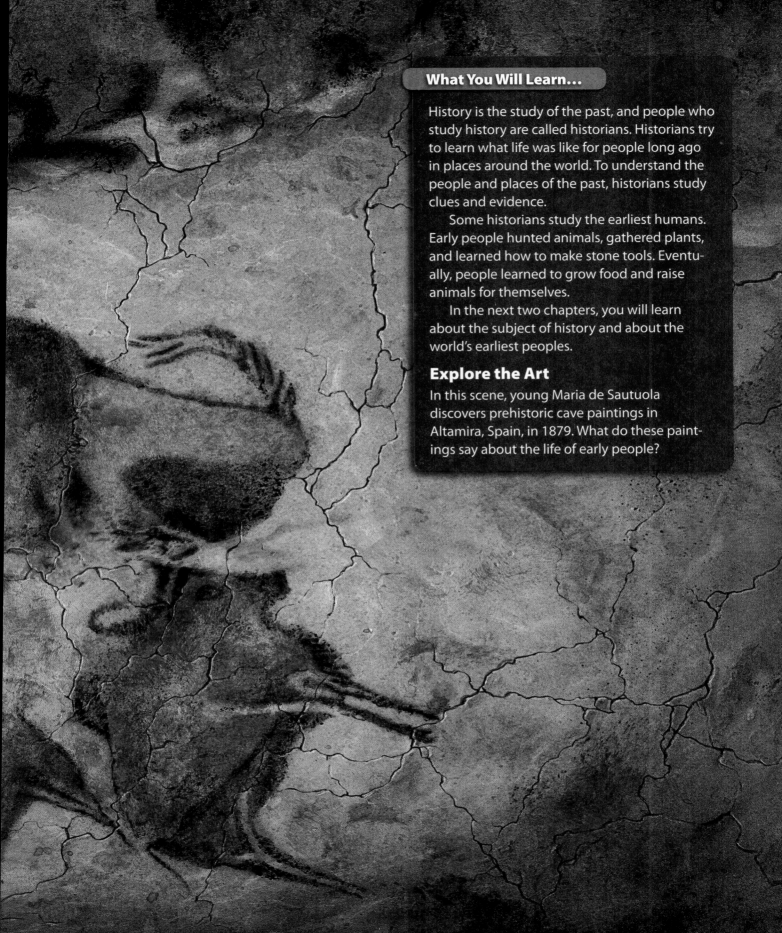

FLORIDA...
The Story Continues

CHAPTER 1, Uncovering the Past

Florida has a rich and diverse story that relates to your own individual story. As you study world history we want you to connect to Florida people, places, and events that are tied to the content and time period you will study in each chapter. The different Florida stories that are included in these features will keep you on the edge of your seat!

In each *Florida. . .The Story Continues* feature we highlight one of the chapter's Sunshine State Standards, "unpacking" that standard to explain what it means in an easy-to-understand manner. In addition to this featured standard, you can find all Sunshine State Standards for world history unpacked in the front of your textbook on pages FL8–FL31.

Some of these features will end with a "Spotlight On" note to remind you that there is additional Florida information related to that chapter in the front of your textbook on pages FL36–FL49. This information relates to world history Sunshine State Standards. You will see a list of these standards at the end of each relevant feature.

EVENTS **Present: Drought uncovers Native American canoes.**

Drought led to an important archaeological discovery in 2000. When water levels dropped in Newnan's Lake east of Gainesville, archaeologists discovered more than 100 Native American canoes. The dates of the canoes ranged from prehistoric times to the early 1900s. Nearly 70 percent of the canoes were between 3,000 and 5,000 years old! Each prehistoric canoe was carved from a single pine tree trunk using shell or rock tools and fire.

PEOPLE **Present: University of Florida paleontologist Bruce McFadden uncovers new facts about *Titanis walleri*, the "terror bird."** Bruce McFadden analyzed rare earth elements in fossils of the *Titanis walleri*. His findings overturned long-held scientific views. Scientists now know that the bird migrated to Florida millions of years earlier than thought and died out long before humans arrived.

PLACES **Present: Britton Hill in Walton County is Florida's highest point.**

Britton Hill is in the Florida panhandle near Lakewood. It rises 345 feet above sea level. This makes it Florida's tallest landform. Britton Hill might be tall for Florida, but not for other states. Britton Hill is the lowest highpoint in the nation!

EVENTS **Present: Florida's size is not what it used to be!** During the last ice age Florida was at least two times larger than it is today. It was also a much drier and cooler place to live. The many rivers, lakes, and wetlands of today did not exist. Sea levels rose as the ice age came to an end some 10,000 years ago. Waves and currents reshaped Florida's landforms. The climate also became much wetter. One result of these changes was the formation of the Everglades about 4,000 to 6,000 years ago.

Unpacking the Florida Standards <···

Read the following to learn what this standard says and what it means. See FL8–FL31 to unpack all of the standards related to this chapter.

Benchmark SS.6.W.1.5 Describe the roles of historians and recognize varying historical interpretations (historiography).

What does it mean?

Analyze how historians work to increase knowledge of the past, and understand that historians sometimes differ in their interpretations of historical events.

 SPOTLIGHT ON

SS.6.G.1.5, SS.6.G.2.1, SS.6.G.2.2, SS.6.G.2.7 See pages FL43–FL46 for content specifically related to these Chapter 1 standards.

Uncovering the Past

> **Essential Question** Why do scholars study the people, events, and ideas of long ago?

Florida Next Generation Sunshine State Standards

LA.6.1.6.1 The student will use new vocabulary that is introduced and taught directly. **LA.6.1.6.2** The student will listen to, read, and discuss familiar and conceptually challenging text. **LA.6.1.6.3** The student will use context clues to determine meanings of unfamiliar words. **SS.6.G.1.4** Utilize tools geographers use to study the world. **SS.6.G.1.5** Use scale, cardinal, and intermediate directions, and estimation of distances between places on current and ancient maps of the world. **SS.6.G.2.1** Explain how major physical characteristics, natural resources, climate, and absolute and relative locations have influenced settlement, interactions, and the economies of ancient civilizations of the world. **SS.6.G.2.2** Differentiate between continents, regions, countries, and cities in order to understand the complexities of regions created by civilizations. **SS.6.G.2.5** Interpret how geographic boundaries invite or limit interaction with other regions and cultures. **SS.6.G.2.7** Interpret choropleths or dot-density maps to explain the distribution of population in the ancient world. **SS.6.W.1.1** Use timelines to identify chronological order of historical events. **SS.6.W.1.2** Identify terms (decade, century, epoch, era, millennium, BC/BCE, AD/CE) and designations of time periods. **SS.6.W.1.3** Interpret primary and secondary sources. **SS.6.W.1.4** Describe the methods of historical inquiry and how history relates to the other social sciences. **SS.6.W.1.5** Describe the roles of historians and recognize varying historical interpretations (historiography). **SS.6.W.1.6** Describe how history transmits culture and heritage and provides models of human character.

FOCUS ON WRITING

A Job Description What is the job of a historian? an archaeologist? a geographer? In this **chapter** you will read about the work of people who study the past—its events, its people, and its places. Then you will write a job description to include in a career-planning guide.

HISTORY

Cult of Djedfre

Online Resource | VIDEO

This photo shows clay warriors that were found in China. Finds like these teach us a lot about the history of ancient places.

Reading Social Studies

| Economics | Geography | Politics | Religion | Society and Culture | Science and Technology |

Focus on Themes This chapter sets the stage for reading the rest of the book. In it you will learn the definitions of many important terms. You will learn how studying history helps you understand the past and the present. You will also read about the study of geography and learn how the world's physical features affected when and where civilization began. Finally, you will begin to think about how **society and culture** and **science and technology** have interacted throughout time.

Specialized Vocabulary of History

Focus on Reading Have you ever done a plié at the barre or sacked the quarterback? You probably haven't if you've never studied ballet or played football. In fact, you may not even have known what those words meant.

Specialized Vocabulary Plié, barre, sack, and quarterback are **specialized vocabulary**, words that are used in only one field. History has its own specialized vocabulary. The charts below list some terms often used in the study of history.

Terms that identify periods of time	
Decade	a period of 10 years
Century	a period of 100 years
Millennium	a period of 1,000 years
Epoch	a long period of time marked by a distinctiive development
Era	a long period of time marked by great events, developments, or figures

Terms used with dates	
circa or c.	a word used to show that historians are not sure of an exact date; it means "about"
BC	a term used to identify dates that occurred long ago, before the birth of Jesus Christ, the founder of Christianity; it means "before Christ." As you can see on the time line below, BC dates get smaller as time passes, so the larger the number the earlier the date.
AD	a term used to identify dates that occurred after Jesus's birth; it comes from a Latin phrase that means "in the year of our Lord." Unlike BC dates, AD dates get larger as time passes, so the larger the number the later the date.
BCE	another way to refer to BC dates; it stands for "before the common era"
CE	another way to refer to AD dates; it stands for "common era"

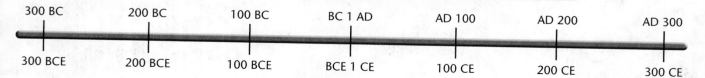

LA.6.1.6.1 The student will use new vocabulary that is introduced and taught directly. **LA.6.1.6.3** The student will use context clues to determine meanings of unfamiliar words. **SS.6.W.1.1** Use timelines to identify chronological order of historical events. **SS.6.W.1.2** Identify terms (decade, century, epoch, era, millennium, BC/BCE, AD/CE) and designations of time periods.

You Try It!

As you read this textbook, you will find many examples of specialized vocabulary terms that historians use. Many of these terms will be highlighted in the text and defined for you as key terms. Others may not be highlighted, but they will still be defined. For some examples, read the passage below. Learning these words as you come across them will help you understand what you read later in the book. For your own reference, you may wish to keep a list of important terms in your notebook.

Vocabulary in Context

We must rely on a variety of sources to learn history. For information on the very first humans, we have fossil remains. A **fossil** is a part or imprint of something that was once alive. Bones and footprints preserved in rock are examples of fossils.

As human beings learned to make things, by accident they also created more sources of information for us. They made what we call **artifacts**, objects created by and used by humans. Artifacts include coins, arrowheads, tools, toys, and pottery.

From Chapter 1, page 10

Answer the following questions about the specialized vocabulary of history.

1. What is a fossil? What is an artifact? How can you tell?

2. Were you born in a BC year or an AD year?

3. Put the following dates in order: AD 2000, 3100 BC, 15 BCE, AD 476, AD 3, CE 1215

4. If you saw that an event happened c. AD 1000, what would that mean?

Key Terms

Chapter 1

Section 1
history *(p. 6)*
culture *(p. 7)*
archaeology *(p. 7)*
fossil *(p. 10)*
artifacts *(p. 10)*
primary source *(p. 10)*
secondary source *(p. 10)*

Section 2
geography *(p. 12)*
landforms *(p. 12)*
climate *(p. 12)*
environment *(p. 13)*
region *(p. 15)*
resources *(p. 16)*

Academic Vocabulary

Success in school is related to knowing academic vocabulary—the words that are frequently used in school assignments and discussions. In this chapter, you will learn the following academic words:

values *(p. 8)*
absolute location *(p. 14)*
relative location *(p. 14)*
features *(p. 14)*

LA.6.1.6.1 The student will use new vocabulary that is introduced and taught directly.

As you read Chapter 1, keep a list in your notebook of specialized vocabulary words that you learn.

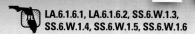
Studying History

LA.6.1.6.1, LA.6.1.6.2, SS.6.W.1.3, SS.6.W.1.4, SS.6.W.1.5, SS.6.W.1.6

What You Will Learn...

Main Ideas

1. History is the study of the past.
2. We can improve our understanding of people's actions and beliefs through the study of history.
3. Historians use clues from various sources to learn about the past.

The Big Idea

Historians use many kinds of clues to understand how people lived in the past.

Key Terms

history, *p. 6*
culture, *p. 7*
archaeology, *p. 7*
fossil, *p. 10*
artifacts, *p. 10*
primary source, *p. 10*
secondary source, *p. 10*

Online Resource
TAKING NOTES

Use the graphic organizer online to take notes about the clues historians use to understand the past.

SS.6.W.1.5 Describe the roles of historians and recognize varying historical interpretations (historiography).

If YOU were there...

You are a student helping scholars uncover the remains of an ancient city. One exciting day you find a jar filled with bits of clay on which strange symbols have been carved. You recognize the marks as letters because for years you have studied the language of the city's people. This is your chance to put your skills to use!

What might you learn from the ancient writings?

BUILDING BACKGROUND Last year you learned about our country's past. Now you begin a study of world history, which started many centuries before the history of the United States. You will find that we learn about world history in many ways.

The Study of the Past

The people of the ancient world didn't build skyscrapers, invent the automobile, or send spaceships to Mars. But they did remarkable things. Among their amazing feats were building huge temples, inventing writing, and discovering planets. Every step we take—in technology, science, education, literature, and all other fields—builds on what people did long ago. We are who we are because of what people did in the past.

What Is History?

History is the study of the past. A battle that happened 5,000 years ago and an election that happened yesterday are both parts of history.

Historians are people who study history. Their main concern is human activity in the past. They want to know how people lived and why they did the things they did. They try to learn about the problems people faced and how they found solutions.

Historians are interested in how people lived their daily lives. How and where did they work, fight, trade, farm, and worship? What did they do in their free time? What games did they play? In other words, historians study the past to understand people's **culture**—the knowledge, beliefs, customs, and values of a group of people.

What Is Archaeology?

An important field that contributes much information about the past is **archaeology** (ahr-kee-AH-luh-jee). It is the study of the past based on what people left behind.

Archaeologists, or people who practice archaeology, explore places where people once lived, worked, or fought. The things that people left in these places may include jewelry, dishes, or weapons. They range from stone tools to huge buildings.

Archaeologists examine the objects they find to learn what they can tell about the past. In many cases, the objects that people left behind are the only clues we have to how they lived.

READING CHECK **Comparing** How are the fields of history and archaeology similar?

THE IMPACT TODAY

Modern technology, including computers and satellite imagery, has allowed archaeologists to more easily locate and study objects from the past.

Studying the Past

Historians and archaeologists study the people and places of the past. For example, by studying the remains of an ancient Egyptian temple (right), they can learn about the lives of the ancient Egyptians (left).

Understanding through History

There are many reasons why people study history. Understanding the past helps us to understand the world today. History can also provide us with a guide to making better decisions in the future.

ACADEMIC VOCABULARY

values ideas that people hold dear and try to live by

Knowing Yourself

History can teach you about yourself. What if you did not know your own past? You would not know which subjects you liked in school or which sports you enjoyed. You would not know what makes you proud or what mistakes not to repeat. Without your own personal history, you would not have an identity.

History is just as important for groups as it is for individuals. What would happen if countries had no record of their past? People would know nothing about how their governments came into being. They would not remember their nation's great triumphs or tragedies. History teaches us about the experiences we have been through as a people. It shapes our identity and teaches us the **values** that we share.

SS.6.W.1.6 Describe how history transmits culture and heritage and provides models of human character.

Knowing Others

Like today, the world in the past included many cultures. History teaches about the cultures that were unlike your own. You learn about other peoples, where they lived, and what was important to them. History teaches you how cultures were similar and how they were different.

History also helps you understand why other people think the way they do. You learn about the struggles people have faced. You also learn how these struggles have affected the way people view themselves and others.

Understanding the World

History can help us understand the world around us. For example, why do these buildings in San Francisco look the way they do? The answer is history. These buildings are in a neighborhood called Chinatown, where Chinese immigrants began settling in the 1800s.

Immigrants painted these houses bright colors like the houses in China. Chinese-style roofs and pillars were also added.

Chinese people who moved to California brought their language with them. By studying the languages spoken in a region, historians can learn who settled there.

8

For example, Native Americans, European settlers, enslaved Africans, and Asian immigrants all played vital roles in our country's history. But the descendants of each group have a different story to tell about their ancestors' contributions.

Learning these stories and others like them that make up history can help you see the viewpoints of other peoples. It can help teach you to respect and understand different opinions. This knowledge helps promote tolerance. History can also help you relate more easily to people of different backgrounds. In other words, knowing about the past can help build social harmony throughout the world today.

Knowing Your World

History can provide you with a better understanding of where you live. You are part of a culture that interacts with the outside world. Even events that happen in other parts of the world affect your culture. History helps you to understand how today's events are shaped by the events of the past.

History is concerned with the entire range of human activities. It is the record of humanity's combined efforts. So while you are studying history, you can also learn more about math, science, religion, government, and many other topics. Political scientists and economists study history to better understand trends that shape government and the economy in the modern world.

Studying the past will also help you develop mental skills. History encourages you to ask important questions. It forces you to analyze the facts you learn. This skill helps you to find the main facts when studying any topic.

History also promotes good decision-making skills. A famous, often repeated saying warns us that those who forget their past are doomed to repeat it. This means

Primary Source

BOOK
History Makers

One way to study history is to study the "big names" of the past, the people who shaped the times in which they lived and became models of human character. In this passage from a collection of essays, historian Barbara W. Tuchman explains why some historians focus their attention on such people.

❚❚They are the captains and kings, saints and fanatics, traitors, rogues and villains, pathfinders and explorers, thinkers and creators, even, occasionally, heroes. They are significant—if not necessarily admirable . . . they *matter*. They are the actors, not the acted upon, and are consequently that much more interesting.**❚❚**

–Barbara W. Tuchman, from *Practicing History: Selected Essays*

ANALYSIS SKILL **ANALYZING PRIMARY SOURCES**

What words does the author use to make history sound interesting?

that people who ignore the results of past decisions often make the same mistakes over and over again.

Individuals and countries both benefit from the wisdom that history can teach. Your own history may have taught you that studying for a test results in better grades. In a similar way, world history has taught that providing young people with education makes them more productive when they become adults.

Historians have been talking about the value of history for centuries. More than 2,000 years ago a great Greek historian named Polybius wrote:

FOCUS ON READING
What does the word *century* mean?

❝The purpose of history is not the reader's enjoyment at the moment of perusal [reading it], but the reformation [improvement] of the reader's soul, to save him from stumbling at the same stumbling block many times over.**❞**

–Polybius, from *The Histories, Book XXXVIII*

READING CHECK **Summarizing** What are some benefits of studying history?

Clues from the Past

This archaeologist is examining ancient pottery in Lebanon to learn about the past.

Using Clues

SS.6.W.1.4 Describe the methods of historical inquiry and how history relates to the other social sciences.

We must rely on a variety of sources to learn history. For information on the very first humans, we have fossil remains. A **fossil** is a part or imprint of something that was once alive. Bones and footprints preserved in rock are examples of fossils.

As human beings learned to make things, by accident they also created more sources of information for us. They made what we call **artifacts**, objects created by and used by humans. Artifacts include coins, arrowheads, tools, toys, and pottery. Archaeologists examine artifacts and the places where the artifacts were found to learn about the past.

Sources of Information

About 5,000 years ago, people invented writing. They wrote laws, poems, speeches, battle plans, letters, contracts, and many other things. In these written sources, historians have found countless clues about how people lived. In addition, people have recorded their messages in many ways over the centuries. Historians have studied writing carved into stone pillars, stamped onto clay tablets, scribbled on turtle shells, typed with typewriters, and sent by computer.

Historical sources are of two types. A **primary source** is an account of an event created by someone who took part in or witnessed the event. Treaties, letters, diaries, laws, court documents, and royal commands are all primary sources. An audio or video recording of an event is also a primary source.

A **secondary source** is information gathered by someone who did not take part in or witness an event. Examples include history textbooks, journal articles, and encyclopedias. The textbook you are reading right now is a secondary source. The historians who wrote it did not take part in the events described. Instead, they gathered information about these events from different sources.

Written records, like this writing from a tomb in Egypt, are valuable sources of information about the past.

Sometimes, archaeologists must carefully reconstruct artifacts from hundreds of broken pieces, like they did with this statue of an Aztec bat god from Mexico.

Sources of Change

Writers of secondary sources don't always agree about the past. Historians form different opinions about the primary sources they study. As a result, historians may not interpret past events in the same way.

For example, one writer may say that a king was a brilliant military leader. Another may say that the king's armies only won their battles because they had better weapons than their enemies did. Sometimes new evidence leads to new conclusions. As historians review and reanalyze information, their interpretations can and do change.

READING CHECK **Contrasting** How are primary and secondary sources different?

SUMMARY AND PREVIEW We benefit from studying the past. Scholars use many clues to help them understand past events. In the next section you will learn how geography connects to history.

Section 1 Assessment

Reviewing Ideas, Terms, and People

1. **a. Identify** What is **history**?
   b. Explain What kinds of things do historians try to discover about people who lived in the past?
   c. Predict What kinds of evidence will historians of the future study to learn about your **culture**?
2. **a. Describe** How does knowing its own history provide a group with a sense of unity?
   b. Elaborate Explain the meaning of the phrase, "Those who forget their past are doomed to repeat it."
3. **a. Identify** What is a **primary source**?
   b. Explain How did the invention of writing affect the sources on which historians rely?
   c. Elaborate Could a photograph be considered a primary source? Why or why not?

Critical Thinking

4. **Categorizing** Using your notes, identify four types of clues to the past and give at least two examples of each.

clues

FOCUS ON WRITING

5. **Understanding What Historians Do** What is the difference between a historian and an archaeologist? Take notes about the work these people do.

LA.6.1.6.1, LA.6.1.6.2, SS.6.G.1.4,
SS.6.G.2.1, SS.6.G.2.2, SS.6.G.2.5,
SS.6.G.2.7, SS.6.W.1.3, SS.6.W.1.4

What You Will Learn...

Main Ideas

1. Geography is the study of places and people.
2. Studying location is important to both physical and human geography.
3. Geography and history are closely connected.

The Big Idea

Physical geography and human geography contribute to the study of history.

Key Terms

geography, *p. 12*
landforms, *p. 12*
climate, *p. 12*
environment, *p. 13*
region, *p. 15*
resources, *p. 16*

Online Resource
TAKING NOTES

Use the graphic organizer online to take notes on physical geography and human geography.

Studying Geography

If YOU were there...

Your parents are historians researching a city that disappeared long ago. You go with them to a library to help search for clues to the city's location and fate. While thumbing through a dusty old book, you find an ancient map stuck between two pages. Marked on the map are rivers, forests, mountains, and straight lines that look like roads. It is a map that shows the way to the lost city!

How can this map help you find the city?

BUILDING BACKGROUND You have read how historians and archaeologists help us learn about the past. Another group of scholars—geographers—also contribute to our study of history.

Studying Places and People

When you hear about an event on the news, the first questions you ask may be, "Where did it happen?" and "Who was there?" Historians ask the same questions about events that happened in the past. That is why they need to study geography. **Geography** is the study of the earth's physical and cultural features. These features include mountains, rivers, people, cities, and countries.

Physical Geography

Physical geography is the study of the earth's land and features. People who work in this field are called physical geographers. They study **landforms**, the natural features of the land's surface. Mountains, valleys, plains, and other such places are landforms.

Physical geographers also study **climate**, the pattern of weather conditions in a certain area over a long period of time. Climate is not the same as weather. Weather is the conditions at a specific time and place. If you say that your city has cold winters, you are talking about climate. If you say it is below freezing and snowing today, you are talking about the weather.

Physical Geography

The study of the earth's physical features and processes, such as mountains, rivers, oceans, rainfall, and climate, including this section of California's coast

Human Geography

The study of the earth's people, including their way of life, homes and cities, beliefs, and travels, such as these children in the African country of Tanzania

Geography

The study of the earth's physical and cultural features

Climate affects many features of a region. For example, it affects plant life. Tropical rain forests require warm air and heavy rain, while a dry climate can create deserts. Climate also affects landforms. For example, constant wind can wear down mountains into flat plains.

Although climate affects landforms, landforms can also affect climate. For example, the Coast Ranges in northern California are mountains parallel to the Pacific coast. As air presses up against these mountains, it rises and cools. Any moisture that the air was carrying falls as rain. Meanwhile, on the opposite side of the range, the Central Valley stays dry. In this way, a mountain range creates two very different climates.

Landforms and climate are part of a place's environment. The **environment** includes all the living and nonliving things that affect life in an area. This includes the area's climate, land, water, plants, soil, animals, and other features.

Human Geography

The other branch of geography is human geography—the study of people and the places where they live. Specialists in human geography study many different things about people and their cultures. What kind of work do people do? How do they get their food? What are their homes like? What religions do they practice?

Human geography also deals with how the environment affects people. For example, how do people who live near rivers protect themselves from floods? How do people who live in deserts survive? Do different environments affect the size of families? Do people in certain environments live longer? Why do some diseases spread easily in some environments but not in others? As you can see, human geographers study many interesting questions about people and this planet.

READING CHECK **Summarizing** What are the two main branches of geography?

Studying Location

Both physical and human geographers study location. Location tells where something is. Every place on Earth has an **absolute location** and many **relative locations**.

No two places in the world are exactly alike. Even small differences between places can lead to major differences in how people live. That is why geographers try to understand the effects that different locations have on human populations, or groups of people.

By comparing locations, geographers learn more about the factors that affected each of them. For example, they may study why a town grew in one location while a town nearby got smaller.

Learning from Maps

To study various locations, geographers use maps. A map is a drawing of an area. Some maps show physical **features**. Others show cities and the boundaries of states or countries. Most maps have symbols to show different things. For example, large dots often stand for cities. Blue lines show where rivers flow. Most maps also include a guide to show direction.

People have been making maps for more than 4,000 years. Maps help with many activities. Planning battles, looking for new lands, and designing new city parks all require good maps. On the first day of class, you may have used a map of your school to find your classrooms.

Studying Maps

By studying and comparing maps, you can see how a place's physical and human features are related.

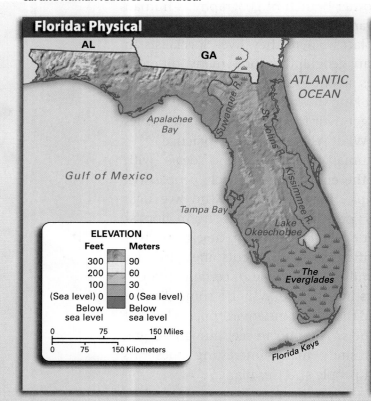

Florida: Physical

ELEVATION

Feet	Meters
300	90
200	60
100	30
(Sea level) 0	0 (Sea level)
Below sea level	Below sea level

0   75   150 Miles
0   75   150 Kilometers

Florida: Climates

Humid subtropical
Humid tropical

0   75   150 Miles
0   75   150 Kilometers

1 What are some of Florida's main physical features? Where are the state's highest elevations?

2 What climates are found in Florida? How are the climate regions related to Florida's physical features?

Learning about Regions

Scholars study areas that vary in size from entire continents to smaller areas, such as a region, a country, or even a single city. A **region** is an area with one or more features that make it different from surrounding areas. These features may be physical, such as forests or grasslands. There may also be differences in climate. For example, a desert area is a type of region. Physical barriers such as mountains and rivers often form a region's boundaries.

Human features can also define regions. An area with many cities is one type of region. An area with only farms is another type. Some regions are identified by the language that people there speak. Other regions are identified by the religion their people practice.

READING CHECK **Categorizing** What are some types of features that can identify a region?

Primary Source

BOOK

What Geography Means

Some people think of geography as the ability to read maps or name state capitals. But as geographer Kenneth C. Davis explains, geography is much more. It is related to almost every branch of human knowledge.

❝Geography doesn't simply begin and end with maps showing the location of all the countries of the world. In fact, such maps don't necessarily tell us much. No— geography poses fascinating questions about who we are and how we got to be that way, and then provides clues to the answers. It is impossible to understand history, international politics, the world economy, religions, philosophy, or 'patterns of culture' without taking geography into account.❞

–Kenneth C. Davis, from *Don't Know Much About Geography*

ANALYSIS SKILL **ANALYZING PRIMARY SOURCES**

Why does the writer think that geography is important?

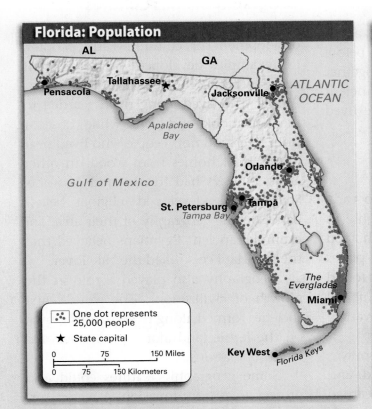

3 Where are Florida's two main population centers? What kind of climate is found in these areas?

4 How are Florida's roads related to its physical features? How are they related to its population centers?

One way you can see how geography has shaped history is by studying the locations of cities. Certain locations have strategic advantages over others, and as a result, people choose to create cities there. For example, the city of Rio de Janeiro, Brazil, has easy access to the ocean and breathtaking scenery.

SS.6.W.1.4 Describe the methods of historical inquiry and how history relates to the other social sciences.

Geography and History

Geography gives us important clues about the people and places that came before us. Like detectives, we can piece together a great deal of information about ancient cultures by knowing where people lived and what the area was like.

Geography Affects Resources

An area's geography was critical to early settlements. People could survive only in areas where they could get enough food and water. Early people settled in places that were rich in **resources**, materials found in the earth that people need and value. All through history, people have used a variety of resources to meet their basic needs.

In early times, essential resources included water, animals, fertile land, and stones for tools. Over time, people learned to use other resources, including metals such as copper, gold, and iron.

Geography Shapes Cultures

Geography also influenced the early development of cultures. Early peoples, for example, developed vastly different cultures because of their environments. People who lived along rivers learned to make fishhooks and boats, while those far from rivers did not. People who lived near forests built homes from wood. In other areas, builders had to use mud or stone. Some people developed religious beliefs based on the geography of their area. For example, ancient Egyptians believed that the god Hapi controlled the Nile River.

Geography also played a role in the growth of civilizations. The world's first societies formed along rivers. Crops grown on the fertile land along these rivers fed large populations.

Some geographic features could also protect areas from invasion. A region surrounded by mountains or deserts, for example, was hard for attackers to reach.

environments in positive and negative ways. People have planted millions of trees. They have created new lakes in the middle of deserts. But people have also created wastelands where forests once grew and built dams that flooded ancient cities. This interaction between humans and their environment has been a major factor in history. It continues today.

READING CHECK **Summarizing** In what ways has geography shaped human history?

SUMMARY AND PREVIEW The field of geography includes physical geography and human geography. Geography has had a major influence on history. In the next chapter you will learn how geography affected the first people.

Geography Influences History

Geography has helped shape history and has affected the growth of societies. People in areas with many natural resources could use their resources to get rich. They could build glorious cities and powerful armies. Features such as rivers also made trade easier. Many societies became rich by trading goods with other peoples.

On the other hand, geography has also caused problems. Floods, for example, have killed millions of people. Lack of rainfall has brought deadly food shortages. Storms have wrecked ships, and with them, the hopes of conquerors. In the 1200s, for example, a people known as the Mongols tried to invade Japan. However, most of the Mongol ships were destroyed by a powerful storm. Japanese history may have been very different if the storm had not occurred.

The relationship between geography and people has not been one-sided. For centuries, people have influenced their

Section 2 Assessment

Reviewing Ideas, Terms, and People

1. **a. Define** What is **geography**?
   b. Summarize What are some of the topics included in human geography?
2. **a. Describe** Identify a **region** near where you live, and explain what sets it apart as a region.
   b. Predict How might a map of a city's **landforms** help an official who is planning a new city park?
3. **a. Recall** Where did early peoples tend to settle?
   b. Compare and Contrast How could a river be both a valuable **resource** and a problem for a region?

Critical Thinking

4. **Comparing and Contrasting**
   Using your note-taking chart, compare and contrast physical and human geography.

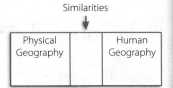

Similarities

Physical Geography		Human Geography

FOCUS ON WRITING

5. **Understanding What Geographers Do** In this section you learned how geographers contribute to the study of history. What is the difference between a physical geographer and a human geographer?

Mapping the Past

Maps are useful tools for historians. By creating a map of how a place used to be, historians can learn where things were located and what the place was like. In other words, by studying a place's geography, we can also learn something about its history.

This map shows the ancient city of Teotihuacán (tay-oh-tee-wah-KAHN) in central Mexico. Teotihuacán reached its height around AD 500. Study this map. What can it tell you about the history of the city?

Pyramid of the Moon

Teotihuacán, c. AD 500

Pyramid of the Moon

Pyramid of the Sun

Houses

San Juan River

Street of the Dead

Citadel

San Lorenzo River

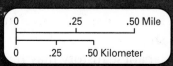

| 0 | .25 | .50 Mile |
| 0 | .25 | .50 Kilometer |

Size and Importance As the map shows, Teotihuacán was a large city. It had many buildings and a large population. From this, you might conclude that the city was important, just as big cities are important today.

Religion The giant buildings that dominate the heart of the city, such as the Pyramid of the Sun, are religious temples. From this, you can conclude that religion was very important to the people of Teotihuacán.

Pyramid of the Sun

Citadel

Street of the Dead

San Juan River

Technology The map shows that this river turns at right angles, just like the city's streets. The people of Teotihuacán must have changed the course of this river. That tells you that they had advanced engineering skills and technology.

GEOGRAPHY SKILLS **INTERPRETING MAPS**

1. **Place** How does the map indicate that Teotihuacán was an important place?
2. **Location** What can you conclude from the fact that large religious buildings are located in the heart of the city?

19

Social Studies Skills

Recognizing Bias

Understand the Skill

Everybody has convictions, or things that they strongly believe. However, if we form opinions about people or events based only on our beliefs, we may be showing bias. Bias is an idea about someone or something based solely on opinions, not facts.

There are many types of bias. Sometimes people form opinions about others based on the group to which that person belongs. For example, some people might believe that all teenagers are selfish or that all politicians are dishonest. These are examples of a type of bias called *stereotyping*. Holding negative opinions of people based on their race, religion, age, gender, or similar characteristics is known as *prejudice*.

We should always be on guard for the presence of personal biases. Such biases can slant how we view, judge, and provide information. Honest and accurate communication requires people to be as free of bias as possible.

Learn the Skill

As you read or write, watch out for biases. One way to identify a bias is to look for facts that support a statement. If a belief seems unreasonable when compared to the facts, it may be a sign of bias.

Another sign of bias is a person's unwillingness to question his or her belief if it is challenged by evidence. People sometimes cling to views that evidence proves are wrong. This is why bias is defined as a "fixed" idea about something. It also points out a good reason why we should try to avoid being biased. Our biases can keep us from considering new ideas and learning new things.

You will meet many peoples from the past as you study world history. Their beliefs, behaviors, and ways of life may seem different or strange to you. It is important to remain unbiased and to keep an open mind. Recognize that "different" does not mean "not as good."

Understand that early peoples did not have the technology or the accumulation of past knowledge that we have today. Be careful to not look down on them just because they were less advanced or might seem "simpler" than we are today. Remember that their struggles, learning, and achievements helped make us what we are today.

The following guidelines can help you to recognize and reduce your own biases. Keep them in mind as you study world history.

1. When discussing a topic, try to think of beliefs and experiences in your own background that might affect how you feel about the topic.

2. Try to not mix statements of fact with statements of opinion. Clearly separate and indicate what you *know* to be true from what you *believe* to be true.

3. Avoid using emotional, positive, or negative words when communicating factual information.

Practice and Apply the Skill

Professional historians try to be objective about the history they study and report. Being *objective* means not being influenced by personal feelings or opinions. Write a paragraph explaining why you think being objective is important in the study of history.

Chapter Review

Visual Summary

Use the visual summary below to help you review the main ideas of the chapter.

QUICK FACTS

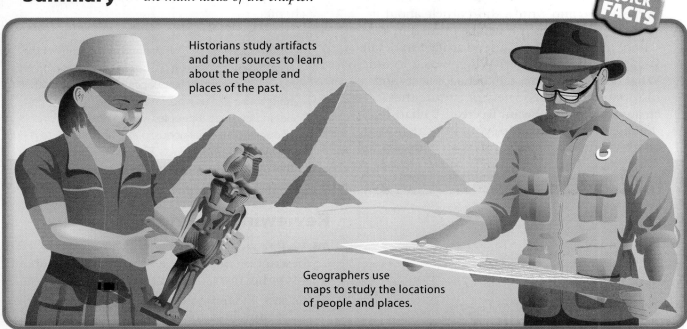

Historians study artifacts and other sources to learn about the people and places of the past.

Geographers use maps to study the locations of people and places.

Reviewing Vocabulary, Terms, and People

*For each statement below, write **T** if it is true or **F** if it is false. If the statement is false, write the correct term that would make the sentence a true statement.*

1. <u>History</u> is the study of the past based on what people left behind.

2. Knowledge, beliefs, customs, and values of a group of people are part of their <u>environment</u>.

3. A handwritten letter from a soldier to his family would be considered a <u>primary source</u>.

4. <u>Geography</u> is the study of the past, whether recent or long ago.

5. Your state probably has many different <u>landforms</u>, such as mountains, plains, and valleys.

6. Weather changes from day to day, but a location's <u>climate</u> does not change as often.

7. <u>Values</u> are ideas that people hold dear and try to live by.

Comprehension and Critical Thinking

SECTION 1 *(Pages 6–11)*

8. **a. Describe** What is history? What is archaeology? How do the two fields work together?

   b. Make Inferences Why may a historian who is still alive disagree with conclusions drawn by a historian who lived a hundred years ago?

   c. Evaluate Do you think primary sources or secondary sources are more valuable to modern historians? Why?

SECTION 2 *(Pages 12–17)*

9. **a. Identify** What are the two main branches of geography, and how does each contribute to our understanding of history?

   b. Analyze If you were asked to divide your state into regions, what features would you use to define those regions? Why?

   c. Predict How might a long period of severe heat or cold affect the history of a city or region?

Using the Internet

10. Activity: Describing Artifacts Archaeologists study the past based on what people have left behind. Go online to explore recent archaeological discoveries. Select one artifact that interests you and write a short article about it. Write your article as if it will be printed in a school magazine. Describe the artifact in detail: What is it? Who made it? Where was it found? What does the artifact tell archaeologists and historians about the society or culture that created it? You may want to create a chart like the one below to organize your information. If possible, include illustrations with your article.

Artifact	
What is it?	
Who made it?	
Where was it found?	
What does it tell us?	

Social Studies Skills

Recognizing Bias Answer the following questions about personal convictions and bias.

11. What is bias?

12. What is the difference between a personal conviction and a bias?

13. Why do historians try to avoid bias in their writing? What methods might they use to do so?

14. Do you think it is possible for a historian to remove all traces of bias from his or her writing? Why or why not?

Reading Skills

15. Specialized Vocabulary of History Read the following passage in which several words have been left blank. Fill in each of the blanks with the appropriate word that you learned in this chapter.

> **"** Although _____ is defined as the study of the past, it is much more. It is a key to understanding our _____, the ideas, languages, religions, and other traits that make us who we are. In the _____ left behind by ancient peoples we can see reflections of our own material goods: plates and dishes, toys, jewelry, and work objects. These objects show us that human _____ has not changed that much.

Reviewing Themes

16. Society and Culture How may a historian's description of a battle reveal information about his or her own society or culture?

17. Science and Technology If hundreds of years from now archaeologists study the things we leave behind, what may they conclude about the role of technology in American society? Explain your answer.

18. Writing Your Job Description Review your notes on the work of historians, archaeologists, and physical and human geographers. Choose one of these jobs and write a description of it. You should begin your description by explaining why the job is important. Then identify the job's tasks and responsibilities. Finally, tell what kind of person would do well in this job. For example, a historian may enjoy reading and an archaeologist may enjoy working outdoors. When you have finished your description, you may be able to add it to a class or school guide for career planning.

Florida Standardized Test Practice

DIRECTIONS: Read each question, and write the letter of the best response.

1

The object with ancient writing that is shown in this photo is a

A primary source and a resource.

B primary source and an artifact.

C secondary source and a resource.

D secondary source and a fossil.

2 Which of the following is the *best* reason for studying history?

A We can learn the dates of important events.

B We can learn interesting facts about famous people.

C We can learn about ourselves and other people.

D We can hear stories about strange things.

3 The study of people and the places where they live is called

A archaeology.

B environmental science.

C human geography.

D history.

4 Which of the following subjects would interest a physical geographer the *least*?

A a place's climate

B a mountain range

C a river system

D a country's highways

5 The type of evidence that archaeologists are best known for working with is a(n)

A artifact.

B primary source.

C secondary source.

D landform.

6 Which statement *best* describes the relationship between people and natural environments?

A Natural environments do not affect how people live.

B People cannot change the environments in which they live.

C Environments influence how people live, and people change their environments.

D People do not live in natural environments.

7 Each of the following is a primary source *except*

A a photograph.

B a diary.

C a treaty.

D an encyclopedia.

FLORIDA...
The Story Continues

CHAPTER 2, The Stone Ages and Early Cultures (5 million years ago–5,000 years ago)

PEOPLE **c. 12,000–13,000 years ago: The first humans come to Florida.** Hunter-gatherers settled in Florida during the last ice age, somewhere between 12,000–13,000 years ago. The land was covered with scrub oaks, pine forests, and grasslands. It was much colder and drier than today. Archaeologists have recorded around 100 sites from this early period. They think there are many more sites buried under the waters off Florida's coasts. These sites were covered when the sea level rose following the last ice age.

PLACES **c. 12,000 years ago: Water is scarce for Florida's first people.** Many Florida rivers were just water holes during the last ice age. When it rained, water gathered in limestone basins and in sinkholes. These water deposits were important watering holes for humans and animals. Florida's first people moved from watering hole to watering hole, much like early humans in Africa did. Hunter-gatherers camped around the watering holes and butchered the animals they hunted.

EVENTS **c. 12,000 years ago: Archaeologists uncover clues about Florida's first people beneath the Aucilla River.** In prehistoric times the Aucilla River was a series of separate watering holes. Archaeologists have excavated many sites along the river. A 7.5 foot mastodon tusk was found at one site in 1993. It has been dated at 12,200 years old. The tusk has eight cut marks that indicate that humans removed the tusk from a mastodon's skull. This lets archaeologists know that humans were hunting mastodon in the area at that time.

PLACES **c. 12,000 years ago: Archaeologists find evidence that humans camped at Little Salt Spring over 12,000 years ago.** Little Salt Spring in Sarasota County is a deep spring. Deep springs were important sources of water for early hunter-gatherers. Shallow limestone basins that filled with rainwater might dry up between rains. A deep spring would not. Because they were reliable sources of water, deep springs like Little Salt Spring were favored camping grounds.

Archaeologists have found many early artifacts at Little Salt Spring. Among these finds were ashes from a campfire located on a ledge deep within the spring. Archaeologists found the remains of a cooked giant land tortoise next to the ashes. Some archaeologists believe that an unlucky hunter fell into the spring and lived long enough to cook his last meal. Archaeologists have dated the ashes at 12,000 years old. This is the earliest evidence of humans in southern Florida.

PEOPLE **c. 12,000 years ago: Florida's first people hunt big game and other animals.** The earliest Floridians used shafts made of ivory to hunt animals. They got the ivory from the tusks of mastodons. They also used stone spear points that they attached to ivory shafts. Many spear points have been found in river bottoms, particularly in limestone areas in northern and central Florida.

Early hunter-gatherers hunted mastodons, mammoths, horses, camels, bison, and giant land tortoises. They also hunted many smaller animals such as deer, panthers, fish, rattlesnakes, rabbits, opossums, raccoons, and different kinds of turtles and frogs. In addition, they collected freshwater shellfish. Many archaeologists suggest that early hunter-gatherers contributed to the extinction of the mastodon, mammoth, and horse by over hunting the animals.

Unpacking the Florida Standards ‹···

Read the following to learn what this standard says and what it means. See FL8–FL31 to unpack all of the standards related to this chapter.

Benchmark SS.6.W.2.1 Compare the lifestyles of hunter-gatherers with those of settlers of early agricultural communities.

What does it mean?
Explain how the hunter-gatherer way of life differed from the lifestyle of cultures that depended on farming.

SPOTLIGHT ON
SS.6.G.2.1 See page FL44 for content specifically related to this Chapter 2 standard.

The Stone Ages and Early Cultures

Essential Question How did humans' ways of living change as they interacted and adapted?

Florida Next Generation Sunshine State Standards

LA.6.1.6.1 The student will use new vocabulary that is introduced and taught directly. **LA.6.1.6.2** The student will listen to, read, and discuss familiar and conceptually challenging text. **LA.6.1.7.1** The student will use background knowledge of subject and related content areas, prereading strategies, graphic representations, and knowledge of text structure to make and confirm complex predictions of content, purpose, and organization of a reading selection. **LA.6.1.7.3** The student will determine the main idea or essential message in grade-level text through inferring, paraphrasing, summarizing, and identifying relevant details. **SS.6.G.1.4** Utilize tools geographers use to study the world. **SS.6.G.2.1** Explain how major physical characteristics, natural resources, climate, and absolute and relative locations have influenced settlement, interactions, and the economies of ancient civilizations of the world. **SS.6.G.2.4** Explain how the geographical location of ancient civilizations contributed to the culture and politics of those societies. **SS.6.G.3.1** Explain how the physical landscape has affected the development of agriculture and industry in the ancient world. **SS.6.G.3.2** Analyze the impact of human populations on the ancient world's ecosystems. **SS.6.G.4.1** Explain how family and ethnic relationships influenced ancient cultures. **SS.6.G.4.2** Use maps to trace significant migrations, and analyze their results. **SS.6.G.4.3** Locate sites in Africa and Asia where archaeologists have found evidence of early human societies, and trace their migration patterns to other parts of the world. **SS.6.W.1.1** Use timelines to identify chronological order of historical events. **SS.6.W.1.2** Identify terms (decade, century, epoch, era, millennium, BC/BCE, AD/CE) and designations of time periods. **SS.6.W.1.3** Interpret primary and secondary sources. **SS.6.W.2.1** Compare the lifestyles of hunter-gatherers with those of settlers of early agricultural communities. **SS.6.W.2.2** Describe how the developments of agriculture and metallurgy related to settlement, population growth, and the emergence of civilization.

FOCUS ON WRITING

A Storyboard Prehistoric humans did not have written alphabets. However, they did carve and paint images on cave walls. In the spirit of these images, you will create a storyboard that uses images to tell the story of prehistoric humans. Remember that a storyboard tells a story with simple sketches and short captions.

4–5 million
Early humanlike creatures called Australopithecus develop in Africa.

5 MILLION YEARS AGO

2.6 million
Hominids make the first stone tools.

SS.6.W.1.1 Use timelines to identify chronological order of historical events.

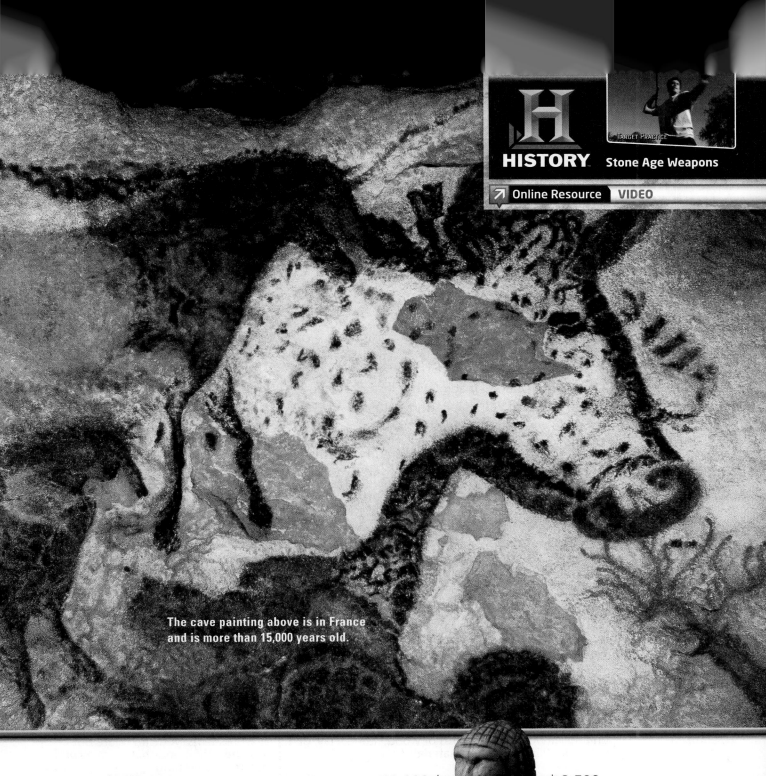

The cave painting above is in France and is more than 15,000 years old.

HISTORY Stone Age Weapons

↗ Online Resource VIDEO

500,000
By this time, hominids live all across Europe.

11,000
Humans occupy all of the continents except Antarctica.

8,500
More than 5,000 people live in Çatal Hüyük, Turkey.

500,000 YEARS AGO

11,000 YEARS AGO

5,000 YEARS AGO

200,000
The first modern humans appear in Africa.

10,000
Ice ages end. People begin to develop agriculture.

25

Reading Social Studies

Focus on Themes In this chapter you will learn about the earliest humans and how they lived. You will read about scientists who work constantly to learn more about this mysterious time. As you read, you will see the beginnings of human **society and culture**—the making of tools, the use of fire, and the creation of language. You will also read about the **geography** of the world and how it shaped where and how early people lived.

Vocabulary Clues

Focus on Reading When you are reading your history textbook, you may often come across a word you do not know. If that word isn't listed as a key term, how do you find out what it means?

Using Context Clues Context means surroundings. Authors often include clues to the meaning of a difficult word in its context. You just have to know how and where to look.

Clue	How It Works	Example	Explanation
Direct Definition	Includes a definition in the same or a nearby sentence	Early hominids, the ancestors of modern humans, migrated from Africa to Asia as early as 2 million years ago	The sentence includes the definition of *hominids* after the word: "the ancestors of modern humans."
Restatement	Uses different words to say the same thing	As early people moved to new lands, they found environments that differed greatly from those in East Africa. Many places were much colder and had strange plants and animals.	The second sentence uses different words and examples to help you understand the word *environments*.
Comparisons or Contrasts	Compares or contrasts the unfamiliar word with a familiar one	Some lived in tents made of animal skins. Others built more permanent structures of wood, stone, clay, or other materials.	By comparing the unfamiliar phrase *permanent structures* to the familiar words *tents,* you can figure out how they differ and that *permanent* means "long-lasting."

You Try It!

The following sentences are from this chapter. Each uses a definition or restatement clue to explain unfamiliar words. See if you can use the context to figure out the meaning of the words in italics.

Vocabulary Clues

1. In fact, the bones belonged to an *Australopithecus*, (aw-stray-loh-PI-thuh-kuhs), one of the earliest ancestors of humans. (p. 28)

2. We *reluctantly* headed back toward camp… I glanced over my right shoulder. (p. 28)

3. Each stone had been struck with another rock to create a sharp, jagged edge along one side. This *process* left one unsharpened side that could be used as a handle. (p. 31)

4. Most experts believe that this *revolution,* or change, first occurred in the societies of Southwest Asia. (p. 41)

After you read the sentences, answer the following questions.

1. In example 1, what does the word *Australopithecus* mean? How do you know?

2. In example 2, what is the meaning of *reluctantly*? How can you use the following sentence to help you understand the word?

3. In example 3, what does the word *process* mean? How can you use the previous sentence to help you understand the word?

4. What is the definition of *revolution* in example 4? What kind of context clue did you find in that sentence?

Key Terms and People

Chapter 2

Section 1
prehistory *(p. 28)*
hominid *(p. 28)*
ancestor *(p. 28)*
tool *(p. 30)*
Paleolithic Era *(p. 31)*
society *(p. 33)*
hunter-gatherers *(p. 33)*

Section 2
migrate *(p. 36)*
ice ages *(p. 36)*
land bridge *(p. 36)*
Mesolithic Era *(p. 38)*

Section 3
Neolithic Era *(p. 41)*
domestication *(p. 41)*
agriculture *(p. 42)*
megaliths *(p. 42)*

Academic Vocabulary

Success in school is related to knowing academic vocabulary—the words that are frequently used in school assignments and discussions. In this chapter, you will learn the following academic words:

distribute *(p. 33)*
development *(p. 42)*

As you read **Chapter 2**, look for words that indicate the order in which events occurred.

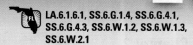
The First People

What You Will Learn...

Main Ideas

1. Scientists study the remains of early humans to learn about prehistory.
2. Hominids and early humans first appeared in East Africa millions of years ago.
3. Stone Age tools grew more complex as time passed.
4. Hunter-gatherer societies developed language, art, and religion.

The Big Idea

Prehistoric people learned to adapt to their environment, to make simple tools, to use fire, and to use language.

Key Terms

prehistory, *p. 28*
hominid, *p. 28*
ancestor, *p. 28*
tool, *p. 30*
Paleolithic Era, *p. 31*
society, *p. 33*
hunter-gatherers, *p. 33*

Online Resource

TAKING NOTES

Use the graphic organizer online to take notes on the advances made by prehistoric humans.

If YOU were there...

You live 200,000 years ago, in a time known as the Stone Age. A local toolmaker has offered to teach you his skill. You watch carefully as he strikes two black rocks together. A small piece flakes off. You try to copy him, but the rocks just break. Finally you learn to strike the rock just right. You have made a sharp stone knife!

How will you use your new skill?

BUILDING BACKGROUND Over millions of years early people learned many new things. Making stone tools was one of the earliest and most valuable skills that they developed. Scientists who study early humans learn a lot about them from the tools and other objects that they made.

Scientists Study Remains

Although humans have lived on the earth for more than a million years, writing was not invented until about 5,000 years ago. Historians call the time before there was writing **prehistory**. To study prehistory, historians rely on the work of archaeologists and anthropologists.

One archaeologist who made important discoveries about prehistory was Mary Leakey. In 1959 she found bones in East Africa that were more than 1.5 million years old. She and her husband, Louis Leakey, believed that the bones belonged to an early **hominid** (HAH-muh-nuhd), an early ancestor of humans. An **ancestor** is a relative who lived in the past.

In fact, the bones belonged to an Australopithecus (aw-stray-loh-PI-thuh-kuhs), one of the earliest ancestors of humans. In 1974 anthropologist Donald Johanson (joh-HAN-suhn) found bones from another early ancestor. He described his discovery:

"We reluctantly headed back toward camp ... I glanced over my right shoulder. Light glinted off a bone. I knelt down for a closer look ... Everywhere we looked on the slope around us we saw more bones lying on the surface."

–Donald Johanson, from *Ancestors: In Search of Human Origins*

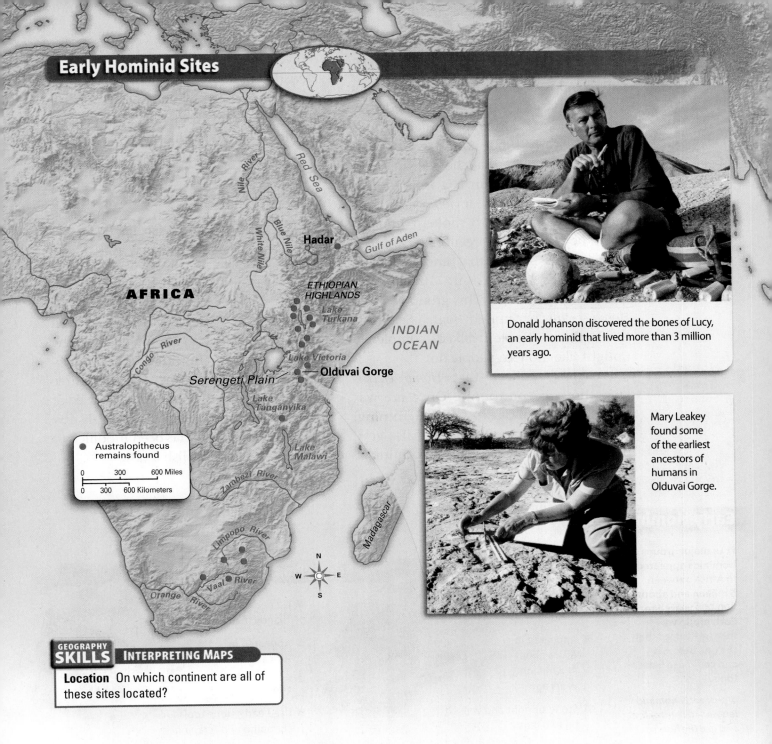

Early Hominid Sites

Hadar

AFRICA

ETHIOPIAN HIGHLANDS

Lake Turkana

INDIAN OCEAN

Lake Victoria

Serengeti Plain

Olduvai Gorge

Lake Tanganyika

Lake Malawi

Madagascar

Limpopo River

Vaal River

Orange River

Zambezi River

Congo River

Nile River

Red Sea

White Nile

Blue Nile

Gulf of Aden

- Australopithecus remains found

0   300   600 Miles
0   300   600 Kilometers

N W E S

Donald Johanson discovered the bones of Lucy, an early hominid that lived more than 3 million years ago.

Mary Leakey found some of the earliest ancestors of humans in Olduvai Gorge.

GEOGRAPHY SKILLS | **INTERPRETING MAPS**

Location On which continent are all of these sites located?

Johanson named his find Lucy. Tests showed that she lived more than 3 million years ago. Johanson could tell from her bones that she was small and had walked on two legs. The ability to walk on two legs was a key step in human development.

In 1994 anthropologist Tim White found even older remains. He believes that the hominid he found may have lived as long as 4.4 million years ago. But some scientists disagree with White's time estimate. Discoveries of ancient bones give us information about early humans and their ancestors, but not all scientists agree on the meaning of these discoveries.

READING CHECK **Drawing Inferences** What can ancient bones tell us about human ancestors?

Hominids and Early Humans

Later groups of hominids appeared about 3 million years ago. As time passed they became more like modern humans.

In the early 1960s Louis Leakey found hominid remains that he called *Homo habilis*, or "handy man." Leakey and his son Richard believed that *Homo habilis* was more closely related to modern humans than Lucy and had a larger brain.

Scientists believe that another group of hominids appeared in Africa about 1.5 million years ago. This group is called *Homo erectus*, or "upright man." Scientists think these people walked completely upright like modern people do.

Scientists believe that *Homo erectus* knew how to control fire. Once fire was started by natural causes, such as lightning, people used it to cook food. Fire also gave them heat and protection against animals.

Eventually hominids developed characteristics of modern humans. Scientists are not sure exactly when or where the first modern humans lived. Many think that they first appeared in Africa about 200,000 years ago. Scientists call these people *Homo sapiens*, or "wise man." Every person alive today belongs to this group.

READING CHECK **Contrasting** How was *Homo erectus* different from *Homo habilis*?

Stone Age Tools

The first humans and their ancestors lived during a long period of time called the Stone Age. To help in their studies, archaeologists divide the Stone Age into three periods based on the kinds of tools used at the time. To archaeologists, a **tool** is any handheld object that has been modified to help a person accomplish a task.

FOCUS ON READING
Dates in a text can help you keep events in order in your mind.

Early Hominids QUICK FACTS

Four major groups of hominids appeared in Africa between 5 million and about 200,000 years ago. Each group was more advanced than the one before it and could use better tools.

Which early hominid learned to control fire and use the hand ax?

Australopithecus

- Name means "southern ape"
- Appeared in Africa about 4–5 million years ago
- Stood upright and walked on two legs
- Brain was about one-third the size of modern humans

Homo habilis

- Name means "handy man"
- Appeared in Africa about 2.4 million years ago
- Used early stone tools for chopping and scraping
- Brain was about half the size of modern humans

An early Stone Age chopper

The first part of the Stone Age is called the **Paleolithic** (pay-lee-uh-LI-thik) **Era**, or Old Stone Age. It lasted until about 10,000 years ago. During this time people used stone tools.

The First Tools

Scientists have found the oldest tools in Tanzania, a country in East Africa. These sharpened stones, about the size of an adult's fist, are about 2.6 million years old. Each stone had been struck with another rock to create a sharp, jagged edge along one side. This process left one unsharpened side that could be used as a handle.

Scientists think that these first tools were mostly used to process food. The sharp edge could be used to cut, chop, or scrape roots, bones, or meat. Tools like these were used for about 2 million years.

Later Tools

Over time people learned to make better tools. For example, they developed the hand ax. They often made this tool out of a mineral called flint. Flint is easy to shape, and tools made from it can be very sharp. People used hand axes to break tree limbs, to dig, and to cut animal hides.

People also learned to attach wooden handles to tools. By attaching a wooden shaft to a stone point, for example, they invented the spear. Because a spear could be thrown, hunters no longer had to stand close to animals they were hunting. As a result, people could hunt larger animals. Among the animals hunted by Stone Age people were deer, horses, bison, and elephantlike creatures called mammoths.

READING CHECK **Summarizing** How did tools improve during the Old Stone Age?

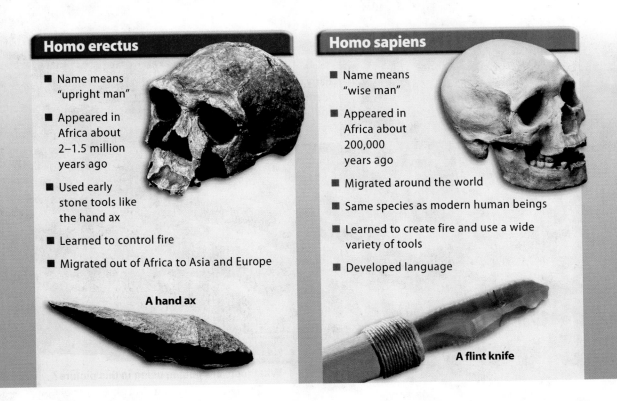

Homo erectus

- Name means "upright man"
- Appeared in Africa about 2–1.5 million years ago
- Used early stone tools like the hand ax
- Learned to control fire
- Migrated out of Africa to Asia and Europe

A hand ax

Homo sapiens

- Name means "wise man"
- Appeared in Africa about 200,000 years ago
- Migrated around the world
- Same species as modern human beings
- Learned to create fire and use a wide variety of tools
- Developed language

A flint knife

Hunter-Gatherers

Early people were hunter-gatherers. They hunted animals and gathered wild plants to survive. Life for these hunter-gatherers was difficult and dangerous. Still, people learned how to make tools, use fire, and even create art.

Hunting
Most hunting was done by men. They worked together to bring down large animals.

Art
People painted herds of animals on cave walls.

Gathering
Most gathering was done by women. They gathered food like wild plants, seeds, fruits, and nuts.

Fire
People learned to use fire to cook their food.

Tools
Early people learned to make tools such as this spear for hunting.

ANALYSIS SKILL **ANALYZING VISUALS**

What tools are people using in this picture?

Hunter-gatherer Societies

As early humans developed tools and new hunting techniques, they formed societies. A **society** is a community of people who share a common culture. These societies developed cultures with languages, religions, and art.

Society

Anthropologists believe that early humans lived in small groups. In bad weather they might have taken shelter in a cave if there was one nearby. When food or water became hard to find, groups of people would have to move to new areas.

The early humans of the Stone Age were **hunter-gatherers**—people who hunt animals and gather wild plants, seeds, fruits, and nuts to survive. Anthropologists believe that most Stone Age hunters were men. They hunted in groups, sometimes chasing entire herds of animals over cliffs. This method was both more productive and safer than hunting alone.

Women in hunter-gatherer societies probably took responsibility for collecting plants to eat. They likely stayed near camps and took care of children.

Language, Art, and Religion

The most important development of early Stone Age culture was language. Scientists have many theories about why language first developed. Some think it was to make hunting in groups easier. Others think it developed as a way for people to form relationships. Still others think language made it easier for people to resolve issues like how to **distribute** food.

Language wasn't the only way early people expressed themselves. They also created art. People carved figures out of stone, ivory, and bone. They painted and carved images of people and animals on cave walls. Scientists still aren't sure why people made art. Perhaps the cave paintings were used to teach people how to hunt, or maybe they had religious meanings.

SS.6.W.2.1 Compare the lifestyles of hunter–gatherers with those of settlers of early agricultural communities.

ACADEMIC VOCABULARY
distribute
to divide among a group of people

LINKING TO TODAY

Stone Tools

Did you know that Stone Age people's tools weren't as primitive as we might think? They made knife blades and arrowheads—like the one shown below—out of volcanic glass called obsidian. The obsidian blades were very sharp. In fact, they could be 100 times sharper and smoother than the steel blades used for surgery in modern hospitals.

Today some doctors are going back to using these Stone Age materials. They have found that blades made from obsidian are more precise than modern scalpels. Some doctors use obsidian blades for delicate surgery on the face because the stone tools leave "nicer-looking" scars.

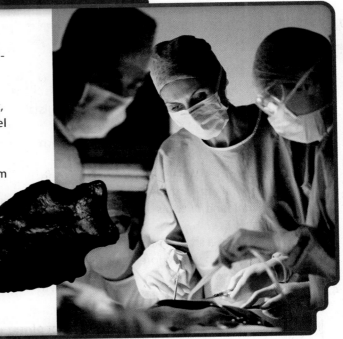

ANALYSIS SKILL **ANALYZING INFORMATION**

How do you think modern obsidian blades are different from Stone Age ones?

Scholars know little about the religious beliefs of early people. Archaeologists have found graves that included food and artifacts. Many scientists think these discoveries are proof that the first human religions developed during the Stone Age.

READING CHECK **Analyzing** What was one possible reason for the development of language?

SUMMARY AND PREVIEW Scientists have discovered and studied the remains of hominids and early humans who lived in East Africa millions of years ago. These Stone Age people were hunter-gatherers who used fire, stone tools, and language. In the next section you will learn how early humans moved out of Africa and populated the world.

Section 1 Assessment

Reviewing Ideas, Terms, and People

1. a. Identify Who found the bones of Lucy?
b. Explain Why do historians need archaeologists and anthropologists to study **prehistory**?

2. a. Recall What is the scientific name for modern humans?
b. Make Inferences What might have been one advantage of walking completely upright?

3. a. Recall What kind of **tools** did people use during the **Paleolithic Era**?
b. Design Design a stone and wood tool you could use to help you with your chores. Describe your tool in a sentence or two.

4. a. Define What is a **hunter-gatherer**?
b. Rank In your opinion, what was the most important change brought by the development of language?

Critical Thinking

5. Evaluate Review the notes in your chart on the advances made by prehistoric humans. Using a graphic organizer like the one here, rank the three advances you think are most important. Next to your organizer, write a sentence explaining why you ranked the advances in that order.

1.
2.
3.

FOCUS ON WRITING

6. Listing Stone Age Achievements Look back through this section and make a list of important Stone Age achievements. Which of these will you include on your storyboard? How will you illustrate them?

The Iceman

The Iceman's dagger and the scabbard, or case, he carried it in

Why was a Stone Age traveler in Europe's highest mountains?

When did he live? about 5,300 years ago

Where did he live? The frozen body of the Iceman was discovered in the snowy Ötztal Alps of Italy in 1991. Scientists nicknamed him Ötzi after this location.

What did he do? That question has been debated ever since Ötzi's body was found. Apparently, he was traveling. At first scientists thought he had frozen to death in a storm. But an arrowhead found in his shoulder suggests that his death was not so peaceful. After he died, his body was covered by glaciers and preserved for thousands of years.

Why is he important? Ötzi is the oldest mummified human ever found in such good condition. His body, clothing, and tools were extremely well preserved, telling us a lot about life during the Stone Ages. His outfit was made of three types of animal skin stitched together. He wore leather shoes padded with grass, a grass cape, a fur hat, and a sort of backpack. He carried an ax with a copper blade as well as a bow and arrows.

Drawing Conclusions Why do you think the Iceman was in the Alps?

Scientists examine the Iceman's body in 1991, before it was removed from the glacier.

LA.6.1.6.2, SS.6.G.1.4, SS.6.G.2.1,
SS.6.G.2.4, SS.6.G.4.2, SS.6.G.4.3,
SS.6.W.1.2, SS.6.W.1.3, SS.6.W.2.1

What You Will Learn...

Main Ideas

1. People moved out of Africa as the earth's climates changed.
2. People adapted to new environments by making clothing and new types of tools.

The Big Idea

As people migrated around the world they learned to adapt to new environments.

Key Terms

migrate, *p. 36*
ice ages, *p. 36*
land bridge, *p. 36*
Mesolithic Era, *p. 38*

 Online Resource

TAKING NOTES

Use the graphic organizer online to take notes on the sequence and paths of migration of early humans.

Early Human Migration

If YOU were there...

Your tribe of hunter-gatherers has lived in this place for as long as anyone can remember. But now there are not enough animals to hunt. Whenever you find berries and roots, you have to share them with people from other tribes. Your leaders think it's time to find a new home in the lands far beyond the mountains. But no one has ever traveled there, and many people are afraid.

How do you feel about moving to a new home?

BUILDING BACKGROUND From their beginnings in East Africa, early humans moved in many directions. Eventually, they lived on almost every continent in the world. People probably had many reasons for moving. One reason was a change in the climate.

People Move Out of Africa

During the Old Stone Age, climate patterns around the world changed, transforming the earth's geography. In response to these changes, people began to **migrate**, or move, to new places.

The Ice Ages

Most scientists believe that about 1.6 million years ago, many places around the world began to experience long periods of freezing weather. These freezing times are called the **ice ages**. The ice ages ended about 10,000 years ago.

During the ice ages huge sheets of ice covered much of the earth's land. These ice sheets were formed from ocean water, leaving ocean levels lower than they are now. Many areas that are now underwater were dry land then. For example, a narrow body of water now separates Asia and North America. But scientists think that during the ice ages, the ocean level dropped and exposed a **land bridge**, a strip of land connecting two continents. Land bridges allowed Stone Age peoples to migrate around the world.

Early Human Migration

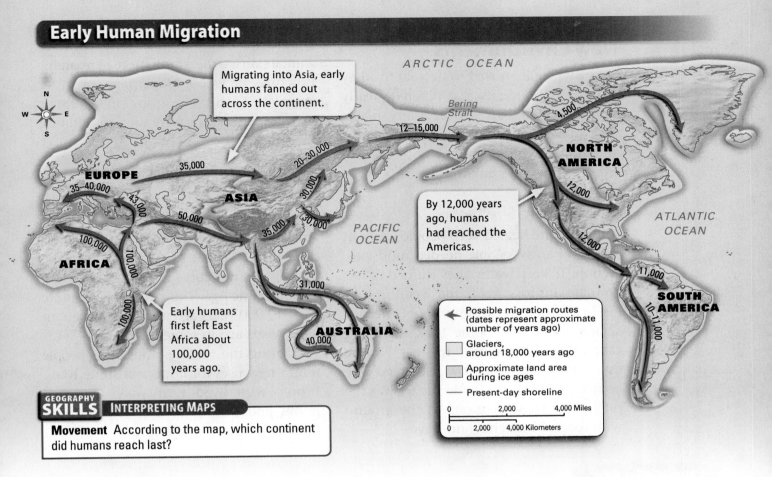

ARCTIC OCEAN

Migrating into Asia, early humans fanned out across the continent.

Bering Strait

12–15,000

4,500

NORTH AMERICA

EUROPE
35–40,000
43,000

35,000

ASIA

20–30,000

30,000

12,000

ATLANTIC OCEAN

50,000

30,000

By 12,000 years ago, humans had reached the Americas.

PACIFIC OCEAN

35,000

100,000

AFRICA

100,000

100,000

31,000

12,000

Early humans first left East Africa about 100,000 years ago.

AUSTRALIA
40,000

11,000

SOUTH AMERICA

10–11,000

100,000

Possible migration routes (dates represent approximate number of years ago)

Glaciers, around 18,000 years ago

Approximate land area during ice ages

Present-day shoreline

0   2,000   4,000 Miles

0   2,000   4,000 Kilometers

GEOGRAPHY SKILLS | **INTERPRETING MAPS**

Movement According to the map, which continent did humans reach last?

Settling New Lands

Scientists agree that migration around the world took hundreds of thousands of years. Early hominids, the ancestors of modern humans, migrated from Africa to Asia as early as 2 million years ago. From there, they spread to Southeast Asia and Europe.

Later, humans also began to migrate around the world, and earlier hominids died out. Look at the map to see the dates and routes of early human migration.

Humans began to migrate from East Africa to southern Africa and southwestern Asia around 100,000 years ago. From there, people moved east across southern Asia. They could then migrate to Australia. Scientists are not sure exactly how the first people reached Australia. Even though ocean levels were lower then, there was always open sea between Asia and Australia.

From southwestern Asia, humans also migrated north into Europe. Geographic features such as high mountains and cold temperatures delayed migration northward into northern Asia. Eventually, however, people from both Europe and southern Asia moved into that region.

From northern Asia, people moved into North America. Scientists disagree on when and how the first people arrived in North America. Most scholars think people must have crossed a land bridge from Asia to North America. Once in North America, these people moved south, following herds of animals and settling South America. By 9000 BC, humans lived on all continents of the world except Antarctica.

READING CHECK **Analyzing** How did the ice ages influence human migration?

SS.6.G.4.2 Use maps to trace significant migrations, and analyze their results.

People Adapt to New Environments

As early people moved to new lands, they found environments that differed greatly from those in East Africa. Many places were much colder and had strange plants and animals. Early people had to learn to adapt to their new environments.

Clothing and Shelter

Although fire helped keep people warm in very cold areas, people needed more protection. To keep warm, they learned to sew animal skins together to make clothing.

In addition to clothing, people needed shelter to survive. Some took shelter in caves. When they moved to areas with no caves, they built their own shelters. One early type of human-made shelter was the pit house. They were pits in the ground with roofs of branches and leaves.

Early people also built homes above the ground. Some lived in tents made of animal skins. Others built more permanent structures of wood, stone, clay, or other materials. Even bones from large animals such as mammoths were used in building shelters.

New Tools and Technologies

People also adapted to new environments with new types of tools. These tools were smaller and more complex than tools from the Old Stone Age. They defined the **Mesolithic** (me-zuh-LI-thik) **Era**, or the Middle Stone Age. This period began more than 10,000 years ago and lasted to about 5,000 years ago in some places.

During the Middle Stone Age, people found new uses for bone and stone tools. People who lived near water invented hooks and fishing spears. Other groups invented the bow and arrow.

Primary Source

POINTS OF VIEW

Views of Migration to the Americas

For many years scientists were fairly certain that the first Americans came from Asia, following big game through an ice-free path in the glaciers.

❝Doubtless it was a formidable [challenging] place . . . an ice-walled valley of frigid winds, fierce snows, and clinging fogs . . . yet grazing animals would have entered, and behind them would have come a rivulet [stream] of human hunters.**❞**

—**Thomas Canby,**
1979, quoted in *Kingdoms of Gold, Kingdoms of Jade* by Brian M. Fagan

New discoveries have challenged beliefs about the first Americans. Some scientists now are not so sure the first Americans came along an ice-free path in the glaciers.

❝There's no reason people couldn't have come along the coast, skirting [going around] the glaciers just the way recreational kayakers do today.**❞**

—**James Dixon,**
quoted in *National Geographic,* December 2000

ANALYSIS SKILL **ANALYZING PRIMARY SOURCES**

Why might a scientist change his or her mind about a long-held belief?

A Mammoth House

Early people used whatever was available to make shelters. In Central Asia, where wood was scarce, some early people made their homes from mammoth bones.

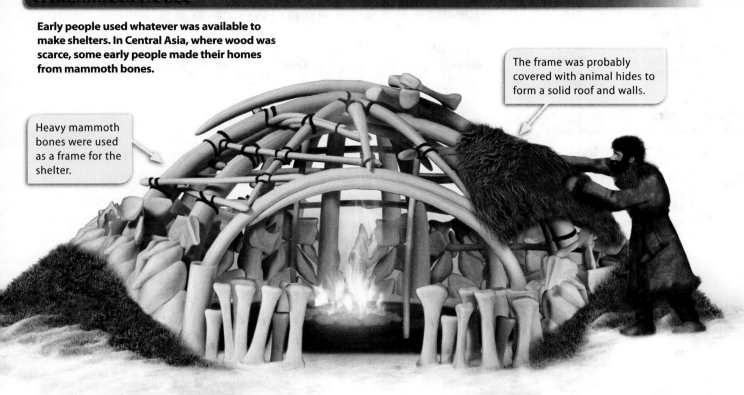

Heavy mammoth bones were used as a frame for the shelter.

The frame was probably covered with animal hides to form a solid roof and walls.

In addition to tools, people developed new technologies to improve their lives. For example, some learned to make canoes by hollowing out logs. They used the canoes to travel on rivers and lakes. They also began to make pottery. The first pets may also have appeared at this time. People kept dogs to help them hunt and for protection. Developments like these, in addition to clothing and shelter, allowed people to adapt to new environments.

READING CHECK Finding Main Ideas
What were two ways people adapted to new environments?

SUMMARY AND PREVIEW Early people adapted to new environments with new kinds of clothing, shelter, and tools. In Section 3 you will read about how Stone Age peoples developed farming.

Section 2 Assessment

Reviewing Ideas, Terms, and People

1. **a. Define** What is a **land bridge**?
   b. Analyze Why did it take so long for early people to reach South America?
2. **a. Recall** What did people use to make tools in the **Mesolithic Era**?
   b. Summarize Why did people have to learn to make clothes and build shelters?

Critical Thinking

3. **Sequencing** Draw the organizer below. Use your notes and sequence chain to show the path of migration around the world.

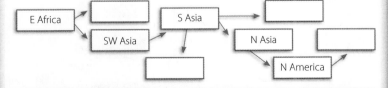

E Africa → □ ; E Africa → SW Asia ; □ ← S Asia → □ ; SW Asia → S Asia ; S Asia → □ ; S Asia → N Asia ; □ ; N Asia → N America ; N America → □

FOCUS ON WRITING

4. **Illustrating** How will you illustrate early migration on your storyboard? Draw some sketches. How does this information relate to your ideas from Section 1?

Beginnings of Agriculture

What You Will Learn...

Main Ideas

1. The first farmers learned to grow plants and raise animals in the New Stone Age.
2. Farming changed societies and the way people lived.

The Big Idea

The development of agriculture brought great changes to human society.

Key Terms

Neolithic Era, *p. 41*
domestication, *p. 41*
agriculture, *p. 42*
megaliths, *p. 42*

Online Resource

TAKING NOTES

Use the graphic organizer online to take notes on the different changes related to the development of agriculture.

If YOU were there...

As a gatherer, you know where to find the sweetest fruits. Every summer, you eat many of these fruits, dropping the seeds on the ground. One day you return to find new plants everywhere. You realize that the plants have grown from your dropped seeds.

How could this discovery change your way of life?

BUILDING BACKGROUND The discovery that plants grew from seeds was one of the major advances of the late Stone Age. Other similar advances led to great changes in the way people lived.

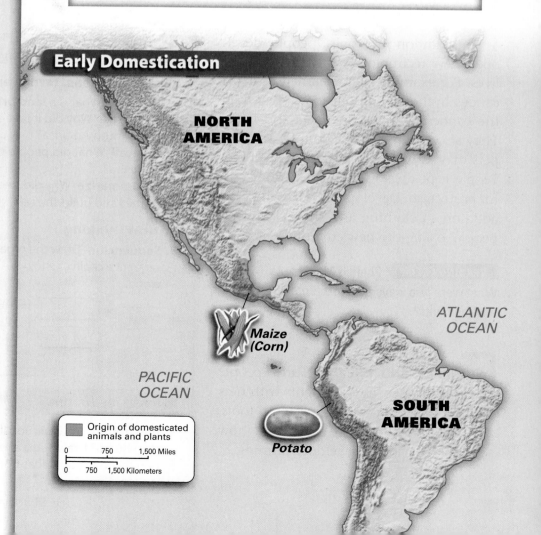

Early Domestication

NORTH AMERICA

Maize (Corn)

ATLANTIC OCEAN

PACIFIC OCEAN

SOUTH AMERICA

Potato

Origin of domesticated animals and plants

0   750   1,500 Miles
0   750   1,500 Kilometers

The First Farmers

After the Middle Stone Age came a period of time that scientists call the **Neolithic** (nee-uh-LI-thik) **Era**, or New Stone Age. It began as early as 10,000 years ago in Southwest Asia. In other places, this era began much later and lasted much longer than it did there.

During the New Stone Age people learned to polish stones to make tools like saws and drills. People also learned how to make fire. Before, they could only use fire that had been started by natural causes such as lightning.

The New Stone Age ended in Egypt and Southwest Asia about 5,000 years ago, when toolmakers began to make tools out of metal. But tools weren't the only major change that occurred during the Neolithic Era. In fact, the biggest changes came in how people produced food.

Plants

After a warming trend brought an end to the ice ages, new plants began to grow in some areas. For example, wild barley and wheat plants started to spread throughout Southwest Asia. Over time, people came to depend on these wild plants for food. They began to settle where grains grew.

People soon learned that they could plant seeds themselves to grow their own crops. Historians call the shift from food gathering to food producing the Neolithic Revolution. Most experts believe that this revolution, or change, first occurred in the societies of Southwest Asia.

Eventually, people learned to change plants to make them more useful. They planted only the largest grains or the sweetest fruits. The process of changing plants or animals to make them more useful to humans is called **domestication**.

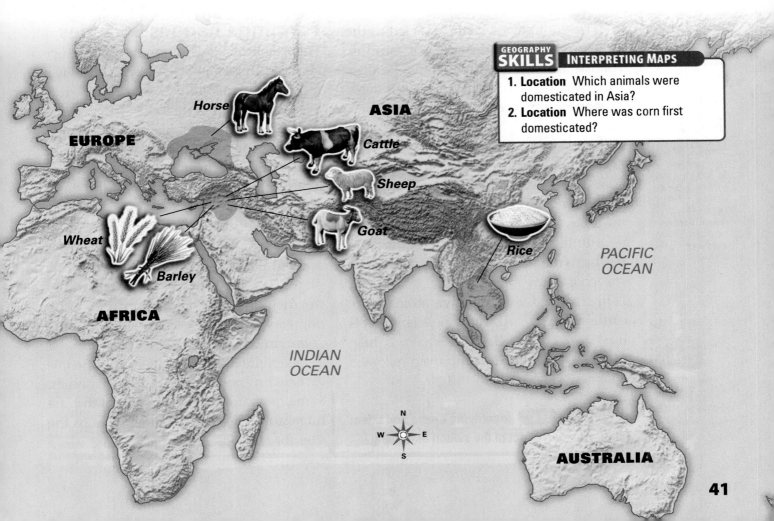

GEOGRAPHY SKILLS **INTERPRETING MAPS**

1. **Location** Which animals were domesticated in Asia?
2. **Location** Where was corn first domesticated?

An Early Farming Society

The village of Çatal Hüyük in modern Turkey is one of the earliest farming villages discovered. Around 8,000 years ago, the village was home to about 5,000–6,000 people living in more than 1,000 houses. Villagers farmed, hunted and fished, traded with distant lands, and worshipped gods in special shrines.

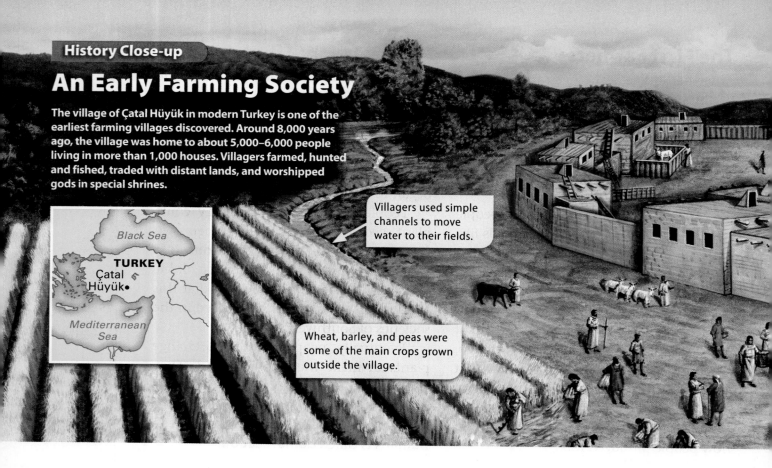

Villagers used simple channels to move water to their fields.

Wheat, barley, and peas were some of the main crops grown outside the village.

Black Sea

TURKEY
Çatal
Hüyük•

Mediterranean Sea

ACADEMIC VOCABULARY

development
creation

SS.6.W.2.1 Compare the lifestyles of hunter–gatherers with those of settlers of early agricultural communities.
SS.6.W.2.2 Describe how the developments of agriculture and metallurgy related to settlement, population growth, and the emergence of civilization.

THE IMPACT TODAY

One megalith, Stonehenge in England, attracts millions of people each year.

The domestication of plants led to the **development** of **agriculture**, or farming. For the first time, people could produce their own food. This development changed human society forever.

Animals

Learning to produce food was a major accomplishment for early people. But learning how to use animals for their own purposes was almost equally important.

Hunters didn't have to follow wild herds anymore. Instead, farmers could keep sheep or goats for milk, food, and wool. Farmers could also use large animals like cattle to carry loads or to pull large tools used in farming. Using animals to help with farming greatly improved people's chances of surviving.

READING CHECK **Identifying Cause and Effect** What was one effect of the switch to farming?

Farming Changes Societies

The Neolithic Revolution brought huge changes to people's lives. With survival more certain, people could focus on activities other than finding food.

Domestication of plants and animals enabled people to use plant fibers to make cloth. The domestication of animals made it possible to use wool from goats and sheep and skins from horses for clothes.

People also began to build permanent settlements. As they started raising crops and animals, they needed to stay in one place. Then, once people were able to control their own food production, the world's population grew. In some areas farming communities developed into towns.

As populations grew, groups of people gathered to perform religious ceremonies. Some put up megaliths. **Megaliths** are huge stones used as monuments or as the sites for religious gatherings.

Houses were made of wood covered with mud. Since they didn't have doors, people entered on ladders through rooftop openings.

Inside their houses, villagers made the earliest known wooden bowls and cups, pottery, and mirrors.

Some houses were built as shrines and had small statues of goddesses and large sculpted bulls' heads.

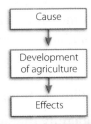

ANALYSIS SKILL **ANALYZING VISUALS**

How did farmers get water to their fields?

Early people probably believed in gods and goddesses associated with the four elements—air, water, fire, and earth—or with animals. For example, one European group honored a thunder god, while another group worshipped bulls. Some scholars also believe that prehistoric peoples also prayed to their ancestors. People in some societies today still hold many of these same beliefs.

READING CHECK **Analyzing** How did farming contribute to the growth of towns?

SUMMARY AND PREVIEW Stone Age peoples adapted to new environments by domesticating plants and animals. These changes led to the development of religion and the growth of towns. In the next chapter you will learn more about early towns.

Section 3 Assessment

Reviewing Ideas, Terms, and People

1. **a. Define** What is **domestication** of a plant or animal?
   b. Make Generalizations How did early people use domesticated animals?
2. **a. Describe** What were gods and goddesses probably associated with in prehistoric religion?
   b. Explain How did domestication of plants and animals lead to the development of towns?

Critical Thinking

3. **Identifying Cause and Effect** Copy the graphic organizer at right. Use it to show one cause and three effects of the development of agriculture.

Cause

↓

Development of agriculture

↓

Effects

FOCUS ON WRITING

4. **Beginnings of Agriculture** Now that you've read about the birth of agriculture, you're ready to plan your storyboard. Look back through your notes from previous sections and the text of this one. Make a list of the events and ideas you will include on your storyboard. Then plan how you will arrange these items.

Social Studies Skills

LA.6.1.7.3 The student will determine the main idea or essential message in grade–level text through inferring, paraphrasing, summarizing, and identifying relevant details.

Analysis | Critical Thinking | Economics | Study

21ST CENTURY

Identifying Central Issues

Understand the Skill

Central issues are the main problems or topics that are related to an event. The issues behind a historical event can be varied and complicated. Central issues in world history usually involve political, social, economic, territorial, moral, or technological matters. The ability to identify the central issue in an event allows you to focus on information that is most important to understanding the event.

Learn the Skill

In this chapter you learned about prehistory. Some of the events you read about may not seem very important. It is hard for people in the computer age to appreciate the accomplishments of the Stone Age. For example, adding wooden handles to stone tools may seem like a simple thing to us. But it was a life-changing advance for people of that time.

This example points out something to remember when looking for central issues. Try not to use only modern-day values and standards to decide what is important about the past. Always think about the times in which people lived. Ask yourself what would have been important to people living then.

The following guidelines will help you to identify central issues. Use them to gain a better understanding of historical events.

1. Identify the subject of the information. What is the information about?

2. Determine the source of the information. Is it a primary source or a secondary source?

3. Determine the purpose of what you are reading. Why has the information been provided?

4. Find the strongest or most forceful statements in the information. These are often clues to issues or ideas the writer thinks are the most central or important.

5. Think about values, concerns, ways of life, and events that would have been important to the people of the times. Determine how the information might be connected to those larger issues.

Practice and Apply the Skill

Apply the guidelines to identify the central issue in the following passage. Then answer the questions.

"What distinguished the Neolithic Era from earlier ages was people's ability to shape stone tools by polishing and grinding. This allowed people to make more specialized tools. Even more important changes took place also. The development of agriculture changed the basic way people lived. Earlier people had been wanderers, who moved from place to place in search of food. Some people began settling in permanent villages. Exactly how they learned that seeds could be planted and made to grow year after year remains a mystery. However, the shift from food gathering to food producing was possibly the most important change ever in history."

1. What is the general subject of this passage?

2. What changes distinguished the Neolithic Era from earlier periods?

3. According to this writer, what is the central issue to understand about the Neolithic Era?

4. What statements in the passage help you to determine the central issue?

Chapter Review

Visual Summary

Use the visual summary below to help you review the main ideas of the chapter.

QUICK FACTS

Hominids developed in Africa and learned how to use tools.

Early humans lived as hunter-gatherers.

Humans migrated around the world, adapting to new environments.

Eventually, people learned how to farm and raise animals.

Reviewing Vocabulary, Terms, and People

For each group of terms below, write a sentence that shows how all the terms in the group are related.

1. prehistory
   ancestor
   hominid

2. domestication
   Neolithic Era
   agriculture

3. Paleolithic Era
   tool
   hunter-gatherers
   develop

4. land bridge
   ice ages
   migrate

5. society
   megaliths
   Neolithic Era

Comprehension and Critical Thinking

SECTION 1 *(Pages 28–34)*

6. **a. Recall** What does *Homo sapiens* mean? When may *Homo sapiens* have first appeared in Africa?

   b. Draw Conclusions If you were an archaeologist and found bead jewelry and stone chopping tools in an ancient woman's grave, what may you conclude?

   c. Elaborate How did stone tools change over time? Why do you think these changes took place so slowly?

SECTION 2 *(Pages 36–39)*

7. **a. Describe** What new skills did people develop to help them survive?

   b. Analyze How did global climate change affect the migration of early people?

   c. Evaluate About 15,000 years ago, where do you think life would have been more difficult— in eastern Africa or northern Europe? Why?

8. **a. Define** What was the Neolithic Revolution?

   b. Make Inferences How did domestication of plants and animals change early societies?

   c. Predict Why do you think people of the Neolithic Era put up megaliths instead of some other kind of monuments?

Reviewing Themes

9. **Geography** What were three ways in which the environment affected Stone Age peoples?

10. **Society and Culture** How did the development of language change hunter-gatherer society?

Using the Internet

11. **Activity: Creating a Skit** In the beginning of the Paleolithic Era, or the Old Stone Age, early humans used modified stones as tools. As the Stone Age progressed, plants and animals became materials for tools too. Go online to research the development of tools and the use of fire. Then create a skit that tells about an early human society discovering fire, creating a new tool, or developing a new way of doing a task.

Reading Skills

Understanding Context Clues *A sentence from the chapter follows each question below. Use the context clues in the sentence to answer each question.*

12. What is the meaning of *era* in the following sentence? After the Middle Stone Age came a period of time that scientists call the Neolithic Era.

13. What word in the following sentence helps you understand the word *transforming*? Climate patterns around the world changed, transforming the earth's geography.

Social Studies Skills

Identifying Central Issues *Read the primary source passage below and then answer the questions that follow.*

> " Almonds provide a striking example of bitter seeds and their change under domestication. Most wild almond seeds contain an intensely bitter chemical called amygdalin, which (as was already mentioned) breaks down to yield the poison cyanide. A snack of wild almonds can kill a person foolish enough to ignore the warning of the bitter taste. Since the first stage in unconscious domestication involves gathering seeds to eat, how on earth did domestication of wild almonds ever reach that first stage? "
>
> –Jared Diamond, from *Guns, Germs, and Steel*

14. What is the main point of this passage?

15. What does the author suggest is the major issue he will address in the text?

FOCUS ON WRITING

16. **Creating Your Storyboard** Use the notes you have taken to plan your storyboard. What images will you include in each frame of the storyboard? How many frames will you need to tell the story of prehistoric people? How will you represent your ideas visually?

   After you have sketched an outline for your storyboard, begin drawing it. Be sure to include all significant adaptations and developments made by prehistoric people, and don't worry if you can't draw that well. If you like, you might want to draw your storyboard in the simple style of prehistoric cave paintings. As the last frame in your storyboard, write a detailed summary to conclude your story.

DIRECTIONS: Read each question, and write the letter of the best response.

1 Use the map to answer the following question.

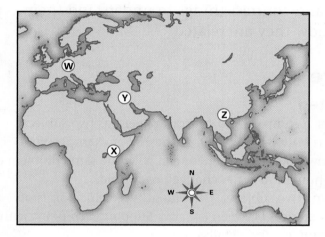

The region in which the first humans lived is shown on the map by the letter

A W.

B X.

C Y.

D Z.

2 The earliest humans lived

A by hunting and gathering their food.

B as herders of sheep and other livestock.

C alone or in pairs.

D in farming villages along rivers and streams.

3 The development of farming brought all of the following changes to the lives of early humans *except*

A the first human-made shelters.

B a larger supply of food.

C the construction of permanent settlements.

D the ability to make cloth.

4 The region of the world that was likely occupied *last* by early humans was

A northern Asia.

B southern Asia.

C North America.

D South America.

5 Hunter-gatherer societies in the Old Stone Age possessed all of the following *except*

A fire.

B art.

C bone tools.

D religious beliefs.

Connecting with Past Learnings

6 You know that history is the study of people and events from the past. To learn about prehistory, historians would likely study all of the following *except*

A graves.

B journals.

C bones.

D art.

7 A skull from a human who lived during the Neolithic Era would be considered a(n)

A tool.

B artifact.

C fossil.

D secondary source.

Assignment

Write a paper comparing and contrasting two early human societies.

TIP **Using a Graphic Organizer**

A Venn diagram can help you see ways that the two societies are similar and different.

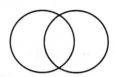

Comparing and Contrasting Societies

Comparing means finding likenesses between or among things. Contrasting means finding differences. You often compare and contrast things to understand them better and see how they are related.

1. Prewrite

Getting Started

Unlike most essays, a compare and contrast paper has two subjects. However, it still has only one big idea, or thesis. For example, your idea may be to show how two societies dealt with the same problem or to show how two human societies changed over time.

Begin by choosing two subjects. Then identify specific points of similarities and differences between the two. Support each point with historical facts, examples, and details.

Organizing Your Information

Choose one of these two ways to organize your points of comparison.

- Present all the points about the first subject and then all the points about the second subject: AAABBB, or block style
- Alternate back and forth between the first subject and the second subject: ABABAB, or point-by-point style

2. Write

This framework will help you use your notes to write a first draft.

A Writer's Framework

Introduction
- Clearly identify your two subjects.
- Give background information readers will need in order to understand your points of comparison between the societies.
- State your big idea, or main purpose in comparing and contrasting these two societies.

Body
- Present your points of comparison in block style or point-by-point style.
- Compare the two societies in at least two ways, and contrast them in at least two ways.
- Use specific historical facts, details, and examples to support each of your points.

Conclusion
- Restate your big idea.
- Summarize the points you have made in your paper.
- Expand on your big idea, perhaps by relating it to your own life, to other societies, or to later historical events.

3. Evaluate and Revise

Evaluating

Use the following questions to discover ways to improve your paper.

Evaluation Questions for a Comparison/Contrast Paper

- Do you introduce both of your subjects in your first paragraph?
- Do you state your big idea, or thesis, at the end of your introduction?
- Do you present two or more similarities and two or more differences between the two societies?

- Do you use either the block style or point-by-point style of organization?
- Do you support your points of comparison with enough historical facts, details, and examples?
- Does your conclusion restate your big idea and summarize your main points?

TIP **Help with Punctuation**

Use the correct punctuation marks before and after clue words within sentences. Usually, a comma comes before *and, but, for, nor, or, so,* and *yet,* with no punctuation after the word. When they are in the middle of a sentence, clue words and phrases such as *however, similarly, in addition, in contrast,* and *on the other hand* usually have a comma before and after them.

Revising

When you are revising your paper, you may need to add comparison-contrast clue words. They will help your readers see the connections between ideas.

Clue Words for Similarities	Clue Words for Differences
also, another, both, in addition, just as, like, similarly, too	although, but, however, in contrast, instead, on the other hand, unlike

4. Proofread and Publish

Proofreading

Before sharing your paper, you will want to polish it by correcting any remaining errors. Look closely for mistakes in grammar, spelling, capitalization, and punctuation. To avoid two common grammar errors, make sure that you have used the correct form of –er or *more* and –est or *most* with adjectives and adverbs when making comparisons.

Publishing

One good way to share your paper is to exchange it with one or more classmates. After reading each other's papers, you can compare and contrast them. How are your papers similar? How do they differ? If possible, share papers with someone whose big idea is similar to yours.

Practice and Apply

Use the steps and strategies outlined in this workshop to write your compare and contrast paper.

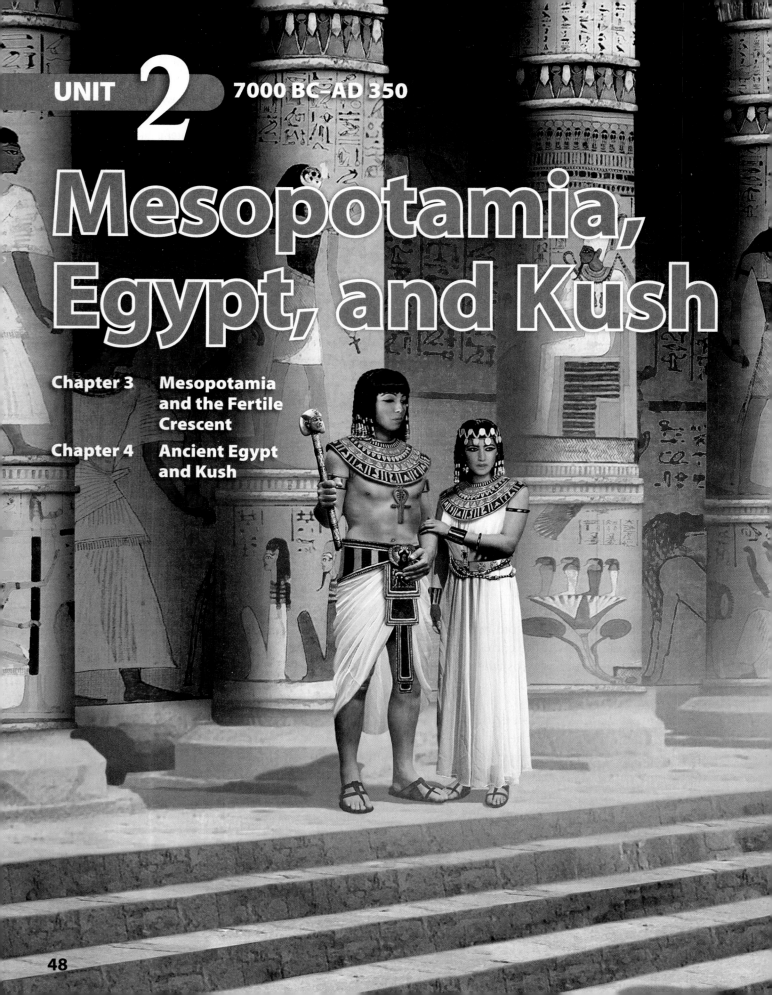

Mesopotamia, Egypt, and Kush

The world's first civilizations developed in Asia and Africa after people learned how to farm. These civilizations began in river valleys, which were perfect places for people to grow crops.

With the development of farming, people no longer had to travel in search of food. Instead, they could settle down in one place. Eventually, people built the first towns and cities and invented government, writing, and the wheel. They also created huge buildings and temples and produced incredible works of art.

In the next two chapters, you will learn about the early civilizations of Mesopotamia, Egypt, and Kush.

Explore the Art

In this scene, the young King Tutankhamen of Egypt stands with his wife at the entrance to a temple. How does this scene show some of the features of Egyptian civilization?

FLORIDA...
The Story Continues

CHAPTER 3, Mesopotamia and the Fertile Crescent (7000–500 BC)

EVENTS **5000–3000 BC: Florida develops its modern climate and environments.** Between 5000 BC and 3000 BC Florida developed the climate and environments it has today. The rising sea level and increased rainfall produced more wetlands, including the Everglades. During the last ice age the Everglades region was a relatively high, dry area with only pockets of water. Over time, it became an area of hammock forests, pinelands, marshes, and cypress. By around 3000 BC the Everglades was a marshland dotted with mangrove and cypress swamps and tree islands.

PLACES **5000–3000 BC: Rivers support population growth and the spread of settlements.** As Florida's climate became wetter, settlements appeared along rivers. One such river was the St. Johns in northeastern Florida. More water allowed people to live more settled lives. Populations increased. Archaeological evidence indicates that people settled throughout the peninsula.

PLACES **c. 5000 BC: The Windover Pond archaeological site provides a glimpse of life 7,000 years ago.** The people who lived around Windover Pond 7,000 years ago created permanent or semi-permanent villages. They buried their dead in the peat at the bottom of the shallow pond. The peat preserved objects that would have normally decayed. Archaeologists have found human remains, woven fiber fabrics and cording, bone and antler tools, and fishing and hunting equipment at the site. They have also found evidence of the people's diet. The people ate otters, rats, squirrels, rabbits, opossums, ducks, wading birds, alligators, turtles, snakes, frogs, fish, shellfish, prickly pears, gourds, hickory nuts, and cattail roots.

EVENTS **c. 3000 BC: Predictable food sources lead to village life.**

Around 3000 BC people increasingly began to settle in villages, even though they remained hunter-gatherers. Archaeological evidence suggests that the availability of large amounts of fish and shellfish played an important role in making this possible. Some sites have yielded bones of more than 50 kinds of fish. Based on shell remains, archaeologists also know that people ate a wide range of fresh and saltwater shellfish. Vast amounts of coquina, scallop, mussel, oyster, and whelk shells have been found at sites around the state. A reliable food source close at

hand enabled hunter-gatherers to begin settling in permanent and semi-permanent villages.

PEOPLE **c. 2000–1000 BC: Villagers learn to make fired clay pottery.**

Archaeological evidence suggests that people in the St. Johns River valley may have been the first Floridians to make pottery. They mixed clay with Spanish moss or palmetto fibers and then fired the pots. The fibers and firing strenthened the clay. The firing also made the pottery waterproof. The practice spread throughout the peninsula, as far south as the Florida Keys, by 1000 BC. The makeup of the clay used in the pottery differed around the state because of the differences in soils. Some archaeologists refer to the appearance of fired clay pottery as the "container revolution" because it changed the way people cooked and stored food.

Photo credits: See Chapter 1 Florida...The Story Continues

Unpacking the Florida Standards <•••

Read the following to learn what this standard says and what it means. See FL8–FL31 to unpack all of the standards related to this chapter.

Benchmark SS.6.G.2.3   Analyze the relationship of physical geography to the development of ancient river valley civilizations. Examples are Tigris and Euphrates [Mesopotamia], Nile [Egypt], Indus and Ganges [Ancient India], and Huang He [Ancient China].

What does it mean?

Explain why physical geography so strongly affected the way that ancient river valley civilizations developed.

 SPOTLIGHT ON

SS.6.E.3.4, SS.6.G.1.2, SS.6.G.1.5 See pages FL39, FL42, and FL43 for content specifically related to these Chapter 3 standards.

Mesopotamia and the Fertile Crescent

Essential Question How did geography influence the development of civilization in Southwest Asia?

Florida Next Generation Sunshine State Standards

SS.6.E.1.1 Identify the factors (new resources, increased productivity, education, technology, slave economy, territorial expansion) that increase economic growth. **SS.6.E.3.4** Describe the relationship among civilizations that engage in trade, including the benefits and drawbacks of voluntary trade. **SS.6.G.1.2** Analyze the purposes of map projections (political, physical, special purpose) and explain the applications of various types of maps. **SS.6.G.1.3** Identify natural wonders of the ancient world. **SS.6.G.1.5** Use scale, cardinal, and intermediate directions, and estimation of distances between places on current and ancient maps of the world. **SS.6.G.1.7** Use maps to identify characteristics and boundaries of ancient civilizations that have shaped the world today. **SS.6.G.2.3** Analyze the relationship of physical geography to the development of ancient river valley civilizations. **SS.6.G.2.6** Explain the concept of cultural diffusion, and identify the influences of different ancient cultures on one another. **SS.6.G.3.1** Explain how the physical landscape has affected the development of agriculture and industry in the ancient world. **SS.6.G.5.1** Identify the methods used to compensate for the scarcity of resources in the ancient world. **SS.6.G.5.2** Use geographic terms and tools to explain why ancient civilizations developed networks of highways, waterways, and other transportation linkages. **SS.6.G.5.3** Use geographic tools and terms to analyze how famine, drought, and natural disasters plagued many ancient civilizations. **SS.6.G.6.2** Compare maps of the world in ancient times with current political maps. **SS.6.W.2.7** Summarize the important achievements of Mesopotamian civilization. **SS.6.W.2.8** Determine the impact of key figures from ancient Mesopotamian civilizations. **SS.6.W.3.1** Analyze the cultural impact the ancient Phoenicians had on the Mediterranean world with regard to colonization (Carthage), exploration, maritime commerce (purple dye, tin), and written communication (alphabet).

FOCUS ON WRITING

A Letter Most elementary students have not read or heard much about ancient Mesopotamia. As you read this chapter, you can gather information about that land. Then you can write a letter to share some of what you have learned with a young child.

CHAPTER EVENTS

WORLD EVENTS

c. 7000 BC Agriculture first develops in Mesopotamia.

7000 BC

c. 3100 BC Menes becomes the first pharaoh of Egypt.

This photo shows the partially reconstructed remains of an ancient temple in Mesopotamia.

c. 2350–2330 BC
Sargon of Akkad conquers Mesopotamia and forms the world's first empire.

c. 1770 BC
Hammurabi of Babylon issues a written code of laws.

c. 1000 BC
Phoenicians trade all around the Mediterranean.

2750 BC   **2000 BC**   **1250 BC**   **500 BC**

c. 2300 BC
The Harappan civilization rises in the Indus Valley.

c. 1500 BC
The Shang dynasty is established in China.

c. 965 BC
Solomon becomes king of Israel.

Reading Social Studies

| Economics | Geography | Politics | Religion | Society and Culture | Science and Technology |

Focus on Themes Chapter three introduces you to a region in Southwest Asia called Mesopotamia, the home of the world's first civilization. You will read about what made this area one where civilizations could begin and grow. You will learn about one group of people—the Sumerians—and their great **technological** inventions. You will also read about other people who invaded Mesopotamia and brought their own rules of governing and **politics** to the area.

Main Ideas in Social Studies

LA.6.1.7.3 The student will determine the main idea or essential message in grade-level text through inferring, paraphrasing, summarizing, and identifying relevant details.
SS.6.W.2.4 Compare the economic, political, social, and religious institutions of ancient river civilizations.

Focus on Reading Have you ever set up a tent? If you have, you know that one pole provides structure and support for the whole tent. A paragraph has a similar structure. One idea—the **main idea**—provides support and structure for the whole paragraph.

Identifying Main Ideas Most paragraphs written about history include a main idea that is stated clearly in a sentence. At other times, the main idea is suggested, not stated. However, that idea still shapes the paragraph's content and the meaning of all of the facts and details in it.

Identifying Main Ideas

1. Read the paragraph. Ask yourself, "What is this paragraph mostly about?"

2. List the important facts and details that relate to that topic.

3. Ask yourself, "What seems to be the most important point the writer is making about the topic?" Or ask, "If the writer could say only one thing about this paragraph, what would it be?" **This is the main idea of the paragraph.**

Having people available to work on different jobs meant that society could accomplish more. Large projects, such as constructing buildings and digging irrigation systems, required specialized workers, managers, and organization. To complete these projects, the Mesopotamians needed structure and rules. Structure and rules could be provided by laws and government.

Topic: The paragraph talks about people, jobs, and structure.

+

Facts and Details:
• People working on different jobs needed structure.
• Laws and government provided this structure.

=

Main Idea: Having people in a society work on many different jobs led to the creation of laws and government.

LA.6.1.7.1 The student will use background knowledge of subject and related content areas, prereading strategies, graphic representations, and knowledge of text structure to make and confirm complex predictions of content, purpose, and organization of a reading selection.

You Try It!

The passage below is from the chapter you are about to read. Read it and then answer the questions below.

Technical Advances

One of the Sumerians' most important developments was the wheel. They were the first people to build wheeled vehicles, including carts and wagons. Using the wheel, Sumerians invented a device that spins clay as a craftsperson shapes it into bowls. This device is called a potter's wheel.

The plow was another important Sumerian invention. Pulled by oxen, plows broke through the hard soil of Sumer to prepare it for planting. This technique greatly increased farm production. The Sumerians also invented a clock that used falling water to measure time.

Sumerian advances improved daily life in many ways. Sumerians built sewers under city streets. They learned to use bronze to make stronger tools and weapons. They even produced makeup and glass jewelry.

Answer the following questions about finding main ideas.

1. Reread the first paragraph. What is its main idea?

2. What is the main idea of the third paragraph? Reread the second paragraph. Is there a sentence that expresses the main idea of the paragraph? What is that main idea? Write a sentence to express it.

3. Which of the following best expresses the main idea of the entire passage?

  a. The wheel was an important invention.

  b. The Sumerians invented many helpful devices.

> **As you read Chapter 3,** find the main ideas of the paragraphs you are studying.

Key Terms and People

Chapter 3

Section 1
Fertile Crescent *(p. 55)*
silt *(p. 55)*
irrigation *(p. 56)*
canals *(p. 56)*
surplus *(p. 56)*
division of labor *(p. 56)*

Section 2
rural *(p. 60)*
urban *(p. 60)*
city-state *(p. 60)*
Gilgamesh *(p. 61)*
Sargon *(p. 61)*
empire *(p. 61)*
polytheism *(p. 62)*
priests *(p. 63)*
social hierarchy *(p. 63)*

Section 3
cuneiform *(p. 65)*
pictographs *(p. 66)*
scribe *(p. 66)*
epics *(p. 66)*
architecture *(p. 68)*
ziggurat *(p. 68)*

Section 4
monarch *(p. 72)*
Hammurabi's Code *(p. 73)*
chariot *(p. 74)*
Nebuchadnezzar *(p. 75)*
alphabet *(p. 77)*

Academic Vocabulary

Success in school is related to knowing academic vocabulary—the words that are frequently used in school assignments and discussions. In this chapter, you will learn the following academic words:

role *(p. 62)*
impact *(p. 63)*

LA.6.1.6.1, SS.6.E.1.1, SS.6.E.2.1,
SS.6.G.1.4, SS.6.G.1.5, SS.6.G.1.6,
SS.6.G.1.7, SS.6.G.2.1, SS.6.G.2.2,
SS.6.G.2.3, SS.6.G.2.4, SS.6.G.3.1, SS.6.G.3.2,
SS.6.G.5.3, SS.6.W.2.3, SS.6.W.2.4

What You Will Learn...

Main Ideas

1. The rivers of Southwest Asia supported the growth of civilization.
2. New farming techniques led to the growth of cities.

The Big Idea

The valleys of the Tigris and Euphrates rivers were the site of the world's first civilizations.

Key Terms

Fertile Crescent, *p. 55*
silt, *p. 55*
irrigation, *p. 56*
canals, *p. 56*
surplus, *p. 56*
division of labor, *p. 56*

Online Resource
TAKING NOTES

Use the graphic organizer online to list the cause-and-effect relationship between each river valley and the civilization that developed around it.

Geography of the Fertile Crescent

If YOU were there...

You are a farmer in Southwest Asia about 6,000 years ago. You live near a slow-moving river, with many shallow lakes and marshes. The river makes the land in the valley rich and fertile, so you can grow wheat and dates. But in the spring, raging floods spill over the riverbanks, destroying your fields. In the hot summers, you are often short of water.

How can you control the waters of the river?

BUILDING BACKGROUND In several parts of the world, bands of hunter-gatherers began to settle down in farming settlements. They domesticated plants and animals. Gradually their cultures became more complex. Most early civilizations grew up along rivers, where people learned to work together to control floods.

Rivers Support the Growth of Civilization

Early peoples settled where crops would grow. Crops usually grew well near rivers, where water was available and regular floods made the soil rich. One region in Southwest Asia was especially well suited for farming. It lay between two rivers.

The Land Between the Rivers

The Tigris and Euphrates rivers are the most important physical features of the region sometimes known as Mesopotamia (mes-uh-puh-TAY-mee-uh). Mesopotamia means "between the rivers" in Greek.

As you can see on the map, the region called Mesopotamia lies between Asia Minor and the Persian Gulf. The region is part of a larger area called the **Fertile Crescent**, a large arc of rich, or fertile, farmland. The Fertile Crescent extends from the Persian Gulf to the Mediterranean Sea.

In ancient times, Mesopotamia was actually made of two parts. Northern Mesopotamia was a plateau bordered on the north and the east by mountains. Southern Mesopotamia was a flat plain. The Tigris and Euphrates rivers flowed down from the hills into this low-lying plain.

The Rise of Civilization

Hunter-gatherer groups first settled in Mesopotamia more than 12,000 years ago. Over time, these people learned how to plant crops to grow their own food. Every year, floods on the Tigris and Euphrates rivers brought **silt**, a mixture of rich soil and tiny rocks, to the land. The fertile silt made the land ideal for farming.

The first farm settlements formed in Mesopotamia as early as 7000 BC. Farmers grew wheat, barley, and other types of grain. Livestock, birds, and fish were also good sources of food. Plentiful food led to population growth, and villages formed. Eventually, these early villages developed into the world's first civilization.

READING CHECK **Summarizing** What made civilization possible in Mesopotamia?

SS.6.G.2.1 Explain how major physical characteristics, natural resources, climate, and absolute and relative locations have influenced settlement, interactions, and the economies of ancient civilizations of the world.
SS.6.G.3.1 Explain how the physical landscape has affected the development of agriculture and industry in the ancient world.

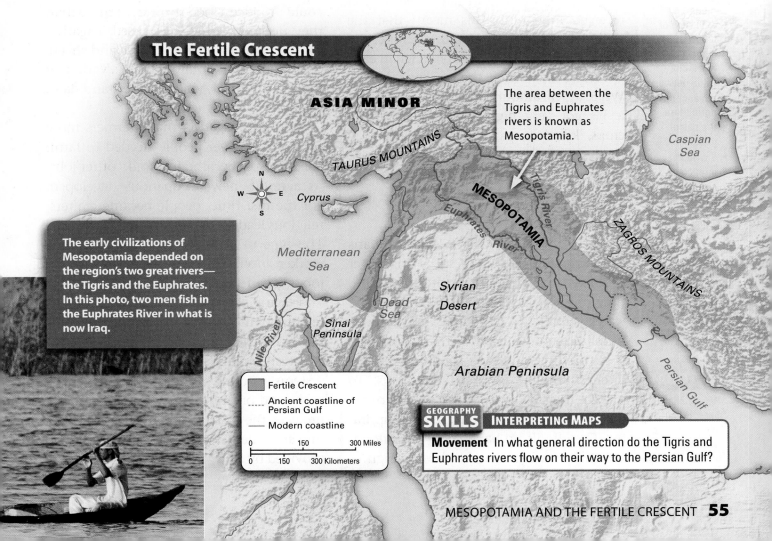

The Fertile Crescent

ASIA MINOR

The area between the Tigris and Euphrates rivers is known as Mesopotamia.

Caspian Sea

TAURUS MOUNTAINS

Cyprus

MESOPOTAMIA

Euphrates River

Tigris River

ZAGROS MOUNTAINS

Mediterranean Sea

The early civilizations of Mesopotamia depended on the region's two great rivers—the Tigris and the Euphrates. In this photo, two men fish in the Euphrates River in what is now Iraq.

Syrian Desert

Dead Sea

Nile River

Sinai Peninsula

Arabian Peninsula

Persian Gulf

Fertile Crescent
Ancient coastline of Persian Gulf
Modern coastline

0   150   300 Miles
0   150   300 Kilometers

GEOGRAPHY SKILLS **INTERPRETING MAPS**

Movement In what general direction do the Tigris and Euphrates rivers flow on their way to the Persian Gulf?

Irrigation and Civilization

Early farmers faced the challenge of learning how to control the flow of river water to their fields in both rainy and dry seasons.

① Early settlements in Mesopotamia were located near rivers. Water was not controlled, and flooding was a major problem.

② Later, people built canals to protect houses from flooding and move water to their fields.

FOCUS ON

What Makes a Civilization? A civilization is defined by these characteristics.

- a central government
- the growth of cities
- a division of labor
- a social hierarchy
- trade networks
- advanced agriculture
- the use of metal tools
- a writing system
- a religious system
- a calendar

SS.6.E.1.1 Identify the factors (new resources, increased productivity, education, technology, slave economy, territorial expansion) that increase economic growth. **SS.6.W.2.3** Identify the characteristics of civilization.

THE IMPACT TODAY

People still build dikes, or earthen walls along rivers or shorelines, to hold back water.

Farming and Cities

Although Mesopotamia had fertile soil, farming wasn't easy there. The region received little rain. This meant that the water levels in the Tigris and Euphrates rivers depended on how much rain fell in eastern Asia Minor where the two rivers began. When a great amount of rain fell there, water levels got very high. Flooding destroyed crops, killed livestock, and washed away homes. When water levels were too low, crops dried up. Farmers knew they needed a way to control the rivers' flow.

Controlling Water

To solve their problems, Mesopotamians used **irrigation**, a way of supplying water to an area of land. To irrigate their land, they dug out large storage basins to hold water supplies. Then they dug **canals**, human-made waterways, that connected these basins to a network of ditches. These ditches brought water to the fields. To protect their fields from flooding, farmers built up the banks of the Tigris and Euphrates. These built-up banks held back floodwaters even when river levels were high.

Food Surpluses

Irrigation increased the amount of food farmers were able to grow. In fact, farmers could produce a food **surplus**, or more than they needed. Farmers also used irrigation to water grazing areas for cattle and sheep. As a result, Mesopotamians ate a variety of foods. Fish, meat, wheat, barley, and dates were plentiful.

Because irrigation made farmers more productive, fewer people needed to farm. Some people became free to do other jobs. As a result, new occupations developed. For the first time, people became crafters, religious leaders, and government workers. The type of arrangement in which each worker specializes in a particular task or job is called a **division of labor**.

Having people available to work on different jobs meant that society could accomplish more. Large projects, such as constructing buildings and digging irrigation systems, required specialized workers, managers, and organization. To complete these projects, the Mesopotamians needed structure and rules. Structure and rules could be provided by laws and government.

3 With irrigation, the people of Mesopotamia were able to grow more food.

4 Food surpluses allowed some people to stop farming and concentrate on other jobs, like making clay pots or tools.

The Appearance of Cities

Over time, Mesopotamian settlements grew in size and complexity. They gradually developed into cities between 4000 and 3000 BC.

Despite the growth of cities, society in Mesopotamia was still based on agriculture. Most people still worked in farming jobs. However, cities were becoming important places. People traded goods there, and cities provided leaders with power bases.

They were the political, religious, cultural, and economic centers of civilization.

READING CHECK **Analyzing** Why did the Mesopotamians create irrigation systems?

SUMMARY AND PREVIEW Mesopotamia's rich, fertile lands supported productive farming, which led to the development of cities. In Section 2 you will learn about some of the first city builders.

Section 1 Assessment

Reviewing Ideas, Terms, and People

1. **a. Identify** Where was Mesopotamia?
   b. Explain How did the **Fertile Crescent** get its name?
   c. Evaluate What was the most important factor in making Mesopotamia's farmland fertile?
2. **a. Describe** Why did farmers need to develop a system to control their water supply?
   b. Explain In what ways did a **division of labor** contribute to the growth of Mesopotamian civilization?
   c. Elaborate How might running large projects prepare people for running a government?

Critical Thinking

3. **Identifying Cause and Effect** Farmers who used the rivers for irrigation were part of a cause-effect chain. Use a chart like this one to show that chain.

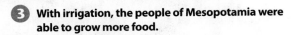

FOCUS ON WRITING

4. **Understanding Geography** Make a list of the words you might use to help young students imagine the land and rivers. Then sketch out a picture or a map to include with your letter.

River Valley Civilizations

All of the world's earliest civilizations had something in common—they all arose in river valleys that were perfect locations for farming. Three key factors made river valleys good for farming. First, the fields that bordered the rivers were flat, which made it easier for farmers to plant crops. Second, the soils were nourished by flood deposits and silt, which made them very fertile. Finally, the river provided the water farmers needed for irrigation.

Natural Highways River travel allowed early civilizations to trade goods and ideas. These people are traveling on the Euphrates River, one of the two main rivers of ancient Mesopotamia.

Mediterranean Sea

Caspian S

MESOPOTAMIA

Tigris River

Euphrates River

Ur

A F R I C A

Memphis

EGYPT

Nile River

Red Sea

A R A B I A N
P E N I N S U L A

From Village to City With the development of agriculture, people settled into farming villages. Over time, some of these villages grew into large cities. These ancient ruins are near Memphis, Egypt.

A S I A

Gift of the River River water was key to farming in early civilizations. This farmer is using water from the Huang He (Yellow River) in China to water her crops.

New Activities Food surpluses allowed people to pursue other activities, like crafts, art, and writing. This tile designer lives in the Indus Valley.

• Harappa

HIMALAYAS

INDUS VALLEY

Indus River

Mohenjo Daro •

Ganges River

INDIA

Arabian Sea

Huang He (Yellow River)

CHINA

Chang Jiang (Yangzi River)

Bay of Bengal

SS.6.G.1.6 Use a map to identify major bodies of water of the world, and explain ways they have impacted the development of civilizations. **SS.6.G.2.3** Analyze the relationship of physical geography to the development of ancient river valley civilizations. **SS.6.W.2.4** Compare the economic, political, social, and religious institutions of ancient river civilizations.

GEOGRAPHY SKILLS **INTERPRETING MAPS**

1. **Human-Environment Interaction** Why did the first civilizations all develop in river valleys?
2. **Location** Where were the four earliest river valley civilizations located?

0		500		1,000 Miles
0	500		1,000 Kilometers	

INDIAN OCEAN

What You Will Learn...

Main Ideas

1. The Sumerians created the world's first advanced society.
2. Religion played a major role in Sumerian society.

The Big Idea

The Sumerians developed the first civilization in Mesopotamia.

Key Terms and People

rural, *p. 60*
urban, *p. 60*
city-state, *p. 60*
Gilgamesh, *p. 61*
Sargon, *p. 61*
empire, *p. 61*
polytheism, *p. 62*
priests, *p. 63*
social hierarchy, *p. 63*

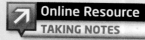

Online Resource
TAKING NOTES

Use the graphic organizer online to take notes on the Sumerian civilization.

The Rise of Sumer

If YOU were there...

You are a crafter living in one of the cities of Sumer. Thick walls surround and protect your city, so you feel safe from the armies of other city-states. But you and your neighbors are fearful of other be-ings—the many gods and spirits that you believe are everywhere. They can bring illness or sandstorms or bad luck.

How might you protect yourself from gods and spirits?

BUILDING BACKGROUND As civilizations developed along rivers, their societies and governments became more advanced. Religion became a main characteristic of these ancient cultures. Kings claimed to rule with the approval of the gods, and ordinary people wore charms and performed rituals to avoid bad luck.

An Advanced Society

In southern Mesopotamia, a people known as the Sumerians (soo-MER-ee-unz) developed the world's first civilization. No one knows where they came from or when they moved into the region. However, by 3000 BC, several hundred thousand Sumerians had settled in Mesopotamia, in a land they called Sumer (SOO-muhr). There they created an advanced society.

The City-States of Sumer

Most people in Sumer were farmers. They lived mainly in **rural**, or countryside, areas. The centers of Sumerian society, however, were the **urban**, or city, areas. The first cities in Sumer had about 10,000 residents. Over time, the cities grew. Historians think that by 2000 BC, some of Sumer's cities had more than 100,000 residents.

As a result, the basic political unit of Sumer combined the two parts. This unit was called a city-state. A **city-state** consisted of a city and all the countryside around it. The amount of coun-tryside controlled by each city-state depended on its military strength. Stronger city-states controlled larger areas.

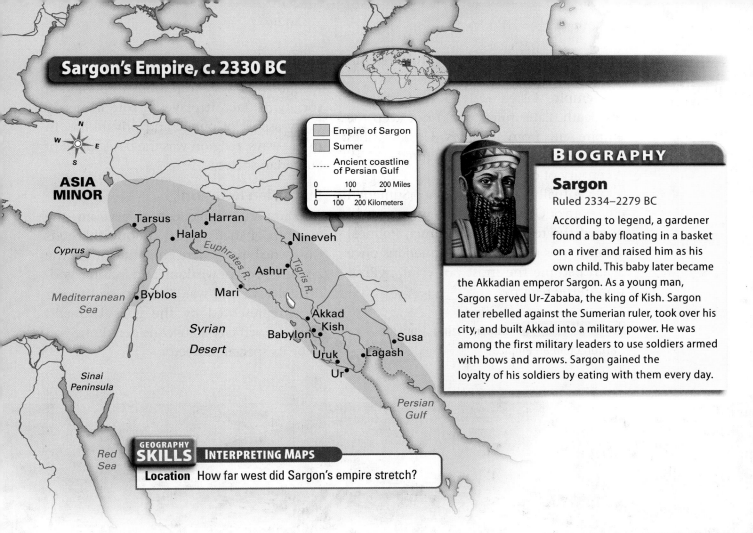

Sargon's Empire, c. 2330 BC

Legend:
- Empire of Sargon
- Sumer
- Ancient coastline of Persian Gulf

0 100 200 Miles
0 100 200 Kilometers

ASIA MINOR

Tarsus
Harran
Halab
Cyprus
Nineveh
Euphrates R.
Ashur
Tigris R.
Mediterranean Sea
Byblos
Mari
Syrian Desert
Akkad
Babylon
Kish
Susa
Uruk
Lagash
Ur
Sinai Peninsula
Persian Gulf
Red Sea

GEOGRAPHY SKILLS | **INTERPRETING MAPS**

Location How far west did Sargon's empire stretch?

City-states in Sumer fought each other to gain more farmland. As a result of these conflicts, the city-states built up strong armies. Sumerians also built strong, thick walls around their cities for protection.

Individual city-states gained and lost power over time. By 3500 BC, a city-state known as Kish had become quite powerful. Over the next 1,000 years, the city-states of Uruk and Ur fought for dominance. One of Uruk's kings, known as **Gilgamesh**, became a legendary figure in Sumerian literature.

Rise of the Akkadian Empire

In time, another society developed along the Tigris and Euphrates. It was created by the Akkadians (uh-KAY-dee-uhns). They lived just north of Sumer, but they were not Sumerians. They even spoke a different language than the Sumerians. In spite of their differences, however, the Akkadians and the Sumerians lived in peace for many years.

That peace was broken in the 2300s BC when **Sargon** sought to extend Akkadian territory. He built a new capital, Akkad (A-kad), on the Euphrates River, near what is now the city of Baghdad. Sargon was the first ruler to have a permanent army. He used that army to launch a series of wars against neighboring kingdoms.

Sargon's soldiers defeated all the city-states of Sumer. They also conquered northern Mesopotamia, finally bringing the entire region under his rule. With these conquests, Sargon established the world's first **empire**, or land with different territories and peoples under a single rule. The Akkadian Empire stretched from the Persian Gulf to the Mediterranean Sea.

SS.6.G.1.7 Use maps to identify characteristics and boundaries of ancient civilizations that have shaped the world today. SS.6.W.2.8 Determine the impact of key figures from ancient Mesopotamian civilizations.

Sargon was emperor, or ruler of his empire, for more than 50 years. However, the empire lasted only a century after his death. Later rulers could not keep the empire safe from invaders. Hostile tribes from the east raided and captured Akkad. A century of chaos followed.

Eventually, however, the Sumerian city-state of Ur rebuilt its strength and conquered the rest of Mesopotamia. Political stability was restored. The Sumerians once again became the most powerful civilization in the region.

READING CHECK **Summarizing** How did Sargon build an empire?

Religion Shapes Society

Religion was very important in Sumerian society. In fact, it played a **role** in nearly every aspect of public and private life. In many ways, religion was the basis for all of Sumerian society.

Sumerian Religion

The Sumerians practiced **polytheism**, the worship of many gods. Among the gods they worshipped were Enlil, the lord of the air; Enki, god of wisdom; and Inanna, goddess of love and war. The sun and moon were represented by the gods Utu and Nanna. Each city-state considered one god to be its special protector.

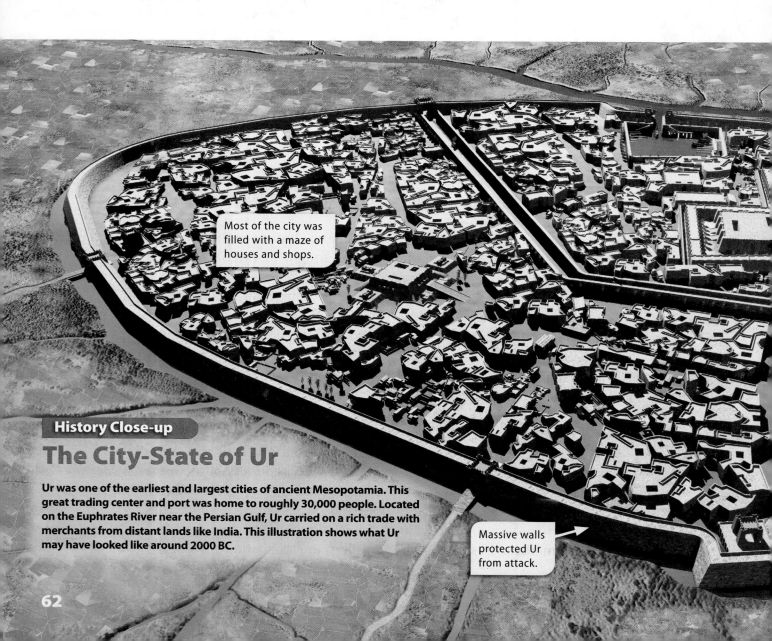

Most of the city was filled with a maze of houses and shops.

History Close-up

The City-State of Ur

Ur was one of the earliest and largest cities of ancient Mesopotamia. This great trading center and port was home to roughly 30,000 people. Located on the Euphrates River near the Persian Gulf, Ur carried on a rich trade with merchants from distant lands like India. This illustration shows what Ur may have looked like around 2000 BC.

Massive walls protected Ur from attack.

The Sumerians believed that their gods had enormous powers. Gods could bring a good harvest or a disastrous flood. They could bring illness, or they could bring good health and wealth. The Sumerians believed that success in every area of life depended on pleasing the gods. Every Sumerian had a duty to serve and to worship the gods.

Priests, people who performed religious ceremonies, had great status in Sumer. People relied on them to help gain the gods' favor. Priests interpreted the wishes of the gods and made offerings to them. These offerings were made in temples, special buildings where priests performed their religious ceremonies.

Sumerian Social Order

Because of their status, priests occupied a high level in Sumer's **social hierarchy**, the division of society by rank or class. In fact, priests were just below kings. The kings of Sumer claimed that they had been chosen by the gods to rule.

Below the priests were Sumer's skilled craftspeople, merchants, and traders. Trade had a great **impact** on Sumerian society. Traders traveled to faraway places and exchanged grain for gold, silver, copper, lumber, and precious stones.

Below traders, farmers and laborers made up the large working class. Slaves were at the bottom of the social order.

ACADEMIC VOCABULARY
impact effect, result

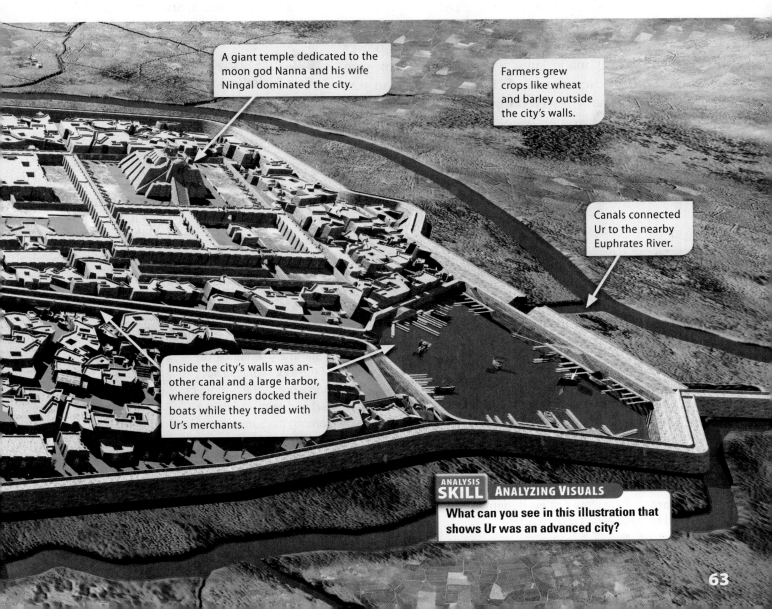

A giant temple dedicated to the moon god Nanna and his wife Ningal dominated the city.

Farmers grew crops like wheat and barley outside the city's walls.

Canals connected Ur to the nearby Euphrates River.

Inside the city's walls was another canal and a large harbor, where foreigners docked their boats while they traded with Ur's merchants.

ANALYSIS SKILL **ANALYZING VISUALS**

What can you see in this illustration that shows Ur was an advanced city?

Sumerian society was divided into different groups. This ancient artifact shows Sumerian leaders celebrating a military victory while a musician plays his instrument.

Men and Women in Sumer

Sumerian men and women had different roles. In general, men held political power and made laws, while women took care of the home and children. Education was usually reserved for men, but some upper-class women were educated as well.

Some educated women were priestesses in Sumer's temples. Some priestesses helped shape Sumerian culture. One, Enheduanna, the daughter of Sargon, wrote hymns to the goddess Inanna. She is the first known female writer in history.

READING CHECK **Analyzing** How did trade affect Sumerian society?

SUMMARY AND PREVIEW In this section you learned about Sumerian city-states, religion, and society. In Section 3, you will read about the Sumerians' achievements.

SS.6.G.4.1 Explain how family and ethnic relationships influenced ancient cultures.

Section 2 Assessment

Reviewing Ideas, Terms, and People

1. **a. Recall** What was the basic political unit of Sumer?
   b. Explain What steps did **city-states** take to protect themselves from their rivals?
   c. Elaborate How do you think Sargon's creation of an **empire** changed the history of Mesopotamia? Defend your answer.
2. **a. Identify** What is **polytheism**?
   b. Draw Conclusions Why do you think **priests** were so influential in ancient Sumerian society?
   c. Elaborate Why would rulers benefit if they claimed to be chosen by the gods?

Critical Thinking

3. **Summarizing** In the right column of your note-taking chart, write a summary sentence for each of the four characteristics. Then add a box at the bottom of the chart and write a sentence summarizing the Sumerian civilization.

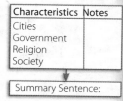

Characteristics	Notes
Cities	
Government	
Religion	
Society	

Summary Sentence:

FOCUS ON WRITING

4. **Gathering Information about Sumer** What aspects of Sumerian society will you include in your letter? What important people, religious beliefs, or social developments do you think the students should learn?

Sumerian Achievements

If YOU were there...

You are a student at a school for scribes in Sumer. Learning all the symbols for writing is very hard. Your teacher assigns you lessons to write on your clay tablet, but you can't help making mistakes. Then you have to smooth out the surface and try again. Still, being a scribe can lead to important jobs for the king. You could make your family proud.

Why would you want to be a scribe?

> **BUILDING BACKGROUND** Sumerian society was advanced in terms of religion and government organization. The Sumerians were responsible for many other achievements, which were passed down to later civilizations.

The Invention of Writing

The Sumerians made one of the greatest cultural advances in history. They developed **cuneiform** (kyoo-NEE-uh-fohrm), the world's first system of writing. But Sumerians did not have pencils, pens, or paper. Instead, they used sharp tools called styluses to make wedge-shaped symbols on clay tablets.

What You Will Learn...

Main Ideas

1. The Sumerians invented the world's first writing system.
2. Advances and inventions changed Sumerian lives.
3. Many types of art developed in Sumer.

The Big Idea

The Sumerians made many advances that helped their society develop.

Key Terms

cuneiform, *p. 65*
pictographs, *p. 66*
scribe, *p. 66*
epics, *p. 66*
architecture, *p. 68*
ziggurat, *p. 68*

↗ **Online Resource**
TAKING NOTES

Use the graphic organizer online to list the achievements and advances made by the Sumerian civilization.

SS.6.W.2.7 Summarize the important achievements of Mesopotamian civilization.

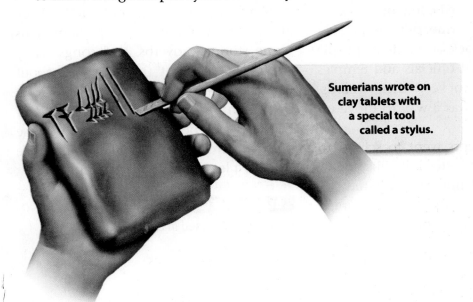

Sumerians wrote on clay tablets with a special tool called a stylus.

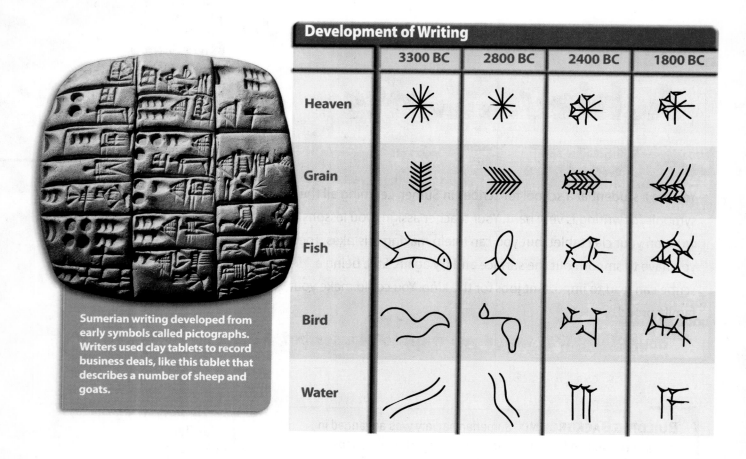

Development of Writing

	3300 BC	2800 BC	2400 BC	1800 BC
Heaven				
Grain				
Fish				
Bird				
Water				

Sumerian writing developed from early symbols called pictographs. Writers used clay tablets to record business deals, like this tablet that describes a number of sheep and goats.

Earlier written communication had used **pictographs**, or picture symbols. Each pictograph represented an object, such as a tree or an animal. But in cuneiform, symbols could also represent syllables, or basic parts of words. As a result, Sumerian writers could combine symbols to express more complex ideas such as "joy" or "powerful."

Sumerians first used cuneiform to keep business records. A **scribe**, or writer, would be hired to keep track of the items people traded. Government officials and temples also hired scribes to keep their records. Becoming a scribe was a way to move up in social class.

Sumerian students went to school to learn to read and write. But, like today, some students did not want to study. A Sumerian story tells of a father who urged his son to do his schoolwork:

" Go to school, stand before your 'school-father,' recite your assignment, open your schoolbag, write your tablet . . . After you have finished your assignment and reported to your monitor [teacher], come to me, and do not wander about in the street. "

–Sumerian essay quoted in *History Begins at Sumer*, by Samuel Noah Kramer

In time, Sumerians put their writing skills to new uses. They wrote works on history, law, grammar, and math. They also created works of literature. Sumerians wrote stories, proverbs, and songs. They wrote poems about the gods and about military victories. Some of these were **epics**, long poems that tell the stories of heroes. Later, people used some of these poems to create *The Epic of Gilgamesh*, the story of a legendary Sumerian king.

READING CHECK Generalizing How was cuneiform first used in Sumer?

Advances and Inventions

Writing was not the only great Sumerian invention. These early people made many other advances and discoveries.

Technical Advances

One of the Sumerians' most important developments was the wheel. They were the first people to build wheeled vehicles, including carts and wagons. Using the wheel, Sumerians invented a device that spins clay as a craftsperson shapes it into bowls. This device is called a potter's wheel.

The plow was another important Sumerian invention. Pulled by oxen, plows broke through the hard clay soil of Sumer to prepare it for planting. The Sumerians also invented a clock that used falling water to measure time. They added sails to their boats to make sailboats.

Sumerian advances improved daily life in many ways. Sumerians built sewers under city streets. They learned to use bronze to make stronger tools and weapons. They even produced makeup and glass jewelry.

Math and Sciences

Another area in which Sumerians excelled was math. In fact, they developed a math system based on the number 60. Based on this system, they divided a circle into 360 degrees. Dividing a year into 12 months—a factor of 60—was another Sumerian idea. Sumerians also calculated the areas of rectangles and triangles.

Sumerian scholars studied science, too. They wrote long lists to record their study of the natural world. These tablets included the names of thousands of animals, plants, and minerals.

The Sumerians also made advances in medicine. They used ingredients from animals, plants, and minerals to produce healing drugs. Items used in these medicines included milk, turtle shells, figs, and salt. The Sumerians even catalogued their medical knowledge, listing treatments according to symptoms and body parts.

READING CHECK **Categorizing** What areas of life were improved by Sumerian inventions?

THE IMPACT TODAY

Like the Sumerians we use a base-60 system when we talk about 60 seconds in a minute and 60 minutes in an hour.

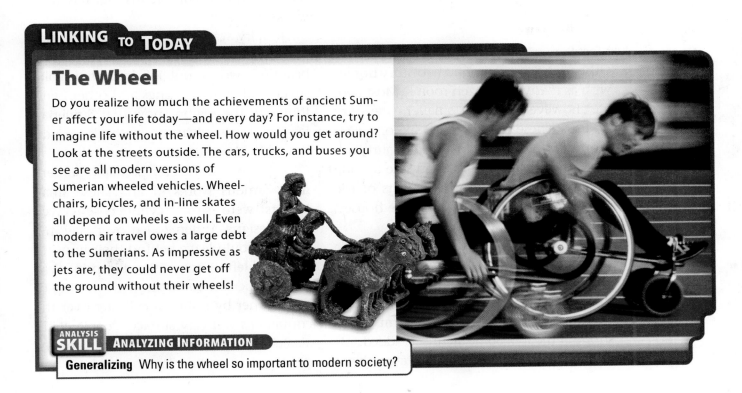

LINKING TO TODAY

The Wheel

Do you realize how much the achievements of ancient Sumer affect your life today—and every day? For instance, try to imagine life without the wheel. How would you get around? Look at the streets outside. The cars, trucks, and buses you see are all modern versions of Sumerian wheeled vehicles. Wheelchairs, bicycles, and in-line skates all depend on wheels as well. Even modern air travel owes a large debt to the Sumerians. As impressive as jets are, they could never get off the ground without their wheels!

ANALYSIS SKILL **ANALYZING INFORMATION**

Generalizing Why is the wheel so important to modern society?

The Sumerians' artistic achievements included beautiful works of gold, wood, and stone.

Cylinder seals like this one were carved into round stones and then rolled over clay to leave their mark.

This stringed musical instrument is called a lyre. It features a cow's head and is made of silver decorated with shell and stone.

The Arts of Sumer

The Sumerians' skills in the fields of art, metalwork, and **architecture**—the science of building—are well known to us. The ruins of great buildings and fine works of art have provided us with wonderful examples of the Sumerians' creativity.

Architecture

Most Sumerian rulers lived in large palaces. Other rich Sumerians had two-story homes with as many as a dozen rooms. Most people, however, lived in smaller, one-story houses. These homes had six or seven rooms arranged around a small courtyard. Large and small houses stood side by side along the narrow, unpaved streets of the city. Bricks made of mud were the houses' main building blocks.

City centers were dominated by their temples, the largest and most impressive buildings in Sumer. A **ziggurat**, a pyramid-shaped temple tower, rose above each city. Outdoor staircases led to a platform and a shrine at the top. Some architects added columns to make the temples more attractive.

The Arts

Sumerian sculptors produced many fine works. Among them are the statues of gods created for temples. Sumerian artists also sculpted small objects out of ivory and rare woods. Sumerian pottery is known more for its quantity than quality. Potters turned out many items, but few were works of beauty.

Jewelry was a popular item in Sumer. The jewelers of the region made many beautiful works out of imported gold, silver, and gems. Earrings and other items found in the region show that Sumerian jewelers knew advanced methods for putting gold pieces together.

Cylinder seals are perhaps Sumer's most famous works of art. These small objects were stone cylinders engraved with designs. When rolled over clay, the designs would leave behind their imprint. Each seal left its own distinct imprint. As a result, a person could show ownership of a container by rolling a cylinder over the container's wet clay surface. People could also use cylinder seals to "sign" documents or to decorate other clay objects.

The Sumerians were the first people in Mesopotamia to build large temples called ziggurats.

This gold dagger was found in a royal tomb. The bull's head is made of gold and silver.

ANALYSIS SKILL **ANALYZING VISUALS**
What animal is shown in two of these works?

Some seals showed battle scenes. Others displayed worship rituals. Some were highly decorative, with hundreds of carefully cut gems. They required great skill to make.

The Sumerians also enjoyed music. Kings and temples hired musicians to play on special occasions. Sumerian musicians played reed pipes, drums, tambourines, and stringed instruments called lyres. Children learned songs in school. People sang hymns to gods and kings. Music and dance provided entertainment in marketplaces and homes.

READING CHECK **Drawing Inferences** What might historians learn from cylinder seals?

SUMMARY AND PREVIEW The Sumerians greatly enriched their society. Next you will learn about the later peoples who lived in Mesopotamia.

Section 3 Assessment

Reviewing Ideas, Terms, and People

1. **a. Identify** What is **cuneiform**?
   b. Analyze Why do you think writing is one of history's most important cultural advances?
   c. Elaborate What current leader would you choose to write an **epic** about, and why?
2. **a. Recall** What were two early uses of the wheel?
   b. Explain Why do you think the invention of the plow was so important to the Sumerians?
3. **a. Describe** What was the basic Sumerian building material?
   b. Make Inferences Why do you think cylinder seals developed into works of art?

Critical Thinking

4. **Identifying Effects** In a chart like this one, identify the effect of each Sumerian advance or achievement you listed in your notes.

Advance/ Achievement	Effect

FOCUS ON WRITING

5. **Evaluating Information** Review the Sumerian achievements you just read about. Then create a list of Sumerian achievements for your letter. Would this list replace some of the information you collected in Section 2?

MESOPOTAMIA AND THE FERTILE CRESCENT **69**

from The Epic of Gilgamesh

translated by N. K. Sandars

About the Reading The Epic of Gilgamesh *is the world's oldest epic, first recorded—carved on stone tablets—in about 2000 BC. The actual Gilgamesh, ruler of the city of Uruk, had lived about 700 years earlier. Over time, stories about this legendary king had grown and changed. In this story, Gilgamesh and his friend Enkidu seek to slay the monster Humbaba, keeper of a distant forest. In addition to his tremendous size and terrible appearance, Humbaba possesses seven splendors, or powers, one of which is fire. Gilgamesh hopes to claim these powers for himself.*

AS YOU READ Notice both the human qualities and the godly qualities of Gilgamesh.

Humbaba came from his strong house of cedar. He nodded his head and shook it, menacing Gilgamesh; and on him he fastened his eye, the eye of death. Then Gilgamesh called to Shamash and his tears were flowing, "O glorious Shamash, I have followed the road you commanded but now if you send no succor how shall I escape?" ❶ Glorious Shamash heard his prayer and he summoned the great wind, the north wind, the whirlwind, the storm and the icy wind, the tempest and the scorching wind; they came like dragons, like a scorching fire, like a serpent that freezes the heart, a destroying flood and the lightning's fork. The eight winds rose up against Humbaba, they beat against his eyes; he was gripped, unable to go forward or back. ❷ Gilgamesh shouted, "By the life of Ninsun my mother and divine Lugulbanda my father . . . my weak arms and my small weapons I have brought to this Land against you, and now I will enter your house." ❸

So he felled the first cedar and they cut the branches and laid them at the foot of the mountain. At the first stroke Humbaba blazed out, but still they advanced. They felled seven cedars and cut and bound the branches and laid them at the foot of the mountain, and seven times Humbaba loosed his glory on them. As the seventh blaze died out they reached his lair. He slapped his thigh in scorn. He approached like a noble wild bull roped on the mountain, a warrior whose elbows were bound together. The tears started to his eyes and he was pale, "Gilgamesh, let me speak. I have never known a mother, no, nor a father who reared me. I was born of the mountain, he reared me, and Enlil made me the keeper of this forest. Let me go free, Gilgamesh, and I will be your servant, you shall be my lord; all the trees of the forest that I tended on the mountain shall be yours. I will cut them down and build you a palace." . . . ❹

Enkidu said, "Do not listen, Gilgamesh: this Humbaba must die. Kill Humbaba first and his servants after." But Gilgamesh said, "If we touch him the blaze and the glory of light will be put out in confusion, the glory and glamour will vanish, its rays will be quenched." Enkidu said to Gilgamesh, "Not so, my friend. First entrap the bird, and where shall the chicks run then? Afterwards we can search out the glory and the glamour, when the chicks run distracted through the grass."

Gilgamesh listened to the word of his companion, he took the ax in his hand, he drew the sword from his belt, and he struck Humbaba with a thrust of the sword to the neck, and Enkidu his comrade struck the second blow. At the third blow Humbaba fell. Then there followed confusion for this was the guardian of the forest whom they had felled to the ground . . .

When he saw the head of Humbaba, Enlil raged at them. "Why did you do this thing? From henceforth may the fire be on your faces, may it eat the bread that you eat, may it drink where you drink." Then Enlil took again the blaze and the seven splendors that had been Humbaba's: he gave the first to the river, and he gave to the lion, to the stone of execration, to the mountain . . . ❺

O Gilgamesh, king and conqueror of the dreadful blaze; wild bull who plunders the mountain, who crosses the sea, glory to him.

GUIDED READING

WORD HELP

execration a cursing
plunders takes by force

❹ **What effect does Humbaba hope his words will have on Gilgamesh?**

❺ The angry air-god Enlil curses the heroes for slaying Humbaba. He takes back the monster's powers and gives them to other creatures and elements of nature.

In your opinion, is Gilgamesh more or less heroic for slaying Humbaba and angering Enlil?

Archaeologists think this statue from the 700s BC represents Gilgamesh.

CONNECTING LITERATURE TO HISTORY

1. **Analyzing** In Sumerian culture, the gods' powers were thought to be enormous. According to this story, what roles do gods play in people's lives?

2. **Making Inferences** Violence was common in Sumerian society. How does the character of Gilgamesh suggest that Sumerian society could be violent?

SECTION 4

LA.6.1.6.2, SS.6.E.1.1,
SS.6.E.1.3, SS.6.E.3.2,
SS.6.E.3.4, SS.6.G.1.3, SS.6.G.1.4, SS.6.G.1.5,
SS.6.G.1.6, SS.6.G.1.7, SS.6.G.2.1, SS.6.G.2.2,
SS.6.G.2.4, SS.6.G.2.5, SS.6.G.2.6, SS.6.G.4.2,
SS.6.G.5.1, SS.6.G.5.2, SS.6.G.6.2, SS.6.W.1.3,
SS.6.W.2.4, SS.6.W.2.7, SS.6.W.2.8, SS.6.W.3.1

What You Will Learn...

Main Ideas

1. The Babylonians conquered Mesopotamia and created a code of law.
2. Invasions of Mesopotamia changed the region's culture.
3. The Phoenicians built a trading society in the eastern Mediterranean region.

The Big Idea

After the Sumerians, many cultures ruled parts of the Fertile Crescent.

Key Terms and People

monarch, p. 72
Hammurabi's Code, p. 73
chariot, p. 74
Nebuchadnezzar, p. 75
alphabet, p. 77

Online Resource
TAKING NOTES

Use the graphic organizer online to keep track of the empires of the Fertile Crescent.

Later Peoples of the Fertile Crescent

If YOU were there...

You are a noble in ancient Babylon, an advisor to the great king Hammurabi. One of your duties is to collect all the laws of the kingdom. They will be carved on a tall block of black stone and placed in the temple. The king asks your opinion about the punishments for certain crimes. For instance, should common people be punished more harshly than nobles?

How will you advise the king?

BUILDING BACKGROUND Many peoples invaded Mesopotamia. A series of kings conquered the lands between the rivers. Each new culture inherited the earlier achievements of the Sumerians. Some of the later invasions of the region also introduced skills and ideas that still influence civilization today, such as a written law code.

The Babylonians Conquer Mesopotamia

Although Ur rose to glory after the death of Sargon, repeated foreign attacks drained its strength. By 2000 BC, Ur lay in ruins. With Ur's power gone, several waves of invaders battled to gain control of Mesopotamia.

The Rise of Babylon

Babylon was home to one such group. That city was located on the Euphrates River near what is today Baghdad, Iraq. Babylon had once been a Sumerian town. By 1800 BC, however, it was home to a powerful government of its own. In 1792 BC, Hammurabi (ham-uh-RAHB-ee) became Babylon's king. He would become the city's greatest **monarch** (MAH-nark), a ruler of a kingdom or empire.

Hammurabi's Code

Hammurabi was a brilliant war leader. His armies fought many battles to expand his power. Eventually, he brought all of Mesopotamia into his empire, called the Babylonian Empire, after his capital.

Hammurabi's skills were not limited to the battlefield, though. He was also an able ruler who could govern a huge empire. He oversaw many building and irrigation projects and improved Babylon's tax collection system to help pay for them. He also brought much prosperity through increased trade. Hammurabi, however, is most famous for his code of laws.

Hammurabi's Code was a set of 282 laws that dealt with almost every part of daily life. There were laws on everything from trade, loans, and theft to marriage, injury, and murder. It contained some ideas that are still found in laws today. Specific crimes brought specific penalties. However, social class did matter. For instance, injuring a rich man brought a greater penalty than injuring a poor man.

Hammurabi's Code was important not only for how thorough it was, but also because it was written down for all to see. People all over the empire could read exactly what was against the law.

Hammurabi ruled for 42 years. During his reign, Babylon became the most important city in Mesopotamia. However, after his death, Babylonian power declined. The kings that followed faced invasions from people Hammurabi had conquered. Before long, the Babylonian Empire came to an end.

READING CHECK **Analyzing** What was Hammurabi's most important accomplishment?

Primary Source

QUICK FACTS

HISTORIC DOCUMENT

Hammurabi's Code

The Babylonian ruler Hammurabi is credited with putting together the earliest known written collection of laws. The code set down rules for both criminal and civil law, and informed citizens what was expected of them.

196. If a man put out the eye of another man, his eye shall be put out.

197. If he break another man's bone, his bone shall be broken.

198. If he put out the eye of a freed man, or break the bone of a freed man, he shall pay one gold mina.

199. If he put out the eye of a man's slave, or break the bone of a man's slave, he shall pay one-half of its value.

221. If a physican heal the broken bone or diseased soft part of a man, the patient shall pay the physician five shekels in money.

222. If he were a freed man he shall pay three shekels.

223. If he were a slave his owner shall pay the physician two shekels.

–Hammurabi, from the Code of Hammurabi, translated by L. W. King

ANALYSIS SKILL **ANALYZING PRIMARY SOURCES**

How do you think Hammurabi's code of laws affected citizens of that time?

Invasions of Mesopotamia

Several other civilizations also developed in and around the Fertile Crescent. As their armies battled each other for fertile land, control of the region passed from one empire to another.

The Hittites and Kassites

FOCUS ON READING
What is the topic of this paragraph? Is the main idea stated in a single sentence?

SS.6.G.6.2 Compare maps of the world in ancient times with current political maps.

A people known as the Hittites built a strong kingdom in Asia Minor, in what is today Turkey. Their success came, in part, from two key military advantages they had over rivals. First, the Hittites were among the first people to master ironworking. This meant that they could make the strongest weapons of the time. Second, the Hittites skillfully used the **chariot**, a wheeled, horse-drawn cart used in battle. The chariots allowed Hittite soldiers to move quickly around a battlefield and fire arrows at their enemy. Using these advantages, Hittite forces captured Babylon around 1595 BC.

Hittite rule did not last long, however. Soon after taking Babylon, the Hittite king was killed by an assassin. The kingdom plunged into chaos. The Kassites, a people who lived north of Babylon, captured the city and ruled for almost 400 years.

The Assyrians

Later, in the 1200s BC, the Assyrians (uh-SIR-ee-unz) from northern Mesopotamia briefly gained control of Babylon. However, their empire was soon overrun by invaders. After this defeat, the Assyrians took about 300 years to recover their strength. Then, starting about 900 BC, they began to conquer all of the Fertile Crescent. They even took over parts of Asia Minor and Egypt.

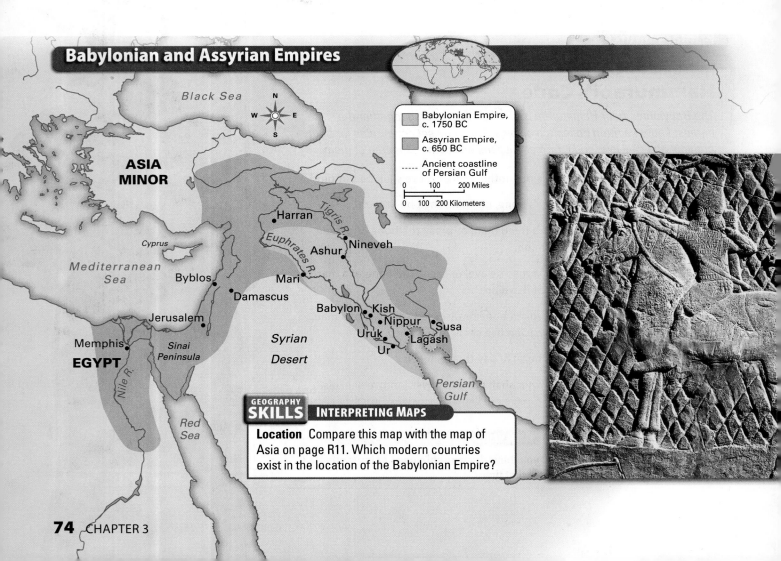

Babylonian and Assyrian Empires

Black Sea

ASIA MINOR

Cyprus

Mediterranean Sea

Harran

Tigris R.

Euphrates R.

Ashur
Nineveh

Byblos
Mari

Damascus

Jerusalem

Babylon
Kish
Nippur
Susa
Uruk
Lagash
Ur

Memphis
Sinai Peninsula

EGYPT

Nile R.

Syrian Desert

Red Sea

Persian Gulf

Babylonian Empire, c. 1750 BC

Assyrian Empire, c. 650 BC

Ancient coastline of Persian Gulf

0   100   200 Miles
0   100   200 Kilometers

GEOGRAPHY SKILLS **INTERPRETING MAPS**

Location Compare this map with the map of Asia on page R11. Which modern countries exist in the location of the Babylonian Empire?

The key to the Assyrians' success was their strong army. Like the Hittites, the Assyrians used iron weapons and chariots. The army was very well organized, and every soldier knew his role.

The Assyrians were fierce in battle. Before attacking, they spread terror by looting villages and burning crops. Anyone who still dared to resist them was killed.

After conquering the Fertile Crescent, the Assyrians ruled from Nineveh (NI-nuh-vuh). They demanded heavy taxes from across the empire. Areas that resisted these demands were harshly punished.

Assyrian kings ruled their large empire through local leaders. Each governed a small area, collected taxes, enforced laws, and raised troops for the army. Roads were built to link distant parts of the empire. Messengers on horseback were sent to deliver orders to faraway officials.

The Chaldeans

In 652 BC a series of wars broke out in the Assyrian Empire over who should rule. These wars greatly weakened the empire.

Sensing this weakness, the Chaldeans (kal-DEE-unz), a group from the Syrian Desert, led other peoples in an attack on the Assyrians. In 612 BC, they destroyed Nineveh and the Assyrian Empire.

In its place, the Chaldeans set up a new empire of their own. **Nebuchadnezzar** (neb-uh-kuhd-NEZ-uhr), the most famous Chaldean king, rebuilt Babylon into a beautiful city. According to legend, his grand palace featured the famous Hanging Gardens. Trees and flowers grew on its terraces and roofs. From the ground the gardens seemed to hang in the air.

The Chaldeans admired Sumerian culture. They studied the Sumerian language and built temples to Sumerian gods.

At the same time, Babylon became a center for astronomy. Chaldeans charted the positions of the stars and kept track of economic, political, and weather events. They also created a calendar and solved complex problems of geometry.

READING CHECK **Sequencing** List in order the peoples who ruled Mesopotamia.

The Assyrian Army
The Assyrian army was the most powerful fighting force the world had ever seen. It was large and well organized, and it featured iron weapons, war chariots, and giant war machines used to knock down city walls.

What kinds of weapons can you see in this carving?

Phoenicia, c. 800 BC

ATLANTIC OCEAN

SPAIN

Strait of Gibraltar

ATLAS MOUNTAINS

The Phoenicians sailed throughout the Mediterranean, building trade networks and founding new cities.

The Phoenicians

At the western end of the Fertile Crescent, along the Mediterranean Sea, was a land known as Phoenicia (fi-NI-shuh). It was not home to a great military power and was often ruled by foreign governments. Nevertheless, the Phoenicians created a wealthy trading society.

The Geography of Phoenicia

Today the nation of Lebanon occupies most of what was once Phoenicia. Mountains border the region to the north and east. The western border is the Mediterranean.

Phoenicia had few resources. One thing it did have, however, was cedar. Cedar trees were prized for their timber, a valuable trade item. But Phoenicia's overland trade routes were blocked by mountains and hostile neighbors. Phoenicians had to look to the sea for a way to trade.

The Expansion of Trade

Motivated by a desire for trade, the people of Phoenicia became expert sailors. They built one of the world's finest harbors at the city of Tyre. Fleets of fast Phoenician trading ships sailed to ports all around the Mediterranean Sea. Traders traveled to Egypt, Greece, Italy, Sicily, and Spain. They even passed through the Strait of Gibraltar to reach the Atlantic Ocean.

The Phoenicians founded several new colonies along their trade routes. Carthage (KAHR-thij), located on the northern coast of Africa, was the most famous of these. It later became one of the most powerful cities on the Mediterranean.

Phoenicia grew wealthy from its trade. Besides lumber, the Phoenicians traded silverwork, ivory carvings, and slaves. Beautiful glass objects also became valuable trade items after crafters invented glass-blowing—the art of heating and shaping glass. In addition, the Phoenicians made purple dye from a type of shellfish. They then traded cloth dyed with this purple color. Phoenician purple fabric was very popular with rich people.

The Phoenicians' most important achievement, however, wasn't a trade good. To record their activities, Phoenician

SS.6.W.3.1 Analyze the cultural impact the ancient Phoenicians had on the Mediterranean world with regard to colonization (Carthage), exploration, maritime commerce (purple dye, tin), and written communication (alphabet).

SS.6.E.3.2 Categorize products that were traded among civilizations, and give examples of barriers to trade of those products.

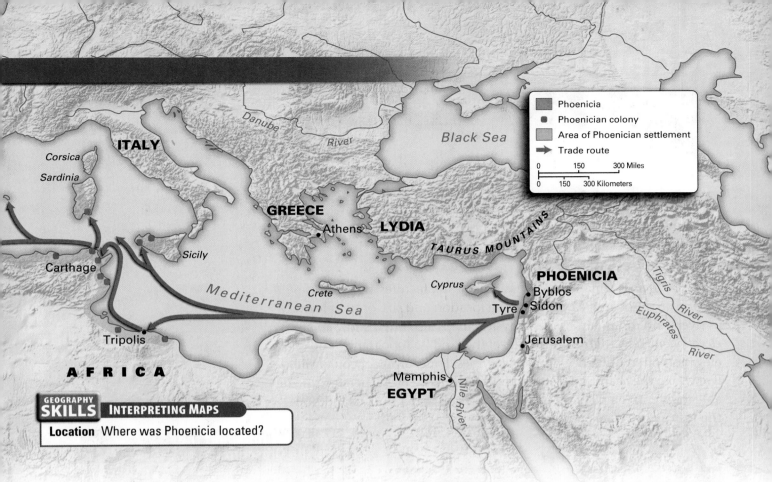

■	Phoenicia
●	Phoenician colony
	Area of Phoenician settlement
→	Trade route

0   150   300 Miles
0   150   300 Kilometers

GEOGRAPHY SKILLS **INTERPRETING MAPS**

Location Where was Phoenicia located?

traders developed one of the world's first alphabets. An **alphabet** is a set of letters that can be combined to form words. This development made writing much easier. It had a major impact on the ancient world and on our own. In fact, the alphabet we use for the English language is based on the Phoenicians', as modified later by the Greeks. Later civilizations, including the Greeks, benefited from the innovations passed along by Phoenician traders.

READING CHECK **Categorize** What goods did the Phoenicians trade?

SUMMARY AND PREVIEW Many different peoples ruled in the Fertile Crescent after the Sumerians. Some made important contributions that are still valued today. In the next chapter you will learn about two remarkable civilizations that developed along the Nile River.

Section 4 Assessment

Reviewing Ideas, Terms, and People

1. **a. Identify** Where was Babylon located?
   b. Analyze What does **Hammurabi's Code** reveal about Babylonian society?
2. **a. Describe** What two advantages did Hittite soldiers have over their opponents?
   b. Rank Which empire discussed in this section do you feel contributed the most to modern-day society? Why?
3. **a. Identify** For what trade goods were the Phoenicians known? For what else were they known?
   b. Analyze How did Phoenicia grow wealthy?

Critical Thinking

4. **Categorizing** Use your note-taking diagram with the names of the empires. List at least one advance or achievement made by each empire.

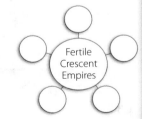

Fertile Crescent Empires

FOCUS ON WRITING

5. **Gathering Information about Later Peoples** Several different peoples contributed to civilization in the Fertile Crescent after the Sumerians. Which ones, if any, will you mention in your letter? What will you say?

MESOPOTAMIA AND THE FERTILE CRESCENT **77**

Social Studies Skills

Interpreting Physical Maps

Understand the Skill

A *physical map* is a map that shows the natural features and landscape, or *topography*, of an area. It shows the location and size of such features as rivers and mountain ranges. Physical maps also often show an area's *elevation*, or how high above sea level the land is. Topography and elevation often influence human activities. For example, people will live where they can find water and defend themselves. Therefore, being able to interpret a physical map can help you better understand how the history of an area unfolded.

Learn the Skill

Follow these steps to interpret a physical map.

1. Read the map's title, distance scale, and legend. These will provide basic information about the map's contents.

2. Note the colors used to show elevation. Use the legend to connect colors on the map to elevations of specific places.

3. Note the shapes of the features, such as how high a mountain range is, how far it stretches, and how long a river is. Note where each feature is in relation to others.

4. Use information from the map to draw conclusions about the effect of the region's topography on settlement and economic activities.

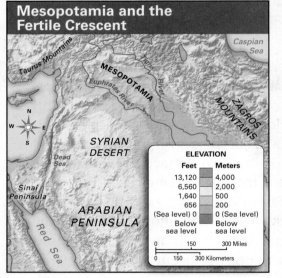

Practice and Apply the Skill

Use the guidelines to answer these questions about the map above.

1. What is the elevation of the western half of the Arabian Peninsula?

2. Describe the topography of Mesopotamia. Why would settlement have occurred here before other places on the map?

3. What feature might have stopped invasions of Mesopotamia?

Chapter Review

Visual Summary

Use the visual summary below to help you review the main ideas of the chapter.

QUICK FACTS

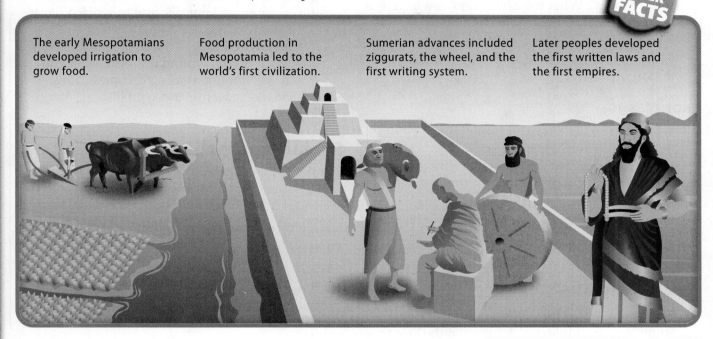

The early Mesopotamians developed irrigation to grow food.

Food production in Mesopotamia led to the world's first civilization.

Sumerian advances included ziggurats, the wheel, and the first writing system.

Later peoples developed the first written laws and the first empires.

Reviewing Vocabulary, Terms, and People

Using your own paper, complete the sentences below by providing the correct term for each blank.

1. Mesopotamian farmers built _____ to irrigate their fields.

2. While city dwellers were urban, farmers lived in _____ areas.

3. The people of Sumer practiced _____, the worship of many gods.

4. Instead of using pictographs, Sumerians developed a type of writing called _____.

5. Horse-drawn _____ gave the Hittites an advantage during battle.

6. The Babylonian king _____ is famous for his code of laws.

7. Another word for effect is _____.

8. Sumerian society was organized in _____, which consisted of a city and the surrounding lands.

Comprehension and Critical Thinking

SECTION 1 *(Pages 54–57)*

9. **a. Describe** Where was Mesopotamia, and what does the name mean?

   b. Analyze How did Mesopotamian irrigation systems allow civilization to develop?

   c. Elaborate Do you think a division of labor is necessary for civilization to develop? Why or why not?

SECTION 2 *(Pages 60–64)*

10. **a. Identify** Who built the world's first empire, and what did that empire include?

   b. Analyze Politically, how was early Sumerian society organized? How did that organization affect society?

   c. Elaborate Why did the Sumerians consider it everyone's responsibility to keep the gods happy?

SECTION 3 *(Pages 65–69)*

11. a. Identify What was the Sumerian writing system called, and why is it so significant?

b. Compare and Contrast What were two ways in which Sumerian society was similar to our society today? What were two ways in which it was different?

c. Evaluate Other than writing and the wheel, which Sumerian invention do you think is most important? Why?

SECTION 4 *(Pages 72–77)*

12. a. Describe What were two important developments of the Phoenicians?

b. Draw Conclusions Why do you think several peoples banded together to fight the Assyrians?

c. Evaluate Do you think Hammurabi was more effective as a ruler or as a military leader? Why?

Reviewing Themes

13. Science and Technology Which of the ancient Sumerians' technological achievements do you think has been most influential in history? Why?

14. Politics Why do you think Hammurabi is so honored for his code of laws?

Reading Skills

Identifying Main Ideas *For each passage, choose the letter that corresponds to the main idea sentence.*

15. (A) Sumerians believed that their gods had enormous powers. (B) Gods could bring a good harvest or a disastrous flood. (C) They could bring illness or they could bring good health and wealth.

16. (A) The wheel was not the Sumerians' only great development. (B) They developed cuneiform, the world's first system of writing. (C) But Sumerians did not have pencils, pens, or paper. (D) Instead, they used sharp reeds to make wedge-shaped symbols on clay tablets.

Using the Internet

17. Activity: Looking at Writing The Sumerians made one of the greatest cultural advances in history by developing cuneiform. This was the world's first system of writing. Go online to research the evolution of language and its written forms. Look at one of the newest methods of writing: text messaging. Then write a paragraph explaining how and why writing was developed and why it was important using text-messaging abbreviations, words, and symbols.

Social Studies Skills

Interpreting Physical Maps *Could you use a physical map to answer the questions below? For each question, answer yes or no.*

18. Are there mountains or hills in a certain region?

19. What languages do people speak in that region?

20. How many people live in the region?

21. What kinds of water features such as rivers or lakes would you find there?

FOCUS ON WRITING

22. Writing Your Letter Use the notes you have taken to create a plan for your letter. You might want to start with a rough outline of two or three main points. For example, one of your main points might be about the land of Mesopotamia. Another might be about the achievements of the Sumerians.

After you have a good plan in mind, you can start to write your letter. As you write, think about the young student who will be reading the letter. What words will he or she understand? How can you capture the student's interest and keep it? If you think it would help the student to see a map or a drawing, create one and attach it to your letter.

Florida Standardized Test Practice

DIRECTIONS: Read each question, and write the letter of the best response.

1 Use the map to answer the following question.

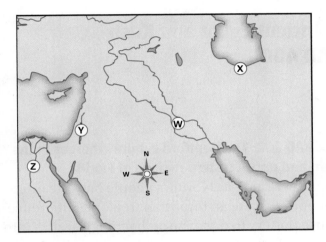

The region known as Mesopotamia is indicated on the map by the letter

A W.

B X.

C Y.

D Z.

2 All of the following ancient civilizations developed in Mesopotamia *except* the

A Akkadians.

B Babylonians.

C Egyptians.

D Sumerians.

3 Which of the following is *not* true of the first writing system?

A It was developed by the Babylonians.

B It began with the use of pictures to represent syllables and objects.

C It was recorded on tablets made of clay.

D It was first used to keep business records.

4 In Sumerian society, people's social class or rank depended on their wealth and their

A appearance.

B religion.

C location.

D occupation.

5 Hammurabi's Code is important in world history because it was an early

A form of writing that could be used to record important events.

B written list of laws that controlled people's daily life and behavior.

C record-keeping system that enabled the Phoenicians to become great traders.

D set of symbols that allowed the Sumerians to communicate with other peoples.

6 What was the most important contribution of the Phoenicians to our civilization?

A purple dye

B their alphabet

C founding of Carthage

D sailing ships

Connecting with Past Learnings

7 In this chapter, you learned about agriculture in Mesopotamia. During what period of prehistory was agriculture first practiced?

A Megalithic Era

B Mesolithic Era

C Paleolithic Era

D Neolithic Era

FLORIDA...
The Story Continues

CHAPTER 4, Ancient Egypt and Kush (4500 BC–AD 400)

PEOPLE **2500 BC–AD 100: The Deptford culture emerges in the northern and northwestern regions of Florida.**
Regional cultures developed as Florida's people became more settled. Styles of pottery were an important regional difference. Archaeologists use pottery to organize archaeological sites into cultural groups. The Deptford culture developed in what is now North and Northwest Florida. The culture's pottery was characterized by a checked design stamped into coiled clay. Most of the people in the northwestern region lived along the coast near salt marshes and streams. The people in the northern region lived along rivers and streams. They all fished and hunted for food. Around 100 BC the Deptford culture began burying their dead in sand mounds. The dead were buried with special items such as copper panpipes, ear spools, and decorative pottery. Copper is not native to Florida. This leads archaeologists to believe that the Deptford people engaged in trade with other cultures of the Southeast.

PEOPLE **c. 1000 BC: The Belle Glades culture emerges around Lake Okeechobee.** The Belle Glades culture developed in the grasslands around the Kissimmee River basin and Lake Okeechobee in southern Florida. By about 500 BC the people were constructing mounds, circular ditches, canals, and other earthworks. Archaeologists believe that many of the earthworks were constructed to control seasonal flooding in the increasingly wet environment. The people appear to have grown corn as early as 400 BC, but the practice stopped around AD 500, most likely because the land became too wet.

PEOPLE **c. 500 BC: The Glades culture lives in southern Florida.**
People of the Glades culture lived in the Everglades and among the mangrove forests and inlets along Florida's southern coast. They lived by fishing and hunting and by gathering plants. Their diet included whales, starfish, sharks, crabs, rays, crayfish, sailfish, and marlin. They also hunted deer, rabbit, raccoons, reptiles, and birds. Lacking a lot of stone, the people made bows and arrows and other tools from wood and shell.

PEOPLE **c. 100 BC: The St. Johns culture constructs sand burial mounds for their dead.** The people of the St. Johns culture lived in the drainage area of the St. Johns River from Brevard County northward to Jacksonville. Each village had one or more leaders that helped organize ceremonies and other activities. Archaeologists believe that villages were organized into kinship groups. When a village became too large, one or more groups formed new villages. Somewhere around 100 BC the people began constructing sand mounds to bury their dead. The St. Johns people buried their dead with exotic trade goods from elsewhere in the Southeast.

PEOPLE **c. AD 200: The Cades Pond culture develops in the north central region of Florida.** About 1,800 years ago the Cades Pond people settled in villages along the lakes, wet prairies, and marshes in what is now Alachua County. Based on the bones and shells found at various sites, archaeologists believe the people relied heavily on the wetland resources of the area. Their diet consisted of such wetland animals as snails, clams, fish, frogs, turtles, snakes, alligators, and water birds. They also ate land animals such as black bears, rabbits, opossums, squirrels, and fox.

Unpacking the Florida Standards <•••

Read the following to learn what this standard says and what it means. See FL8–FL31 to unpack all of the standards related to this chapter.

Benchmark SS.6.G.2.4 Explain how the geographical location of ancient civilizations contributed to the culture and politics of those societies. Examples are Egypt, Rome, Greece, China, Kush.

What does it mean?
Identify the ways in which geography shaped the cultures and governments of ancient civilizations.

 SPOTLIGHT ON
SS.6.E.1.2, SS.6.E.1.3, SS.6.E.3.2, SS.6.E.3.3, SS.6.G.2.2 See pages FL37, FL38, and FL44 for content specifically related to these Chapter 4 standards.

Ancient Egypt and Kush

Essential Question How was the success of the Egyptian civilization tied to the Nile River?

Florida Next Generation Sunshine State Standards

MA.6.A.3.1 Write and evaluate mathematical expressions that correspond to given situations. **SS.6.E.1.2** Describe and identify traditional and command economies as they appear in different civilizations. **SS.6.E.1.3** Describe the following economic concepts as they relate to early civilization: scarcity, opportunity cost, supply and demand, barter, trade, productive resources (land, labor, capital, entrepreneurship). **SS.6.E.3.2** Categorize products that were traded among civilizations, and give examples of barriers to trade of those products. **SS.6.E.3.3** Describe traditional economies (Egypt, Greece, Rome, Kush) and elements of those economies that led to the rise of a merchant class and trading partners. **SS.6.G.2.2** Differentiate between continents, regions, countries, and cities in order to understand the complexities of regions created by civilizations. **SS.6.G.2.4** Explain how the geographical location of ancient civilizations contributed to the culture and politics of those societies. **SS.6.G.2.5** Interpret how geographic boundaries invite or limit interaction with other regions and cultures. **SS.6.G.3.1** Explain how the physical landscape has affected the development of agriculture and industry in the ancient world. **SS.6.G.3.2** Analyze the impact of human populations on the ancient world›s ecosystems. **SS.6.G.4.1** Explain how family and ethnic relationships influenced ancient cultures. **SS.6.G.5.1** Identify the methods used to compensate for the scarcity of resources in the ancient world. **SS.6.G.5.3** Use geographic tools and terms to analyze how famine, drought, and natural disasters plagued many ancient civilizations. **SS.6.W.1.1** Use timelines to identify chronological order of historical events. **SS.6.W.1.2** Identify terms (decade, century, epoch, era, millennium, BC/BCE, AD/CE) and designations of time periods. **SS.6.W.1.3** Interpret primary and secondary sources. **SS.6.W.2.4** Compare the economic, political, social, and religious institutions of ancient river civilizations. **SS.6.W.2.5** Summarize important achievements of Egyptian civilization. **SS.6.W.2.6** Determine the contributions of key figures from ancient Egypt. **SS.6.W.3.18** Describe the rise and fall of the ancient east African kingdoms of Kush and Axum and Christianity's development in Ethiopia.

FOCUS ON WRITING

Riddles In ancient times, according to legend, a sphinx—an imaginary creature like the one whose sculpture is found in Egypt—demanded the answer to a riddle. People died if they couldn't answer the riddle correctly. After you read this chapter, you will write two riddles. The answer to one of your riddles will be "Egypt." The answer to your other riddle will be "Kush."

CHAPTER EVENTS

c. 4500 BC Agricultural communities develop in Egypt.

4000 BC

WORLD EVENTS

This photo shows an ancient temple of Ramses II, one of Egypt's most powerful rulers.

HISTORY The Egyptian Empire Is Born

↗ Online Resource VIDEO

c. 3100 BC
Menes unites Upper and Lower Egypt, establishing the First Dynasty.

c. 2300 BC
The kingdom of Kush sets up its capital at Kerma.

c. 1237 BC
Ramses the Great dies.

c. 730–700 BC
Kush conquers Egypt and establishes the 25th Dynasty.

c. AD 350
Aksum destroys Meroë.

3000 BC   **2000 BC**   **1000 BC**   **400 AD**

c. 3500 BC
The Sumerians create the world's first writing system.

c. 1200 BC
The Olmec form the first urban civilization in the Americas.

c. 1027 BC
The Chou Dynasty begins in China.

c. 500 BC
Buddhism begins to develop in India.

AD 330
Constantinople becomes the capital of the Roman Empire.

Reading Social Studies

Focus on Themes As you read this chapter, you will learn about the ancient kingdoms of Egypt and Kush. You will see that the **geography** of the areas helped these kingdoms to develop. You will also learn how Egypt conquered and ruled Kush and then how Kush conquered and ruled Egypt. You will learn how the **economies** of these kingdoms, based on trade, grew strong. Finally you will learn about the importance of **religion** to the people of both of these ancient societies.

Causes and Effects in History

Focus on Reading Have you heard the saying, "We have to understand the past to avoid repeating it"? That is one reason we look for causes and effects in history.

Identifying Causes and Effects A **cause** is something that makes another thing happen. An **effect** is the result of something else that has happened. Most historical events have a number of causes as well as a number of effects. You can understand history better if you look for causes and effects of events.

1. *Because the Egyptians had captured and destroyed the city of Kerma, the kings of Kush ruled from the city of Napata.* (p. 109)

Cause
Capture of Kerma → **Effect** Kings ruled from Napata

> Sometimes writers use words that signal a cause or an effect. Here are some:
>
> **Cause**—*reason, basis, because, motivated, as*
>
> **Effect**—*therefore, as a result, for that reason, so*

2. *Piankhi fought the Egyptians because he believed that the gods wanted him to rule all of Egypt.* (p. 110)

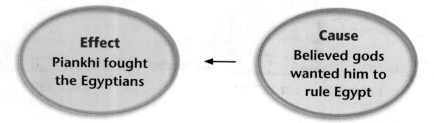

Effect
Piankhi fought the Egyptians ← **Cause** Believed gods wanted him to rule Egypt

LA.6.1.6.1 The student will use new vocabulary that is introduced and taught directly. **SS.6.W.2.4** Compare the economic, political, social, and religious institutions of ancient river civilizations.

Key Terms and People

You Try It!

The following selections are from the chapter you are about to read. As you read each, identify which phrase or sentence describes a cause and which describes an effect.

Finding Causes and Effects

1. "During the mid-1000s BC the New Kingdom in Egypt was ending. As the power of Egypt's pharaohs declined, Kushite leaders regained control of Kush. Kush once again became independent." (p. 109)
2. "A series of inept pharaohs left Egypt open to attack." (p. 109)
3. "The Assyrians' iron weapons were better than the Kushites' bronze weapons. Although the Kushites were skilled archers, they could not stop the invaders (p. 111)
4. "Iron ore and wood for furnaces were easily available, so the iron industry grew quickly." (p. 111)

After you read the sentences, answer the following questions.

1. In selection 1, is "Kush once again became independent" the cause of the Egyptians growing weaker or the effect?

2. In selection 2, what left Egypt open to attack? Is that the cause of why Egypt was easily attacked or the effect?

3. In selection 3, who is using the iron weapons, the Assyrians or the Kushites? What was the effect of using the weapons?

4. In selection 4, does the word *so* signal a cause or an effect?

As you read Chapter 4, look for words that signal causes or effects. Make a chart to keep track of these causes and effects.

Chapter 4

Section 1
cataracts *(p. 87)*
delta *(p. 87)*
Menes *(p. 89)*
pharaoh *(p. 89)*
dynasty *(p. 89)*

Section 2
Old Kingdom *(p. 90)*
Khufu *(p. 91)*
nobles *(p. 91)*
afterlife *(p. 92)*
mummies *(p. 93)*
elite *(p. 93)*
pyramids *(p. 94)*
engineering *(p. 94)*

Section 3
Middle Kingdom *(p. 96)*
New Kingdom *(p. 97)*
trade routes *(p. 97)*
Queen Hathepsut *(p. 98)*
Ramses the Great *(p. 98)*

Section 4
hieroglyphics *(p. 102)*
papyrus *(p. 102)*
Rosetta Stone *(p.103)*
sphinxes *(p. 104)*
obelisk *(p. 104)*
King Tutankhamen *(p. 106)*

Section 5
Piankhi *(p. 110)*
trade network *(p. 111)*
merchants *(p. 111)*
exports *(p. 111)*
imports *(p. 111)*
King Ezana *(p. 113)*

Academic Vocabulary
acquire *(p. 91)*
method *(p. 93)*
contracts *(p. 100)*

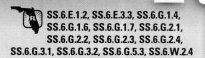
SS.6.E.1.2, SS.6.E.3.3, SS.6.G.1.4, SS.6.G.1.6, SS.6.G.1.7, SS.6.G.2.1, SS.6.G.2.2, SS.6.G.2.3, SS.6.G.2.4, SS.6.G.3.1, SS.6.G.3.2, SS.6.G.5.3, SS.6.W.2.4

What You Will Learn...

Main Ideas

1. Egypt was called the gift of the Nile because the Nile River gave life to the desert.
2. Civilization developed along the Nile after people began farming in this region.
3. Strong kings unified all of Egypt.

The Big Idea

The water, fertile soils, and protected setting of the Nile Valley allowed a great civilization to arise in Egypt around 3200 BC.

Key Terms and People

cataracts, *p. 87*
delta, *p. 87*
Menes, *p. 89*
pharaoh, *p. 89*
dynasty, *p. 89*

Online Resource
TAKING NOTES

Use the graphic organizer online to take notes on characteristics of the Nile River and the way it affected Egypt.

Geography and Ancient Egypt

If YOU were there...

Your family are farmers in the Nile Valley. Each year when the river's floodwaters spread rich soil on the land, you help your father plant barley. When you are not in the fields, you spin fine linen thread from flax you have grown. Sometimes you and your friends hunt birds in the tall grasses along the riverbanks.

Why do you like living in the Nile Valley?

BUILDING BACKGROUND Mesopotamia was not the only place where an advanced civilization grew up along a great river. The narrow valley of the Nile River in Egypt also provided fertile land that drew people to live there. The culture that developed in Egypt was more stable and long-lasting than those in Mesopotamia.

The Gift of the Nile

Geography played a key role in the development of Egyptian civilization. The Nile River brought life to Egypt. The river was so important to people in this region that the Greek historian Herodotus (hi-RAHD-du-tus) called Egypt the gift of the Nile.

Location and Physical Features

The Nile is the longest river in the world. It begins in central Africa and runs 4,000 miles north to the Mediterranean Sea. Egyptian civilization developed along a 750-mile stretch of the Nile in northern Africa.

Ancient Egypt included two regions, a southern region and a northern region. The southern region was called Upper Egypt. It was so named because it was located upriver in relation to the Nile's flow. Lower Egypt, the northern region, was located downriver. The Nile sliced through the desert of Upper Egypt. There, it created a fertile river valley about 13 miles wide. On either side of the Nile lay hundreds of miles of bleak desert.

As you can see on the map to the right, the Nile rushed through rocky, hilly land south of Egypt. At several points, this terrain caused **cataracts**, or strong rapids, to form. The first cataract, 720 miles south of the Mediterranean, marked the southern border of Upper Egypt. Five more cataracts lay farther south. These rapids made sailing that portion of the Nile very difficult.

In Lower Egypt, the Nile divided into several branches that fanned out and flowed into the Mediterranean Sea. These branches formed a **delta**, a triangle-shaped area of land made of soil deposited by a river. In ancient times, swamps and marshes covered much of the Nile Delta. Some two thirds of Egypt's fertile farmland was located in the Nile Delta.

The Floods of the Nile

Because it received so little rain, most of Egypt was desert. Each year, however, rainfall far to the south of Egypt in the highlands of east Africa caused the Nile to flood. The Nile floods were easier to predict than those of the Tigris and Euphrates rivers in Mesopotamia. Almost every year, the Nile flooded Upper Egypt in midsummer and Lower Egypt in the fall, coating the land around the river with a rich silt.

The silt from the Nile made the soil ideal for farming. The silt also made the land a dark color. That is why the Egyptians called their country the black land. They called the dry, lifeless desert beyond the river valley the red land.

Each year, Egyptians eagerly awaited the flooding of the Nile. For them the river's floods were a life-giving miracle. Without the floods, people never could have settled in Egypt.

READING CHECK **Summarizing** Why was Egypt called the gift of the Nile?

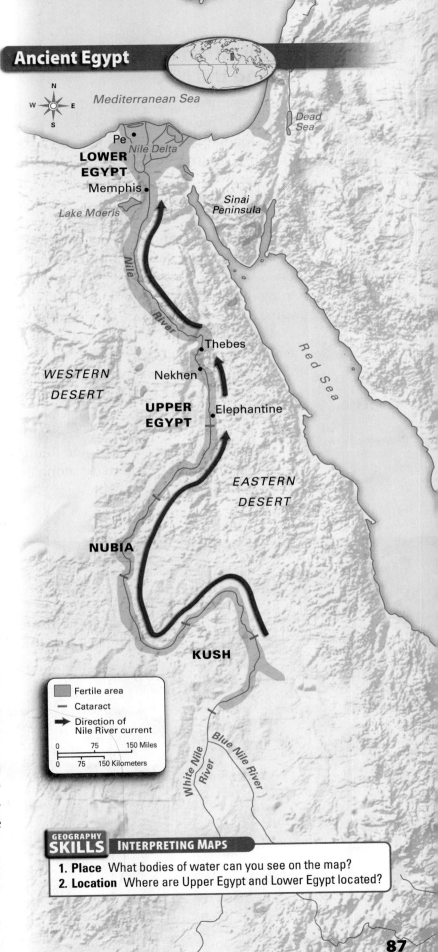

Ancient Egypt

Mediterranean Sea

Dead Sea

Pe

Nile Delta

LOWER EGYPT

Memphis

Lake Moeris

Sinai Peninsula

Nile River

Red Sea

Thebes

WESTERN DESERT

Nekhen

UPPER EGYPT

Elephantine

EASTERN DESERT

NUBIA

KUSH

■ Fertile area
— Cataract
→ Direction of Nile River current

0   75   150 Miles
0   75   150 Kilometers

White Nile River

Blue Nile River

GEOGRAPHY SKILLS **INTERPRETING MAPS**

1. **Place** What bodies of water can you see on the map?
2. **Location** Where are Upper Egypt and Lower Egypt located?

Civilization Develops Along the Nile

SS.6.G.2.4 Explain how the geographical location of ancient civilizations contributed to the culture and politics of those societies.

Hunter-gatherer groups moved into the Nile Valley more than 12,000 years ago. They found plants, wild animals, and fish there to eat. In time these people learned how to farm, and they settled along the Nile in small villages.

As in Mesopotamia, farmers in Egypt developed an irrigation system. They built basins to collect water during the yearly floods and to store this precious resource long afterward. They also built a series of canals that could be used in the dry months to direct water from the basins to the fields where it was needed.

The Nile provided early Egyptian farmers with an abundance of food. The farmers grew wheat, barley, fruits, and vegetables, and raised cattle and sheep. The river also provided many types of fish, and hunters trapped wild geese and ducks along its

SS.6.G.2.5 Interpret how geographic boundaries invite or limit interaction with other regions and cultures.

banks. Like the Mesopotamians, Egyptians enjoyed a varied diet.

In addition to a stable food supply, the Nile Valley offered another valuable advantage. It had natural barriers that made Egypt hard to invade. The desert to the west was too big and harsh to cross. To the north, the Mediterranean Sea kept many enemies away. The Red Sea provided protection against invasion as well. Cataracts in the Nile made it difficult for outsiders to sail in from the south.

Protected from invaders, the villages of Egypt grew. Wealthy farmers emerged as village leaders, and strong leaders gained control over several villages. By 3200 BC, the villages had banded together and developed into two kingdoms. One was called Lower Egypt and the other was called Upper Egypt.

READING CHECK **Summarizing** What attracted early settlers to the Nile Valley?

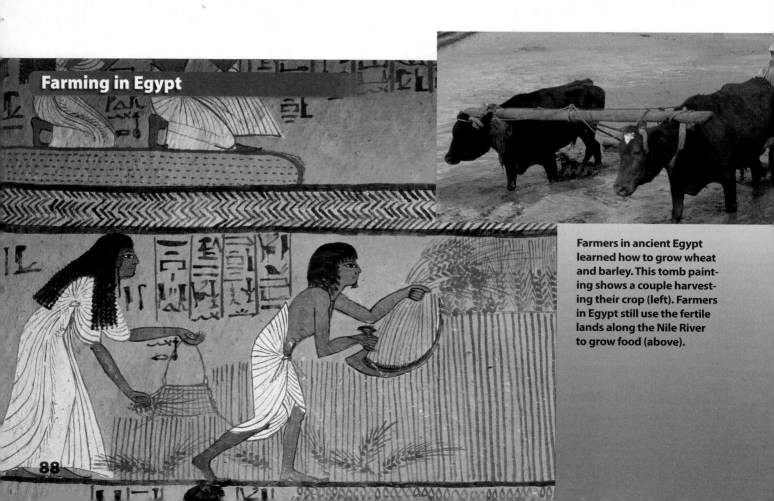

Farming in Egypt

Farmers in ancient Egypt learned how to grow wheat and barley. This tomb painting shows a couple harvesting their crop (left). Farmers in Egypt still use the fertile lands along the Nile River to grow food (above).

Kings Unify Egypt

The king of Lower Egypt ruled from a town called Pe. He wore a red crown to symbolize his authority. Nekhen was the capital city of Upper Egypt. In this kingdom, the king wore a cone-shaped white crown.

Around 3100 BC a leader named **Menes** (MEE-neez), also known as Narmer, rose to power in Upper Egypt. He sought to finish what an earlier king, Scorpion, had started. He wanted to unify Upper and Lower Egypt.

The armies of Menes invaded and took control of Lower Egypt. Menes then united the two kingdoms. He married a princess from Lower Egypt to strengthen his control over the unified country. As Egypt's ruler, Menes wore both the white crown of Upper Egypt and the red crown of Lower Egypt. This symbolized his leadership over the two kingdoms. Later, he combined the two crowns into a double crown.

Historians consider Menes to be Egypt's first **pharaoh** (FEHR-oh), the title used by the rulers of Egypt. The title *pharaoh* means "great house." Menes also founded Egypt's first dynasty. A **dynasty** is a series of rulers from the same family.

Menes built a new capital city at the southern tip of the Nile Delta. The city was later named Memphis. For centuries, Memphis was the political and cultural center of Egypt. Many government offices were located there, and the city bustled with artistic activity.

The First Dynasty lasted for about 200 years. Pharaohs who came after Menes also wore the double crown to symbolize their rule over Upper and Lower Egypt. They extended Egyptian territory southward along the Nile and into southwest Asia. Eventually, however, rivals appeared to challenge the First Dynasty for power. These challengers took over Egypt and established the Second Dynasty.

READING CHECK Drawing Inferences

Why do you think Menes wanted to rule over both kingdoms of Egypt?

SUMMARY AND PREVIEW Civilization in ancient Egypt began in the fertile, protected Nile River Valley. People there formed two kingdoms that were later united under one ruler. In the next section, you will learn how Egypt grew and changed under later rulers in a period known as the Old Kingdom.

SS.6.W.2.6 Determine the contributions of key figures from ancient Egypt.

Section 1 Assessment

Reviewing Ideas, Terms, and People

1. **a. Recall** What were the two regions that made up ancient Egypt?
   b. Make Inferences Why was the Nile Delta well suited for settlement?
   c. Predict How might the Nile's **cataracts** have both helped and hurt Egypt?

2. **a. Describe** What foods did the Egyptians eat?
   b. Analyze What role did the Nile play in supplying Egyptians with these foods?
   c. Elaborate How did the desert on both sides of the Nile help ancient Egypt?

3. **a. Identify** Who was the first **pharaoh** of Egypt?
   b. Draw Conclusions Why did the pharaohs of the First Dynasty wear a double crown?

Critical Thinking

4. **Comparing and Contrasting** Use your notes on the Nile River to complete a Venn diagram like the one shown. List the differences and similarities between the Nile River in Egypt and the Tigris and Euphrates rivers in Mesopotamia.

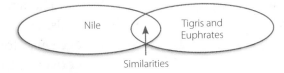

Nile — Tigris and Euphrates — Similarities

FOCUS ON WRITING

5. **Thinking about Geography and Early History** In this section, you read about Egypt's geography and early history. What could you put into your riddle about geography and historical events that would be a clue to the answer?

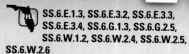
The Old Kingdom

What You Will Learn...

Main Ideas

1. In early Egyptian society, pharaohs ruled as gods and were at the top of the social structure.
2. Religion shaped Egyptian life.
3. The pyramids of Egypt were built as tombs for the pharaohs.

The Big Idea

Egyptian government and religion were closely connected during the Old Kingdom.

Key Terms and People

Old Kingdom, *p. 90*
Khufu, *p. 91*
nobles, *p. 91*
afterlife, *p. 92*
mummies, *p. 93*
elite, *p. 93*
pyramids, *p. 94*
engineering, *p. 94*

 Online Resource
TAKING NOTES

Use the graphic organizer online to take notes on government and religion in the Old Kingdom.

If YOU were there...

You are a peasant farmer in ancient Egypt. To you, the pharaoh is a god, a descendent of the sun god, Re. You depend on his strength and wisdom. For part of the year, you are busy planting crops in your fields. But at other times, you work for the pharaoh. You are currently helping to build a great tomb in which the pharaoh and many of his belongings will be buried when he dies.

How do you feel about working for the pharaoh?

BUILDING BACKGROUND As in other ancient cultures, Egyptian society was based on a strict order of social classes. A small group of royalty, nobles, and priests ruled Egypt. They depended on the rest of the population to supply foods, crafts, and labor. Few people questioned this arrangement of society.

Early Egyptian Society

The First and Second Dynasties ruled Egypt for about four centuries. Around 2700 BC, the Third Dynasty rose to power. Its rule began the **Old Kingdom**, a period in Egyptian history that lasted from about 2700 BC to 2200 BC.

Rule by Pharaohs

During the Old Kingdom, the Egyptians continued to develop their political system. This system was based on the belief that the pharaoh was both a king and a god.

The ancient Egyptians believed that Egypt belonged to the gods. They believed that the pharaoh had come to earth to manage Egypt for the rest of the gods. As a result, he had absolute power over all the land and people in Egypt. But the pharaoh's status as a god came with many responsibilities. People blamed him if crops did not grow well or if disease struck. They also demanded that the pharaoh make trade profitable and prevent wars.

During the Old Kingdom, the duties of the pharaohs grew. To help carry out these duties, the pharaohs hired government officials. Most officials came from the pharaoh's family.

The most famous pharaoh of the Old Kingdom was **Khufu** (KOO-foo), who ruled in the 2500s BC. Egyptian legend says that he was cruel, but historical records tell us that the people who worked for him were well fed. Khufu is best known for the monuments that were built to him.

The Social Structure

By 2200 BC, Egypt had about 2 million people. At the top of Egyptian society was the pharaoh. Just below him were the upper classes, which included priests and key government officials. Many of these priests and officials were **nobles**, or people from rich and powerful families.

Below the nobles was a middle class of lesser government officials, scribes, craftspeople, and merchants. Egypt's lower class, about 80 percent of the population, was made up mostly of farmers. During flood season, when they could not work the fields, farmers worked on the pharaoh's building projects. Below farmers in the social order were slaves and servants.

Egypt and Its Neighbors

Although well-protected by its geography, Egypt was not isolated. Other cultures had influenced it for centuries. For example, Sumerian designs are found in Egyptian art. Egyptian pottery also reflects styles from Nubia, a region south of Egypt.

During the Old Kingdom, Egypt began trading with its neighbors. Traders returned from Nubia with gold, ivory, slaves, and stone. Traders traveled to Punt, an area on the Red Sea, to **acquire** incense and myrrh (MUHR). These two items were used to make perfume and medicine. Trade with Syria provided Egypt with wood.

READING CHECK **Generalizing** How was society structured in the Old Kingdom?

ACADEMIC VOCABULARY
acquire (uh-KWYR) to get

SS.6.E.3.3 Describe traditional economies (Egypt, Greece, Rome, Kush) and elements of those economies that led to the rise of a merchant class and trading partners.

Egyptian Society

Pharaoh
The pharaoh ruled Egypt as a god.

Nobles
Officials and priests helped run the government and temples.

Scribes and Craftspeople
Scribes wrote and craftspeople produced goods.

Farmers, Servants, and Slaves
Most Egyptians were farmers. Below them were servants and slaves.

ANALYSIS SKILL **ANALYZING VISUALS**
Which group helped run the government and temples?

Osiris, god of the underworld, waited to judge the souls of the dead.

The god Anubis weighed each dead person's heart against the feather of truth. If they weighed the same amount, the person was allowed into the underworld.

Religion and Egyptian Life

The ancient Egyptians had strong religious beliefs. Worshipping the gods was a part of their everyday lives. Many Egyptian religious customs focused on what happened after people died.

The Gods of Egypt

Like Mesopotamians, Egyptians practiced polytheism. Before the First Dynasty, each village worshipped its own gods. During the Old Kingdom, however, Egyptian officials tried to give some sort of structure to religious beliefs. Everyone was expected to worship the same gods, though how they worshipped the gods might differ from one region of Egypt to another.

The Egyptians built temples to the gods all over the kingdom. The temples collected payments from both the government and worshippers. These payments allowed the temples to grow more influential.

Over time, certain cities became centers for the worship of certain gods. In Memphis, for example, people prayed to Ptah, the creator of the world.

The Egyptians had gods for nearly everything, including the sun, the sky, and the earth. Many gods mixed human and animal forms. For example, Anubis, the god of the dead, had a human body but a jackal's head. Other major gods included

- Re, or Amon-Re, the sun god
- Osiris, the god of the underworld
- Isis, the goddess of magic, and
- Horus, a sky god, god of the pharaohs

Emphasis on the Afterlife

Much of Egyptian religion focused on the **afterlife**, or life after death. The Egyptians believed that the afterlife was a happy place. Paintings from Egyptian tombs show the afterlife as an ideal world where all the people are young and healthy.

The Egyptian belief in the afterlife stemmed from their idea of *ka* (KAH), or a person's life force. When a person died, his or her *ka* left the body and became a spirit. The *ka,* however, remained linked to the

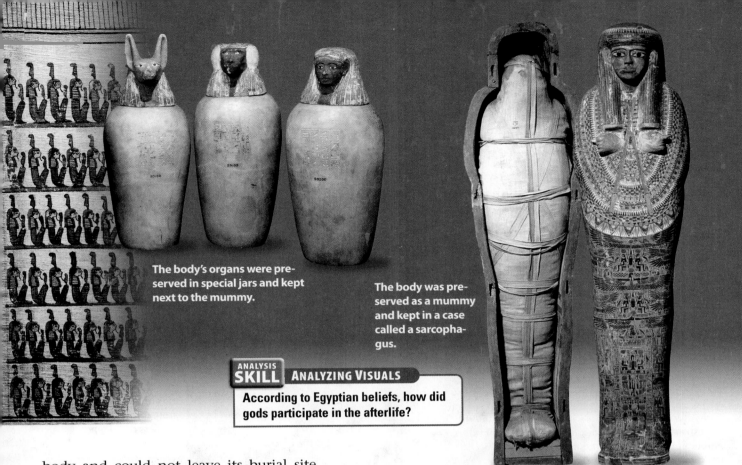

The body's organs were preserved in special jars and kept next to the mummy.

The body was preserved as a mummy and kept in a case called a sarcophagus.

According to Egyptian beliefs, how did gods participate in the afterlife?

body and could not leave its burial site. The *ka* had all the same needs that the person had when he or she was living.

To fulfill the *ka's* needs, people filled tombs with objects for the afterlife. These objects included furniture, clothing, tools, jewelry, and weapons. Relatives of the dead were expected to bring food and beverages to their loved ones' tombs so the *ka* would not be hungry or thirsty.

Burial Practices

Egyptian ideas about the afterlife shaped their burial practices. Egyptians believed that a body had to be prepared for the afterlife before it could be buried. This meant the body had to be preserved. If the body decayed, its spirit could not recognize it. That would break the link between the body and spirit. The *ka* would then be unable to receive the food and drink it needed to have a good afterlife.

To keep the *ka* from suffering, the Egyptians developed a **method** called

embalming. Embalming allowed bodies to be preserved for many, many years as **mummies**, specially treated bodies wrapped in cloth. A body that was not embalmed would decay quickly.

Embalming was a complex process that took several weeks. When finished, embalmers wrapped the body with linen cloths and bandages. The mummy was then placed in a coffin. Relatives often wrote magic spells inside the coffin to help the mummy receive food and drink.

Only royalty and other members of Egypt's **elite** (AY-leet), or people of wealth and power, could afford to have mummies made. Peasant families buried their dead in shallow graves at the edge of the desert. The hot dry sand and lack of moisture preserved the bodies naturally.

READING CHECK Analyzing How did religious beliefs affect Egyptian burial practices?

ACADEMIC VOCABULARY
method
a way of doing something

The Pyramids

FOCUS ON READING
What group of words in this paragraph signals an effect?

Egyptians believed that burial sites, especially royal tombs, were very important. As a result, they built spectacular monuments in which to bury their rulers. The most spectacular of all were the **pyramids**, huge stone tombs with four triangle-shaped walls that met in a point on top.

The Egyptians began to build pyramids during the Old Kingdom. Many of these huge structures are still standing. The first known pyramid was designed by the priest and architect Imhotep in the 2600s BC. The largest is the Great Pyramid of Khufu near the town of Giza. It covers more than 13 acres at its base and stands 481 feet high. This single pyramid took more than 2 million limestone blocks to build. Historians are still not sure exactly how Egyptians built the pyramids. They are, however, amazing feats of **engineering**, the application of scientific knowledge for practical purposes.

Burial in a pyramid demonstrated a pharaoh's importance. The size was a symbol

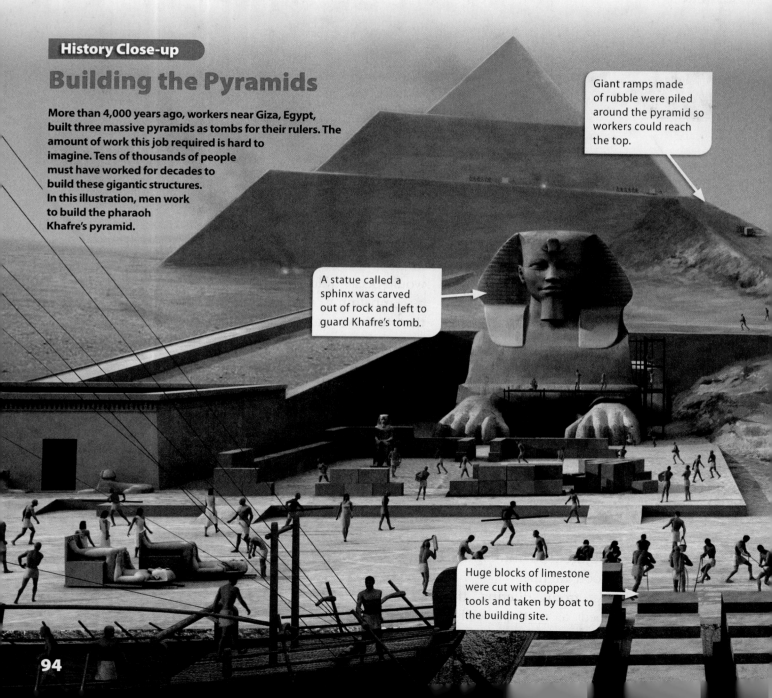

History Close-up

Building the Pyramids

More than 4,000 years ago, workers near Giza, Egypt, built three massive pyramids as tombs for their rulers. The amount of work this job required is hard to imagine. Tens of thousands of people must have worked for decades to build these gigantic structures. In this illustration, men work to build the pharaoh Khafre's pyramid.

Giant ramps made of rubble were piled around the pyramid so workers could reach the top.

A statue called a sphinx was carved out of rock and left to guard Khafre's tomb.

Huge blocks of limestone were cut with copper tools and taken by boat to the building site.

of the pharaoh's greatness. The pyramid's shape, pointing to the skies, symbolized the pharaoh's journey to the afterlife. The Egyptians wanted the pyramids to be spectacular because they believed that the pharaoh, as their link to the gods, controlled everyone's afterlife. Making the pharaoh's spirit happy was a way of ensuring a happy afterlife for every Egyptian.

READING CHECK **Identifying Points of View** Why were pyramids so important to the people of ancient Egypt?

SUMMARY AND PREVIEW During the Old Kingdom, new political and social orders were created in Egypt, and many of the pyramids were built. In Section 3, you will learn about life in later periods, the Middle and New Kingdoms.

Teams of workers dragged the stones on wooden sleds to the pyramid.

ANALYSIS SKILL **ANALYZING VISUALS**

How did workers get their stone blocks to the pyramids?

Section 2 Assessment

Reviewing Ideas, Terms, and People

1. a. **Recall** To what does the term **Old Kingdom** refer?
   b. **Analyze** Why was the pharaoh's authority never questioned?
   c. **Elaborate** How did trade benefit the Egyptians?
2. a. **Describe** What did Egyptians mean by the **afterlife**?
   b. **Analyze** Why was embalming important to the Egyptians?
3. a. **Identify** What is **engineering**?
   b. **Elaborate** What does the building of the **pyramids** tell us about Egyptian society?

Critical Thinking

4. **Generalizing** Using your notes, complete this graphic organizer with three statements about the relationship between government and religion in the Old Kingdom.

Government and Religion
1.
2.
3.

FOCUS ON WRITING

5. **Noting Characteristics of the Old Kingdom** The Old Kingdom developed special characteristics related to religion and social structure. Write down any of those characteristics you might want to include in your riddle.

SS.6.E.1.1, SS.6.E.1.2, SS.6.E.1.3,
SS.6.E.2.1, SS.6.E.3.2, SS.6.E.3.3,
SS.6.G.1.4, SS.6.G.1.5, SS.6.G.1.6,
SS.6.G.2.2, SS.6.G.4.1, SS.6.G.5.1, SS.6.G.5.3,
SS.6.W.1.2, SS.6.W.1.3, SS.6.W.2.4, SS.6.W.2.6

What You Will Learn...

Main Ideas

1. The Middle Kingdom was a period of stable government between periods of disorder.
2. In the New Kingdom, Egyptian trade and military power reached their peak, but Egypt's greatness did not last.
3. Work and daily life were different for each of Egypt's social classes.

The Big Idea

During the Middle and New Kingdoms, order and greatness were restored in Egypt.

Key Terms and People

Middle Kingdom, *p. 96*
New Kingdom, *p. 97*
trade routes, *p. 97*
Queen Hatshepsut, *p. 98*
Ramses the Great, *p. 98*

Online Resource
TAKING NOTES

Use the graphic organizer online to take notes on life in Egypt during the Middle and New Kingdoms.

The Middle and New Kingdoms

If YOU were there...

You are an official serving Queen Hatshepsut of Egypt. You admire her, but some people think that a woman should not rule. She calls herself king, and she dresses like a pharaoh—even wearing a fake beard. That was your idea! You wish you could help more.

What could Hatshepsut do to show her authority?

BUILDING BACKGROUND The power of the pharaohs expanded during the Old Kingdom. Society was orderly, based on great differences between social classes. But rulers and dynasties changed, and Egypt changed with them. In time, these changes led to new eras in Egyptian history, eras called the Middle and New Kingdoms.

The Middle Kingdom

At the end of the Old Kingdom, the wealth and power of the pharaohs declined. Building and maintaining pyramids cost a lot of money. Pharaohs could not collect enough taxes to keep up with the expenses. At the same time, ambitious nobles used their government positions to take power from the pharaohs.

In time, nobles gained enough power to challenge the pharaohs. By about 2200 BC, the Old Kingdom had fallen. For the next 160 years, local nobles battled each other for power in Egypt. The kingdom had no central ruler. Chaos within Egypt disrupted trade with foreign lands and caused farming to decline. The people faced economic hardship and famine.

Finally, around 2050 BC, a powerful pharaoh named Mentuhotep II defeated his rivals. Once again all of Egypt was united. Mentuhotep's rule began the **Middle Kingdom**, a period of order and stability that lasted until about 1750 BC.

Toward the end of the Middle Kingdom, however, Egypt again experienced internal disorder. Its pharaohs could not hold the kingdom together. There were other problems in Egypt as well. In the mid-1700s BC, a group from Southwest Asia called the Hyksos (HIK-sohs) invaded. They used horses, chariots, and advanced weapons to conquer Lower Egypt, which they ruled for 200 years.

The Egyptians did not like being occupied by the Hyksos. The people of Egypt resented having to pay taxes to foreign rulers. Eventually, the Egyptians fought back. In the mid-1500s BC, Ahmose (AHM-ohs) of Thebes drove the Hyksos out of Egypt. Once the Hyksos were gone, Ahmose declared himself king of all Egypt.

READING CHECK **Summarizing** What problems caused the end of the Middle Kingdom?

The New Kingdom

Ahmose's rise to power marked the beginning of Egypt's 18th Dynasty. More importantly, it was the beginning of the **New Kingdom**, the period during which Egypt reached the height of its power and glory. During the New Kingdom, which lasted from about 1550 BC to 1050 BC, conquest and trade brought tremendous wealth to the pharaohs.

Building an Empire

After battling the Hyksos, Egyptian leaders feared future invasions. To prevent such invasions from occurring, they decided to take control of all possible invasion routes into the kingdom. In the process, these leaders turned Egypt into an empire.

Egypt's first target was the homeland of the Hyksos. After taking over that area, the army continued north and conquered Syria. As you can see from the map on the next page, Egypt had taken over the entire eastern shore of the Mediterranean. It had also defeated the kingdom of Kush, south of Egypt. By the 1400s BC, Egypt was the leading military power in the region. Its empire extended from the Euphrates River to southern Nubia.

Military conquests made Egypt rich. The kingdoms it conquered regularly sent treasures to their Egyptian conquerors. For example, the kingdom of Kush in Nubia sent annual payments of gold, leopard skins, and precious stones to the pharaohs. Assyrian, Babylonian, and Hittite kings also sent expensive gifts to Egypt in an effort to maintain good relations.

Growth and its Effects on Trade

Conquest also brought Egyptian traders into contact with more distant lands. Egypt's trade expanded along with its empire. Profitable **trade routes**, or paths followed by traders, developed. Many of the lands that Egypt took over also had valuable resources for trade. The Sinai Peninsula, for example, had large supplies of turquoise and copper.

BIOGRAPHY

Queen Hatshepsut
Ruled c. 1472–1458 BC

Hatshepsut was married to the pharaoh Thutmose II, her half-brother. He died young, leaving the throne to Thutmose III, his son by another woman. Since Thutmose III was still very young, Hatshepsut took over power. Many people did not think women should rule, but Hatshepsut dressed as a man and called herself king. After Hatshepsut died, her stepson took back power and destroyed all of the monuments Hatshepsut had built during her rule.

Analyze Why do you think some Egyptians objected to the idea of being ruled by a woman?

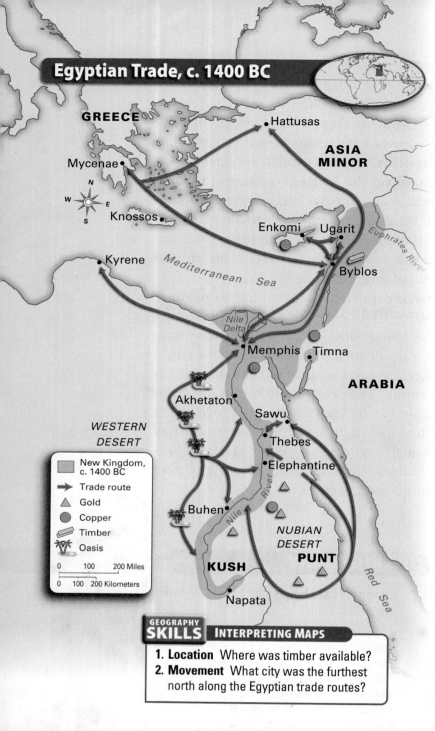

Egyptian Trade, c. 1400 BC

GREECE
Hattusas
Mycenae
ASIA MINOR
Knossos
Enkomi Ugarit
Euphrates River
Kyrene
Mediterranean Sea
Byblos
Nile Delta
Memphis Timna
ARABIA
Akhetaton
Sawu
WESTERN DESERT
Thebes
Elephantine

Legend:
- New Kingdom, c. 1400 BC
- → Trade route
- △ Gold
- ● Copper
- ▱ Timber
- 🌴 Oasis

0   100   200 Miles
0   100   200 Kilometers

Buhen
Nile River
NUBIAN DESERT
KUSH PUNT
Red Sea
Napata

GEOGRAPHY SKILLS **INTERPRETING MAPS**
1. **Location** Where was timber available?
2. **Movement** What city was the furthest north along the Egyptian trade routes?

SS.6.E.2.1 Evaluate how civilizations through clans, leaders, and family groups make economic decisions for that civilization providing a framework for future city–state or nation development.

One ruler who worked to increase Egyptian trade was **Queen Hatshepsut.** She sent Egyptian traders south to trade with the kingdom of Punt on the Red Sea and north to trade with the people of Asia Minor and Greece.

Hatshepsut and later pharaohs used the wealth that they earned from trade to support the arts and architecture. Hatshepsut especially is remembered for the many impressive monuments and temples built during her reign. The best known of these structures was a magnificent temple built for her near the city of Thebes (THEEBZ).

Invasions of Egypt

Despite its great successes, Egypt's military might did not go unchallenged. In the 1200s BC the pharaoh Ramses (RAM-seez) II, or **Ramses the Great**, came to power. Ramses, whose reign was one of the longest in Egyptian history, fought the Hittites, a group from Asia Minor. The two powers fought fiercely for years, but neither could defeat the other. Ramses and the Hittite leader eventually signed a peace treaty. Afterwards, the Egyptians and the Hittites became allies.

Egypt faced threats in other parts of its empire as well. To the west, a people known as the Tehenu invaded the Nile Delta. Ramses fought them off and built a series of forts to strengthen the western frontier. This proved to be a wise decision because the Tehenu invaded again a century later. Faced with Egypt's strengthened defenses, however, the Tehenu were defeated once more.

Soon after Ramses the Great died, invaders called the Sea Peoples sailed into southwest Asia. Little is known about these people. Historians are not even sure who they were. All we know is that they were strong warriors who had crushed the Hittites and destroyed cities in southwest Asia. Only after 50 years of fighting were the Egyptians able to turn them back.

Egypt survived, but its empire in Asia was gone. Shortly after the invasions of the Hittites and the Sea Peoples, the New Kingdom came to an end. Egypt once again fell into a period of violence and disorder. Egypt would never again regain its power.

READING CHECK **Identifying Cause and Effect** What caused the growth of trade in the New Kingdom?

Work and Daily Life

Although Egyptian dynasties rose and fell, daily life for Egyptians did not change very much. But as the population grew, society became more complex. A complex society requires people to take on different jobs.

Scribes

Other than priests and government officials, no one in Egypt was more honored than scribes. They worked for the government and for temples. Scribes kept records and accounts for the state. They also wrote and copied religious and literary texts. Scribes did not pay taxes, and many became wealthy.

Artisans, Artists, and Architects

Below scribes on the social scale were artisans whose jobs required advanced skills. Among the artisans who worked in Egypt were sculptors, builders, carpenters, jewelers, metal workers, and leather workers. Most of Egypt's artisans worked for the government or for temples. They made statues, furniture, jewelry, pottery, footwear, and other items.

Architects and artists were also admired in Egypt. Architects designed the temples and royal tombs for which Egypt is famous. Talented architects could rise to become high government officials. Artists, often employed by the state or the temples, produced many different works. Artists often worked in the pharaohs' tombs painting detailed pictures.

Soldiers

After the Middle Kingdom, Egypt created a professional army. The military offered a chance to rise in status. Soldiers received land as payment and could keep treasure they captured in war. Those who excelled could be promoted to officer positions.

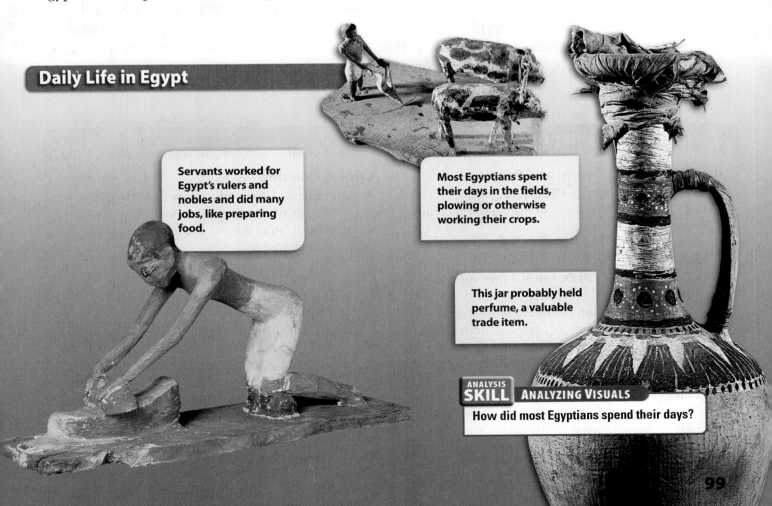

Daily Life in Egypt

Servants worked for Egypt's rulers and nobles and did many jobs, like preparing food.

Most Egyptians spent their days in the fields, plowing or otherwise working their crops.

This jar probably held perfume, a valuable trade item.

ANALYSIS SKILL **ANALYZING VISUALS**
How did most Egyptians spend their days?

Farmers and Other Peasants

Egypt's farmers and other peasants were toward the bottom of the social scale. They made up the vast majority of Egypt's population. Peasant farmers used wooden hoes or cow-drawn plows to prepare the land before the Nile flooded. After the floodwaters had drained away, they planted seeds. Farmers worked together to gather the harvest.

ACADEMIC VOCABULARY
contracts
binding legal agreements

Farmers had to give crops to the pharaoh as taxes. All peasants, including farmers, were subject to special duty. The pharaoh could demand at any time that people work on projects such as building pyramids, mining gold, or fighting in wars.

Slaves

The few slaves in Egypt were considered lower than farmers. They worked on farms, on building projects, and in households. Slaves had some legal rights and in some cases could earn their freedom.

Family Life in Egypt

Most Egyptian families lived in their own homes. Men were expected to marry young so that they could start having children. Most Egyptian women were devoted to their homes and their families. Some, however, had jobs outside the home. A few served as priestesses, and some worked as administrators and artisans. Unlike most women in the ancient world, Egyptian women had certain legal rights. These included the right to own property, make **contracts**, and divorce their husbands.

Children played with toys, took part in ballgames, and hunted. Most boys and girls received an education. At school they learned morals, writing, math, and sports. At age 14, most boys left school to enter their father's profession.

READING CHECK **Categorizing** What types of jobs did people perform in ancient Egypt?

SUMMARY AND PREVIEW Egypt's power and wealth peaked during the New Kingdom. As society became more complex, people in different classes worked at different jobs. Next, you will learn about Egyptian achievements.

Section 3 Assessment

Reviewing Ideas, Terms, and People

1. **a. Recall** What was the **Middle Kingdom**?
   b. Analyze How did Ahmose manage to become king of all Egypt?
2. **a. Identify** Which group of invaders did **Ramses the Great** defeat?
   b. Describe What did **Queen Hatshepsut** do as pharaoh of Egypt?
   c. Predict What do you think is a more reliable source of wealth—trade or payments from conquered kingdoms? Why?
3. **a. Identify** What job employed the most people in ancient Egypt?
   b. Analyze What rights did Egyptian women have?
   c. Evaluate Why do you think scribes were so honored in Egyptian society?

Critical Thinking

4. **Categorizing** Using your notes, fill in the pyramids below with information about political and military factors that led to the rise and fall of the Middle and New Kingdoms.

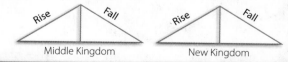

FOCUS ON WRITING

5. **Developing Key Ideas from the Middle and New Kingdoms** Your riddle should contain some information about the later pharaohs and daily life in Egypt. Decide which key ideas you should include in your riddle and add them to your list.⊠

Ramses the Great

How Could a Ruler Achieve Fame That Would Last 3,000 Years?

When did he live? the late 1300s and early 1200s BC

Where did he live? As pharaoh, Ramses lived in a city he built on the Nile Delta. The city's name, Pi-Ramesse, means the "house of Ramses."

What did he do? From a young age, Ramses was trained as a ruler and a fighter. Made an army captain at age 10, he began military campaigns even before he became pharaoh. During his reign, Ramses greatly increased the size of his kingdom.

Why is he so important? Many people consider Ramses the last great Egyptian pharaoh. He accomplished great things, but the pharaohs who followed could not maintain them. Both a great warrior and a great builder, he is known largely for the massive monuments he built. The temples at Karnak, Luxor, and Abu Simbel stand as 3,000-year-old symbols of the great pharaoh's power.

Drawing Conclusions Why do you think Ramses built great monuments all over Egypt?

KEY IDEAS

● **Ramses** had a poem praising him carved into the walls of five temples, including Karnak. One verse of the poem praises Ramses as a great warrior and the defender of Egypt.

Gracious lord and bravest king, savior-guard
Of Egypt in the battle, be our ward;
Behold we stand alone, in the hostile Hittite ring,
Save for us the breath of life,
Give deliverance from the strife,
Oh! protect us Ramses Miamun!
Oh! save us, mighty king!

—Pen-ta-ur, from *The Victory of Ramses over the Khita,* in *The World's Story,* edited by Eva March Tappan

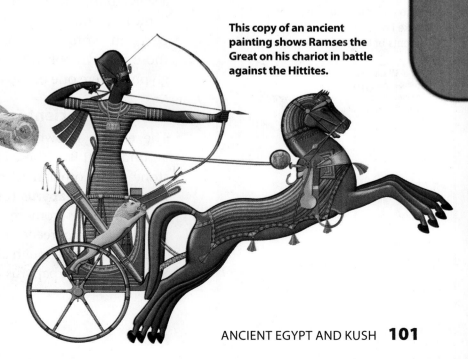

This copy of an ancient painting shows Ramses the Great on his chariot in battle against the Hittites.

Egyptian Achievements

What You Will Learn...

Main Ideas

1. The Egyptians developed a writing system using hieroglyphics.
2. The Egyptians created magnificent temples, tombs, and works of art.

The Big Idea

The Egyptians made lasting achievements in writing, architecture, and art.

Key Terms and People

hieroglyphics, *p. 102*
papyrus, *p. 102*
Rosetta Stone, *p. 103*
sphinxes, *p. 104*
obelisk, *p. 104*
King Tutankhamen, *p. 106*

Online Resource
TAKING NOTES

Use the graphic organizer online to take notes on the many achievements of the ancient Egyptians.

SS.6.W.2.5 Summarize important achievements of Egyptian civilization.

If YOU were there...

You are an artist in ancient Egypt. A noble has hired you to decorate the walls of his family tomb. You are standing inside the new tomb, studying the bare walls that you will decorate. No light reaches this chamber, but your servant holds a lantern high. You've met the noble only briefly but think that he is someone who loves his family, the gods, and Egypt.

What will you include in your painting?

BUILDING BACKGROUND The Egyptians had a rich and varied history, but most people today remember them for their cultural achievements, such as their unique writing system. In addition, Egyptian art, including the tomb paintings mentioned above, is admired by millions of tourists in museums around the world.

Egyptian Writing

If you were reading a book and saw pictures of folded cloth, a leg, a star, a bird, and a man holding a stick, would you know what it meant? You would if you were an ancient Egyptian. In the Egyptian writing system, or **hieroglyphics** (hy-ruh-GLIH-fiks), those five symbols together meant "to teach." Egyptian hieroglyphics were one of the world's first writing systems.

Writing in Ancient Egypt

The earliest known examples of Egyptian writing are from around 3300 BC. These early Egyptian writings were carved in stone or on other hard material. Later, the Egyptians learned how to make **papyrus** (puh-PY-ruhs), a long-lasting, paper-like material made from reeds. The Egyptians made papyrus by pressing layers of reeds together and pounding them into sheets. These sheets were tough and durable, yet easy to roll into scrolls. Scribes wrote on papyrus using brushes and ink.

Egyptian Writing

Egyptian hieroglyphics used picture symbols to represent sounds.

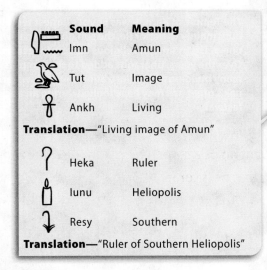

	Sound	Meaning
	Imn	Amun
	Tut	Image
	Ankh	Living

Translation—"Living image of Amun"

	Sound	Meaning
	Heka	Ruler
	Iunu	Heliopolis
	Resy	Southern

Translation—"Ruler of Southern Heliopolis"

ANALYSIS SKILL **ANALYZING VISUALS**

What does the symbol for ruler look like?

The hieroglyphic writing system used more than 600 symbols, mostly pictures of objects. Each symbol represented one or more sounds in the Egyptian language. For example, a picture of an owl represented the same sound as our letter *M*.

Hieroglyphics could be written either horizontally or vertically. They could be written from right to left or from left to right. These options made hieroglyphics flexible to write but difficult to read. The only way to tell which way a text is written is to look at individual symbols.

The Rosetta Stone

Historians and archaeologists have known about hieroglyphics for centuries, but for a long time they didn't know how to read them. In fact, it was not until 1799 when a lucky discovery by a French soldier gave historians the key they needed to read ancient Egyptian writing.

That key was the **Rosetta Stone**, a stone slab inscribed with hieroglyphics. In addition to hieroglyphics, the Rosetta Stone had text in Greek and a later form of Egyptian. Because the text in all three languages was the same, scholars who knew Greek figured out what the hieroglyphics said.

Egyptian Texts

Because papyrus did not decay in Egypt's dry climate, many Egyptian texts survive. Historians today can read Egyptian government and historical records, science texts, their calendar, and medical manuals. Literary works have also survived. We can read stories, poems, and mythological tales. Some texts, such as *The Book of the Dead*, tell about the afterlife. Others include love poems and stories about gods and kings.

READING CHECK **Comparing** How is our writing system similar to hieroglyphics?

THE IMPACT TODAY

An object that helps solve a difficult mystery is sometimes called a Rosetta Stone.

Temples, Tombs, and Art

The Egyptians are famous for their architecture and art. The walls of Egypt's magnificent temples and tombs are covered with impressive paintings and carvings.

Egypt's Great Temples

You have already read about the Egyptians' most famous structures, the pyramids. But the Egyptians also built massive temples. Those that survive are among the most spectacular sites in Egypt today.

The Egyptians believed that temples were the homes of the gods. People visited the temples to worship, offer the gods gifts, and ask for favors.

Many Egyptian temples shared similar features. Rows of stone **sphinxes**—imaginary creatures with the bodies of lions and the heads of other animals or humans—lined the path leading to the entrance. The entrance itself was a huge, thick gate. On either side of the gate might stand an **obelisk** (AH-buh-lisk), a tall, four-sided pillar that is pointed on top.

Inside, temples were lavishly decorated, as you can see in the drawing of the Temple of Karnak. Huge columns supported the temple's roof. In many cases, these columns were covered with paintings and hieroglyphics, as were the temple walls. Statues of gods and pharaohs often stood along the walls as well. The sanctuary, the most sacred part of the building, was at the far end of the temple.

The Temple of Karnak is only one of Egypt's great temples. Others were built by Ramses the Great at Abu Simbel and Luxor. Part of what makes the temple at Abu Simbel so impressive is that it is carved out of sandstone cliffs. At the temple's entrance, four 66-foot-tall statues show Ramses as pharaoh. Nearby are some smaller statues of his family.

THE IMPACT TODAY

The Washington Monument, in Washington, DC, was built in the shape of an obelisk.

The Temple of Karnak

The Temple of Karnak was Egypt's largest temple. Built mainly to honor Re, the sun god, Karnak was one of Egypt's major religious centers for centuries. Over the years, pharaohs added to the temple's many buildings. This illustration shows how Karnak's great hall may have looked during an ancient festival.

Karnak's interior columns and walls were painted brilliant colors.

ANALYSIS SKILL **ANALYZING VISUALS**

What features of Egyptian architecture can you see in this illustration?

Massive columns, some more than 80 feet high, supported the temple's high roof.

High windows let light and air into the temple.

In the annual Opet festival, priests carried statues of the gods and sacred boats from the temple to the Nile River.

Only the pharaoh and priests were allowed inside the temple, which was considered the home of the gods.

Egyptian Art

The ancient Egyptians were masterful artists. Egyptians painted lively, colorful scenes on canvas, papyrus, pottery, plaster, and wood. Detailed works also covered the walls of temples and tombs. The temple art was created to honor the gods, while the tomb art was intended for the enjoyment of the dead in the afterlife.

The subjects of Egyptian paintings vary widely. Some paintings show important historical events, such as the crowning of kings and the founding of temples. Others illustrate major religious rituals. Still other paintings show scenes from everyday life, such as farming or hunting.

Egyptian painting has a distinctive style. People's heads and legs are always seen from the side, but their upper bodies and shoulders are shown straight on. In addition, people do not always appear the same size. Important figures such as pharaohs appear huge in comparison to others. In contrast, Egyptian animals were usually drawn realistically.

Painting was not the only art form in which Egyptians excelled. For example, the Egyptians were skilled stoneworkers. Many tombs included huge statues and detailed carvings on the walls.

The Egyptians also made beautiful objects out of gold and precious stones. They made jewelry for both women and men. This included necklaces, collars, and bracelets. The Egyptians also used gold to make burial items for their pharaohs.

Over the years, treasure hunters emptied many pharaohs' tombs. At least one tomb, however, was not disturbed. In 1922 archaeologists found the tomb of **King Tutankhamen** (too-tang-KAHM-uhn), or King Tut. This tomb was filled with treasures, including jewelry, robes, a burial mask, and ivory statues. King Tut's treasures have taught us much about Egyptian burial practices and beliefs.

READING CHECK **Summarizing** What types of artwork were contained in Egyptian tombs?

SUMMARY AND PREVIEW Ancient Egyptians developed one of the best known cultures in the ancient world. Next, you will learn about a culture that developed in the shadow of Egypt—Kush.

Section 4 Assessment

Reviewing Ideas, Terms, and People

1. **a. Identify** What are **hieroglyphics**?
   b. Contrast How was hieroglyphic writing different from our writing today? from cuneiform used by the Mesopotamians?
   c. Evaluate Why was finding the **Rosetta Stone** so important to scholars?
2. **a. Describe** What were two ways the Egyptians decorated their temples?
   b. Analyze Why were tombs filled with art, jewelry, and other treasures?
   c. Draw Conclusions Why do you think pharaohs like Ramses the Great built huge temples?

Critical Thinking

3. **Summarizing** Draw a chart like the one below. Under each heading, write a statement that summarizes Egyptian achievements in that field.

Writing	Architecture	Art

FOCUS ON WRITING

4. **Adding Up What You Know about Egypt** Look at the notes you have taken at the end of each section. Think about what clues you might include when you write your riddle about Egypt.

Ancient Kush

If YOU were there...

You live along the Nile River, where it moves quickly through swift rapids. A few years ago, armies from the powerful kingdom of Egypt took over your country. Some Egyptians have moved here. They bring new customs, and many people are imitating them. Now your sister has a new baby and wants to give it an Egyptian name! This upsets many people in your family.

How do you feel about following Egyptian customs?

> **BUILDING BACKGROUND** Egypt dominated the lands along the Nile, but it was not the only ancient culture to develop along the river. Another kingdom called Kush arose to the south of Egypt. Through trade, conquest, and political dealings, the histories of Egypt and Kush became closely tied together.

The Geography of Early Nubia

South of Egypt, a group of people settled in the region we now call Nubia. These Africans established the first great kingdom in the interior of Africa. We know this kingdom by the name the Egyptians gave it—Kush. The development of Kushite society was greatly influenced by the geography of Nubia, especially the role played by the Nile River.

SECTION **5**

SS.6.E.1.1, SS.6.E.1.2, SS.6.E.1.3, SS.6.E.2.1, SS.6.E.3.2, SS.6.E.3.3, SS.6.G.1.3, SS.6.G.1.4, SS.6.G.1.5, SS.6.G.1.6, SS.6.G.2.2, SS.6.G.2.4, SS.6.G.2.6, SS.6.G.3.2, SS.6.G.4.1, SS.6.G.5.1, SS.6.G.5.3, SS.6.W.1.3, SS.6.W.2.4, SS.6.W.3.18

What You Will Learn...

Main Ideas

1. The geography of early Nubia helped civilization develop there.
2. Kush and Egypt traded, but they also fought.
3. Later Kush became a trading power with a unique culture.
4. Both internal and external factors led to the decline of Kush.

The Big Idea

The kingdom of Kush, which arose south of Egypt in a land called Nubia, developed an advanced civilization with a large trading network.

Key Terms and People

Piankhi, *p. 110*
trade network, *p. 111*
merchants, *p. 111*
exports, *p. 111*
imports, *p. 111*
Queen Shanakhdakheto, *p. 113*
King Ezana, *p. 113*

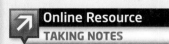

Online Resource
TAKING NOTES

Use the graphic organizer online to take notes on the rise and fall of Kush.

The ruins of ancient Kushite pyramids stand behind those reconstructed to look the way they did when originally built.

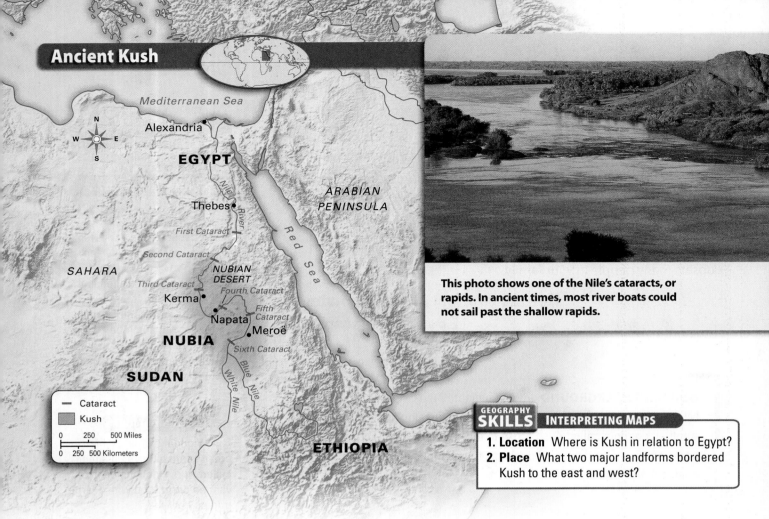

Ancient Kush

Mediterranean Sea

Alexandria

EGYPT

ARABIAN
PENINSULA

Thebes

First Cataract

Red Sea

Second Cataract

SAHARA

NUBIAN
DESERT

Third Cataract

Fourth Cataract

Kerma

Fifth
Cataract

Napata

Meroë

NUBIA

Sixth Cataract

SUDAN

White Nile

Blue Nile

ETHIOPIA

— Cataract

Kush

0   250   500 Miles

0   250   500 Kilometers

This photo shows one of the Nile's cataracts, or rapids. In ancient times, most river boats could not sail past the shallow rapids.

GEOGRAPHY SKILLS | **INTERPRETING MAPS**

1. **Location** Where is Kush in relation to Egypt?
2. **Place** What two major landforms bordered Kush to the east and west?

SS.6.W.3.18 Describe the rise and fall of the ancient east African kingdoms of Kush and Axum and Christianity's development in Ethiopia.

The Land of Nubia

Today desert covers much of Nubia, but in ancient times the region was more fertile than it is now. Rain flooded the Nile every year, providing a rich layer of silt to nearby lands. The kingdom of Kush developed in this fertile area.

Ancient Nubia was rich in minerals such as gold, copper, and stone. These resources played a major role in the area's history and contributed to its wealth.

Early Civilization in Nubia

Like all early civilizations, the people of Nubia depended on agriculture for their food. Fortunately for them, the Nile's floods allowed the Nubians to plant both summer and winter crops. Among the crops they grew were wheat, barley, and other grains.

Besides farmland, the banks of the Nile also provided grazing land for livestock. As a result, farming villages thrived all along the Nile by 3500 BC.

Over time some farmers grew richer than others. These farmers became village leaders. Sometime around 2000 BC, one of these leaders took control of other villages and made himself king of the region. His new kingdom was called Kush.

The kings of Kush ruled from their capital at Kerma (KAR-muh). This city was located on the Nile just south of the third cataract. Because the Nile's cataracts made parts of the river hard to pass through, they were natural barriers against invaders. For many years the cataracts kept Kush safe from the more powerful Egyptian kingdom to the north.

As time passed, Kushite society grew more complex. Besides farmers and herders, some Kushites became priests and artisans. Early Kush was influenced by cultures to the south. Later, Egypt played a greater role in Kush's history.

READING CHECK **Finding Main Ideas** How did geography help civilization grow in Nubia?

Kush and Egypt

Kush and Egypt were neighbors. Sometimes the neighbors lived in peace with each other and helped each other prosper. For example, Kush became a major supplier of both slaves and raw materials to Egypt. The Kushites sent materials such as gold, copper, and stone to Egypt. The Kushites also sent the Egyptians ebony, a type of dark, heavy wood, and ivory, the hard white material that makes up elephant tusks.

Egypt's Conquest of Kush

Relations between Kush and Egypt were not always peaceful, however. As Kush grew wealthy from trade, its army grew stronger as well. Egypt's rulers soon feared that Kush would grow even more powerful and attack Egypt.

To prevent such an attack from occurring, the pharaoh Thutmose I sent an army to take control of Kush around 1500 BC. The pharaoh's army conquered all of Nubia north of the Fifth Cataract. As a result, Kush became part of Egypt.

After his army's victory, the pharaoh destroyed Kerma, the Kushite capital. Later pharaohs—including Ramses the Great—built huge temples in what had been Kushite territory.

Effects of the Conquest

Kush remained an Egyptian territory for about 450 years. During that time, Egypt's influence over Kush grew tremendously. Many Egyptians settled in Kush. Egyptian became the language of the region. Many Kushites used Egyptian names and wore Egyptian-style clothing. They also adopted Egyptian religious practices.

A Change in Power

During the mid-1000s BC the New Kingdom in Egypt was ending. As the power of Egypt's pharaohs declined, Kushite leaders regained control of Kush. Kush once again became independent.

We know almost nothing about the history of the Kushites from the time they gained independence until 200 years later. Kush is not mentioned in any historical records that describe those centuries.

The Conquest of Egypt

By around 850 BC Kush had regained its strength. It was once again as strong as it had been before it had been conquered by Egypt. Because the Egyptians had captured and destroyed the city of Kerma, the kings of Kush ruled from the city of Napata. Built by the Egyptians, Napata was on the Nile, about 100 miles southeast of Kerma.

As Kush grew stronger, Egypt was further weakened. A series of inept pharaohs

BIOGRAPHY

Piankhi (PYAN-kee)
c. 751–716 BC

Also known as Piye, Piankhi was among Kush's most successful military leaders. A fierce warrior on the battlefield, the king was also deeply religious. Piankhi's belief that he had the support of the gods fueled his passion for war against Egypt. His courage inspired his troops on the battlefield. Piankhi loved his horses and was buried with eight of his best steeds.

Drawing Conclusions How did Piankhi's belief that he was supported by the gods affect his plans for Egypt?

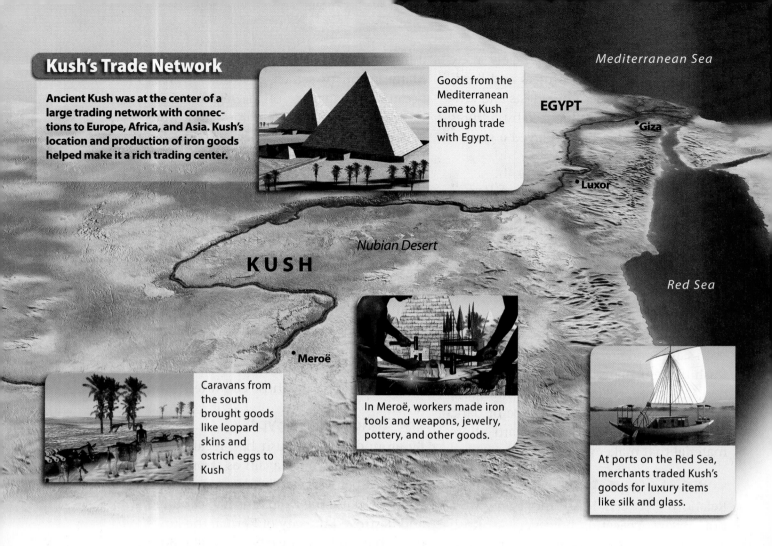

Kush's Trade Network

Ancient Kush was at the center of a large trading network with connections to Europe, Africa, and Asia. Kush's location and production of iron goods helped make it a rich trading center.

Goods from the Mediterranean came to Kush through trade with Egypt.

Caravans from the south brought goods like leopard skins and ostrich eggs to Kush

In Meroë, workers made iron tools and weapons, jewelry, pottery, and other goods.

At ports on the Red Sea, merchants traded Kush's goods for luxury items like silk and glass.

left Egypt open to attack. In the 700s BC a Kushite king, Kashta, seized on Egypt's weakness and attacked it. By about 751 BC he had conquered Upper Egypt. He then established relations with Lower Egypt.

After Kashta died, his son **Piankhi** (PYAN-kee) continued to attack Egypt. The armies of Kush captured many cities, including Egypt's ancient capital. Piankhi fought the Egyptians because he believed that the gods wanted him to rule all of Egypt. By the time he died in about 716 BC, Piankhi had accomplished this task. His kingdom extended north from Napata to the Nile Delta.

The Kushite Dynasty

After Piankhi died, his brother Shabaka (SHAB-uh-kuh) took control of the kingdom.

Shabaka then declared himself pharaoh. This declaration began the 25th Dynasty, or Kushite Dynasty, in Egypt.

Shabaka and later rulers of his dynasty believed that they were heirs of the great pharaohs of Egypt's past. They tried to restore old Egyptian cultural practices and renew faded traditions. Some of these practices and traditions had been abandoned during Egypt's period of weakness. For example, Shabaka was buried in a pyramid. The Egyptians had stopped building pyramids for their rulers centuries before.

The Kushite rulers of Egypt built new temples to Egyptian gods and restored old temples. They also worked to preserve Egyptian writings. As a result, Egyptian culture thrived during the 25th Dynasty.

The End of Kushite Rule in Egypt

The Kushite Dynasty remained strong in Egypt for about 40 years. In the 670s BC, however, the powerful army of the Assyrians from Mesopotamia invaded Egypt. The Assyrians' iron weapons were better than the Kushites' bronze weapons. Although the Kushites were skilled archers, they could not stop the invaders. The Kushites were steadily pushed southward. In just 10 years the Assyrians had driven the Kushite forces completely out of Egypt.

READING CHECK **Analyzing** How did internal problems in Egypt benefit Kush?

Later Kush

After they lost control of Egypt, the people of Kush devoted themselves to agriculture and trade, hoping to make their country rich again. Within a few centuries, the kingdom of Kush had indeed become prosperous and powerful once more.

Kush's Iron Industry

The economic center of Kush during this period was at Meroë (MER-oh-wee), the kingdom's new capital. Meroë's location helped Kush's economy to grow. Large deposits of gold could be found nearby, as could forests of ebony and other wood. More importantly, the area around Meroë was full of rich iron ore deposits. In this location, the Kushites developed Africa's first iron industry. Iron ore and wood for furnaces were easily available, so the iron industry grew quickly.

The Expansion of Trade

In time, Meroë became the center of a large **trade network**, a system of people in different lands who trade goods. The Kushites sent goods down the Nile to Egypt. From there, Egyptian and Greek **merchants**, or

traders, carried goods to ports on the Mediterranean and Red seas and to southern Africa. These goods may have eventually reached India, and perhaps China.

Kush's **exports**—items sent out to other regions—included gold, pottery, iron tools, slaves, and ivory. Kushite merchants also exported leopard skins, ostrich feathers, and elephants. In return, the Kushites received **imports**—goods brought in from other regions—such as fine jewelry and luxury items from Egypt, Asia, and other lands along the Mediterranean Sea.

Kushite Culture

As Kushite trade grew, merchants came into contact with people from other cultures. As a result, the people of Kush combined customs from other cultures with their own unique Kushite culture.

The most obvious influence on Kushite culture was Egypt. Many buildings in Meroë, especially temples, resembled those in Egypt. Many people in Kush worshipped Egyptian gods and wore Egyptian clothing. Kushite rulers used the title *pharaoh* and were buried in pyramids.

Many elements of Kushite culture were not borrowed. Kushite houses and daily life were unique. One Greek geographer noted some Kushite differences.

> "The houses in the cities are formed by interweaving split pieces of palm wood or of bricks. ... They hunt elephants, lions, and panthers. There are also serpents ... and there are many other kinds of wild animals."
>
> –Strabo, *The Geographies*

In addition to Egyptian gods, the people of Kush worshipped their own gods. They also developed their own written language, Meroitic. Unfortunately, historians are not yet able to understand Meroitic.

READING CHECK **Categorize** List three Kush exports and three Kush imports.

History Close-up

Rulers of Kush

Like the Egyptians, the people of Kush considered their rulers to be gods. Kush's culture was similar to Egypt's, but there were also important differences.

Like the Egyptians, Kush's rulers built pyramids, but they were much smaller and the style was different.

Kush was ruled by a few different powerful queens. Queens seem to have been more important in Kush than in Egypt.

Stone carvings were made to commemorate important buildings and events, just like in Egypt. Kush's writing system was similar to Egyptian hieroglyphics, but scholars have been unable to understand most of it.

ANALYSIS SKILL **ANALYZING VISUALS**

What can you see in the illustration that is similar to Egyptian culture?

The Decline of Kush

The Kushite kingdom centered at Meroë reached its height in the first century BC. Four centuries later, Kush collapsed. Events both inside and outside the empire led to its downfall.

Loss of Resources

A series of problems weakened its economy. One problem was that cattle were allowed to overgraze. Then wind blew the soil away, causing farmers to produce less food. Without this soil, farmers could not produce enough food for Kush's people.

In addition, ironmakers caused deforestation. They used up the forests near Meroë. As wood became scarce, furnaces shut down. Kush could no longer produce enough weapons or trade goods. As a result, Kush's military and economic power declined.

Aksum Conquers Kush

Kush was also weakened by a loss of trade. Foreign merchants set up new trade routes that went around Kush. One such trade route bypassed Kush in favor of Aksum (Axum) (AKH-soom), a kingdom located along the Red Sea in what is today Ethiopia and Eritrea. In the first two centuries AD, Aksum grew wealthy from trade. Aksum's wealth and power, however, came at the expense of Kush. As Kush's power declined, Aksum became the most powerful state in the region.

By the AD 300s, Kush had lost much of its wealth and military might. The king of Aksum saw an opportunity and sent an army to conquer his former trade rival. In about AD 350, the Aksumite army of **King Ezana** (AY-zah-nah) destroyed Meroë and took over Kush.

In the late 300s, the rulers of Aksum became Christian. Around two hundred years later, the Nubians also converted. Their new religion reshaped culture throughout Nubia, and the last influence of Kush disappeared.

READING CHECK **Summarizing** What factors led to the decline of Kush?

SUMMARY AND PREVIEW From their capital at Meroë, the people of Kush controlled a powerful trading network. Next, you will learn about a land that may have traded with Kush—India.

THE IMPACT TODAY

Much of the population of Ethiopia, which includes what used to be Aksum, is still Christian today.

SS.6.G.3.2 Analyze the impact of human populations on the ancient world's ecosystems.

Section 5 Assessment

Reviewing Ideas, Terms, and People

1. **a. Recall** On which river did Kush develop?
   b. Evaluate How did Nubia's natural resources influence the early history of Kush?
2. **a. Identify** Who was **Piankhi** and why was he important to the history of Kush?
   b. Analyze What were some elements of Egyptian culture that became popular in Kush?
   c. Draw Conclusions Why is the 25th Dynasty significant in the history of both Egypt and Kush?
3. **a. Describe** What advantages did the location of Meroë offer to the Kushites?
   b. Compare How were Kushite and Egyptian cultures similar?
4. **a. Identify** Who conquered Kush in the AD 300s?

   b. Evaluate What was the impact of new trading routes on Kush?

Critical Thinking

5. **Identifying Cause and Effect** Create a chart like this one. Using your notes, list an effect for each cause.

Cause	Effect
Thutmose I invades Kush.	
Power of Egyptian pharaohs declines.	
Piankhi attacks Egypt.	

FOCUS ON WRITING

6. **Taking Notes on Kush** Review this section and take notes on those people, places, and events that would make good clues for your riddle about Kush.

Social Studies Skills

SS.6.W.1.3 Interpret primary and secondary sources.

Assessing Primary and Secondary Sources

Understand the Skill

Primary sources in history are materials created by people who lived during the times they describe. Examples include letters, diaries, and photographs. *Secondary sources* are accounts written later by someone who was not present. They are designed to teach about or discuss a historical topic. This textbook is an example of a secondary source.

Together, primary and secondary sources can present a good picture of a historical period or event. However, they must be used carefully to make sure that the picture they present is accurate.

Learn the Skill

Here are some questions to ask to help you judge the accuracy of primary and secondary sources.

1. **What is it?** Is it a firsthand account or is it based on information provided by others? In other words, is it primary or secondary?

2. **Who wrote it?** For a primary source, what was the author's connection to what he or she was writing about? For a secondary source, what makes the author an authority on this subject?

3. **Who is the audience?** Was the information meant for the public? Was it meant for a friend or for the writer alone? The intended audience can influence what the writer has to say.

4. **What is the purpose?** Authors of either primary or secondary sources can have reasons to exaggerate—or even lie—to suit their own goals or purposes. Look for evidence of emotion, opinion, or bias in the source. These might influence the accuracy of the account.

5. **Does other evidence support the source?** Look for other information that supports the source's account. Compare different sources whenever possible.

Practice and Apply the Skill

Below are two passages about the military in ancient Egypt. Read them both and use the guidelines to answer the questions that follow.

> "The pharaohs began . . . leading large armies out of a land that had once known only small police forces and militia. The Egyptians quickly extended their military and commercial influence over an extensive region that included the rich provinces of Syria . . . and the numbers of Egyptian slaves grew swiftly."
>
> –C. Warren Hollister, from *Roots of the Western Tradition*

> "Let me tell you how the soldier fares . . . how he goes to Syria, and how he marches over the mountains. His bread and water are borne [carried] upon his shoulders like the load of [a donkey]; they make his neck bent as that of [a donkey], and the joints of his back are bowed [bent]. His drink is stinking water . . . When he reaches the enemy, he is trapped like a bird, and he has no strength in his limbs."
>
> –from *Wings of the Falcon: Life and Thought of Ancient Egypt,* translated by Joseph Kaster

1. Which quote is a primary source, and which is a secondary source?

2. Is there evidence of opinion, emotion, or bias in the second quote? Explain why or why not.

3. Which information is more likely to be accurate on this subject? Explain your answer.

Chapter Review

Visual Summary

Use the visual summary below to help you review the main ideas of the chapter.

QUICK FACTS

Egypt
Egyptian civilization developed along the Nile River. There, powerful pharaohs ruled a diverse society whose achievements included building impressive pyramids and developing a writing system.

Kush
Kush developed farther south along the Nile. Ruled by their own kings and queens, the Kushites had extensive interaction with the Egyptians and blended Egyptian influences into their own advanced culture.

Reviewing Vocabulary, Terms, and People

For each group of terms below, circle the letter of the term that does not relate to the others. Then write a sentence that explains how the other two terms are related.

1. **a.** cataract
    b. delta
    c. dynasty
2. **a.** afterlife
    b. mummies
    c. engineering
3. **a.** hieroglyphics
    b. Rosetta Stone
    c. obelisk
4. **a.** exports
    b. imports
    c. papyrus

Comprehension and Critical Thinking

SECTION 1 *(pages 86–89)*

5. a. Describe Besides crops, what foods did the Nile provide?

b. Analyze Why did Menes wear a double crown?

c. Predict What do you think happened in the years when the Nile River did not flood?

SECTION 2 *(pages 90–95)*

6. a. Identify In what type of structure were pharaohs buried?

b. Analyze How were beliefs in the afterlife linked to items placed in tombs?

c. Elaborate Why did nobles and commoners alike obey the pharaoh?

SECTION 3 *(pages 96–100)*

7 a. Describe What factors contributed to Egypt's wealth during the New Kingdom?

b. Analyze How might a young Egyptian rise in social status?

c. Elaborate What caused the New Kingdom to fall?

SECTION 4 *(pages 102–106)*

8. a. Identify What is a sphinx?

b. Describe What was the name of the Egyptian system of writing and how does it differ from our system of writing?

c. Elaborate Why is the temple at Karnak so famous?

SECTION 5 *(pages 107–113)*

9. a. Describe Where did Kushite civilization develop?

b. Draw Conclusions Why did Egypt want to gain control of Kush?

c. Evaluate Why was the 25th Dynasty so important for both Kush and Egypt?

Reviewing Themes

10. Geography Do you think that societies like those in Egypt and Kush could have grown up anywhere besides the Nile River Valley? Why or why not?

11. Religion How did religious beliefs shape both Egyptian and Kushite culture?

12. Economics What led to the creation of Africa's first iron industry in Kush?

Using the Internet

13. Activity: Creating Art The Egyptians developed an incredibly artistic civilization. Their architecture included innovative pyramids and temples. Artisans created beautiful paintings, carvings, and jewelry. Go online to research the main features of Egyptian art and architecture. Then imagine you are an Egyptian artisan. Create a piece of art to place inside a pharaoh's tomb. Include hieroglyphics telling the pharaoh about your art.

Reading Skills

Causes and Effects in History Read the following passage and answer the questions.

> Much of Egyptian religion is focused on the afterlife. The Egyptians believed that the afterlife was a happy place. Their belief in the afterlife stemmed from their idea of *ka*, or a person's life force. When a person died, his or her *ka* left the body and became a spirit. The *ka*, however, remained linked to the body and could not leave its burial site. The *ka* had all the same needs that the person had when he or she was living. To fulfill the *ka's* needs, people filled tombs with objects for the afterlife.

14. What is the cause of the Egyptian custom of putting objects in tombs?

15. According to the passage, what is an effect of the Egyptian belief in *ka*?

Social Studies Skills

16. Assessing Primary and Secondary Sources Write three questions you would want to ask about a primary source and three questions you would want to ask about a secondary source that deals with the history of Egypt and Kush.

FOCUS ON WRITING

17. Writing Riddles Choose five details about Egypt and write a sentence about each detail. End each sentence with a "me" statement. For example, a sentence about the United States might say, "In the north, Canada borders me." End your riddle with "Who am I?" Repeat this for a riddle about Kush.

FOCUS ON MATHEMATICS

18. Mathematical Expressions You are a worker helping to build a pyramid in ancient Egypt. Your team begins with 100 stone blocks to use in the pyramid, and you receive 5 more blocks per day. Write and solve a mathematical expression to reflect how many blocks you will have after 10 days of deliveries.

Florida Standardized Test Practice

DIRECTIONS: Read each question and write the letter of the best response.

1

> Oh great god and ruler, the gift of Re,
>   God of the Sun.
> Oh great protector of Egypt and its people.
> Great one who has saved us from the horrible
>   Tehenu.
> You, who have turned back the Hittites.
> You, who have fortified our western border to
>   forever protect us from our enemies.
> We bless you, oh great one.
> We worship and honor you, oh great pharaoh.

A tribute such as the one above would have been written in honor of which Egyptian ruler?

A Khufu

B Ramses the Great

C King Tutankhamen

D Queen Hatshepsut

2 **The Nile helped civilization develop in Egypt and Nubia in all of the following ways *except* by**

A providing a source of food and water.

B allowing farming to develop.

C enriching the soil along its banks.

D protecting against invasion from the west.

3 **The most fertile soil in Egypt was located in the**

A Nile Delta.

B desert.

C cataracts.

D far south.

4 **Which of the following statements about the relationship of Egypt and Kush is *NOT* true?**

A Egypt ruled Kush for many centuries.

B Kush was an important trading partner of Egypt.

C Egypt sent the first people to colonize Kush.

D Kush ruled Egypt for a period of time.

5 **How did Egypt influence Kush?**

A Egypt taught Kush how to raise cattle.

B Egypt helped Kush develop its irrigation system.

C Egypt taught Kush to make iron products.

D Kush learned about pyramids from Egypt.

Connecting with Past Learnings

6 **In this chapter, you learned about hieroglyphics, one of the world's first writing systems. In Chapter 3, you read about another ancient writing system called**

A Sumerian.

B Hammurabi.

C ziggurat.

D cuneiform.

7 **In Chapter 3 you read about Sargon I, who first united Mesopotamia under one ruler. Which Egyptian ruler's accomplishments were most similar to Sargon's?**

A King Ezana's

B Khufu's

C Menes's

D Hatshepsut's

A Description of a Historical Place

If a picture is worth a thousand words, then a thousand words could add up to a good description. Writers turn to description when they want to explain what a place is like—what you would see if you were there, or what you might hear, smell, or touch.

Assignment

Write a description of a place—a city, village, building, or monument—in ancient Mesopotamia, Egypt, or Kush.

TIP **Organizing Details**

Organize the details you gather in one of these ways.

- **Spatial Order** Arrange details according to where they are. You can describe things from right to left, top to bottom, or faraway to close up.
- **Chronological Order** Arrange details in the order they occurred or in the order that you experienced them.
- **Order of Importance** Arrange details from the most to least important or vice versa.

1. Prewrite

Picking a Subject and a Main Idea

Think about the civilizations of ancient Mesopotamia, Egypt, and Kush. Which civilization seems most interesting to you? What villages, cities, or buildings seem interesting? Select one place and use this textbook, the Internet, or sources in your library to find out more about it.

You also need to decide on your point of view about your subject. For example, was this place scary, exciting, or overwhelming?

Choosing Details

As you conduct your research, look for details to show your readers what it would have been like to actually be in that place.

- **Sensory Details** What color(s) do you associate with your subject? What shape or shapes do you see? What sounds would you hear if you were there? What could you touch—rough walls, dry grass, a smooth, polished stone?
- **Factual Details** How big was this place? Where was it located? When did it exist? If people were there, what were they doing?

When you choose the details to use in your description, think about your point of view on this place. If it was exciting, choose details that will help you show that.

2. Write

This framework will help you use your notes to write a first draft.

A Writer's Framework

Introduction
- Identify your subject and your point of view on it.
- Give your readers any background information that they might need.

Body
- Describe your subject, using sensory and factual details.
- Follow a consistent and logical order.

Conclusion
- Briefly summarize the most important details about the place.
- Reveal your point of view about the place.

3. Evaluate and Revise

Evaluating
Use the following questions to discover ways to improve your paper.

Evaluation Questions for a Description of a Place

- Do you immediately catch the reader's interest?
- Do you use sensory and factual details that work together to create a vivid picture of your subject?
- Do you clearly state your point of view or most important idea?

- Is the information organized clearly?
- Do you end the description by summarizing the most important details?

TIP **Showing Location** When describing the physical appearance of something, make sure you use precise words and phrases to explain where a feature is located. Some useful words and phrases for explaining location are *below, beside, down, on top, over, next to, to the right,* and *to the left.*

Revising
We often help others understand or imagine something by making a comparison. Sometimes we compare two things that are really very much alike. For example, "The city grew like San Diego did. It spread along a protected harbor." At other times we compare two things that are not alike. These comparisons are called figures of speech, and they can help your readers see something in an interesting way.

- Similes compare two unlike things by using words such as *like* or *so*. **EXAMPLE** *The city center curved around the harbor like a crescent moon.*
- Metaphors compare two unlike things by saying one is the other. **EXAMPLE** *The city was the queen of the region.*

When you evaluate and revise your description, look for ways you can make your subject clearer by comparing it to something else.

4. Proofread and Publish

- Make sure you use commas correctly with a list of details. **EXAMPLE** *The temple was 67 feet high, 35 feet wide, and 40 feet deep.*
- Share your paper with students who wrote about a similar place. What details do your descriptions share? How are they different?
- Find or create a picture of the place you have described. Ask a classmate or a family member to read your description and compare it to the picture.

Practice and Apply
Use the steps and strategies outlined in this workshop to write your description of a place in ancient Mesopotamia, Egypt, or Kush.

UNIT 3

2300 BC–AD 500

Civilization in India and China

Chapter 5   Ancient India
Chapter 6   Ancient China

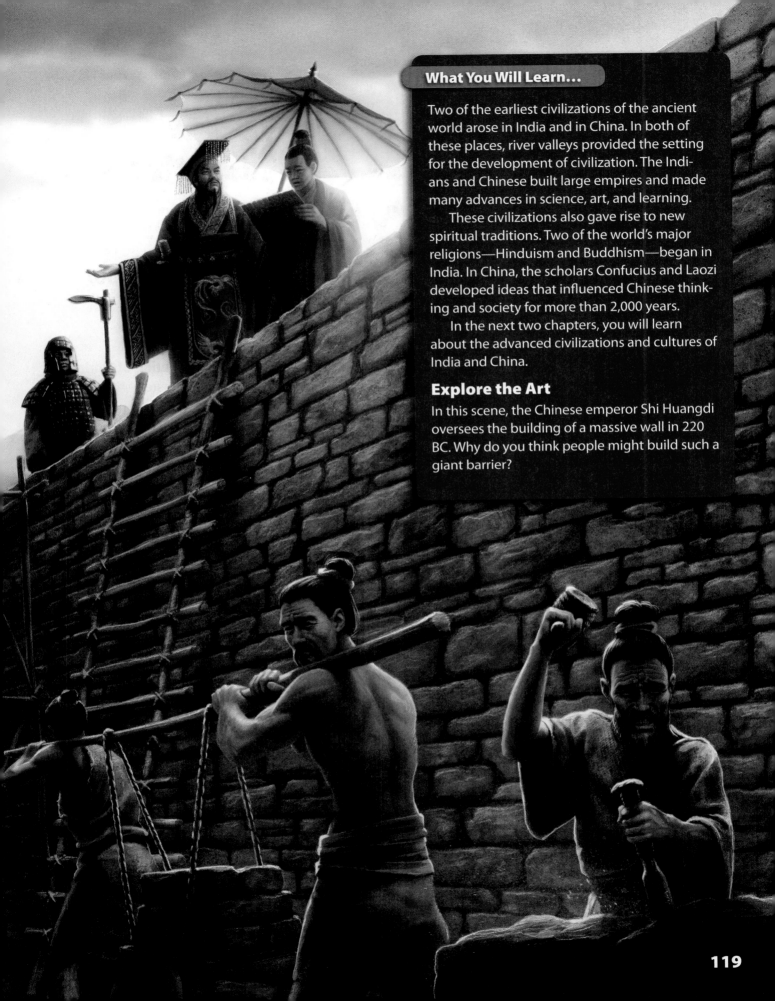

What You Will Learn...

Two of the earliest civilizations of the ancient world arose in India and in China. In both of these places, river valleys provided the setting for the development of civilization. The Indians and Chinese built large empires and made many advances in science, art, and learning.

These civilizations also gave rise to new spiritual traditions. Two of the world's major religions—Hinduism and Buddhism—began in India. In China, the scholars Confucius and Laozi developed ideas that influenced Chinese thinking and society for more than 2,000 years.

In the next two chapters, you will learn about the advanced civilizations and cultures of India and China.

Explore the Art

In this scene, the Chinese emperor Shi Huangdi oversees the building of a massive wall in 220 BC. Why do you think people might build such a giant barrier?

FLORIDA...
The Story Continues

CHAPTER 5, Ancient India (2300 BC–AD 500)

PEOPLE **1990–Present: The Asian Indian population of Florida grows.** Asian Indians are one of the fastest-growing population groups in Florida. According to the U.S. Census the Asian Indian population of Florida stood at about 30,000 in 1990. By 2000 that number had risen to more than 70,000. In 2010 the government estimated that nearly 129,000 Asian Indians lived in the state. That was an 82 percent increase since 2000. Many Asian Indians have settled in Alachua County, the Greater Orlando area, Hillsborough County, and the Florida Gold Coast (Monroe, Miami-Dade, Broward, and Palm Beach counties).

PLACES **1996: The Hindu Temple of Florida is built in Tampa.** The Hindu Temple of Florida is built in a traditional Hindu architectural style. A grand staircase leads to the main gate on the second floor of the temple. There are two sets of 18 steps—a step for each of the 18 chapters of the Bhagavad-Gita, the Hindu holy book. Shri Jay and Shri Vijay—the gatekeepers—stand guard at the bottom of the stairs. The pyramid-like gate tower soars 70 feet into the air. Its surface is decorated with detailed sculptures. The inner and outer walls of the temple are also decorated with elephants, peacocks, lotus flowers, and other sculptures. A team of 10 shilpis—temple sculptors—came from India to decorate the temple. It took them years to complete the work. The temple is dedicated to five deities: Ganesha, the remover of obstacles; Siva, god of destruction; Lakshmi, goddess of wealth; Subramanya, eliminator of lust, anger and ego; and Satyanarayana , a form of Lord Vishnu, preserver of the universe. The statues of the deities were made in India.

PLACES **1999: Construction begins on the Shiva Vishnu Temple of South Florida in Broward County.** Dr. Ganapati Sthapati is a well-known temple architect from India. He designed the Shiva Vishnu Temple of South Florida in the traditional Dravidian temple style of South India. It is the same style of architecture as the Hindu Temple of Florida. Twelve shilpis came from India to add the sculptures. This process is known as Indianization. Being a shilpi is an ancient Indian profession. The designs and methods the shilpi use are guided by Hindu tradition.

EVENTS **Present: Florida Hindus celebrate Diwali.** Diwali is the Hindu Festival of Lights. According to North Indian tradition, Diwali celebrates the victory of the Hindu god Rama over the evil king Ravana. When Rama returned home after killing Ravana, villagers heralded his return with lamps. Each year during Diwali, Hindus light clay oil lamps in memory of the event. In other parts of India the festival honors Lakshmi, the goddess of wealth. Lights are used to welcome Lakshmi into the home. Each year Diwali celebrations are held in Hindu temples and homes throughout Florida.

PLACES **Present: Florida is home to many Buddhist centers.** The Kadampa Meditation Center in Sarasota is one of the main U.S. centers of the New Kadampa Tradition of Buddhism. Kadampa Buddhism is a Mahayana Buddhist school founded by the Indian Buddhist master Atisha (AD 982–1054). Atisha's followers are known as Kadampas. *Ka* refers to Buddha's teachings, and *dam* to Atisha's special instructions known as the stages of the path to enlightenment.

Unpacking the Florida Standards ⟨···

Read the following to learn what this standard says and what it means. See FL8–FL31 to unpack all of the standards related to this chapter.

Benchmark SS.6.W.4.2 Explain the major beliefs and practices associated with Hinduism and the social structure of the caste system in ancient India. Examples are Brahman, reincarnation, dharma, karma, ahimsa, moksha.

What does it mean?

Understand the key aspects of Hinduism and analyze how Hinduism affected the development of ancient India. Describe the caste system that developed in India.

SPOTLIGHT ON

SS.6.G.2.2 See page FL44 for content specifically related to this Chapter 5 standard.

Ancient India

Essential Question How do India's rich history and culture affect the world today?

Florida Next Generation Sunshine State Standards

SS.6.G.2.2 Differentiate between continents, regions, countries, and cities in order to understand the complexities of regions created by civilizations. **SS.6.G.2.3** Analyze the relationship of physical geography to the development of ancient river valley civilizations. **SS.6.G.2.4** Explain how the geographical location of ancient civilizations contributed to the culture and politics of those societies. **SS.6.G.2.5** Interpret how geographic boundaries invite or limit interaction with other regions and cultures. **SS.6.G.2.6** Explain the concept of cultural diffusion, and identify the influences of different ancient cultures on one another. **SS.6.G.3.1** Explain how the physical landscape has affected the development of agriculture and industry in the ancient world. **SS.6.G.4.2** Use maps to trace significant migrations, and analyze their results. **SS.6.G.4.4** Map and analyze the impact of the spread of various belief systems in the ancient world. **SS.6.W.1.1** Use timelines to identify chronological order of historical events. **SS.6.W.2.4** Compare the economic, political, social, and religious institutions of ancient river civilizations. **SS.6.W.4.1** Discuss the significance of Aryan and other tribal migrations on Indian civilization. **SS.6.W.4.2** Explain the major beliefs and practices associated with Hinduism and the social structure of the caste system in ancient India. **SS.6.W.4.3** Recognize the political and cultural achievements of the Mauryan and Gupta empires. **SS.6.W.4.4** Explain the teachings of Buddha, the importance of Asoka, and how Buddhism spread in India, Ceylon, and other parts of Asia. **SS.6.W.4.5** Summarize the important achievements and contributions of ancient Indian civilization.

FOCUS ON WRITING

An Illustrated Poster Ancient India was a fascinating place. It was the home of amazing cities, the site of strong empires, and the birthplace of major religions. As you read this chapter, think about how you could illustrate one aspect of Indian culture in a poster. When you finish the chapter, you will design such a poster, which will include captions that explain the illustrations you have drawn.

CHAPTER EVENTS

c. 2300 BC The Harappan civilization develops.

2300 BC

WORLD EVENTS

2200 BC The Old Kingdom ends in Egypt.

In this photo, crowds of Hindus gather to bathe in the sacred Ganges River.

1500s BC
Aryans begin migrating into India.

c. 1250 BC
Hinduism begins to develop in India.

c. 563 BC
Prince Siddhartha Gautama, or the Buddha, is born in northern India.

c. AD 320
Candra Gupta I founds the Gupta Empire.

1500 BC | 1000 BC | 500 BC | BC 1 AD | AD 500

c. 1500 BC
The Shang dynasty is established in China.

334 BC
Alexander the Great begins his conquests.

AD 391 All non-Christian religions are banned in the Roman Empire.

ANCIENT INDIA **121**

Reading Social Studies

| Economics | Geography | Politics | Religion | Society and Culture | Science and Technology |

Focus on Themes This chapter outlines and describes the development of India. You will read about India's first civilization, the Harappan civilization, so advanced that the people had indoor bathrooms and their own writing system. You will also learn about the **society and culture** that restricted who Indian people could talk with or marry. Finally, you will read about the **religions** and empires that united India and about the art and literature that Indians created.

Inferences about History

Focus on Reading What's the difference between a good guess and a weak guess? A good guess is an educated guess. In other words, the guess is based on some knowledge or information. That's what an **inference** is, an educated guess.

Making Inferences About What You Read Making inferences is similar to drawing conclusions. You use almost the same process to make an inference: combine information from your reading—what's "inside the text"—with what you already know—what's "outside the text"—and make an educated guess about what it all means. Once you have made several inferences, you may be able to draw a conclusion that ties them all together.

Steps for Making Inferences
1. Ask a question.
2. Note information "inside the Text."
3. Note information "outside the Text."
4. **Use both sets of information to make an educated guess, or inference.**

Question: Why did Aryan priests have rules for performing sacrifices?	
Inside the Text	**Outside the Text**
Sacred texts tell how to perform sacrifices.	Other religions have duties only priests can perform.
Priests sacrificed animals in fire.	Many ancient societies believed sacrifices helped keep the gods happy.
Sacrifices were offered to the gods.	

Inference: The Aryans believed that performing a sacrifice incorrectly might anger the gods.

LA.6.1.6.1 The student will use new vocabulary that is introduced and taught directly. **LA.6.1.7.3** The student will determine the main idea or essential message in grade-level text through inferring, paraphrasing, summarizing, and identifying relevant details. **SS.6.W.2.4** Compare the economic, political, social, and religious institutions of ancient river civilizations.

Key Terms and People

You Try It!

The following passage is from the chapter you are about to read. Read the passage and then answer the questions that follow.

Harappan Achievements

Harappan civilization was very advanced. Most houses had bathrooms with indoor plumbing. Artisans made excellent pottery, jewelry, ivory objects, and cotton clothing. They used high-quality tools and developed a system of weights and measures.

From Chapter 5, p. 128

Harappans also developed India's first writing system. However, scholars have not yet learned to read this language, so we know very little about Harappan society. Historians think that the Harappans had kings and strong central governments, but they aren't sure. As in Egypt, the people may have worshipped the king as a god.

Harappan civilization ended by the early 1700s BC, but no one is sure why.

Answer the following questions to make inferences about Harappan society.

1. Do you think the Harappan language was closely related to the languages spoken in India today? Consider the information inside the text and things you have learned outside the text to make an inference about the Harappan language.

2. What have you just learned about Harappan achievements? Think back to other civilizations you have studied that made similar achievements. What allowed those civilizations to make their achievements? From this, what can you infer about earlier Harappan society?

> **As you read Chapter 5,** use the information you find in the text to make inferences about Indian society.

Chapter 5

Section 1
subcontinent *(p. 124)*
monsoons *(p. 125)*
Sanskrit *(p. 129)*

Section 2
caste system *(p. 131)*
Hinduism *(p. 133)*
reincarnation *(p. 133)*
karma *(p. 134)*
Jainism *(p. 134)*
nonviolence *(p. 135)*
Sikhism, *(p. 135)*

Section 3
fasting *(p. 137)*
meditation *(p.137)*
the Buddha *(p. 137)*
Buddhism *(p. 138)*
nirvana *(p. 138)*
missionaries *(p.140)*

Section 4
Candragupta Maurya *(p. 142)*
Asoka *(p. 143)*
Candra Gupta II *(p. 144)*

Section 5
metallurgy *(p. 150)*
alloys *(p. 150)*
Hindu-Arabic numerals *(p. 150)*
inoculation *(p. 150)*
astronomy *(p. 151)*

Academic Vocabulary
Success in school is related to knowing academic vocabulary—the words that are frequently used in school assignments and discussions. In this chapter, you will learn the following academic words:

establish *(p. 144)*
process *(p.150)*

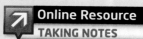

SS.6.G.1.3, SS.6.G.1.4, SS.6.G.1.5, SS.6.G.1.6, SS.6.G.1.7, SS.6.G.2.1, SS.6.G.2.3, SS.6.G.2.4, SS.6.G.2.5, SS.6.G.2.6, SS.6.G.3.1, SS.6.G.4.2, SS.6.W.2.4, SS.6.W.4.1, SS.6.W.4.5

What You Will Learn...

Main Ideas

1. The geography of India includes high mountains, great rivers, and heavy seasonal rain.
2. Harappan civilization developed along the Indus River.
3. The Aryan migration to India changed the region's civilization.

The Big Idea

Indian civilization first developed on the Indus River.

Key Terms

subcontinent, *p. 124*
monsoons, *p. 125*
Sanskrit, *p. 129*

Online Resource
TAKING NOTES

Use the graphic organizer online to take notes on India's geography and its two earliest civilizations, the Harappan and Aryan civilizations.

SECTION 1

Geography and Early India

If YOU were there...

Your people are nomadic herders in southern Asia about 1200 BC. You live in a river valley with plenty of water and grass for your cattle. Besides looking after cattle, you spend time learning songs and myths from the village elders. They say these words hold your people's history. One day, it will be your duty to teach them to your own children.

Why is it important to pass on these words?

BUILDING BACKGROUND Like Mesopotamia and Egypt, India was home to one of the world's first civilizations. Like other early civilizations, the one in India grew up in a river valley. But the society that eventually developed in India was very different from the ones that developed elsewhere.

Geography of India

Look at a map of Asia in the atlas of this book. Do you see the large, roughly triangular landmass that juts out from the center of the southern part of the continent? That is India. It was the location of one of the world's earliest civilizations.

Landforms and Rivers

India is huge. In fact, it is so big that many geographers call it a subcontinent. A **subcontinent** is a large landmass that is smaller than a continent. Subcontinents are usually separated from the rest of their continents by physical features. If you look at the map on the next page, for example, you can see that mountains largely separate India from the rest of Asia.

Among the mountains of northern India are the Himalayas, the highest mountains in the world. To the west are the Hindu Kush. Though these mountains made it hard to enter India, invaders have historically found a few paths through them.

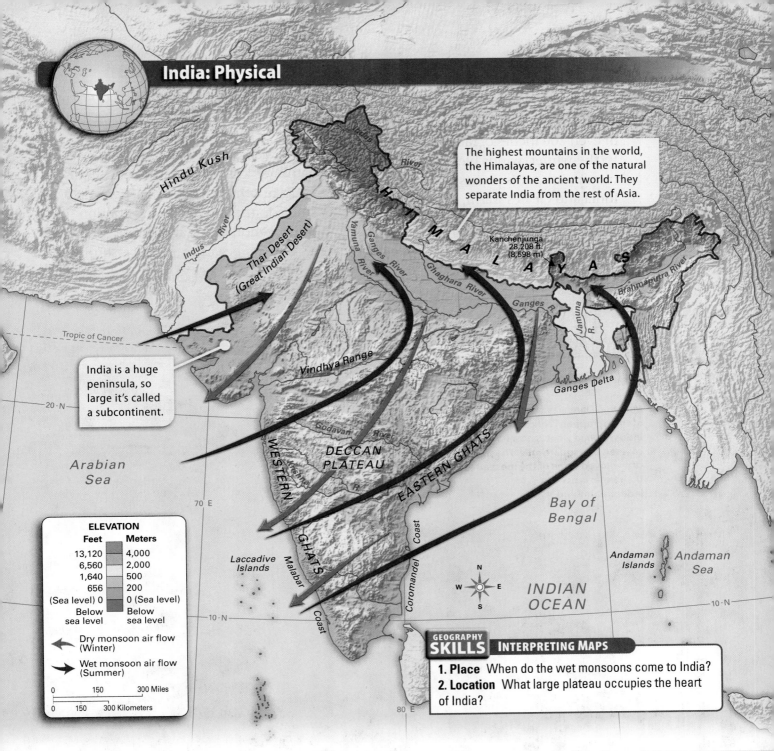

India: Physical

The highest mountains in the world, the Himalayas, are one of the natural wonders of the ancient world. They separate India from the rest of Asia.

India is a huge peninsula, so large it's called a subcontinent.

Kanchenjunga
28,208 ft.
(8,598 m)

Hindu Kush

Indus River

Thar Desert (Great Indian Desert)

Yamuna River

Ganges River

Ghaghara River

H I M A L A Y A S

Brahmaputra River

Ganges R.

Jamuna R.

Tropic of Cancer

Vindhya Range

Ganges Delta

Godavari River

DECCAN PLATEAU

20°N

Arabian Sea

WESTERN GHATS

EASTERN GHATS

R.

70°E

Bay of Bengal

Laccadive Islands

Malabar Coast

Coromandel Coast

Andaman Islands

Andaman Sea

INDIAN OCEAN

10°N

10°N

Coast

80°E

ELEVATION

Feet	Meters
13,120	4,000
6,560	2,000
1,640	500
656	200
(Sea level) 0	0 (Sea level)
Below sea level	Below sea level

← Dry monsoon air flow (Winter)

→ Wet monsoon air flow (Summer)

0   150   300 Miles
0   150   300 Kilometers

N
W   E
S

GEOGRAPHY SKILLS   INTERPRETING MAPS

1. **Place** When do the wet monsoons come to India?
2. **Location** What large plateau occupies the heart of India?

To the west of the Himalayas is a vast desert. Much of the rest of India is covered by fertile plains and rugged plateaus.

Several major rivers flow out of the Himalayas. The valleys of two of these rivers, the Indus and the Ganges, provided fertile farmland that allowed early civilizations to develop. When heavy snows in the Himalayas melted, the rivers flooded.

As in Mesopotamia and Egypt, the flooding left behind a layer of fertile silt. The silt created ideal farmland for early settlers.

Climate

Most of India has a hot and humid climate. This climate is heavily influenced by India's **monsoons**, seasonal wind patterns that cause wet and dry seasons.

SS.6.G.1.3 Identify natural wonders of the ancient world.

In the summer, monsoon winds blow into India from the Indian Ocean, bringing heavy rains that can cause terrible floods. Some parts of India receive as much as 100 or even 200 inches of rain during this time. In the winter, winds blow down from the mountains. This forces moisture out of India and creates warm, dry winters.

READING CHECK **Drawing Conclusions**
How do you think monsoons affected settlement in India?

Harappan Civilization

Historians call the civilization that grew up in the Indus River Valley the Harappan (huh-RA-puhn) civilization. In addition, many Harappan settlements were found along the Saras-vati River, located southeast of the Indus.

Like other ancient societies you have studied, the Harappan civilization grew as irrigation and agriculture improved. As farmers began to produce surpluses of food, towns and cities appeared in India.

History Close-up

Life in Mohenjo Daro

Mohenjo Daro was one of the two major cities of the Harappan civilization. Located next to the Indus River in what is now Pakistan, the city probably covered one square mile. The people who lived in the city enjoyed some of the most advanced comforts of their time, including indoor plumbing.

Harappan merchants used a standard set of weights to measure goods such as precious stones.

India's First Cities

The Harappan civilization was named after the modern city of Harappa (huh-RA-puh), Pakistan. It was near this city that ruins of the civilization were first discovered. From studying these ruins, archaeologists think that the civilization thrived between 2300 and 1700 BC.

The greatest sources of information we have about Harappan civilization are the ruins of two large cities, Harappa and Mohenjo Daro (mo-HEN-joh DAR-oh). The two cities lay on the Indus more than 300 miles apart but were remarkably similar.

Both Harappa and Mohenjo Daro were well planned. Each stood near a towering fortress. From these fortresses, defenders could look down on the cities' brick streets, which crossed at right angles and were lined with storehouses, workshops, market stalls, and houses. In addition, both cities had many public wells.

Next to the city was a huge citadel, or fortress, to guard against invasions.

The houses of Mohenjo Daro had flat roofs. Many had staircases that allowed people to climb to the roof from the street.

The city's streets were paved and well drained. They met at right angles, creating a grid pattern.

Harappan Civilization

HIMALAYAS

Harappa

Mohenjo Daro

Indus River

Sarasvati River

Thar Desert

Arabian Sea

Harappan civilization

• Major settlement

0   100   200 Miles

0 100 200 Kilometers

ANALYSIS SKILL **ANALYZING VISUALS**

What in this picture suggests that Mohenjo Daro was a well-planned city?

Harappan Achievements

Harappan civilization was very advanced. Most houses had bathrooms with indoor plumbing. Artisans made excellent pottery, jewelry, ivory objects, and cotton clothing. They used high-quality tools and developed a system of weights and measures.

Harappans also developed India's first writing system. However, scholars have not yet learned to read this language, so we know very little about Harappan society. Historians think that the Harappans had kings and strong central governments, but they aren't sure. As in Egypt, the people may have worshipped the king as a god.

SS.6.W.4.1 Discuss the significance of Aryan and other tribal migrations on Indian civilization.

Harappan civilization ended by the early 1700s BC, but no one is sure why. Perhaps invaders destroyed the cities or natural disasters, like floods or earthquakes, caused the civilization to collapse.

READING CHECK **Analyzing** Why don't we know much about Harappan civilization?

Harappan Art

Like other ancient peoples, the Harappans made small seals like the one below that were used to stamp goods. They also used clay pots like the one at right as burial urns.

Aryan Migration

Not long after the Harappan civilization crumbled, a new group arrived in the Indus Valley. They were called the Aryans (AIR-ee-uhnz). They were originally from the area around the Caspian Sea in Central Asia. Over time, however, they became the dominant group in India.

Arrival and Spread

The Aryans first arrived in India in the 2000s BC. Historians and archaeologists believe that the Aryans crossed into India through mountain passes in the northwest. Over many centuries, they spread east and south into central India. From there they moved even farther east into the Ganges River Valley.

Much of what we know about Aryan society comes from religious writings known as the Vedas (VAY-duhs). These are collections of poems, hymns, myths, and rituals that were written by Aryan priests. You will read more about the Vedas later in this chapter.

Government and Society

As nomads, the Aryans took along their herds of animals as they moved. But over time, they settled in villages and began to farm. Unlike the Harappans, they did not build big cities.

The Aryan political system was also different from the Harappan system. The Aryans lived in small communities, based mostly on family ties. No single ruling authority existed. Instead, each group had its own leader, often a skilled warrior.

Aryan villages were governed by rajas (RAH-juhz). A raja was a leader who ruled a village and the land around it. Villagers farmed some of this land for the raja. They used other sections as pastures for their cows, horses, sheep, and goats.

Although many rajas were related, they didn't always get along. Sometimes rajas joined forces before fighting a common enemy. Other times, however, rajas went to war against each other. In fact, Aryan groups fought each other nearly as often as they fought outsiders.

Language

The first Aryan settlers did not read or write. Because of this, they had to memorize the poems and hymns that were important in their culture, such as the Vedas. If people forgot these poems and hymns, the works would be lost forever.

The language in which these Aryan poems and hymns were composed was **Sanskrit**, the most important language of ancient India. At first, Sanskrit was only a spoken language. Eventually, however, people figured out how to write it down so they could keep records. These Sanskrit records are a major source of information about Aryan society. Sanskrit is no longer spoken today, but it is the root of many modern South Asian languages.

READING CHECK **Identifying** What source provides much of the information we have about the Aryans?

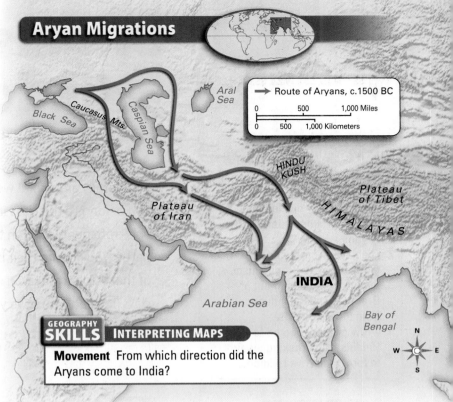

Aryan Migrations

Route of Aryans, c.1500 BC

GEOGRAPHY SKILLS **INTERPRETING MAPS**

Movement From which direction did the Aryans come to India?

SUMMARY AND PREVIEW The earliest civilizations in India were centered in the Indus Valley. First the Harappans and then the Aryans lived in this fertile valley. In the next section, you will learn about a new religion that developed in the Indus Valley after the Aryans settled there—Hinduism.

THE IMPACT TODAY

Hindi, the most widely spoken Indian language, is based on Sanskrit.

Section 1 Assessment

Reviewing Ideas, Terms, and People

1. **a. Define** What are **monsoons**?
   b. Contrast How does northern India differ from the rest of the region?
   c. Elaborate Why is India called a **subcontinent**?
2. **a. Recall** Where did Harappan civilization develop?
   b. Analyze What is one reason that scholars do not completely understand some important parts of Harappan society?
3. **a. Identify** Who were the Aryans?
   b. Contrast How was Aryan society different from Harappan society?

Critical Thinking

4. **Drawing Conclusions** Using your notes, draw conclusions about the effect of geography on Indian society. Record your conclusions in a diagram like this one.

Geography of India →	Harappan society
→	Aryan society

FOCUS ON WRITING

5. **Illustrating Geography and Early Civilizations** This section described two possible topics for your poster: geography and early civilizations. Which of them is more interesting to you? Write down some ideas for a poster about your chosen topic.

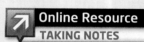
Origins of Hinduism

What You Will Learn...

Main Ideas

1. Indian society divided into distinct groups under the Aryans.
2. The Aryans practiced a religion known as Brahmanism.
3. Hinduism developed out of Brahmanism and influences from other cultures.
4. A few groups reacted to Hinduism by breaking away to form their own religions.

The Big Idea

Hinduism, the largest religion in India today, developed out of ancient Indian beliefs and practices.

Key Terms

caste system, *p. 131*
Hinduism, *p. 133*
reincarnation, *p. 133*
karma, *p. 134*
Jainism, *p. 134*
nonviolence, *p. 135*
Sikhism, *p. 135*

Online Resource
TAKING NOTES

Use the graphic organizer online to take notes on Hinduism. Pay attention to the religion's origins, its teachings, and other religions that developed alongside it.

SS.6.W.4.2 Explain the major beliefs and practices associated with Hinduism and the social structure of the caste system in ancient India.

If YOU were there...

Your family are skillful weavers who make beautiful cotton cloth. You belong to the class in Aryan society who are traders, farmers, and craftspeople. Often the raja of your town leads the warriors into battle. You admire their bravery but know you can never be one of them. To be an Aryan warrior, you must be born into that noble class. Instead, you have your own duty to carry out.

How do you feel about remaining a weaver?

BUILDING BACKGROUND As the Aryans moved into India, they developed a strict system of social classes. As the Aryans' influence spread through India, so did their class system. Before long, this class system was a key part of Indian society.

Indian Society Divides

As Aryan society became more complex, their society became divided into groups. For the most part, these groups were organized by people's occupations. Strict rules developed about how

The *Varnas*   QUICK FACTS

Kshatriyas
Kshatriyas were rulers and warriors.

Brahmins
Brahmins were India's priests and were seen as the highest *varna*.

people of different groups could interact. As time passed, these rules became stricter and became central to Indian society.

The *Varnas*

According to the Vedas, there were four main *varnas*, or social divisions, in Aryan society. These *varnas* were:

- Brahmins (BRAH-muhns), or priests,
- Kshatriyas (KSHA-tree-uhs), or rulers and warriors,
- Vaisyas (VYSH-yuhs), or farmers, craftspeople, and traders, and
- Sudras (SOO-drahs), or laborers and non-Aryans.

The Brahmins were seen as the highest ranking because they performed rituals for the gods. This gave the Brahmins great influence over the other *varnas*.

The Caste System

As the rules of interaction between *varnas* got stricter, the Aryan social order became more complex. In time, each of the four *varnas* in Aryan society was further divided into many castes, or groups. This **caste system** divided Indian society into groups based on a person's birth, wealth, or occupation. At one time, some 3,000 separate castes existed in India.

The caste to which a person belonged determined his or her place in society. However, this ordering was by no means permanent. Over time, individual castes gained or lost favor in society as caste members gained wealth or power. On rare occasions, people could change caste.

Both men and women belonged to castes. Early in the Aryan period, women had most of the same rights as men. They could, for example, own property and receive an education. Over time, however, laws were passed to limit these rights.

By the late Aryan period, a segment of early Indian society had developed that did not belong to any caste. This group was called the untouchables. They could hold only certain, often unpleasant, jobs.

Caste Rules

To keep their classes distinct, the Aryans developed sutras, or guides, which listed all the rules for the caste system. For example, people were not allowed to marry anyone from a different class. It was even forbidden for people from one class to eat with people from another. People who broke the caste rules could be banned from their homes and their castes, which would make them untouchables. Because of these rules, people spent almost all of their time with others in their same class.

READING CHECK **Drawing Inferences** How did a person become a member of a caste?

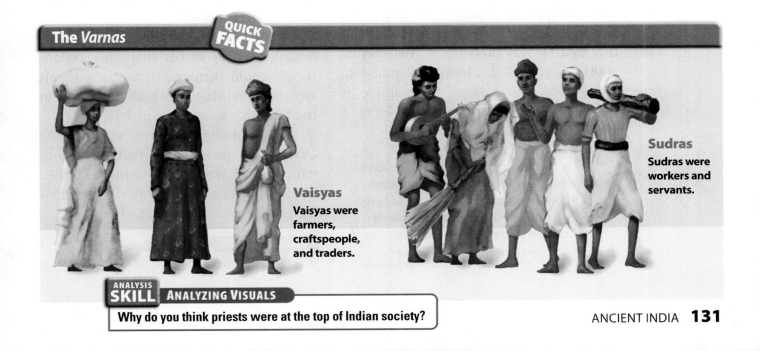

The *Varnas* QUICK FACTS

Vaisyas
Vaisyas were farmers, craftspeople, and traders.

Sudras
Sudras were workers and servants.

Why do you think priests were at the top of Indian society?

ANCIENT INDIA **131**

Hindu Gods and Beliefs

Hindus believe in many gods, but they believe that all the gods are aspects of a single universal spirit called Brahman. Three aspects of Brahman are particularly important in Hinduism—Brahma, Siva, and Vishnu.

Major Beliefs of Hinduism

QUICK FACTS

- A universal spirit called Brahman created the universe and everything in it. Everything in the world is just a part of Brahman.

- Every person has a soul or *atman* that will eventually join with Brahman.

- People's souls are reincarnated many times before they can join with Brahman.

- A person's karma affects how he or she will be reincarnated.

The god Brahma represents the creator aspect of Brahman. His four faces symbolize the four Vedas.

Brahmanism

Religion had been an important part of Aryan life even before the Aryans moved to India. Eventually, in India, religion took on even more meaning. Because Aryan priests were called Brahmins, their religion is often called Brahmanism.

The Vedas

Aryan religion was based on the Vedas. There are four Vedas, each containing sacred hymns and poems. The oldest of the Vedas, the *Rigveda*, was probably written before 1000 BC. It includes hymns of praise to many gods. This passage, for example, is the opening of a hymn praising Indra, a god of the sky and war.

> "The one who is first and possessed of wisdom when born; the god who strove to protect the gods with strength; the one before whose force the two worlds were afraid because of the greatness of his virility [power]: he, O people, is Indra."
>
> –from the *Rigveda*, in *Reading about the World, Volume I*, edited by Paul Brians, et al

Later Vedic Texts

Over the centuries, Aryan Brahmins wrote down their thoughts about the Vedas. In time these thoughts were compiled into collections called Vedic texts.

One collection of Vedic texts describes Aryan religious rituals. For example, it describes how sacrifices should be performed. Priests placed animals, food, or drinks to be sacrificed in a fire. The Aryans believed that the fire would carry these offerings to the gods.

A second collection of Vedic texts describes secret rituals that only certain people could perform. In fact, the rituals were so secret that they had to be done in the forest, far from other people.

The final group of Vedic texts are the Upanishads (oo-PAHN-ee-shads), most of which were written by about 600 BC. These writings are reflections on the Vedas by religious students and teachers.

READING CHECK **Finding Main Ideas** What are the Vedic texts?

Siva, the destroyer aspect of Brahman, is usually shown with four arms and three eyes. Here he is shown dancing on the back of a demon he has defeated.

Vishnu is the preserver aspect of Brahman. In his four arms, he carries a conch shell, a mace, and a discus, symbols of his power and greatness.

Hinduism Develops

The Vedas, the Upanishads, and the other Vedic texts remained the basis of Indian religion for centuries. Eventually, however, the ideas of these sacred texts began to blend with ideas from other cultures. People from Persia and other kingdoms in Central Asia, for example, brought their ideas to India. In time, this blending of ideas created a religion called **Hinduism**, the largest religion in India today.

Hindu Beliefs

The Hindus believe in many gods. Among them are three major gods: Brahma the Creator, Siva the Destroyer, and Vishnu the Preserver. At the same time, however, Hindus believe that each god is part of a single universal spirit called Brahman. They believe that Brahman created the world and preserves it. Gods like Brahma, Siva, and Vishnu represent different aspects of Brahman. In fact, Hindus believe that everything in the world is part of Brahman.

Life and Rebirth

According to Hindu teachings, everyone has a soul, or *atman*, inside them. This soul holds the person's personality, the qualities that make them who they are. Hindus believe that a person's ultimate goal should be to reunite that soul with Brahman, the universal spirit.

Hindus believe that their souls will eventually join Brahman because the world we live in is an illusion. Brahman is the only reality. The Upanishads taught that people must try to see through the illusion of the world. Since it is hard to see through illusions, it can take several lifetimes. That is why Hindus believe that souls are born and reborn many times, each time in a new body. This process of rebirth is called **reincarnation**.

Hinduism and the Caste System

According to the traditional Hindu view of reincarnation, a person who has died is reborn in a new physical form.

THE IMPACT
TODAY

More than 800 million people in India practice Hinduism today.

The type of form depends upon his or her **karma**, the effects that good or bad actions have on a person's soul. Evil actions will build bad karma. A person with bad karma will be born into a lower caste or life form.

In contrast, good actions build good karma. People with good karma are born into a higher caste in their next lives. In time, good karma will bring salvation, or freedom from life's worries and the cycle of rebirth. This salvation is called *moksha*.

Hinduism taught that each person had a *dharma,* or set of spiritual duties, to fulfill. Fulfilling one's *dharma* required accepting one's station in life. By teaching people to accept their stations, Hinduism helped preserve the caste system.

READING CHECK **Summarizing** What determined how a person would be reborn?

Groups React to Hinduism

Although Hinduism was widely followed in India, not everyone agreed with its beliefs. Some unsatisfied people and groups looked for new religious ideas. Two such groups were the Jains (JYNZ), believers in a religion called Jainism (JY-niz-uhm), and the Sikhs (SEEKS), believers in Sikhism (SEEK-iz-uhm).

Jainism

Jainism is based on the teachings of a man named Mahavira, who is believed to have been born around 599 BC. Mahavira was raised as a Hindu. As an adult, however, he thought Hinduism put too much emphasis on rituals. Instead of ritual, his teachings emphasize four basic principles: injure no life, tell the truth, do not steal, and own

LINKING TO TODAY

Nonviolence

In modern times, nonviolence has been a powerful tool for social protest. Mohandas Gandhi led a long nonviolent struggle against British rule in India. This movement helped India win its independence in 1947. About 10 years later, Martin Luther King Jr. adopted Gandhi's nonviolent methods in his struggle to win civil rights for African Americans. Then, in the 1960s, Cesar Chavez organized a campaign of nonviolence to protest the treatment of farm workers in California. These three leaders proved that people can bring about social change without using violence. As Chavez once explained, "Nonviolence is not inaction. It is not for the timid or the weak. It is hard work. It is the patience to win."

**Mohandas Gandhi (top),
Martin Luther King Jr. (above),
and Cesar Chavez (right)**

ANALYSIS SKILL **ANALYZING INFORMATION**

How did these three leaders prove that nonviolence is a powerful tool for social change?

no property. In their efforts not to injure anyone or anything, the Jains practice **nonviolence**, or the avoidance of violent actions. The Sanskrit word for this nonviolence is *ahimsa* (uh-HIM-sah). Many Hindus also practice *ahimsa*.

The Jains' emphasis on nonviolence comes from their belief that everything is alive and part of the cycle of rebirth. Jains are very serious about not injuring or killing any creature—humans, animals, insects, or even plants. They do not believe in animal sacrifice, unlike the ancient Brahmins. Because they don't want to hurt living creatures, Jains are vegetarians. They do not eat any food that comes from animals.

Sikhism

Founded centuries later than Jainism, **Sikhism** has its roots in the teachings of the Guru Nanak, who lived in the AD 1400s. The title *guru* is Sanskrit for "teacher." Like Mahavira, Nanak was raised a Hindu but grew dissatisfied with the religion's teachings. He began to travel and came into contact with many other religions, including Islam. His teachings blended ideas from Hinduism with ideas from Islam and other religions. Over time, these teachings were explained and expanded by nine other gurus.

Sikhism is monotheistic. Sikhs believe in only one God, who has no physical form but can be sensed in the creation. For Sikhs, the ultimate goal is to be reunited with God after death. To achieve this goal, one must meditate to find spiritual enlightenment. Because they believe that achieving enlightenment may take several lifetimes, Sikhs also believe in reincarnation. Sikhism teaches that people should live truthfully and treat all people equally, regardless of gender, social class, or any other factor.

Sikhs pray several times each day. They are expected to wear five items at all times as signs of their religion: long hair, a small comb, a steel bracelet, a sword, and a special undergarment. In addition, all Sikh men wear turbans, as do many women.

READING CHECK Finding Main Ideas
What are two religions that developed out of Hinduism?

SUMMARY AND PREVIEW You have learned about three religions that developed in India—Hinduism, Jainism, and Sikhism. In Section 3, you will learn about another religion that began there—Buddhism.

Section 2 Assessment

Reviewing Ideas, Terms, and People
1. a. **Identify** What is the **caste system**?
   b. **Explain** Why did strict caste rules develop?
2. a. **Identify** What does the Rigveda include?
   b. **Analyze** What role did sacrifice play in Aryan society?
3. a. **Define** What is **karma**?
   b. **Sequence** How did Brahmanism develop into **Hinduism**?
   c. **Elaborate** How does Hinduism reinforce followers' willingness to remain within their castes?
4. a. **Recall** What are the four main teachings of **Jainism**?
   b. **Draw Conclusions** How do you think Guru Nanak's travels influenced the development of **Sikhism**?

Critical Thinking
5. **Analyzing Causes** Draw a graphic organizer like this one. Using your notes, explain how Hinduism developed from Brahmanism, and how Jainism and Sikhism developed from Hinduism.

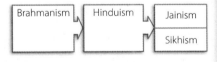

FOCUS ON WRITING

6. **Illustrating Hinduism** Now you have a new possible topic for your poster. How might you explain a complex religion like Hinduism?

Origins of Buddhism

What You Will Learn...

Main Ideas

1. Siddhartha Gautama searched for wisdom in many ways.
2. The teachings of Buddhism deal with finding peace.
3. Buddhism spread far from where it began in India.

The Big Idea

Buddhism began in India and became a major religion.

Key Terms and People

fasting, *p. 137*
meditation, *p. 137*
the Buddha, *p. 137*
Buddhism, *p. 138*
nirvana, *p. 138*
missionaries, *p. 140*

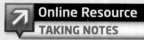
Online Resource
TAKING NOTES

Use the graphic organizer online to take notes on the basic ideas of Buddhism and on Buddhism's spread.

If **YOU** were there...

You are a trader traveling in northern India in about 520 BC. As you pass through a town, you see a crowd of people sitting silently in the shade of a huge tree. A man sitting at the foot of the tree begins to speak about how one ought to live. His words are like nothing you have heard from the Hindu priests.

Will you stay to listen? Why or why not?

BUILDING BACKGROUND The Jains were not the only ones to break from Hinduism. In the 500s BC a young Indian prince attracted many people to his teachings about how people should live.

Siddhartha's Search for Wisdom

In the late 500s BC a restless young man, dissatisfied with the teachings of Hinduism, began to ask his own questions about life and religious matters. In time, he found answers. These answers attracted many followers, and the young man's ideas became the foundation of a major new religion in India.

The Quest for Answers

The restless young man was Siddhartha Gautama (si-DAHR-tuh GAU-tuh-muh). Born around 563 BC in northern India, near the Himalayas, Siddhartha was a prince who grew up in luxury. Born a Kshatriya, a member of the warrior class, Siddhartha never had to struggle with the problems that many people of his time faced. However, Siddhartha was not satisfied. He felt that something was missing in his life.

Siddhartha looked around him and saw how hard other people had to work and how much they suffered. He saw people grieving for lost loved ones and wondered why there was so much pain in the world. As a result, Siddhartha began to ask questions about the meaning of human life.

The Great Departure

In this painting, Prince Siddhartha leaves his palace to search for the true meaning of life, an event known as the Great Departure. Special helpers called *ganas* hold his horse's hooves so he won't awaken anyone.

Before Siddhartha reached age 30, he left his home and family to look for answers. His journey took him to many regions in India. Wherever he traveled, he had discussions with priests and people known for their wisdom. Yet no one could give convincing answers to Siddhartha's questions.

The Buddha Finds Enlightenment

Siddhartha did not give up. Instead, he became even more determined to find the answers he was seeking. For several years, he wandered in search of answers.

Siddhartha wanted to free his mind from daily concerns. For a while, he did not even wash himself. He also started **fasting**, or going without food. He devoted much of his time to **meditation**, the focusing of the mind on spiritual ideas.

According to legend, Siddhartha spent six years wandering throughout India. He eventually came to a place near the town of Gaya, close to the Ganges River. There, he sat down under a tree and meditated.

After seven weeks of deep meditation, he suddenly had the answers that he had been looking for. He realized that human suffering comes from three things:

- wanting what we like but do not have,
- wanting to keep what we like and already have, and
- not wanting what we dislike but have.

Siddhartha spent seven more weeks meditating under the tree, which his followers later named the Tree of Wisdom. He then described his new ideas to five of his former companions. His followers later called this talk the First Sermon.

Siddhartha Gautama was about 35 years old when he found enlightenment under the tree. From that point on, he would be called **the Buddha** (BOO-duh), or the "Enlightened One." The Buddha spent the rest of his life traveling across northern India and teaching people his ideas.

READING CHECK **Summarizing** What did the Buddha conclude about the cause of suffering?

THE IMPACT TODAY

Buddhists from all over the world still travel to India to visit the Tree of Wisdom and honor the Buddha.

Subsets of the Eightfold Path are the Three Qualities. The Three Qualities are wisdom (including Right Thought and Right Intent), virtue (including Right Speech, Right Action, and Right Livelihood), and meditation (including Right Mindfulness and Right Concentration).

SS.6.W.4.4 Explain the teachings of Buddha, the importance of Asoka, and how Buddhism spread in India, Ceylon, and other parts of Asia.

Teachings of Buddhism

As he traveled, the Buddha gained many followers, especially among India's merchants and artisans. He even taught his views to a few kings. These followers were the first believers in **Buddhism**, a religion based on the teachings of the Buddha.

The Buddha was raised Hindu, and many of his teachings reflected Hindu ideas. Like Hindus, he believed that people should act morally and treat others well. In one of his sermons, he said:

> "Let a man overcome anger by love. Let him overcome the greedy by liberality [giving], the liar by truth. This is called progress in the discipline [training] of the Blessed."
> –The Buddha, quoted in *The History of Nations: India*

Four Noble Truths

At the heart of the Buddha's teachings were four guiding principles. These became known as the Four Noble Truths:

1. Suffering and unhappiness are a part of human life. No one can escape sorrow.

2. Suffering comes from our desires for pleasure and material goods. People cause their own misery because they want things they cannot have.

3. People can overcome desire and ignorance and reach **nirvana** (nir-VAH-nuh), a state of perfect peace. Reaching nirvana frees the soul from suffering and from the need for further reincarnation.

4. People can overcome ignorance and desire by following an eightfold path that leads to wisdom, enlightenment, and salvation.

The chart on the next page shows the steps in the Eightfold Path. The Buddha believed that this path was a middle way between human desires and denying oneself any pleasure. He believed that people should overcome their desire for material goods. They should, however, be reasonable, and not starve their bodies or cause themselves unnecessary pain.

This giant statue of the Buddha is just south of the town of Gaya in Bodh Gaya, India—the place where Buddhists believe Siddhartha reached enlightenment.

The Eightfold Path

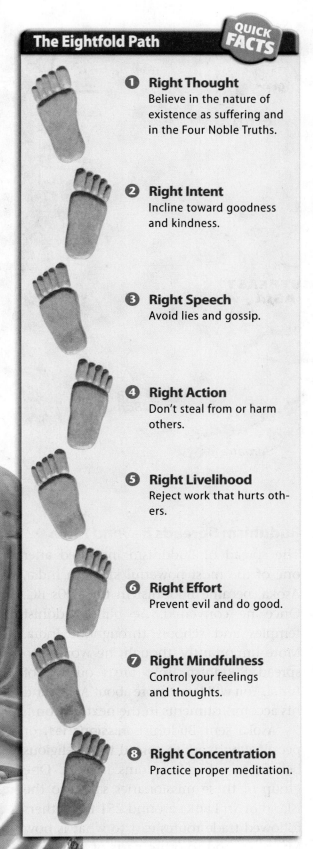

1 **Right Thought**
Believe in the nature of existence as suffering and in the Four Noble Truths.

2 **Right Intent**
Incline toward goodness and kindness.

3 **Right Speech**
Avoid lies and gossip.

4 **Right Action**
Don't steal from or harm others.

5 **Right Livelihood**
Reject work that hurts others.

6 **Right Effort**
Prevent evil and do good.

7 **Right Mindfulness**
Control your feelings and thoughts.

8 **Right Concentration**
Practice proper meditation.

Challenging Hindu Ideas

Some of the Buddha's teachings challenged traditional Hindu ideas. For example, the Buddha rejected many of the ideas contained in the Vedas, such as animal sacrifice. He told people that they did not have to follow these texts.

The Buddha challenged the authority of the Hindu priests, the Brahmins. He did not believe that they or their rituals were necessary for enlightenment. Instead, he taught that it was the responsibility of each individual to work for his or her own salvation. Priests could not help them. However, the Buddha did not reject the Hindu teaching of reincarnation. He taught that people who failed to reach nirvana would have to be reborn time and time again until they achieved it.

The Buddha was opposed to the caste system. He didn't think that people should be confined to a particular place in society. Everyone who followed the Eightfold Path properly, he said, would achieve nirvana. It didn't matter what *varna* or caste they had belonged to in life as long as they lived the way they should.

The Buddha's opposition to the caste system won him support from the masses. Many of India's herdsmen, farmers, artisans, and untouchables liked hearing that their low social rank would not be a barrier to enlightenment. Unlike Hinduism, Buddhism made them feel that they had the power to change their lives.

The Buddha also gained followers among the higher classes. Many rich and powerful Indians welcomed his ideas about avoiding extreme behavior while seeking salvation. By the time of his death around 483 BC, the Buddha's influence was spreading rapidly throughout India.

READING CHECK **Comparing** How did Buddha's teachings agree with Hinduism?

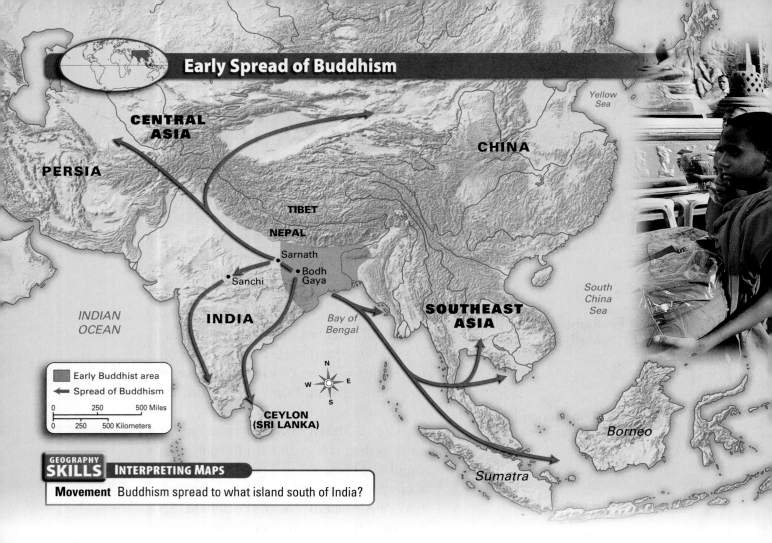

Early Spread of Buddhism

GEOGRAPHY SKILLS **INTERPRETING MAPS**

Movement Buddhism spread to what island south of India?

SS.6.G.4.4 Map and analyze the impact of the spread of various belief systems in the ancient world.

Buddhism Spreads

Buddhism continued to attract followers after the Buddha's death. After spreading through India, the religion began to spread to other areas as well.

Buddhism Spreads in India

According to Buddhist tradition, 500 of the Buddha's followers gathered together shortly after he died. They wanted to make sure that the Buddha's teachings were remembered correctly.

In the years after this council, the Buddha's followers spread his teachings throughout India. The ideas spread very quickly, because Buddhist teachings were popular and easy to understand. Within 200 years of the Buddha's death, his teachings had spread through most of India.

Buddhism Spreads Beyond India

The spread of Buddhism increased after one of the most powerful kings in India, Asoka, became Buddhist in the 200s BC. Once he converted, he built Buddhist temples and schools throughout India. More importantly, though, he worked to spread Buddhism into areas outside of India. You will learn more about Asoka and his accomplishments in the next section.

Asoka sent Buddhist **missionaries**, or people who work to spread their religious beliefs, to other kingdoms in Asia. One group of these missionaries sailed to the island of Sri Lanka around 251 BC. Others followed trade routes east to what is now Myanmar and to other parts of Southeast Asia. Missionaries also went north to areas near the Himalayas.

Young Buddhist students carry gifts in Sri Lanka, one of the many places outside of India where Buddhism spread.

Members of the Theravada branch tried to follow the Buddha's teachings exactly as he had stated them. Mahayana Buddhists, though, believed that other people could interpret the Buddha's teachings to help people reach nirvana. Both branches have millions of believers today, but Mahayana is by far the larger branch.

READING CHECK **Sequencing** How did Buddhism spread from India to other parts of Asia?

SUMMARY AND PREVIEW Buddhism, one of India's major religions, grew more popular once it was adopted by rulers of India's great empires. You will learn more about those empires in the next section.

Missionaries also introduced Buddhism to lands west of India. They founded Buddhist communities in Central Asia and Persia. They even taught about Buddhism as far away as Syria and Egypt.

Buddhism continued to grow over the centuries. Eventually it spread via the Silk Road into China, then Korea and Japan. Through their work, missionaries taught Buddhism to millions of people.

A Split within Buddhism

Even as Buddhism spread through Asia, however, it began to change. Not all Buddhists could agree on their beliefs and practices. Eventually disagreements between Buddhists led to a split within the religion. Two major branches of Buddhism were created—Theravada and Mahayana.

Section 3 Assessment

Reviewing Ideas, Terms, and People
1. **a. Identify** Who was **the Buddha**, and what does the term Buddha mean?
   b. Summarize How did Siddhartha Gautama free his mind and clarify his thinking as he searched for wisdom?
2. **a. Identify** What is **nirvana**?
   b. Contrast How are Buddhist teachings different from Hindu teachings?
   c. Elaborate Why do Buddhists believe that following the Eightfold Path leads to a better life?
3. **a. Describe** Into what lands did **Buddhism** spread?
   b. Summarize What role did **missionaries** play in spreading Buddhism?

Critical Thinking
4. **Finding Main Ideas** Draw a diagram like this one. Use it and your notes to identify and describe Buddhism's Four Noble Truths. Write a sentence explaining how these Truths are central to Buddhism.

FOCUS ON WRITING

5. **Considering Indian Religions** Look back over what you've just read and the notes you took about Hinduism earlier. Perhaps you will want to focus your poster on ancient India's two major religions. Think about how you could design a poster around this theme.

Indian Empires

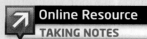
If YOU were there...

You are a merchant in India in about 240 BC. You travel from town to town on your donkey, carrying bolts of colorful cloth.

In the heat of summer, you are grateful for the banyan trees along the road. They shelter you from the blazing sun. You stop at wells for cool drinks of water and rest houses for a break in your journey. You know these are all the work of your king, Asoka.

How do you feel about your king?

BUILDING BACKGROUND For centuries after the Aryan invasion, India was divided into small states. Each state had its own ruler and India had no central government. Then, in the 300s BC, a foreign conqueror, Alexander the Great, took over part of northwestern India. His armies soon left, but his influence continued to affect Indian society. Inspired by Alexander's example, a strong leader soon united India for the first time.

Mauryan Empire Unifies India

In the 320s BC a military leader named **Candragupta Maurya** (kuhn-druh-GOOP-tuh MOUR-yuh) seized control of the entire northern part of India. By doing so, he founded the Mauryan Empire. Mauryan rule lasted for about 150 years.

The Mauryan Empire

Candragupta Maurya ruled his empire with the help of a complex government. It included a network of spies and a huge army of some 600,000 soldiers. The army also had thousands of war elephants and thousands of chariots. In return for the army's protection, farmers paid a heavy tax to the government.

In 301 BC Candragupta decided to become a Jainist monk. To do so, he had to give up his throne. He passed the throne to his son, who continued to expand the empire. Before long, the Mauryas ruled all of northern India and much of central India as well.

Asoka

Around 270 BC Candragupta's grandson **Asoka** (uh-SOH-kuh) became king. Asoka was a strong ruler, the strongest of all the Mauryan emperors. He extended Mauryan rule over most of India. In conquering other kingdoms, Asoka made his own empire both stronger and richer.

For many years, Asoka watched his armies fight bloody battles against other peoples. A few years into his rule, however, Asoka converted to Buddhism. When he did, he swore that he would not launch any more wars of conquest.

After converting to Buddhism, Asoka had the time and resources to improve the lives of his people. He had wells dug and roads built throughout the empire. Along these roads, workers planted shade trees and built rest houses for weary travelers. He also encouraged the spread of Buddhism in India and the rest of Asia. As you read in the previous section, he sent missionaries to lands all over Asia.

Asoka died in 233 BC, and the empire began to fall apart soon afterward. His sons fought each other for power, and invaders threatened the empire. In 184 BC the last Mauryan king was killed by one of his own generals. India divided into smaller states once again.

FOCUS ON READING
What can you infer about the religious beliefs of Asoka's sons?

READING CHECK **Finding Main Ideas** How did the Mauryans gain control of most of India?

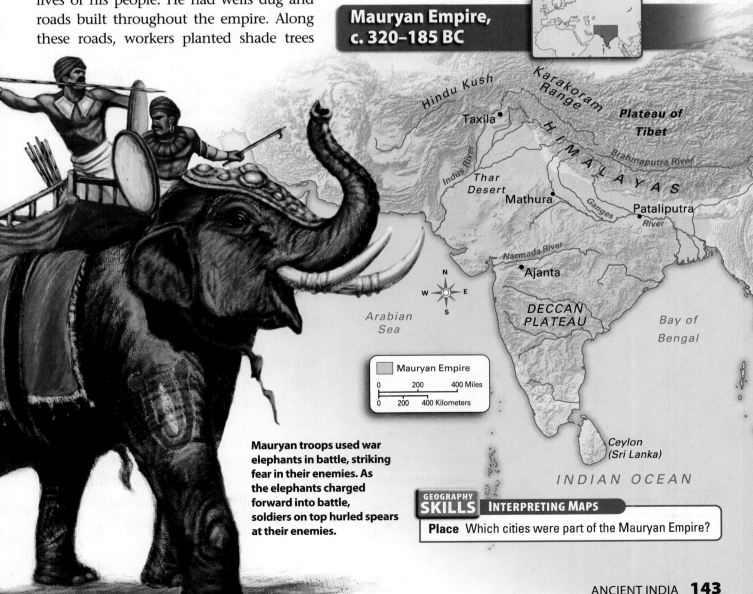

Mauryan Empire, c. 320–185 BC

Hindu Kush

Karakoram Range

Taxila

Plateau of Tibet

Brahmaputra River

HIMALAYAS

Indus River

Thar Desert

Mathura

Ganges

Pataliputra

River

Narmada River

Ajanta

Arabian Sea

DECCAN PLATEAU

Bay of Bengal

Mauryan Empire

0   200   400 Miles
0   200   400 Kilometers

Ceylon (Sri Lanka)

INDIAN OCEAN

Mauryan troops used war elephants in battle, striking fear in their enemies. As the elephants charged forward into battle, soldiers on top hurled spears at their enemies.

GEOGRAPHY SKILLS **INTERPRETING MAPS**

Place Which cities were part of the Mauryan Empire?

Gupta Rulers Promote Hinduism

After the collapse of the Mauryan Empire, India remained divided for about 500 years. During that time, Buddhism continued to prosper and spread in India, and so the popularity of Hinduism declined.

A New Hindu Empire

ACADEMIC VOCABULARY

establish to set up or create

Eventually, however, a new dynasty was **established** in India. It was the Gupta (GOOP-tuh) dynasty, which took over India around AD 320. Under the Guptas, India was once again united, and it once again became prosperous.

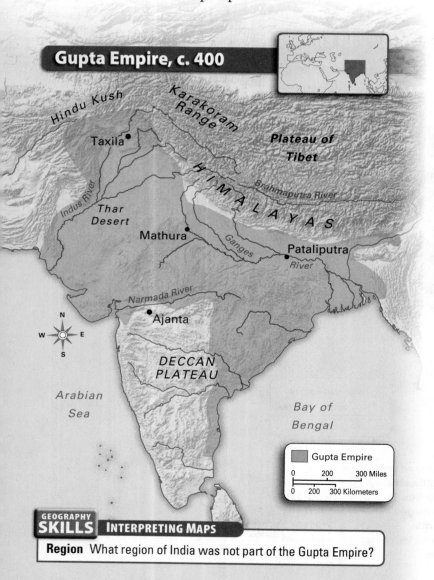

Gupta Empire, c. 400

Hindu Kush

Karakoram Range

Taxila

Plateau of Tibet

HIMALAYAS

Brahmaputra River

Indus River

Thar Desert

Mathura

Ganges River

Pataliputra

Narmada River

Ajanta

DECCAN PLATEAU

Arabian Sea

Bay of Bengal

Gupta Empire

0   200   300 Miles

0   200   300 Kilometers

GEOGRAPHY SKILLS INTERPRETING MAPS

Region What region of India was not part of the Gupta Empire?

The first Gupta emperor was Candra Gupta I. Although their names are similar, he was not related to Candragupta Maurya. From his base in northern India, Candra Gupta's armies invaded and conquered neighboring lands. Eventually he brought much of the northern part of India under his control.

Candra Gupta was followed as emperor by his son, Samudra Gupta, a brilliant military leader. He continued his father's wars of conquest, fighting battles against many neighboring peoples. Through these wars, Samudra Gupta added more territory to his empire. By the time he died, for example, he had taken control of nearly all of the Ganges River valley.

Indian civilization flourished under the Gupta rulers. These rulers were Hindu, so Hinduism became India's major religion. The Gupta kings built many Hindu temples, some of which became models for later Indian architecture. They also promoted a revival of Hindu writings and worship practices.

Although they were Hindus, the Gupta rulers also supported the religious beliefs of Buddhism and Jainism. They promoted Buddhist art and built Buddhist temples. They also established a university at Nalanda that became one of Asia's greatest centers for Buddhist studies.

Gupta Society

In 375 Emperor **Candra Gupta II** took the throne in India. Gupta society reached its high point during his rule. Under Candra Gupta II, the empire continued to grow, eventually stretching all the way across northern India. At the same time, the empire's economy strengthened, and people prospered. They created fine works of art and literature. Outsiders admired the empire's wealth and beauty.

Gupta Art
This Gupta painting of a palace scene shows some of India's different castes. Gupta rulers supported Hinduism and the caste system.

Gupta kings believed the social order of the Hindu caste system would strengthen their rule. They also thought it would keep the empire stable. As a result, the Gupta considered the caste system an important part of Indian society.

Gupta rule remained strong in India until the late 400s. At that time the Huns, a group from Central Asia, invaded India from the northwest. Their fierce attacks drained the Gupta Empire of its power and wealth. As the Hun armies marched farther into India, the Guptas lost hope.

By the middle of the 500s, Gupta rule had ended, and India had divided into small kingdoms yet again.

READING CHECK **Summarizing** What was the Gupta dynasty's position on religion?

SUMMARY AND PREVIEW The Mauryas and Guptas united much of India in their empires. Next you will learn about their many achievements.

Section 4 Assessment

Reviewing Ideas, Terms, and People

1. **a. Identify** Who created the Mauryan Empire?
   b. Summarize What happened after **Asoka** became a Buddhist?
   c. Elaborate Why do you think many people consider Asoka the greatest of all Mauryan rulers?
2. **a. Recall** What religion did most of the Gupta rulers belong to?
   b. Compare and Contrast How were the rulers **Candragupta Maurya** and Candra Gupta I alike, and how were they different?

Critical Thinking

3. **Categorizing** Draw a chart like this one. Fill it with information about India's rulers.

Ruler	Dynasty	Accomplishments

FOCUS ON WRITING

4. **Comparing Indian Empires** Another possible topic for your poster would be a comparison of the Mauryan and Gupta empires. Make a chart in your notebook that shows such a comparison.

Asoka

How can one decision change a man's entire life?

When did he live? before 230 BC

Where did he live? Asoka's empire included much of northern and central India.

What did he do? After fighting many bloody wars to expand his empire, Asoka gave up violence and converted to Buddhism.

KEY EVENTS

- **c. 270 BC** Asoka becomes the Mauryan emperor.

- **c. 261 BC** Asoka's empire reaches its greatest size.

- **c. 261 BC** Asoka becomes a Buddhist.

- **c. 251 BC** Asoka begins to send Buddhist missionaries to other parts of Asia.

Why is he important? Asoka is one of the most respected rulers in Indian history and one of the most important figures in the history of Buddhism. As a devout Buddhist, Asoka worked to spread the Buddha's teachings. In addition to sending missionaries around Asia, he built huge columns carved with Buddhist teachings all over India. Largely through his efforts, Buddhism became one of Asia's main religions.

Generalizing How did Asoka's life change after he became Buddhist?

This Buddhist shrine, located in Sanchi, India, was built by Asoka.

Indian Achievements

SS.6.G.2.6, SS.6.W.1.3, SS.6.W.2.4, SS.6.W.4.3, SS.6.W.4.5

If YOU were there...

You are a traveler in western India in the 300s. You are visiting a cave temple that is carved into a mountain cliff. Inside the cave it is cool and quiet. Huge columns rise all around you. You don't feel you're alone, for the walls and ceilings are covered with paintings. They are filled with lively scenes and figures. In the center is a large statue with calm, peaceful features.

How does this cave make you feel?

BUILDING BACKGROUND The Mauryan and Gupta empires united most of India politically. During these empires, Indian artists, writers, scholars, and scientists made great advances. Some of their works are still studied and admired today.

Religious Art

The Indians of the Mauryan and Gupta periods created great works of art, many of them religious. Many of their paintings and sculptures illustrated either Hindu and Buddhist teachings. Magnificent temples—both Hindu and Buddhist—were built all around India. They remain some of the most beautiful buildings in the world today.

Temples

Early Hindu temples were small stone structures. They had flat roofs and contained only one or two rooms. In the Gupta period, though, temple architecture became more complex. Gupta temples were topped by huge towers and were covered with carvings of the god worshipped inside.

Buddhist temples of the Gupta period are also impressive. Some Buddhists carved entire temples out of mountainsides. The most famous such temple is at Ajanta. Its builders filled the caves with beautiful wall paintings and sculpture.

What You Will Learn...

Main Ideas

1. Indian artists created great works of religious art.
2. Sanskrit literature flourished during the Gupta period.
3. The Indians made scientific advances in metalworking, medicine, and other sciences.

The Big Idea

The people of ancient India made great contributions to the arts and sciences.

Key Terms

metallurgy, *p. 150*
alloys, *p. 150*
Hindu-Arabic numerals, *p. 150*
inoculation, *p. 150*
astronomy, *p. 151*

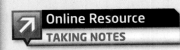

Online Resource

TAKING NOTES

Use the graphic organizer online to take notes on the achievements of ancient India.

SS.6.W.4.5 Summarize the important achievements and contributions of ancient Indian civilization.

This Hindu temple is covered with incredibly detailed carvings and decorations. Many individual sculptures are images of important Hindu gods, like the statue of Vishnu above.

Another type of Buddhist temple was the stupa. Stupas had domed roofs and were built to house sacred items from the life of the Buddha. Many of them were covered with detailed carvings.

Paintings and Sculpture

The Gupta period also saw the creation of great works of art, both paintings and statues. Painting was a greatly respected profession, and India was home to many skilled artists. However, we don't know the names of many artists from this period. Instead, we know the names of many rich and powerful members of Gupta society who paid artists to create works of beauty and significance.

Most Indian paintings from the Gupta period are clear and colorful. Some of them show graceful Indians wearing fine jewelry and stylish clothes. Such paintings offer us a glimpse of the Indians' daily and ceremonial lives.

Artists from both of India's major religions, Hinduism and Buddhism, drew on their beliefs to create their works. As a result, many of the finest paintings of ancient India are found in temples. Hindu painters drew hundreds of gods on temple walls and entrances. Buddhists covered the walls and ceilings of temples with scenes from the life of the Buddha.

Indian sculptors also created great works. Many of their statues were made for Buddhist cave temples. In addition to the temples' intricately carved columns, sculptors carved statues of kings and the Buddha. Some of these statues tower over the cave entrances. Hindu temples also featured impressive statues of their gods. In fact, the walls of some temples, such as the one pictured above, were completely covered with carvings and images.

READING CHECK **Summarizing** How did religion influence ancient Indian art?

Sanskrit Literature

Sanskrit was the main language of the ancient Aryans. During the Mauryan and Gupta periods, many works of Sanskrit literature were created. These works were later translated into many other languages.

Religious Epics

The greatest of these Sanskrit writings are two religious epics, the *Mahabharata* (muh-HAH-BAH-ruh-tuh) and the *Ramayana* (rah-MAH-yuh-nuh). Still popular in India, the *Mahabharata* is one of the world's longest literary works. It is a story about the struggle between two families for control of a kingdom. Included within the story are many long passages about Hindu beliefs. The most famous is called the *Bhagavad Gita* (BUG-uh-vuhd GEE-tah).

The *Ramayana*, according to Hindu tradition written prior to the *Mahabharata*, tells about a prince named Rama. In truth, the prince was the god Vishnu in human form. He had become human so he could rid the world of demons. He also had to rescue his wife, a princess named Sita. For centuries, the characters of the *Ramayana* have been seen as models for how Indians should behave. For example, Rama is seen as the ideal ruler, and his relationship with Sita as the ideal marriage.

Other Works

Writers in the Gupta period also created plays, poetry, and other types of literature. One famous writer of this time was Kalidasa (kahl-ee-DAHS-uh). His work was so brilliant that Candra Gupta II hired him to write plays for the royal court.

Sometime before 500, Indian writers also produced a book of stories called the *Panchatantra* (PUHN-chuh-TAHN-truh). The stories in this collection were intended to teach lessons. They praise people for cleverness and quick thinking. Each story ends with a message about winning friends, losing property, waging war, or some other idea. For example, the message below warns listeners to think about what they are doing before they act.

" The good and bad of given schemes
Wise thought must first reveal:
The stupid heron saw his chicks
Provide a mongoose meal. "
–from the *Panchatantra*, translated by Arthur William Ryder

Eventually, translations of this collection spread throughout the world. It became popular even as far away as Europe.

READING CHECK **Categorizing** What types of literature did writers of ancient India create?

In this illustration of the *Ramayana*, the monkey king sends the monkey general Hanuman to find Sita. Hanuman helped Rama defeat the demons and win back Sita. Many Indians view him as a model of devotion and loyalty.

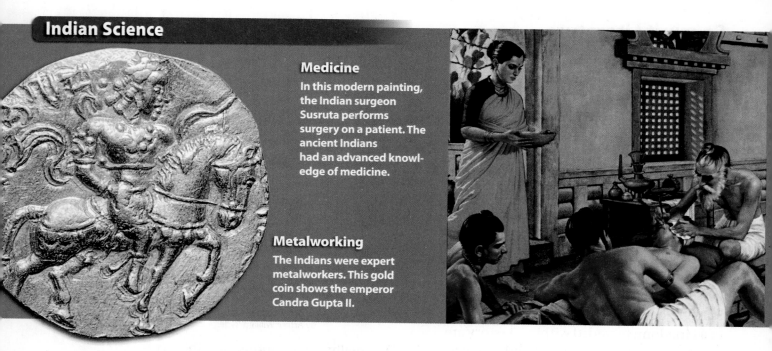

Medicine

In this modern painting, the Indian surgeon Susruta performs surgery on a patient. The ancient Indians had an advanced knowledge of medicine.

Metalworking

The Indians were expert metalworkers. This gold coin shows the emperor Candra Gupta II.

Scientific Advances

Indian achievements were not limited to art, architecture, and literature. Indian scholars also made important advances in metalworking, math, and the sciences.

Metalworking

The ancient Indians were pioneers of **metallurgy** (MET-uhl-uhr-jee), the science of working with metals. Their knowledge allowed them to create high-quality tools and weapons. The Indians also knew **processes** for mixing metals to create **alloys**, mixtures of two or more metals. Alloys are sometimes stronger or easier to work with than pure metals.

Metalworkers made their strongest products out of iron. Indian iron was very hard and pure. These features made the iron a valuable trade item.

During the Gupta dynasty, metalworkers built the famous Iron Pillar near Delhi. Unlike most iron, which rusts easily, this pillar is very resistant to rust. The tall column still attracts crowds of visitors. Scholars study this column even today to learn the Indians' secrets.

ACADEMIC VOCABULARY

process a series of steps by which a task is accomplished

THE IMPACT TODAY

People still get inoculations against many diseases.

Mathematics and Other Sciences

Gupta scholars also made advances in math and science. In fact, they were among the most advanced mathematicians of their day. They developed many elements of our modern math system. The very numbers we use today are called **Hindu-Arabic numerals** because they were created by Indian scholars and brought to Europe by Arabs. The Indians were also the first people to create the zero. Although it may seem like a small thing, modern math wouldn't be possible without the zero.

The ancient Indians were also very skilled in the medical sciences. As early as the AD 100s, doctors were writing their knowledge down in textbooks. Among the skills these books describe is making medicines from plants and minerals.

Besides curing people with medicines, Indian doctors knew how to protect people against disease. The Indians practiced **inoculation** (i-nah-kyuh-LAY-shuhn), or injecting a person with a small dose of a virus to help him or her build up defenses to a disease. By fighting off this small dose, the body learns to protect itself.

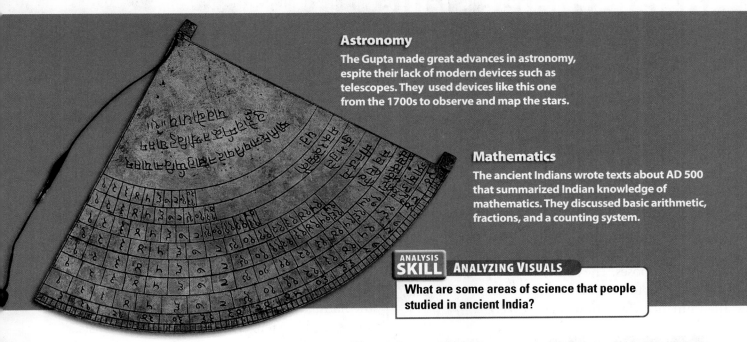

Astronomy

The Gupta made great advances in astronomy, espite their lack of modern devices such as telescopes. They used devices like this one from the 1700s to observe and map the stars.

Mathematics

The ancient Indians wrote texts about AD 500 that summarized Indian knowledge of mathematics. They discussed basic arithmetic, fractions, and a counting system.

ANALYSIS SKILL ANALYZING VISUALS

What are some areas of science that people studied in ancient India?

For people who were injured, Indian doctors could perform surgery. Surgeons repaired broken bones, treated wounds, removed infected tonsils, reconstructed broken noses, and even reattached torn earlobes! If they could find no other cure for an illness, doctors would cast magic spells to help people recover.

Indian interest in **astronomy**, the study of stars and planets, dates back to early times as well. Indian astronomers knew of seven of the planets in our solar system. They knew that the sun was a star and that the planets revolved around it. They also knew that the earth was a sphere and that it rotated on its axis. In addition, they could predict eclipses of the sun and the moon.

READING CHECK Finding Main Ideas What were two Indian achievements in mathematics?

SUMMARY AND PREVIEW From a group of cities on the Indus River, India grew into a major empire whose people made great achievements. In the next chapter, you'll read about another civilization that experienced similar growth—China.

Section 5 Assessment

Reviewing Ideas, Terms, and People

1. **a. Describe** What did Hindu temples of the Gupta period look like?
   b. Analyze How can you tell that Indian artists were well respected?
   c. Evaluate Why do you think Hindu and Buddhist temples contained great works of art?
2. **a. Identify** What is the *Bhagavad Gita*?
   b. Explain Why were the stories of the *Panchatantra* written?
   c. Elaborate Why do you think people are still interested in ancient Sanskrit epics today?
3. **a. Define** What is **metallurgy**?
   b. Explain Why do we call the numbers we use today **Hindu-Arabic numerals**?

Critical Thinking

4. **Categorizing** Draw a chart like this one. Identify the scientific advances that fall into each category below.

Metallurgy	Math	Medicine	Astronomy

FOCUS ON WRITING

5. **Highlighting Indian Achievements** Make a list of Indian achievements that you could include on a poster. Now look back through your notes from this chapter. Which will you choose as the subject of your poster?

Social Studies Skills

Analysis | Critical Thinking | Economics | Study

Interpreting Diagrams

Understand the Skill

Diagrams are drawings that illustrate or explain objects or ideas. Different types of diagrams have different purposes. The ability to interpret diagrams will help you to better understand historical objects, their functions, and how they worked.

Learn the Skill

Use these guidelines to interpret a diagram:

1 Read the diagram's title or caption to find out what it represents. If a legend is present, study it as well to understand any symbols and colors in the diagram.

2 Most diagrams include labels that identify the object's parts or explain relationships between them. Study these parts and labels carefully.

3 If any written information or explanation accompanies the diagram, compare it to the drawing as you read.

The diagram below is of the Great Stupa at Sanchi in India, which is thought to contain the Buddha's remains. Like most stupas, it was shaped like a dome.

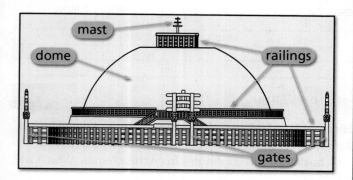

The Sanchi stupa is surrounded by a stone railing with four gates called *torenas*. About halfway up the side of the mound is a second railing next to a walkway. Worshippers move along this walkway in a clockwise direction to honor the Buddha. The stupa is topped by a cube called the *harmika*. Rising from the harmika is a mast or spire. These parts and their shapes all have religious meaning for Buddhists.

Practice and Apply the Skill

Here is another diagram of the Sanchi stupa. Interpret both diagrams on this page to answer the questions that follow.

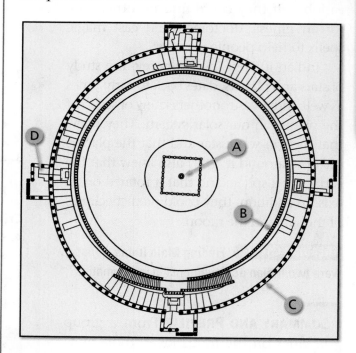

1. Which letter in this diagram labels the *torenas*?

2. What part of the stupa does the letter A label?

3. The walkway and railing are labeled by which letter?

Chapter Review

Visual Summary

Use the visual summary below to help you review the main ideas of the chapter.

QUICK FACTS

The Harappan civilization began in the Indus River Valley.

Hinduism and Buddhism both developed in India.

Indians made great advances in art, literature, science, and other fields.

Reviewing Vocabulary, Terms and People

Fill in the blanks with the correct term or name from this chapter.

1. _____ are winds that bring heavy rainfall.

2. A _____ is a division of people into groups based on birth, wealth, or occupation.

3. Hindus believe in _____, the belief that they will be reborn many times after death.

4. _____ founded the Mauryan Empire.

5. The focusing of the mind on spiritual things is called _____.

6. People who work to spread their religious beliefs are called _____.

7. People who practice _____ use only peaceful ways to achieve change.

8. _____ converted to Buddhism while he was ruler of the Mauryan Empire.

9. A mixture of metals is called an _____.

Comprehension and Critical Thinking

SECTION 1 *(Pages 124–129)*

10. **a. Describe** What caused floods on the Indus River, and what was the result of those floods?

    b. Contrast How was Aryan culture different from Harappan culture?

    c. Elaborate Why is the Harappan culture considered a civilization?

SECTION 2 *(Pages 130–135)*

11. **a. Identify** Who were the Brahmins, and what role did they play in Aryan society?

    b. Analyze How do Hindus believe karma affects reincarnation?

    c. Elaborate Hinduism has been called both a polytheistic religion—one that worships many gods—and a monotheistic religion—one that worships only one god. Why do you think this is so?

SECTION 3 (Pages 136–141)

12. a. Describe What did the Buddha say caused human suffering?

b. Analyze How did Buddhism grow and change after the Buddha died?

c. Elaborate Why did the Buddha's teachings about nirvana appeal to many people of lower castes?

SECTION 4 (Pages 142–145)

13. a. Identify What was Candragupta Maurya's greatest accomplishment?

b. Compare and Contrast What was one similarity between the Mauryas and the Guptas? What was one difference between them?

c. Predict How might Indian history have been different if Asoka had not become a Buddhist?

SECTION 5 (Pages 147–151)

14. a. Describe What kinds of religious art did the ancient Indians create?

b. Make Inferences Why do you think religious discussions are included in the *Mahabharata?*

c. Evaluate Which of the ancient Indians' achievements do you think is most impressive? Why?

Reviewing Themes

15. Religion What is one teaching that Buddhism and Hinduism share? What is one idea about which they differ?

16. Society and Culture How did the caste system affect the lives of most people in India?

Using the Internet

17. Activity: Making a Brochure In this chapter, you learned about India's diverse geographical features and the ways in which geography influenced India's history. Go online to research the geography and civilizations of India, taking notes as you go. Finally, use the interactive brochure template to present what you have found.

Reading Skills

18. Inferences about History Based on what you learned about the Gupta period, what inference can you draw about religious tolerance in ancient India? Draw a box like the one below to help you organize your thoughts.

Question:	
Inside the Text:	Outside the Text:
Inference:	

Social Studies Skills

19. Understanding Diagrams Look back over the diagram of the Buddhist temple in the skills activity at the end of this chapter. Using this diagram as a guide, draw a simple diagram of your house or school. Be sure to include labels of important features on your diagram. An example has been provided for you below.

Bedroom	Bathroom	Kitchen
Hallway		
Bedroom	Bedroom	Living Room

FOCUS ON WRITING

20. Designing Your Poster Now that you have chosen a subject for your poster, it's time to create it. On a large sheet of paper or poster board, write a title that identifies your subject. Then draw pictures, maps, or diagrams that illustrate it.

Next to each picture, write a short caption. Each caption should be two sentences long. The first sentence should identify what the picture, map, or diagram shows. The second sentence should explain why the picture is important to the study of Indian history.

Florida Standardized Test Practice

DIRECTIONS: Read each question, and write the letter of the best response.

1 Use the map to answer the following question.

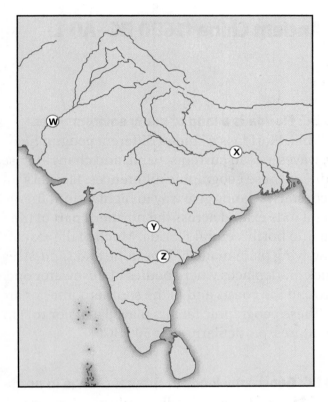

Civilization grew on the Indian subcontinent along the river marked on the map by the letter

A W.

B X.

C Y.

D Z.

2 The people of which *varna* in early India had the hardest lives?

A Brahmins

B Kshatriyas

C Sudras

D Vaisyas

3 What is the *main* goal of people who follow Buddhism as it was taught by the Buddha?

A wealth

B rebirth

C missionary work

D reaching nirvana

4 The Mauryan emperor Asoka is known for all of the following *except*

A expanding the empire across most of India.

B spreading Hinduism.

C working to improve his people's lives.

D practicing nonviolence.

5 Early India's contributions to world civilization included

A developing the world's first calendar.

B creating what is now called algebra.

C inventing the plow and the wheel.

D introducing zero to the number system.

Connecting with Past Learnings

6 In this chapter you learned about two great epics, the *Mahabharata* and the *Ramayana*. Which of the following is also an epic poem that you have studied?

A Hammurabi's Code

B the *Book of the Dead*

C *Gilgamesh*

D the Pyramid Texts

7 As you learned earlier in this course, the ancient Egyptians held elaborate religious rituals. Which of these Indian religions also involved many rituals, including sacrifices?

A Buddhism

B Brahmanism

C Jainism

D Mauryanism

FLORIDA...
The Story Continues

CHAPTER 6, Ancient China (1600 BC–AD 1)

PLACES **c. 500 BC: Florida is a land of many environments.**
Like China, Florida is a land of different geographic regions. Water, waves, ocean currents, wind, and changes in sea level have produced these geographic differences. Florida's northwestern coastal lowlands give way to highlands in the interior. The highlands extend across the northern part of the state and down into north-central Florida. Much of the rest of the state is a low-lying plain made of limestone and sand. Areas of peat and muck mark places where bodies of freshwater once stood. Areas around the coasts and in the southern interior are often swampy. These geographic factors played a major role in shaping early cultures, particularly after 500 BC.

PLACES **c. 500 BC: Geography leads to cultural change in northern Florida.** In the panhandle sandy beaches and dunes covered the coastal areas. In the interior low rolling hills of red clay were drained by the Apalachicola and Escambia rivers. Forests of mainly pine covered the land. The rolling hills continued across northern Florida and down into the north-central area of the peninsula. The Aucilla, Suwannee, Sante Fe, and other rivers flowed through these areas. In the panhandle, the Apalachicola River connected to the Flint and Chattahoochee rivers to form a waterway north. Farther east, the Suwannee served the same purpose. These waterways helped spur contact with Native American cultures living in the Mississippi River Valley eastward to Georgia. Contact brought trade and new ideas. As a result the people of northern Florida developed many different cultures.

c. 500 BC: Life in eastern and central Florida is centered in the St. Johns River basin. The geography of the St. Johns River basin was one of wetlands and pine forest in the eastern region. Along the coast the rivers and streams of the basin flowed into the Atlantic Ocean. Farther south people lived along the marshes of the Indian River. Central Florida was a land of lakes. The cultures of the St. Johns region changed after 500 BC, but not as much as the cultures of northern Florida. The St. Johns River was a major transportation route for the people of the region. However, the river only flowed within the region. This meant that the St. Johns cultures had less contact with cultures outside of Florida.

PLACES **c. 500 BC: Water shapes the cultures of Florida's Central Gulf Coast.** The area from the Aucilla River south to Charlotte Bay was a land of bays and inlets, saltwater marshes, and freshwater wetlands. Tampa Bay was the largest of the bays. The flat coastal region was a soggy place. The region's wet geography led the people to develop cultures that were different from their neighbors to the north and east.

PLACES **c. 500 BC: Southern Florida is a water world.** South Florida was even wetter than the Central Gulf Coast. It was a land of coastal mangrove forests and saltwater marshes. In the interior the Kissimmee River and Lake Okeechobee basins were a wet world of lakes, ponds, cypress swamps, wet prairies, and pine and palmetto flatlands. Farther south the Everglades was an expanse of sawgrass marshes dotted with islands of trees. People in southern Florida settled wherever there was dry land. Most archaeological sites have been found along the coast, on river banks, and on drier areas around Lake Okeechobee.

Unpacking the Florida Standards ‹···

Read the following to learn what this standard says and what it means. See FL8–FL31 to unpack all of the standards related to this chapter.

Benchmark SS.6.W.4.10 Explain the significance of the silk roads and maritime routes across the Indian Ocean to the movement of goods and ideas among Asia, East Africa, and the Mediterranean Basin.

What does it mean?

Analyze how the major east-west silk roads and sea routes led to the exchange not only of goods, but also ideas between eastern and western civilizations.

SPOTLIGHT ON

SS.6.E.1.2, SS.6.E.3.3 See pages FL37 and FL38 for content specifically related to these Chapter 6 standards.

Ancient China

Essential Question How do the people, events, and ideas that shaped ancient China continue to influence the world?

Florida Next Generation Sunshine State Standards

LA.6.1.2 The student will listen to, read, and discuss familiar and conceptually challenging text. **SS.6.E.1.2** Describe and identify traditional and command economies as they appear in different civilizations. **SS.6.E.3.3** Describe traditional economies (Egypt, Greece, Rome, Kush) and elements of those economies that led to the rise of a merchant class and trading partners. **SS.6.G.2.6** Explain the concept of cultural diffusion, and identify the influences of different ancient cultures on one another. **SS.6.G.3.1** Explain how the physical landscape has affected the development of agriculture and industry in the ancient world. **SS.6.G.3.2** Analyze the impact of human populations on the ancient world's ecosystems. **SS.6.G.4.1** Explain how family and ethnic relationships influenced ancient cultures. **SS.6.G.4.4** Map and analyze the impact of the spread of various belief systems in the ancient world. **SS.6.G.5.1** Identify the methods used to compensate for the scarcity of resources in the ancient world. **SS.6.G.5.2** Use geographic terms and tools to explain why ancient civilizations developed networks of highways, waterways, and other transportation linkages. **SS.6.G.5.3** Use geographic tools and terms to analyze how famine, drought, and natural disasters plagued many ancient civilizations. **SS.6.G.6.2** Compare maps of the world in ancient times with current political maps. **SS.6.W.1.1** Use timelines to identify chronological order of historical events. **SS.6.W.1.2** Identify terms (decade, century, epoch, era, millennium, BC/BCE, AD/CE) and designations of time periods. **SS.6.W.1.3** Interpret primary and secondary sources. **SS.6.W.2.4** Compare the economic, political, social, and religious institutions of ancient river civilizations. **SS.6.W.4.4** Explain the teachings of Buddha, the importance of Asoka, and how Buddhism spread in India, Ceylon, and other parts of Asia. **SS.6.W.4.6** Describe the concept of the Mandate of Heaven and its connection to the Zhou and later dynasties. **SS.6.W.4.7** Explain the basic teachings of Laozi, Confucius, and Han Fei Zi. **SS.6.W.4.8** Describe the contributions of classical and post classical China. **SS.6.W.4.9** Identify key figures from classical and post classical China. **SS.6.W.4.10** Explain the significance of the silk roads and maritime routes across the Indian Ocean to the movement of goods and ideas among Asia, East Africa, and the Mediterranean Basin.

FOCUS ON SPEAKING

Oral Presentation In this chapter you will read about China's fascinating early years. Choose one person or event from that history. You will then tell your classmates why the person or event was important to the history of China.

CHAPTER EVENTS

c. 1500s BC The Shang dynasty is established in China.

1600 BC

WORLD EVENTS

c. 1480 BC Queen Hatshepsut rules Egypt.

China was one of the earliest world civilizations. Rivers played key roles in the economy and the development of Chinese society.

1100s BC
The Zhou dynasty begins.

551 BC
Confucius is born in China.

221 BC
Shi Huangdi unites China under the Qin dynasty.

206 BC
The Han dynasty begins its rule of China.

1200 BC

800 BC

400 BC

BC 1 AD

c. 965 BC
Solomon becomes king of the Israelites.

c. 500 BC
Buddhism begins to emerge in India.

c. 100 BC
The overland Silk Road connects China and Southwest Asia.

ANCIENT CHINA **157**

Reading Social Studies

Focus on Themes This chapter will describe the early development of China—how Chinese civilization began and took shape under early dynasties. You will see how these dynasties controlled the government and **politics**. You will also see how the Chinese, influenced by the philosopher Confucius, established traditions such as the importance of families. They also encouraged art and learning, helping to shape the **society and culture** that would last for centuries in China.

Summarizing Historical Texts

Focus on Reading When you are reading a history book, how can you be sure that you understand everything? One way is to briefly restate what you've read in a summary.

Writing a Summary A **summary** is a short restatement of the most important ideas in a text. The example below shows three steps used in writing a summary. First underline important details. Then write a short summary of each paragraph. Finally, combine these paragraph summaries into a short summary of the whole passage.

> The first dynasty for which we have clear evidence is the Shang, which was firmly established by the 1500s BC. Strongest in the Huang He Valley, the Shang ruled a broad area of northern China. Shang rulers moved their capital several times, probably to avoid floods or attack by enemies.
>
> The king was at the center of Shang political and religious life. Nobles served the king as advisors and helped him rule. Less important officials were also nobles. They performed specific governmental and religious duties.

Summary of Paragraph 1
China's first dynasty, the Shang, took power in northern China in the 1500s BC.

Summary of Paragraph 2
Shang politics and religion were run by the king and nobles.

Combined Summary
The Shang dynasty, which ruled northern China by the 1500s BC, was governed by a king and nobles.

You Try It!

The following passage is from the chapter you are about to read. As you read it, think about what you would include in a summary.

Early Settlements

From Chapter 6 p. 162

Archaeologists have found remains of early Chinese villages. One village near the Huang He had more than 40 houses. Many of them were partly underground and may have had straw-covered roofs. The site also included animal pens, storage pits, and a cemetery.

Some of the villages along the Huang He grew into large towns. Walls surrounded these towns to defend them against floods and hostile neighbors. In towns like these, the Chinese left many artifacts, such as arrowheads, fishhooks, tools, and pottery. Some village sites even contained pieces of cloth.

After you read the passage, answer the following questions.

1. Read the following summaries and decide which one is the better summary statement. Explain your answer.
    a) Archaeologists have found out interesting things about the early settlements of China. For example, they have discovered that the Chinese had homes with straw-covered roofs, pens for their animals, and even cemeteries. Also, they have found that larger villages were surrounded by walls for defense. Finally, they have found tools like arrowheads and fishhooks.
    b) Archaeologists have found remains of early Chinese villages, some of which grew into large walled settlements. Artifacts found there help us understand Chinese culture.

2. What are three characteristics of a good summary?

Key Terms and People

Chapter 6

Section 1
jade *(p. 163)*
oracle *(p. 164)*

Section 2
lords *(p. 167)*
peasants *(p. 167)*
Confucius *(p. 169)*
ethics *(p. 169)*
Confucianism *(p. 169)*
Daoism *(p. 170)*
Laozi *(p. 170)*
Legalism *(p. 170)*
Han Fei Zi *(p. 171)*

Section 3
Shi Huangdi *(p. 172)*
Great Wall *(p. 175)*

Section 4
sundial *(p. 182)*
seismograph *(p. 182)*
acupuncture *(p. 183)*

Section 5
silk *(p. 187)*
Silk Road *(p. 187)*
diffusion *(p. 189)*

Academic Vocabulary

Success in school is related to knowing academic vocabulary—the words that are frequently used in school assignments and discussions. In this chapter, you will learn the following academic words:

vary *(p. 161)*
structure *(p. 168)*
innovation *(p. 182)*
procedure *(p. 187)*

As you read **Chapter 6,** think about how you would summarize the material you are reading.

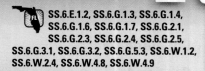

SECTION **1**

SS.6.E.1.2, SS.6.G.1.3, SS.6.G.1.4,
SS.6.G.1.6, SS.6.G.1.7, SS.6.G.2.1,
SS.6.G.2.3, SS.6.G.2.4, SS.6.G.2.5,
SS.6.G.3.1, SS.6.G.3.2, SS.6.G.5.3, SS.6.W.1.2,
SS.6.W.2.4, SS.6.W.4.8, SS.6.W.4.9

What You Will Learn...

Main Ideas

1. China's physical geography made farming possible but travel and communication difficult.
2. Civilization began in China along the Huang He and Chang Jiang rivers.
3. China's first dynasties helped Chinese society develop and made many other achievements.

The Big Idea

Chinese civilization began with the Shang dynasty along the Huang He.

Key Terms

jade, *p. 163*
oracle, *p. 164*

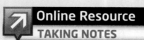

Online Resource
TAKING NOTES

Use the graphic organizer online to take notes on China's geography and its early civilizations.

Geography and Early China

If YOU were there...

You live along a broad river in China in about 1400 BC. Your grandfather is a farmer. He tells you wonderful stories about an ancient king. Long ago, this legendary hero tamed the river's raging floods. He even created new rivers. Without him, no one could farm or live in this rich land.

Why is this legend important to your family?

BUILDING BACKGROUND Like other river civilizations, the Chinese people had to learn to control floods and irrigate their fields. China's geographical features divided the country into distinct regions.

China's Physical Geography

Geography played a major role in the development of Chinese civilization. China has many different geographical features. Some features separated groups of people within China. Others separated China from the rest of the world.

A Vast and Varied Land

China covers an area of nearly 4 million square miles, about the same size as the United States. One of the physical barriers that separates China from its neighbors is a harsh desert, the Gobi (GOH-bee). It spreads over much of China's north. East of the Gobi are low-lying plains. These plains, which cover most of eastern China, form one of the world's largest farming regions. The Pacific Ocean forms the country's eastern boundary.

More than 2,000 miles to the west, rugged mountains make up the western frontier. In the southwest the Plateau of Tibet has several mountain peaks that reach more than 26,000 feet. From the plateau, smaller mountain ranges spread eastward. The most important of these ranges is the Qinling Shandi (CHIN-LING shahn-DEE). It separates northern China from southern China.

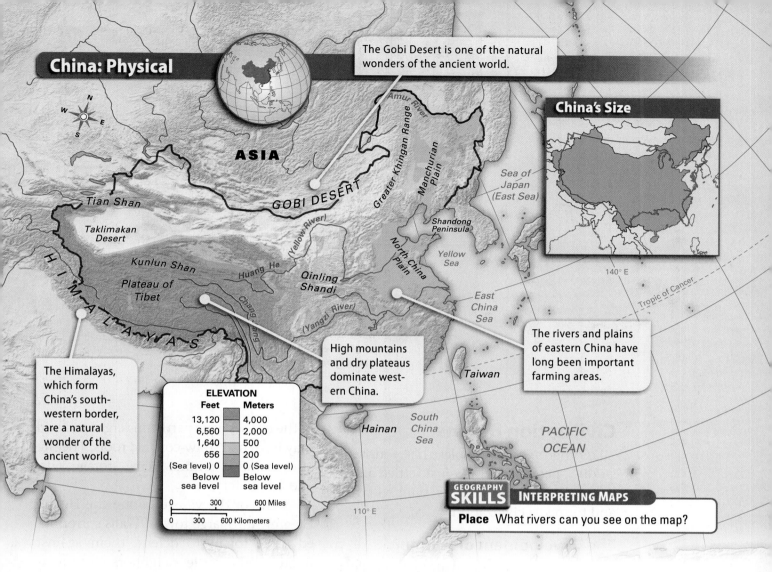

China: Physical

The Gobi Desert is one of the natural wonders of the ancient world.

ASIA

GOBI DESERT

Tian Shan

Taklimakan Desert

Kunlun Shan

Plateau of Tibet

HIMALAYAS

Amur River

Greater Khingan Range

Manchurian Plain

(Yellow River)

Huang He

Qinling Shandi

Chang Jiang

(Yangzi River)

Shandong Peninsula

North China Plain

Yellow Sea

East China Sea

Hainan

South China Sea

Taiwan

PACIFIC OCEAN

Sea of Japan (East Sea)

China's Size

140° E

Tropic of Cancer

110° E

The Himalayas, which form China's southwestern border, are a natural wonder of the ancient world.

High mountains and dry plateaus dominate western China.

The rivers and plains of eastern China have long been important farming areas.

ELEVATION

Feet		Meters
13,120		4,000
6,560		2,000
1,640		500
656		200
(Sea level) 0		0 (Sea level)
Below sea level		Below sea level

0   300   600 Miles
0   300   600 Kilometers

GEOGRAPHY SKILLS ⟩ **INTERPRETING MAPS**

Place What rivers can you see on the map?

Weather and temperature patterns **vary** widely across China. In the northeast, the climate is cold and dry. Winter temperatures drop well below 0°F. Rivers there are frozen for more than half of the year. In the northwest, the deserts are very dry. But on the eastern plains of China, heavy rains fall. The tropical southeast is the wettest region. Monsoons can bring 250 inches of rain each year. That's enough water to cover a two-story house!

The Rivers of China

Two great rivers flow from west to east in China. The Huang He, or Yellow River, stretches for nearly 3,000 miles across northern China. The river often floods, and the floods leave behind layers of silt on the surrounding countryside. Because these floods can be very destructive, the river is sometimes called China's Sorrow. Over the years, millions of people have died in Huang He floods.

To the south, the Chang Jiang, or Yangzi River, cuts through central China. It flows from the mountains of Tibet to the Pacific Ocean. The Chang Jiang is the longest river in Asia.

In early China, the two rivers helped link people in the eastern part of the country with those in the west. At the same time, the mountains between the rivers limited contact.

READING CHECK ⟩ **Summarizing** What geographical features limited travel in China?

ACADEMIC VOCABULARY

vary to be different

SS.6.G.5.3 Use geographic tools and terms to analyze how famine, drought, and natural disasters plagued many ancient civilizations.

China is a large country with many different types of environments.

How do these photos show China's diverse geography?

1 In northern China, the Huang He, or Yellow River, has long been the center of civilization. The silt in the river gives it a yellow look.

Civilization Begins

Like other ancient peoples that you have studied, people in China first settled along rivers. There they farmed, built villages, and formed a civilization.

The Development of Farming

Farming in China started along the Huang He and Chang Jiang. The rivers' floods deposited fertile silt. These silt deposits made the land ideal for growing crops.

As early as 7000 BC farmers grew rice in the middle Chang Jiang Valley. North, along the Huang He, the land was better for growing cereals such as millet and wheat.

Along with farming, the early Chinese people increased their diets in other ways. They fished and hunted with bows and arrows. They also domesticated animals such as pigs and sheep. With more sources of food, the population grew.

Early Settlements

Archaeologists have found remains of early Chinese villages. One village site near the Huang He had more than 40 houses. Many of the houses were partly underground and may have had straw-covered roofs. The site also included animal pens, storage pits, and a cemetery.

Some of the villages along the Huang He grew into large towns. Walls surrounded these towns to defend them against floods and hostile neighbors. In towns like these, the Chinese left many artifacts, such as arrowheads, fishhooks, tools, and pottery. Some village sites even contained pieces of cloth.

Separate cultures developed in southern and northeastern China. These included the Sanxingdui (sahn-shing-DWAY) and Hongshan peoples. Little is known about them, however. As the major cultures along the Huang He and Chang Jiang grew, they absorbed other cultures.

Over time, Chinese culture became more advanced. After 3000 BC people used potter's wheels to make more types of pottery. These people also learned to dig water wells. As populations grew, villages spread out over larger areas in both northern and southeastern China.

2 Southern China receives more rain than northern China, and farmers can grow several crops of rice a year.

3 Western China's high mountains and wide deserts make travel difficult and isolate China's population centers in the east.

Burial sites have provided information about the culture of this period. Like the Egyptians, the early Chinese filled their tombs with objects. Some tombs included containers of food, suggesting a belief in an afterlife. Some graves contained many more items than others. These differences show that a social order had developed. Often the graves of rich people held beautiful jewelry and other objects made from **jade**, a hard gemstone.

READING CHECK **Generalizing** What were some features of China's earliest settlements?

China's First Dynasties

Societies along the Huang He grew and became more complex. They eventually formed the first Chinese civilization.

The Xia Dynasty

According to ancient stories, a series of kings ruled early China. Around 2200 BC one of them, Yu the Great, is said to have founded the Xia (SHAH) dynasty.

Writers told of terrible floods during Yu's lifetime. According to these accounts, Yu dug channels to drain the water to the ocean. This labor took him more than 10 years and is said to have created the major waterways of north China.

Archaeologists have not yet found evidence that the tales about the Xia are true. However, the stories of Xia rulers were important to the ancient Chinese because they told of kings who helped people solve problems by working together. The stories also explained the geography that had such an impact on people's lives.

The Shang Dynasty

The first dynasty for which we have clear evidence is the Shang, which was firmly established by the 1500s BC. Strongest in the Huang He Valley, the Shang ruled a broad area of northern China. Shang rulers moved their capital several times, probably to avoid floods or attack by enemies.

The king was at the center of Shang political and religious life. Nobles served the king as advisors and helped him rule.

FOCUS ON

Classical China
The start of the Shang dynasty marks the beginning of classical China. Historians say the classical age of China lasts from the Shang dynasty to the fall of the Han dynasty in AD 220.

SS.6.W.4.9 Identify key figures from classical and post classical China.

Less important officials were also nobles. They performed specific governmental and religious duties.

The social order became more organized under the Shang. The royal family and the nobles were at the highest level. Nobles owned much land, and they passed on their wealth and power to their sons. Warrior leaders from the far regions of the empire also had high rank in society. Most people in the Shang ruling classes lived in large homes in cities.

Artisans settled outside the city walls. They lived in groups based on what they made for a living. Some artisans made weapons. Other artisans made pottery, tools, or clothing. Artisans were at a middle level of importance in Shang society.

Farmers ranked below artisans in the social order. Farmers worked long hours but had little money. Taxes claimed much of what they earned. Slaves, who filled society's lowest rank, were an important source of labor during the Shang period.

The Shang made many advances, including China's first writing system. This system used more than 2,000 symbols to express words or ideas. Although the system has gone through changes over the years, the Chinese symbols used today are based on those of the Shang period.

Shang writing has been found on thousands of cattle bones and turtle shells. Priests had carved questions about the future on bones or shells, which were then heated, causing them to crack. The priests believed they could "read" these cracks to predict the future. The bones were called oracle bones because an **oracle** is a prediction.

In addition to writing, the Shang also made other achievements. Artisans made beautiful bronze containers for cooking and

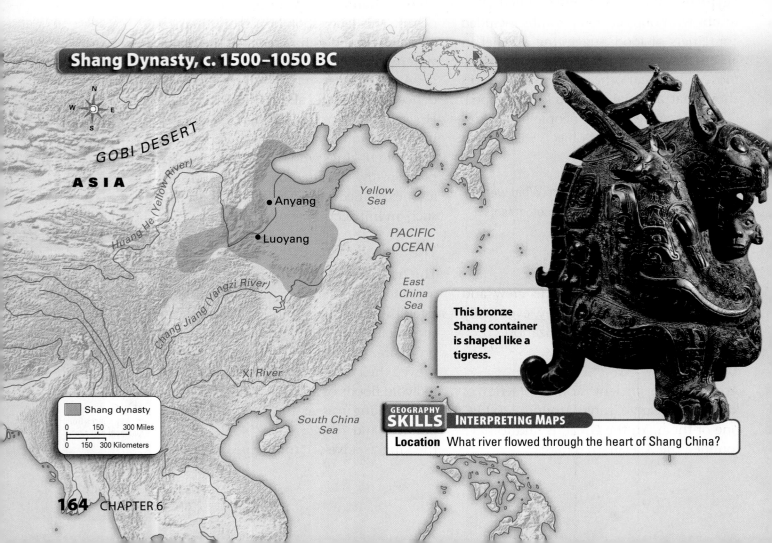

Shang Dynasty, c. 1500–1050 BC

GOBI DESERT

ASIA

Huang He (Yellow River)

- Anyang
- Luoyang

Yellow Sea

PACIFIC OCEAN

East China Sea

Chang Jiang (Yangzi River)

Xi River

South China Sea

Shang dynasty

0   150   300 Miles
0   150   300 Kilometers

This bronze Shang container is shaped like a tigress.

GEOGRAPHY SKILLS INTERPRETING MAPS

Location What river flowed through the heart of Shang China?

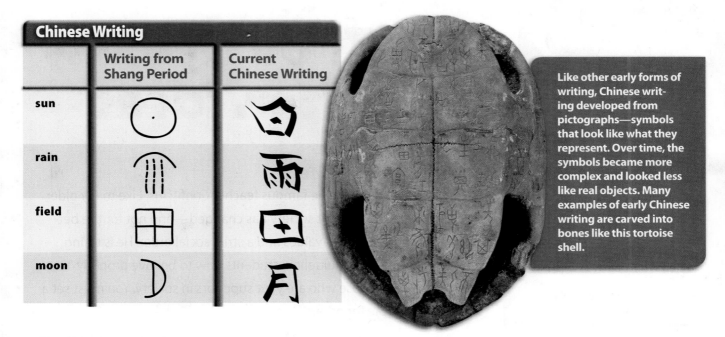

Chinese Writing

	Writing from Shang Period	Current Chinese Writing
sun		
rain		
field		
moon		

Like other early forms of writing, Chinese writing developed from pictographs—symbols that look like what they represent. Over time, the symbols became more complex and looked less like real objects. Many examples of early Chinese writing are carved into bones like this tortoise shell.

religious ceremonies. They also made axes, knives, and ornaments from jade. The military developed war chariots, powerful bows, and bronze body armor. Shang astrologers also made an important contribution. They developed a calendar based on the cycles of the moon.

READING CHECK **Contrasting** What is a major historical difference between the Xia and Shang dynasties?

SUMMARY AND PREVIEW China is a vast land with a diverse geography. Ancient Chinese civilization developed in the fertile valleys of the Huang He and Chang Jiang. Civilization there advanced under Shang rule. People developed a social order, a writing system, and made other achievements. In the next section you will learn about new ideas in China during the rule of the Zhou dynasty.

Section 1 Assessment

Reviewing Ideas, Terms, and People

1. **a. Identify** Name China's two major rivers.
   b. Analyze How did China's geography affect its development?
2. **a. Identify** In which river valley did China's civilization begin?
   b. Explain What made China's river valleys ideal for farming?
   c. Elaborate What do Chinese artifacts reveal about China's early civilization?
3. **a. Describe** How do historians know about the Xia dynasty?
   b. Draw Conclusions What does the use of **oracle** bones tell us about the early Chinese?

Critical Thinking

4. **Comparing and Contrasting** Draw a chart like this one. Use it and your notes to compare and contrast the Xia and Shang dynasties.

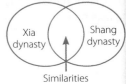

Xia dynasty   Shang dynasty

Similarities

FOCUS ON SPEAKING

5. **Thinking about Events** Look back over the section to note the important events of China's earliest times. Think about what it is that makes one event more important than another. Write down your ideas in a notebook.

LA.6.1.7.3, SS.6.E.1.2, SS.6.E.2.1,
SS.6.G.1.4, SS.6.G.1.5, SS.6.G.1.7,
SS.6.G.2.2, SS.6.W.1.1, SS.6.W.1.2,
SS.6.W.1.3, SS.6.W.2.4, SS.6.W.4.6, SS.6.W.4.7,
SS.6.W.4.8, SS.6.W.4.9

What You Will Learn...

Main Ideas

1. The Zhou dynasty expanded China but then declined.
2. Confucius offered ideas to bring order to Chinese society.
3. Daoism and Legalism also gained followers.

The Big Idea

The Zhou dynasty brought political stability and new ways to deal with political and social changes in ancient China.

Key Terms and People

lords, p. 167
peasants, p. 167
Confucius, p. 169
ethics, p. 169
Confucianism, p. 169
Daoism, p. 170
Laozi, p. 170
Legalism, p. 170

Online Resource
TAKING NOTES

Use the graphic organizer online to take notes on changes that occurred during the Zhou dynasty.

The Zhou Dynasty and New Ideas

If YOU were there...

You are a student of the famous teacher Confucius. Like many older Chinese, he thinks that society has changed—and not for the better. He believes in old values and a strict social order. He is trying to teach you and your fellow students how to behave properly. You must respect those who are your superiors in society. You must set a good example for others.

How will these teachings affect your life?

BUILDING BACKGROUND The people of the Shang dynasty made many advances, including beautiful metalwork, a writing system, and a calendar. The next dynasty, the Zhou, established other Chinese traditions. Some of these traditions included the importance of family and social order. Later thinkers looked back with admiration to the values of the Zhou period.

The Zhou Dynasty

In the 1100s BC the leaders of a people who came to be known as the Zhou (JOH) ruled over a kingdom in China. They joined with other nearby tribes and attacked and overthrew the Shang dynasty. The Zhou dynasty lasted longer than any other dynasty in Chinese history.

Time Line

The Zhou Dynasty

1100s BC
The Zhou dynasty begins.

551 BC
Confucius is born.

1200 BC	800 BC	400 BC

771 BC
Invaders reach the Zhou capital.

481 BC
Civil war spreads across China during the Warring States period.

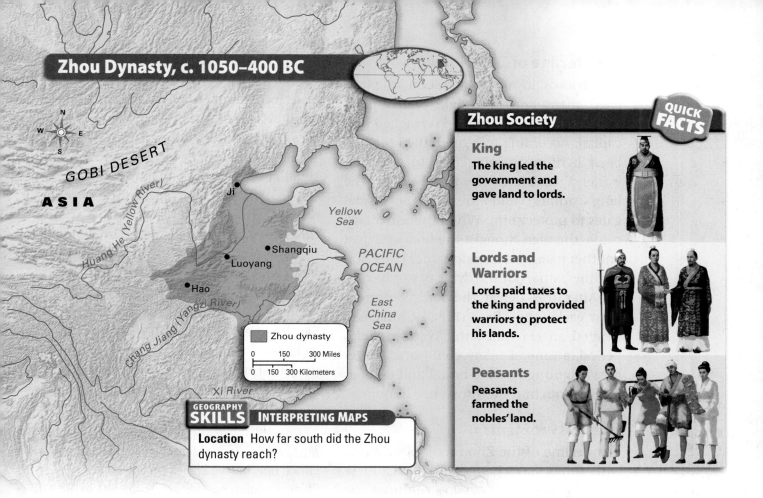

Zhou Dynasty, c. 1050–400 BC

GOBI DESERT

ASIA

Huang He (Yellow River)

Ji

Yellow Sea

Shangqiu
Luoyang

PACIFIC OCEAN

Hao

Chang Jiang (Yangzi River)

East China Sea

Zhou dynasty

0   150   300 Miles
0   150   300 Kilometers

Xi River

GEOGRAPHY SKILLS | INTERPRETING MAPS

Location How far south did the Zhou dynasty reach?

Zhou Society QUICK FACTS

King
The king led the government and gave land to lords.

Lords and Warriors
Lords paid taxes to the king and provided warriors to protect his lands.

Peasants
Peasants farmed the nobles' land.

The Zhou Political System

The Zhou kings claimed to possess the mandate of heaven. According to this idea, heaven gave power to the king or leader, and no one ruled without heaven's permission. If a king was found to be bad, heaven would support another leader.

The Zhou came from an area to the west of the Shang kingdom. Early Zhou rulers used the mandate of heaven to justify their rebellion against the Shang. Later Zhou rulers expanded their territory to the northwest and the east. Zhou soldiers then moved south, eventually expanding their rule to the Chang Jiang.

The Zhou established a new political order. They granted land to others in return for loyalty, military support, and other services. The Zhou king was at the highest level. He granted plots of land to **lords**, or people of high rank. Lords paid taxes and provided soldiers to the king as needed. **Peasants**, or farmers with small farms, were at the bottom of the order. Each peasant family received a small plot of land and had to farm additional land for the noble. The system was described in the *Book of Songs*:

" Everywhere under vast Heaven
There is no land that is not the king's
Within the borders of those lands
There are none who are not the king's servants. "
–from the Zhou *Book of Songs*

The Zhou system brought order to China. Ruling through lords helped the Zhou control distant areas and helped ensure loyalty to the king. Over time, however, the political order broke down. Lords passed their power to their sons, who were less loyal to the king. Local rulers gained power. They began to reject the authority of the Zhou kings.

SS.6.W.4.6 Describe the concept of the Mandate of Heaven and its connection to the Zhou and later dynasties.

The Decline of Zhou Power

As the lords' loyalty to the Zhou king lessened, many refused to fight against invasions. In 771 BC invaders reached the capital. According to legend, the king had been lighting warning fires to entertain a friend. Each time the fires were lit, the king's armies would rush to the capital gates to protect him. When the real attack came, the men thought the fires were just another joke, and no one came. The Zhou lost the battle, but the dynasty survived.

After this defeat the lords began to fight each other. By 481 BC, China had entered an era called the Warring States period, a time of many civil wars. Armies grew. Fighting became brutal and cruel as soldiers fought for territory, not honor.

Internal Problems

The decline of the Zhou took place along with important changes in the Chinese family **structure**. For many centuries the family had been the foundation of life in China. Large families of several generations formed powerful groups. When these families broke apart, they lost their power. Close relatives became rivals.

Bonds of loyalty even weakened within small families, especially among the upper classes. Sons plotted against each other over inheritances. A wealthy father sometimes tried to maintain peace by dividing his land among his sons. But this created new problems. Each son could build up his wealth and then challenge his brothers. Some sons even killed their own fathers. During the Warring States period, China lacked a strong government to stop the power struggles within the ruling-class families. Chinese society fell into a period of disorder.

READING CHECK Identifying Cause and Effect How did the Zhou's decline affect Chinese society?

The Warring States Period

During China's Warring States period, thousands of armies fought each other to gain territory. The armies used new weapons and battle techniques in the civil wars that lasted more than 200 years.

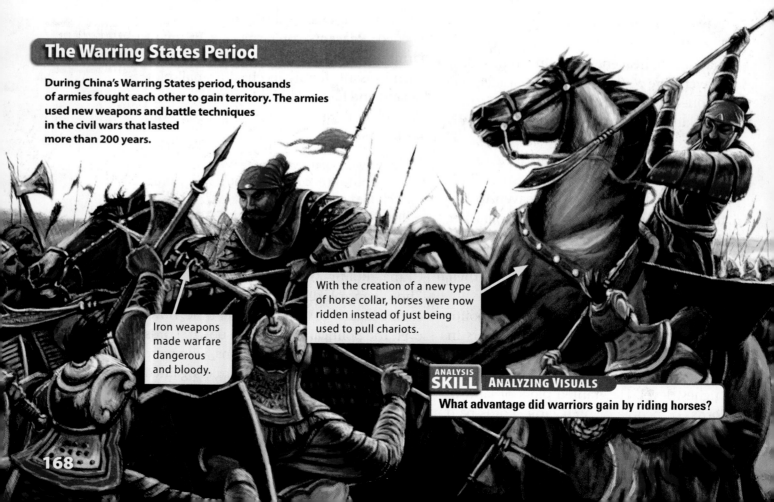

Iron weapons made warfare dangerous and bloody.

With the creation of a new type of horse collar, horses were now ridden instead of just being used to pull chariots.

ANALYSIS SKILL **ANALYZING VISUALS**

What advantage did warriors gain by riding horses?

Confucius and Society

During the late Zhou period, thinkers came up with ideas about how to restore order to China. One such person, **Confucius**, became the most influential teacher in Chinese history. Confucius is a Western form of the Chinese title of "Master Kong" or "Kongfuzi."

Confucius felt that China was overrun with rude and dishonest people. Upset by the disorder and people's lack of decency, Confucius said that the Chinese needed to return to **ethics**, or moral values. The ideas of Confucius are known as **Confucianism**.

Confucius wanted China to return to ideas and practices from a time when people knew their proper roles in society. These are basic guidelines that Confucius thought would restore family order and social harmony:

- Fathers should display high moral values to inspire their families.
- Children should respect their parents and ancestors, an idea known as *filial piety*.
- All family members should be loyal to each other.

Confucius's ideas about government were similar to his ideas about family:

- Moral leadership, not laws, brought order to China.
- A king should lead by example, inspiring good behavior in all of his subjects.
- The lower classes would learn by following the example of their superiors. Confucius expressed this idea when he told kings:

> "Lead the people by means of government policies and regulate them through punishments, and they will be evasive and have no sense of shame. Lead them by means of virtue . . . and they will have a sense of shame and moreover have standards."
>
> –Confucius, from *The Analects*

SS.6.W.4.7 Explain the basic teachings of Laozi, Confucius, and Han Fei Zi.

BIOGRAPHY

Confucius
551–479 BC

Confucius, whose Chinese title is Kongfuzi, grew up in extreme poverty. Confucius was a dedicated student into his teenage years. Little is known about how he received his formal education, but he mastered many subjects, including music, mathematics, poetry, and history. He served in minor government positions, then he became a teacher. He never knew his teachings would transform Chinese life and thought.

Drawing Inferences How do you think Confucius's government jobs helped shape his teachings?

HISTORY

VIDEO
Confucius: Words of Wisdom

Online Resource

As Confucius traveled to many different regions, he earned the reputation of a respected teacher. His ideas were passed down through his students and later compiled into a book called *The Analects*.

Because Confucianism focuses on morality, family, society, and government, people often think of it as a philosophy or way of thinking. But it is much more. Confucianism is a unique teaching that is both philosophical and religious. It has been a guiding force in human behavior and religious understanding in China.

Confucius believed that when people behaved well and acted morally, they were simply carrying out what heaven expected of them. Over the centuries Confucius's ideas about virtue, kindness, and learning became the dominant beliefs in China.

READING CHECK Identifying Points of View
What did Confucius believe about good behavior?

HISTORIC DOCUMENT
The Analects

The followers of Confucius placed their teacher's sayings together in a work called in Chinese the Lun Yü *and in English* The Analects. *The word* analects *means "writings that have been collected."*

❝ Yu, shall I teach you what knowledge is? When you know a thing, say that you know it; when you do not know a thing, admit that you do not know it. That is knowledge.**❞**

❝ Is there any one word that can serve as a principle for . . . life? Perhaps the word is reciprocity [fairness]: Do not do to others what you would not want others to do to you.**❞**

❝ I do not enlighten anyone who is not eager to learn, nor encourage anyone who is not anxious to put his ideas into words.**❞**

–Confucius, from *The Analects*

ANALYSIS SKILL **ANALYZING PRIMARY SOURCES**
What are some of the qualities that Confucius valued?

Main Ideas of Confucianism

- People should be respectful and loyal to their family members.

- Leaders should be kind and lead by example.

- Learning is a process that never ends.

- Heaven expects people to behave well and act morally.

Daoism and Legalism

Other beliefs besides Confucianism influenced China during the Zhou period. Two in particular attracted many followers.

Daoism

Daoism (DOW-ih-zum) takes its name from *Dao,* meaning "the way." **Daoism** stressed living in harmony with the Dao, the guiding force of all reality. In Daoist teachings, the Dao gave birth to the universe and all things in it. Daoism developed in part as a reaction to Confucianism. Daoists didn't agree with the idea that active, involved leaders brought social harmony. Instead, they wanted the government to stay out of people's lives.

Daoists believed that people should avoid interfering with nature or each other. They should be like water and simply let things flow in a natural way. For Daoists, the ideal ruler was a wise man who was in harmony with the Dao. He would govern so effortlessly that his people would not even know they were being governed.

Daoists taught that the universe is a balance of opposites: female and male, light and dark, low and high. In each case, opposing forces should be in harmony.

While Confucianism focused its followers' attention on the human world, Daoists paid more attention to the natural world. Daoists regarded humans as just a part of nature, not better than any other thing. In time the Dao, as represented by nature, became so important to the Daoists that they worshipped it.

Laozi (LOWD-zuh) was the most famous Daoist teacher. He taught that people should not try to gain wealth, nor should they seek power. Laozi is credited with writing the basic text of Daoism, *The Way and Its Power.* Later writers created many legends about Laozi's achievements.

Legalism

Legalism, the belief that people were bad by nature and needed to be controlled, contrasted with both Confucianism and Daoism. Unlike the other two beliefs, Legalism was a political philosophy without religious concerns. Instead, it dealt only with government and social control. Followers of Legalism disagreed with the moral preaching of Confucius. Legalists also rejected Daoism because it didn't stress respect for authority.

Legalists, such as **Han Fei Zi** (HAHN-fay-zuh), felt that society needed strict laws to keep people in line and that punishments should fit crimes. For example, they believed that citizens should be held responsible for each other's conduct. A guilty person's relatives and neighbors should also be punished. This way, everyone would obey the laws.

Unity and efficiency were also important to Legalists. They wanted appointed officials, not nobles, to run China. Legalists wanted the empire to continue to expand. Therefore, they urged the state to always be prepared for war.

Confucianism, Daoism, and Legalism competed for followers. All three beliefs became popular, but the Legalists were the first to put their ideas into practice throughout China.

> **READING CHECK** **Contrasting** How did Daoism and Legalism differ in their theories about government?

BIOGRAPHY

Laozi
c. 500s or 400s BC

Scholars have found little reliable information about Laozi's life. Some believe that his book on Daoism was actually the work of several different authors. Most ancient sources of information about Laozi are myths. For example, one legend states that when Laozi was born, he was already an old man. In Chinese *Laozi* can mean "Old Baby." Over the years, many Daoists have worshipped Laozi as a supernatural being.

Drawing Inferences What do you think it meant to say Laozi was born "old"?

SUMMARY AND PREVIEW When the Zhou dynasty crumbled, political and social chaos erupted. In response, the new teachings of Confucianism, Daoism, and Legalism emerged. In the next section you will learn how the Qin dynasty applied the teachings of Legalism.

Section 2 Assessment

Reviewing Ideas, Terms, and People

1. **a. Identify** What is the mandate of heaven?
   b. Explain Describe the political order used by the Zhou kings to rule distant lands.
   c. Elaborate What happened when nobles began to reject the Zhou king's authority?
2. **a. Identify** Who was **Confucius**?
   b. Analyze Why did many of the teachings of Confucius focus on the family?
3. **a. Identify** Who was the most famous Daoist teacher?
   b. Summarize What were the main ideas of **Daoism**?
   c. Elaborate What might be some disadvantages of **Legalism**?

Critical Thinking

4. **Finding Main Ideas**
   Draw a chart like the one here. Use it and your notes on the Zhou dynasty to list two main ideas about each set of beliefs.

Confucianism	
Daoism	
Legalism	

FOCUS ON SPEAKING

5. **Exploring the Importance of Historical Figures** Many important people in history are rulers or conquerors. People who think and teach, however, have also played major roles in history. How did thinkers and teachers shape China's history? Write some ideas in your notebook.

The Qin Dynasty

LA.6.1.6.1, SS.6.E.1.1, SS.6.G.1.4,
SS.6.G.1.7, SS.6.G.2.2, SS.6.G.5.2,
SS.6.W.1.1, SS.6.W.1.2, SS.6.W.2.4,
SS.6.W.4.6, SS.6.W.4.8, SS.6.W.4.9

What You Will Learn...

Main Ideas

1. The first Qin emperor created a strong but strict government.
2. A unified China was created through Qin policies and achievements.

The Big Idea

The Qin dynasty unified China with a strong government and a system of standardization.

Key Terms and People

Shi Huangdi, *p. 172*
Great Wall, *p. 175*

Online Resource
TAKING NOTES

Use the graphic organizer online to take notes on the achievements and policies of Shi Huangdi. Note how he affected life in China.

SS.6.W.4.9 Identify key figures from classical and post classical China.

If YOU were there...

You are a scholar living in China in about 210 BC. You have a large library of Chinese literature, poetry, and philosophy. The new emperor is a harsh ruler with no love for learning. He says you must burn all the books that disagree with his ideas. The idea horrifies you. But if you do not obey, the punishment may be severe.

Will you obey the order to burn your books? Why or why not?

BUILDING BACKGROUND Different dynasties held very different ideas about how to rule. As the Zhou period declined, putting new ideas into effect brought great changes.

The Qin Emperor's Strong Government

The Warring States period marked a time in China when several states battled each other for power. One state, the Qin (CHIN), built a strong army that defeated the armies of the rivaling states. Eventually, the Qin dynasty united the country under one government.

Shi Huangdi Takes the Throne

In 221 BC, the Qin king Ying Zheng succeeded in unifying China. He gave himself the title **Shi Huangdi** (SHEE hwahng-dee), which means "first emperor." Shi Huangdi followed Legalist political beliefs. He created a strong government with strict laws and harsh punishments.

Time Line

The Qin Dynasty

c. 213 BC
Shi Huangdi orders book burnings.

c. 206 BC
The Qin dynasty collapses.

225 BC | 215 BC | 205 BC

221 BC
Emperor Shi Huangdi unifies China, beginning the Qin dynasty.

210 BC
Shi Huangdi dies.

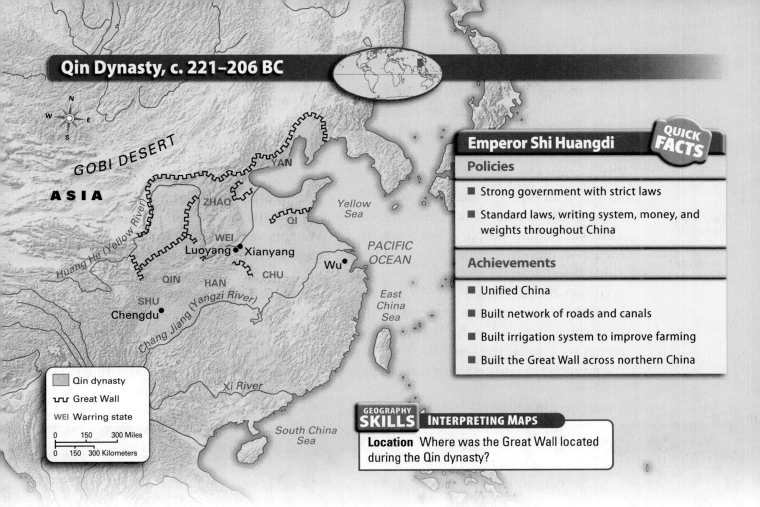

Qin Dynasty, c. 221–206 BC

GOBI DESERT

ASIA

Huang He (Yellow River)

YAN

ZHAO

QI

WEI

Luoyang • Xianyang

QIN

HAN

CHU

Wu •

SHU

Chengdu •

Chang Jiang (Yangzi River)

Xi River

Yellow Sea

PACIFIC OCEAN

East China Sea

South China Sea

Qin dynasty
ᒐᒐᒐ Great Wall
WEI Warring state

0   150   300 Miles
0   150   300 Kilometers

Emperor Shi Huangdi

QUICK FACTS

Policies

■ Strong government with strict laws

■ Standard laws, writing system, money, and weights throughout China

Achievements

■ Unified China

■ Built network of roads and canals

■ Built irrigation system to improve farming

■ Built the Great Wall across northern China

GEOGRAPHY SKILLS INTERPRETING MAPS

Location Where was the Great Wall located during the Qin dynasty?

Shi Huangdi demanded that everyone follow his policies. He ordered the burning of all writings that did not agree with Legalism. The only other books that were saved dealt with farming, medicine, and predicting the future. Many scholars opposed the book burnings. The emperor responded to the opposition by burying 460 scholars alive.

Shi Huangdi also used his armies to expand the empire. First, they occupied the lands around both of China's major rivers. Then his soldiers turned north and advanced almost to the Gobi Desert. To the south, they invaded more lands and advanced as far as the Xi River.

Shi Huangdi ensured that there would not be any future revolts in his new territories. When his soldiers conquered a city, he had them destroy its walls and take all the weapons.

China under the Qin

Shi Huangdi changed China's old political system. He claimed all the power and did not share it with the lords. He even took land away from them and forced thousands of nobles to move with their families to the capital so he could keep an eye on them. He also forced thousands of commoners to work on government building projects. Workers faced years of hardship, danger, and often, death.

To control China, Shi Huangdi divided it into districts, each with its own governor. Districts were subdivided into counties that were governed by appointed officials. This organization helped the emperor enforce his tax system. It also helped the Qin enforce a strict chain of command.

READING CHECK **Summarizing** How did Shi Huangdi strengthen the government?

A Unified China

Qin rule brought other major changes to China. Under Shi Huangdi, new policies and achievements united the Chinese people.

Qin Policies

FOCUS ON READING

How might you summarize the new Qin policies?

As you read earlier, mountains and rivers divided China into distinct regions. Customs varied, and people in each area had their own money, writing styles, and laws. Shi Huangdi wanted all Chinese people to do things the same way.

Early in his reign, the emperor set up a uniform system of law. Rules and punishments were to be the same in all parts of the empire. Shi Huangdi also standardized the written language. People everywhere were required to write using the same set of symbols. People from different regions could now communicate with each other in writing. This gave them a sense of shared culture and a common identity.

Next, the emperor set up a new money system. Standardized gold and copper coins became the currency used in all of China. Weights and measures were also standardized. Even the axle width of carts had to be the same. With all these changes and the unified writing system, trade between different regions became much easier. The Qin government strictly enforced these new standards. Any citizen who disobeyed the laws would face severe punishment.

Guardians of Shi Huangdi's Tomb

In 1974 archaeologists found the tomb of Emperor Shi Huangdi near Xi'an and made an amazing discovery. Buried close to the emperor was an army of more than 6,000 life-size terracotta, or clay, soldiers. They were designed to be with Shi Huangdi in the afterlife. In other nearby chambers of the tomb there were another 1,400 clay figures of cavalry and chariots.

MONGOLIA
Huang He (Yellow River)
Xi'an • Shi Huangdi's Tomb
CHINA
Chang Jiang (Yangzi River)

Qin Achievements

New, massive building projects also helped to unify the country. Under Shi Huangdi's rule, the Chinese built a network of roads that connected the capital to every part of the empire. These roads made travel easier for everyone. Each of these new roads was the same width, 50 paces wide. This design helped the army move quickly and easily to put down revolts in distant areas.

China's water system was also improved. Workers built canals to connect the country's rivers. Like the new roads, the canals improved transportation throughout the country. Using the new canals and rivers together made it easier and faster to ship goods from north to south. In addition, the Qin built an irrigation system to make more land good for farming. Parts of that system are still in use today.

Shi Huangdi also wanted to protect the country from invasion. Nomads from the north were fierce warriors, and they were a real threat to China. Hoping to stop them from invading, the emperor built the **Great Wall**, a barrier that linked earlier walls across China's northern frontier. The first section of the wall had been built in the 600s BC to keep invading groups out of China. The Qin connected earlier pieces of the wall to form a long, unbroken structure. Building the wall required years of labor from hundreds of thousands of workers. Many of them died building the wall.

SS.6.G.5.2 Use geographic terms and tools to explain why ancient civilizations developed networks of highways, waterways, and other transportation linkages.

THE IMPACT TODAY

The Great Wall is a major tourist attraction today.

HISTORY

VIDEO
The First Emperor of China

↗ Online Resource

Each terra-cotta soldier was different, with its own facial features, hairstyle, and unique expression. Here, a computer model shows what a soldier might have looked like when it was created.

The Great Wall has been added to and rebuilt many times since Shi Huangdi ruled China.

Rebel forces formed across the country. Each claimed to have received the mandate of heaven to replace the emperor. One of these groups attacked the Qin capital, and the new emperor surrendered. The palace was burned to the ground. Qin authority had disappeared. With no central government, the country fell into civil war.

READING CHECK **Recall** What massive building projects did Shi Huangdi order to unify China?

The Fall of the Qin

Shi Huangdi's policies unified China. However, his policies also stirred resentment. Many peasants, scholars, and nobles hated his harsh ways.

Still, Shi Huangdi was powerful enough to hold the country together. When he died in 210 BC China was unified, but that didn't last. Within a few years, the government began to fall apart.

SUMMARY AND PREVIEW Qin emperor Shi Huangdi's policies and achievements unified China, but his harsh rule led to resentment. After his death, the dynasty fell apart. In the next section you will learn about the Han dynasty that came to power after the end of the Qin.

Section 3 Assessment

Reviewing Ideas, Terms, and People

1. **a. Identify** What does the title **Shi Huangdi** mean?
   b. Explain After unifying China, why did Shi Huangdi divide the country into military districts?
   c. Rate Which of the following acts do you think best showed how powerful Shi Huangdi was—burning books, forcing nobles to move, or forcing commoners to work on government projects? Explain your answer.
2. **a. Recall** Why was the **Great Wall** built?
   b. Summarize What actions did Shi Huangdi take to unify China and standardize things within the empire?
   c. Evaluate In your opinion, was Shi Huangdi a good ruler? Explain your answer.

Critical Thinking

3. **Evaluating** Using your notes and a diagram like this one, rank the effectiveness of the emperor's achievements and policies in unifying China.

Most important   Least important

| 1. | 2. | 3. |

FOCUS ON SPEAKING

4. **Evaluating Contributions to History** When evaluating a person's contribution to history, it is important to consider both the person's good impact and bad impact. In what ways was Shi Huangdi great? What negative impact did he have on China? Write down your ideas.

Emperor Shi Huangdi

If you were a powerful ruler, how would you protect yourself?

When did he live? c. 259–210 BC

Where did he live? Shi Huangdi built a new capital city at Xianyang, now called Xi'an (SHEE-AHN), in eastern China.

What did he do? Shi Huangdi didn't trust people. Several attempts were made on his life, and the emperor lived in fear of more attacks. He was constantly seeking new ways to protect himself and extend his life. By the time Shi Huangdi died, he didn't even trust his own advisors. Even in death, he surrounded himself with protectors: the famous terra-cotta army.

Why is he important? Shi Huangdi was one of the most powerful rulers in Chinese history. The first ruler to unify all of China, he is also remembered for his building programs. He built roads and canals throughout China and expanded what would become the Great Wall.

Drawing Conclusions Why do you think Shi Huangdi feared for his life?

KEY EVENTS

● **246 BC** Shi Huangdi becomes emperor. Because he is still young, a high official rules in his name.

● **238 BC** He exiles the official, whom he suspects of plotting against him, and rules alone.

● **227 BC** An assassination attempt adds fuel to the emperor's paranoia.

● **221 BC** Shi Huangdi unites all of China under his rule.

HISTORY VIDEO
Omens in Ancient China

Online Resource

This painting shows Shi Huangdi's servants burning books and attacking scholars.

SS.6.E.1.2, SS.6.G.1.4, SS.6.G.1.5,
SS.6.G.1.7, SS.6.G.2.2, SS.6.G.4.1,
SS.6.G.6.2, SS.6.W.1.1, SS.6.W.1.2,
SS.6.W.2.4, SS.6.W.4.6, SS.6.W.4.8, SS.6.W.4.9

What You Will Learn...

Main Ideas

1. Han dynasty government was based on the ideas of Confucius.
2. Family life was supported and strengthened in Han China.
3. The Han made many achievements in art, literature, and learning.

The Big Idea

The Han dynasty created a new form of government that valued family, art, and learning.

Key Terms

sundial, p. 182
seismograph, p. 182
acupuncture, p. 183

Online Resource
TAKING NOTES

Use the graphic organizer online to take notes on Han government, family life, and achievements.

The Han Dynasty

If YOU were there...

You are a young Chinese student from a poor family. Your family has worked hard to give you a good education so that you can get a government job and have a great future. Your friends laugh at you. They say that only boys from wealthy families win the good jobs. They think it is better to join the army.

Will you take the exam or join the army? Why?

BUILDING BACKGROUND Though it was harsh, the rule of the first Qin emperor helped to unify northern China. With the building of the Great Wall, he strengthened defenses on the northern frontier. But his successor could not hold on to power. The Qin gave way to a remarkable new dynasty that would last for 400 years.

Han Dynasty Government

When the Qin dynasty collapsed in 207 BC, several different groups battled for power. After several years of fighting, an army led by Liu Bang (lee-oo bang) won control. Liu Bang became the first emperor of the Han dynasty. This Chinese dynasty lasted for more than 400 years.

The Rise of a New Dynasty

Liu Bang, a peasant, was able to become emperor in large part because of the Chinese belief in the mandate of heaven. He was the first common person to become emperor. He earned people's

Time Line

The Han Dynasty

206 BC
The Han dynasty begins.

AD 220
The Han dynasty falls.

200 BC | BC 1 AD | AD 200

140 BC
Wudi becomes emperor and tries to strengthen China's government.

AD 25
The Han move their capital east to Luoyang.

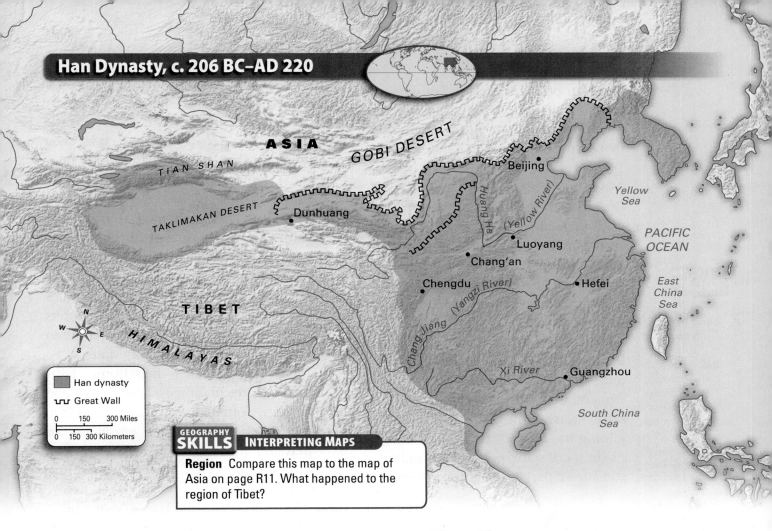

ASIA

GOBI DESERT

TIAN SHAN

TAKLIMAKAN DESERT

Dunhuang

Beijing

Huang He (Yellow River)

Yellow Sea

PACIFIC OCEAN

Luoyang

Chang'an

Chengdu

(Yangzi River)

Hefei

East China Sea

TIBET

HIMALAYAS

Chang Jiang

Xi River

Guangzhou

South China Sea

Han dynasty

Great Wall

0   150   300 Miles

0   150   300 Kilometers

GEOGRAPHY SKILLS **INTERPRETING MAPS**

Region Compare this map to the map of Asia on page R11. What happened to the region of Tibet?

loyalty and trust. In addition, he was well liked by both soldiers and peasants, which helped him to maintain control.

Liu Bang's rule was different from the strict Legalism of the Qin. He wanted to free people from harsh government policies. He lowered taxes for farmers and made punishments less severe. He gave large blocks of land to his supporters.

In addition to setting new policies, Liu Bang changed the way government worked. He set up a government structure that built on the foundation begun by the Qin. He also relied on educated officials to help him rule.

Wudi Creates a New Government

In 140 BC Emperor Wudi (WOO-dee), also spelled Wu-ti, took the throne. He wanted to create a stronger central government.

He took land from the lords, raised taxes, and placed the supply of grain under the control of the government.

Under Wudi, Confucianism became China's official government philosophy. Government officials were expected to practice Confucianism. Wudi even began a university to teach Confucian ideas.

If a person passed an exam on Confucian teachings, he could get a good position in the government. However, not just anyone could take the test. The exams were only open to people who had been recommended for government service already. As a result, wealthy or influential families continued to control the government.

READING CHECK **Analyzing** How was the Han government based on the ideas of Confucius?

Family Life

The Han period was a time of great social change in China. Class structure became more rigid. Confucian ideas about the family became important in Chinese society.

Social Classes

Based on the Confucian system, people were divided into four classes. The upper class was made up of the emperor, his court, and scholars who held government positions. The second class, the largest, was made up of the peasants. Next were artisans who produced items for daily life and some luxury goods. Merchants occupied the lowest class because they did not produce anything. They only bought and sold what others made. The military was not an official class in the Confucian system. Still, joining the army offered men a chance to rise in social status because the military was considered part of the government.

This Han artifact is an oil lamp held by a servant.

Lives of Rich and Poor

The classes only divided people into social rank. They did not indicate wealth or power. For instance, even though peasants made up the second highest class, they were poor. On the other hand, some merchants were wealthy and powerful despite being in the lowest class.

People's lifestyles varied according to wealth. The emperor and his court lived in a large palace. Less important officials lived in multilevel houses built around courtyards. Many of these wealthy families owned large estates and employed laborers to work the land. Some families even hired private armies to defend their estates.

The wealthy filled their homes with expensive decorations. These included paintings, pottery, bronze lamps, and jade figures. Rich families hired musicians for entertainment. Even the tombs of dead family members were filled with beautiful, expensive objects.

Most people in the Han dynasty, however, didn't live like the wealthy. Nearly 60 million people lived in China during the Han dynasty, and about 90 percent of them were peasants who lived in the countryside. Peasants put in long, tiring days working the land. Whether it was in the millet fields of the north or in the rice paddies of the south, the work was hard. In the winter, peasants were also forced to work on building projects for the government. Heavy taxes and bad weather forced many farmers to sell their land and work for rich landowners. By the last years of the Han dynasty, only a few farmers were independent.

Chinese peasants lived simple lives. They wore plain clothing made of fiber from a native plant. The main foods they ate were cooked grains like barley. Most peasants lived in small villages. Their small, wood-framed houses had walls made of mud or stamped earth.

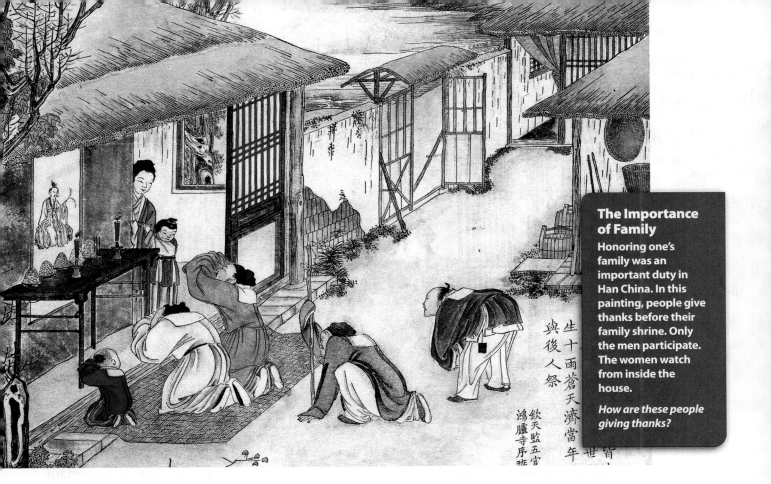

The Importance of Family
Honoring one's family was an important duty in Han China. In this painting, people give thanks before their family shrine. Only the men participate. The women watch from inside the house.

How are these people giving thanks?

生十　兩蒼天濟當年
與後人祭

欽天監五官
鴻臚寺序班

The Revival of the Family

Since Confucianism was the official government philosophy during Wudi's reign, Confucian teachings about the family were also honored. Children were taught from birth to respect their elders. Disobeying one's parents was a crime. Even emperors had a duty to respect their parents.

Confucius had taught that the father was the head of the family. Within the family, the father had absolute power. It was a woman's duty to obey her husband, and children had to obey their father.

Han officials believed that filial piety was central to keeping order: If a family was strong and obeyed the father, then it would obey the emperor and order would be maintained. Since the Han stressed respect for elders, some men even gained government jobs based on the respect they showed their parents.

Children were encouraged to serve their parents. They were also expected to honor dead parents with ceremonies and offerings. All family members were expected to care for family burial sites.

Chinese parents valued boys more highly than girls. This was because sons carried on the family line and took care of their parents when they were old. On the other hand, daughters became part of their husband's family. According to a Chinese proverb, "Raising daughters is like raising children for another family." Some women, however, still gained power. They could actually influence their sons' families. An older widow could even become the head of the family.

READING CHECK **Identifying Cause and Effect**
Why did the family take on such importance during the Han dynasty?

Han Achievements

During the Han dynasty, the Chinese made many advances in art and learning. Some of these advances are shown here.

Science

This is a model of an ancient Chinese seismograph. When an earthquake struck, a lever inside caused a ball to drop from a dragon's mouth into a toad's mouth, indicating the direction from which the earthquake had come.

SS.6.W.4.8 Describe the contributions of classical and post classical China.

ACADEMIC VOCABULARY

innovation a new idea, method, or device

Han Achievements

Han rule was a time of great accomplishments. Art and literature thrived, and inventors developed many useful devices.

Art and Literature

The Chinese of the Han period produced many works of art. They became experts at figure painting—a style of painting that includes portraits of people. Portraits often showed religious figures and Confucian scholars. Han artists also painted realistic scenes from everyday life. Their creations covered the walls of palaces and tombs.

In literature, Han China is known for its poetry. Poets developed new styles of verse, including the *fu* style which was the most popular. *Fu* poets combined prose and poetry to create long works of literature. Another style, called *shi*, featured short lines of verse that could be sung. Han rulers hired poets known for the beauty of their verse.

Han writers also produced important works of history. One historian by the name of Sima Qian wrote a complete history of all the dynasties through the early Han. His format and style became the model for later historical writings.

Inventions and Advances

The Han Chinese invented one item that we use every day—paper. They made it by grinding plant fibers, such as mulberry bark and hemp, into a paste. Then they let it dry in sheets. Chinese scholars produced "books" by pasting several pieces of paper together into a long sheet. Then they rolled the sheet into a scroll.

The Han also made other **innovations** in science. These included the sundial and the seismograph. A **sundial** uses the position of shadows cast by the sun to tell the time of day. The sundial was an early type of clock. A **seismograph** is a device that measures the strength of an earthquake. Han emperors were very interested

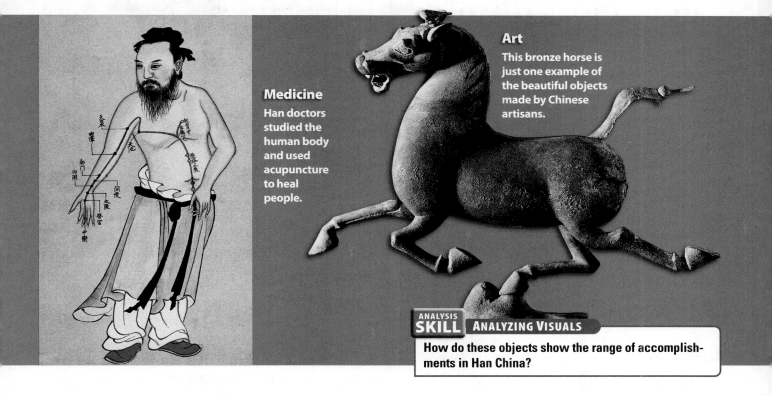

Medicine
Han doctors studied the human body and used acupuncture to heal people.

Art
This bronze horse is just one example of the beautiful objects made by Chinese artisans.

ANALYSIS SKILL ANALYZING VISUALS

How do these objects show the range of accomplishments in Han China?

in knowing about the movements of the earth. They believed that earthquakes were signs of future evil events.

Another Han innovation, acupuncture (AK-yoo-punk-cher), improved medicine. **Acupuncture** is the practice of inserting fine needles through the skin at specific points to cure disease or relieve pain. Many Han inventions in science and medicine are still used today.

READING CHECK Categorizing What advances did the Chinese make during the Han period?

SUMMARY AND PREVIEW Han rulers moved away from Legalism and based their government on Confucianism. This strengthened family bonds in Han China. In addition, art and learning thrived under Han rule. In the next section you will learn about China's contact beyond its borders.

Section 4 Assessment

Reviewing Ideas, Terms, and People

1. **a. Identify** Whose teachings were the foundation for government during the Han dynasty?
   b. Summarize How did Emperor Wudi create a strong central government?
   c. Evaluate Do you think that an exam system is the best way to make sure that people are fairly chosen for government jobs? Why or why not?
2. **a. Describe** What was the son's role in the family?
   b. Contrast How did living conditions for the wealthy differ from those of the peasants during the Han dynasty?
3. **Identify** What device did the Chinese invent to measure the strength of earthquakes?

Critical Thinking

4. **Analyzing** Use your notes to complete this diagram about how Confucianism influenced Han government and family.

Government
↑↓
Confucianism
↑↓
Family

FOCUS ON SPEAKING

5. **Analyzing Impact on History** Sometimes a ruler has the biggest impact on history. Other times, ideas that develop within a society have a greater impact. Which had a greater impact on Han China? Why?

from The Shiji

by Sima Qian

Translated by Burton Watson

WORD HELP

intervals periods of time
dispatched sent
envoy representative

❶ Henan (HUH-NAHN) is a region of eastern China. It is a productive agricultural region.

❷ The Xiongnu were a tribe of nomads. They lived in the north and often raided towns near China's border.

❸ *Why do you think the emperor invites Bu Shi to work for the government?*

About the Reading *The* Shiji, *also called the* Records of the Grand Historian, *is a history that describes more than two thousand years of Chinese culture. The author, Sima Qian (soo-MAH chee-EN), held the title Grand Historian under the Han emperor Wudi. He spent 18 years of his life writing the* Shiji. *His hard work paid off, and his history was well received. In fact, the* Shiji *was so respected that it served as the model for every later official history of China. This passage describes a man named Bu Shi, who attracted the emperor's attention through his generosity and good deeds. Eventually, the emperor invited him to live in the imperial palace.*

AS YOU READ Ask yourself why Sima Qian included Bu Shi in his history.

Bu Shi was a native of Henan, where his family made a living by farming and animal raising. **❶** When his parents died, Bu Shi left home, handing over the house, the lands, and all the family wealth to his younger brother, who by this time was full grown. For his own share, he took only a hundred or so of the sheep they had been raising, which he led off into the mountains to pasture. In the course of ten years or so, Bu Shi's sheep had increased to over a thousand and he had bought his own house and fields. His younger brother in the meantime had failed completely in the management of the farm, but Bu Shi promptly handed over to him a share of his own wealth. This happened several times. Just at that time the Han was sending its generals at frequent intervals to attack the Xiongnu. **❷** Bu Shi journeyed to the capital and submitted a letter to the throne, offering to turn over half of his wealth to the district officials to help in the defense of the border. The emperor dispatched an envoy to ask if Bu Shi wanted a post in the government. **❸**

"From the time I was a child," Bu Shi replied, "I have been an animal raiser. I have had no experience in government and would certainly not want such a position" . . .

"If that is the case," said the envoy, "then what is your objective in making this offer?"

Bu Shi replied, "The Son of Heaven has set out to punish the Xiongnu. ❹ In my humble opinion, every worthy man should be willing to fight to the death to defend the borders, and every person with wealth ought to contribute to the expense . . ."

The emperor discussed the matter with the chancellor, but the latter said, "The proposal is simply not in accord with human nature! ❺ Such eccentric people are of no use in guiding the populace, but only throw the laws into confusion. I beg Your Majesty not to accept his offer!"

For this reason the emperor put off answering Bu Shi for a long time, and finally after several years had passed, turned down the offer, whereupon Bu Shi went back to his fields and pastures . . .

The following year a number of poor people were transferred to other regions . . . At this point Bu Shi took two hundred thousand cash of his own and turned the sum over to the governor of Henan to assist the people who were emigrating to other regions . . . At this time the rich families were all scrambling to hide their wealth; only Bu Shi, unlike the others, had offered to contribute to the expenses of the government. ❻ The emperor decided that Bu Shi was really a man of exceptional worth after all . . . Because of his simple, unspoiled ways and his deep loyalty, the emperor finally appointed him grand tutor to his son Liu Hong, the king of Qi.

GUIDED READING

WORD HELP

objective goal
chancellor high official
accord agreement
eccentric someone who acts strangely
populace people
tutor private teacher

❹ The Chinese people believed that their emperor was the "Son of Heaven." They thought he received his power from heavenly ancestors.

❺ The "latter" means the one mentioned last. In this case, the latter is the chancellor.

❻ *What is Bu Shi's attitude toward his wealth? How is it different from the attitude of the rich families?*

In this painting from the 1600s, government officials deliver a letter.

CONNECTING LITERATURE TO HISTORY

1. **Drawing Conclusions** Like many Chinese historians, Sima Qian wanted to use history to teach lessons. What lessons could the story of Bu Shi be used to teach?

2. **Analyzing** The Emperor Wudi based his government on the teachings of Confucius. What elements of Confucianism can you see in this story?

FL SS.6.E.1.1, SS.6.E.1.3, SS.6.E.3.2, SS.6.E.3.4, SS.6.G.1.4, SS.6.G.1.7, SS.6.G.2.1, SS.6.G.2.6, SS.6.G.4.4, SS.6.G.5.1, SS.6.G.5.2, SS.6.W.2.4, SS.6.W.4.4, SS.6.W.4.8, SS.6.W.4.10

What You Will Learn...

Main Ideas

1. Farming and manufacturing grew during the Han dynasty.
2. Trade routes linked China with the Middle East and Rome.
3. Buddhism came to China from India and gained many followers.

The Big Idea

Trade routes led to the exchange of new products and ideas among China, Rome, and other lands.

Key Terms

silk, *p. 187*
Silk Road, *p. 187*
diffusion, *p. 189*

 **Online Resource**
TAKING NOTES

Use the graphic organizer online to take notes on Chinese products and trade routes and on the arrival of Buddhism in China.

Han Contacts with Other Cultures

If YOU were there...

You are a trader traveling along the Silk Road to China. This is your first journey, but you have heard many stories about the country. You know the trip will be hard, through mountains and deserts and terrible weather. While you expect to make a good profit from silk, you are also curious about China and its people.

What do you expect to find in China?

BUILDING BACKGROUND During the Han dynasty Chinese society returned its focus to Confucian ideas, and new inventions were developed. In addition, increased trade allowed other countries to learn about the rich culture of China.

Farming and Manufacturing

Many advances in manufacturing took place during the Han dynasty. As a result, productivity increased and the empire prospered. These changes paved the way for China to make contact with people of other cultures.

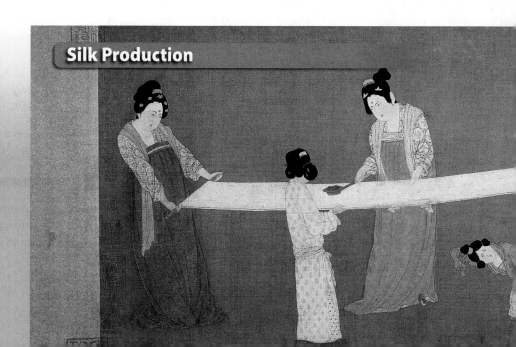
Silk Production

By the Han period, the Chinese had become master ironworkers. They manufactured iron swords and armor that made the army more powerful.

Farmers also gained from advances in iron. The iron plow and the wheelbarrow, a single-wheeled cart, increased farm output. With a wheelbarrow a farmer could haul more than 300 pounds all by himself. With an iron plow, he could till more land and raise more food.

Another item that increased in production during the Han dynasty was **silk**, a soft, light, highly valued fabric. For centuries, Chinese women had known the complicated methods needed to raise silkworms, unwind the silk threads of their cocoons, and then prepare the threads for dyeing and weaving. The Chinese were determined to keep their **procedure** for making silk a secret. Revealing these secrets was punishable by death.

During the Han period, weavers used foot-powered looms to weave silk threads into beautiful fabric. Garments made from this silk were very expensive.

READING CHECK **Finding Main Ideas** How did advances in technology affect farming and silk production?

Trade Routes

Chinese goods, especially silk and fine pottery, were highly valued by people in other lands. During the Han period, the value of these goods to people outside China helped increase trade.

Expansion of Trade

Trade increased partly because Han armies conquered lands deep in Central Asia. Leaders there told the Han generals that people who lived still farther west wanted silk. At the same time, Emperor Wudi wanted strong, sturdy Central Asian horses for his army. China's leaders saw that they could make a profit by bringing silk to Central Asia and trading the cloth for the horses. The Central Asian peoples would then take the silk west and trade it for other products they wanted.

The Silk Road

Traders used a series of overland routes to take Chinese goods to distant buyers. The most famous trade route was known as the **Silk Road**. This 4,000-mile-long network of routes stretched westward from China across Asia's deserts and mountain ranges, through the Middle East, until it reached the Mediterranean Sea.

PHOTOGRAPH © 2012 MUSEUM OF FINE ARTS, BOSTON

The technique for making silk was a well-kept secret in ancient China, as silk was a valuable trade good in distant lands. Workers made silk from the cocoons of silkworms, just as they do today.

Chinese traders did not travel the entire Silk Road. Upon reaching Central Asia, they sold their goods to local traders who would take them the rest of the way.

Traveling the Silk Road was difficult. Hundreds of men and camels loaded down with valuable goods, including silks and jade, formed groups. They traveled the Silk Road together for protection. Armed guards were hired to protect traders from bandits who stole cargo and water, a precious necessity. Weather presented other dangers. Traders faced icy blizzards, desert heat, and blinding sandstorms.

Named after the most famous item transported along it, the Silk Road was worth its many risks. Silk was so popular in Rome, for example, that China grew wealthy from that trade relationship alone. Traders returned from Rome with silver, gold, precious stones, and horses.

READING CHECK **Categorize** What goods did China export along the Silk Road?

Buddhism Comes to China

When the Chinese people came into contact with other civilizations, they exchanged ideas along with trade goods. Among these ideas was a new religion. In the first century AD Buddhism spread from India to China along the Silk Road and other trade routes.

Arrival of a New Religion

Over time, the Han government became less stable. People ignored laws, and violence was common. As rebellions flared up, millions of peasants went hungry. Life became violent and uncertain. Many Chinese looked to Daoism or Confucianism to find out why they had to suffer so much, but they didn't find helpful answers.

Buddhism seemed to provide more hope than the traditional Chinese beliefs did. It offered rebirth and relief from suffering. This promise was a major reason the Chinese people embraced Buddhism.

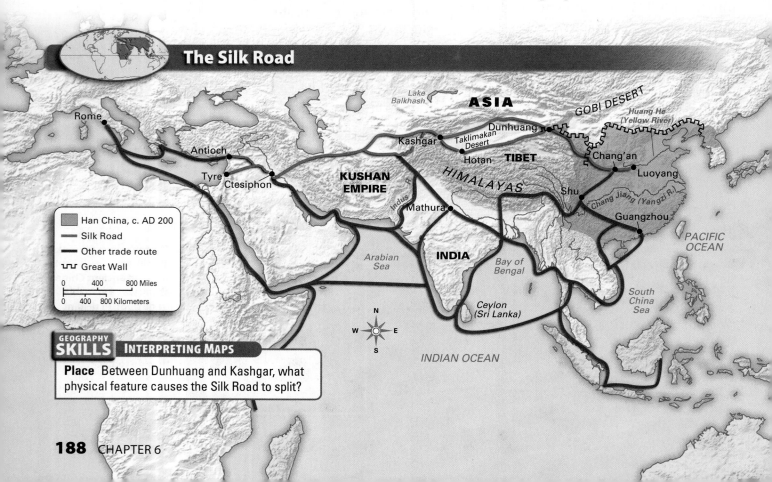

The Silk Road

Han China, c. AD 200
Silk Road
Other trade route
Great Wall

0   400   800 Miles
0 400 800 Kilometers

GEOGRAPHY SKILLS **INTERPRETING MAPS**

Place Between Dunhuang and Kashgar, what physical feature causes the Silk Road to split?

Impact on China

At first, Indian Buddhists had trouble explaining their religion to the Chinese. Then they used ideas found in Daoism to help describe Buddhist beliefs. Many people grew curious about Buddhism.

Before long, Buddhism caught on in China with both the poor and the upper classes. By AD 200, Buddhist altars stood in the emperor's palace.

Buddhism's introduction to China is an example of **diffusion**, the spread of ideas, goods, and technology from one culture to another. Elements of Chinese culture changed in response to the new faith. For example, scholars translated Buddhist texts into Chinese. Many Chinese became Buddhist monks and nuns. Artists carved towering statues of Buddha into mountain walls.

READING CHECK **Finding Main Ideas** How did Chinese people learn of Buddhism?

SUMMARY AND PREVIEW Under the Han, trade brought new goods and ideas, including Buddhism, to China. In the next chapter you'll read about the religion of another people—the Jews.

This giant Buddha statue in China is among the largest in the world. It was carved from a hillside and looks down over the meeting place of three rivers.

SS.6.G.2.6 Explain the concept of cultural diffusion, and identify the influences of different ancient cultures on one another.

Section 5 Assessment

Reviewing Ideas, Terms, and People

1. **a. Describe** How did wheelbarrows help farmers?
   b. Summarize How was **silk** made in ancient China?
   c. Elaborate Why did the Chinese keep silk-making methods a secret?

2. **a. Identify** Where did the **Silk Road** begin and end?
   b. Elaborate What information would you use to support the argument that the silk trade must have been very valuable?

3. **a. Identify** What is **diffusion**?
   b. Make Generalizations What Buddhist beliefs appealed to millions of Chinese peasants?

Critical Thinking

4. **Categorizing** Copy the chart here. Use it and your notes on trade to identify goods and ideas that were exchanged along the Silk Road, both into and out of China.

Into China

Trade Along the Silk Road

Out of China

FOCUS ON SPEAKING

5. **Evaluating the Importance of Events** Not all the important events in history are wars or invasions. What peaceful events in this section changed Chinese history? Write down some ideas.

The Silk Road

The Silk Road was a long trade route that stretched across the heart of Asia. Along this route, an active trade developed between China and Southwest Asia by about 100 BC. By AD 100, the Silk Road connected Han China in the east with the Roman Empire in the west.

The main goods traded along the Silk Road were luxury goods—ones that were small, light, and expensive. These included goods like silk, spices, and gold. Because they were small and valuable, merchants could carry these goods long distances and still sell them for a large profit. As a result, people in both the east and the west were able to buy luxury goods that were unavailable at home.

GAUL

SPAIN

EUROPE

Aral Sea

Rome

ROMAN EMPIRE

Black Sea

Caspian Sea

Merv

Byzantium

Carthage

GREECE

Asia Minor

Antioch

Ecbatana

Mediterranean Sea

Ctesiphon

Babylon

Alexandria

PERSIA

Petra

Persepolis

AFRICA

Goods from the West Roman merchants like this man grew rich from Silk Road trade. Merchants in the west traded goods like those you see here—wool, amber, and gold.

Aden

A S I A

Goods from the East Chinese merchants also got rich from Silk Road trade. Valuable Asian goods included silk cloth, jade objects, and spices like cinnamon, nutmeg, and ginger that didn't grow in Europe.

• Kaifeng

• Wuwei

Chang'an •

HAN EMPIRE

Chengdu •

TAKLIMAKAN DESERT

• Kashgar

HIMALAYAS

• Bagram

A Network of Roads The Silk Road was actually a network of roads that linked trading centers in Asia. Most merchants only traveled a small part of the Silk Road, selling their goods along the way to other traders from distant lands.

Kandahar

South China Sea

India

N
W E
S

Silk Road
Other trade routes
Han Empire
Roman Empire
Scale varies on this map.

GEOGRAPHY SKILLS ▶ **INTERPRETING MAPS** ▶

1. **Place** What two empires did the Silk Road connect by AD 100?
2. **Movement** What were some goods traded along the Silk Road?

N D I A N   O C E A N

Social Studies Skills

Conducting Internet Research

Understand the Skill

The Internet is a huge network of computers that are linked together. You can connect to this network from a personal computer or from a computer at a public library or school. Once connected, you can go to places called Web sites. Web sites consist of one or more Web pages. Each page contains information that you can view on the computer screen.

Governments, businesses, individuals, and many different types of organizations such as universities, news organizations, and libraries have Web sites. Most library Web sites allow users to search their card catalog electronically. Many libraries also have databases on their Web sites. A database is a large collection of related information that is organized by topic.

The Internet can be a very good reference source. It allows you to gather information on almost any topic without ever having to leave your chair. However, finding the information you need can sometimes be difficult. Having the skill to use the Internet efficiently increases its usefulness.

Learn the Skill

There are millions of Web sites on the Internet. This can make it hard to locate specific information. The following steps will help you in doing research on the Internet.

1. **Use a search engine.** This is a Web site that searches other sites. Type a word or phrase related to your topic into the search engine. It will list Web pages that might contain information on your topic. Clicking on an entry in this list will bring that page to your screen.

2. **Study the Web page.** Read the information to see if it is useful. You can print the page on the computer's printer or take notes. If you take notes, be sure to include the page's URL. This is its location or "address" on the Internet. You need this as the source of the information.

3. **Use hyperlinks.** Many Web pages have connections, called hyperlinks, to related information on the site or on other Web sites. Clicking on these links will take you to those pages. You can follow their links to even more pages, collecting information as you go.

4. **Return to your results list.** If the information or hyperlinks on a Web page are not useful, return to the list of pages that your search engine produced and repeat the process.

The Internet is a useful tool. But remember that information on the Internet is no different than printed resources. It must be evaluated with the same care and critical thinking as other resources.

Practice and Apply the Skill

Answer the following questions to apply the guidelines to Internet research on ancient China.

1. How would you begin if you wanted information about the Qin Dynasty from the Internet?

2. What words might you type into a search engine to find information about Confucianism?

3. Use a school computer to research the Great Wall of China. What kinds of pages did your search produce? Evaluate the usefulness of each type.

Chapter Review

Visual Summary

Use the visual summary below to help you review the main ideas of the chapter.

QUICK FACTS

Chinese civilization began along the Huang He (Yellow River).

During the Zhou dynasty, armies fought for power, and the ideas of Confucius spread.

The Qin dynasty unified China with a strong government.

During the Han dynasty, China made advances in learning, and Buddhism spread.

Reviewing Vocabulary, Terms, and People

Match the "I" statement with the person or thing that might have made the statement. Not all of the choices will be used.

a. jade

b. innovation

c. lord

d. oracle

e. peasant

f. Confucius

g. Daoism

h. Shi Huangdi

i. seismograph

j. wheelbarrow

k. Great Wall

l. Legalism

1. "I stressed the importance of living in harmony with nature."

2. "I took a name that means 'first emperor.'"

3. "I stressed that people needed to be controlled with strict laws."

4. "I am a beautiful, hard gemstone that the Chinese made into many objects."

5. "I was built to keep invaders from attacking China."

6. "I can measure the strength of an earthquake."

7. "I am a person of high rank."

8. "I am a new idea, method, or device."

9. "I emphasized the importance of moral values and respect for the family."

10. "I am a farmer who tills a small plot of land."

Comprehension and Critical Thinking

SECTION 1 *(Pages 160–165)*

11. **a. Identify** In what region did the Shang dynasty develop?

 b. Analyze How did China's geography contribute to the country's isolation?

 c. Evaluate Considering the evidence, do you think the Xia dynasty was really China's first dynasty or a myth? Explain your answer.

SECTION 2 (Pages 166–171)

12. a. Identify Which Chinese philosophy encouraged strict laws and severe punishments to keep order?

b. Analyze How would Confucianism benefit Chinese emperors?

c. Evaluate Would you be happier under a government influenced by Legalism or by Daoism? In which type of government would there be more order? Explain your answers.

SECTION 3 (Pages 172–176)

13. a. Describe What were the main reasons for the fall of the Qin dynasty?

b. Make Inferences Why did Shi Huangdi's armies destroy city walls and take weapons from people they conquered?

c. Evaluate Shi Huangdi was a powerful ruler. Was his rule good or bad for China? Why?

SECTION 4 (Pages 178–183)

14. a. Identify During the Han dynasty, who belonged to the first and second social groups?

b. Analyze What was the purpose of the exam system during Wudi's rule?

c. Elaborate What inventions show that the Chinese studied nature?

SECTION 5 (Pages 186–189)

15. a. Identify What factors led to the growth of trade during the Han dynasty?

b. Calculate Your caravan has traveled 500 miles of the Silk Road in 25 days. The goods you are carrying still have 3,500 miles to travel. Write a mathematical expression to determine how many more days it will take to complete the route if the subsequent traders can travel at the same rate.

Reviewing Themes

16. Politics Why might historians differ in their views of Shi Huangdi's success as a ruler?

17. Society and Culture How did Confucianism affect people's roles in their family, in government, and in society?

Using the Internet

18. Activity: Solving Problems Confucius was one of the most influential teachers in Chinese history. His ideas suggested ways to restore order in Chinese society. Go online to research Confucianism. Take note of the political and cultural problems Confucianism tried to address. Then investigate some of the current political and cultural problems in the United States. Could Confucianism solve problems in the United States? Prepare a persuasive argument to support your answer.

Reading Skills

19. Summarizing Historical Texts From the chapter, choose a subsection under a blue headline. For each paragraph within that subsection, write a sentence that summarizes the paragraph's main idea. Continue with the other subsections under the blue heading to create a study guide.

Social Studies Skills

20. Conducting Internet Research Find a topic in the chapter about which you would like to know more. Use the Internet to explore your topic. Compare the sources you find to determine which seem most complete and reliable. Write a short paragraph about your results.

FOCUS ON SPEAKING

21. Giving Your Oral Presentation You have chosen a person or event and know why your choice was important to Chinese history. Now you must convince your classmates.

First, write a brief description of what the person did or what happened during the event. Then summarize why your person or event is important to Chinese history.

When you give your oral presentation, use vivid language to create pictures in your listeners' minds. Also, use a clear but lively tone of voice.

Florida Standardized Test Practice

DIRECTIONS: Read each question, and write the letter of the best response.

1

> The connecting link between serving one's father and serving one's mother is love. The connecting link between serving one's father and serving one's prince is reverence [respect]. Thus the mother [brings forth] love, while the prince brings forth reverence. But to the father belong both—love and reverence . . . Likewise, to serve one's elders reverently paves the way for civic obedience.

The observation and advice in this passage *best* express the teachings of

A Buddhism.

B Confucianism.

C Daoism.

D Legalism.

2 Which feature of China's physical geography did *not* separate its early people from the rest of the world?

A the Gobi

B the Huang-He

C the Pacific Ocean

D the Tibetan Plateau

3 How did the Qin emperor Shi Huangdi unify and control China in the 200s BC?

A He created districts and counties that were governed by appointed officials.

B He gave land to China's nobles so that they would be loyal to him.

C He dissolved the army so that it could not be used against him by his enemies.

D He established the Silk Road to get goods from far away.

4 Which of the following developments in China is an example of diffusion?

A the growth of manufacturing and trade

B the building of the Great Wall

C the spread of Buddhism from India

D the procedure for making silk

5 Which dynasty's rulers created a government based on the ideas of Confucius?

A the Shang dynasty

B the Zhou dynasty

C the Qin dynasty

D the Han dynasty

Connecting with Past Learnings

6 In your studies of ancient India, you learned about the Hindu belief in rebirth. Which belief system that influenced early China also emphasized rebirth?

A Buddhism

B Confucianism

C Daoism

D Legalism

7 What characteristic did early civilization in Mesopotamia share with early civilization in China?

A Both developed paper.

B Both were influenced by Buddhism.

C Both built ziggurats.

D Both first developed in river valleys.

China and the Great Wall

Today, the Great Wall of China is an impressive symbol of the Asian giant's power, genius, and endurance. It wasn't always so. For much of its history, the Chinese people saw the Great Wall as a symbol of cruelty and oppression. This is just one way in which the wall differs from what we think we know. In contrast to popular notions, the wall that draws tourists to Beijing by the millions was not built 2,000 years ago. Nor is the Great Wall a single wall. Instead, it was patched together from walls built over many centuries. And for all its grandeur, the wall failed to keep China safe from invasion.

Explore facts and fictions about the Great Wall online. You can find more information, video clips, primary sources, activities, and more online.

A Land of Walls Within Walls

Watch the video to learn how the Great Wall fits within the ancient Chinese tradition of wall-building.

The Great Wall of China

Watch the video to learn the history and significance of the magnificent, mysterious walls that snake across northern China.

The Human Costs of Building

Watch the video to learn about the miseries that awaited the men who built the wall.

Twentieth-Century China

Watch the video to examine the role that the wall has played in modern Chinese history.

Why Things Happen

Assignment

Write an expository essay explaining one of these topics:

- Why the Aryans developed the caste system
- Why Confucius is considered the most influential teacher in Chinese history

TIP **Organizing Information**

Essays that explain why should be written in a logical order. Consider using one of these:

- **Chronological order**, the order in which things happened
- **Order of importance**, the order of the least important reason to the most important, or vice versa.

Why do civilizations so often develop in river valleys? Why did early people migrate across continents? You learn about the forces that drive history when you ask why things happened. Then you can share what you learned by writing an expository essay, explaining why events turned out as they did.

1. Prewrite

Considering Topic and Audience

Choose one of the two topics in the assignment, and then start to think about your big idea. Your big-idea statement might start out like this:

- The Aryans developed the caste system to . . .
- Confucius is considered the most influential teacher in Chinese history because he . . .

Collecting and Organizing Information

You will need to collect information that answers the question *Why*. To begin, review the information in this unit of your textbook. You can find more information on your topic in the library or on the Internet.

You should not stop searching for information until you have at least two or three answers to the question *Why*. These answers will form the points to support your big idea. Then take another look at your big idea. You may need to revise it or add to it to reflect the information you have gathered.

2. Write

Here is a framework that can help you write your first draft.

A Writer's Framework

Introduction
- Start with an interesting fact or question.
- Identify your big idea.
- Include any important background information.

Body
- Include at least one paragraph for each point supporting your big idea.
- Include facts and details to explain and illustrate each point.
- Use chronological order or order of importance.

Conclusion
- Summarize your main points.
- Using different words, restate your big idea.

3. Evaluate and Revise

Evaluating

Effective explanations require clear, straightforward language. Use the following questions to discover ways to improve your draft.

Evaluation Questions for an Expository Essay

- Does your essay begin with an interesting fact or question?
- Does the introduction identify your big idea?
- Have you developed at least one paragraph to explain each point?
- Is each point supported with facts and details?

- Have you organized your points clearly and logically?
- Did you explain any unusual words?
- Does the conclusion summarize your main points?
- Does the conclusion restate your big idea in different words?

Revising

Reread your draft. See whether each point is connected logically to the main idea and the other points you are making. If needed, add transitions—words and phrases that show how ideas fit together.

To connect points and information in time, use words like *after*, *before*, *first*, *later*, *soon*, *eventually*, *over time*, *as time passed*, and *then*. To show order of importance, use transitional words and phrases like *first*, *last*, *mainly*, *to begin with*, and *more important*.

4. Proofread and Publish

Proofreading

If you create a bulleted or numbered list, be sure to capitalize and punctuate the list correctly.

- **Capitalization:**   It is always acceptable to capitalize the first word of each item in the list.
- **Punctuation:**   (1) If the items are sentences, put a period at the end of each. (See the list in the tip above.) (2) If the items are not complete sentences, you usually do not need any end punctuation.

Publishing

Share your explanation with students from another class. After they read it, ask them to summarize your explanation. How well did they undertand the points you wanted to make?

● Practice and Apply

Use the steps and strategies in this workshop to write your explanation.

TIP **Using Lists** To make an explanation easier to follow, look for information that can be presented in a list.

Sentence/Paragraph Form Confucius gave the Chinese people guidelines for behavior. He felt that fathers should display high moral values, and he thought it was important that women obey their husbands. Children were to be obedient and respectful.

List Form
Confucius gave the Chinese people guidelines for behavior:

- Fathers should display high moral values.
- Wives should obey their husbands.
- Children should obey and respect their parents.

Foundations of Western Ideas

The foundations of Western civilization can be traced back more than 2,000 years to the eastern Mediterranean region. There, the ancient Hebrews, their descendants, and the ancient Greeks developed many of the ideas and traditions that have shaped the world today.

The Jewish religion, Judaism, is based on a belief in one God and basic ideas about right and wrong. The ancient Greeks created the world's first democracy. The Greeks also revolutionized science and mathematics and created some of the world's most famous art and literature.

In the next three chapters, you will learn how the Hebrews and Greeks helped shape the world you live in today.

Explore the Art
In this scene, the daughter of a Greek king warns her father not to trust a general who needs help in a war. What does this scene show about life in ancient Greece?

FLORIDA...
The Story Continues

CHAPTER 7, The Hebrews and Judaism (2000 BC–AD 70)

PEOPLE **1763: The first Jewish settlers come to Florida.**
According to the earliest records, the first Jewish settlers came to Pensacola in 1763 from New Orleans. By 1821 the Jewish population was still quite small—only about 30 to 40 people. Hoping to attract Jewish settlers fleeing persecution in Europe, Moses Elias Levy (1782–1854) purchased a large tract of land near Micanopy in 1821 to start a colony. He named his colony Pilgrimage Plantation. To his disappointment, few settlers came. The colony was destroyed in 1835 during the Second Seminole War. Today Florida's Jewish population is about 750,000—the third largest in the nation.

PEOPLE **1838–1839: David Levy Yulee helps write the Florida State Constitution.** Floridians voted for statehood in 1838. The territorial governor called for the election of delegates to a constitutional convention. David Levy Yulee (1810–1886) was one of the delegates. Yulee was the son of Moses Elias Levy, the founder of Pilgrimage Plantation. The Levy family had originally come from Morocco. David Levy adopted the honorary Moorish title Yulee that his family had once used. Yulee was the person most responsible for getting Florida admitted to the Union. Some voters wanted to split the territory into two states. Yulee fought for a single state. He also lobbied members of Congress to vote for Florida's admission. Florida became the twenty-seventh state in 1845. Yulee went on to serve as one of the state's first two U.S. senators, and the first Jewish member of the U.S. Senate. The city of Yulee in northeastern Florida is named in his honor. Levy County on the Gulf Coast is named for his family.

PLACES **1990: The Holocaust Memorial opens in Miami Beach.** In 1984 a group of Holocaust survivors decided to create a memorial to honor the 6 million Jewish victims of the Holocaust. Sculptor and architect Kevin Treister was asked to design the memorial. The memorial was opened to the public in 1990. It includes sculptures, granite slabs showing images of the Holocaust, and a meditation garden.

PLACES **1995: The Jewish Museum of Florida opens in Miami Beach.** The Jewish Museum of Florida grew out of the MOSAIC project, a research project that documented the state's Jewish history. Beginning in 1985 Marcia Jo Zerivitz traveled the state collecting information and artifacts about Jewish life in Florida since 1763. She used the information and artifacts to create the MOSAIC: Jewish Life in Florida exhibit.

Zerivitz took the exhibit to 13 cities from 1990 to 1994. The exhibit then became the basis for the museum.

PEOPLE **2004: Debbie Wasserman Schultz becomes the first Jewish woman from Florida elected to the U.S. House of Representatives.** In 2004, voters from the Twentieth Congressional District elected Debbie Wasserman Schultz (1966–) to the U.S. House of Representatives. It was the first time voters had elected a Jewish woman to serve the state in the U.S. House of Representatives. Representative Wasserman Schultz was sworn in on January 4, 2005. The Twentieth Congressional District stretches from Miami Beach to Fort Lauderdale. Before being elected to the U.S. House of Representatives, Wasserman Schultz served in the Florida state legislature, first as a representative and later as a senator.

Unpacking the Florida Standards ‹•••

Read the following to learn what this standard says and what it means. See FL8–FL31 to unpack all of the standards related to this chapter.

Benchmark SS.6.W.2.9 Identify key figures and basic beliefs of the Israelites and determine how these beliefs compared with those of others in the geographic area. Examples are Abraham, Moses, monotheism, law, emphasis on individual worth and responsibility.

What does it mean?
Name leading ancient Israelites and explain their significance. Know the fundamental beliefs of the ancient Israelites and compare these beliefs to those of other nearby peoples.

 SPOTLIGHT ON
SS.6.G.1.5, SS.6.G.2.1, SS.6.G.2.2, SS.6.G.2.7 See pages FL43–FL46 for content specifically related to these Chapter 7 standards.

The Hebrews and Judaism

Essential Question How did the Hebrews and their descendants defend themselves and maintain their beliefs?

Florida Next Generation Sunshine State Standards

LA.6.1.6.1 The student will use new vocabulary that is introduced and taught directly. **LA.6.1.7.3** The student will determine the main idea or essential message in grade-level text through inferring, paraphrasing, summarizing, and identifying relevant details. **SS.6.G.1.4** Utilize tools geographers use to study the world. **SS.6.G.1.5** Use scale, cardinal, and intermediate directions, and estimation of distances between places on current and ancient maps of the world. **SS.6.G.1.7** Use maps to identify characteristics and boundaries of ancient civilizations that have shaped the world today. **SS.6.G.2.1** Explain how major physical characteristics, natural resources, climate, and absolute and relative locations have influenced settlement, interactions, and the economies of ancient civilizations of the world. **SS.6.G.2.2** Differentiate between continents, regions, countries, and cities in order to understand the complexities of regions created by civilizations. **SS.6.G.2.4** Explain how the geographical location of ancient civilizations contributed to the culture and politics of those societies. **SS.6.G.2.6** Explain the concept of cultural diffusion, and identify the influences of different ancient cultures on one another. **SS.6.G.2.7** Interpret choropleths or dot-density maps to explain the distribution of population in the ancient world. **SS.6.G.4.1** Explain how family and ethnic relationships influenced ancient cultures. **SS.6.G.4.2** Use maps to trace significant migrations, and analyze their results. **SS.6.G.4.4** Map and analyze the impact of the spread of various belief systems in the ancient world. **SS.6.G.5.3** Use geographic tools and terms to analyze how famine, drought, and natural disasters plagued many ancient civilizations. **SS.6.W.1.1** Use timelines to identify chronological order of historical events. **SS.6.W.1.3** Interpret primary and secondary sources. **SS.6.W.1.6** Describe how history transmits culture and heritage and provides models of human character. **SS.6.W.2.9** Identify key figures and basic beliefs of the Israelites and determine how these beliefs compared with those of others in the geographic area.

FOCUS ON WRITING

A Web Site Have you ever designed your own Web site? If not, here's your chance to create one. As you read this chapter, you'll gather information about Jewish history, beliefs, values, and culture. Then you will write a description of how you would present this same information on a Web site.

In this photo, hundreds of people pray at the Western Wall, part of the Temple complex, the holiest site in the world of Judaism. The wall was built around 19 BC.

CHAPTER EVENTS

c. 2000 BC Abraham leaves Mesopotamia.

2000 BC

WORLD EVENTS

c. 1750 BC Hammurabi issues his law code.

HISTORY

Moses at Mount Sinai

Online Resource   VIDEO

c. 1000 BC
David becomes king of Israel.

586 BC
The Jews are enslaved in Babylon.

AD 70
The Romans destroy the Second Temple in Jerusalem.

1475 BC   950 BC   425 BC   AD 100

c. 1240–1224 BC
Ramses the Great rules Egypt.

c. 563 BC
The Buddha is born in India.

27 BC
Augustus becomes the first Roman emperor.

THE HEBREWS AND JUDAISM   **199**

Reading Social Studies

Focus on Themes In this chapter, you will read about the Hebrews and their descendents, the Israelites and Jews, and the religion called Judaism. You will learn about Jewish beliefs, texts such as the Torah and the Dead Sea Scrolls, and leaders such as Abraham and Moses. As you read, pay close attention to how people's beliefs affected where and how they lived. In the process, you will discover that the lives of the early Jews revolved around their **religious** beliefs and practices.

Facts and Opinions about the Past

Focus on Reading Why is it important to know the difference between a fact and an opinion? Separating facts from opinions about historical events helps you know what really happened.

Identifying Facts and Opinions Something is a **fact** if there is a way to prove it or disprove it. For example, research can prove or disprove the following statement: "The ancient Jews recorded their laws." But research can't prove the following statement because it is just an **opinion**, or someone's belief: "Everyone should read the records of the ancient Jews."

Use the process below to decide whether a statement is fact or opinion.

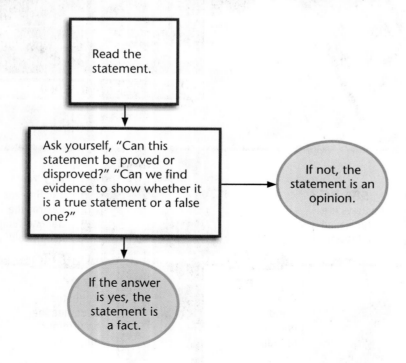

Read the statement.

Ask yourself, "Can this statement be proved or disproved?" "Can we find evidence to show whether it is a true statement or a false one?"

If not, the statement is an opinion.

If the answer is yes, the statement is a fact.

You Try It!

The following passage tells about boys who, years ago, found what came to be called the Dead Sea Scrolls. All the statements in this passage are facts. What makes them facts and not opinions?

Scrolls Reveal Past Beliefs

Until 1947 no one knew about the Dead Sea Scrolls. In that year, young boys looking for a lost goat near the Dead Sea found a small cave. One of the boys went in to explore and found several old jars filled with moldy scrolls.

From Chapter 7, pages 212–213

Scholars were very excited about the boy's find. Eager to find more scrolls, they began to search the desert. Over the next few decades, searchers found several more groups of scrolls.

Careful study revealed that most of the Dead Sea Scrolls were written between 100 BC and AD 50. The scrolls included prayers, commentaries, letters, and passages from the Hebrew Bible. These writings help historians learn about the lives of many Jews during this time.

Identify each of the following as a fact or an opinion and then explain your choice.

1. Boys discovered the Dead Sea Scrolls in 1947.

2. The discovery of the scrolls is one of the most important discoveries ever.

3. All religious leaders should study the Dead Sea Scrolls.

4. The Dead Sea Scrolls were written between 100 BC and AD 50.

Academic Vocabulary

Success in school is related to knowing academic vocabulary— the words that are frequently used in school assignments and discussions. In this chapter, you will learn the following academic word:

principles *(p. 210)*

As you read Chapter 7, look for clues that will help you determine which statements are facts.

LA.6.1.6.1, LA.6.1.7.3, SS.6.G.1.4,
SS.6.G.1.5, SS.6.G.1.7, SS.6.G.2.1,
SS.6.G.2.2, SS.6.G.2.4, SS.6.G.4.1,
SS.6.G.4.2, SS.6.G.5.3, SS.6.W.1.1, SS.6.W.1.3,
SS.6.W.1.6, SS.6.W.2.9

What You Will Learn...

Main Ideas

1. Abraham led the Hebrews to Canaan and to a new religion, and Moses led the Israelites out of slavery in Egypt.
2. Strong kings united the Israelites to fight off invaders.
3. Invaders conquered and ruled the Israelites after their kingdom broke apart.
4. Some women in Israelite society made great contributions to their history.

The Big Idea

Originally desert nomads, the Hebrews established a great kingdom called Israel.

Key Terms and People

Judaism, *p. 202*
Abraham, *p. 202*
Moses, *p. 203*
Exodus, *p. 203*
Ten Commandments, *p. 204*
David, *p. 205*
Solomon, *p. 205*
Diaspora, *p. 206*

Online Resource
TAKING NOTES

Use the graphic organizer online to take notes on the stages of Hebrew and later Jewish history from its beginnings in Canaan to Roman rule.

The Early Hebrews

If YOU were there...

You and your family are herders, looking after large flocks of sheep. Your grandfather is the leader of your tribe. One day your grandfather says that your whole family will be moving to a new country where there is more water and food for your flocks. The trip will be long and difficult.

How do you feel about moving to a faraway land?

BUILDING BACKGROUND Like the family described above, the early Hebrews moved to new lands in ancient times. According to Jewish tradition, their history began when God told an early Hebrew leader to travel west to a new land.

Abraham and Moses Lead Their People

Sometime between 2000 and 1500 BC a new people appeared in Southwest Asia. They were the Hebrews (HEE-brooz), ancestors of the Israelites and Jews. The early Hebrews were simple herders, but they developed a culture that became a major influence on later civilizations.

Much of what is known about their early history comes from the work of archaeologists and from accounts written by Jewish scribes. These accounts describe the early history of the Jews' ancestors and the laws of **Judaism** (JOO-dee-i-zuhm), their religion. In time these accounts became the Hebrew Bible. The Hebrew Bible is largely the same as the Old Testament of the Christian Bible.

The Beginnings in Canaan and Egypt

The Hebrew Bible traces the Hebrews back to a man named **Abraham**. One day, the Hebrew Bible says, God told Abraham to leave his home in Mesopotamia. He was to take his family on a long journey to the west. God promised to lead Abraham to a new land and make his descendants into a mighty nation.

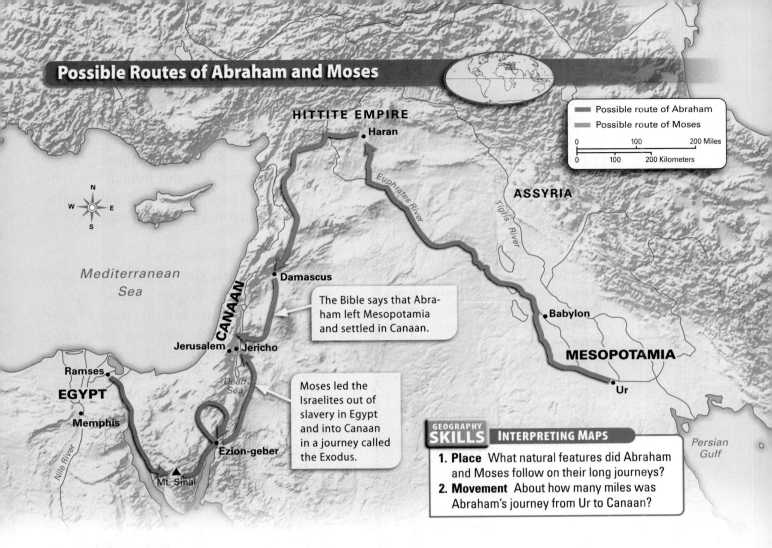

Possible Routes of Abraham and Moses

HITTITE EMPIRE

Haran

ASSYRIA

Euphrates River

Tigris River

Mediterranean Sea

CANAAN

Damascus

The Bible says that Abraham left Mesopotamia and settled in Canaan.

Babylon

Jerusalem • Jericho

MESOPOTAMIA

Ramses

Dead Sea

Moses led the Israelites out of slavery in Egypt and into Canaan in a journey called the Exodus.

Ur

EGYPT

Memphis

Nile River

Ezion-geber

Mt. Sinai

Persian Gulf

Possible route of Abraham
Possible route of Moses

0   100   200 Miles
0   100   200 Kilometers

GEOGRAPHY SKILLS INTERPRETING MAPS

1. **Place** What natural features did Abraham and Moses follow on their long journeys?
2. **Movement** About how many miles was Abraham's journey from Ur to Canaan?

Abraham left Mesopotamia and settled in Canaan (KAY-nuhn), on the Mediterranean Sea. Some of his descendants, the Israelites, lived in Canaan for many years. Later, however, some Israelites moved to Egypt, perhaps because of famine in Canaan.

The Israelites lived well in Egypt, and their population grew. This growth worried Egypt's ruler, the pharaoh. He feared that the Israelites might soon become too powerful. To stop this from happening, the pharaoh made the Israelites slaves.

The Exodus

According to the Hebrew Bible, a leader named **Moses** appeared among the Israelites in Egypt. In the 1200s BC, God told Moses to lead the Israelites out of Egypt. Moses went to the pharaoh and demanded that the Israelites be freed. The pharaoh refused. Soon afterward a series of terrible plagues, or disasters, struck Egypt.

The plagues frightened the pharaoh so much that he agreed to free the Israelites. Overjoyed with the news of their release, Moses led his people out of Egypt in a journey called the **Exodus**. To the Israelites, the release from slavery proved that God was protecting and watching over them. They believed that they had been set free because God loved them.

The Exodus is a major event in Jewish history, but other people recognize its significance as well. Throughout history, for example, enslaved people have found hope in the story. Before the Civil War, American slaves sang about Moses to keep their hopes of freedom alive.

For many years after their release, the Israelites traveled through the desert. When they reached a mountain called Sinai, the Hebrew Bible says, God gave Moses two stone tablets. On the tablets was written a code of moral laws known as the **Ten Commandments**:

"I the Lord am your God who brought you out of the land of Egypt, the house of bondage: You shall have no other gods besides Me.

You shall not make for yourself a sculptured image, or any likeness of what is in the heavens above, or on the earth below, or in the waters under the earth. You shall not bow down to them or serve them. For I the Lord your God am an impassioned God. . . .

You shall not swear falsely by the name of the Lord your God; for the Lord will not clear one who swears falsely by His name.

Remember the sabbath day and keep it holy. . . .

Honor your father and your mother, that you may long endure on the land that the Lord your God is assigning to you.

You shall not murder.

You shall not commit adultery.

You shall not steal.

You shall not bear false witness against your neighbor.

You shall not covet your neighbor's house: you shall not covet your neighbor's wife, or his male or female slave, or his ox or his ass, or anything that is your neighbor's."

—Exodus 20:2–14

By accepting the Ten Commandments, the Israelites agreed to worship only God. They also agreed to value human life, self-control, and justice. The commandments shaped the development of their society.

The Return to Canaan

According to the Hebrew Bible, the Israelites eventually reached Canaan, where they fought the people living there to gain control of the land. After they conquered Canaan and settled down, the Israelites built their own society.

In Canaan, the 12 Israelite tribes lived in small, scattered communities. These communities had no central government. Instead, each community selected judges as leaders to enforce laws and settle disputes. Before long, though, a threat arose that called for a new kind of leadership.

READING CHECK **Identifying Cause and Effect**
Why did Abraham leave Mesopotamia?

Time Line

Hebrew and Israelite History

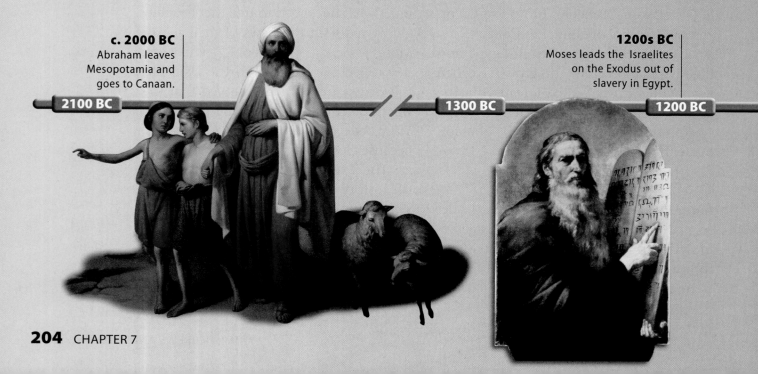

c. 2000 BC
Abraham leaves Mesopotamia and goes to Canaan.

2100 BC

1300 BC

1200s BC
Moses leads the Israelites on the Exodus out of slavery in Egypt.

1200 BC

Kings Unite the Israelites

The new threat to the Israelites came from the Philistines (FI-li-steenz), who lived along the Mediterranean coast. In the mid-1000s BC the Philistines invaded the Israelites' lands.

Frightened by these powerful invaders, the Israelites banded together under a single ruler who could lead them in battle. That ruler was a man named Saul, who became the first king of Israel. Saul had some success as a military commander, but he wasn't a strong king. He never won the total support of tribal and religious leaders. They often disputed his decisions.

King David

After Saul died, a man once out of favor with Saul became king. That king's name was **David**. As a young man, David had been a shepherd. The Hebrew Bible tells how David slew the Philistine giant Goliath, which brought him to the attention of the king. David was admired for his military skills and as a poet; many of the Psalms are attributed to him. For many years, David lived in the desert, gathering support from local people. When Saul died, David used this support to become king.

Unlike Saul, David was well loved by the Israelites. He won the full support of Israel's tribal leaders. David defeated the Philistines and fought and won wars against many other peoples of Canaan. He established the capital of Israel in Jerusalem.

King Solomon

David's son **Solomon** (SAHL-uh-muhn) took the throne in about 965 BC. Like his father, Solomon was a strong king. He expanded the kingdom and made nearby kingdoms, including Egypt and Phoenicia, his allies. Trade with these allies made Israel very rich. With these riches, Solomon built a great Temple to God in Jerusalem. This Temple became the center of the Israelites' religious life and a symbol of their faith.

READING CHECK **Finding Main Ideas** Why did the Israelites unite under a king?

FOCUS ON READING

Are the sentences in this paragraph facts or opinions? How can you tell?

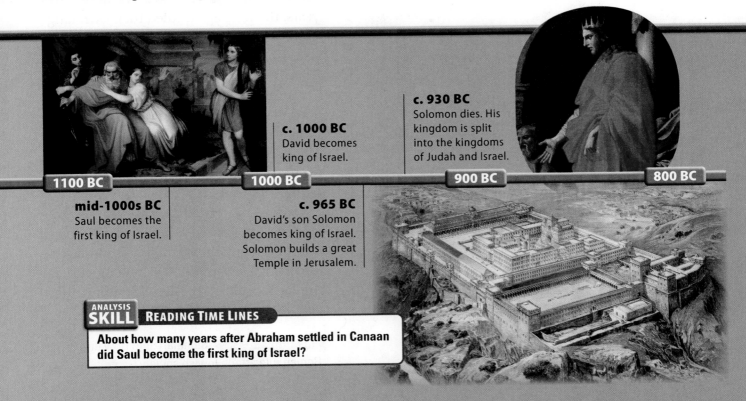

c. 1000 BC
David becomes king of Israel.

c. 930 BC
Solomon dies. His kingdom is split into the kingdoms of Judah and Israel.

| 1100 BC | 1000 BC | 900 BC | 800 BC |

mid-1000s BC
Saul becomes the first king of Israel.

c. 965 BC
David's son Solomon becomes king of Israel. Solomon builds a great Temple in Jerusalem.

ANALYSIS SKILL **READING TIME LINES**

About how many years after Abraham settled in Canaan did Saul become the first king of Israel?

THE HEBREWS AND JUDAISM **205**

Invaders Conquer and Rule

After Solomon's death in about 930 BC, revolts broke out over who should be king. Within a year, conflict tore Israel apart. Israel split into two kingdoms called Israel and called Judah (JOO-duh). The people of Judah became known as Jews.

The two new kingdoms lasted for a few centuries. In the end, however, both were conquered. The Assyrians defeated Israel around 722 BC. The kingdom fell apart because most of its people were dispersed. Judah lasted longer, but before long it was defeated by the Chaldeans.

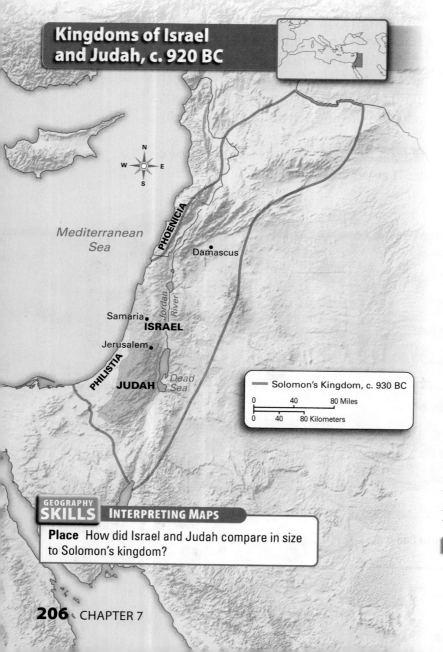

Kingdoms of Israel and Judah, c. 920 BC

Mediterranean Sea

PHOENICIA

Damascus

Jordan River

Samaria

ISRAEL

Jerusalem

PHILISTIA

JUDAH

Dead Sea

Solomon's Kingdom, c. 930 BC

0   40   80 Miles

0   40   80 Kilometers

GEOGRAPHY SKILLS | **INTERPRETING MAPS**

Place How did Israel and Judah compare in size to Solomon's kingdom?

The Dispersal of the Jews

The Chaldeans captured Jerusalem and destroyed Solomon's Temple in 586 BC. They marched thousands of Jews to their capital, Babylon, to work as slaves. The Jews called this enslavement the Babylonian Captivity. It lasted about 50 years.

In the 530s BC a people called the Persians conquered the Chaldeans and let the Jews return to Jerusalem. But many never took this opportunity to return home. Instead, some moved to other parts of the Persian Empire. Scholars call the dispersal of the Jews outside of Israel and Judah the **Diaspora** (dy-AS-pruh).

The rest of the Jews did return home to Jerusalem. There they rebuilt Solomon's Temple, which became known as the Second Temple. The Jews remained under Persian control until the 330s BC, when the Persians were conquered by invaders.

Independence and Conquest

Tired of foreign rule, a Jewish family called the Maccabees (MA-kuh-beez) led a successful revolt in the 160s BC. For about 100 years, the Jews again ruled their own kingdom. Their independence, however, didn't last. In 63 BC the Jews were conquered again, this time by the Romans.

Although Jewish leaders added to the Second Temple under Roman rule, life was difficult. Heavy taxes burdened the people. The Romans were brutal masters who had no respect for the Jewish religion and way of life.

Some rulers tried to force the Jews to worship the Roman Emperor. The Roman rulers even appointed the high priests, the leaders of the Temple. This was more than the Jews could bear. They called on their people to rebel against the Romans.

READING CHECK **Summarizing** How did Roman rule affect Jewish society?

Women in Israelite Society

Israelite government and society were dominated by men, as were most ancient societies. Women and men had different roles. Men made most decisions, and a woman's husband was chosen by her father. However, a daughter could not be forced into marriage. A family's property was inherited by the eldest son, who provided for all children and for women without husbands.

Some Israelite and Jewish women, however, made great contributions to their society. The Hebrew Bible describes them. Some were political and military leaders, such as Queen Esther and the judge Deborah. According to the Hebrew Bible, these women saved their people from their enemies. Other women, such as Miriam, the sister of Moses, were spiritual leaders.

Some women in the Hebrew Bible were seen as examples of how Israelite and Jewish women should behave. For example, Ruth, who left her people to care for her mother-in-law, was seen as a model of human character. Ruth's story was told as an example of how people should treat their family members.

READING CHECK **Generalizing** What was life like for most Israelite women?

Ruth and Naomi

The story of Ruth and Naomi comes from the Book of Ruth, one of the books of the Hebrew Bible. According to this account, Ruth was not an Israelite, though her husband was. After he died, Ruth and her mother-in-law, Naomi, resettled in Israel. Inspired by Naomi's faith in God, Ruth joined Naomi's family and adopted her beliefs. She dedicated her life to supporting Naomi.

Drawing Inferences What lessons might the story of Ruth be used to teach?

SUMMARY AND PREVIEW The history of the Jews and their ancestors began some 3,500 to 4,000 years ago. The instructions that Jews believe God gave to the early Hebrews and Israelites shaped their religion, Judaism. In the next section, you will learn about the main teachings of Judaism.

Section 1 Assessment

Reviewing Ideas, Terms, and People

1. **a. Identify** Who was **Abraham**?
   b. Evaluate Why was the Exodus a significant event in Israelite history?
2. **Summarize** How did **David** and **Solomon** strengthen the kingdom of Israel?
3. **Describe** What happened during the Babylonian Captivity?
4. **a. Describe** Who had more rights in Israelite society, men or women?
   b. Make Inferences How did Ruth and Naomi set an example for other Israelites?

Critical Thinking

5. **Evaluating** Review your notes on the chapter. In a chart like this one, note the contributions of the four most important people.

Key Figure	Contribution

FOCUS ON WRITING

6. **Taking Notes about Early Jewish History** Make a list of events and people that played key roles in early Jewish history. Look for ways to group your facts into features on your Web page.

Jewish Beliefs and Texts

What You Will Learn...

Main Ideas

1. Belief in God, commitment to education and justice, and observance of the law anchor Jewish society.
2. Jewish beliefs are listed in the Torah, the Hebrew Bible, and the Commentaries.
3. The Dead Sea Scrolls reveal many past Jewish beliefs.
4. The ideas of Judaism have helped shape later cultures.

The Big Idea

The central ideas and laws of Judaism are contained in sacred texts such as the Torah.

Key Terms

monotheism, p. 208
Torah, p. 210
synagogue, p. 210
prophets, p. 211
Talmud, p. 212
Dead Sea Scrolls, p. 212

Online Resource
TAKING NOTES

Use the graphic organizer online to record notes on Jewish beliefs and texts.

SS.6.W.2.9 Identify key figures and basic beliefs of the Israel-ites and determine how these beliefs compared with those of others in the geographic area.

If YOU were there...

You live in a small town in ancient Israel. Some people in your town treat strangers very badly. But you have been taught to be fair and kind to everyone, including strangers. One day, you tell one of your neighbors he should be kinder to strangers. He asks you why you feel that way.

How will you explain your belief in kindness?

BUILDING BACKGROUND The idea that people should be fair and kind to everyone in the community is an important Jewish teaching. Sometimes, their teachings set the Jews apart from other people in society. But at the same time, their shared beliefs tie all Jews together as a religious community.

Jewish Beliefs Anchor Their Society

Religion is the foundation upon which the Jews base their whole society. In fact, much of Jewish culture is based directly on Jewish beliefs. The central concepts of Judaism are belief in God, education, justice and righteousness, and observance of religious and moral law.

Belief in One God

Most importantly, Jews believe in one God. The Hebrew name for God is YHWH, which is never pronounced by Jews, as it is considered too holy. The belief in only one God is called **monotheism**. Many people believe that Judaism was the world's first monotheistic religion. It is certainly the oldest such religion that is still widely practiced today.

In the ancient world where most people worshipped many gods, the Jews' worship of only God set them apart. This worship also shaped Jewish society. The Jews believed that God had guided their history through his relationships with Abraham, Moses, and other leaders.

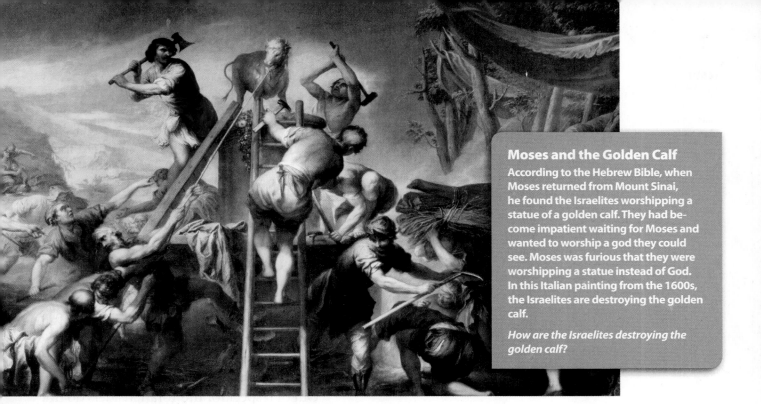

Education

Another central element of Judaism is education and study. Teaching children the basics of Judaism has always been important in Jewish society. In ancient Jewish communities, older boys—but not girls—studied with professional teachers to learn their religion. Even today, education and study are central to Jewish life.

Justice and Righteousness

Also central to the Jews' religion are the ideas of justice and righteousness. To Jews, justice means kindness and fairness in dealing with other people. Everyone deserves justice, even strangers and criminals. Jews are expected to give aid to those who need it, including the poor, the sick, and orphans. Jews are also expected to be fair in business dealings.

Righteousness refers to doing what is proper. Jews are supposed to behave properly, even if others around them do not. For the Jews, righteous behavior is more important than formal ceremonies.

Observance of Religious and Moral Law

Observance of the law is closely related to justice and righteousness. Moral and religious laws have guided Jews through their history and continue to do so today. Jews believe that God gave them these laws to follow.

The most important Jewish laws are the Ten Commandments. The commandments, however, are only part of Jewish law. Jews believe that Moses recorded a whole system of laws that God had set down for them to obey. Named for Moses, this system is called Mosaic law.

Like the Ten Commandments, Mosaic laws guide many areas of Jews' daily lives. For example, Mosaic law governs how people pray and celebrate holidays. The laws forbid Jews to work on holidays or on the Sabbath, the seventh day of each week. The Sabbath is a day of rest because, in Jewish tradition, God created the world in six days and rested on the seventh. The Jewish Sabbath begins at sundown Friday and ends at nightfall Saturday, the seventh day of the week.

Among the Mosaic laws are rules about the foods that Jews can eat and rules that must be followed in preparing them. For example, the laws state that Jews cannot eat pork or shellfish, which are thought to be unclean. Other laws say that meat has to be killed and prepared in a way that makes it acceptable for Jews to eat. Today foods that have been so prepared are called kosher (KOH-shuhr), or fit.

In many Jewish communities today, people still strictly follow Mosaic law. They are called Orthodox Jews. Other Jews choose not to follow many of the ancient laws. They are known as Reform Jews. A third group, the Conservative Jews, falls between the other two groups. These are the three largest groups of Jews in the world today.

READING CHECK **Generalizing** What are the most important beliefs of Judaism?

Texts List Jewish Beliefs

The laws and **principles** of Judaism are described in several sacred texts, or writings. Among the main texts are the Torah, the Hebrew Bible, and the Commentaries.

The Torah

The ancient Jews recorded most of their laws in five books. Together these books are called the **Torah**, the most sacred text of Judaism. In addition to laws, the Torah includes a history of the Jews until the death of Moses.

Readings from the Torah are central to Jewish religious services today. Nearly every **synagogue** (SI-nuh-gawg), or Jewish house of worship, has at least one Torah. Out of respect for the Torah, readers do not touch it. They use special pointers to mark their places in the text.

Hebrew Texts

The Torah

Using a special pointer called a *yad*, this girl is reading aloud from the Torah. The Torah is the most sacred of Hebrew writings. Jews believe its contents were revealed to Moses by God. The Torah plays a central role in many Jewish ceremonies, like this one.

The Hebrew Bible

The Torah is the first of three parts of a group of writings called the Hebrew Bible, or Tanakh (tah-NAHK). The second part is made up of eight books that describe the messages of Jewish prophets. **Prophets** are people who are said to receive messages from God to be taught to others.

The final part of the Hebrew Bible is 11 books of poetry, songs, stories, lessons, and history. For example, the Book of Daniel tells about a prophet named Daniel, who lived during the Babylonian Captivity. According to the book, Daniel angered the king who held the Jews as slaves. As punishment, the king had Daniel thrown into a den of lions. The story tells that Daniel's faith in God kept the lions from killing him, and he was released. Jews tell this story to show the power of faith.

Also in the final part of the Hebrew Bible are the Proverbs, short expressions of Jewish wisdom. Many of these sayings are attributed to Israelite leaders, especially King Solomon. For example, Solomon is supposed to have said, "A good name is to be chosen rather than great riches." In other words, it is better to be seen as a good person than to be rich and not respected.

The third part of the Hebrew Bible also includes the Book of Psalms. Psalms are poems or songs of praise to God. Many of these are attributed to King David. One of the most famous psalms is the Twenty-third Psalm. It includes lines often read today during times of difficulty:

" The Lord is my shepherd; I lack nothing.
 He makes me lie down in green pastures;
    He leads me to water in places of repose;
    He renews my life;
    He guides me in right paths as befits His name. "
—Psalms 23:1–3

The Hebrew Bible
These beautifully decorated pages are from a Hebrew Bible. The Hebrew Bible, sometimes called the Tanakh, includes the Torah and other ancient writings.

The Commentaries
The Talmud is a collection of commentaries and discussions about the Torah and the Hebrew Bible. The Talmud is a rich source of information for discussion and debate. Rabbis and religious scholars like these young men study the Talmud to learn about Jewish history and laws.

ANALYSIS
SKILL ANALYZING VISUALS
How does the Torah look different from the Hebrew Bible and the commentaries?

The Dead Sea Scrolls

The Dead Sea Scrolls were found in this cave, and in similar caves, near Qumran. The hot, dry desert climate preserved the 2,000-year-old scrolls remarkably well.

Why might historians have had trouble reading the Dead Sea Scrolls?

Commentaries

For centuries scholars have studied the Torah and Jewish laws. Because some laws are hard to understand, the scholars write commentaries to explain them.

Many such commentaries are found in the **Talmud** (TAHL-moohd), a set of commentaries and lessons for everyday life. The writings of the Talmud were produced between AD 200 and 600. Many Jews consider them second only to the Hebrew Bible in their significance to Judaism.

READING CHECK **Analyzing** What texts do Jews consider sacred?

Scrolls Reveal Past Beliefs

Besides the Torah, the Hebrew Bible, and the Commentaries, many other documents also explain ancient Jewish beliefs. Among the most important are the **Dead Sea Scrolls**, writings by Jews who lived about 2,000 years ago.

Until 1947 no one knew about the Dead Sea Scrolls. In that year, young boys looking for a lost goat near the Dead Sea found a small cave. One of the boys went in to explore and found several old jars filled with moldy scrolls.

Scholars were very excited about the boy's find. Eager to find more scrolls, they began to search the desert. Over the next few decades, searchers found several more groups of scrolls.

Careful study revealed that most of the Dead Sea Scrolls were written between 100 BC and AD 50. The scrolls included prayers, commentaries, letters, and passages from the Hebrew Bible. These writings help historians learn about the lives of many Jews during this time.

READING CHECK Finding Main Ideas What did the Dead Sea Scrolls contain?

Judaism and Later Cultures

For centuries, Jewish ideas have greatly influenced other cultures, especially those in Europe and the Americas. Historians call European and American cultures the Western world to distinguish them from the Asian cultures to the east of Europe.

Because Jews lived all over the Western world, people of many cultures learned of Jewish ideas. In addition, these ideas helped shape the largest religion of Western society today, Christianity. Jesus, whose teachings are the basis of Christianity, was Jewish, and many of his teachings reflected Jewish ideas. These ideas were carried forward into Western civilization by both Jews and Christians. Judaism also influenced the development of another major religion, Islam. The first people to adopt Islam believed that they, like the Jews, were descendants of Abraham.

How are Jewish ideas reflected in our society? Many people still look to the Ten Commandments as a guide to how they should live. For example, people are expected to honor their parents, families, and neighbors and not to lie or cheat. In addition, many people do not work on weekends in honor of the Sabbath. Although not all these ideas were unique

to Judaism, it was through the Jews that they entered Western culture.

Not all of the ideas adopted from Jewish teachings come from the Ten Commandments. Other Jewish ideas can also be seen in how people live today. For example, people give money or items to charities to help the poor and needy. This concept of charity is based largely on Jewish teachings.

READING CHECK Summarizing How have Jewish ideas helped shape modern laws?

SUMMARY AND PREVIEW Judaism is based on the belief in and obedience to God as described in the Torah and other sacred texts. In the next section you will learn how religion helped unify Jews even when they were forced out of Jerusalem.

Section 2 Assessment

Reviewing Ideas, Terms, and People

1. **a. Define** What is **monotheism**?
   b. Explain What is the Jewish view of justice and righteousness?
2. **a. Identify** What are the main sacred texts of Judaism?
   b. Predict Why do you think the commentaries are so significant to many Jews?
3. **Recall** Why do historians study the Dead Sea Scrolls?
4. **Describe** How are Jewish teachings reflected in Western society today?

Critical Thinking

5. **Finding Main Ideas** Using the information in your notes, identify four basic beliefs of Judaism and explain them in a diagram like the one shown here.

Jewish Beliefs

FOCUS ON WRITING

6. **Thinking about Basic Values and Teachings** While the information in Section 1 was mostly historical, this section has different kinds of topics. As you write down this information for your Web site, what links do you see between these topics and items already on the list you started in Section 1?

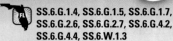
What You Will Learn...

Main Ideas

1. Revolt, defeat, and migration led to great changes in Jewish culture.
2. Because Jews settled in different parts of the world, two cultural traditions formed.
3. Jewish traditions and holy days celebrate their history and religion.

The Big Idea

Although many Jews were forced out of Israel by the Romans, shared beliefs and customs helped Jews maintain their religion.

Key Terms

Zealots, *p. 214*
rabbis, *p. 216*
Passover, *p. 219*
High Holy Days, *p. 219*

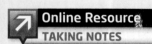

Online Resource

TAKING NOTES

Use the graphic organizer online to take notes on events that threatened the survival of Jewish society, and notes on beliefs and customs that helped strengthen it.

Judaism over the Centuries

If YOU were there...

Foreign soldiers have taken over your homeland and are forcing you to obey their laws. So, some people are urging you to stand up and fight for freedom. But your conquerors come from a huge, powerful empire. If your people revolt, you have little chance of winning.

Will you join the rebellion? Why or why not?

BUILDING BACKGROUND By about AD 60, many Jews in Jerusalem had to decide whether they would join a rebellion against their foreign conquerors. For a little over a century, Jerusalem had been ruled by Rome. The Romans had a strong army, but their disrespect for Jewish traditions angered many Jews.

Revolt, Defeat, and Migration

The teachings of Judaism helped unite the ancient Jews. After the conquest of Israel by the Romans, many events threatened to tear Jewish society apart.

One threat to Jewish society was foreign rule. By the beginning of the first century AD, many Jews in Jerusalem had grown tired of foreign rule. If they could regain their independence, these Jews thought they could re-create the kingdom of Israel.

Revolt against Rome

The most rebellious of these Jews were a group called the **Zealots** (ZE-luhts). This group didn't think that Jews should answer to anyone but God. As a result, they refused to obey Roman officials. The Zealots urged their fellow Jews to rise up against the Romans. Tensions between Jews and Romans increased. Finally, in AD 66, the Jews revolted. Led by the Zealots, they fought fiercely.

In the end, the Jews' revolt against the Romans was not successful. The revolt lasted four years and caused terrible damage. By the time the fighting ended, Jerusalem lay in ruins. The war had wrecked buildings and cost many lives. Even more devastating to the Jews was the fact that the Romans burned the Second Temple during the last days of fighting in AD 70:

" As the flames went upward, the Jews made a great clamor [shout], such as so mighty an affliction [ordeal] required, and ran together to prevent it; and now they spared not their lives any longer, nor suffered any thing to restrain their force, since that holy house was perishing. "

–Flavius Josephus, *The Wars of the Jews*

After the Temple was destroyed, most Jews lost their will to fight and surrendered. But a few refused to give up their fight. That small group of about 1,000 Zealots locked themselves in a mountain fortress called Masada (muh-SAH-duh).

Intent on smashing the revolt, the Romans sent 15,000 soldiers to capture these Zealots. However, Masada was hard to reach. The Romans had to build a huge ramp of earth and stones to get to it. For two years, the Zealots refused to surrender, as the ramp grew. Finally, as the Romans broke through Masada's walls, the Zealots took their own lives. They refused to become Roman slaves.

THE IMPACT TODAY

The western retaining wall of the Second Temple survived the fire and still stands. Thousands of Jews each year visit the wall.

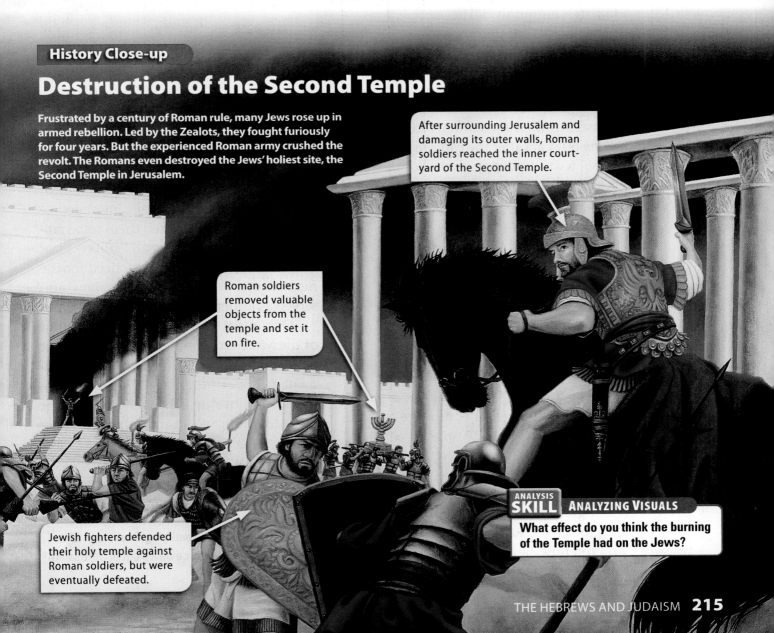

History Close-up

Destruction of the Second Temple

Frustrated by a century of Roman rule, many Jews rose up in armed rebellion. Led by the Zealots, they fought furiously for four years. But the experienced Roman army crushed the revolt. The Romans even destroyed the Jews' holiest site, the Second Temple in Jerusalem.

After surrounding Jerusalem and damaging its outer walls, Roman soldiers reached the inner courtyard of the Second Temple.

Roman soldiers removed valuable objects from the temple and set it on fire.

Jewish fighters defended their holy temple against Roman soldiers, but were eventually defeated.

ANALYSIS SKILL **ANALYZING VISUALS**

What effect do you think the burning of the Temple had on the Jews?

Results of the Revolt

With the capture of Masada in AD 73, the Jewish revolt was over. As punishment for the Jews' rebellion, the Romans killed much of Jerusalem's population. They took many of the surviving Jews to Rome as slaves. The Romans dissolved the Jewish power structure and took over the city.

Besides those taken as slaves, thousands of Jews left Jerusalem after the destruction of the Second Temple. With the Temple destroyed, they didn't want to live in Jerusalem anymore. Many moved to Jewish communities in other parts of the Roman Empire. One common destination was Alexandria in Egypt, which had a large Jewish community. The populations of these Jewish communities grew after the Romans destroyed Jerusalem.

A Second Revolt

Some Jews, however, chose not to leave Jerusalem when the Romans conquered it. Some 60 years after the capture of Masada, these Jews, unhappy with Roman rule, began another revolt. Once again, however, the Roman army defeated the Jews. After this rebellion in the 130s the Romans banned all Jews from the city of Jerusalem. Roman officials declared that any Jew caught in or near the city would be killed. As a result, Jewish migration throughout the Mediterranean region increased.

Migration and Discrimination

The Sephardim are descended from Jews who migrated to Spain and Portugal during the Diaspora, or dispersal, of the Jews. This Sephardic rabbi is working on part of a Torah scroll.

ATLANTIC OCEAN

PORTUGAL

SPAIN

AFRICA

For Jews not living in Jerusalem, the nature of Judaism changed. Because the Jews no longer had a single temple at which to worship, local synagogues became more important. At the same time, leaders called **rabbis** (RAB-yz), or religious teachers, took on a greater role in guiding Jews in their religious lives. Rabbis were responsible for interpreting the Torah and teaching.

This change was largely due to the actions of Yohanan ben Zaccai, a rabbi who founded a school at Yavneh, near Jerusalem. In this school, he taught people about Judaism and trained them to be rabbis. Influenced by Yohanan, rabbis' ideas shaped how Judaism was practiced for the next several centuries. Many rabbis also served as leaders of Jewish communities.

Over many centuries, Jews moved out of the Mediterranean region to other parts of the world. In many cases this movement was not voluntary. The Jews were forced to move by other religious groups who discriminated against them or were unfair to them. Jews were forced to leave their cities and find new places to live. As a result, some Jews settled in Europe and Asia, and much later, the United States.

READING CHECK Identifying Cause and Effect
Why did the Romans force Jews out of Jerusalem?

THE IMPACT TODAY
The United States today has a larger Jewish population than any other country in the world.

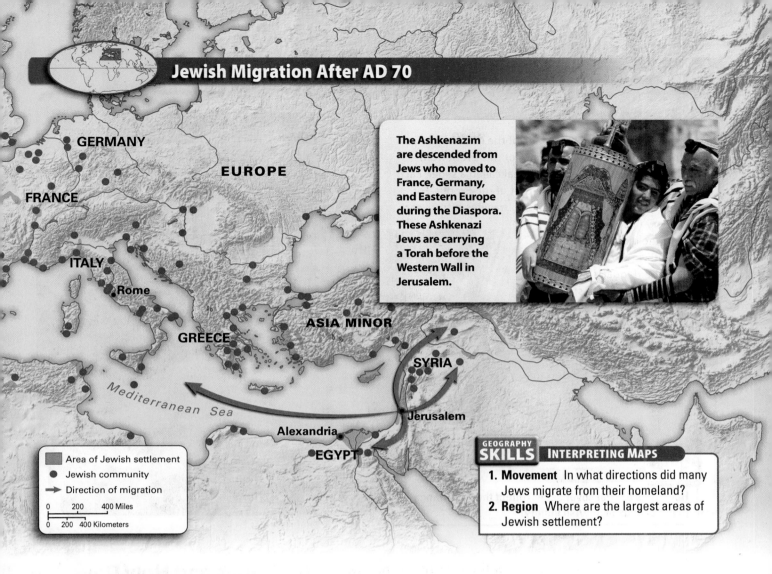

Jewish Migration After AD 70

GERMANY

FRANCE

EUROPE

ITALY

Rome

GREECE

ASIA MINOR

SYRIA

Mediterranean Sea

Jerusalem

Alexandria

EGYPT

The Ashkenazim are descended from Jews who moved to France, Germany, and Eastern Europe during the Diaspora. These Ashkenazi Jews are carrying a Torah before the Western Wall in Jerusalem.

Area of Jewish settlement
Jewish community
Direction of migration

0   200   400 Miles
0   200   400 Kilometers

GEOGRAPHY SKILLS | **INTERPRETING MAPS**

1. **Movement** In what directions did many Jews migrate from their homeland?
2. **Region** Where are the largest areas of Jewish settlement?

Two Cultural Traditions

As you read earlier, the dispersal of Jews around the world is called the Diaspora. It began with the Babylonian Captivity in the 500s BC. After that time, Jewish communities developed all around the world.

Jews everywhere shared the basic beliefs of Judaism. For example, all Jews still believed in God and tried to obey his laws as set forth in the sacred texts. But communities in various parts of the world had different customs. As a result, the Jewish communities in different parts of the world began to develop their own languages, rituals, and cultures. These differences led to the creation of two main cultural traditions, both of which still exist today.

The Jews in Eastern Europe

One of the two traditions, the Ashkenazim (ahsh-kuh-NAH-zuhm), is made up of descendants of Jews who moved to France, Germany, and eastern Europe during the Diaspora. For the most part, these Jews had communities separate from their non-Jewish neighbors. Therefore, they developed their own customs that were unlike those of their neighbors. As an example, they developed their own language, Yiddish. Yiddish is similar to German but is written in the Hebrew alphabet.

The Jews in Spain and Portugal

Another Jewish cultural tradition developed during the Diaspora in what are now Spain and Portugal in Western Europe.

THE IMPACT TODAY

Some Yiddish words have entered the English language. For example, *schlep* means "to carry."

A Passover Meal

Passover honors the Exodus, one of the most important events in Jewish history. In honor of this event from their past, Jews share a special meal called a seder. Each item in the seder symbolizes a part of the Exodus. For example, bitter herbs represent the Israelites' bitter years of slavery in Egypt. Before eating the meal, everyone reads prayers from a book called the Haggadah (huh-GAH-duh). It tells the story of the Exodus and reminds everyone present of the Jews' history. The small picture shows a seder in a copy of a Haggadah from the 1300s.

ANALYSIS SKILL **ANALYZING INFORMATION**

How does the Passover seder reflect the importance of the Exodus in Jewish history?

The descendants of the Jews there are called the Sephardim (suh-FAHR-duhm). They also have a language of their own—Ladino. It is a mix of Spanish, Hebrew, and Arabic. Unlike the Ashkenazim, the Sephardim mixed with the region's non-Jewish residents. As a result, Sephardic religious and cultural practices borrowed elements from other cultures. Known for their writings and their philosophies, the Sephardim produced a golden age of Jewish culture in the AD 1000s and 1100s. During this period, for example, Jewish poets wrote beautiful works in Hebrew and other languages. Jewish scholars also made great advances in mathematics, astronomy, medicine, and philosophy.

READING CHECK **Summarizing** What are the two main Jewish cultural traditions?

Traditions and Holy Days

Jewish culture is one of the oldest in the world. Because their roots go back so far, many Jews feel a strong connection with the past. They also feel that understanding their history will help them better follow Jewish teachings. Their traditions and holy days help them understand and celebrate their history.

Hanukkah

One Jewish tradition is celebrated by Hanukkah, which falls in December. It honors the rededication of the Second Temple during the revolt of the Maccabees.

The Maccabees wanted to celebrate a great victory that had convinced their non-Jewish rulers to let them keep their religion. According to legend, though, the Maccabees didn't have enough lamp oil to perform the rededication ceremony. Miraculously, the oil they had—enough to burn for only one day—burned for eight full days.

Today Jews celebrate this event by lighting candles in a special candleholder called a menorah (muh-NOHR-uh). Its eight branches represent the eight days through which the oil burned. Many Jews also exchange gifts on each of the eight nights.

Passover

More important than Hanukkah to Jews, Passover is celebrated in March or April. **Passover** is a time for Jews to remember the Exodus, the journey of the Israelites out of slavery in Egypt.

According to Jewish tradition, the Israelites left Egypt so quickly that bakers didn't have time to let their bread rise. Therefore, during Passover Jews eat only matzo, a flat, unrisen bread. They also celebrate the holy day with ceremonies and a ritual meal called a seder (SAY-duhr). During the seder, participants recall and reflect upon the events of the Exodus.

High Holy Days

Ceremonies and rituals are also part of the **High Holy Days**, the two most sacred of all Jewish holy days. They take place each year in September or October. The first two days of the celebration, Rosh Hashanah (rahsh uh-SHAH-nuh), celebrate the beginning of a new year in the Jewish calendar.

On Yom Kippur (yohm ki-POOHR), which falls soon afterward, Jews ask God to forgive their sins. Jews consider Yom Kippur to be the holiest day of the entire year. Because it is so holy, Jews don't eat or drink anything for the entire day. Many of the ceremonies they perform for Yom Kippur date back to the days of the Second

Temple. These ceremonies help many Jews feel more connected to their long past, to the days of Abraham and Moses.

READING CHECK Finding Main Ideas What name is given to the two most important Jewish holy days?

SUMMARY AND PREVIEW The Jewish culture is one of the oldest in the world. Over the course of their long history, the Jews' religion and customs have helped them maintain a sense of identity and community. This sense has helped the Jewish people endure many hardships. In the next chapter you will learn about another people who made major contributions to Western culture. These were the Greeks.

Section 3 Assessment

Reviewing Ideas, Terms, and People

1. **a. Recall** Who won the battle at Masada?
   b. Evaluate How did the defeat by the Romans affect Jewish history?
2. **a. Identify** What language developed in the Jewish communities of eastern Europe?
   b. Contrast How did communities of Ashkenazim differ from communities of Sephardim?
3. **Identify** What event does **Passover** celebrate?

Critical Thinking

4. **Evaluating** Review your notes. Then use a graphic organizer like the one shown to describe the belief or custom that you think may have had the biggest role in strengthening Jewish society.

Major Belief or Custom

FOCUS ON WRITING

5. **Organizing Your Information** Add notes about what you've just read to the notes you have already collected. Now that you have all your information, organize it into categories that will be windows, links, and other features on your Web page.

Social Studies Skills

Analysis **Critical Thinking** **Economics** **Study**

Identifying Short- and Long-Term Effects

Understand the Skill

Many events of the past are the result of other events that took place earlier. When something occurs as the result of things that happened earlier, it is an effect of those things.

Some events take place soon after the things that cause them. These events are short-term effects. Long-term effects can occur decades or even hundreds of years after the events that caused them. Recognizing cause-and-effect relationships will help you to better understand the connections between historical events.

Learn the Skill

As you learned in Chapter 5, "clue words" can reveal cause-and-effect connections between events. Often, however, no such words are present. Therefore, you should always be looking for what happened as a result of an action or event.

Short-term effects are usually fairly easy to identify. They are often closely linked to the event that caused them. Take this sentence, for example:

"After Solomon's death around 930 BC, revolts broke out over who should be king."

It is clear from this information that a short-term effect of Solomon's death was political unrest.

Now, consider this other passage:

"Some Israelites . . . moved to Egypt . . . The Israelites lived well in Egypt and their population grew. But this growing population worried Egypt's ruler, the pharaoh. He feared that the Israelites would soon become too powerful. To prevent this from happening, the pharaoh made the Israelites slaves."

Look carefully at the information in the passage. No clue words exist. However, it shows that one effect of the Israelites' move to Egypt was the growth of their population. It takes time for a population to increase, so this was a long-term effect of the Israelites' move.

Recognizing long-term effects is not always easy, however, because they often occur well after the event that caused them. Therefore, the long-term effects of those events may not be discussed at the time. This is why you should always ask yourself why an event might have happened as you study it.

For example, many of our modern laws are based on the Ten Commandments of the ancient Israelites. Religion is a major force in history that makes things happen. Other such forces include economics, science and technology, geography, and the meeting of peoples with different cultures. Ask yourself if one of these forces is a part of the event you are studying. If so, the event may have long-term effects.

Practice and Apply the Skill

Review the information in Chapter 7 and answer the following questions.

1. What were the short-term effects of King Solomon's rule of the Israelites? What long-term benefit resulted from his rule?

2. What was the short-term effect of the destruction of the Temple at Jerusalem in AD 70? What effect has that event had on the world today?

Chapter Review

Visual Summary

Use the visual summary below to help you review the main ideas of the chapter.

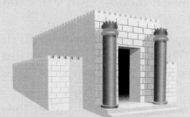

The early Hebrews settled in Canaan.

In Canaan the Israelites formed the kingdom of Israel and built a great Temple to God.

The Romans destroyed the Second Temple in Jerusalem and forced the Jews to leave.

Jewish religion and traditions have united the Jews over the centuries.

Reviewing Vocabulary, Terms, and People

For each group of terms below, write a sentence that shows how the terms in the group are related.

1. Abraham
   Judaism

2. Moses
   Exodus

3. David
   Solomon

4. Torah
   Talmud

5. Passover
   High Holy Days

6. Moses
   Ten Commandments

7. Passover
   Exodus

8. monotheism
   Judaism

9. synagogues
   rabbis

10. principles
    Torah

Comprehension and Critical Thinking

SECTION 1 *(Pages 202–207)*

11. a. Describe How did Abraham and Moses shape the history of the Hebrews and Israelites?

b. Compare and Contrast What did Saul, David, and Solomon have in common? How did they differ?

c. Evaluate Of Esther, Deborah, Miriam, and Ruth, which do you think provided the best example of how people should treat their families? Explain your answer.

SECTION 2 *(Pages 208–213)*

12. a. Identify What are the basic beliefs of Judaism?

b. Analyze What do the various sacred Jewish texts contain?

c. Elaborate How are Jewish ideas observed in modern Western society?

SECTION 3 *(Pages 214–219)*

13. a. Describe What happened as a result of tensions between the Romans and the Jews?

b. Analyze What led to the creation of the two main Jewish cultural traditions?

c. Predict In the future, what role do you think holy days and other traditions will play in Judaism? Explain your answer.

Reading Skills

Identifying Facts and Opinions *Identify each of the following statements as a fact or an opinion.*

14. Much of what we know about Jewish history comes from the work of archaeologists.

15. Archaeologists should spend more time studying Jewish history.

16. The Exodus is one of the most fascinating events in world history.

17. Until 1947, scholars did not know about the Dead Sea Scrolls.

18. Hanukkah is a Jewish holy day that takes place every December.

Social Studies Skills

19. Identifying Short- and Long-Term Effects *Identify both the short-term and long-term effects of each of the following events.*

	Short-Term Effects	Long-Term Effects
the Exodus		
the Babylonian Captivity		
the expulsion of the Jews from Jerusalem		

Using the Internet

20. Activity: Interpreting Maps Migration and conflict were key factors shaping Jewish history and culture. The Exodus, the Babylonian Captivity, and the revolts against Rome forced Israelites and later Jews to adapt their culture and settle in regions outside Israel. Go online to research the birthplace of Judaism and the Jews' movements into other parts of the world. Create an annotated map. Your map should include a legend as well as labels to identify events and explain their impact on the Jewish people.

Reviewing Themes

21. Religion How did monotheism shape the history of the Jews?

22. Religion Do you agree or disagree with this statement: "The history of Judaism is also the history of the Hebrew and Jewish people." Why?

23. Religion How does Mosaic law affect the daily lives of Jewish people?

FOCUS ON WRITING

24. Designing Your Web Site Look back at your notes and how you've organized them. Have you included all important facts and details? Will people be able to find information easily?

What will appear in menus or as hot links, and elsewhere on the page? What images will you include? Draw a rough diagram or sketch of your page. Be sure to label the parts of your page.

Most of the information in your textbook is presented chronologically, by the year or era. How did you present the information?

DIRECTIONS: Read each question, and write the letter of the best response.

1 **Use the map to answer the following question.**

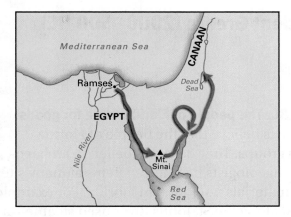

The map above illustrates

A the Babylonian Captivity.

B the Exodus.

C Abraham's migration to Canaan.

D the capture of Jerusalem by the Romans.

2 **The Jews believe that the Ten Commandments were given by God to**

A Moses.

B Abraham.

C King David.

D King Solomon.

3 **The ancient Jews probably were the first people to**

A conduct religious ceremonies.

B have a code of laws.

C practice monotheism.

D hold religious beliefs.

4 **The basic teachings and laws that guide the Jewish people are found in the**

A Talmud.

B Torah.

C Book of the Dead.

D Dead Sea Scrolls.

5 **Which group was *most* responsible for the migration of Jews out of Jerusalem to other parts of the Mediterranean region?**

A the Israelites

B the Philistines

C the Egyptians

D the Romans

Connecting with Past Learnings

6 **Moses transmitted a set of laws for the Israelites to follow. What other ancient leader is famous for issuing a code of laws?**

A Gilgamesh

B Tutankhamen

C Asoka

D Hammurabi

7 **Jewish teachings required people to honor and respect their parents. This was an idea also common in China. In his writings, who else encouraged people to respect their parents?**

A Chandragupta Maurya

B Shi Huangdi

C Confucius

D Abraham

FLORIDA...
The Story Continues

CHAPTER 8, Ancient Greece (2000–500 BC)

EVENTS **2000–500 BC: The people of Florida trade for goods.**
Archaeologists believe that the people of Florida traded with faraway groups. They base this belief on archaeological evidence. Archaeologists have found items at many sites that are made from materials not found in Florida. For example, the people who lived along the St. Johns River used steatite—a soft talc-like stone—to weight their throwing sticks. Florida does not have deposits of steatite. The closest source is the area around Atlanta, Georgia. The St. Johns people must have traded with groups farther north to get the steatite. The St. Johns people were not the only ones who traded for steatite. Archaeologists have found items made of steatite at sites around the Tampa Bay area as well.

PLACES **2000–500 BC: Water routes help connect cultures.**
Many of Florida's native people lived along the coasts and along rivers. Water provided a highway between groups. Archaeologists point to differences in cultural traits between groups as evidence of the importance of water routes in shaping culture. For example, archaeologists have found that groups from the Choctawhatchee Bay area in the Florida panhandle had more cultural traits in common with people from New Orleans than with people who lived around the St. Johns River. New Orleans and the St. Johns River are about the same distance from Choctawhatchee Bay. However, ancient people would have had to make the trip to the St. Johns River overland. They could have traveled to New Orleans by canoe. That would have been a much easier trip.

PEOPLE **1905: Greek divers come to Tarpon Springs to harvest the sponge beds.** Divers hunting for turtles accidently discovered huge sponge beds off the coast of Tarpon Springs in 1873. By 1900 Tarpon Springs was the largest sponge port in the United States. John Cocoris, a sponge buyer from New York, believed the industry could run more efficiently. People were using large hooks to haul the sponges into boats. He knew the Greeks had a better way. They used divers in special suits to harvest sponges from deep waters. Cocoris brought in 500 divers from Greece. More soon followed. Tarpon Springs developed a thriving Greek culture.

EVENTS **Present: Florida has a representative government.** Floridians elect officials to make state laws and to enforce them. State representatives are elected to two-year terms. State senators are elected to four-year terms. Members of the state legislature make the laws. They meet for a 60-day session each year. Special sessions are called when needed. Voters also elect the governor, who serves a four-year term. The governor sees that the laws are carried out.

PLACES **Present: The names for several Florida cities are taken from Greek mythology.** Greek mythology and ancient Greek history provide the names for many places in Florida. Apollo Beach and Apollo Annex are named after Apollo, the Greek god of the sun. Arcadia is named for a famous place in ancient Greece. The name for Olympia Heights is based on Olympus, the home of the ancient Greek gods. Zephyr Hills is named after Zephyr, the West Wind. Lake Helen is named after Helen of Troy, the beautiful woman who caused the Trojan War. Marathon and Marathon Shores are named for Marathon, the site of an ancient Greek battle.

Unpacking the Florida Standards ‹···

Read the following to learn what this standard says and what it means. See FL8–FL31 to unpack all of the standards related to this chapter.

Benchmark SS.6.W.3.5 Summarize the important achievements and contributions of ancient Greek civilization. Examples are art and architecture, athletic competitions, the birth of democracy and civic responsibility, drama, history, literature, mathematics, medicine, philosophy, science, warfare.

What does it mean?

Identify the major accomplishments and contributions of Greek civilization.

 SPOTLIGHT ON
SS.6.G.2.1, SS.6.G.2.2 See page FL44 for content specifically related to these Chapter 8 standards.

Ancient Greece

Essential Question What factors shaped government in Greece?

Florida Next Generation Sunshine State Standards

LA.6.1.6.3 The student will use context clues to determine meanings of unfamiliar words. **LA.6.1.7.1** The student will use background knowledge of subject and related content areas, prereading strategies, graphic representations, and knowledge of text structure to make and confirm complex predictions of content, purpose, and organization of a reading selection. **SS.6.C.1.1** Identify democratic concepts developed in ancient Greece that served as a foundation for American constitutional democracy. **SS.6.C.2.1** Identify principles (civic participation, role of government) from ancient Greek and Roman civilizations which are reflected in the American political process today, and discuss their effect on the American political process. **SS.6.G.1.6** Use a map to identify major bodies of water of the world, and explain ways they have impacted the development of civilizations. **SS.6.G.1.7** Use maps to identify characteristics and boundaries of ancient civilizations that have shaped the world today. **SS.6.G.2.1** Explain how major physical characteristics, natural resources, climate, and absolute and relative locations have influenced settlement, interactions, and the economies of ancient civilizations of the world. **SS.6.G.2.2** Differentiate between continents, regions, countries, and cities in order to understand the complexities of regions created by civilizations. **SS.6.G.3.1** Explain how the physical landscape has affected the development of agriculture and industry in the ancient world. **SS.6.G.4.2** Use maps to trace significant migrations, and analyze their results. **SS.6.G.5.1** Identify the methods used to compensate for the scarcity of resources in the ancient world. **SS.6.G.5.3** Use geographic tools and terms to analyze how famine, drought, and natural disasters plagued many ancient civilizations. **SS.6.W.1.1** Use timelines to identify chronological order of historical events. **SS.6.W.1.3** Interpret primary and secondary sources. **SS.6.W.3.2** Explain the democratic concepts (polis, civic participation and voting rights, legislative bodies, written constitutions, rule of law) developed in ancient Greece. **SS.6.W.3.3** Compare life in Athens and Sparta (government and the status of citizens, women and children, foreigners, helots). **SS.6.W.3.5** Summarize the important achievements and contributions of ancient Greek civilization. **SS.6.W.3.6** Determine the impact of key figures from ancient Greece.

FOCUS ON WRITING

A Myth Like most people, the Greeks enjoyed good stories. But they also took their stories seriously. They used stories called myths to explain everything from the creation of the world to details of everyday life. Reading this chapter will provide you with ideas you can use to create your own myth.

CHAPTER EVENTS

c. 2000 BC The Minoan civilization prospers in Crete.

2000 BC

WORLD EVENTS

c. 2000 BC The main part of Stonehenge is built in England.

In this photo you see the ruins of the temple at Delphi. It was one of the most sacred places in ancient Greece.

c. 1200 BC
The Greeks and Trojans fight the Trojan War.

c. 750 BC
The Greeks begin to build city-states.

c. 500 BC
Athens becomes the world's first democracy.

| 1700 BC | 1400 BC | 1100 BC | 800 BC | 500 BC |

c. 1200 BC
The Olmec civilization develops in the Americas.

c. 900 BC
The Phoenicians dominate trade in the Mediterranean.

753 BC
According to legend, Rome is founded.

ANCIENT GREECE **225**

Reading Social Studies

Focus on Themes In this chapter, you will read about the civilizations of ancient Greece. Whether reading about the Minoans and Mycenaeans or the Spartans and Athenians, you will see that where the people lived affected how they lived.

You will also read how the government of these ancient people changed over the years. By the end of this chapter, you will have learned a great deal about the **geography** and the **politics** of the ancient Greeks.

Greek and Latin Word Roots

Focus on Reading Sometimes when you read an unusual word, you can figure out what it means by using the other words around it. Other times you might need to consult a dictionary. But sometimes, if you know what the word's root parts mean, you can figure out its meaning. The charts below show you several English words that have Greek and Latin roots.

Common Latin Roots		
Root	**Meaning**	**Sample words**
-aud-	hear	audience, audible
liter-	writing	literature, literary
re-	again	repeat, redo
-script-	write	script, manuscript
sub-	below	submarine, substandard
trans-	across	transport, translate

Common Greek Roots		
Root	**Meaning**	**Sample words**
acr-	top	acropolis, acrophobia
-archy	rule	monarchy, erchitect
-cracy	power	democracy
dem-	people	demonstrate, democrat
olig-	few	oligarchy
-ology	study of	biology, geology

LA.6.1.6.3 The student will use context clues to determine meanings of unfamiliar words.

Key Terms and People

You Try It!

Each of the following sentences is taken from the chapter you are about to read. After you've read the sentences, answer the questions at the bottom of the page.

Getting to the Root of the Word

1. Because the Greeks loved myths and stories, it is no surprise that they created great works of <u>literature</u>. (*p. 246*)
2. Writers have <u>retold</u> ancient stories, sometimes set in modern times. (*p. 248*)
3. The town around the <u>acropolis</u> was surrounded by walls for added protection. (*p. 232*)
4. Athens developed the world's first <u>democracy</u>. (*p. 238*)
5. Minoan ships <u>transported</u> goods such as wood, olive oil, and pottery. (*p. 230*)

Answer the following questions about the underlined words. Use the Common Roots charts on the opposite page for help.

1. Which of the underlined words has a root word that means "writing?" How does knowing the root word help you figure out what the word means?

2. What two root words make up the word *democracy*? How do the root words help you figure out the meaning of *democracy*?

3. In the second sentence, what do you think *retold* means? How could this be related to the root *re-*?

4. What's the root word in *transported*? What does *transported* mean? How is that definition related to the meaning of the root word?

5. The root word *phobia* means "fear of," and the word *acrophobia* means "fear of heights." How is the word *acrophobia* related to the word *acropolis* in the third sentence?

6. How many more words can you think of that use the roots in the charts on the opposite page? Make a list and share it with your classmates.

Academic Vocabulary

Success in school is related to knowing academic vocabulary— the words that are frequently used in school assignments and discussions. In this chapter, you will learn the following academic word:

influence (*p. 230*)

As you read Chapter 8, pay close attention to the highlighted words. Many of those words are Greek or come from Greek roots. Refer to the chart on the opposite page to help you understand what those words mean.

Geography and the Early Greeks

SS.6.E.1.3, SS.6.E.3.2, SS.6.E.3.3, SS.6.E.3.4, SS.6.G.1.4, SS.6.G.1.6, SS.6.G.1.7, SS.6.G.2.1, SS.6.G.2.2, SS.6.G.2.4, SS.6.G.2.5, SS.6.G.3.1, SS.6.G.4.2, SS.6.G.5.1, SS.6.G.5.3, SS.6.W.3.2

What You Will Learn...

Main Ideas

1. Geography helped shape early Greek civilization.
2. Trading cultures developed in the Minoan and Mycenaean civilizations.
3. The Greeks created city-states for protection and security.

The Big Idea

Greece's geography and its nearness to the sea strongly influenced the development of trade and the growth of city-states.

Key Terms

polis, *p. 232*
classical, *p. 232*
acropolis, *p. 232*

Online Resource
TAKING NOTES

Use the graphic organizer online to take notes on how Greece's geography affected the development of trade and city-states.

If **YOU** were there...

You live on the rocky coast of a bright blue sea. Across the water you can see dozens of islands and points of land jutting out into the sea. Rugged mountains rise steeply behind your village. It is hard to travel across the mountains in order to visit other villages or towns. Near your home on the coast is a sheltered cove where it's easy to anchor a boat.

What could you do to make a living here?

BUILDING BACKGROUND The paragraph you just read could be describing many parts of Greece, a peninsula in southern Europe. Greece's mountain ranges run right up to the coast in many places, making travel and farming difficult. Although it does not seem like the easiest place in the world to live, Greece was home to some of the ancient world's greatest civilizations.

Greece is a land of rugged mountains, rocky coastlines, and beautiful islands. The trees you see are olive trees. Olives were grown by the early Greeks for food and oil.

Geography Shapes Greek Civilization

The Greeks lived on rocky, mountainous lands surrounded by water. The mainland of Greece is a peninsula, an area of land that is surrounded on three sides by water. But the Greek peninsula is very irregular. It's one big peninsula made up of a series of smaller peninsulas. The land and sea intertwine like your hand and fingers in a bowl of water. In addition, there are many islands. Look at the map of Greece and notice the rugged coastline.

In your mind, picture those peninsulas and islands dominated by mountains that run almost to the sea. Just a few small valleys and coastal plains provide flat land for farming and villages. Now you have an image of Greece, a land where one of the world's greatest civilizations developed.

Mountains and Settlements

Because mountains cover much of Greece, there are few flat areas for farmland. People settled in those flat areas along the coast and in river valleys. They lived in villages and towns separated by mountains and seas.

Travel across the mountains and seas was difficult, so communities were isolated from one another. As a result, the people created their own governments and ways of life. Even though they spoke the same language, Greek communities saw themselves as separate countries.

Seas and Ships

Since travel inland across the rugged mountains was so difficult, the early Greeks turned to the seas. On the south was the huge Mediterranean Sea, to the west was the Ionian (eye-OH-nee-uhn) Sea, and to the east was the Aegean (ee-JEE-uhn) Sea.

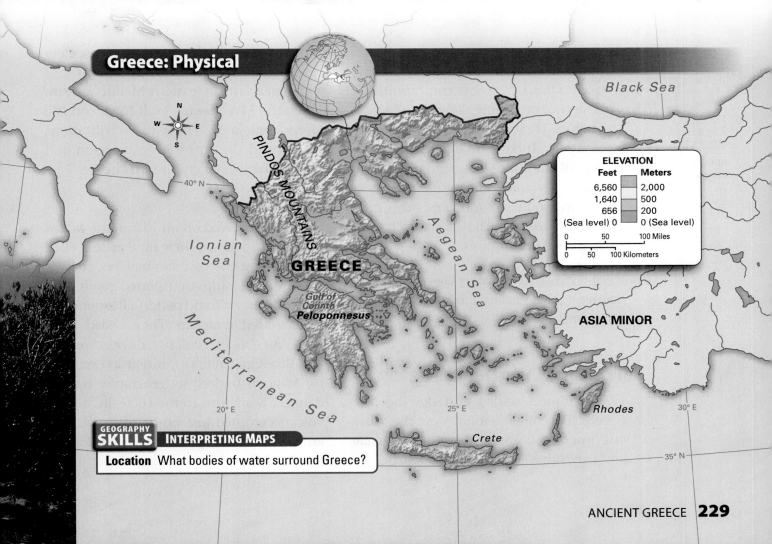

Greece: Physical

Black Sea

PINDOS MOUNTAINS

40° N

Ionian Sea

GREECE

Gulf of Corinth

Peloponnesus

Aegean Sea

ASIA MINOR

Mediterranean Sea

20° E

25° E

30° E

Rhodes

Crete

35° N

ELEVATION

Feet	Meters
6,560	2,000
1,640	500
656	200
(Sea level) 0	0 (Sea level)

0　50　100 Miles

0　50　100 Kilometers

GEOGRAPHY SKILLS INTERPRETING MAPS

Location What bodies of water surround Greece?

Early Trading Cultures

The Minoans and Mycenaeans were expert shipbuilders and seafarers. They sailed throughout the eastern Mediterranean to trade.

For what did the Minoans and Mycenaeans use their ships?

The Minoans

The Minoans traded goods like this vase decorated with an octopus. Trade made the Minoans rich enough to build magnificent buildings. These are the ruins of a great palace in the Minoan city of Knossos, on the island of Crete.

It's not surprising that the early Greeks used the sea as a source for food and as a way of trading with other communities.

The Greeks became skilled shipbuilders and sailors. Their ships sailed to Asia Minor (present-day Turkey), to Egypt, and to the islands of the Mediterranean and Aegean seas. As they traveled around these seas, they found sources of food and other products they needed. They also exchanged ideas with other cultures.

READING CHECK Drawing Conclusions
How did mountains affect the location of Greek settlements?

Trading Cultures Develop

Many cultures settled and developed in Greece. Two of the earliest were the Minoans (muh-NOH-uhnz) and the Mycenaeans (my-suh-NEE-uhns). By 2000 BC the Minoans had built an advanced society on the island of Crete. Crete lay south of the Aegean in the eastern Mediterranean. Later, the Mycenaeans built towns on the Greek mainland. These two civilizations **influenced** the entire Aegean region and helped shape later cultures in Greece.

The Minoans

Because they lived on an island, the Minoans spent much of their time at sea. They were among the best shipbuilders of their time. Minoan ships transported goods such as wood, olive oil, and pottery all around the eastern Mediterranean. They traded these goods for copper, gold, silver, and jewels.

Although Crete's location was excellent for Minoan traders, its geography had its dangers. Sometime in the 1600s BC a huge volcano erupted just north of Crete. This eruption created a giant wave that flooded much of Crete. In addition, the eruption

ACADEMIC VOCABULARY

influence change, or have an effect on

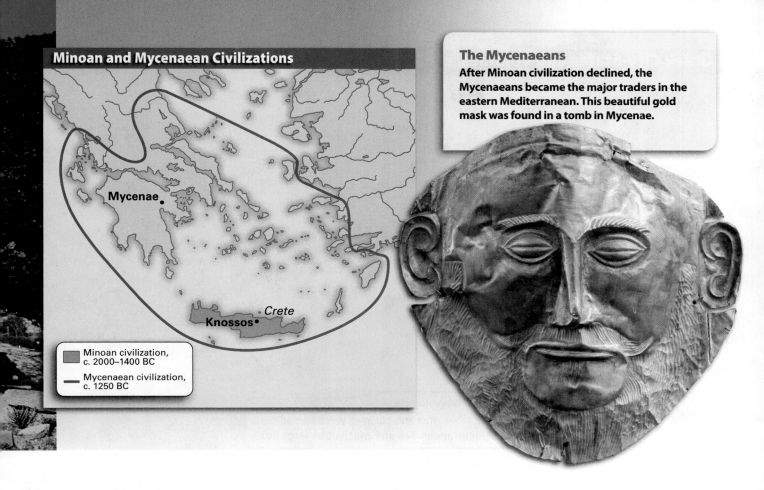

Minoan and Mycenaean Civilizations

Mycenae.

Knossos• •Crete

Minoan civilization,
c. 2000–1400 BC

Mycenaean civilization,
c. 1250 BC

The Mycenaeans

After Minoan civilization declined, the Mycenaeans became the major traders in the eastern Mediterranean. This beautiful gold mask was found in a tomb in Mycenae.

threw up huge clouds of ash, ruining crops and burying cities. This eruption may have led to the end of Minoan civilization.

The Mycenaeans

Although they lived in what is now Greece and influenced Greek society, historians don't consider the Minoans to be Greek. This is because the Minoans didn't speak the Greek language. The first people to speak Greek, and therefore the first to be considered Greek, were the Mycenaeans.

While the Minoans were sailing the Mediterranean, the Mycenaeans were building fortresses all over the Greek mainland. The largest and most powerful fortress was Mycenae (my-SEE-nee), after which the Mycenaeans were named.

By the mid-1400s, Minoan society had declined. That decline allowed the Mycenaeans to take over Crete and become the major traders in the eastern Mediterranean.

They set up colonies in northern Greece and Italy from which they shipped goods to markets around the Mediterranean and Black seas.

The Mycenaeans didn't think trade had to be conducted peacefully. They often attacked other kingdoms. Some historians think the Mycenaeans attacked the city of Troy, possibly starting the legendary Trojan War, which is featured in many works of literature.

Mycenaean society began to fall apart in the 1200s BC when invaders from Europe swept into Greece. At the same time, earthquakes destroyed many cities. As Mycenaean civilization crumbled, Greece slid into a period of warfare and disorder, a period called the Dark Age.

READING CHECK Finding Main Ideas
To what regions did Minoan and Mycenaean traders travel?

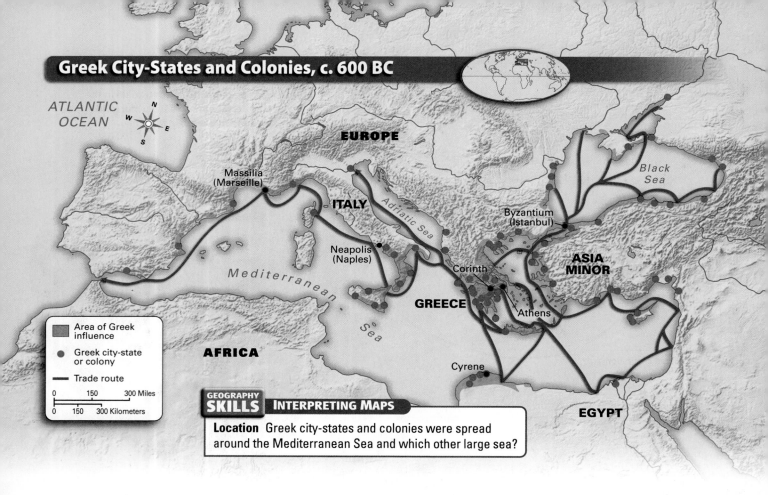

ATLANTIC OCEAN

N
W   E
S

EUROPE

Massilia (Marseille)

ITALY

Adriatic Sea

Black Sea

Byzantium (Istanbul)

Neapolis (Naples)

Mediterranean

Corinth

ASIA MINOR

GREECE

Athens

Sea

AFRICA

Cyrene

EGYPT

Legend:
- Area of Greek influence
- ● Greek city-state or colony
- — Trade route

0   150   300 Miles
0   150   300 Kilometers

GEOGRAPHY SKILLS — INTERPRETING MAPS

Location Greek city-states and colonies were spread around the Mediterranean Sea and which other large sea?

Greeks Create City-States

The Greeks of the Dark Age left no written records. All that we know about the period comes from archaeological findings.

About 300 years after the Mycenaean civilization crumbled, the Greeks started to join together in small groups for protection and stability. Over time, these groups set up independent city-states. The Greek word for a city-state is **polis** (PAH-luhs). The creation of city-states marks the beginning of what is known as Greece's classical age. A **classical** age is one that is marked by great achievements.

Life in a City-State

A Greek city was usually built around a strong fortress. This fortress often stood on top of a high hill called the **acropolis** (uh-KRAH-puh-luhs). The town around the acropolis was surrounded by walls for added protection.

Not everyone who lived in the city-state actually lived inside the city walls. Farmers, for example, usually lived near their fields outside the walls. In times of war, however, women, children, and elderly people all gathered inside the city walls for protection. As a result, they remained safe while the men of the polis formed an army to fight off its enemies.

Life in the city often focused on the marketplace, or agora (A-guh-ruh) in Greek. Farmers brought their crops to the market to trade for goods made by craftsmen in the town. Because it was a large open space, the market also served as a meeting place. People held both political and religious assemblies in the market. It often contained shops as well.

The city-state became the foundation of Greek civilization. Besides providing security for its people, the city gave them an identity. People thought of themselves

SS.6.W.3.2 Explain the democratic concepts (polis, civic participation and voting rights, legislative bodies, written constitutions, rule of law) developed in ancient Greece.

FOCUS ON READING

How do Greek roots give you clues to the meaning of *acropolis*?

as residents of a city, not as Greeks. Because the city-state was so central to their lives, the Greeks expected people to participate in its affairs, especially in its economy and its government.

City-States and Colonization

Life in Greece eventually became more settled. People no longer had to fear raiders swooping down on their cities. As a result, they were free to think about things other than defense. Some Greeks began to dream of becoming rich through trade. Others became curious about neighboring lands around the Mediterranean Sea. Some also worried about how to deal with Greece's growing population. Despite their different reasons, all these people eventually reached the same idea: the Greeks should establish colonies.

Before long, groups from city-states around Greece began to set up colonies in distant lands. After they were set up, Greek colonies became independent. In other words, each colony became a new polis. In fact, some cities that began as colonies began to create colonies of their own. Eventually Greek colonies spread all around the Mediterranean and Black seas. Many big cities around the Mediterranean today began as Greek colonies. Among them are Istanbul (is-tahn-BOOL) in Turkey, Marseille (mahr-SAY) in France, and Naples in Italy.

Patterns of Trade

Although the colonies were independent, they often traded with city-states in Greece. The colonies sent metals such as copper and iron back to mainland Greece. In return, the Greek city-states sent wine, olive oil, and other products.

Trade made the city-states much richer. Because of their locations, some city-states became great trading centers. By 550 BC the Greeks had become the greatest traders in the whole Aegean region. Greek ships sailed to Egypt and cities around the Black Sea.

READING CHECK **Analyzing** Why did the Greeks develop city-states?

SUMMARY AND PREVIEW In this section you learned about the creation of city-states and how they affected Greek society. In the next section you will read about how the government of one city-state changed as people became more interested in how they were ruled.

SS.6.E.3.3 Describe traditional economies (Egypt, Greece, Rome, Kush) and elements of those economies that led to the rise of a merchant class and trading partners.

Section 1 Assessment

Reviewing Ideas, Terms, and People
1. **a. Identify** What kinds of landforms are found in Greece?
   b. Interpret How did the sea help shape early Greek society?
   c. Predict How might the difficulty of mountain travel have been a benefit to the Greeks?
2. **a. Recall** What was the first major civilization to develop in Greece?
   b. Compare How were the Minoans and Mycenaeans similar?
3. **a. Define** What is a **polis**?
   b. Elaborate Why do you think the Greeks built their cities around a high **acropolis**?

Critical Thinking
4. **Summarizing** Using your notes, write one descriptive sentence about Greece's geography and one about city-states. Then write a sentence summarizing the influence of geography on city-states.

| Geography | → | City-States | → | Summary |

FOCUS ON WRITING

5. **Thinking About Geographical Features as Characters** Have you ever thought about physical features as having personalities? For example, you might describe a strong, blustery wind as angry. Think about the physical features of Greece you read about in this section. What kinds of personalities might they have? Write your ideas down in your notebook.

Natural Disaster!

Nature is a powerful force. Throughout history, great natural disasters have affected civilizations. One natural disaster was so devastating that it may have contributed to the destruction of the entire Minoan civilization.

In the 1600s BC a volcano on the Greek island of Thera erupted. The colossal explosion was one of the largest in history. It was so powerful that people could see and hear it from hundreds of miles away. In a moment of nature's fury, the history of the Mediterranean world was changed forever.

BLACK SEA

Troy

ANATOLIA

Mycenae

PELOPONNESUS

Knossos

CRETE

For centuries, the Minoans had thrived on the island of Crete. The Minoans were great sea traders who often sailed to the island of Thera, just 70 miles away.

The eruption of Thera produced fast-moving waves called tsunami (soo-NAH-mee) in the Mediterranean Sea. Scientists today estimate that the waves may have traveled at about 200 miles an hour.

MEDITERRANEAN SEA

N
W   E
S

LIBYA

SS.6.G.5.3 Use geographic tools and terms to analyze how famine, drought, and natural disasters plagued many ancient civilizations.

Three Stages of
Disaster

The ancient island of Thera is known as Santorini today. The huge gap on the island's western side and the water in the middle are evidence of the explosion more than 3,500 years ago.

Stage 1

Warning Signs Following a series of earthquakes, the volcano begins to shoot ash into the sky. People flee the island in fear.

Stage 2

Explosion Ash and rock are flung into the air and sweep down the volcano's sides, destroying everything in their path. Cracks through the island rock begin to form from the powerful explosions.

Aleppo

Stage 3

Collapse The volcano collapses and falls into the sea, creating massive waves. The powerful waves slam into Crete, flooding coastal areas.

CYPRUS

The explosion produced a massive cloud of ash that smothered crops, cities, and people. For years afterward, the ash dimmed the sunlight, making it difficult for farmers to grow their crops.

GEOGRAPHY SKILLS **INTERPRETING MAPS**

1. **Location** What direction did the ash cloud travel after the island's eruption?
2. **Human-Environment Interaction** How might the effects of the ash cloud have influenced Minoan civilization?

Jericho

E G Y P T

Government in Athens

If YOU were there...

For many years, your city has been ruled by a small group of rich men. They have generally been good leaders. They have built new buildings and protected the city from enemies. But now a new leader wants to let all free men help run the government. It won't matter whether they are rich or poor. Some people, however, worry about giving power to ordinary people.

What do you think of this new government?

BUILDING BACKGROUND The decision to change a city's government was not unusual in Greece. Many cities tried several forms of government before people were satisfied. To see how these changes came about, we can look at one city whose government changed many times—Athens.

Aristocrats and Tyrants Rule

Greece is the birthplace of **democracy**, a type of government in which people rule themselves. The word democracy comes from Greek words meaning "rule of the people." But Greek city-states didn't start as democracies, and not all became democratic.

Government in Athens QUICK FACTS

Oligarchy

Early Athens was governed by a small group of powerful aristocrats. This type of government is called an oligarchy. Oligarchy means "rule by a few."

Rule by a Few People

Even Athens, the city where democracy was born, began with a different kind of government. In early Athens, kings ruled the city-state. Later, a group of rich landowners, or **aristocrats** (uh-RIS-tuh-krats), took power. A government in which only a few people have power is called an **oligarchy** (AH-luh-gar-kee).

The aristocrats dominated Athenian society. As the richest men in town, they ran the city's economy. They also served as its generals and judges. Common people had little say in the government.

In the 600s BC a group of rebels tried to overthrow the aristocrats. They failed. Possibly as a result of their attempt, however, a man named Draco (DRAY-koh) created a new set of laws for Athens. These laws were very harsh. For example, Draco's laws made minor crimes such as loitering punishable by death.

The people of Athens thought Draco's laws were too strict. In the 590s BC a man named Solon (SOH-luhn) created a set of laws that were much less harsh and gave more rights to nonaristocrats. Under Solon's constitution, all free men living in Athens became **citizens**, people who had the right to participate in government. But his efforts were not enough for the Athenians. They were ready to end the rule of the aristocracy.

The Rise of the Tyrants

Because the Athenians weren't pleased with the rule of the aristocrats, they wanted a new government. In 546 BC a noble named Peisistratus (py-SIS-truht-uhs) overthrew the oligarchy. He became the ruler of Athens. Peisistratus was called a **tyrant**, which meant a leader who held power through the use of force.

Today the word *tyrant* means a ruler who is harsh, but the word had a different meaning in ancient Greece. Athenian tyrants were usually good leaders. Tyrants were able to stay in power because they had strong armies and because the people supported them.

Peisistratus brought peace and prosperity to the city. He began new policies meant to unify the city. He created new festivals and built temples and monuments. During his rule, many improvements were made in Athens.

After Peisistratus died, his son took over as tyrant. Many aristocrats, however, were unhappy because their power was gone. Some of these aristocrats convinced a rival city-state to attack Athens. As a result of this invasion, the tyrants lost power and, for a short time, aristocrats returned to power in Athens.

READING CHECK **Finding Main Ideas** What was a tyrant in ancient Greece?

SS.6.W.3.6 Determine the impact of key figures from ancient Greece.

FOCUS ON READING
How do Greek roots give you clues to the meaning of *oligarchy*?

THE IMPACT TODAY
Today very harsh laws or rules are called "draconian" after Draco.

Tyranny
Peisistratus overthrew the oligarchy in 546 BC, and Athens became a tyranny. Tyranny means "rule by a tyrant"—a strong leader who has power.

Democracy
Around 500 BC Athens became a democracy. Democracy means "rule by the people." For the first time in history, a government was based on the votes of its free citizens.

Democracy in Action

Ancient Athens was the birthplace of democracy—the system of government in which the people rule themselves. Democracy was perhaps the greatest achievement of ancient Athens. In time, it became the Greeks' greatest gift to the world.

Only free male citizens of Athens were members of the assembly with the right to vote. Women, slaves, and foreigners could not participate.

In Athenian democracy, people debated issues in the open air, and these debates were noisy affairs.

Voting was usually done by a show of hands, but sometimes assembly members wrote their votes on broken pieces of pottery. Then officials collected these pottery pieces and counted the votes.

SS.6.C.1.1 Identify democratic concepts developed in ancient Greece that served as a foundation for American constitutional democracy.

Athens Creates Democracy

Around 500 BC a new leader named Cleisthenes (KLYS-thuh-neez) gained power in Athens. Although he was a member of one of the most powerful families in Athens, Cleisthenes didn't want aristocrats to run the government. He thought they already had too much influence. By calling on the support of the people, Cleisthenes was able to overthrow the aristocracy. Then he wrote a new constitution and established a completely new form of government.

Under Cleisthenes' leadership, Athens developed the world's first democracy. For this reason, he is sometimes called the father of democracy.

Democracy under Cleisthenes

Under Cleisthenes, all citizens in Athens had the right to participate in the assembly, or gathering of citizens, that created the city's laws. The assembly met outdoors on a hillside so that everyone could attend the meetings. During meetings, people stood before the crowd and gave speeches on political issues. Every citizen had the right to speak his opinion. In fact, the Athenians encouraged people to speak. They loved to hear speeches and debates. After the speeches were over, the assembly voted. Voting was usually done by a show of hands, but sometimes the Athenians used secret ballots.

The Athenian assembly met on a hill called the Pnyx (pah-NIKS). Sometimes, more than 6,000 men crowded onto the small hill.

Men spoke before the assembly to support or argue against different issues. Persuasive speakers often convinced others to pass laws they supported.

Men in the crowd often argued with speakers.

ANALYSIS SKILL **ANALYZING VISUALS**
How did people vote in ancient Athens?

The number of people who voted in the assembly changed from day to day. For major decisions, however, the assembly needed about 6,000 people to vote. But it wasn't always easy to gather that many people together in one place.

According to one Greek writer, the government sent slaves to the market to round up more citizens if necessary. In one of the writer's plays, slaves walked through the market holding a long rope between them. The rope was covered in red dye and would mark the clothing of anyone it touched. Any citizen with red dye on his clothing had to go to the assembly meeting or pay a large fine.

Because the assembly was so large, it was sometimes difficult to make decisions. The Athenians therefore selected citizens to be city officials and to serve on a smaller council. These officials decided which laws the assembly should discuss. This helped the government run more smoothly.

Changes in Athenian Democracy

As time passed, citizens gained more powers. For example, they served on juries to decide court cases. Juries had anywhere from 200 to 6,000 people, although juries of about 500 people were much more common. Most juries had an odd number of members to prevent ties.

THE IMPACT TODAY

Like the ancient Greeks, we use juries to decide court cases. But our modern juries have only 12 people.

SPEECH
Pericles' Funeral Oration

In 430 BC Pericles addressed the people of Athens at a funeral for soldiers who had died in battle. In his speech, Pericles tried to comfort the Athenians by reminding them of the greatness of their government.

Pericles is praising the Athenians for creating a democracy.

"Our form of government does not enter into rivalry with the institutions of others. We do not copy our neighbors, but are an example to them. It is true that we are called a democracy, for the administration is in the hands of the many and not of the few . . . There is no exclusiveness [snobbery] in our public life, and . . . we are not suspicious of one another. . . . "

–Pericles, quoted in Thucydides,

Athenian government was open to all free men, not just a few.

ANALYSIS SKILL **ANALYZING PRIMARY SOURCES**

How do you think Pericles felt Athenian government compared to other cities' governments?

Athens remained a democracy for about 170 years. It reached its height under a brilliant elected leader named **Pericles** (PER-uh-kleez). He led the government from about 460 BC until his death in 429 BC.

Pericles encouraged the Athenians to take pride in their city. He believed that participating in government was just as important as defending Athens in war. To encourage people to participate in government, Pericles began to pay people who served in public offices or on juries. Pericles also encouraged the people of Athens to introduce democracy into other parts of Greece.

End of Democracy in Athens

Eventually, the great age of Athenian democracy came to an end. In the mid-330s BC Athens was conquered by the Macedonians from north of Greece. After the conquest, Athens fell under strong Macedonian influence.

Even after being conquered by Macedonia, Athens kept its democratic government. But it was a democracy with very limited powers. The Macedonian king ruled his country like a dictator, a ruler who held all the power. No one could make any decisions without his approval.

In Athens, the assembly still met to make laws, but it had to be careful not to upset the king. The Athenians didn't dare make any drastic changes to their laws without the king's consent. They weren't happy with this situation, but they feared the king's powerful army. Before long, though, the Athenians lost even this limited democracy. In the 320s BC a new king took over Greece and ended Athenian democracy forever.

READING CHECK **Summarizing** How were citizens involved in the government of Athens?

Ancient Democracy Differs from Modern Democracy

Like ancient Athens, the United States has a democratic government in which the people hold power. But our modern democracy is very different from the ancient Athenians' democracy.

Direct Democracy

All citizens in Athens could participate directly in the government. We call this form of government a direct democracy. It is called direct democracy because each person's decision directly affects the outcome of a vote. In Athens, citizens gathered together to discuss issues and vote on them. Each person's vote counted, and the majority ruled.

The United States is too large for direct democracy to work for the whole country. For example, it would be impossible for all citizens to gather in one place for a debate. Instead, the founders of the United States set up another kind of democracy.

Representative Democracy

The democracy created by the founders of the United States is a representative democracy, or republic. In this system, the citizens elect officials to represent them in the government. These elected officials then meet to make the country's laws and to enforce them. For example, Americans elect senators and representatives to Congress, the body that makes the country's laws. Americans don't vote on each law that Congress passes but trust their chosen representatives to vote for them.

READING CHECK **Contrasting** How are direct democracy and representative democracy different?

Democracy Then and Now

QUICK FACTS

In Athenian Direct Democracy...	In American Representative Democracy...
■ All citizens met as a group to debate and vote directly on every issue.	■ Citizens elect representatives to debate and vote on issues for them.
■ There was no separation of powers. Citizens created laws, enforced laws, and acted as judges.	■ There is a separation of powers. Citizens elect some people to create laws, others to enforce laws, and others to be judges.
■ Only free male citizens could vote. Women and slaves could not vote.	■ Men and women who are citizens have the right to vote.

SUMMARY AND PREVIEW In this section, you learned about the development and decline of democracy in Athens. You also learned how Athenian democracy influenced the government of the United States. In the next section, you will learn about the beliefs and culture of the ancient Greeks and how they affect our culture and literature today.

SS.6.C.2.1 Identify principles (civic participation, role of government) from ancient Greek and Roman civilizations which are reflected in the American political process today, and discuss their effect on the American political process.

Section 2 Assessment

Reviewing Ideas, Terms, and People

1. **a. Define** What are **aristocrats**?
   b. Contrast How were **oligarchy** and **tyranny** different?
2. **a. Describe** Describe the **democracy** created by Cleisthenes.
   b. Analyze How did **Pericles** change Athenian democracy?
3. **a. Identify** What type of democracy did Athens have?
   b. Develop In what situations would a representative democracy work better than a direct democracy?

Critical Thinking

4. **Finding Main Ideas** Draw a chart like the one shown. Using your notes, identify who held power in each type of government. Then write a sentence explaining what role common people had in each government.

Oligarchy	Tyranny	Democracy

FOCUS ON WRITING

5. **Connecting Personalities and Governments** Think back to the personalities you assigned to natural features in Section 1. What if people with these same personalities were working to create a government? What kind would they create? Would they rule as tyrants or build a democracy? Write your thoughts in your notebook.

Greek Mythology and Literature

What You Will Learn...

Main Ideas

1. The Greeks created myths to explain the world.
2. Ancient Greek literature provides some of the world's greatest poems and stories.
3. Greek literature lives on and influences our world even today.

The Big Idea

The ancient Greeks created great myths and works of literature that influence the way we speak and write today.

Key Terms and People

mythology, *p. 243*
Homer, *p. 246*
Sappho, *p. 247*
Aesop, *p. 247*
fables, *p. 247*

Online Resource
TAKING NOTES

Use the graphic organizer online to record characteristics of Greek myths and literature.

If **YOU** were there...

As a farmer in ancient Greece, your way of life depends on events in nature. The crops you grow need sunshine and rain, though thunder and lightning scare you. When you look up at the night sky, you wonder about the twinkling lights you see there. You know that at certain times of the year, the weather will turn cold and gray and plants will die. Then, a few months later, green plants will grow again.

How might you explain these natural events?

BUILDING BACKGROUND The Greeks lived in a time long before the development of modern science. To them, natural events like thunderstorms and changing seasons were mysterious. Today we can explain what causes these events. But to the Greeks, they seemed like the work of powerful gods.

Hephaestus

Hestia

Demeter

Poseidon

Dionysus

Myths Explain the World

The ancient Greeks believed in many gods. These gods were at the center of Greek **mythology**—a body of stories about gods and heroes that try to explain how the world works. Each story, or myth, explained natural or historical events.

Greek Gods

People today have scientific explanations for events like thunder, earthquakes, and volcanic eruptions. The ancient Greeks did not. They believed their gods caused these events to happen, and they created myths to explain the gods' actions.

Among the most important Greek gods were the ones in the picture below:

- Zeus, king of the gods
- Hera, queen of the gods
- Poseidon, god of the sea
- Hades, god of the underworld
- Demeter, goddess of agriculture
- Hestia, goddess of the hearth
- Athena, goddess of wisdom
- Apollo, god of the sun
- Artemis, goddess of the moon
- Ares, god of war
- Aphrodite, goddess of love
- Hephaestus, god of metalworking
- Dionysus, god of celebration
- Hermes, the messenger god

HISTORY

VIDEO
The Panathenaia
⬈ Online Resource

Olympian Gods

Hermes

Zeus

Athena

Ares

Apollo

Aphrodite

Hera

Artemis

Hades

ANALYSIS SKILL **ANALYZING VISUALS**

What can you see that indicates the Olympian gods have superhuman powers?

Gods and Mythology

The Greeks saw the work of the gods in events all around them. For example, the Greeks lived in an area where volcanic eruptions were common. To explain these eruptions, they told stories about the god Hephaestus (hi-FES-tuhs), who lived underground. The fire and lava that poured out of volcanoes, the Greeks said, came from the huge fires of the god's forge. At this forge he created weapons and armor for the other gods.

The Greeks did not think the gods spent all their time creating disasters, though. They also believed the gods caused daily events. For example, they believed the goddess of agriculture, Demeter (di-MEE-tuhr), created the seasons. According to Greek myth, Demeter had a daughter who was kidnapped by another god. The desperate goddess begged the god to let her daugh-ter go, and eventually he agreed to let her return to her mother for six months every year. During the winter, Demeter is separated from her daughter and misses her. In her grief, she doesn't let plants grow. When her daughter comes home, the goddess is happy, and summer comes to Greece. To the Greeks, this story explained why winter came every year.

To keep the gods happy, the Greeks built great temples to honor them all around Greece. In return, however, they expected the gods to give them help when they needed it. For example, many Greeks in need of advice traveled to Delphi, a city in central Greece. There they spoke to the oracle, a female priest of Apollo to whom they thought the god gave answers. The oracle at Delphi was so respected that Greek leaders sometimes asked her for advice about how to rule their cities.

Theseus the Hero
According to legend, Athens had to send 14 people to Crete every year to be eaten by the Minotaur, a terrible monster. But Theseus, a hero from Athens, traveled to Crete and killed the Minotaur, freeing the people of Athens from this burden.

Let the Games Begin!

One way the ancient Greeks honored their gods was by holding sporting contests like the one shown on the vase. The largest took place every four years at Olympia, a city in southern Greece. Held in honor of Zeus, this event was called the Olympic Games. Athletes competed in footraces, chariot races, boxing, wrestling, and throwing events. Only men could compete. The Greeks held these games every four years for more than 1,000 years, until the AD 320s.

In modern times, people began to hold the Olympics again. The first modern Olympics took place in Athens in 1896. Since then, athletes from many nations have assembled in cities around the world to compete. Today the Olympics include 28 sports, and both men and women participate. They are still held every four years. In 2004 the Olympic Games once again returned to their birthplace, Greece.

ANALYSIS SKILL **ANALYZING INFORMATION**

How do you think the modern Olympics are similar to the ancient Games? How do you think they are different?

Heroes and Mythology

Not all Greek myths were about gods. Many told about the adventures of great heroes. Some of these heroes were real people, while others were not. The Greeks loved to tell the stories of heroes who had special abilities and faced terrible monsters. The people of each city had their favorite hero, usually someone from there.

The people of Athens, for example, told stories about the hero Theseus. According to legend, he traveled to Crete and killed the Minotaur, a terrible monster that was half human and half bull. People from northern Greece told myths about Jason and how he sailed across the seas in search of a great treasure, fighting enemies the whole way.

Perhaps the most famous of all Greek heroes was a man called Hercules. The myths explain how Hercules fought many monsters and performed nearly impossible tasks. For example, he fought and killed the hydra, a huge snake with nine heads and poisonous fangs. Every time Hercules cut off one of the monster's heads, two more heads grew in its place. In the end, Hercules had to burn the hydra's neck each time he cut off a head to keep a new head from growing. People from all parts of Greece enjoyed stories about Hercules and his great deeds.

READING CHECK **Finding Main Ideas** How did the Greeks use myths to explain the world around them?

Ancient Greek Literature

Because the Greeks loved myths and stories, it is no surprise that they created great works of literature. Early Greek writers produced long epic poems, romantic poetry, and some of the world's most famous stories.

Homer and Epic Poetry

Among the earliest Greek writings are two great epic poems, the *Iliad* and the *Odyssey*, by a poet named **Homer**. Like most epics, both poems describe the deeds of great heroes. The heroes in Homer's poems fought in the Trojan War. In this war, the Mycenaean Greeks fought the Trojans, people of the city called Troy.

The *Iliad* tells the story of the last years of the Trojan War. It focuses on the deeds of the Greeks, especially Achilles (uh-KIL-eez), the greatest of all Greek warriors. It describes in great detail the battles between the Greeks and their Trojan enemies.

The *Odyssey* describes the challenges that the Greek hero Odysseus (oh-DI-see-uhs) faced on his way home from the war. For 10 years after the war ends, Odysseus tries to get home, but many obstacles stand in his way. He has to fight his way past terrible monsters, powerful magicians, and even angry gods.

Both the *Iliad* and the *Odyssey* are great tales of adventure. But to the Greeks Homer's poems were much more than just entertainment. They were central to the ancient Greek education system. People memorized long passages of the poems as part of their lessons. They admired Homer's poems and the heroes described in them as symbols of Greece's great history.

Homer's poems influenced later writers. They copied his writing styles and borrowed some of the stories and ideas he wrote about in his works. Homer's poems are considered some of the greatest literary works ever produced.

BIOGRAPHY

Homer
800s–700s BC

Historians know nothing about Homer, the greatest poet of the ancient world. Some don't think such a person ever lived. The ancient Greeks believed he had, though, and seven different cities claimed to be his birthplace. According to ancient legend, Homer was blind and recited the *Iliad* and the *Odyssey* aloud. It wasn't until much later that the poems were written down.

Making Predictions Why might scholars not be sure that Homer existed?

In Homer's *Odyssey*, the half woman and half bird Sirens sang sweet songs that made passing sailors forget everything and crash their ships. To get past the Sirens, Odysseus plugged his crew's ears with wax and had himself tied to his ship's mast.

Lyric Poetry

Other poets wrote poems that were often set to music. During a performance, the poet played a stringed instrument called a lyre while reading a poem. These poets were called lyric poets after their instrument, the lyre. Today, the words of songs are called lyrics after these ancient Greek poets.

Most poets in Greece were men, but the most famous lyric poet was a woman named **Sappho** (SAF-oh). Her poems were beautiful and emotional. Most of her poems were about love and relationships with her friends and family.

Fables

Other Greeks told stories to teach people important lessons. **Aesop** (EE-sahp), for example, is famous for his fables. **Fables** are short stories that teach the reader lessons about life or give advice on how to live.

In most of Aesop's fables, animals are the main characters. The animals talk and act like humans. One of Aesop's most famous stories is the tale of the ants and the grasshopper:

"The ants were spending a fine winter's day drying grain collected in the summertime. A Grasshopper, perishing [dying] with famine [hunger], passed by and earnestly [eagerly] begged for a little food. The Ants inquired [asked] of him, "Why did you not treasure up food during the summer?" He replied, "I had not leisure enough. I passed the days in singing." They then said in derision: "If you were foolish enough to sing all the summer, you must dance supperless to bed in the winter."
–Aesop, from "The Ants and the Grasshopper"

The lesson in this fable is that people shouldn't waste time instead of working. Those who do, Aesop says, will be sorry.

Another popular fable by Aesop, "The Tortoise and the Hare," teaches that it is better to work slowly and carefully than to hurry and make mistakes. "The Boy Who Cried Wolf" warns readers not to play pranks on others. Since we still read these fables, you may be familiar with them.

READING CHECK **Summarizing** Why did the Greeks tell fables?

SS.6.W.3.5
Summarize the important achievements and contributions of ancient Greek civilization.

Greek Literature Lives

The works of ancient Greek writers such as Homer, Sappho, and Aesop are still alive and popular today. In fact, Greek literature has influenced modern language, literature, and art. Did you know that some of the words you use and some of the stories you hear come from ancient Greece?

Language

Probably the most obvious way we see the influence of the Greeks is in our language. Many English words and expressions come from Greek mythology. For example, we call a long journey an "odyssey" after Odysseus, the wandering hero of Homer's poem. Something very large and powerful is called "titanic." This word comes from the Titans, a group of large and powerful gods in Greek myth.

Many places around the world today are also named after figures from Greek myths. For example, Athens is named for Athena, the goddess of wisdom. Africa's Atlas Mountains were named after a giant from Greek mythology who held up the sky. The name of the Aegean Sea comes from Aegeus, a legendary Greek king. Europe itself was named after a figure from Greek myth, the princess Europa. Even places in space bear names from mythology. For example, Jupiter's moon Io was named after a goddess's daughter.

Literature and the Arts

Greek myths have inspired artists for centuries. Great painters and sculptors have used gods and heroes as the subjects of their works. Writers have retold ancient stories, sometimes set in modern times. Moviemakers have also borrowed stories from ancient myths. Hercules, for example, has been the subject of dozens of films. These films range from early classics to a Walt Disney cartoon.

Mythological references are also common in today's popular culture. Many sports teams have adopted the names of powerful figures from myths, like Titans or

Greek Influence on Language	
In Greek Literature and Mythology...	**Today...**
■ Achilles was a great warrior who was killed when an arrow struck his heel.	■ An "Achilles heel" is a person's weak spot.
■ Hercules was the strongest man on earth who completed 12 almost impossible tasks.	■ When a person has a really hard job to do it is called a "Herculean" task.
■ A fox wanted to eat some grapes but he couldn't reach the branch they were on, so he said, "Those grapes are probably sour anyway."	■ When people pretend they don't want something after they find out they can't have it, they are said to have "sour grapes."
■ King Midas was granted one wish by the god Dionysus, so he wished that everything he touched turned to gold.	■ A person who seems to get rich easily is said to have a "Midas touch."
■ Tantalus was punished for offending the gods. He had to stand up to his chin in water and he was always thirsty, but if he tried to drink the water it went away.	■ Something is "tantalizing" if you want it but it's just out of your reach.

Greek Names Today

The influence of Greek stories and culture can still be seen in names. Astronomers named one of Jupiter's moons Io (EYE-oh) after a woman from Greek mythology. Sports teams also use Greek names. This college mascot is dressed like a Trojan warrior.

Trojans. Businesses frequently use images or symbols from mythology in their advertising. Although people no longer believe in the Greek gods, mythological ideas can still be seen all around us.

READING CHECK Finding Main Ideas
How did Greek myths influence later language and art?

SUMMARY AND PREVIEW The myths, stories, and poems of ancient Greece have shaped how people today speak, read, and write. Like democracy, these myths, stories, and poems are part of ancient Greece's gift to the world. In the next chapter you will learn more about life and culture in ancient Greece.

Section 3 Assessment

Reviewing Ideas, Terms, and People

1. **a. Define** What is **mythology**?
   b. Summarize Why did the ancient Greeks create myths?
2. **a. Identify** What are **Homer**'s most famous works?
   b. Contrast How are **fables** different from myths?
3. **a. Recall** In what areas have Greek myths influenced our culture?
   b. Analyze Why do you think mythological references are popular with sports teams and businesses today?
   c. Evaluate Why do you think Greek literature has been so influential throughout history?

Critical Thinking

4. **Analyzing** Using your notes and a chart like this, explain the influence of myths and literature on the world today.

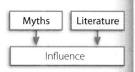

FOCUS ON WRITING

5. **Putting Your Ideas Together** Look at your notes from the previous sections. Think about the personalities you gave physical features and government leaders. Now imagine that those personalities belonged to gods. What stories might be told about these gods? Write down some ideas.

ANCIENT GREECE **249**

The Epic Poetry of Homer

from the *Iliad*

as translated by Robert Fitzgerald

About the Reading *The Iliad describes one part of a ten-year war between the Greeks and the city of Troy. As the poem opens, the Greek hero Achilles (uh-KIL-eez) has left the battle to wait for help from the gods. When he learns that his best friend Patroclus is dead, however, Achilles springs back into action. In this passage, the angry Achilles sprints across the plain toward Troy—and Hector, the Trojan warrior who has killed his friend.*

AS YOU READ Look for words and actions that tell you Achilles is a hero.

GUIDED READING

WORD HELP

main strength
resolute determined
imploring begging

❶ To what is Achilles being compared?

❷ Priam, Hector's father, knows that the gods have protected and strengthened Achilles.

❸ Achilles' armor was made by the god of metalworking.

Why might the very sight of this armor make Priam afraid?

Then toward the town with might and main
he ran magnificent, like a racing chariot horse
that holds its form at full stretch on the plain. ❶
So light-footed Achilles held the pace.
And aging Priam was the first to see him
sparkling on the plain, bright as that star
in autumn rising, whose unclouded rays
shine out amid a throng of stars at dusk—
the one they call Orion's dog, most brilliant... ❷
So pure and bright the bronze gear blazed upon
him as he ran. The old man gave a cry. ❸ With
both his hands thrown up on high he struck his
head, then shouted, groaning, appealing to his
dear son. Unmoved, Lord Hector stood in the
gateway, resolute to fight Achilles.

         Stretching out his hands,
old Priam said, imploring him:

                "No, Hector!
... don't try to hold your ground against this man,
or soon you'll meet the shock of doom..."

The painting on this vase shows people fighting in the Trojan War.

from the *Odyssey*

About the Reading *The* Odyssey *takes place after the Trojan War has ended. It describes the adventures of another hero, Odysseus (oh-DIS-ee-uhs), as he makes his way home to his kingdom of Ithaca. His voyage is full of obstacles—including the two sea monsters described in this passage. The idea for these monsters probably came from an actual strait in the Mediterranean Sea, where a jagged cliff rose on one side and dangerous whirlpools churned on the other.*

AS YOU READ Try to picture the action in your mind.

> And all this time,
> in travail, sobbing, gaining on the current,
> we rowed into the strait—Scylla to port
> and on our starboard beam Charybdis, dire
> gorge of the salt sea tide. ❶ By heaven! when she
> vomited, all the sea was like a cauldron
> seething over intense fire, when the mixture
> suddenly heaves and rises.
>
>   The shot spume
> soared to the landside heights, and fell like rain.
> But when she swallowed the sea water down
> we saw the funnel of the maelstrom, heard
> the rock bellowing all around, and dark
> sand raged on the bottom far below. ❷
> My men all blanched against the gloom, our eyes
> were fixed upon that yawning mouth in fear
> of being devoured.
>
>   Then Scylla made her strike,
> whisking six of my best men from the ship.
> I happened to glance aft at ship and oarsmen
> and caught sight of their arms and legs, dangling
> high overhead. Voices came down to me
> in anguish, calling my name for the last time . . . ❸
>   We rowed on.
> The Rocks were now behind; Charybdis, too,
> and Scylla dropped astern.

GUIDED READING

WORD HELP

travail pain
dire gorge terrible throat
spume foam or froth
maelstrom whirlpool
blanched grew pale
anguish great suffering

❶ Odysseus is the speaker. He is referring to himself and his crew.

Why might the crew be sobbing?

❷ Three times a day, the monster Charybdis (cuh-RIB-duhs) takes in water and then spits it out.

❸ Like many Greek monsters, Scylla (SIL-uh) is part human and part animal. She has the body of a woman, six heads with snake-like necks, and twelve feet.

CONNECTING LITERATURE TO HISTORY

1. **Comparing** Many Greek myths were about heroes who had special abilities. What heroic abilities or traits do Achilles, Hector, and Odysseus share?

2. **Analyzing** The Greeks used myths to explain the natural world. How does the *Odyssey* passage illustrate this?

Social Studies Skills

Analyzing Costs and Benefits

Understand the Skill

Everything you do has both costs and benefits connected to it. *Benefits* are what you gain from something. *Costs* are what you give up to obtain benefits. For example, if you buy a video game, the benefits of your action include the game itself and the enjoyment of playing it. The most obvious cost is what you pay for the game. However, there are also costs that do not involve money. One of these costs is the time you spend playing the game. This is a cost because you give up something else, such as doing your homework or watching a TV show, when you choose to play the game.

The ability to analyze costs and benefits is a valuable life skill as well as a useful tool in the study of history. Weighing an action's benefits against its costs can help you decide whether or not to take it.

Learn the Skill

Analyzing the costs and benefits of historical events will help you to better understand and evaluate them. Follow these guidelines to do a cost-benefit analysis of an action or decision in history.

1. First determine what the action or decision was trying to accomplish. This step is needed in order to determine which of its effects were benefits and which were costs.

2. Then look for the positive or successful results of the action or decision. These are its benefits.

3. Consider the negative or unsuccessful effects of the action or decision. Also think about what positive things would have happened if it had *not* occurred. All these things are its costs.

4. Making a chart of the costs and benefits can be useful. By comparing the list of benefits to the list of costs you can better understand the action or decision and evaluate it.

For example, you learned in Chapter 8 that because of Greece's geography, the early Greeks settled near the sea. A cost-benefit analysis of their dependence on the sea might produce a chart like this one.

Benefits	Costs
Sea was a source of some food.	Would have paid more attention to agriculture than they did.
Didn't have to depend on Greece's poor soil for food.	Had to rely on trade with other peoples for some food and other necessities.
Became great shipbuilders and sailors	
Became great traders and grew rich from trade	
Settled colonies through-out the region	

Based on this chart, one might conclude that the Greeks' choice of where to settle was a good one.

Practice and Apply the Skill

In 546 BC a noble named Peisistratus overthrew the oligarchy and ruled Athens as a tyrant. Use information from the chapter and the guidelines above to do a cost-benefit analysis of this action. Then write a paragraph explaining whether or not it was good for the people of Athens.

Visual Summary

Use the visual summary below to help you review the main ideas of the chapter.

QUICK FACTS

The early Greeks developed trading cultures and independent city-states.

Athens had the world's first direct democracy.

The stories of Greek literature and mythology have influenced language and culture today.

Reviewing Vocabulary, Terms, and People

Unscramble each group of letters below to spell a term that matches the given definition.

1. **olpsi**—a Greek city-state
2. **iciznets**—people who have the **right** to participate in government
3. **ntaryt**—a person who rules alone, usually through military force
4. **comdeyacr**—rule by the people
5. **bleafs**—stories that teach lessons
6. **tsrarciotas**—rich landowners
7. **coiglhary**—rule by a few people
8. **siclalacs**—referring to a period of great achievements

Comprehension and Critical Thinking

SECTION 1 *(Pages 228–233)*

9. **a. Describe** How did geography affect the development of the Greek city-states?

   b. Compare and Contrast What did the Minoans and Mycenaeans have in common? How were the two civilizations different?

   c. Elaborate How did the concept of the polis affect the growth of Greek colonies?

SECTION 2 *(Pages 236–241)*

10. **a. Identify** What roles did Draco, Solon, and Peisistratus play in the history of Greek government?

   b. Contrast The Greeks tried many forms of government before they created a democracy. How did these various forms of government differ?

   c. Evaluate Do you agree or disagree with this statement: "Representative democracy works better than direct democracy in large countries." Defend your answer.

11. a. Recall Who were some of the main gods of Greek mythology? Who were some of the main heroes?

b. Analyze What are some of the topics that appear in ancient Greek literature, such as the *Iliad* and the *Odyssey*?

c. Predict Do you think the language and literature of ancient Greece will play roles in Western civilization in years to come? Why or why not?

Reading Skills

Greek Word Origins *Look at the list of Greek words and their meanings below. Then answer the questions that follow.*

archos (ruler)	*monos* (single)
bios (life)	*oligos* (few)
geo (earth)	*pente* (five)
micros (small)	*treis* (three)

12. Which of the following words means rule by a single person?

a. oligarchy   **c.** pentarchy

b. monarchy   **d.** triarchy

13. Which of the following words means the study of life?

a. biology   **c.** archaeology

b. geology   **d.** pentology

14. Is something that is *microscopic* very small or very large?

Using the Internet

15. Activity: Comparing Greek Governments Greek government had many forms: tyranny, oligarchy, direct democracy, and monarchy. Go online to research Greek government, and then create a three-dimensional model, a drawing, or a diagram to illustrate what a person's life under each type of government might have looked like. Include information about the type of government you are representing.

Social Studies Skills

16. Analyzing Costs and Benefits Under Cleisthenes' leadership, Athens developed the world's first democracy. Create a chart comparing costs and benefits of this event. Then write a sentence explaining whether or not it was good for the people of Athens.

Cleisthenes' Leadership

Costs	Benefits

Reviewing Themes

17. Geography How do you think Greek society would have been different if Greece were a land-locked country?

18. Geography How did Crete's physical geography both help and hurt the development of Minoan civilization?

19. Politics Why was citizenship so important in Athens?

FOCUS ON WRITING

20. Writing Your Myth First, decide if your main character is going to be a god or if it will be a human who interacts with the gods. Think about the situations and decisions that your character will face, and how he or she will react to them.

Now it's time to write your myth down. Write a paragraph of seven to eight sentences about your character. You may want to include terrible monsters or heroes with great powers. Don't forget that a myth is supposed to explain something about the world.

Florida Standardized Test Practice

DIRECTIONS: Read each question, and write the letter of the best response.

1

> . . . that multitude of gleaming helms and bossed shields issued from the ships, with plated cuirasses [armor] and ashwood spears. Reflected glintings flashed to heaven, as the plain in all directions shone with glare of bronze and shook with trampling feet of men. Among them Prince Achilles armed. One heard his teeth grind hard together, and his eyes blazed out like licking fire, for unbearable pain had fixed upon his heart. Raging at Trojans, he buckled on the arms Hephaestus forged.

The content of this passage suggests that it was written by

A Homer.

B Zeus.

C Apollo.

D Cleisthenes.

2 **What type of ancient Greek literature would *most* likely describe the deeds of a great hero?**

A fable

B epic poem

C lyric poem

D oration

3 **Which was the main cause for the independence of city-states in ancient Greece?**

A the Greeks' location on the sea

B the threat of warlike neighbors to the north

C the geography of mountainous peninsulas

D the spread of Minoan culture

4 **Athens was ruled by a single person under the type of government known as**

A direct democracy.

B representative democracy.

C oligarchy.

D tyranny.

5 **The citizens' assembly in ancient Athens was an example of**

A trial by jury.

B rule by aristocrats.

C direct democracy.

D representative democracy.

Connecting with Past Learnings

6 **Recently you learned about Hebrew history and beliefs. The ancient Hebrew and Greek civilizations shared all of the following characteristics *except***

A great written works.

B democratic governments.

C strong political leaders.

D influence on later civilizations.

7 **You know that early towns in India were controlled by small groups of priests. Like ancient Greek government, this early Indian government was an example of**

A oligarchy.

B tyranny.

C monarchy.

D democracy.

ANCIENT GREECE

The Acropolis of Athens symbolizes the city and represents the architectural and artistic legacy of ancient Greece. *Acropolis* means "highest city" in Greek, and there are many such sites in Greece. Historically, an acropolis provided shelter and defense against a city's enemies. The Acropolis of Athens—the best known of them all—contained temples, monuments, and artwork dedicated to the Greek gods. Archaeological evidence indicates that the Acropolis was an important place to inhabitants from much earlier eras. However, the structures that we see today on the site were largely conceived by the statesman Pericles during the Golden Age of Athens in the 5th century B.C.

Explore the Acropolis of ancient Greece and learn about the legacy of Greek civilization. You can find a wealth of information, video clips, primary sources, activities, and more online.

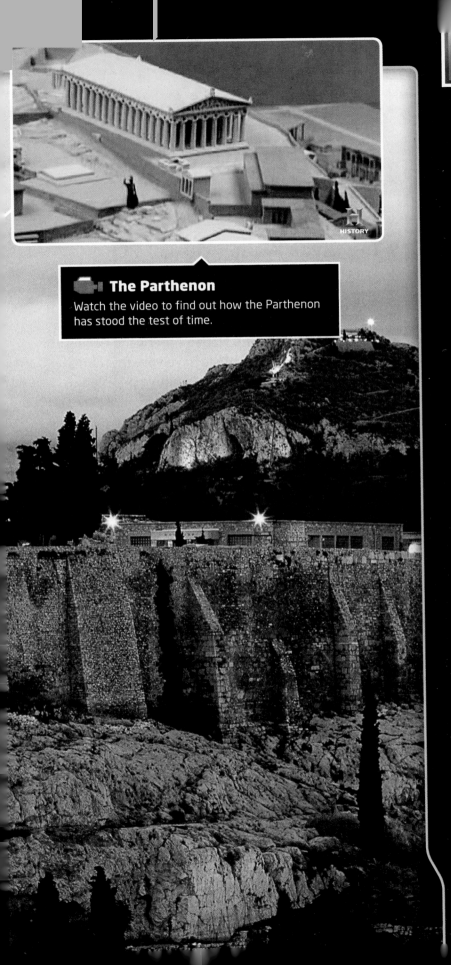

The Parthenon
Watch the video to find out how the Parthenon has stood the test of time.

At War with the Persians
Watch the video to find out how Athens emerged as the principal Greek city-state at the conclusion the Persian Wars.

Athena as Divine Guardian
Watch the video to learn how, according to Greek mythology, Athena became the protector of Ather

Origins of Western Culture
Watch the video to learn how the origins of Weste civilization can be traced to ancient Greece.

FLORIDA...
The Story Continues

CHAPTER 9, The Greek World (550–30 BC)

PEOPLE **c. 550 BC–AD 1500: Florida's Native Americans develop their war skills.** Archaeologists have very few clues about the nature of warfare among Florida's native people in 550 BC. They assume that fighting likely took place on a small scale between villages. What is known is that by the time the first Europeans arrived in the early 1500s, the Native American people of Florida were skilled fighters. The Spanish quickly learned to respect the bravery and determination of Timucua, Calusa, and Apalachee warriors. In the years between 500 BC and AD 1500, Native American populations grew and societies became more complex. Warfare between groups increased. By 1500, war chiefs held positions of power in many of Florida's Native American societies.

PEOPLE **c. 550 BC–AD 1500: The people of North and Central Florida are fierce fighters.** In AD 1500 the Timucua lived on land that had been home to the people of the St. Johns and Deptford cultures in 550 BC. The Timucua went to war for personal glory and to gain property. Timucua fighters prepared for war with special ceremonies and by filing their nails into sharp points. The Timucua used their sharp nails in hand-to-hand combat. A warrior cut an enemy's forehead to blind the person with his own blood. The Timucua also used bows and arrows and heavy clubs. A warrior tied his long hair into a knot to hold his arrows. The Timucua tipped their arrows with flaming Spanish moss to burn down the houses of their enemies. Victorious Timucua warriors brought back their enemies' legs, arms, and scalps as trophies.

PEOPLE **c. 550 BC–1500: The people of Southwest Florida view war as a way of life.**   In AD 1500 the Calusa lived on land that had been home to the people of the Caloosahatchee culture in 550 BC. The Caloosahatchee were the Calusa's direct ancestors. The Calusa worshipped three gods—one of them a god of war. Spanish reports indicate that the Calusa were skilled fighters and that warfare was a way of life for them. They used bows and arrows, clubs, spears, and blowguns against their enemies.

EVENTS **c. 550 BC–AD 1500: The chunky stone game trains warriors.**
Like other peoples of the Southeast, the Native Americans of Florida played a game called chunky stone. The game consisted of rolling a stone disk across the ground. Several players threw their spears or shot their arrows at the spot they thought the rolling stone would stop. The person who was the closest won.

PLACES **Present: Florida buildings show the influence of Greek architecture.**   Greek Revival architecture was popular in the late 1700s and early 1800s. The style grew out of a renewed interest in ancient Greece. The Greek Revival style is noted for its use of the large columns, porches, and domes found in ancient Greek architecture.

Many of the grand houses built in the years following Florida's statehood are in the Greek Revival style. Great Oaks mansion in Greenwood in the Florida panhandle is an example of this type of architecture. The house is on the National Register of Historic Places. Although built much later, the Florida State Supreme Court Building in Tallahassee has many features common in Greek Revival architecture. The front of the building has rows of massive columns and a large covered porch. A huge dome tops the center of the building.

Unpacking the Florida Standards ‹···

Read the following to learn what this standard says and what it means. See FL8–FL31 to unpack all of the standards related to this chapter.

Benchmark SS.6.W.3.5 **Summarize the important achievements and contributions of ancient Greek civilization. Examples are art and architecture, athletic competitions, the birth of democracy and civic responsibility, drama, history, literature, mathematics, medicine, philosophy, science, warfare.**

What does it mean?
Identify the major accomplishments and contributions of Greek civilization.

SPOTLIGHT ON
SS.6.G.1.5, SS.6.G.2.1, SS.6.G.2.2, SS.6.G.2.7 See pages FL43–FL46 for content specifically related to these Chapter 9 standards.

The Greek World

Essential Question What advances did the Greeks make that still influence the world today?

Florida Next Generation Sunshine State Standards

MA.6.A.2.2 Interpret and compare ratios and rates. **SS.6.G.1.4** Utilize tools geographers use to study the world. **SS.6.G.1.5** Use scale, cardinal, and intermediate directions, and estimation of distances between places on current and ancient maps of the world. **SS.6.G.2.4** Explain how the geographical location of ancient civilizations contributed to the culture and politics of those societies. **SS.6.G.2.6** Explain the concept of cultural diffusion, and identify the influences of different ancient cultures on one another. **SS.6.G.2.7** Interpret choropleths or dot-density maps to explain the distribution of population in the ancient world. **SS.6.G.4.1** Explain how family and ethnic relationships influenced ancient cultures. **SS.6.G.4.2** Use maps to trace significant migrations, and analyze their results. **SS.6.G.4.4** Map and analyze the impact of the spread of various belief systems in the ancient world. **SS.6.G.5.2** Use geographic terms and tools to explain why ancient civilizations developed networks of highways, waterways, and other transportation linkages. **SS.6.G.5.3** Use geographic tools and terms to analyze how famine, drought, and natural disasters plagued many ancient civilizations. **SS.6.G.6.2** Compare maps of the world in ancient times with current political maps. **SS.6.W.1.1** Use timelines to identify chronological order of historical events. **SS.6.W.1.3** Interpret primary and secondary sources. **SS.6.W.1.6** Describe how history transmits culture and heritage and provides models of human character. **SS.6.W.2.9** Identify key figures and basic beliefs of the Israelites and determine how these beliefs compared with those of others in the geographic area. **SS.6.W.3.3** Compare life in Athens and Sparta (government and the status of citizens, women and children, foreigners, helots). **SS.6.W.3.4** Explain the causes and effects of the Persian and Peloponnesian Wars. **SS.6.W.3.5** Summarize the important achievements and contributions of ancient Greek civilization. **SS.6.W.3.6** Determine the impact of key figures from ancient Greece. **SS.6.W.3.7** Summarize the key achievements, contributions, and figures associated with The Hellenistic Period.

FOCUS ON WRITING

A Poem Ancient Greek poets often wrote poems in praise of great leaders, victorious military commanders, star athletes, and other famous people. As you read this chapter, you will learn about the accomplishments of Greek and Persian kings, generals, writers, thinkers, and scientists. As you read, you'll choose the one person you most admire and write a five-line poem praising that person.

CHAPTER EVENTS

c. 550 BC Cyrus the Great founds the Persian Empire.

550 BC

WORLD EVENTS

c. 551 BC Confucius is born in China.

The ruins shown in this photo are from the Parthenon, a beautiful temple built to celebrate a Greek victory in war.

HISTORY

Peter on the Parthenon

↗ Online Resource VIDEO

431 BC
The Peloponnesian War begins.

334–323 BC
Alexander the Great builds his empire.

30 BC
Rome conquers Egypt, ending the Hellenistic Age.

450 BC   350 BC   250 BC   150 BC   50 BC

343 BC
The last Egyptian ruler of Egypt is overthrown.

c. 325 BC
The Mauryan Empire is founded in India.

c. 160 BC
The Maccabees regain Jewish independence.

THE GREEK WORLD **257**

Reading Social Studies

| Economics | Geography | Politics | Religion | Society and Culture | Science and Technology |

Focus on Themes In this chapter, you will learn about Persia's attempt to take over Greece. You will also read about two great Greek cities, Sparta and Athens, and how they both worked to protect Greece from this invader. Finally, you will discover how, even though another invader conquered Greece, Greek influence continued to spread. Without a doubt, you need to understand the **politics** of the time in order to understand the Greek world and its **society and culture**.

Comparing and Contrasting Historical Facts

Focus on Reading Comparing and contrasting are good ways to learn. That's one reason historians use comparison and contrast to explain people and events in history.

Understanding Comparison and Contrast To **compare** is to look for likenesses, or similarities. To **contrast** is to look for differences. Sometimes writers point out similarities and differences. Other times you have to look for them yourself. You can use a diagram like this one to keep track of similarities and differences as you read.

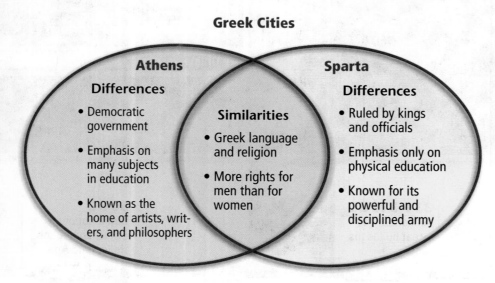

Greek Cities

Athens

Differences
- Democratic government
- Emphasis on many subjects in education
- Known as the home of artists, writers, and philosophers

Similarities
- Greek language and religion
- More rights for men than for women

Sparta

Differences
- Ruled by kings and officials
- Emphasis only on physical education
- Known for its powerful and disciplined army

Clues for Comparison-Contrast

Writers sometimes signal comparisons or contrasts with words like these:

Comparison—*similarly, like, in the same way, too*

Contrast—*however, unlike, but, while, although, in contrast*

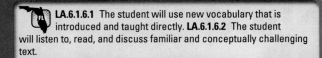

LA.6.1.6.1 The student will use new vocabulary that is introduced and taught directly. LA.6.1.6.2 The student will listen to, read, and discuss familiar and conceptually challenging text.

21ST CENTURY

Key Terms and People

You Try It!

The following passage is from the chapter you are getting ready to read. As you read the passage, look for word clues about similarities and differences.

Boys and Men in Athens

From a young age, Athenian boys from rich families worked to improve both their bodies and their minds. Like Spartan boys, Athenian boys had to learn to run, jump, and fight. But this training was not as harsh or as long as the training in Sparta.

Unlike Spartan men, Athenian men didn't have to devote their whole lives to the army. All men in Athens joined the army, but only for two years. They helped defend the city between the ages of 18 and 20. Older men only had to serve in the army in times of war.

After you read the passage, answer the following questions.

1. What does the word *like* (line 3 of the passage) compare or contrast?

2. Which boys had harsher training, Athenian boys or Spartan boys? What comparison or contrast signal word helped you answer this question?

3. What other comparison or contrast words do you find in the passage? How do these words or phrases help you understand the passage?

4. How are the similarities and differences organized in the passage—alternating back and forth between topics (ABAB) or first one topic and then the next (AABB)?

Academic Vocabulary

Success in school is related to knowing academic vocabulary— the words that are frequently used in school assignments and discussions. In this chapter, you will learn the following academic word:

strategy (p. 262)

As you read Chapter 9, think about the organization of the ideas. Look for comparison and contrast signal words.

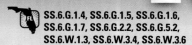

SS.6.G.1.4, SS.6.G.1.5, SS.6.G.1.6, SS.6.G.1.7, SS.6.G.2.2, SS.6.G.5.2, SS.6.W.1.3, SS.6.W.3.4, SS.6.W.3.6

What You Will Learn...

Main Ideas

1. Persia became an empire under Cyrus the Great.
2. The Persian Empire grew stronger under Darius I.
3. The Persians fought Greece twice in the Persian Wars.

The Big Idea

Over time the Persians came to rule a great empire which eventually brought them into conflict with the Greeks.

Key Terms and People

Cyrus the Great, *p. 261*
cavalry, *p. 262*
Darius I, *p. 262*
Persian Wars, *p. 263*
Xerxes I, *p. 264*

Online Resource

TAKING NOTES

Use the graphic organizer online to take notes on Persia and its conflicts with Greece.

Greece and Persia

If YOU were there...

You're a great military leader and the ruler of a great empire. You control everything in the nations you've conquered. One of your advisers urges you to force conquered people to give up their customs. He thinks they should adopt your way of life. But another adviser disagrees. Let them keep their own ways, she says, and you'll earn their loyalty.

Whose advice do you take? Why?

BUILDING BACKGROUND Among the rulers who faced decisions like the one described above were the rulers of the Persian Empire. Created in 550 BC, the empire grew quickly. Within about 30 years, the Persians had conquered many peoples, and Persian rulers had to decide how these people would be treated.

Persia Becomes an Empire

While the Athenians were taking the first steps toward creating a democracy, a new power was rising in the East. This power, the Persian Empire, would one day attack Greece. But early in their history, the Persians were an unorganized nomadic people. It took the skills of leaders like Cyrus the Great and Darius I to change that situation. Under these leaders, the Persians created a huge empire, one of the mightiest of the ancient world.

Cyrus the Great

Early in their history, the Persians often fought other peoples of Southwest Asia. Sometimes they lost. In fact, they lost a fight to a people called the Medes (MEEDZ) and were ruled by them for about 150 years. In 550 BC, however, Cyrus II (SY-ruhs) led a Persian revolt against the Medes. His revolt was successful. Cyrus won independence for Persia and conquered the Medes. His victory marked the beginning of the Persian Empire.

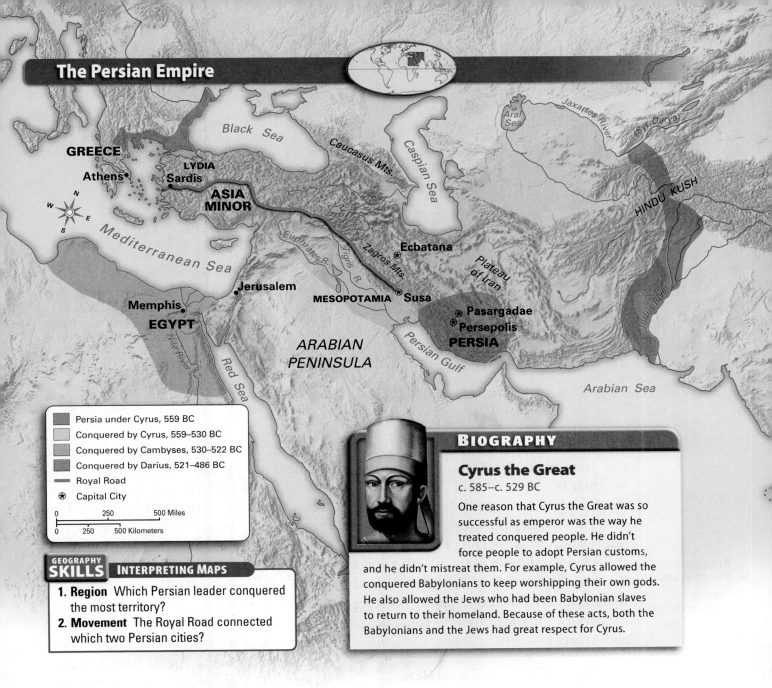

GREECE
Athens
LYDIA
Sardis
ASIA MINOR
Black Sea
Caucasus Mts.
Caspian Sea
Aral Sea
Jaxartes River
(Syr Darya)
HINDU KUSH
Mediterranean Sea
Euphrates R.
Tigris R.
Zagros Mts.
Ecbatana
Plateau of Iran
Indus River
Jerusalem
MESOPOTAMIA
Susa
Pasargadae
Persepolis
PERSIA
Memphis
EGYPT
Nile River
ARABIAN PENINSULA
Persian Gulf
Arabian Sea
Red Sea

Persia under Cyrus, 559 BC
Conquered by Cyrus, 559–530 BC
Conquered by Cambyses, 530–522 BC
Conquered by Darius, 521–486 BC
Royal Road
Capital City

0   250   500 Miles
0   250   500 Kilometers

GEOGRAPHY SKILLS | **INTERPRETING MAPS**

1. **Region** Which Persian leader conquered the most territory?
2. **Movement** The Royal Road connected which two Persian cities?

BIOGRAPHY

Cyrus the Great
c. 585–c. 529 BC

One reason that Cyrus the Great was so successful as emperor was the way he treated conquered people. He didn't force people to adopt Persian customs, and he didn't mistreat them. For example, Cyrus allowed the conquered Babylonians to keep worshipping their own gods. He also allowed the Jews who had been Babylonian slaves to return to their homeland. Because of these acts, both the Babylonians and the Jews had great respect for Cyrus.

As you can see on the map, Cyrus conquered much of Southwest Asia, including nearly all of Asia Minor, during his rule. Included in this region were several Greek cities that Cyrus took over. He then marched south to conquer Mesopotamia.

Cyrus also added land to the east. He led his army into central Asia to the Jaxartes River, which we now call the Syr Darya. When he died around 529 BC, Cyrus ruled the largest empire the world had ever seen.

Cyrus let the people he conquered keep their own customs. He hoped this would make them less likely to rebel. He was right. Few people rebelled against Cyrus, and his empire remained strong. Because of his great successes, historians call him **Cyrus the Great**.

The Persian Army

Cyrus was successful in his conquests because his army was strong. It was strong because it was well organized and loyal.

Persia Under Darius

Sitting on a throne, the emperor Darius meets with an officer of his empire. Darius restored order to the Persian Empire and then expanded it. His army included royal guards like the two shown here.

Why do you think Darius appears larger than the official he is meeting with?

ACADEMIC
VOCABULARY
strategy
a plan for fighting
a battle or war

At the heart of the Persian army were the Immortals, 10,000 soldiers chosen for their bravery and skill. In addition to the Immortals, the army had a powerful cavalry. A **cavalry** is a unit of soldiers who ride horses. Cyrus used his cavalry to charge the enemy and shoot at them with arrows. This **strategy** weakened the enemy before the Immortals attacked. Working together, the cavalry and the Immortals could defeat almost any foe.

READING CHECK Finding Main Ideas
Who created the Persian Empire?

The Persian Empire Grows Stronger

Cyrus's son Cambyses continued to expand the Persian Empire after Cyrus died. For example, he conquered Egypt and added it to the empire. Soon afterward, though, a rebellion broke out in Persia. During this rebellion, Cambyses died. His death left Persia without a clear leader.

Within four years a young prince named **Darius I** (da-RY-uhs) claimed the throne and killed all his rivals for power. Once he was securely in control, Darius worked to restore order in Persia. He also improved Persian society and expanded the empire.

Political Organization

Darius organized the empire by dividing it into 20 provinces. Then he chose governors called satraps (SAY-traps) to rule the provinces for him. The satraps collected taxes for Darius, served as judges, and put down rebellions within their territories. Satraps had great power within their provinces, but Darius remained the empire's real ruler. His officials visited each province to make sure the satraps were loyal to Darius. He called himself king of kings to remind other rulers of his power.

Persian Society

After Darius restored order to the empire, he made many improvements to Persian society. For example, he built many roads.

Darius had roads built to connect various parts of the empire. Messengers used these roads to travel quickly throughout Persia. One road, called the Royal Road, was more than 1,700 miles long. Even Persia's enemies admired these roads and the Persian messenger system. For example, one Greek historian wrote:

> "Nothing mortal travels so fast as these Persian messengers ... these men will not be hindered from accomplishing at their best speed the distance which they have to go, either by snow, or rain, or heat, or by the darkness of night."
>
> –Herodotus, from *History of the Persian Wars*

Darius also built a new capital for the empire. It was called Persepolis. Darius wanted his capital to reflect the glory of his empire, so he filled the city with beautiful works of art. For example, 3,000 carvings like the ones on the previous page line the city's walls. Statues throughout the city glittered with gold, silver, and precious jewels.

During Darius's rule, the prophet Zoroaster founded a new religion in the Persian Empire. This religion, which was called Zoroastrianism, taught that there were two forces fighting for control of the universe. One force was good, and the other was evil. Its priests urged people to help the side of good in its struggle. This religion remained popular in Persia for many centuries.

Persian Expansion

Like Cyrus, Darius wanted the Persian Empire to grow. In the east, he conquered the entire Indus Valley. He also tried to expand the empire westward into Europe. However, before Darius could move very far into Europe, he had to deal with a revolt in the empire.

READING CHECK **Summarizing** How did Darius I change Persia's political organization?

The Persians Fight Greece

In 499 BC several Greek cities in Asia Minor rebelled against Persian rule. To help their fellow Greeks, a few city-states in mainland Greece sent soldiers to join the fight against the Persians.

The Persians put down the revolt, but Darius was still angry with the Greeks. Although the cities that had rebelled were in Asia, Darius was enraged that other Greeks had given them aid. He swore to get revenge on the Greeks.

The Battle of Marathon

Nine years after the Greek cities rebelled, Darius invaded Greece. He and his army sailed to the plains of Marathon near Athens. This invasion began a series of wars between Persia and Greece that historians call the **Persian Wars**.

The Athenian army had only about 11,000 soldiers, while the Persians had about 15,000. However, the Greeks won the battle because they had better weapons and clever leaders.

SS.6.W.3.4 Explain the causes and effects of the Persian and Peloponnesian Wars.

The Persian Wars
This Greek vase shows a Persian soldier (at left) and a Greek soldier in a fight to the death. During the Persian Wars, the Greeks fiercely defended their homeland against massive invasions by the Persians.

With what kinds of weapons are the two soldiers fighting?

The Persian Wars

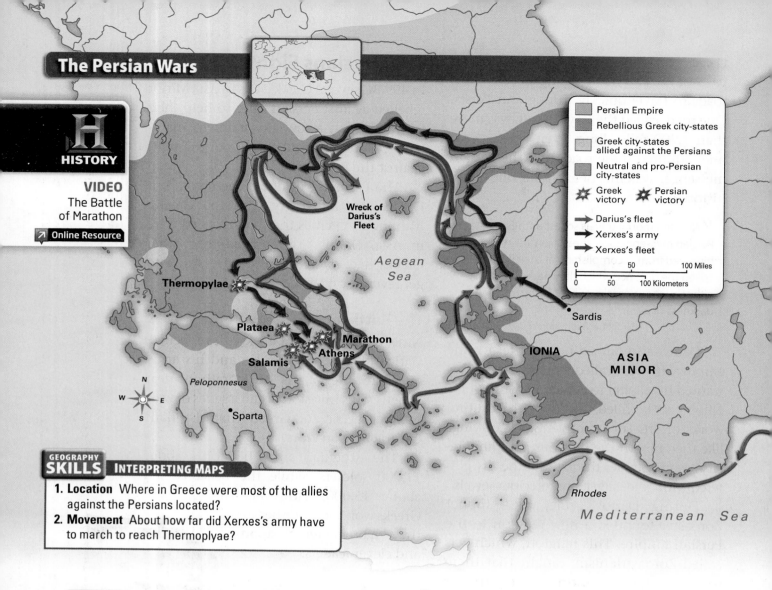

HISTORY

VIDEO
The Battle
of Marathon

↗ Online Resource

Persian Empire
Rebellious Greek city-states
Greek city-states allied against the Persians
Neutral and pro-Persian city-states
✦ Greek victory   ✦ Persian victory
→ Darius's fleet
→ Xerxes's army
→ Xerxes's fleet

0   50   100 Miles
0   50   100 Kilometers

Wreck of Darius's Fleet

Aegean Sea

Thermopylae ✦
Plataea ✦
Salamis ✦   ✦ Athens   ✦ Marathon
Peloponnesus
•Sparta

•Sardis
IONIA
ASIA MINOR

Rhodes

Mediterranean Sea

GEOGRAPHY SKILLS | INTERPRETING MAPS

1. **Location** Where in Greece were most of the allies against the Persians located?
2. **Movement** About how far did Xerxes's army have to march to reach Thermoplyae?

THE IMPACT TODAY

Athletes today re-create the Greek messenger's run in 26-mile races called marathons.

According to legend, a messenger ran from Marathon to Athens—a distance of just over 26 miles—to bring news of the great victory. After crying out "Rejoice! We conquer!" the exhausted runner fell to the ground and died.

The Second Invasion of Greece

Ten years after the Battle of Marathon, Darius's son **Xerxes I** (ZUHRK-seez) tried to conquer Greece again. In 480 BC the Persian army set out for Greece. This time they were joined by the Persian navy.

The Greeks prepared to defend their homeland. This time Sparta, a powerful city-state in southern Greece, joined with Athens. The Spartans had the strongest army

in Greece, so they went to fight the Persian army. Meanwhile, the Athenians sent their powerful navy to attack the Persian navy.

To slow the Persian army, the Spartans sent about 1,400 soldiers to Thermopylae (thuhr-MAH-puh-lee), a narrow mountain pass. The Persians had to cross through this pass to attack Greek cities. For three days, the small Greek force held off the Persian army. Then the Persians asked a traitorous Greek soldier to lead them through another pass. A large Persian force attacked the Spartans from behind. Surrounded, the brave Spartans and their allies fought to their deaths. After winning the battle, the Persians swept into Athens, attacking and burning the city.

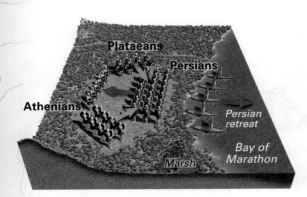

Marathon

At Marathon, the Greeks defeated a larger Persian force by luring the Persians into the middle of their forces. The Athenians then surrounded and defeated the Persians.

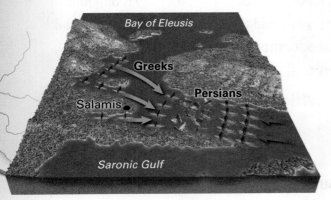

Salamis

At Salamis, the Greeks destroyed the Persian navy by attacking in a narrow strait where the Persian ships could not maneuver well.

Although the Persians won the battle, the Greeks quickly regained the upper hand. A few days after Athens was burned, the Athenians defeated the Persian navy through a clever plan devised by their leader, Themistocles. They led the larger Persian navy into the narrow straits of Salamis. The Persians had so many ships that they couldn't steer well in the narrow strait. As a result, the smaller Athenian boats easily sank many Persian ships. Those ships that were not destroyed soon returned home.

Soon after the Battle of Salamis, an army of soldiers from all over Greece beat the Persians at Plataea (pluh-TEE-uh). This battle ended the Persian Wars. Defeated, the Persians left Greece.

For the Persians, this defeat was humiliating, but it was not a major blow. Their empire remained strong for more than a century after the war. For the Greeks, though, the defeat of the Persians was a triumph. They had saved their homeland.

READING CHECK **Analyzing** Why did Darius and Xerxes want to conquer Greece?

SUMMARY AND PREVIEW Athens and Sparta fought together against Persia. Their friendship didn't last long, though. In the next section, you will learn what happened when they became enemies.

Section 1 Assessment

Reviewing Ideas, Terms, and People

1. **a. Describe** Describe the empire of **Cyrus the Great**.
   b. Make Generalizations Why did peoples conquered by Cyrus the Great seldom rebel?
2. **a. Identify** How did **Darius I** change Persia's political organization?
   b. Make Generalizations How did Persia's roads help improve the empire's organization?
3. **a. Explain** Why did Persia want to invade Greece?
   b. Predict How might the **Persian Wars** have ended if the Spartans had not slowed the Persians at Thermopylae?

Critical Thinking

4. **Categorizing** Review your notes on major events. Using a chart like the one below, list the battles you have identified in the first column. In the other columns identify who fought, who won, and what happened as a result of each battle.

Battle	Armies	Winner	Result

FOCUS ON WRITING

5. **Taking Notes on Persian Leaders** Draw a table with three columns. In the first column, write the names of each leader mentioned in this section. In the second column, list each person's military accomplishments. In the third column, list any other accomplishments.

LA.6.1.6.2, SS.6.G.1.4, SS.6.G.1.5,
SS.6.G.1.6, SS.6.G.1.7, SS.6.G.4.1,
SS.6.W.1.3, SS.6.W.3.3, SS.6.W.3.4,
SS.6.W.3.6

What You Will Learn...

Main Ideas

1. The Spartans built a military society to provide security and protection.
2. The Athenians admired the mind and the arts in addition to physical abilities.
3. Sparta and Athens fought over who should have power and influence in Greece.

The Big Idea

The two most powerful city-states in Greece, Sparta and Athens, had very different cultures and became bitter enemies in the 400s BC.

Key Terms

alliance, *p. 270*
Peloponnesian War, *p. 271*

Online Resource
TAKING NOTES

Use the graphic organizer online to take notes on Athens and Sparta.

SS.6.W.3.3 Compare life in Athens and Sparta (government and the status of citizens, women and children, foreigners, helots).

Sparta and Athens

If YOU were there...

Your father, a wandering trader, has decided it is time to settle down. He offers the family a choice between two cities. In one city, everyone wants to be athletic, tough, and strong. They're good at enduring hardships and following orders. The other city is different. There, you'd be admired if you could think deeply and speak persuasively, if you knew a lot about astronomy or history, or if you sang and played beautiful music.

Which city do you choose? Why?

BUILDING BACKGROUND Two of the greatest city-states in Greece were Sparta and Athens. Sparta, like the first city mentioned above, had a culture that valued physical strength and military might. The Athenian culture placed more value on the mind. However, both city-states had military strength, and they both played important roles in the defense of ancient Greece.

Spartans Build a Military Society

Spartan society was dominated by the military. According to Spartan tradition, their social system was created between 900 and 600 BC by a man named Lycurgus (ly-KUHR-guhs) after a slave revolt. To keep such a revolt from happening again, he increased the military's role in society. The Spartans believed that military power was the way to provide security and protection for their city. Daily life in Sparta reflected this belief.

Boys and Men in Sparta

Daily life in Sparta was dominated by the army. Even the lives of children reflected this domination. When a boy was born, government officials came to look at him. If he was not healthy, the baby was taken outside of the city and left to die. Healthy boys were trained from an early age to be soldiers.

As part of their training, boys ran, jumped, swam, and threw javelins to increase their strength. They also learned to endure the hardships they would face as soldiers. For example, boys weren't given shoes or heavy clothes, even in winter. They also weren't given much food. Boys were allowed to steal food if they could, but if they were caught, they were whipped. At least one boy chose to die rather than admit to his theft:

> "One youth, having stolen a fox and hidden it under his coat, allowed it to tear out his very bowels [organs] with its claws and teeth and died rather than betray his theft."
>
> –Plutarch, from *Life of Lycurgus*

To this boy—and to most Spartan soldiers—courage and strength were more important than one's own safety.

Soldiers between the ages of 20 and 30 lived in army barracks and only occasionally visited their families. Spartan men stayed in the army until they turned 60.

The Spartans believed that the most important qualities of good soldiers were self-discipline and obedience. To reinforce self-discipline they required soldiers to live tough lives free from comforts. For example, the Spartans didn't have luxuries like soft furniture and expensive food. They thought such comforts made people weak. Even the Spartans' enemies admired their discipline and obedience.

Girls and Women in Sparta

Because Spartan men were often away at war, Spartan women had more rights than other Greek women. Some women owned land in Sparta and ran their households when their husbands were gone. Unlike women in other Greek cities, Spartan women didn't spend time spinning cloth or weaving. They thought of those tasks as the jobs of slaves, unsuitable for the wives and mothers of soldiers.

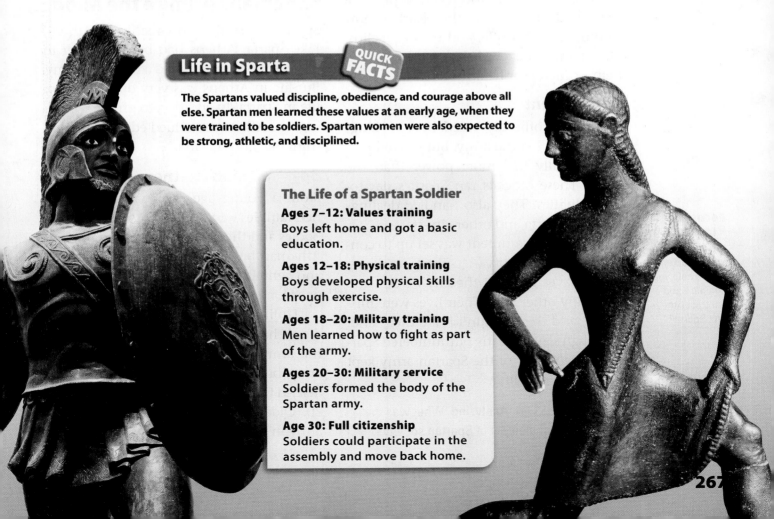

Life in Sparta

QUICK FACTS

The Spartans valued discipline, obedience, and courage above all else. Spartan men learned these values at an early age, when they were trained to be soldiers. Spartan women were also expected to be strong, athletic, and disciplined.

The Life of a Spartan Soldier

Ages 7–12: Values training
Boys left home and got a basic education.

Ages 12–18: Physical training
Boys developed physical skills through exercise.

Ages 18–20: Military training
Men learned how to fight as part of the army.

Ages 20–30: Military service
Soldiers formed the body of the Spartan army.

Age 30: Full citizenship
Soldiers could participate in the assembly and move back home.

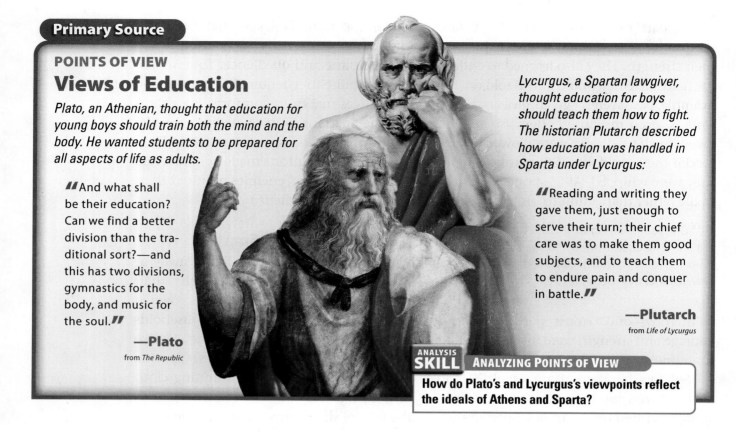

POINTS OF VIEW

Views of Education

Plato, an Athenian, thought that education for young boys should train both the mind and the body. He wanted students to be prepared for all aspects of life as adults.

❝And what shall be their education? Can we find a better division than the traditional sort?—and this has two divisions, gymnastics for the body, and music for the soul.❞

—Plato
from *The Republic*

Lycurgus, a Spartan lawgiver, thought education for boys should teach them how to fight. The historian Plutarch described how education was handled in Sparta under Lycurgus:

❝Reading and writing they gave them, just enough to serve their turn; their chief care was to make them good subjects, and to teach them to endure pain and conquer in battle.❞

—Plutarch
from *Life of Lycurgus*

ANALYSIS SKILL | **ANALYZING POINTS OF VIEW**

How do Plato's and Lycurgus's viewpoints reflect the ideals of Athens and Sparta?

Spartan women also received physical training. Like the men, they learned how to run, jump, wrestle, and throw javelins. The Spartans believed this training would help women bear healthy children.

Government

Sparta was officially ruled by two kings who jointly led the army. But elected officials actually had more power than the kings. These officials ran Sparta's day-to-day activities. They also handled dealings between Sparta and other city-states.

Sparta's government was set up to control the city's helots (HEL-uhts), or slaves. These slaves grew all the city's crops and did many other jobs. Their lives were miserable, and they couldn't leave their land. Although slaves greatly outnumbered Spartan citizens, fear of the Spartan army kept them from rebelling.

FOCUS ON READING

How can the words *like* and *unlike* help you compare and contrast Athens and Sparta?

READING CHECK **Analyzing** What was the most important element of Spartan society?

Athenians Admire the Mind

Sparta's main rival in Greece was Athens. Like Sparta, Athens had been a leader in the Persian Wars and had a powerful army. But life in Athens was very different from life in Sparta. In addition to physical training, the Athenians valued education, clear thinking, and the arts.

Boys and Men in Athens

From a young age, Athenian boys from rich families worked to improve both their bodies and their minds. Like Spartan boys, Athenian boys had to learn to run, jump, and fight. But this training was not as harsh or as long as the training in Sparta.

Unlike Spartan men, Athenian men didn't have to devote their whole lives to the army. All men in Athens joined the army, but for only two years. They helped defend the city between the ages of 18 and 20. Older men only had to serve in the army in times of war.

In addition to their physical training, Athenian students, unlike the Spartans, also learned other skills. They learned to read, write, and count as well as sing and play musical instruments. Boys also learned about Greek history and legend. For example, they studied the *Iliad*, the *Odyssey*, and other works of Greek literature.

Boys from very rich families often continued their education with private tutors. These tutors taught their students about philosophy, geometry, astronomy, and other subjects. They also taught the boys how to be good public speakers. This training prepared boys for participation in the Athenian assembly.

Very few boys had the opportunity to receive this much education, however. Boys from poor families usually didn't get any education, although most of them could read and write at least a little. Most of the boys from poor families became farmers and grew food for the city's richer citizens. A few went to work with craftspeople to learn other trades.

Girls and Women in Athens

While many boys in Athens received good educations, girls didn't. In fact, girls received almost no education. Athenian men didn't think girls needed to be educated. A few girls were taught how to read and write at home by private tutors. However, most girls only learned household tasks like weaving and sewing.

Despite Athens's reputation for freedom and democracy, women there had fewer rights than women in many other city-states. Athenian women could not

- serve in any part of the city's government, including the assembly and juries,
- leave their homes, except on special occasions,
- buy anything or own property, or
- disobey their husbands or fathers.

In fact, women in Athens had almost no rights at all.

READING CHECK Identifying Cause and Effect
Why did girls in Athens receive little education?

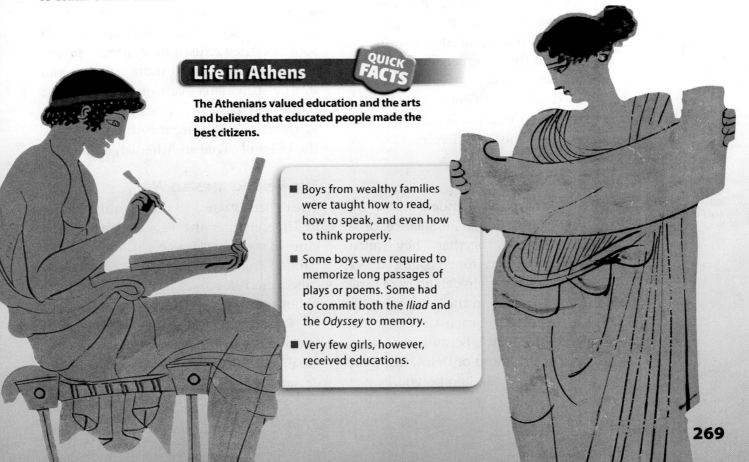

Life in Athens QUICK FACTS

The Athenians valued education and the arts and believed that educated people made the best citizens.

- Boys from wealthy families were taught how to read, how to speak, and even how to think properly.

- Some boys were required to memorize long passages of plays or poems. Some had to commit both the *Iliad* and the *Odyssey* to memory.

- Very few girls, however, received educations.

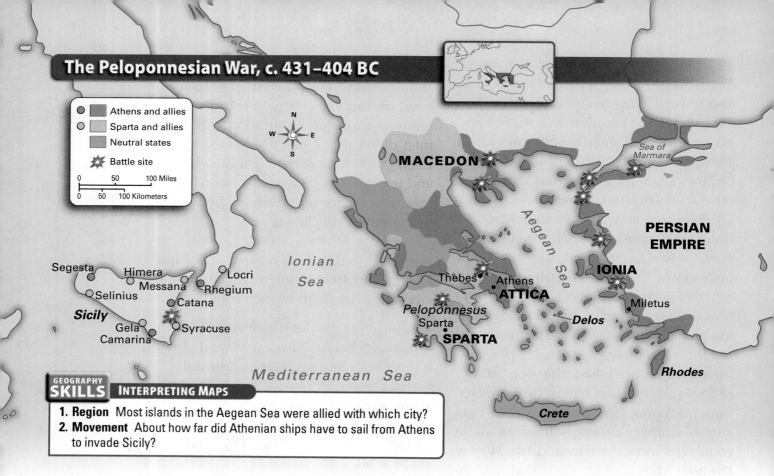

The Peloponnesian War, c. 431–404 BC

Legend:
- Athens and allies
- Sparta and allies
- Neutral states
- Battle site

0 50 100 Miles
0 50 100 Kilometers

MACEDON

Sea of Marmara

Aegean Sea

PERSIAN EMPIRE

IONIA

Ionian Sea

Segesta
Himera
Messana
Selinius
Locri
Rhegium
Catana
Sicily
Gela
Camarina
Syracuse

Thebes
Athens
ATTICA
Peloponnesus
Sparta
SPARTA

Miletus

Delos

Rhodes

Mediterranean Sea

Crete

Sparta and Athens Fight

As you learned earlier, Sparta and Athens worked together to win the Persian Wars. The Spartans fought most of the battles on land, and the Athenians fought at sea. After the war, the powerful Athenian fleet continued to protect Greece from the Persian navy. As a result, Athens had a great influence over much of Greece.

SS.6.W.3.4 Explain the causes and effects of the Persian and Peloponnesian Wars.

Athenian Power

After the Persian Wars ended in 480 BC, many city-states formed an **alliance**, or an agreement to work together. They wanted to punish the Persians for attacking Greece. They also agreed to help defend each other and to protect trade in the Aegean Sea. To pay for this defense, each city-state gave money to the alliance. Because the money was kept on the island of Delos, historians call the alliance the Delian League.

With its navy protecting the islands, Athens was the strongest member of the league. As a result, the Athenians began to treat other league members as their subjects. They refused to let members quit the league and forced more cities to join it. The Athenians even used the league's money to pay for buildings in Athens. Without even fighting, the Athenians made the Delian League an Athenian empire.

The Peloponnesian War

The Delian League was not the only alliance in Greece. After the Persian Wars, many cities in southern Greece, including Sparta, banded together as well. This alliance was called the Peloponnesian League after the peninsula on which the cities were located.

The growth of Athenian power worried many cities in the Peloponnesian League. Finally, to stop Athens's growth, Sparta declared war.

This declaration of war began the **Peloponnesian War**, a war between Athens and Sparta that threatened to tear all of Greece apart. In 431 BC the Spartan army marched north to Athens. They surrounded the city, waiting for the Athenians to come out and fight. But the Athenians stayed in the city, hoping that the Spartans would leave. Instead, the Spartans began to burn the crops in the fields around Athens. They hoped that Athens would run out of food and be forced to surrender.

The Spartans were in for a surprise. The Athenian navy escorted merchant ships to Athens, bringing plenty of food to the city. The navy also attacked Sparta's allies, forcing the Spartans to send troops to defend other Greek cities. At the same time, though, disease swept through Athens, killing thousands. For 10 years neither side could gain an advantage over the other. Eventually, they agreed to a truce. Athens kept its empire, and the Spartans went home.

A few years later, in 415 BC, Athens tried again to expand its empire. It sent its army and navy to conquer the island of Sicily. This effort failed. The entire Athenian army was defeated by Sicilian allies of Sparta and taken prisoner. Even worse, these Sicilians also destroyed most of the Athenian navy.

Taking advantage of Athens's weakness, Sparta attacked Athens, and the war started up once more. Although the Athenians fought bravely, the Spartans won. They cut off the supply of food to Athens completely. In 404 BC, the people of Athens, starving and surrounded, surrendered. The Peloponnesian War was over, and Sparta was in control.

Fighting Among the City-States

With the defeat of Athens, Sparta became the most powerful city-state in Greece. For about 30 years, the Spartans controlled nearly all of Greece, until other city-states started to resent them. This resentment led to a period of war. Control of Greece shifted from city-state to city-state. The fighting went on for many years, which weakened Greece and left it open to attack from outside.

READING CHECK Identifying Cause and Effect What happened to Greece after the Peloponnesian War?

SUMMARY AND PREVIEW In this section you read about conflicts among city-states for control of Greece. In the next section, you will learn what happened when all of Greece was conquered by a foreign power.

Section 2 Assessment

Reviewing Ideas, Terms, and People

1. **a. Recall** How long did Spartan men stay in the army?
   b. Summarize How did the army affect life in Sparta?
2. **a. Identify** What skills did rich Athenian boys learn in school?
   b. Elaborate How might the government of Athens have influenced the growth of its educational system?
3. **a. Identify** Which city-state won the Peloponnesian War?
   b. Explain Why did many city-states form an **alliance** against Athens?

Critical Thinking

4. **Comparing and Contrasting** Look through your notes on Athens and Sparta to find similarities and differences between the two city-states. Use a graphic organizer like the one on the right to organize the information.

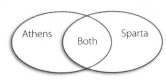

FOCUS ON WRITING

5. **Analyzing Greek Accomplishments** Think about the characteristics you would expect to be admired in Sparta and Athens. Write down some of these characteristics in your notebook. How do they relate to the Persian leaders you listed before?

LA.6.1.7.3, SS.6.G.1.4, SS.6.G.1.5, SS.6.G.1.7, SS.6.G.2.2, SS.6.G.2.6, SS.6.G.6.2, SS.6.W.3.6, SS.6.W.3.7

What You Will Learn...

Main Ideas

1. Macedonia conquered Greece in the 300s BC.
2. Alexander the Great built an empire that united much of Europe, Asia, and Egypt.
3. The Hellenistic kingdoms formed from Alexander's empire blended Greek and other cultures.

The Big Idea

Alexander the Great built a huge empire and helped spread Greek culture into Egypt and Asia.

Key Terms and People

Philip II, *p. 272*
phalanx, *p. 273*
Alexander the Great, *p. 274*
Hellenistic, *p. 275*

Online Resource
TAKING NOTES

Use the graphic organizer online to take notes on Alexander the Great and how he spread Greek culture.

Alexander the Great

If YOU were there...

You are a soldier in the most powerful army in the world. In just eight years, you and your fellow soldiers have conquered an enormous empire. Now your general wants to push farther into unknown lands in search of greater glory. But you're thousands of miles from home, and you haven't seen your family in years.

Do you agree to go on fighting? Why or why not?

BUILDING BACKGROUND The world's most powerful army in the 300s BC was from Macedonia, a kingdom just north of Greece. The Greeks had long dismissed the Macedonians as unimportant. They thought of the Macedonians as barbarians because they lived in small villages and spoke a strange form of the Greek language. But the Greeks underestimated the Macedonians, barbarians or not.

Macedonia Conquers Greece

In 359 BC **Philip II** became king of Macedonia. Philip spent the first year of his rule fighting off invaders who wanted to take over his kingdom. Once he defeated the invaders, he was ready to launch invasions of his own.

Philip's main target was Greece. The leaders of Athens, knowing they were the target of Philip's powerful army, called for all Greeks to join together. Few people responded.

As a result, the armies of Athens and its chief ally Thebes were easily defeated by the Macedonians. Having witnessed this defeat, the rest of the Greeks agreed to make Philip their leader.

Philip's Military Strength

Philip defeated the Greeks because he was a brilliant military leader. He borrowed and improved many of the strategies Greek armies used in battle. For example, Philip's soldiers, like the Greeks, fought as a phalanx (FAY-langks). A **phalanx** was a group of warriors who stood close together in a square. Each soldier held a spear pointed outward to fight off enemies. As soldiers in the front lines were killed, others stepped up from behind to fill their spots.

Philip improved upon the Greeks' idea. He gave his soldiers spears that were much longer than those of his opponents. This allowed his army to attack effectively in any battle. Philip also sent cavalry and archers into battle to support the phalanx.

After conquering Greece, Philip turned his attention to Persia. He planned to march east and conquer the Persian Empire, but he never made it. He was murdered in 336 BC while celebrating his daughter's wedding. When Philip died, his throne—and his plans—passed to his son, Alexander.

READING CHECK **Summarizing** How was Philip II able to conquer Greece?

Alexander Builds an Empire

When Philip died, the people in the Greek city of Thebes rebelled. They thought that the Macedonians would not have a leader strong enough to keep the kingdom together. They were wrong.

Controlling the Greeks

Although he was only 20 years old, Philip's son Alexander was as strong a leader as his father had been. He immediately went south to end the revolt in Thebes.

The Phalanx
With men holding 16-foot-long spears, a phalanx marches into battle.

Why were the soldiers' spears so long?

Within a year, Alexander had destroyed Thebes and enslaved the Theban people. He used Thebes as an example to other Greeks of what would happen if they turned against him. Then, confident that the Greeks would not rebel again, he set out to build an empire.

Alexander's efforts to build an empire made him one of the greatest conquerors in history. These efforts earned him the name **Alexander the Great**.

Building a New Empire

Like his father, Alexander was a brilliant commander. In 334 BC he attacked the Persians, whose army was much larger than his own. But Alexander's troops were well trained and ready for battle. They defeated the Persians time after time.

According to legend, Alexander visited a town called Gordium in Asia Minor while he was fighting the Persians. There he heard an ancient tale about a knot tied by an ancient king. The tale said that whoever untied the knot would rule all of Asia. According to the legend, Alexander pulled out his sword and cut right through the knot. Taking this as a good sign, he and his army set out again.

THE IMPACT TODAY

We still use the phrase "cutting the Gordian knot" to mean solving a difficult problem easily.

If you look at the map, you can follow the route Alexander took on his conquests. After defeating the Persians near the town of Issus, Alexander went to Egypt, which was part of the Persian Empire. The Persian governor had heard of his skill in battle. He surrendered without a fight in 332 BC and crowned Alexander pharaoh.

After a short stay in Egypt, Alexander set out again. Near the town of Gaugamela (gaw-guh-MEE-luh), he defeated the Persian army for the last time. After the battle, the Persian king fled. The king soon died, killed by one of his nobles. With the king's death, Alexander became the ruler of what had been the Persian Empire.

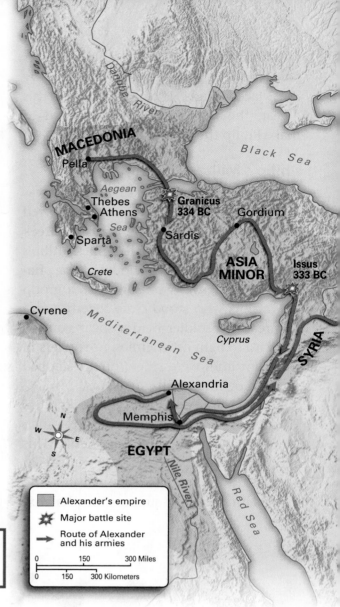

Marching Home

Still intent on building his empire, Alexander led his army through Central Asia. In 327 BC Alexander crossed the Indus River and wanted to push deeper into India. But his exhausted soldiers refused to go any farther. Disappointed, Alexander began the long march home.

Alexander left India in 325 BC, but he never made it back to Greece. In 323 BC, on his way back, Alexander visited the city of Babylon and got sick. He died a few days later at age 33. After he died, Alexander's body was taken to Egypt and buried in a golden coffin.

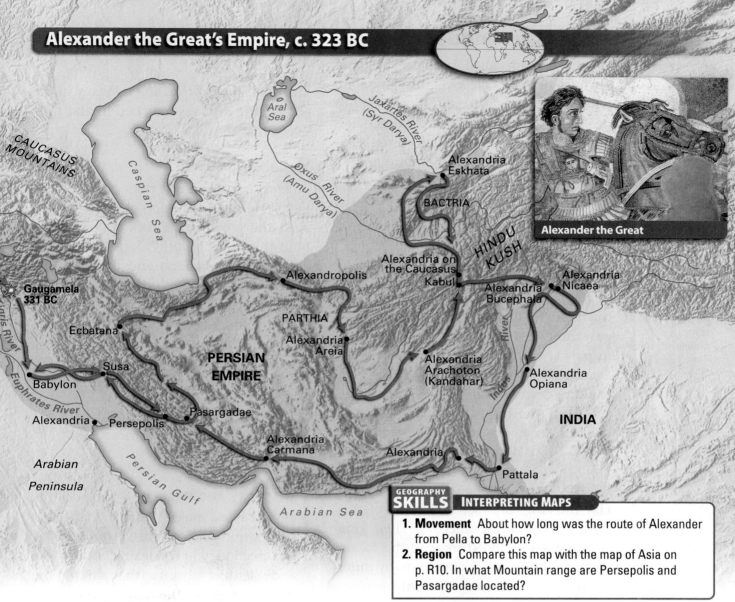

Alexander the Great's Empire, c. 323 BC

CAUCASUS MOUNTAINS

Caspian Sea

Aral Sea

Jaxartes River (Syr Darya)

Oxus River (Amu Darya)

Alexandria Eskhata

BACTRIA

HINDU KUSH

Alexandria on the Caucasus

Kabul

Alexandria Nicaea

Alexandria Bucephala

Alexandropolis

Gaugamela 331 BC

Tigris River

Ecbatana

PARTHIA

Alexandria Areia

Indus River

Euphrates River

Susa

Babylon

Alexandria

Persepolis

Pasargadae

PERSIAN EMPIRE

Alexandria Arachoton (Kandahar)

Alexandria Opiana

Arabian Peninsula

Persian Gulf

Alexandria Carmana

INDIA

Alexandria

Pattala

Arabian Sea

Alexander the Great

GEOGRAPHY SKILLS | INTERPRETING MAPS

1. **Movement** About how long was the route of Alexander from Pella to Babylon?
2. **Region** Compare this map with the map of Asia on p. R10. In what Mountain range are Persepolis and Pasargadae located?

Spreading Greek Culture

Alexander's empire was the largest the world had ever seen. An admirer of Greek culture, he worked to spread Greek influence throughout his empire by founding cities in the lands he conquered.

Alexander modeled his new cities after the cities of Greece. He named many of them Alexandria, after himself. He built temples and theaters like those in Greece. He then encouraged Greek settlers to move to the new cities. These settlers spoke Greek, which became common throughout the empire. In time, Greek art, literature, and science spread into surrounding lands.

Even as he supported the spread of Greek culture, however, Alexander encouraged conquered people to keep their own customs and traditions. As a result, a new blended culture developed in Alexander's empire. It combined elements of Persian, Egyptian, Syrian, and other cultures with Greek ideas. Because this new culture was not completely Greek, or Hellenic, historians call it **Hellenistic**, or Greek-like. It wasn't purely Greek, but it was heavily influenced by Greek ideas.

READING CHECK **Sequencing** What steps did Alexander take to create his empire?

Hellenistic Kingdoms

When Alexander died, he didn't have an obvious heir to take over his kingdom, and no one knew who was in power. With no clear direction, Alexander's generals fought for power. In the end, three powerful generals divided the empire among themselves. One became king of Macedonia and Greece, one ruled Syria, and the third claimed Egypt.

Hellenistic Macedonia

As you might expect, the kingdom of Macedonia and Greece was the most Greek of the three. However, it also had the weakest government. The Macedonian kings had to put down many revolts by the Greeks. Damaged by the revolts, Macedonia couldn't defend itself. Armies from Rome, a rising power from the Italian Peninsula, marched in and conquered Macedonia in the mid-100s BC.

Hellenistic Syria

Like the kings of Macedonia, the rulers of Syria faced many challenges. Their kingdom, which included most of the former Persian Empire, was home to many different peoples with many different customs.

Unhappy with Hellenistic rule, many of these people rebelled against their leaders. Weakened by years of fighting, the kingdom slowly broke apart. Finally in the 60s BC the Romans marched in and took over Syria.

Hellenistic Egypt

Ptolemy I was the first ruler of Hellenistic Egypt. He and other rulers of Egypt encouraged the growth of Greek culture. They built the ancient world's largest library in the city of Alexandria and the Museum, a place for scholars and artists to meet. Through their efforts, Alexandria became a great center of culture and learning. The Egyptian kingdom lasted longer than the other Hellenistic kingdoms. However, in 30 BC it too was conquered by Rome.

READING CHECK Analyzing Why were three kingdoms created from Alexander's empire?

SUMMARY AND PREVIEW Alexander the Great caused major political changes in Greece and the Hellenistic world. In the next section, you will learn about artistic and scientific advances that affected the lives of people in the same areas.

Section 3 Assessment

Reviewing Ideas, Terms, and People

1. **Identify** What king conquered Greece in the 300s BC?
2. **a. Describe** What territories did **Alexander the Great** conquer?
   b. Interpret Why did Alexander destroy Thebes?
   c. Calculate If Alexander's armies marched 10 miles in 5 hours, what rate were they marching at?
3. **a. Recall** What three kingdoms were created out of Alexander's empire after his death?
   b. Explain Why were these kingdoms called **Hellenistic**?

Critical Thinking

4. **Generalizing** Review your notes on Alexander. Then, write one sentence explaining why he is an important historical figure.

Building an Empire	Spreading Culture

Why Alexander was important

FOCUS ON WRITING

5. **Evaluating Alexander** Add Alexander the Great to the table you created earlier. Remember that although Alexander was a military man, not all of his accomplishments were in battle.

Greek Achievements

If YOU were there...

Everyone in Athens has been talking about a philosopher and teacher named Socrates, so you decide to go and see him for yourself. You find him sitting under a tree, surrounded by his students. "Teach me about life," you say. But instead of answering, he asks you, "What is life?" You struggle to reply. He asks another question, and another. If he's such a great teacher, you wonder, shouldn't he have all the answers? Instead, all he seems to have are questions.

What do you think of Socrates?

> **BUILDING BACKGROUND** Socrates was only one of the brilliant philosophers who lived in Athens in the 400s BC. The city was also home to some of the world's greatest artists and writers. In fact, all over Greece men and women made great advances in the arts and sciences. Their work inspired people for centuries.

The Arts

Among the most notable achievements of the ancient Greeks were those they made in the arts. These arts included sculpture, painting, architecture, and writings.

Statues and Paintings

The ancient Greeks were master artists. Their paintings and statues have been admired for hundreds of years. Examples of these works are still displayed in museums around the world.

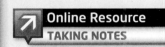

Hellenistic sculpture is admired for its realism, natural look, and details.

277

Greek statues are so admired because the sculptors tried to make them look perfect. Like Classical Greek artists, Hellenistic sculptors wanted their statues to show how beautiful people could be. These sculptors carefully studied the human body, especially when it was moving. Then, using what they had learned, they carved stone and marble statues. As a result, many Hellenistic statues look as though they could come to life at any moment.

Hellenistic painting is also admired for its realism and detail. For example, Greek artists painted detailed scenes on vases, pots, and other vessels. These vessels often show scenes from myths or athletic competitions.

Many of the scenes were created using only two colors, black and red. Sometimes artists used black glaze to paint scenes on red vases. Other artists covered whole vases with glaze and then scraped parts away to let the red background show through.

Greek Architecture

If you went to Greece today, you would see the ruins of many ancient buildings. Old columns still hold up parts of broken roofs, and ancient carvings decorate fallen walls. These remains give us an idea of the beauty of ancient Greek buildings.

The Greeks took great care in designing

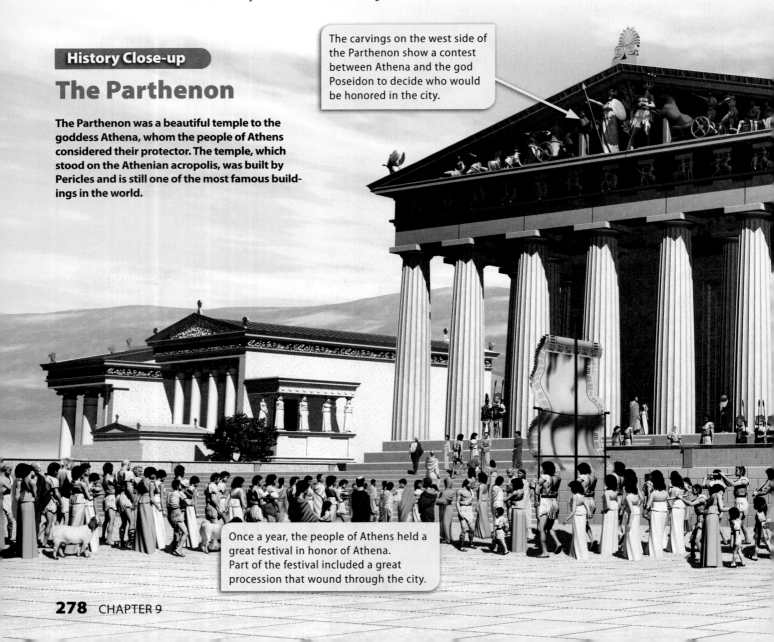

History Close-up

The Parthenon

The Parthenon was a beautiful temple to the goddess Athena, whom the people of Athens considered their protector. The temple, which stood on the Athenian acropolis, was built by Pericles and is still one of the most famous buildings in the world.

The carvings on the west side of the Parthenon show a contest between Athena and the god Poseidon to decide who would be honored in the city.

Once a year, the people of Athens held a great festival in honor of Athena. Part of the festival included a great procession that wound through the city.

their buildings, especially their temples. Rows of tall columns surrounded the temples, making the temples look stately and inspiring. Greek designers were very careful when they measured these columns. They knew that columns standing in a long row often looked as though they curved in the middle. To prevent this optical illusion, they made their columns bulge slightly in the middle. As a result, Greek columns look perfectly straight.

Ancient Greek designers took such care because they wanted their buildings to reflect the greatness of their cities. The most impressive of all ancient Greek buildings was the Parthenon (PAHR-thuh-nahn) in Athens, pictured below. This temple to Athena was built in the 400s BC on the Athenian acropolis. It was designed to be magnificent not only outside, but inside as well. As you can see, the interior was decorated with carvings and columns.

New Forms of Writing

Sculpture, painting, and architecture were not the only Greek art forms. The Greeks also excelled at writing. In fact, Greek writers created many new writing forms, including drama and history.

The Greeks created drama, or plays, as

FOCUS ON 🏴

The Golden Mean
When the sculptor Phidias built the Parthenon, he used the mathematical ratio called the Golden Mean or the Golden Ratio. The Golden Ratio, which says that the length of a rectangle will be 1.618 times longer than the width of the rectangle, is found throughout Greek architecture.

MA.6.A.2.2 Interpret and compare ratios and rates.

Inside the Parthenon was a magnificent statue of Athena by the sculptor Phidias, whom many people considered the greatest sculptor in all of Greece.

The Parthenon's 46 columns are a type called Doric columns. These simple columns have no decoration at the top.

ANALYSIS SKILL ANALYZING VISUALS

Why do you think people are bringing animals and goods with them to the temple?

279

THE IMPACT
TODAY

The Hellenis-
tic historian
Plutarch, like the
historian Thucy-
dides, wanted
to use history to
teach lessons.
His work *Parallel
Lives* includes
biographies of fa-
mous Greek and
Roman states-
men chosen as
examples of how,
or how not, to
live. This work is
the best source
we have today for
many historical
figures.

part of their religious ceremonies. Actors and singers performed scenes in honor of the gods and heroes. These plays became a popular form of entertainment.

In the 400s BC Athenian writers created many of the greatest plays of the ancient world. Some writers produced tragedies, which described the hardships faced by Greek heroes. Among the best tragedy writers were Aeschylus (ES-kuh-luhs) and Sophocles (SAHF-uh-kleez). For example, Sophocles wrote about a Greek hero who mistakenly killed his own father. Other Greek dramatists focused on comedies, which made fun of people and ideas. One famous comedy writer was Aristophanes (ar-uh-STAHF-uh-neez). He used his comedy to make serious points about war, courts of law, and famous people.

The Greeks were also among the first people to write about history. They were interested in the lessons history could teach. One of the greatest of the Greek historians was Thucydides (thoo-SID-uh-deez). His history of the Peloponnesian War was based in part on his experiences as an Athenian soldier. Even though he was from Athens, Thucydides tried to be **neutral** in his writing. He studied the war and tried to figure out what had caused it. Many later historians modeled their works after his.

READING CHECK **Summarizing** What were some forms of art found in ancient Greece?

Philosophy

The ancient Greeks worshipped gods and goddesses whose actions explained many of the mysteries of the world. But by around 500 BC a few people had begun to think about other explanations. We call these people philosophers. Thales is regarded as the first philosopher in the Greek tradition. He influenced many other Greek philosophers. They believed in the power of the human mind to think, explain, and understand life.

Primary Source

BOOK
The Death of Socrates

In 399 BC Socrates was arrested and charged with corrupting the young people of Athens and ignoring religious traditions. He was sentenced to die by drinking poison. Socrates spent his last hours surrounded by his students. One of them, Plato, later described the event in detail.

Socrates himself does not protest against his sentence but willingly drinks the poison.

The students and friends who have visited Socrates, including the narrator, are much less calm than he is.

❝Then raising the cup to his lips, quite readily and cheerfully he drank off the poison. And hitherto most of us had been able to control our sorrow; but now when we saw him drinking . . . my own tears were flowing fast; so that I covered my face and wept . . . Socrates alone retained his calmness: What is this strange outcry? he said . . . I have been told that a man should die in peace. Be quiet then, and have patience.**❞**

–Plato, from *Phaedo*

ANALYSIS SKILL **ANALYZING PRIMARY SOURCES**

How does Socrates tell his students to act when they see him drink the poison?

Socrates

Among the greatest of these thinkers was a man named **Socrates** (SAHK-ruh-teez). He believed that people must never stop looking for knowledge.

Socrates was a teacher as well as a thinker. Today we call his type of teaching the Socratic method. Socrates taught by asking questions. His questions were about human qualities such as love and courage. He would ask, "What is courage?" When people answered, he challenged their answers with more questions.

Socrates wanted to make people think and question their own beliefs. But he made people angry, even frightened. They accused him of questioning the authority of the gods. For these reasons, he was arrested and condemned to death. His friends and students watched him calmly accept his death. He took the poison he was given, drank it, and died.

Plato

Plato (PLAYT-oh) was a student of Socrates. Like Socrates, he was a teacher as well as a philosopher. Plato created a school, the Academy, to which students, philosophers, and scientists could come to discuss ideas.

Although Plato spent much of his time running the Academy, he also wrote many works. The most famous of these works was called *The Republic*. It describes Plato's idea of an ideal society. This society would be based on justice and fairness to everyone. To ensure this fairness, Plato argued, society should be run by philosophers. He thought that only they could understand what was best for everyone.

Aristotle

Perhaps the greatest Greek thinker was **Aristotle** (ar-uh-STAH-tuhl), Plato's student. He taught that people should live lives of moderation, or balance. For example,

BIOGRAPHY

Euclid
c. 300 BC

Euclid is considered one of the world's greatest mathematicians. He lived and taught in Alexandria, Egypt, a great center of learning. Euclid wrote about the relationship between mathematics and other fields, including astronomy and music. But it is for geometry that he is best known. In fact, his works were so influential that the branch of geometry we study in school—the study of flat shapes and lines—is called Euclidean geometry.

Drawing Conclusions Why do you think a branch of geometry is named after Euclid?

people should not be greedy, but neither should they give away everything they own. Instead, people should find a balance between these two extremes.

Aristotle believed that moderation was based on **reason**, or clear and ordered thinking. He thought that people should use reason to govern their lives. In other words, people should think about their actions and how they will affect others.

Aristotle also made great advances in the field of logic, the process of making inferences. He argued that you could use facts you knew to figure out new facts. For example, if you know that Socrates lives in Athens and that Athens is in Greece, you can conclude that Socrates lives in Greece. Aristotle's ideas about logic helped inspire many later Greek scientists.

READING CHECK **Generalizing** What did ancient Greek philosophers like Socrates, Plato, and Aristotle want to find out?

FOCUS ON

Hellenistic Philosophy New philosophies emerged during the Hellenistic Period. **Epicureans** believed that people should focus on happiness and avoid pain. **Stoics** taught the importance of reason and duty above all other things. **Cynics** thought that people should live in harmony with nature, and that people should be free and take care of themselves.

FOCUS ON

Hellenistic Science Many Hellenistic scientists made important discoveries. Aristarchus figured out how to measure the sizes and distances of the sun and the moon. Another scientist, Erasistratus of Ceos, figured out that the heart makes the blood move throughout the human body.

Science

Aristotle's works inspired many Greek scientists. They began to look closely at the world to see how it worked.

Mathematics

Some Greeks spent their lives studying mathematics. One of these people was **Euclid** (YOO-kluhd). He was interested in geometry, the study of lines, angles, and shapes. In fact, many of the geometry rules we learn in school today come straight from Euclid's writings.

Other Greek mathematicians included a geographer who used mathematics to accurately calculate the size of the earth. Years later, in the AD 300s and 400s, a woman named Hypatia (hy-PAY-shuh) taught about mathematics and astronomy.

Medicine and Engineering

Not all Greek scientists studied numbers. Some studied other areas of science, such as medicine and engineering.

Greek doctors studied the human body to understand how it worked. In trying to cure diseases and keep people healthy, Greek doctors made many discoveries.

The greatest Greek doctor was **Hippocrates** (hip-AHK-ruh-teez). He wanted to figure out what caused diseases so he could better treat them. Hippocrates is better known today, though, for his ideas about how doctors should behave.

Greek engineers also made great discoveries. Some devices they invented are still used today. For example, farmers in many countries still use water screws to bring water to their fields. This device, which brings water from a lower level to a higher one, was invented by the Helenistic scientist Archimedes (ahr-kuh-MEED-eez) in the 200s BC. Greek inventors could be playful as well as serious. For example, one inventor created mechanical toys like birds, puppets, and coin-operated machines.

READING CHECK **Summarizing** What advances did Greek scientists make in medicine?

SUMMARY AND PREVIEW Through their art, philosophy, and science, the Greeks have greatly influenced Western civilization. In the next chapter, you will learn about another group that has helped shape the Western world—the Romans.

Section 4 Assessment

Reviewing Ideas, Terms, and People

1. **a. Identify** What two types of drama did the Greeks invent?
   b. Compare What ratio was used in ancient Greek buildings? Name a rectangular building you know that appears to use the same ratio. How could you find out if the building uses the same ratio?
   c. Elaborate How did studying the human body help Greek artists make their statues look real?
2. **Describe** How did **Socrates** teach? What is this method of teaching called?
3. **a. Identify** In what fields did **Hippocrates** and **Euclid** make their greatest achievements?
   b. Make Inferences Why do some people call Greece the birthplace of the Western world?

Critical Thinking

4. **Summarizing** Add a box to the bottom of your note-taking chart. Use it to summarize Greek contributions in the arts, philosophy, and science.

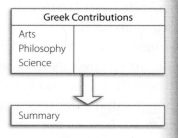

Greek Contributions	
Arts Philosophy Science	

Summary

FOCUS ON WRITING

5. **Taking Notes about Artists and Thinkers** Add the artists and thinkers from this section to your chart. Because these people were not military leaders, all of your notes will go in the third column of your chart.

Greek Philosophers— Socrates, Plato, and Aristotle

What would the world be like if no one believed in the importance of knowledge and truth?

When did they live? the 400s and 300s BC

Where did they live? Athens

What did they do? They thought. Socrates, Plato, and Aristotle thought about the world and searched for knowledge, wisdom, and truth. Between them they created the Socratic method of learning, the first political science book, and a method of scientific reasoning.

Why are they important? In most of the ancient world, strong fighters won all the glory. But in Athens, great thinkers and wise men were honored. People listened to them and followed their advice. Even today, people admire the ideas of Socrates, Plato, and Aristotle. Their teachings are at the root of modern philosophy and science.

Making Inferences Do you think these philosophers would have been as influential if they had lived in a different city? Why or why not?

This drawing shows how one artist imagined Plato (left), Aristotle (center), and Socrates (right) to look.

HISTORY

VIDEO
The Death of a Philosopher
↗ Online Resource

Social Studies Skills

Analysis | Critical Thinking | Economics | **Study**

Interpreting Charts and Tables

Understand the Skill

Charts present information visually to make it easier to understand. Different kinds of charts have different purposes. *Organizational charts* can show relationships among the parts of something. *Flow-charts* show steps in a process or cause-and-effect relationships. *Classification charts* group information so it can be easily compared. *Tables* are a type of classification chart that organize information into rows and columns for easy comparison. The ability to interpret charts helps you to analyze information and understand relationships.

Learn the Skill

Use these basic steps to interpret a chart:

1 Identify the type of chart and read its title in order to understand its purpose and subject.

2 Note the parts of the chart. Read the headings of rows and columns to determine the categories and types of information. Note any other labels that accompany the information presented in the chart. Look for any lines that connect its parts. What do they tell you?

3 Study the chart's details. Look for relationships in the information it presents. If it is a classification chart, analyze and compare all content in the rows and columns. In flowcharts and organizational charts, read all labels and other information. Follow and analyze directional arrows or lines.

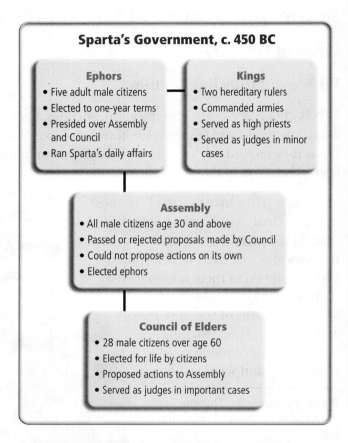

Sparta's Government, c. 450 BC

Ephors
- Five adult male citizens
- Elected to one-year terms
- Presided over Assembly and Council
- Ran Sparta's daily affairs

Kings
- Two hereditary rulers
- Commanded armies
- Served as high priests
- Served as judges in minor cases

Assembly
- All male citizens age 30 and above
- Passed or rejected proposals made by Council
- Could not propose actions on its own
- Elected ephors

Council of Elders
- 28 male citizens over age 60
- Elected for life by citizens
- Proposed actions to Assembly
- Served as judges in important cases

Practice and Apply the Skill

Apply the strategies given to interpret the chart above and answer the following questions.

1. What type of chart is this and what is its purpose?

2. In what ways were the ephors and the Assembly connected?

3. How did the roles of the Assembly and the Council of Elders differ?

4. What position in Spartan government had no direct relationship with the Assembly?

Chapter Review

Visual Summary

Use the visual summary below to help you review the main ideas of the chapter.

Sparta and Athens fought together to defeat Persia in the Persian Wars.

Spartan culture centered on the military, while Athenian culture emphasized government and the arts.

Alexander the Great built a huge empire and spread Greek culture.

The ancient Greeks made lasting contributions to architecture, philosophy, science, and many other fields.

Reviewing Vocabulary, Terms, and People

Choose one word from each word pair to correctly complete each sentence below.

1. A ruler named _____ created the Persian Empire. **(Cyrus the Great/Xerxes I)**

2. A _____ was a group of soldiers that stood in a square to fight. **(cavalry/phalanx)**

3. _____ built the largest empire the world had ever seen. **(Alexander the Great/Aristotle)**

4. The _____ War(s) pitted two city-states against each other. **(Persian/Peloponnesian)**

5. The philosopher _____ taught people by asking them questions. **(Darius/Socrates)**

6. The greatest medical scholar of ancient Greece was _____. **(Philip II/Hippocrates)**

7. Aristotle taught the importance of _____ in his writings. **(reason/alliance)**

8. _____ was a great mathematician. **(Plato/Euclid)**

Comprehension and Critical Thinking

SECTION 1 *(Pages 260–265)*

9. **a. Identify** Who were Cyrus the Great, Darius I, and Xerxes I?

   b. Analyze How did the Greeks use strategy to defeat a larger fighting force?

   c. Elaborate What were some factors that led to the success of the Persian Empire?

SECTION 2 *(Pages 266–271)*

10. **a. Describe** What was life like for Spartan women? for Athenian women?

   b. Compare and Contrast How was the education of Spartan boys different from the education of Athenian boys? What did the education of both groups have in common?

   c. Evaluate Do you agree or disagree with this statement: "The Athenians brought the Peloponnesian War on themselves." Defend your argument.

SECTION 3 *(Pages 272–276)*

11. a. Describe How did Philip II improve the phalanx?

b. Analyze How did the cultures that Alexander conquered change after his death?

c. Predict How might history have been different if Alexander had not died so young?

SECTION 4 *(Pages 277–282)*

12. a. Identify What is the Parthenon? For which goddess was it built?

b. Compare What did Socrates, Plato, and Aristotle have in common?

c. Evaluate Why do you think Greek accomplishments in the arts and sciences are still admired today?

Reviewing Themes

13. Politics Why did the Persians and the Greeks react differently to the end of the Persian Wars?

14. Politics How were the government and the army related in Sparta?

15. Society and Culture How were the roles of women different in Athens and Sparta?

Using the Internet

16. Activity: Writing a Dialogue While rulers such as Alexander and Cyrus fought to gain land, thinkers like Socrates may have questioned their methods. Go online to research Socrates' views on rulers. Write a dialogue between Socrates and a student on whether it was right to invade another country. Socrates should ask at least 10 questions to his student.

Social Studies Skills

17. Interpreting Charts and Tables Create a chart in your notebook that identifies key Greek achievements in architecture, art, writing, philosophy, and science. Complete the chart with details from this chapter.

Reading Skills

18. Comparing and Contrasting Historical Facts Complete the chart below to compare and contrast two powerful leaders you studied in this chapter, Cyrus the Great and Alexander the Great.

Compare	**List two characteristics that Cyrus and Alexander shared.**
	a. _____
	b. _____

Contrast	**How did Cyrus's and Alexander's backgrounds differ?**	
	Cyrus	Alexander
	c. _____	d. _____
	What happened to their empires after they died?	
	Cyrus	Alexander
	e. _____	f. _____

19. Writing Your Poem Look back over your notes from this chapter. Ask yourself which of the accomplishments you noted are the most significant. Do you admire people for their ideas? their might? their leadership? their brilliance?

Choose one person whose accomplishments you admire. Look back through the chapter for more details about the person's accomplishments. Then write a poem in praise of your chosen figure. Your poem should be five lines long. The first line should identify the subject of the poem. The next three lines should note his or her accomplishments, and the last line should sum up why he or she is respected.

Florida Standardized Test Practice

DIRECTIONS: Read each question and write the letter of the best response.

1

> The freedom which we enjoy in our government extends also to our ordinary life . . . Further, we provide plenty of means for the mind to refresh itself from business. We celebrate games and sacrifices all the year round . . . Where our rivals from their very cradles by a painful discipline seek after manliness . . . we live exactly as we please and yet are just as ready to encounter every legitimate danger.

The information in this passage suggests that the person who wrote it probably lived in

A Athens.

B Persia.

C Sparta.

D Troy.

2 The Athenians' main rivals were from

A Sparta.

B Rome.

C Macedonia.

D Alexandria.

3 Which people were the chief enemies of the Greeks in the 400s BC?

A the Romans

B the Persians

C the Egyptians

D the Macedonians

4 All of the following were Greek philosophers *except*

A Aristotle.

B Plato.

C Socrates.

D Zoroaster.

5 Hellenistic culture developed as a result of the activities of which person?

A Darius I

B Philip II

C Cyrus the Great

D Alexander the Great

Connecting with Past Learnings

6 Cyrus the Great and Alexander the Great both built huge empires. What other leader that you have studied in this course also created an empire?

A Moses

B Shi Huangdi

C Confucius

D Hatshepsut

7 In this chapter you have read about many great philosophers and thinkers. Which of the following people you have studied was *not* a philosopher or thinker?

A Socrates

B Ramses the Great

C Confucius

D Siddhartha Gautama

A Social Studies Report

Assignment

Collect information and write an informative report on a topic related to the Hebrews or the ancient Greeks.

The purpose of a social studies report is to share information. Often, this information comes from research. You begin your research by asking questions about a subject.

1. Prewrite

Choosing a Subject

You could ask many questions about the unit you have just studied.

> • Why was Ruth an important person in the history of the Jewish religion?
> • What was the role of mythology in the lives of the ancient Greeks?
> • What were the most important accomplishments of Alexander the Great?

Jot down some topics that interested you. Then, brainstorm a list of questions about one or more of these topics. Make sure your questions are narrow and focused. Choose the question that seems most interesting.

Finding Historical Information

Use at least three sources besides your textbook to find information on your topic. Good sources include

- books, maps, magazines, newspapers
- television programs, movies, videos
- Internet sites, CD-ROMs, DVDs

Keep track of your sources of information by writing them in a notebook or on cards. Give each source a number as shown below.

TIP **Narrowing a Topic**
Broad: Sparta
Less Broad: Women and Girls in Sparta
Focus Question: What was life like for women and girls in Sparta?

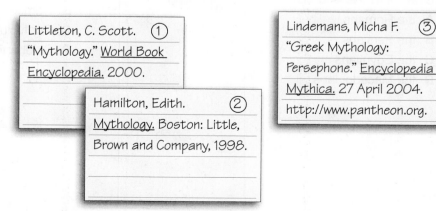

Littleton, C. Scott. ①
"Mythology." World Book Encyclopedia. 2000.

Hamilton, Edith. ②
Mythology. Boston: Little, Brown and Company, 1998.

Lindemans, Micha F. ③
"Greek Mythology: Persephone." Encyclopedia Mythica. 27 April 2004.
http://www.pantheon.org.

Taking Notes

Take notes on important facts and details from your sources. Historical writing needs to be accurate. Carefully record all names, dates, and other information from sources. Copy any direct quotation word for word and enclose the words in quotation marks. Along with each note, include the number of its source and its page number.

Stating the Big Idea of Your Report

You can easily turn your original question into the big idea for your report. If your question changes a bit as you do your research, rewrite it before turning it into a statement. The big idea of a report is often, but not always, stated in the first paragraph.

Organizing Your Ideas and Information

Sort your notes into topics and subtopics. Put them in an order that is logical, that will make sense to your reader. We often use one of these ways to organize information:

- placing events and details in the order they happened
- grouping causes with their effects
- grouping information by category, usually in the order of least to most important

Here is a partial outline for a paper on Greek mythology.

Big Idea: The ancient Greeks told myths to explain the world.
I. Purpose of mythology in ancient Greece
  A. Greeks' questions about the world around them
  B. Greeks' use of myths for answers
II. Myths about everyday events in the Greeks' lives
  A. The myth of Hestia, goddess of the home
  B. The myth of Hephaestus, god of crafts and fire
III. Myths about the natural world of the Greeks
  A. The myth of Apollo, god of the sun
  B. The myth of Persephone, goddess of the seasons

TIP **Statement or Question**
Your big idea statement can be a statement of the point you want to make in your paper.

The ancient Greeks used mythology to explain nature.

It can also be a question, similar to your original research question.

How did the ancient Greeks use mythology to explain their lives?

TIP **Making the Most of Your Outline** If you write each of your topics and subtopics as a complete sentence, you can use those sentences to create your first draft.

2. Write

It is good to write a first draft fairly quickly, but it's also helpful to organize it as you go. Use the following framework as a guide.

A Writer's Framework

Introduction	Body	Conclusion
■ Start with a quotation or interesting historical detail. ■ State the big idea of your report. ■ Provide any historical background readers need in order to understand your big idea.	■ Present your information under at least three main ideas. ■ Write at least one paragraph for each of these main ideas. ■ Add supporting details, facts, or examples to each paragraph.	■ Restate your main idea, using slightly different words. ■ Close with a general comment about your topic or tell how the historical information in your report relates to later historical events.

Studying a Model

Here is a model of a social studies report. Study it to see how one student developed a social studies paper. The first and the concluding paragraphs are shown in full. The paragraphs in the body of the paper are summarized.

INTRODUCTORY PARAGRAPH

Attention grabber

Statement of Big Idea

The ancient Greeks faced many mysteries in their lives. How and why did people fall in love? What made rain fall and crops grow? What are the planets and stars, and where did they come from? Through the myths they told about their heroes, gods, and goddesses, the Greeks answered these questions. They used mythology to explain all things, from everyday events to forces of nature to the creation of the universe.

Body Paragraphs

The first body paragraph opens with a statement about how the Greeks used myths to explain their daily lives. Then two examples of those kinds of myths are given. The student summarizes myths about Aphrodite, goddess of love, and Hephaestus, god of crafts and fire.

In the next paragraph, the student shows how the Greeks used myths to explain the natural world. The example of such a story is Persephone and her relationship to the seasons.

The last paragraph in the body contains the student's final point, which is about creation myths. The two examples given for these myths are stories about Helios, god of the sun, and Artemis, goddess of the moon.

CONCLUDING PARAGRAPH

First two sentences restate the thesis

Last three sentences make a general comment about the topic, Greek myths.

The Greeks had a huge number of myths. They needed that many to explain all of the things that they did and saw. Besides explaining things, myths also gave the Greeks a feeling of power. By praying and sacrificing to the gods, they believed they could affect the world around them. All people want to have some control over their lives, and their mythology gave the Greeks that feeling of control.

Notice that each paragraph is organized in the same way as the entire paper. Each paragraph expresses a main idea and includes information to support that main idea. One big difference is that not every paragraph requires a conclusion. Only the last paragraph needs to end with a concluding statement.

3. Evaluate and Revise

It is important to evaluate your first draft before you begin to revise it. Follow the steps below to evaluate and revise your draft.

Evaluating and Revising an Informative Report

1. Does the introduction grab the readers' interest and state the big idea of your report?
2. Does the body of your report have at least three paragraphs that develop your big idea? Is the main idea in each paragraph clearly stated?
3. Have you included enough information to support each of your main ideas? Are all facts, details, and examples accurate? Are all of them clearly related to the main ideas they support?
4. Is the report clearly organized? Does it use chronological order, order of importance, or cause and effect?
5. Does the conclusion restate the big idea of your report? Does it end with a general comment about your topic?
6. Have you included at least three sources in your bibliography? Have you included all the sources you used and not any you did not use?

4. Proofread and Publish

Proofreading

To correct your report before sharing it, check the following:

- the spelling and capitalization of all proper names for specific people, places, things, and events
- punctuation marks around any direct quotation
- punctuation and capitalization in your bibliography

Publishing

Choose one or more of these ideas to share your report.

- Create a map to accompany your report. Use a specific color to highlight places and routes that are important in your report.
- File a copy of your report in your school's library for other students' reference. Include illustrations to go with the report.
- If your school has a Web site, you might post your report there. See if you can link to other sources on your topic.

TIP **Bibliography**

- Underline the titles of all books, television programs, and Web sites.
- Use quotation marks around titles of articles and stories.

Practice and Apply

Use the steps and strategies outlined in this workshop to research and write an informative report.

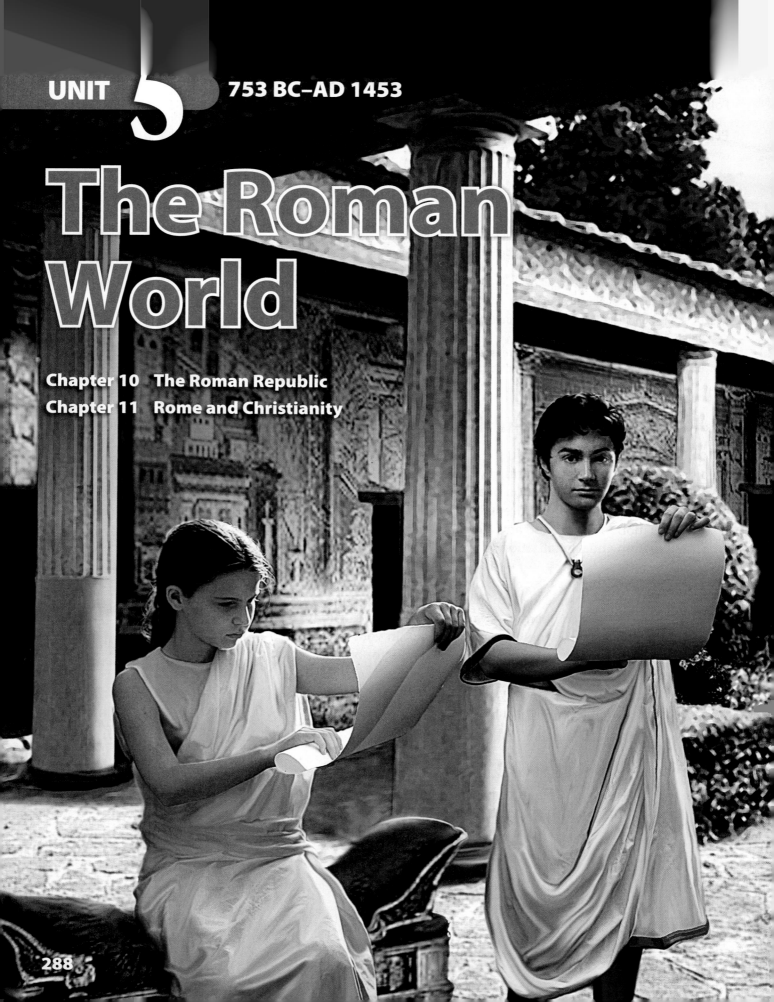

The Roman World

What You Will Learn...

From a small town in Italy, Rome grew to become the center of one of the world's greatest empires. Like the Greeks, whom they admired, the Romans had a lasting influence on world history.

The legacy of Rome was great. The Romans made many huge advances in engineering and architecture, and they developed advanced systems of written laws and government. In the first century AD, a new religion called Christianity appeared and spread throughout the empire.

In the next two chapters, you will learn about the rise of Rome, the growth and spread of Christianity, and the ultimate division and decline of one of the world's greatest empires.

Explore the Art
In this scene, a Roman tutor teaches two young students how to read. What does this scene suggest about life in ancient Rome?

FLORIDA...
The Story Continues

CHAPTER 10, The Roman Republic (753–27 BC)

PLACES **c. 500 BC: The council house serves as the center of ceremonial and political life for Florida's native people.**

Historic descriptions of the council houses of the Timucua shed light on what council houses might have looked like around 500 BC. The Timucua had a large circular council house. The chief and his council met in the building. The building had other uses as well. The people used the building for ceremonies, and the men of the village used it as a lodge. The building also served as a place for visitors to stay. At the center of the council house was a hearth surrounded by a dance floor. Rows of benches lined the walls. Where people sat in the council house depended on their status. Some council houses could hold only about 300 people. Others were large enough to hold 3,000 people. Since populations were smaller in 500 BC, it is unlikely that council house would have been as large then.

EVENTS **Present: Florida's current constitution is its sixth.**

Like other states, Florida has revised its constitution through the years as needed. The state's first constitution was written in 1838 while Florida was still a territory. A written constitution was one of the requirements of becoming a state. The constitutional convention's 56 delegates established a government that consisted of a one-term governor, a two-house legislature, and department administrators selected by the legislature. Since that time the constitution has been revised five times. The constitution was first revised in 1861 when Florida seceded from the Union during the Civil War. It was revised again in 1865 at the end of the Civil War and again in 1868 and 1885. The last revision was adopted in 1968. It is

Florida's current constitution. The Constitution of the State of Florida outlines the duties, power, and structure of the government and the rights of citizens.

PEOPLE **Present: The Florida governor has the power to veto laws.**

The Roman Tribunes had the right to veto, or prohibit, actions by other government officials. Similarly, the governor of Florida has the right to veto laws passed by the Florida legislature. When a bill comes before the governor, the governor can sign the bill, approve it without signing it, or veto it. A vetoed bill cannot become law unless the bill is sent back to both houses of the legislature and is passed by a two-thirds vote. The governor also has the right to veto certain items in bills dealing with spending money without vetoing the entire bill. This is called a line-item veto. The right to veto is the governor's strongest constitutional power.

PEOPLE **Present: Good government requires civic participation.**

People's willingness to participate in government is as important in Florida as it was in ancient Rome. Romans believed that participating in their government was their civic duty as citizens of Rome. Florida's people carry out their civic duty when they vote, run for office, and obey laws.

EVENTS **Present: The Florida state government has checks and balances.** The Constitution of the State of Florida divides the powers of state government into three branches: the executive, the legislative, and the judicial. The branches are separate and relatively independent. The branches are only relatively independent because each branch of government shares in the powers of the other two. This means that each branch can also limit the powers of the other branches. This ability to limit the powers of other branches serves as a check and balance.

Unpacking the Florida Standards <···

Read the following to learn what this standard says and what it means. See FL8–FL31 to unpack all of the standards related to this chapter.

Benchmark SS.6.C.1.2 **Identify how the government of the Roman Republic contributed to the development of democratic principles (separation of powers, rule of law, representative government, civic duty).**

What does it mean?

Explain how a number of key principles developed by the Roman Republic contributed to the development of modern democracy.

 SPOTLIGHT ON

SS.6.E.3.1, SS.6.E.3.2, SS.6.E.3.4, SS.6.G.2.1 See pages FL38, FL39, and FL44 for content specifically related to these Chapter 10 standards.

The Roman Republic

Essential Question How did Rome become the dominant power in the Mediterranean region?

Florida Next Generation Sunshine State Standards

SS.6.C.1.2 Identify how the government of the Roman Republic contributed to the development of democratic principles (separation of powers, rule of law, representative government, civic duty). **SS.6.C.2.1** Identify principles (civic participation, role of government) from ancient Greek and Roman civilizations which are reflected in the American political process today, and discuss their effect on the American political process. **SS.6.E.3.1** Identify examples of mediums of exchange (currencies) used for trade (barter) for each civilization, and explain why international trade requires a system for a medium of exchange between trading both inside and among various regions. **SS.6.E.3.2** Categorize products that were traded among civilizations, and give examples of barriers to trade of those products. **SS.6.E.3.4** Describe the relationship among civilizations that engage in trade, including the benefits and drawbacks of voluntary trade. **SS.6.G.2.1** Explain how major physical characteristics, natural resources, climate, and absolute and relative locations have influenced settlement, interactions, and the economies of ancient civilizations of the world. **SS.6.G.2.4** Explain how the geographical location of ancient civilizations contributed to the culture and politics of those societies. **SS.6.G.3.1** Explain how the physical landscape has affected the development of agriculture and industry in the ancient world. **SS.6.G.5.1** Identify the methods used to compensate for the scarcity of resources in the ancient world. **SS.6.W.3.8** Determine the impact of significant figures associated with ancient Rome. **SS.6.W.3.9** Explain the impact of the Punic Wars on the development of the Roman Empire. **SS.6.W.3.10** Describe the government of the Roman Republic and its contribution to the development of democratic principles (separation of powers, rule of law, representative government, civic duty). **SS.6.W.3.11** Explain the transition from Roman Republic to empire and Imperial Rome, and compare Roman life and culture under each one. **SS.6.W.3.14** Describe the key achievements and contributions of Roman civilization. **SS.6.W.3.16** Compare life in the Roman Republic for patricians, plebeians, women, children, and slaves.

FOCUS ON SPEAKING

A Legend The ancient Romans created many legends about their early history. They told of heroes and kings who performed great deeds to build and rule their city. As you read this chapter, look for people or events that could be the subjects of legends. When you finish studying this chapter, you will create and present a legend about one of the people or events that you have studied.

CHAPTER EVENTS

753 BC According to legend, Rome is founded.

800 BC

WORLD EVENTS

c. 700 BC The Assyrians conquer Israel.

The Roman Forum, the ruins of which are shown above, was a public meeting place at the heart of Rome.

c. 600 BC
The Etruscans take over Rome.

509 BC
The Roman Republic is founded.

264–146 BC
Rome and Carthage fight in the Punic Wars.

27 BC
Augustus becomes Rome's first emperor.

600 BC

490 BC
The Persians invade Greece.

400 BC

334–323 BC
Alexander the Great builds his empire.

200 BC

c. 221–206 BC
The Qin dynasty rules China.

BC 1 AD

291

Reading Social Studies

Focus on Themes In this chapter, you will read about the Roman Republic, about how Rome's location and **geography** helped it become a major power in the ancient world. You will also read about the city's **politics** and discover how its three-pronged government affected all of society. Finally, you will read about the wars the Roman Republic fought as it expanded its boundaries. You will see how this growth led to problems that were difficult to solve.

Outlining and History

Focus on Reading How can you make sense of all the facts and ideas in a chapter? One way is to take notes in the form of an outline.

Outlining a Chapter Here is an example of a partial outline for Section 1 of this chapter. Compare the outline to the information on pages 294–297. Notice how the writer looked at the heads in the chapter to determine the main and supporting ideas.

> The writer picked up the first heading in the chapter (page 294) as the first main idea. She identified it with Roman numeral I.

Section 1, Geography and the Rise of Rome
I. The Geography of Italy
   A. Physical features—many types of features
      1. Mountain ranges
      2. Hills
      3. Rivers
   B. Climate—warm summers, mild winters
II. Rome's Legendary Origins
   A. Aeneas
      1. Trojan hero
      2. Sailed to Italy and became ruler
   B. Romulus and Remus
      1. Twin brothers
      2. Decided to build city
         a. Romulus killed Remus
         b. City named for Romulus
   C. Rome's Early Kings

> The writer saw two smaller heads under the bigger head on pages 294–295 and listed them as A and B.

> The writer identified two facts that supported II.A (the head on page 296). She listed them as numbers 1 and 2.

> The writer decided it was important to note some individual facts under B.2. That's why she added a and b.

Outlining a Few Paragraphs When you need to outline only a few paragraphs, you can use the same outline form. Just look for the main idea of each paragraph and give each one a Roman numeral. Supporting ideas within the paragraph can be listed with A, B, and so forth. You can use Arabic numbers for specific details and facts.

LA.6.1.7.1 The student will use background knowledge of subject and related content areas, prereading strategies, graphic representations, and knowledge of text structure to make and confirm complex predictions of content, purpose, and organization of a reading selection. **LA.6.1.7.3** The student will determine the main idea or essential message in grade-level text through inferring, paraphrasing, summarizing, and identifying relevant details.

You Try It!

Read the following passage from this chapter. Then fill in the blanks to complete the outline below.

Growth of Territory

Roman territory grew mainly in response to outside threats. In about 387 BC a people called the Gauls attacked Rome and took over the city. The Romans had to give the Gauls a huge amount of gold to leave the city.

From Chapter 10, page 308

Inspired by the Gauls' victory, many of Rome's neighboring cities also decided to attack. With some difficulty, the Romans fought off these attacks. As Rome's attackers were defeated, the Romans took over their lands. As you can see on the map, the Romans soon controlled all of the Italian Peninsula except far northern Italy.

One reason for the Roman success was the organization of the army. Soldiers were organized in legions . . . This organization allowed the army to be very flexible.

Complete this outline based on the passage you just read.

I. Roman territory grew in response to outside threats.

  A. Gauls attacked Rome in 387 BC.
    1. Took over the city
    2. _____
  B. The Gauls' victory inspired other people to attack Rome.
    1. _____
    2. Romans took lands of defeated foes.
    3. _____

II. _____

  A. Soldiers were organized in legions.
  B. _____

Key Terms and People

Chapter 10

Section 1
Aeneas *(p. 296)*
Romulus and Remus *(p. 297)*
republic *(p. 298)*
dictators *(p. 298)*
Cincinnatus *(p. 298)*
plebeians *(p. 299)*
patricians *(p. 299)*

Section 2
magistrates *(p. 303)*
consuls *(p. 303)*
Roman Senate *(p. 303)*
veto *(p. 304)*
Latin *(p. 304)*
checks and balances *(p. 305)*
Forum *(p. 305)*

Section 3
legions *(p. 309)*
Punic Wars *(p. 309)*
Hannibal *(p. 310)*
Gaius Marius *(p. 312)*
Lucius Cornelius Sulla *(p. 313)*
Spartacus *(p. 313)*

Academic Vocabulary

Success in school is related to knowing academic vocabulary—the words that are frequently used in school assignments and discussions. In this chapter, you will learn the following academic words:

primary *(p. 303)*
purpose *(p. 312)*

As you read Chapter 10, identify the main ideas you would use in an outline of this chapter.

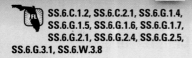

SECTION 1

SS.6.C.1.2, SS.6.C.2.1, SS.6.G.1.4,
SS.6.G.1.5, SS.6.G.1.6, SS.6.G.1.7,
SS.6.G.2.1, SS.6.G.2.4, SS.6.G.2.5,
SS.6.G.3.1, SS.6.W.3.8

What You Will Learn...

Main Ideas

1. The **geography** of Italy made land travel difficult but helped the Romans prosper.
2. Ancient historians were very interested in Rome's legendary history.
3. Once a monarchy, the Romans created a republic.

The Big Idea

Rome's location and government helped it become a major power in the ancient world.

Key Terms and People

Aeneas, *p. 296*
Romulus and Remus, *p. 297*
republic, *p. 298*
dictators, *p. 298*
Cincinnatus, *p. 298*
plebeians, *p. 299*
patricians, *p. 299*

Online Resource
TAKING NOTES

Use the graphic organizer online to take notes on Italy's **geography** and the rise of Rome.

Geography and the Rise of Rome

If YOU were there...

You are the ruler of a group of people looking for a site to build a new city. After talking with your advisors, you have narrowed your choice to two possible sites. Both locations have plenty of water and good soil for farming, but they are otherwise very different. One is on top of a tall rocky hill overlooking a shallow river. The other is on a wide open field right next to the sea.

Which site will you choose for your city? Why?

BUILDING BACKGROUND From a small town on the Tiber River, Rome grew into a mighty power. Rome's **geography**—its central location and good climate—were important factors in its success and growth. The city's rise as a military power began when the Romans went to war and conquered neighboring Italian tribes.

The Geography of Italy

Rome eventually became the center of one of the greatest civilizations of the ancient world. In fact, the people of Rome conquered many of the territories you have studied in this book, including Greece, Egypt, and Asia Minor.

Italy, where Rome was built, is a peninsula in southern Europe. If you look at the map, you can see that Italy looks like a high-heeled boot sticking out into the Mediterranean Sea.

Physical Features

Look at the map again to find Italy's two major mountain ranges. In the north are the Alps, Europe's highest mountains. Another range, the Apennines (A-puh-nynz), runs the length of the Italian Peninsula. This rugged land made it hard for ancient people to cross from one side of the peninsula to the other. In addition, some of Italy's mountains, such as Mount Vesuvius, are volcanic. Their eruptions could devastate Roman towns.

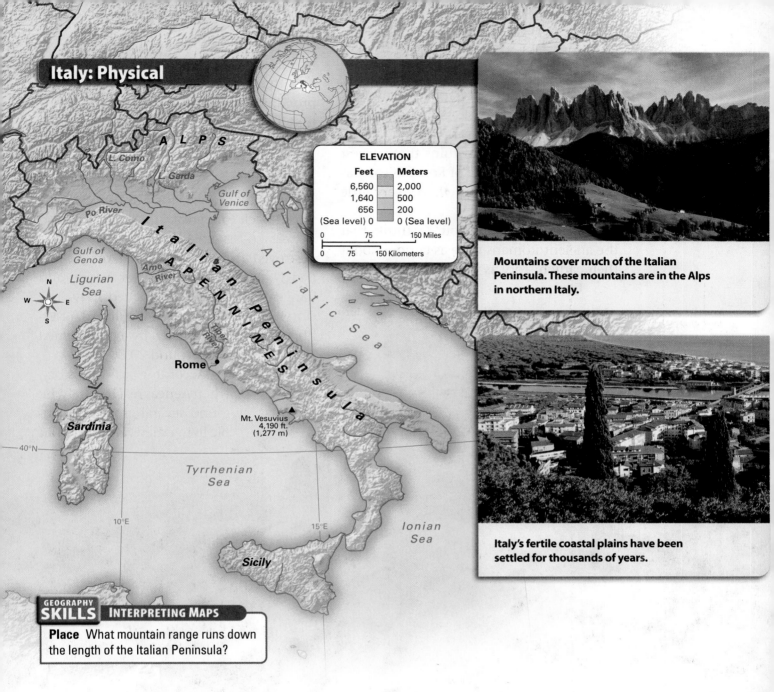

Italy: Physical

L. Como
L. Garda
ALPS
Gulf of Venice
Po River
Gulf of Genoa
Arno River
Ligurian Sea
Italian Peninsula
APENNINES
Adriatic Sea
Tiber River
Rome
Mt. Vesuvius
4,190 ft.
(1,277 m)
Sardinia
Tyrrhenian Sea
Sicily
Ionian Sea
40°N
10°E
15°E

ELEVATION

Feet		Meters
6,560		2,000
1,640		500
656		200
(Sea level) 0		0 (Sea level)

0   75   150 Miles
0   75   150 Kilometers

Mountains cover much of the Italian Peninsula. These mountains are in the Alps in northern Italy.

Italy's fertile coastal plains have been settled for thousands of years.

GEOGRAPHY SKILLS | **INTERPRETING MAPS**

Place What mountain range runs down the length of the Italian Peninsula?

Not much of Italy is flat. Most of the land that isn't mountainous is covered with hills. Throughout history, people have built cities on these hills for defense. As a result, many of the ancient cities of Italy—including Rome—sat atop hills. Rome was built on seven hills.

Several rivers flow out of Italy's mountains. Because these rivers were a source of fresh water, people also built their cities near them. For example, Rome lies on the Tiber (TY-buhr) River.

Climate

Most of Italy, including the area around Rome, has warm, dry summers and mild, rainy winters. This climate is similar to that of southern California. Italy's mild climate allows people to grow a wide variety of crops. Grains, citrus fruits, grapes, and olives all grow well there. A plentiful food supply was one key factor in Rome's early growth.

READING CHECK Drawing Conclusions
How did Rome's location affect its early history?

Rome's Legendary Origins

Rome's early history is wrapped in mystery. No written records exist, and we have little evidence of the city's earliest days. All we have found are ancient ruins that suggest people lived in the area of Rome as early as the 800s BC. However, we know very little about how they lived.

SS.6.W.3.8 Determine the impact of significant figures associated with ancient Rome.

Would it surprise you to think that the ancient Romans were as curious about their early history as we are today? Rome's leaders wanted their city to have a glorious past that would make the Roman people proud. Imagining that glorious past, they told legends, or stories, about great heroes and kings who built the city.

Aeneas

The Romans believed their history could be traced back to a great Trojan hero named **Aeneas** (i-NEE-uhs). When the Greeks destroyed Troy in the Trojan War, Aeneas fled with his followers. After a long and dangerous journey, he reached Italy. The story of this trip is told in the *Aeneid* (i-NEE-id), an epic poem written by a poet named Virgil (VUHR-juhl) around 20 BC.

According to the story, when Aeneas reached Italy, he found several groups of people living there. He formed an

Legendary Founding of Rome

QUICK FACTS

Roman historians traced their city's history back to legendary figures such as Aeneas, Romulus, and Remus.

Aeneas

According to the *Aeneid*, Aeneas carried his father from the burning city of Troy and then searched for a new home for the Trojans. After traveling around the Mediterranean, Aeneas finally settled in Italy.

alliance with one of these groups, a people called the Latins. Together they fought the other people of Italy. After defeating these opponents, Aeneas married the daughter of the Latin king. Aeneas, his son, and their descendants became prominent rulers in Italy.

Romulus and Remus

Among the descendants of Aeneas were the founders of Rome. According to Roman legends, these founders were twin brothers named **Romulus** (RAHM-yuh-luhs) and **Remus** (REE-muhs). In the story, these boys led exciting lives. When they were babies, they were put in a basket and thrown into the Tiber River. They didn't drown, though, because a wolf rescued them. The wolf cared for the boys for many years. Eventually, a shepherd found the boys and adopted them.

After they grew up, Romulus and Remus decided to build a city to mark the spot where the wolf had rescued them. While they were planning the city, Remus mocked one of his brother's ideas. In a fit of anger, Romulus killed Remus. He then built the city and named it Rome after himself.

Rome's Early Kings

According to ancient historians, Romulus was the first king of Rome, taking the throne in 753 BC. Modern historians believe that Rome could have been founded within 50 years before or after that date.

Roman records list seven kings who ruled the city. Not all of them were Roman. Rome's last three kings were Etruscans (i-TRUHS-kuhnz), members of a people who lived north of Rome. The Etruscans, who had been influenced by Greek colonies in Italy, lived in Italy before Rome was founded.

The Etruscan kings made great contributions to Roman society. They built huge temples and Rome's first sewer. Many historians think that the Romans learned their alphabet and numbers from the Etruscans.

The last Roman king was said to have been a cruel man who had many people killed, including his own advisors. Finally, a group of nobles rose up against him. According to tradition, he was overthrown in 509 BC. The nobles, who no longer wanted kings, created a new government.

READING CHECK **Drawing Conclusions** Why did early Romans want to get rid of the monarchy?

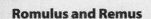

Romulus and Remus
The Romans believed that the twins Romulus and Remus were descendants of Aeneas. In Roman legend, Romulus and Remus were rescued and raised by a wolf. Romulus later killed Remus and built the city of Rome.

The Early Republic

The government of the United States today is a republic.

The government the Romans created in 509 BC was a republic. In a **republic**, people elect leaders to govern them. Each year the Romans elected officials to rule the city. These officials had many powers but only stayed in power for one year. This system was supposed to keep any one person from becoming too powerful in the government.

But Rome was not a democracy. The city's elected officials nearly all came from a small group of wealthy and powerful men. These wealthy and powerful Romans held all the power, and other people had little to no say in how the republic was run.

Challenges from Outside

Shortly after the Romans created the republic, they found themselves at war. For about 50 years the Romans were at war with other peoples of the region. For the most part the Romans won these wars. But they lost several battles, and the wars destroyed many lives and much property.

During particularly difficult wars, the Romans chose **dictators**—rulers with almost absolute power—to lead the city. To keep them from abusing their power, dictators could only stay in power for six months. When that time was over, the dictator gave up his power.

One of Rome's famous dictators was **Cincinnatus** (sin-suh-NAT-uhs), who gained power in 458 BC. Although he was a farmer, the Romans chose him to defend the city against a powerful enemy that had defeated a large Roman army.

Cincinnatus quickly defeated the city's enemies. Immediately, he resigned as dictator and returned to his farm, long before his six-month term had run out.

The victory by Cincinnatus did not end Rome's troubles. Rome continued to fight its neighbors on and off for many years.

Italy, 500 BC

Romans
Etruscans
Greeks
Carthaginians

0   30   60 Miles
0   30   60 Kilometers

Ligurian Sea

Rome

Tyrrhenian Sea

Mediterranean Sea

Adriatic Sea

Ionian Sea

Carthage

GEOGRAPHY SKILLS **INTERPRETING MAPS**

Location What group lived mostly north of Rome?

BIOGRAPHY

Cincinnatus
c. 519 BC–?

Cincinnatus is the most famous dictator from the early Roman Republic. Because he wasn't eager to hold on to his power, the Romans considered Cincinnatus an ideal leader. They admired his abilities and his loyalty to the republic. The early citizens of the United States admired the same qualities in their leaders. In fact, some people called George Washington the "American Cincinnatus" when he refused to run for a third term as president. The people of the state of Ohio also honored Cincinnatus by naming one of their major cities, Cincinnati, after him.

Challenges within Rome

Enemy armies weren't the only challenge facing Rome. Within the city, Roman society was divided into two groups. Many of Rome's **plebeians** (pli-BEE-uhnz), or common people, were calling for changes in the government. They wanted more of a say in how the city was run.

Rome was run by powerful nobles called **patricians** (puh-TRI-shuhnz). Only patricians could be elected to office, so they held all political power.

The plebeians were peasants, craftspeople, traders, and other workers. Some of these plebeians, especially traders, were as rich as patricians. Even though the plebeians outnumbered the patricians, they couldn't take part in the government.

In 494 BC the plebeians formed a council and elected their own officials, an act that frightened many patricians. They feared that Rome would fall apart if the two groups couldn't cooperate. The patricians decided that it was time to change the government.

READING CHECK **Contrasting** How were patricians and plebeians different?

Roman Society

QUICK FACTS

Patricians	Plebeians
■ Wealthy, powerful citizens	■ Common people
■ Nobles	■ Peasants, craftspeople, traders, other workers
■ Small minority of the population	■ Majority of the population
■ Once controlled all aspects of government	■ Gained right to participate in government
■ After 218 BC, not allowed to participate in trade or commerce	■ Only Romans who could be traders, so many became wealthy

SS.6.W.3.16 Compare life in the Roman Republic for patricians, plebeians, women, children, and slaves.

SUMMARY AND PREVIEW In this section you read about the location and founding of Rome, its early rule by kings, and the creation of the city's republican government. In the next section you'll learn more about that government, its strengths and weaknesses, how it worked, and how it changed over time.

Section 1 Assessment

Reviewing Ideas, Terms, and People

1. **a. Describe** Where is Italy located?
   b. Explain How did mountains affect life in Italy?
   c. Predict How do you think Rome's location on the Mediterranean affected its history as it began to grow into a world power?
2. **a. Identify** What brothers supposedly founded the city of Rome?
   b. Summarize What role did **Aeneas** play in the founding of Rome?
3. **a. Describe** What type of government did the Romans create in 509 BC?
   b. Contrast How were **patricians** and **plebeians** different?

Critical Thinking

4. **Categorizing** As you review your notes, separate the legends from the historical events in Rome's founding and growth. Then use a diagram like the one below to list the key legendary events.

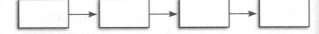

FOCUS ON SPEAKING

5. **Gathering Background Ideas** In this section you read about several legends the Romans told about their own history. Look back at the text to get some ideas about what you might include in your own legend. Write some ideas in your notebook.

from the Aeneid

by Virgil

Translated by Robert Fitzgerald

About the Reading *Virgil wrote the* Aeneid *to record the glorious story of Rome's founding and to celebrate the Rome of his day. At the center of the poem stands the hero Aeneas, survivor of the Trojan War and son of the goddess Venus. After wandering for seven years, Aeneas finally reaches southern Italy—then known as Ausonia. Here, Aeneas's friend Ilioneus leads a group of representatives to visit a nearby Latin settlement.*

AS YOU READ Try to identify each group's goals and desires.

GUIDED READING

WORD HELP

tranquilly calmly
astray off course
broached crossed
moored anchored
constraint force
gale storm

❶ Both "Teucrians" and "sons of Dardanus" are ways of referring to Trojans.

❷ Ilioneus says that the Trojans are not lost. A sea-mark is similar to a landmark, a feature sailors use to find their way.

How does Ilioneus address the king? Why do you think he does so?

Latinus
Called the Teucrians before him, saying
Tranquilly as they entered:
   "Sons of Dardanus—
You see, we know your city and your nation,
As all had heard you laid a westward course—
Tell me your purpose. ❶ What design or need
Has brought you through the dark blue sea so far
To our Ausonian coast? Either astray
Or driven by rough weather, such as sailors
Often endure at sea, you've broached the river,
Moored ship there. Now do not turn away
From hospitality here. Know that our Latins
Come of Saturn's race, that we are just—
Not by constraint or laws, but by our choice
And habit of our ancient god . . ."
Latinus then fell silent, and in turn
Ilioneus began:
   "Your majesty,
Most noble son of Faunus, no rough seas
Or black gale swept us to your coast, no star
Or clouded seamark put us off our course. ❷

Aeneas, from an Italian painting of the 1700s

We journey to your city by design
And general consent, driven as we are
From realms in other days greatest by far
The Sun looked down on, passing on his way
From heaven's far eastern height. ❸ Our line's from Jove,
In his paternity the sons of Dardanus
Exult, and highest progeny of Jove
Include our king himself—Trojan Aeneas,
Who sent us to your threshold . . . ❹
So long on the vast waters, now we ask
A modest settlement of the gods of home,
A strip of coast that will bring harm to no one,
Air and water, open and free to all . . .
Our quest was for your country. Dardanus
Had birth here, and Apollo calls us back,
Directing us by solemn oracles
To Tuscan Tiber . . . ❺ Here besides
Aeneus gives you from his richer years
These modest gifts, relics caught up and saved
From burning Troy . . ."
                    Latinus heard
Ilioneus out, his countenance averted,
Sitting immobile, all attention, eyes
Downcast but turning here and there. The embroidered
Purple and the scepter of King Priam
Moved him less in his own kingliness
Than long thoughts on the marriage of his daughter,
As he turned over in his inmost mind
Old Faunus' prophecy.
                    "This is the man,"
he thought, "foretold as coming from abroad
To be my son-in-law, by fate appointed,
Called to reign here with equal authority—
The man whose heirs will be brilliant in valor
And win the mastery of the world." ❻

GUIDED READING

WORD HELP

progeny offspring
threshold door
oracle person who gives advice
averted turned away
immobile unmoving

❸ Ilioneus explains that the Trojans have come to Italy "by design"—both on purpose and with help from the gods.

❹ Aeneas and Dardanus, the founder of Troy, were both believed to be descendants of Jove, the king of the gods.

❺ The Romans believed that Troy's founder Dardanus was born in Italy.

What does Ilioneus ask the king to give the Trojans?

❻ Virgil included this vision of Rome's great future to point out the city's greatness to his readers.

CONNECTING LITERATURE TO HISTORY

1. Analyzing Rome's leaders wanted their city to have a glorious past that would make the Roman people proud. What details in this passage would make Roman readers proud of their past?

2. Drawing Conclusions When Aeneas reached Italy, he formed an alliance with the Latins. Think about how Virgil portrays the Latins in this passage. What words or phrases would you use to describe them? Why might such people make good allies?

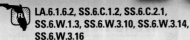
What You Will Learn...

Main Ideas

1. Roman government was made up of three parts that worked together to run the city.
2. Written laws helped keep order in Rome.
3. The Roman Forum was the heart of Roman society.

The Big Idea

Rome's tripartite government and written laws helped create a stable society.

Key Terms

magistrates, *p. 303*
consuls, *p. 303*
Roman Senate, *p. 303*
veto, *p. 304*
Latin, *p. 304*
checks and balances, *p. 305*
Forum, *p. 305*

Online Resource
TAKING NOTES

Use the graphic organizer online to take notes about how government, written laws, and the Forum contributed to the development of Roman society.

SS.6.C.1.2 Identify how the government of the Roman Republic contributed to the development of democratic principles (separation of powers, rule of law, representative government, civic duty). **SS.6.W.3.10** Describe the government of the Roman Republic and its contribution to the development of democratic principles (separation of powers, rule of law, representative government, civic duty).

Government and Society

If YOU were there...

You have just been elected as a government official in Rome. Your duty is to represent the plebeians, the common people. You hold office for only one year, but you have one important power—you can stop laws from being passed. Now city leaders are proposing a law that will hurt the plebeians. If you stop the new law, it will hurt your future in politics. If you let it pass, it will hurt the people you are supposed to protect.

Will you let the new law pass? Why or why not?

BUILDING BACKGROUND Government in Rome was often a balancing act. Like the politician above, leaders had to make compromises and risk the anger of other officials to keep the people happy. To keep anyone from gaining too much power, the Roman government divided power among many different officials.

Roman Government

When the plebeians complained about Rome's government in the 400s BC, the city's leaders knew they had to do something. If the people stayed unhappy, they might rise up and overthrow the whole government.

To calm the angry plebeians, the patricians made some changes to Rome's government. For example, they created new offices that could only be held by plebeians. The people who held these offices protected the plebeians' rights and interests. Gradually, the distinctions between patricians and plebeians began to disappear, but that took a very long time.

As a result of the changes the patricians made, Rome developed a tripartite (try-PAHR-tyt) government, or a government with three parts. Each part had its own responsibilities and duties. To fulfill its duties, each part of the government had its own powers, rights, and privileges.

Magistrates

The first part of Rome's government was made up of elected officials, or **magistrates** (MA-juh-strayts). The two most powerful magistrates in Rome were called **consuls** (KAHN-suhlz). The consuls were elected each year to run the city and lead the army. There were two consuls so that no one person would be too powerful.

Below the consuls were other magistrates. Rome had many different types of magistrates. Each was elected for one year and had his own duties and powers. Some were judges. Others managed Rome's finances or organized games and festivals.

Senate

The second part of Rome's government was the Senate. The **Roman Senate** was a council of wealthy and powerful Romans that advised the city's leaders. It was originally created to advise Rome's kings. After the kings were gone, the Senate continued to meet to advise consuls.

Unlike magistrates, senators—members of the Senate—held office for life. By the time the republic was created, the Senate had 300 members. At first most senators were patricians, but as time passed many wealthy plebeians became senators as well. Because magistrates became senators after completing their terms in office, most didn't want to anger the Senate and risk their future jobs.

As time passed the Senate became more powerful. It gained influence over magistrates and took control of the city's finances. By 200 BC the Senate had great influence in Rome's government.

Assemblies and Tribunes

The third part of Rome's government, the part that protected the common people, had two branches. The first branch was made up of assemblies. Both patricians and plebeians took part in these assemblies. Their **primary** job was to elect the magistrates who ran the city of Rome.

FOCUS ON READING

If you were outlining the discussion on this page, what headings would you use?

ACADEMIC VOCABULARY

primary main, most important

Government of the Roman Republic QUICK FACTS		
Magistrates	**Senate**	**Assemblies and Tribunes**
■ Consuls led the government and army, judged court cases ■ Served for one year ■ Had power over all citizens, including other officials	■ Advised the consuls ■ Served for life ■ Gained control of financial affairs	■ Represented the common people, approved or rejected laws, declared war, elected magistrates ■ Roman citizens could take part in assemblies all their adult lives, tribunes served for one year ■ Could veto the decisions of consuls and other magistrates

Do as the Romans Do

The government of the Roman Republic was one of its greatest strengths. When the founders of the United States sat down to plan our government, they copied many elements of the Roman system. Like the Romans, we elect our leaders. Our government also has three branches—the president, Congress, and the federal court system. The powers of these branches are set forth in our Constitution, just like the Roman officials' powers were. Our government also has a system of checks and balances to prevent any one branch from becoming too strong. For example, Congress can refuse to give the president money to pay for programs. Like the Romans, Americans have a civic duty to participate in the government to help keep it as strong as it can be.

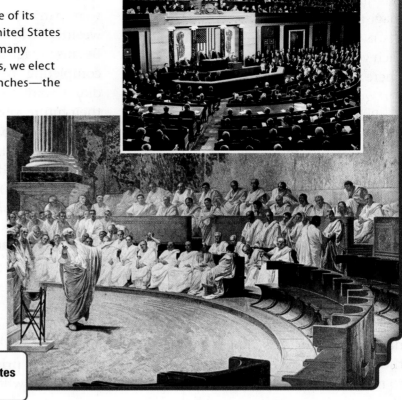

ANALYSIS SKILL **ANALYZING INFORMATION**

Why do you think the founders of the United States borrowed ideas from Roman government?

THE IMPACT TODAY

Like tribunes, the president of the United States has the power to veto actions by other government officials.

SS.6.C.2.1 Identify principles (civic participation, role of government) from ancient Greek and Roman civilizations which are reflected in the American political process today, and discuss their effect on the American political process.

The second branch was made up of a group of elected officials called tribunes. Elected by the plebeians, tribunes had the ability to **veto** (VEE-toh), or prohibit, actions by other officials. Veto means "I forbid" in **Latin**, the Romans' language. This veto power made tribunes very powerful in Rome's government. To keep them from abusing their power, each tribune remained in office only one year.

Civic Duty

Rome's government would not have worked without the participation of the people. People participated in the government because they felt it was their civic duty, or their duty to the city. That civic duty included doing what they could to make sure the city prospered. For example,

they were expected to attend assembly meetings and to vote in elections. Voting in Rome was a complicated process, and not everyone was allowed to do it. Those who could, however, were expected to take part in all elections.

Wealthy and powerful citizens also felt it was their duty to hold public office to help run the city. In return for their time and commitment, these citizens were respected and admired by other Romans.

Checks and Balances

In addition to limiting terms of office, the Romans put other restrictions on their leaders' power. They did this by giving government officials the ability to restrict the powers of other officials. For example, one consul could block the actions of the other.

Laws proposed by the Senate had to be approved by magistrates and ratified by assemblies. We call these methods to balance power **checks and balances**. Checks and balances keep any one part of a government from becoming stronger or more influential than the others.

Checks and balances made Rome's government very complicated. Sometimes quarrels arose when officials had different ideas or opinions. When officials worked together, however, Rome's government was strong and efficient, as one Roman historian noted:

> "In unison [together] they are a match for any and all emergencies, the result being that it is impossible to find a constitution that is better constructed. For whenever some common external danger should come upon them and should compel [force] them to band together in counsel [thought] and in action, the power of their state becomes so great that nothing that is required is neglected [ignored]."
>
> –Polybius, from *The Constitution of the Roman Republic*

READING CHECK **Finding Main Ideas** What were the three parts of the Roman government?

Written Laws Keep Order

Rome's officials were responsible for making the city's laws and making sure that people followed them. At first these laws weren't written down. The only people who knew all the laws were the patricians who had made them.

Many people were unhappy with this situation. They did not want to be punished for breaking laws they didn't even know existed. As a result, they began to call for Rome's laws to be written down and made accessible to everybody.

Rome's first written law code was produced in 450 BC on 12 bronze tables, or tablets. These tables were displayed in the **Forum**, Rome's public meeting place. Because of how it was displayed, this code was called the Law of the Twelve Tables.

Over time, Rome's leaders passed many new laws. Still, throughout their history, the Romans looked to the Law of the Twelve Tables as a symbol of Roman law and of their rights as Roman citizens.

READING CHECK **Drawing Inferences** Why did many people want a written law code?

Primary Source

HISTORIC DOCUMENT
Law of the Twelve Tables

The Law of the Twelve Tables governed many parts of Roman life. Some laws were written to protect the rights of all Romans. Others only protected the patricians. The laws listed here should give you an idea of the kinds of laws the tables included.

A Roman who did not appear before a government official when called or did not pay his debts could be arrested.

Women—even as adults—were legally considered to be children.

No one in Rome could be executed without a trial.

[from Table I] If anyone summons a man before the magistrate, he must go. If the man summoned does not go, let the one summoning him call the bystanders to witness and then take him by force.

[from Table III] One who has confessed a debt, or against whom judgment has been pronounced, shall have thirty days to pay it. After that forcible seizure of his person is allowed . . . unless he pays the amount of the judgment.

[from Table V] Females should remain in guardianship even when they have attained their majority.

[from Table IX] Putting to death of any man, whosoever he might be, unconvicted is forbidden.

–Law of the Twelve Tables, translated in *The Library of Original Sources* edited by Oliver J. Thatcher

ANALYSIS SKILL **ANALYZING PRIMARY SOURCES**

How are these laws similar to and different from our laws today?

The Roman Forum

The Forum was the center of life in ancient Rome. The city's most important temples and government buildings were located there, and Romans met there to talk about the issues of the day. The word *forum* means "public place."

The Roman Forum

The Roman Forum, the place where the Law of the Twelve Tables was kept, was the heart of the city of Rome. It was the site of important government buildings and temples. Government and religion were only part of what made the Forum so important, though. It was also a popular meeting place for Roman citizens. People met there to shop, chat, and gossip.

HISTORY

The Glory of Rome's Forum

↗ Online Resource

The Temple of Jupiter stood atop the Capitoline Hill, overlooking the Forum.

Important government records were stored in the Tabularium.

Roman citizens often wore togas, loose-fitting garments wrapped around the body. Togas were symbols of Roman citizenship.

Public officials often addressed people from this platform.

ANALYSIS SKILL ANALYZING VISUALS

What can you see in this illustration that indicates the Forum was an important place?

The Forum lay in the center of Rome, between two major hills. On one side was the Palatine (PA-luh-tyn) Hill, where Rome's richest people lived. Across the forum was the Capitoline (KA-pet-uhl-yn) Hill, where Rome's grandest temples stood. Because of this location, city leaders could often be found in or near the forum, mingling with the common people. These leaders used the Forum as a speaking area, delivering speeches to the crowds.

But the Forum also had attractions for people not interested in speeches. Various shops lined the open square, and fights between gladiators were sometimes held there. Public ceremonies were commonly held in the Forum as well. As a result, the forum was usually packed with people.

READING CHECK **Generalizing** How was the Forum the heart of Roman society?

SUMMARY AND PREVIEW In this section you read about the basic structure of Roman government. In the next section you'll see how that government changed as Rome's territory grew and its influence expanded.

The Senate met here in the curia, or Senate House.

Section 2 Assessment

Reviewing Ideas, Terms, and People
1. **a. Identify** Who were the **consuls**?
   b. Explain Why did the Romans create a system of **checks and balances**?
   c. Elaborate How do you think the **Roman Senate** gained power?
2. **a. Recall** What was Rome's first written law code called?
   b. Draw Conclusions Why did Romans want their laws written down?
3. **a. Describe** What kinds of activities took place in the Roman **Forum**?

Critical Thinking
4. **Analyzing** Review your notes on Roman government. Use this diagram to note information about the powers of the parts of Rome's government.

Magistrates

Senate

Assemblies and Tribunes

FOCUS ON SPEAKING

5. **Choosing a Topic** You've just read about Roman laws and government. Would anything related to these topics make good subjects for your legend? Write some ideas in your notebook.

The Late Republic

LA.6.1.7.3, SS.6.E.1.1, SS.6.E.1.3,
SS.6.E.3.1, SS.6.E.3.2, SS.6.E.3.3,
SS.6.E.3.4, SS.6.G.1.4, SS.6.G.1.7,
SS.6.G.2.2, SS.6.G.2.6, SS.6.G.5.1, SS.6.W.3.8,
SS.6.W.3.9, SS.6.W.3.11

What You Will Learn...

Main Ideas

1. The late republic period saw the growth of territory and trade.
2. Through wars, Rome grew beyond Italy.
3. Several crises struck the republic in its later years.

The Big Idea

The later period of the Roman Republic was marked by wars of expansion and political crises.

Key Terms and People

legions, *p. 309*
Punic Wars, *p. 309*
Hannibal, *p. 310*
Gaius Marius, *p. 312*
Lucius Cornelius Sulla, *p. 313*
Spartacus, *p. 313*

Online Resource
TAKING NOTES

Use the graphic organizer online to take notes on Rome's expansion and on crises in the later years of the Republic.

If YOU were there...

You are a farmer in Italy during the Roman Republic. You are proud to be a Roman citizen, but times are hard. Rich landowners are buying farmland, and many farmers like you have lost their jobs. Some are moving to the city, but you've heard that there are not many jobs there, either. You've also heard that a famous general is raising an army to fight in Asia. That seems very far away, but it would mean good pay.

What might convince you to join the army?

BUILDING BACKGROUND The Roman army played a vital part in the expansion of the republic. Roman soldiers were well trained and defeated many of the city's enemies. As they did so, the Romans took over new lands. As the army conquered these new lands, traders moved in, seeking new products and markets that could make them rich.

Growth of Territory and Trade

After about 400 BC the Roman Republic grew quickly, both geographically and economically. Within 200 years the Roman army had conquered nearly all of Italy. Meanwhile Roman traders had begun to ship goods back and forth around the Mediterranean in search of new products and wealth.

Growth of Territory

Roman territory grew mainly in response to outside threats. In about 387 BC a people called the Gauls attacked Rome and took over the city. The Romans had to give the Gauls a huge amount of gold to leave the city.

Inspired by the Gauls' victory, many of Rome's neighboring cities also decided to attack. With some difficulty, the Romans fought off these attacks. As Rome's attackers were defeated, the Romans took over their lands. As you can see on the map, the Romans soon controlled all of the Italian Peninsula except far northern Italy.

One reason for the Roman success was the organization of the army. Soldiers were organized in **legions** (LEE-juhnz), or groups of up to 6,000 soldiers. Each legion was divided into centuries, or groups of 100 soldiers. This organization allowed the army to be very flexible. It could fight as a large group or as several small ones. This flexibility allowed the Romans to defeat most enemies.

Farming and Trade

Before Rome conquered Italy, most Romans were farmers. As the republic grew, many people left their farms for Rome. In place of these small farms, wealthy Romans built large farms in the countryside. These farms were worked by slaves who grew one or two crops. The owners of the farms didn't usually live on them. Instead, they stayed in Rome or other cities and let others run the farms for them.

Roman trade also expanded as the republic grew. Rome's farmers couldn't grow enough food to support the city's increasing population, so merchants brought food from other parts of the Mediterranean. These merchants also brought metal goods and slaves to Rome. To pay for these goods, the Romans made coins out of copper, silver, and other metals. Roman coins began to appear in markets all around the Mediterranean.

READING CHECK Identifying Cause and Effect Why did the Romans conquer their neighbors?

Rome Grows Beyond Italy

As Rome's power grew other countries came to see the Romans as a threat to their own power and declared war on them. In the end the Romans defeated their opponents, and Rome gained territory throughout the Mediterranean.

The Roman Republic, 509–270 BC

Roman lands in 509 BC
Roman lands in 270 BC

0   75   150 Miles
0   75   150 Kilometers

Ligurian Sea

Adriatic Sea

Rome

Tyrrhenian Sea

Ionian Sea

Mediterranean Sea

Carthage

N S E W

GEOGRAPHY SKILLS INTERPRETING MAPS

Location What seas bordered Roman lands in 270 BC?

The Punic Wars

The fiercest of the wars Rome fought were the **Punic** (PYOO-nik) **Wars**, a series of wars against Carthage, a city in northern Africa. The word *Punic* means "Phoenician" in Latin. As you learned earlier in this book, the Phoenicians were an ancient civilization that had built the city of Carthage.

Rome and Carthage went to war three times between 264 and 146 BC. The wars began when Carthage sent its armies to Sicily, an island just southwest of Italy. In response, the Romans also sent an army to the island. Before long, war broke out between them. After almost 20 years of fighting, the Romans forced their enemies out and took control of Sicily.

SS.6.E.3.3 Describe traditional economies (Egypt, Greece, Rome, Kush) and elements of those economies that led to the rise of a merchant class and trading partners.

In 218 BC Carthage tried to attack Rome itself. An army led by the brilliant general **Hannibal** set out for Rome. Although he forced the Romans right to the edge of defeat, Hannibal was never able to capture Rome itself. In the meantime, the Romans sent an army to attack Carthage. Hannibal rushed home to defend his city, but his troops were defeated at Zama (ZAY-muh) in the battle illustrated below.

By the 140s BC many senators had grown alarmed that Carthage was growing powerful again. They convinced Rome's consuls to declare war on Carthage, and once again the Romans sent an army to Africa and destroyed Carthage. After this victory, the Romans burned the city, killed most of its people, and sold the rest of the people into slavery. They also took control of northern Africa.

History Close-up

Rome Battles Carthage

During the Second Punic War, Hannibal invaded Italy, as you can see on the map. But Rome's leaders sent an army under their general Scipio Africanus (SIP-ee-oh af-ri-KAY-nuhs) to attack Carthage itself, forcing Hannibal to return and defend his city. The two generals met at Zama, where Scipio defeated Hannibal's army in the last great battle of the Second Punic War.

Rome

Carthage

Carthage
Roman Republic
0   150   300 Miles
0   150   300 Kilometers

Battle of Zama, 202 BC
Hannibal's route
Scipio's route

N W E S

The Romans had the advantage in cavalry, which helped them win the battle.

Some Roman soldiers blew trumpets and yelled to distract the war elephants.

Later Expansion

During the Punic Wars, Rome took control of Sicily, Corsica, Spain, and North Africa. As a result, Rome controlled most of the western Mediterranean region.

In the years that followed, Roman legions marched north and east as well. In the 120s Rome conquered the southern part of Gaul. By that time, Rome had also conquered Greece and parts of Asia.

Although the Romans took over Greece, they were greatly changed by the experience. We would normally expect the victor to change the conquered country. Instead, the Romans adopted ideas about literature, art, philosophy, religion, and education from the Greeks.

READING CHECK **Summarizing** How did the Romans gain territory?

SS.6.W.3.9 Explain the impact of the Punic Wars on the development of the Roman Empire.

BIOGRAPHY

Hannibal
247–183 BC

Many historians consider Hannibal to be one of the greatest generals of the ancient world. From an early age, he hated Rome. In 218 BC he began the Second Punic War by attacking one of Rome's allies in Spain. After the war he became the leader of Carthage, but later he was forced by the Romans to flee the city. He went to Asia and joined with a king fighting the Romans there. The king was defeated, and Hannibal killed himself so that he wouldn't become a Roman prisoner.

HISTORY
Carthage: Defeat at Zama

↗ Online Resource

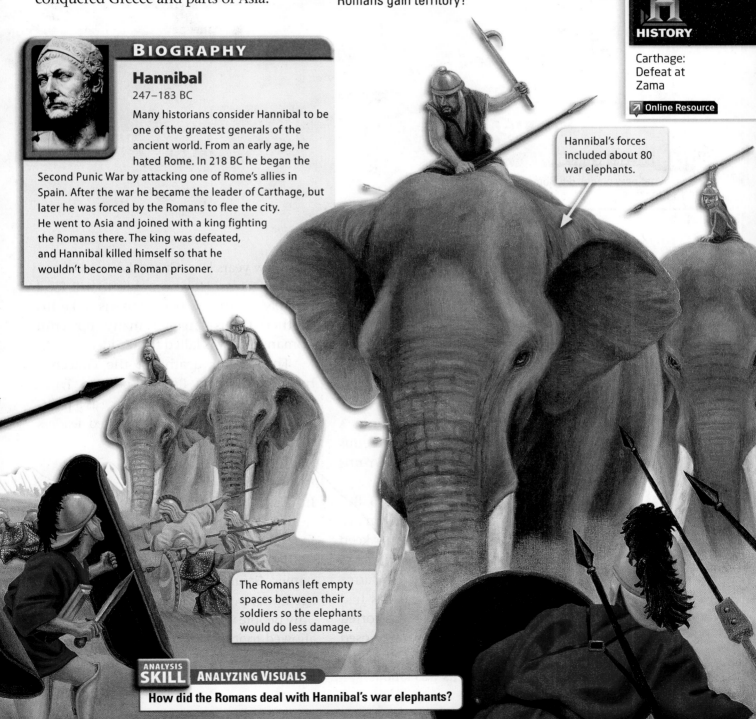

Hannibal's forces included about 80 war elephants.

The Romans left empty spaces between their soldiers so the elephants would do less damage.

ANALYSIS SKILL **ANALYZING VISUALS**

How did the Romans deal with Hannibal's war elephants?

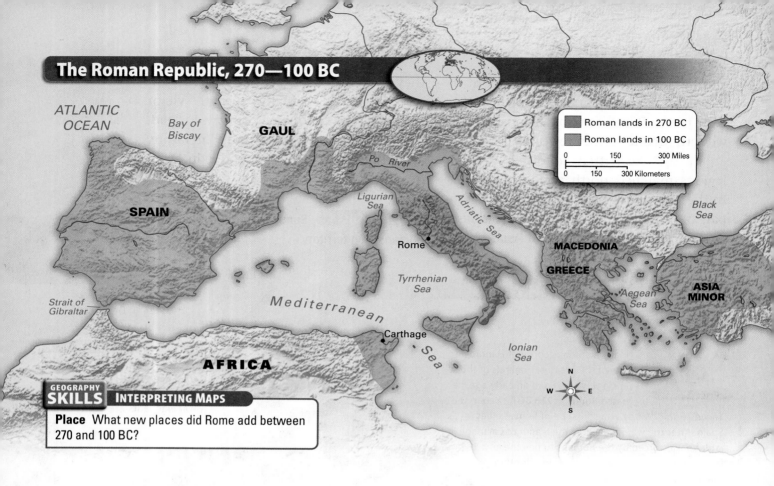

Roman lands in 270 BC
Roman lands in 100 BC

0   150   300 Miles
0   150   300 Kilometers

ATLANTIC OCEAN

Bay of Biscay

GAUL

Po River

Ligurian Sea

Adriatic Sea

Black Sea

SPAIN

Rome

Tyrrhenian Sea

MACEDONIA

GREECE

Aegean Sea

ASIA MINOR

Strait of Gibraltar

Mediterranean Sea

Carthage

Ionian Sea

AFRICA

N W E S

GEOGRAPHY SKILLS **INTERPRETING MAPS**

Place What new places did Rome add between 270 and 100 BC?

Crises Strike the Republic

As the Romans' territory grew, problems arose in the republic. Rich citizens were getting richer, and many leaders feared that violence would erupt between rich and poor.

Tiberius and Gaius Gracchus

Among the first leaders to address Rome's problems were brothers named Tiberius (ty-BIR-ee-uhs) and Gaius Gracchus (GY-uhs GRAK-uhs). Both served as tribunes.

Tiberius, who took office in 133 BC, wanted to create farms for poor Romans. The **purpose** of these farms was to keep the poor citizens happy and prevent rebellions. Tiberius wanted to create his farms on public land that wealthy citizens had illegally taken over. The public supported this idea, but the wealthy citizens opposed it. Conflict over the idea led to riots in the city, during which Tiberius was killed.

ACADEMIC VOCABULARY

purpose the reason something is done

A few years later Gaius also tried to create new farms. He also began to sell food cheaply to Rome's poor citizens. Like his brother, Gaius angered many powerful Romans and was killed for his ideas.

The violent deaths of the Gracchus brothers changed Roman politics. From that time on people saw violence as a political weapon. They often attacked leaders with whom they disagreed.

Marius and Sulla

In the late 100s BC another social change nearly led to the end of the republic. In 107 BC the Roman army desperately needed more troops. In response, a consul named **Gaius Marius** (MER-ee-uhs) encouraged poor people to join the army. Before, only people who owned property had been allowed to join. As a result of this change, thousands of poor and unemployed citizens joined Rome's army.

Because Marius was a good general, his troops were more loyal to him than they were to Rome. The army's support gave Marius great political power. Following his example, other ambitious politicians also sought their armies' support.

One such politician, **Lucius Cornelius Sulla** (LOO-shuhs kawr-NEEL-yuhs SUHL-uh), became consul in 88 BC. Sulla soon came into conflict with Marius, a conflict that led to a civil war in Rome. A civil war is a war between citizens of the same country. In the end Sulla defeated Marius. He later named himself dictator and used his power to punish his enemies.

Spartacus

Not long after Sulla died, another crisis arose to challenge Rome's leaders. Thousands of slaves led by a former gladiator, **Spartacus** (SPAHR-tuh-kuhs), rose up and demanded freedom.

Spartacus and his followers defeated an army sent to stop them and took over much of southern Italy. Eventually, though, Spartacus was killed in battle. Without his leadership, the revolt fell apart. Victorious, the Romans executed 6,000 rebellious

BIOGRAPHY

Lucius Cornelius Sulla
138–78 BC

Although the two eventually became enemies, Sulla learned much of what he knew about military affairs from Gaius Marius. He had been an assistant to Marius before he became consul. Sulla changed Rome's government forever when he became dictator, but he actually had many traditional ideas. For example, he believed the Senate should be the main ruling group in Rome, and he increased its power during his rule.

Analyzing Information Do you think Sulla was a traditional Roman leader? Why or why not?

slaves as an example to others who thought about rebelling. The rebellion was over, but the republic's problems were not.

READING CHECK **Predicting** How do you think Marius and Sulla influenced later leaders?

SUMMARY AND PREVIEW You have read about crises that arose in the late Roman Republic. These crises eventually led to changes in Roman society, as you will see in the next chapter.

Section 3 Assessment

Reviewing Ideas, Terms, and People

1. **a. Define** What was a Roman **legion**?
   b. Explain Why did the Romans decide to conquer all of Italy?
   c. Elaborate How did the growth of territory help increase Roman trade?
2. **a. Recall** Who fought in the **Punic Wars**?
   b. Summarize What led to the beginning of the Punic Wars?
   c. Elaborate Why do you think the Romans borrowed many ideas from Greek culture?
3. **a. Identify** Who was **Spartacus**?
   b. Explain How did the deaths of the Gracchus brothers change Roman politics?

Critical Thinking

4. **Summarizing** Draw a diagram like the one here. Use your notes on crises Rome faced to list three crises during the later period of the republic. Then list two facts about each crisis.

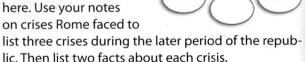

FOCUS ON SPEAKING

5. **Selecting Characters** In this section you learned about many major figures in Roman history. Choose one of them to be the subject of your legend. Now look back at your notes. How will you make the subject of your legend interesting for your listeners?

Social Studies Skills

Interpreting Culture Maps

Understand the Skill

A culture map is a special type of political map. As you know, physical maps show natural features, such as mountains and rivers. Political maps show the human features of an area, such as boundaries, cities, and roads. The human features shown on a culture map are cultural ones, such as the languages spoken or religions practiced in an area. Historians often use culture maps in their work. Therefore, being able to interpret them is important for understanding history.

Learn the Skill

Follow these guidelines to interpret a culture map.

1. Use map basics. Read the title to identify the subject. Note the labels, legend, and scale. Pay extra attention to special symbols for cultural features. Be sure you understand what these symbols represent.

2. Study the map as a whole. Note the location of the cultural symbols and features. Ask yourself how they relate to the rest of the map.

3. Connect the information on the map to any written information about the subject in the text.

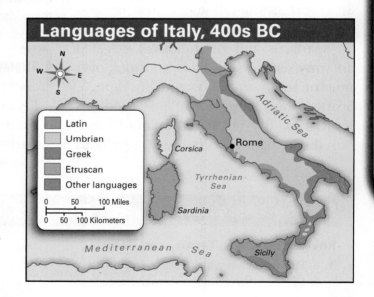

Languages of Italy, 400s BC

Legend:
- Latin
- Umbrian
- Greek
- Etruscan
- Other languages

0   50   100 Miles
0   50   100 Kilometers

Adriatic Sea
Corsica
Rome
Tyrrhenian Sea
Sardinia
Mediterranean Sea
Sicily

Practice and Apply the Skill

Apply the guidelines to the map on this page and answer the following questions.

1. What makes this map a culture map?

2. What language was most widely spoken on the Italian Peninsula? What other language was widely spoken?

3. Where was Greek spoken? Why did the people there talk in Greek?

4. What language did the Romans speak?

Chapter Review

Visual Summary

Use the visual summary below to help you review the main ideas of the chapter.

The Romans created many legends about their city's glorious history.

The early Romans set up a type of government called a republic.

The Roman Republic conquered lands in Italy and around the Mediterranean.

Reviewing Vocabulary, Terms, and People

Match each numbered definition with the correct lettered vocabulary term.

a. republic
b. plebeians
c. Spartacus
d. legions
e. Aeneas
f. consuls

g. Forum
h. dictator
i. veto
j. Roman Senate
k. patricians
l. primary

1. Rome's public meeting place
2. groups of about 6,000 soldiers
3. the legendary Trojan founder of Rome
4. main, most important
5. a government in which people elect leaders
6. a council that advised Rome's leaders
7. a leader with absolute power for six months
8. the common people of Rome
9. the two most powerful officials in Rome
10. leader of a slave rebellion
11. prohibit
12. noble, powerful Romans

Comprehension and Critical Thinking

SECTION 1 *(Pages 294–299)*

13. **a. Describe** What are two legends that describe Rome's founding? How are the two legends connected?

   b. Compare and Contrast What roles did the plebeians and the patricians take in the early Roman government? In what other ways were the two groups different?

   c. Predict How do you think Italy's geography and Rome's location would affect the spread of Rome's influence?

SECTION 2 (Pages 302–307)

14. a. Describe What were the three parts of Rome's government?

b. Analyze How do checks and balances protect the rights of the people? How do written laws do the same thing?

c. Elaborate What are some places in modern society that serve purposes similar to those of the Roman Forum?

SECTION 3 (Pages 308–313)

15. a. Identify What difficulties did Hannibal, Lucius Cornelius Sulla, and Spartacus cause for Rome?

b. Analyze How did Roman occupations, economics, and society change during the Late Republic?

c. Evaluate Some historians say that Rome and Carthage were destined to fight each other. Why do you think they say this?

Reviewing Themes

16. Politics Why did Roman magistrates only hold office for one year?

17. Geography How do you think Rome's location helped the Romans in their quest to conquer the entire Mediterranean region?

Using the Internet

18. Activity: Explaining Roman Society A key reason the Roman Republic fell was because the Roman people gave up on it. The army, once Rome's protector, let itself be turned against the Roman people. The Senate gave up on debate and compromise when it turned to political violence. Go online to research the fall of the Roman Republic. Then create an exhibit for a local history museum. Make sure your exhibit contains information about key figures in the Roman military and government. Use words and pictures to explain the political, religious, and social structures that made Rome an empire and what caused its eventual downfall.

Reading Skills

19. Outlining and History Look back at the discussion "Crises Strike the Republic" in the last section of this chapter. Prepare an outline that will help clarify the people, events, and ideas of this discussion. Before you prepare your outline, decide what your major headings will be. Then choose the details that will appear below each heading. Remember that most outlines follow this basic format:

> I. Main Idea
>   A. Supporting Idea
>   B. Supporting Idea
>   1. Detail
>   2. Detail
> II. Main Idea
>   A. Supporting Idea

Social Studies Skills

Interpreting Culture Maps *Look at the culture map on page 314. Then answer the following questions.*

20. What was the main language spoken in Italy during the 400s BC?

21. Which language do you think was spoken by the fewest people? Why do you think this?

FOCUS ON SPEAKING

22. Presenting Your Legend Now that you've chosen the subject for your legend, it's time to write and present it. As you write your legend, focus on exciting details that will bring the subject to life in your listeners' minds. Once you've finished writing, share your legend with the class. Try to make your legend exciting as you present it. Remember to alter the tone and volume of your voice to convey the appropriate mood.

DIRECTIONS: Read each question, and write the letter of the best response.

1 Use the map to answer the following question.

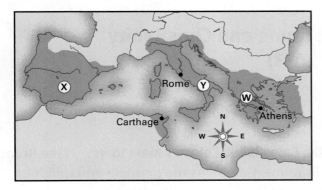

The order in which Rome expanded its control in the Mediterranean region is shown by which of the following sequences of letters?

A Y–W–X

B X–W–Y

C Y–X–W

D W–X–Y

2 Which was the *least* important reason for the growth of Rome's power and influence in the Mediterranean region?

A religion

B trade

C military organization

D wars and conquests

3 According to Roman legend, the city of Rome was founded by

A Latin peoples who moved to Italy from ancient Egypt.

B two men named Romulus and Remus who were raised by a wolf.

C the gods of Greece, who were looking for a new home.

D a Greek warrior named Achilles who had fled from the destruction of Troy.

4 Roman nobles were called

A patricians.

B plebeians.

C tribunes.

D magistrates.

5 Which of the following characteristics did *not* apply to Roman government?

A system of checks and balances

B sense of civic duty

C written code of laws

D equality of all people

Connecting with Past Learnings

6 You learned earlier in this course about other ancient peoples who, like the Romans, founded their civilizations along rivers. These peoples include all of the following *except* the

A Chinese.

B Egyptians.

C Sumerians.

D Hebrews.

7 Virgil's *Aeneid* is similar to what other piece of ancient literature that you've learned about in this course?

A the *Shiji*

B the *Book of the Dead*

C *The Odyssey*

D the *Bhagavad Gita*

FLORIDA...
The Story Continues

CHAPTER 11, Rome and Christianity (50 BC–AD 1453)

PLACES **c. 1400s: Calos is the Calusa's main town.** Like Rome to the Romans, Calos was the political and religious center of the Calusa of Florida's southwestern coast. It was where the head chief lived and major religious and political ceremonies took place. Archaeologists believe that Calos was located on Mound Key in Estero Bay. The island is a shell midden. A midden is a special type of archaeological site. It is basically a prehistoric garbage dump! As people prepared their food, they threw away the scraps. Most Florida middens are made of shells, since shellfish represented a large part of people's diet. There is evidence that a canal once cut across the island. The site includes several flat-topped ceremonial mounds. During the time of the Calusa, buildings of wood and thatch sat atop the mounds. From Calos, the Calusa chief ruled as many as 20,000 people occupying more than 50 villages. His political influence extended across most of southern Florida.

PLACES **c. 1797: The Cathedral Basilica of St. Augustine is built.** In 1586 St. Augustine was attacked and burned to the ground. Citizens rebuilt the town and the parish church. The church was again destroyed in 1702. This time the people of St. Augustine decided to hold services in the chapel of La Soledad Hospital. Finally, in 1786, the Spanish crown ordered the construction of a new church. The cornerstone was laid in 1793, and the cathedral was completed in 1797. Fire damaged the cathedral in 1887. Donations from around the nation enabled the cathedral to be rebuilt and enlarged.

PLACES **1821: Trinity Episcopal Parish is established in St. Augustine.**
Trinity Episcopal Parish is the oldest Protestant church in Florida. It is located in downtown St. Augustine. The parish was established in 1821, soon after Florida became a U.S. territory. The first church building was begun in 1830. It was constructed of coquina shell and measured 36 feet by 50 feet.

EVENTS **1905–1912: Henry Flagler builds an overseas railroad.** Henry Flagler was convinced that Florida had potential as a tourist haven. Like the Romans, what he needed was a way to get people where they wanted to go. Rather than roads, Flagler built railroads. Between 1885 and 1896, he put together a hotel and railroad empire that stretch from Jacksonville to Miami. Not satisfied, he decided to extend his Florida East Coast Railway all the way to Key West.

The only thing that stood in his way was a lot of water! Construction of the railway bridge began in 1905. By 1909 only seven miles remained—the seven miles from Knights Key to Key West. Spanning the distance was a daunting engineering feat. By 1912, workers had succeeded!

EVENTS **1941–1942: Florida Keys aqueduct brings water to the Keys.**
Only some keys had wells large enough to supply people with sufficient water. As the population grew, the problem grew. It was impossible to catch enough rainwater to meet people's needs. To solve the problem, the United States Navy and the state of Florida began construction on the Florida Keys Aqueduct in 1941. The original pipeline carried water from Florida City across the Everglades all the way to Key West—a distance of nearly 130 miles. The water took about six days to reach Key West!

Unpacking the Florida Standards ‹•••

Read the following to learn what this standard says and what it means. See FL8–FL31 to unpack all of the standards related to this chapter.

Benchmark SS.6.W.3.12 Explain the causes for the growth and longevity of the Roman Empire. Examples are centralized and efficient government, religious toleration, expansion of citizenship, the legion, the extension of road networks.

What does it mean?
Analyze why the Roman Empire was able to extend its territorial control and why the empire maintained its power for so long.

SPOTLIGHT ON
SS.6.E.1.3, SS.6.E.3.2, SS.6.E.3.4, SS.6.G.2.1 See pages FL38, FL39, and FL44 for content specifically related to these Chapter 11 standards.

Rome and Christianity

Essential Question Why did the Roman Empire fall, and what is its legacy?

FL Florida Next Generation Sunshine State Standards

SS.6.E.1.1 Identify the factors (new resources, increased productivity, education, technology, slave economy, territorial expansion) that increase economic growth. **SS.6.E.1.3** Describe the following economic concepts as they relate to early civilization: scarcity, opportunity cost, supply and demand, barter, trade, productive resources (land, labor, capital, entrepreneurship). **SS.6.E.3.2** Categorize products that were traded among civilizations, and give examples of barriers to trade of those products. **SS.6.E.3.4** Describe the relationship among civilizations that engage in trade, including the benefits and drawbacks of voluntary trade. **SS.6.G.1.7** Use maps to identify characteristics and boundaries of ancient civilizations that have shaped the world today. **SS.6.G.2.1** Explain how major physical characteristics, natural resources, climate, and absolute and relative locations have influenced settlement, interactions, and the economies of ancient civilizations of the world. **SS.6.G.2.5** Interpret how geographic boundaries invite or limit interaction with other regions and cultures. **SS.6.G.4.4** Map and analyze the impact of the spread of various belief systems in the ancient world. **SS.6.G.5.1** Identify the methods used to compensate for the scarcity of resources in the ancient world. **SS.6.W.1.3** Interpret primary and secondary sources. **SS.6.W.3.8** Determine the impact of significant figures associated with ancient Rome. **SS.6.W.3.11** Explain the transition from Roman Republic to empire and Imperial Rome, and compare Roman life and culture under each one. **SS.6.W.3.12** Explain the causes for the growth and longevity of the Roman Empire. **SS.6.W.3.13** Identify key figures and the basic beliefs of early Christianity and how these beliefs impacted the Roman Empire. **SS.6.W.3.14** Describe the key achievements and contributions of Roman civilization. **SS.6.W.3.15** Explain the reasons for the gradual decline of the Western Roman Empire after the Pax Romana. **SS.6.W.3.17** Explain the spread and influence of the Latin language on Western Civilization.

FOCUS ON WRITING

Note Cards for a Screenplay Imagine that you are a research assistant for a movie studio that is planning to make a movie about the Roman Empire. Your job is to find out about the important people, places, and events in the history of the empire and to report this information to a group of writers who will create a screenplay. As you read this chapter, look for descriptions of the people, places, and events of the Roman world from the 70s BC to the end of the Eastern Roman Empire.

CHAPTER EVENTS

44 BC Julius Caesar is assassinated.

27 BC Augustus becomes Rome's first emperor.

25 BC

WORLD EVENTS

HISTORY

Online Resource   VIDEO

This photo shows the Colosseum, an impressive example of ancient Roman architecture that still influences the design of stadiums around the world.

c. AD 30
Jesus is crucified.

AD 312
Emperor Constantine ends the persecution of Christians.

AD 476
The last Roman emperor in the West is overthrown.

AD 1453
The Byzantine Empire ends.

BC 1 AD

c. AD 65
Buddhism is introduced to China.

250

AD 250
The Maya Classic Age begins in Mexico.

500

AD 570
Muhammad is born in Mecca.

1450

ROME AND CHRISTIANITY **319**

Reading Social Studies

Economics | Geography | Politics | Religion | Society and Culture | Science and Technology

Focus on Themes This chapter describes the development of Rome as it grew from a republic into a strong and vast empire. First, you will learn about the **geographic** expansion of the empire. You will read about powerful leaders such as Julius Caesar, Marc Antony, and Augustus. Finally, you will learn about how the people of the Roman Empire lived and worked. You will read about their many contributions to literature, language, law, and **science and technology.**

Online Research

Focus on Reading Finding information on the World Wide Web can be easy. Just enter a word or two into a search engine and you will instantly find dozens—if not hundreds—of sites full of information.

Evaluating Web Sites However, looking through all those sites can be overwhelming. In addition, not all Web sites have good or accurate information. How do you know which sites are the ones you want? You have to evaluate, or judge, the sites. You can use an evaluation form like the one below to evaluate a Web site.

Evaluating Web-Based Resources

Name of site: _____ Topic of site _____
URL: _____ Date of access: _____

Scroll through the site then answer the questions below.

I. Evaluating the author of the site
   A. Who is the author? What are his or her qualifications?
   B. Is there a way to contact the author?

II. Evaluating the content of the site
   A. Is the site's topic related to the topic you are studying?
   B. Is there enough information at this site to help you?
   C. Is there too much information for you to read or understand?
   D. Does the site include pictures or illustrations to help you understand the information?
   E. Does the site discuss more than one point of view about the topic?
   F. Does the site express the author's opinions rather than facts?
   G. Does the site provide references for any of its information, including quotes?
   H. Are there links to other sites that have valuable information?

III. Evaluating the overall design and quality
   A. Is the site easy to navigate or to find information on?
   B. When was the site last updated?

IV. My overall impression
   A. I think this site has good information that will help me with my research. _____
   B. I think this site either is too hard or too easy or has information I can't verify. _____

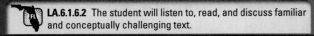
LA.6.1.6.2 The student will listen to, read, and discuss familiar and conceptually challenging text.

You Try It!

The information below is an example of a student's evaluation of a fictional Web site on Julius Caesar. Review the student's answers to the questions on the previous page and then answer the questions at the bottom of the page.

Web Site Evaluation

I. Evaluating the author
  A. Author is listed as Klee O. Patra. She has read many books about Julius Caesar.
  B. No information is listed for contacting the author.

II. Evaluating content of the site
  A. Yes. It is about Julius Caesar.
  B. There appears to be a great deal of information about Julius Caesar.
  C. No, it looks easy to understand.
  D. There are pictures, but most are from movies. There are no maps or historical images.
  E. No.
  F. Yes, it is all about how she loves Caesar.
  G. I can't find any references.
  H. There are two links, but they are both dead.

III. Evaluating overall design and quality
  A. No. It takes a long time to find any specific information. Also, the layout of the page is confusing.
  B. It was last updated in July 1998.

Study the evaluation then answer the following questions.

1. What do you know about the author of this site? Based on the evaluation information, do you think she is qualified to write about Caesar?

2. Does the content of the site seem valuable and reliable? Why?

3. The site has not been updated for many years, but that may not be a major problem for a site about Julius Caesar. Why? When might recent updates be more important?

4. Overall, would you say this site would be helpful? Why or why not?

Key Terms and People

Chapter 11

Section 1
Cicero (p. 322)
Julius Caesar (p. 323)
Pompey (p. 323)
Augustus (p. 324)
currency (p. 326)
Pax Romana (p. 326)
aqueduct (p. 327)
Romance languages (p. 328)
civil law (p. 328)

Section 2
Christianity (p. 334)
Jesus of Nazareth (p. 334)
Bible (p. 335)
crucifixion (p. 336)
Resurrection (p. 336)
disciples (p. 336)
Paul (p. 337)
Constantine (p. 338)

Section 3
Diocletian (p. 340)
Attila (p. 341)
corruption (p. 342)
Justinian (p. 342)
Theodora (p. 343)
Byzantine Empire (p. 343)

Academic Vocabulary

Success in school is related to knowing academic vocabulary—the words that are frequently used in school assignments and discussions. In this chapter, you will learn the following academic word:

efficient (p. 342)

As you read Chapter 11, think about what topics would be interesting to research on the Web. If you do some research on the Web, remember to evaluate the site and its contents.

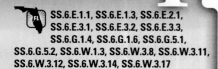
What You Will Learn...

Main Ideas

1. Disorder in the Roman Republic created an opportunity for Julius Caesar to gain power.
2. The Republic ended when Augustus became Rome's first emperor.
3. The Roman Empire grew to control the entire Mediterranean world.
4. The Romans accomplished great things in science, engineering, architecture, art, literature, and law.

The Big Idea

After changing from a republic to an empire, Rome grew politically and economically, and developed a culture that influenced later civilizations.

Key Terms and People

Cicero, *p. 322*
Julius Caesar, *p. 323*
Pompey, *p. 323*
Marc Antony, *p. 324*
Augustus, *p. 324*
Pax Romana, *p. 326*
aqueduct, *p. 327*
Romance languages, *p. 328*
civil law, *p. 328*

Online Resource
TAKING NOTES

Use the graphic organizer online to take notes on Rome's change from a republic to an empire and the accomplishments of the empire.

From Republic to Empire

If YOU were there...

You are a friend of a famous Roman Senator. Your friend is worried about the growing power of military men in Rome's government. Some other Senators want to take violent action to stop generals from taking over as dictators. Your friend wants your advice: Is violence justified to save the Roman Republic?

What advice will you give your friend?

BUILDING BACKGROUND By the first century BC, the government of the Roman Republic was in trouble. Politicians looked for ways to solve the problems. Philosophers offered ideas, too. In the end, however, the Republic could not survive the great changes that were taking place in Rome.

Disorder in the Republic

Rome in the 70s BC was a dangerous place. Politicians and generals went to war to increase their power even as political order broke down in Rome. There were politically inspired riots to restore the power of the tribunes. All the while, more and more people from throughout the republic flooded into the city, further adding to the confusion.

Calls for Change

Some Romans tried to stop the chaos in Rome's government. One such person was **Cicero** (SIS-uh-roh), a philosopher and gifted orator, or public speaker. In his speeches, Cicero called on upperclass Romans to work together to make Rome a better place. One way to do this, he argued, was to limit the power of generals. Cicero wanted the Romans to give more support to the Senate and to restore checks and balances on government.

But the government did not change. Many Romans didn't agree with Cicero. Others were too busy to listen. Meanwhile, several generals were working to take over the government. The most powerful of these generals was **Julius Caesar** (JOOL-yuhs SEE-zuhr).

Caesar's Rise to Power

Caesar was a great general. Romans admired him for his bravery and skill in battle. His soldiers respected him for treating them well. Between 58 BC and 50 BC Caesar conquered nearly all of Gaul—an area that is today the country of France. He wrote about this conquest in great detail. In this description of one battle, notice how he refers to himself as Caesar:

> "Caesar, having divided his forces . . . and having hastily [quickly] constructed some bridges, enters their country in three divisions, burns their houses and villages, and gets possession of a large number of cattle and men."
>
> —Julius Caesar, *The Gallic Wars*

Caesar's military successes made him a key figure in Roman politics. In addition to being a strong leader, Caesar was an excellent speaker. He won many supporters with his speeches in the forum.

Caesar also had powerful friends. Before he went to Gaul, he made an alliance with two of Rome's most influential men, **Pompey** (PAHM-pea) and Crassus (KRAS-uhs). Together the three ruled Rome.

Challenges to Caesar

The partnership lasted about 10 years. But after his conquests in Gaul, Caesar was so popular that even his friends were jealous of him. In 50 BC Pompey's allies in the Senate ordered Caesar to give up command of his armies. They wanted Pompey to control Rome alone.

Caesar refused. Instead he led his troops back toward Rome for a confrontation. Once his men crossed the Rubicon River, the boundary between Gaul and Italy, Caesar knew that there was no turning back.

SS.6.W.3.8 Determine the impact of significant figures associated with ancient Rome.

THE IMPACT TODAY

People now use the phrase "crossing the Rubicon" when they do something that can't be undone.

Julius Caesar conquered Gaul and added it to the empire. This painting from the late 1800s shows a Gallic leader surrendering to Caesar by dropping his weapons at Caesar's feet.

323

War was certain since Roman law said no general could enter Italy with his army.

Pompey and his allies fled Italy. They didn't think they had enough troops to defeat Caesar. But Caesar's army chased Pompey's forces for a year. They finally defeated Pompey in Greece in 48 BC. Pompey was killed by orders of an Egyptian king.

After Caesar returned to Rome in 45 BC, he made himself dictator for life. Although Caesar worked to improve Roman society, many people resented the way he gained power. They were also concerned that Caesar wanted to become king of Rome.

The Senators were especially angry with Caesar. He had reduced their powers, and they feared his growing strength. On March 15—a date known as the Ides of March—in 44 BC a group of Senators attacked Caesar in the Senate and stabbed him to death.

READING CHECK **Sequencing** How did Caesar gain power in Rome?

SS.6.W.3.11 Explain the transition from Roman Republic to empire and Imperial Rome, and compare Roman life and culture under each one.

The End of the Republic

After Caesar's assassination, two great leaders emerged to take control of Roman politics. One was Caesar's former assistant, **Marc Antony**. The other was Caesar's adopted son Octavian (ahk-TAY-vee-uhn), later called **Augustus** (aw-GUHS-tuhs).

Antony and Octavian

One priority for Antony and Octavian was punishing the men who killed Caesar. The murderers had thought they would become heroes. Instead they were forced to flee for their lives. Rome was shocked by Caesar's murder. Many people loved Caesar, and riots broke out after his death. In order to end the chaos that followed Caesar's assassination, the Senate had to act quickly to restore order.

At Caesar's funeral, Antony delivered a famous speech that turned even more Romans against the killers. Shortly afterward, he and Octavian set out with an army to try to avenge Caesar's death.

Their army caught up to the killers near Philippi (FI-luh-py) in northern Greece. In 42 BC Antony and Octavian soundly defeated their opponents. After the battle, the last of Caesar's murderers killed themselves.

Octavian Becomes Emperor

After the Battle of Philippi, Octavian returned to Italy. Antony went east to fight Rome's enemies. In 40 BC Antony married Octavian's sister, Octavia. Eight years later, however, he divorced her to marry Cleopatra, the queen of Egypt. Octavian saw this divorce as an insult to his sister and to himself.

Antony's behavior led to civil war in Rome. In 31 BC Octavian sent a fleet to attack Antony. Antony sailed out to meet it, and the two forces met just west of Greece in the Battle of Actium (AK-shee-uhm). Antony's fleet was defeated, but he escaped back to Egypt with Cleopatra. There the two committed suicide so they wouldn't be taken prisoner by Octavian.

Octavian then became Rome's sole ruler. Over the next few years he gained nearly limitless power. He took the title *princeps* (PRIN-seps), or first citizen.

In 27 BC Octavian announced that he was giving up his power to the Senate, but, in reality, he kept all his power. The Senate gave him a new name—Augustus, which means "revered one." Modern historians consider the naming of Augustus to mark the end of the Roman Republic and the beginning of the Roman Empire.

READING CHECK **Summarizing** How did the Roman Republic become an empire?

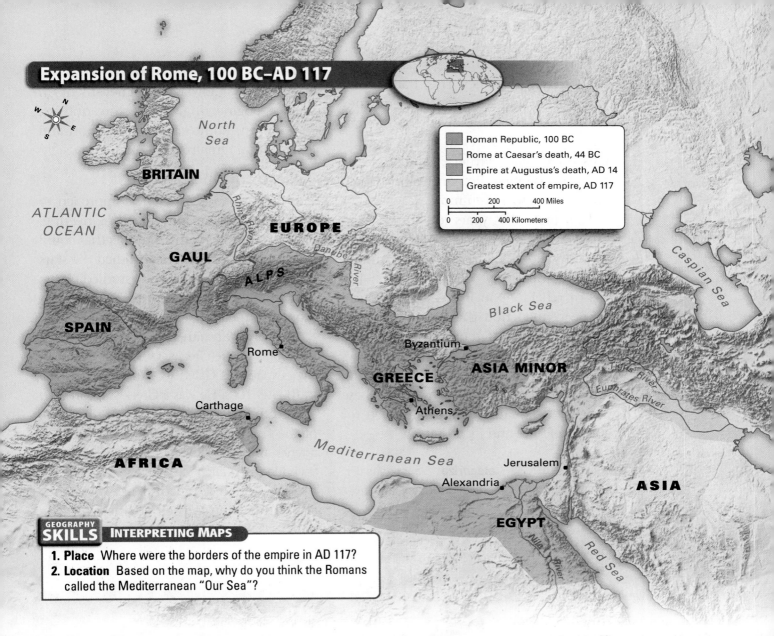

Expansion of Rome, 100 BC–AD 117

	Roman Republic, 100 BC
	Rome at Caesar's death, 44 BC
	Empire at Augustus's death, AD 14
	Greatest extent of empire, AD 117

0   200   400 Miles
0   200   400 Kilometers

North Sea
BRITAIN
ATLANTIC OCEAN
EUROPE
Rhine River
GAUL
Danube River
ALPS
SPAIN
Rome
Black Sea
Byzantium
GREECE
ASIA MINOR
Caspian Sea
Athens
Carthage
Tigris River
Euphrates River
AFRICA
Mediterranean Sea
Jerusalem
Alexandria
ASIA
EGYPT
Nile River
Red Sea

GEOGRAPHY SKILLS INTERPRETING MAPS

1. **Place** Where were the borders of the empire in AD 117?
2. **Location** Based on the map, why do you think the Romans called the Mediterranean "Our Sea"?

Rome's Growing Empire

When Rome became an empire, it already controlled most of the Mediterranean world. Augustus and the emperors who followed him further expanded the empire. Some emperors conquered territories to control hostile neighbors. Other Roman leaders wanted to gain control of gold, farmland, and other resources.

By the early AD 100s the Romans had taken over Gaul and much of central Europe. By the reign of the Emperor Hadrian (117–138), the Romans had conquered most of Britain. Rome also controlled Asia Minor, Mesopotamia, the eastern coast of the Mediterranean, and all of the north African coast.

The Roman conquests promoted trade. People in Rome needed raw materials that were lacking in Italy. Many of the materials, though, could be found in Rome's provinces, the administrative districts of the empire outside Italy. Traders brought metals, cloth, and food from the provinces to the city. They also brought more exotic goods, like spices and silk from Asia and animals from Africa. In return, the Romans sent goods made by artisans to the provinces. These goods included jewelry, glass, and clothing.

SS.6.W.3.12 Explain the causes for the growth and longevity of the Roman Empire.

FOCUS ON

One reason Rome was so successful in its conquests was the discipline and adaptability of its army, which was organized into legions. Legions could be combined to face large armies or broken into smaller units when more flexibility was needed in battle.

FOCUS ON

**Mediums of
Exchange** A
medium of
exchange is any
item that is com-
monly accepted
in exchange for
goods and servic-
es. Every medium
is assigned a basic
value. Goods and
services are then
priced accord-
ing to that value.
Today, money is
the most com-
mon medium of
exchange. In the
past, gold and
silver were often
used in this way.

To pay for their trade goods, Romans used currency, or money. They traded coins made of gold and silver for the items they wanted. These coins allowed the Romans to trade with people even if they had no items their trade partners wanted. Nearly everyone accepted Roman coins, which helped trade grow even more.

The first 200 years of the Roman Empire was a time of general peace and prosperity. Rome had a stable government and a well-run army. There were no major wars or rebellions in the empire. We call this peaceful period the **Pax Romana**, or Roman peace. It lasted until the AD 180s.

During the Pax Romana, the empire's population grew. Trade increased, making many Romans wealthy. As a result of these changes, the quality of life improved for people in Rome and its provinces.

READING CHECK **Categorize** What goods did Romans get from their provinces in Asia and in Africa?

SS.6.E.3.1 Identify examples of mediums of exchange (currencies) used for trade (barter) for each civilization, and explain why international trade requires a system for a medium of exchange between trading both inside and among various regions.

Rome's Accomplishments

The Romans made lasting achievements in science, engineering, architecture, and art. In addition, Rome's literary tradition and legal system remain influential today.

Science and Engineering

The Romans took a practical approach to their study of science and engineering. Roman scientists wanted results that could benefit their society. They studied the stars to produce a calendar. They studied plants and animals to learn how to obtain better crops and meat.

To improve health, Roman doctors studied the works of the Greeks. One great doctor in the empire was Galen (GAY-luhn), who lived in the AD 100s. He was a Greek surgeon who studied the body. Galen described the valves of the heart and noted differences between arteries and veins. For centuries doctors based their ideas on Galen's teachings.

The Romans' practical use of science also can be seen in their engineering. The

The Roman Arch

The Romans were the first people to make wide use of the arch. The photograph at right shows a Roman aqueduct supported by hundreds of arches. Below is a drawing showing how Roman engineers built their tall and strong arches.

How did the Romans support arches during their construction?

Romans were great builders. They developed new materials to help their structures last. For example, the Romans made cement by mixing a mineral called lime with volcanic rock and ash. The resulting material dried to be very hard and watertight.

More important than the materials they used, though, were the designs the Romans had for their structures. They built their roads in layers. Each layer was made of a different material. This layered construction made the road highly durable. Many Roman roads have not worn down even after centuries of traffic.

The Romans also created lasting structures by using arches. Because of its rounded shape, an arch can support much more weight than other shapes can. This strength has allowed many arched Roman bridges to last until the present.

The Romans also used arches in their aqueducts (A-kwuh-duhkts). An **aqueduct** is a raised channel used to carry water from mountains into cities. Because they crossed deep valleys, Roman aqueducts needed to be strong. Many still stand today.

Roman builders also learned how to combine arches to create vaults. A vault is a set of arches that supports the roof of a building. The Romans used vaults to create huge, open areas within buildings.

Architecture and Art

The Romans weren't interested only in practicality. They also admired beauty. This appreciation can be seen in the new designs of architecture and art that they created.

Roman architecture also copied some older Greek designs. For example, the Romans used columns to make their public buildings look impressive. The Romans also copied the Greeks by covering many of their buildings with marble.

Their engineering techniques allowed the Romans to make new architectural

Roman Accomplishments	QUICK FACTS
Government	**Architecture**
■ Importance of written laws	■ Large and strong buildings
■ Equal treatment for all citizens	■ Columns and open spaces
■ Rights and duties of citizens	**Art**
Engineering	■ Realistic statues
■ Excellent, durable roads	■ Lifelike portraits
■ Strong bridges	**Philosophy**
■ Aqueducts to move water	■ Focused on improving people's lives
■ Building designs that inspired later societies	■ Stoic philosophy emphasizing people's civic duty

advances. The vault let them build huge structures, much larger than anything the Greeks could build. One such structure was the Colosseum in Rome—a huge building built for gladiator fights. Many other Roman structures are topped with domes.

Roman artists were known for their beautiful mosaics, paintings, and statues. Mosaics and paintings were used to decorate Roman buildings. Most Roman paintings were frescoes. A fresco is a type of painting done on plaster. Many Roman painters were particularly skilled at creating portraits, or pictures of people. Roman sculptors were also very talented. They studied what the Greeks had done and tried to re-create this brilliance.

Literature and Language

Rich in art and architecture, Rome was also home to many of the greatest authors in the ancient world. One such author was Virgil, who wrote a great epic about the founding of Rome, the *Aeneid* (ih-NEE-uhd). Others were Ovid, who wrote poems about Roman mythology, and Horace, whose poems encouraged people to enjoy life.

The Glory of the Colosseum

↗ Online Resource

FOCUS ON

The Romans also wrote philosophy. One of the most famous Roman philosophers was the emperor Marcus Aurelius (121–180), who was a Stoic. Stoics emphasized self control, contentment, and living simply in harmony with nature.

FOCUS ON READING

What key words would you use to search for Web information on a subject discussed in this paragraph?

SS.6.W.3.17 Explain the spread and influence of the Latin language on Western Civilization.

THE IMPACT TODAY

The Latin language has influenced many contemporary languages. Many legal and medical terms we use today have Latin roots. Latin was the language of education and Christianity in Europe for centuries after the fall of Rome.

In addition, Roman writers produced histories, speeches, and dramas that are still studied and enjoyed today.

Virgil, Ovid, and other poets wrote in Latin, the language of government and law. People throughout the Roman world wrote, conducted business, and kept records in Latin. In the eastern half of the empire, Greek was just as important.

Latin later developed into many different languages. These languages are called **Romance languages.** They include Italian, French, Spanish, Portuguese, and Romanian.

Latin also influenced other languages. Many non-Romance languages, including English, contain Latin words. Words like *et cetera, circus,* and *veto* were all originally Latin terms. Latin words are also common in scientific terms and mottoes.

Law

Rome's greatest influence may have been in the field of law. Roman law was enforced across much of Europe. Even after the empire fell, Roman laws continued to exist in the kingdoms that followed.

Over time, Roman law inspired a system called civil law. **Civil law** is a legal system based on a written code of laws, like the one created by the Romans.

Most countries in Europe today have civil law traditions. In the 1500s and 1600s, colonists from some of these countries carried civil law around the world. As a result, many countries in Africa, Asia, and the Americas have legal systems influenced by Roman law.

READING CHECK Finding the Main Idea
How did Roman literature and language influence later societies?

SUMMARY AND PREVIEW Augustus made the Roman Republic into an empire. The empire grew during its first 200 years, and the Romans made many lasting contributions to the world. In the next section, you will learn about an influential development that changed life in Rome—Christianity.

Section 1 Assessment

Reviewing Ideas, Terms, and People

1. **a. Recall** To whom did **Cicero** want to give power?
   b. Making Inferences Why did many Senators consider **Julius Caesar** a threat?
   c. Evaluate What role did the military play in Caesar's rise to power?

2. **a. Identify** Who took over Rome after Caesar's death?
   b. Summarize How did Octavian take power from **Marc Antony**?
   c. Evaluate Why is it significant that Octavian did not take the title of dictator?

3. **a. Identify** What areas of the world did the Romans take over?
   b. Elaborate Why did trade increase during the **Pax Romana**?

4. **a. Recall** What type of law is based on the Roman law code?
   b. Draw Conclusions Latin is no longer spoken. Why do you think people still study it?

Critical Thinking

5. **Analyzing** Review your notes on Rome's accomplishments. Describe how the effects of one Roman accomplishment in each of the fields below is being felt today.

Engineering	
Language	
Law	
Literature	

FOCUS ON WRITING

6. **Taking Notes for a Screenplay** In your notebook, create a three-columned chart labeled "Characters," "Setting," and "Plot." Under the columns, write notes about the people and events from this section that you think would make good material for a movie.

Augustus

What would you do if you had great power?

When did he live? 63 BC–AD 14

Where did he live? Rome

What did he do? As the leader of Rome, Augustus made many improvements in the city. He created a fire department and a police force to protect the city's people. He built new aqueducts and repaired old ones to increase Rome's water supply. Augustus also worked on improving and expanding Rome's road network.

Why is he important? As Rome's first emperor, Augustus is one of the most significant figures in Roman history. Almost singlehandedly, he changed the nature of Roman government forever. But Augustus is also known for the great monuments he had built around Rome. He built a new forum that held statues, monuments, and a great temple to the god Mars. In writing about his life, Augustus declared, "I found Rome a city of brick and left it a city of marble."

Identifying Points of View Why do you think many Romans greatly admired Augustus?

Augustus was responsible for the construction of many impressive buildings in Rome.

KEY EVENTS

- **45 BC** Julius Caesar adopts Octavian as his son and heir.

- **44 BC** Octavian moves to Rome when Caesar dies.

- **42 BC** Octavian and Antony defeat Brutus.

- **31 BC** Octavian defeats Antony.

- **27 BC** Octavian takes the name Augustus and becomes emperor of Rome.

Roman Roads

The Romans are famous for their roads. They built a road network so large and well constructed that parts of it remain today, roughly 2,000 years later. Roads helped the Romans run their empire. Armies, travelers, messengers, and merchants all used the roads to get around. They stretched to every corner of the empire in a network so vast that people even today say that "all roads lead to Rome."

Roman roads stretched as far north as Scotland.

The Romans built about 50,000 miles of roads. That's enough to circle the earth—twice!

EUROPE

In the west, roads crisscrossed Spain.

PYRENEES

ITALY

Rome

SS.6.G.5.2 Use geographic terms and tools to explain why ancient civilizations developed networks of highways, waterways, and other transportation linkages.

Roman roads in the south connected different parts of northern Africa.

Mediterranean Sea

N
W   E
S

AFRICA

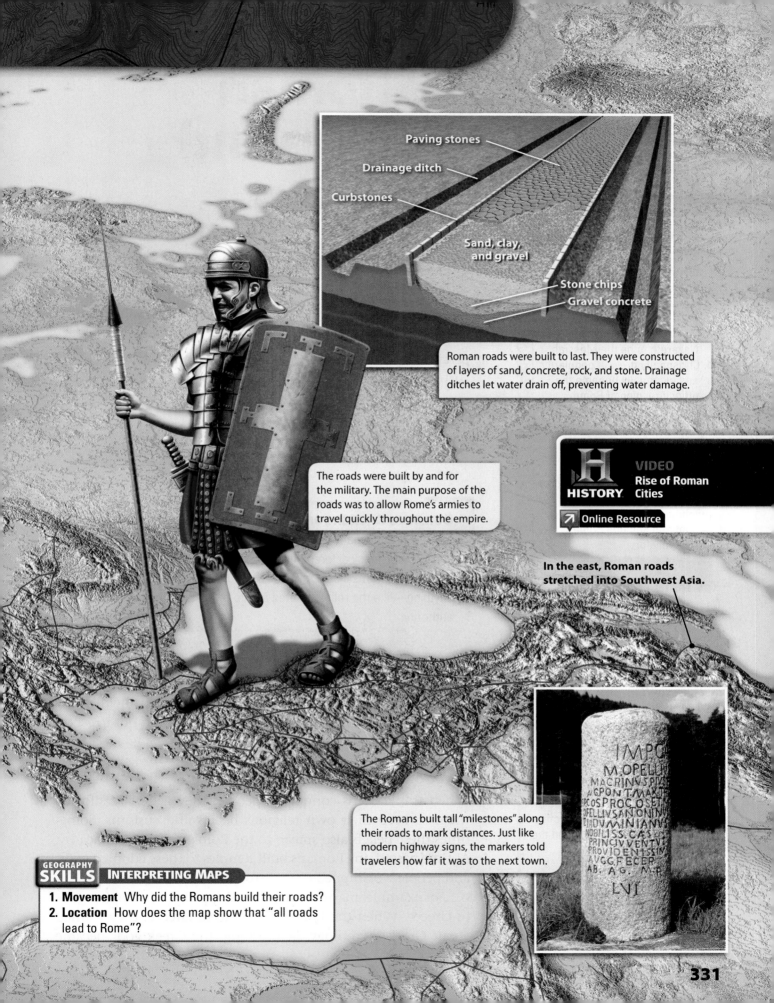

Paving stones

Drainage ditch

Curbstones

Sand, clay, and gravel

Stone chips

Gravel concrete

Roman roads were built to last. They were constructed of layers of sand, concrete, rock, and stone. Drainage ditches let water drain off, preventing water damage.

The roads were built by and for the military. The main purpose of the roads was to allow Rome's armies to travel quickly throughout the empire.

HISTORY VIDEO **Rise of Roman Cities**

↗ Online Resource

In the east, Roman roads stretched into Southwest Asia.

The Romans built tall "milestones" along their roads to mark distances. Just like modern highway signs, the markers told travelers how far it was to the next town.

GEOGRAPHY
SKILLS **INTERPRETING MAPS**

1. **Movement** Why did the Romans build their roads?
2. **Location** How does the map show that "all roads lead to Rome"?

331

LA.6.1.6.2, LA.6.1.7.3, SS.6.G.1.4,
SS.6.G.1.7, SS.6.G.2.6, SS.6.G.4.4,
SS.6.W.1.3, SS.6.W.3.8, SS.6.W.3.11,
SS.6.W.3.12, SS.6.W.3.13, SS.6.W.3.14

What You Will Learn...

Main Ideas

1. Despite its general religious tolerance, Rome came into conflict with the Jews.
2. A new religion, Christianity, grew out of Judaism.
3. Many considered Jesus of Nazareth to be the Messiah.
4. Christianity grew in popularity and eventually became the official religion of Rome.

The Big Idea

People in the Roman Empire practiced many religions before Christianity, based on the teachings of Jesus of Nazareth, spread and became Rome's official religion.

Key Terms and People

Christianity, *p. 334*
Jesus of Nazareth, *p. 334*
Messiah, *p. 334*
crucifixion, *p. 336*
Resurrection, *p. 336*
Apostles, *p. 337*
Paul of Tarsus, *p. 337*
Constantine, *p. 338*

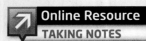

Online Resource
TAKING NOTES

Use the graphic organizer online to take notes on the religious practices in Rome, Jesus's teachings, and the early history of Christianity.

The Roman Empire and Religion

If YOU were there...

You are a Roman soldier stationed in one of the empire's provinces. You are proud that you've helped bring Roman culture to this place far from the city of Rome. But one group of local people refuses to take part in official Roman holidays and rituals, saying it is against their religious beliefs. Other than that, they seem peaceful. Even so, some soldiers think this group is dangerous.

What will you do about this group?

BUILDING BACKGROUND As the Roman Empire expanded, it came to include many people who spoke many different languages and followed many different religions. While Roman officials were generally tolerant of local religions and cultures, they did not allow anything—like the religion noted above—that might threaten their authority.

Religious Tolerance and Conflict

The Romans were a very religious people. They held many festivals in honor of their gods. However, they did not insist on imposing their beliefs on others.

Freedom of Worship

When the Romans conquered people, they generally allowed them to keep their own religious beliefs and customs. Sometimes these beliefs also spread to the Romans who lived nearby. As time passed, the Romans built temples to these adopted gods, and people worshipped them throughout the empire.

For example, many Romans worshipped the Olympian gods of Greece. When the Romans conquered Greece, they learned about Greek mythology. Before long, the Greek gods became the main gods of Rome as well, although they were known by different names. In the same way, many Romans also adopted gods and beliefs from the Egyptians, Gauls, and Persians.

In their religious lives, the Romans were very practical. They were not sure which gods did or did not exist. To avoid offending any gods, the Romans prayed to a wide variety of gods and goddesses.

The only time the Romans banned a religion was when the rulers of Rome considered it a political problem. In these cases, government officials took steps to prevent problems. Sometimes they placed restrictions on when and where members of a religion could meet. Judaism was one religion that some Roman leaders came to consider a political problem.

Clashes with the Jews

Unlike the Romans, the Jews did not worship many gods. They believed that their God was the only god. Some Romans thought the Jews insulted Rome's gods by not praying to them.

Still, the Romans did not attempt to ban Judaism in the empire. At first, they allowed the Jews to keep their religion and practice it. The Jews, however, created political conflict by rebelling against Roman rule. Judea, the territory in which most Jews lived, had been conquered by Rome in 63 BC. Since then, many Jews had resented Roman rule. They did not want to answer to outsiders. As a result, the Jews rebelled against the Romans in AD 66–70. There were other disturbances as well, but each time the Jews were defeated.

The Romans built many temples to honor their many gods. Temples built to honor all the gods were called pantheons, and the most famous of these is the Pantheon in Rome, first built in the 20s BC. Its huge dome awes visitors even today.

The Roman general Titus captured Jerusalem in AD 70. To celebrate this victory, the Romans built an arch decorated with scenes like this one of Roman soldiers carrying a stolen menorah from Jerusalem's holy Second Temple.

By the early 100s the Romans had become more hostile toward the Jews. Treated harshly and taxed heavily, the Jews grew increasingly bitter. Matters worsened when the emperor Hadrian banned the practice of certain Jewish rituals. He thought this ban would end the Jewish people's desire for independence and cause them to give up Judaism.

Instead Hadrian's actions made the Jews even more upset. Once again they rebelled. This time, Hadrian decided to end the rebellions once and for all.

The Roman army crushed the Jewish revolt and destroyed Jerusalem in 135. Soon after, they forced the remaining Jews to leave the city. Then the Romans built a new city on the ruins of Jerusalem and brought settlers from other parts of the empire to live there. Jews were forbidden to enter this new city more than once a year. Driven out of their ancient city, many Jews moved into other parts of the Roman world.

READING CHECK Drawing Conclusions
Why did the Romans consider Judaism a threat?

A New Religion

At the beginning of the first century AD, what would become a new religion appeared in Judea. Called **Christianity**, this religion was based on the life and teachings of **Jesus of Nazareth**. Christianity was rooted in the ideas and traditions of Judaism, but it developed as a separate faith.

At the time that Jesus was born, around the end of the first century BC, there were several groups of Jews in Judea. The largest of these groups was stricter than the others in its religious practices. Its members were particularly careful about obeying the laws of Moses, whom you read about in Chapter 7. Jews believe that Moses gave them a set of laws to follow.

In keeping with their observance of the laws, Jews led structured lives. For example, they performed daily rituals and avoided eating certain foods.

Many Jews followed the laws closely because Jewish prophets had said a new leader would appear among them. Many thought this leader was more likely to appear if they were strict in their religious behavior.

According to the prophecy, the Jews' new leader would be a descendant of King David. When he came, he would restore the greatness of King David's ancient kingdom, Israel. The prophets called this leader the **Messiah** (muh-SY-uh), which means "God's anointed one" in Hebrew. In other words, the Jews believed that God would choose the Messiah that would lead them.

When the Romans took over Judea in 63 BC, many Jews believed that the Messiah would soon appear. Jewish prophets wandered through Judea, announcing that the Messiah was coming. Many Jews anxiously awaited his arrival.

READING CHECK Summarizing Why were Jews waiting for the Messiah to arrive?

Jesus of Nazareth

Jesus of Nazareth, the man Christians believe was the Jewish Messiah, lived at the very beginning of the first century AD. Although Jesus was one of the most influential figures in all of world history, we know relatively little about his life. Most of what we know is contained in the Christian Bible, the holy book of the religion of Christianity.

The Christian Bible is made up of two parts. The first part, the Old Testament, is largely the same as the Hebrew Bible. It tells the history and ideas of the Hebrew and Jewish people. The second part, the New Testament, is sacred to Christians. The New Testament contains accounts of the life and teachings of Jesus and the early history of Christianity. The New Testament also contains letters written by some followers of Jesus.

The Birth of Jesus

According to the New Testament, Jesus was born in a town called Bethlehem (BETH-li-hem). In our dating system, the birth of Jesus marks the shift from BC to AD. Jesus's mother, Mary, was married to a carpenter named Joseph. But Christians believe God, not Joseph, was Jesus's father.

As a young man, Jesus lived in the town of Nazareth and probably studied with Joseph to become a carpenter. Like most young Jewish men of the time, he also studied the laws and teachings of Judaism. By the time he was about 30, Jesus had begun to travel and teach about religion. Stories of his teachings and actions make up the beginning of the Bible's New Testament. According to the Bible, Jesus created excitement wherever he went.

SS.6.W.3.13 Identify key figures and the basic beliefs of early Christianity and how these beliefs impacted the Roman Empire.

LINKING TO TODAY

Christian Holidays

For centuries, Christians have honored key events in Jesus's life. Some of these events inspired holidays that Christians celebrate today.

The most sacred holiday for Christians is Easter, which is celebrated each spring. Easter is a celebration of the Resurrection, Jesus's rising from the dead. Christians usually celebrate Easter by attending church services. Many people also celebrate by dyeing eggs because eggs are seen as a symbol of new life.

Another major Christian holiday is Christmas. It honors Jesus's birth and is celebrated every December 25. Although no one knows on what date Jesus was actually born, Christians have placed Christmas in December since the 200s. Today, people celebrate with church services and the exchange of gifts. Some, like people in the picture at right, reenact scenes of Jesus's birth.

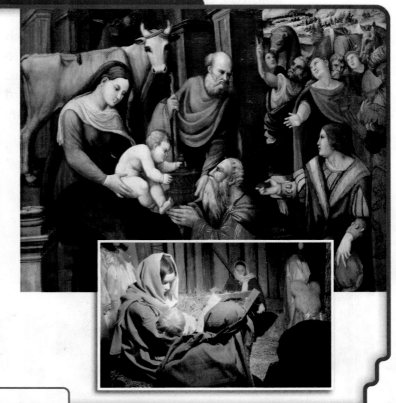

ANALYSIS SKILL ANALYZING INFORMATION

Why do you think Christians celebrate events in Jesus's life?

Crucifixion and Resurrection

As a teacher, Jesus attracted many followers. As he traveled the Judean countryside, he greatly influenced many who listened to his message. According to the New Testament, his teachings challenged the authority of political leaders. Roman leaders arrested Jesus while he was in Jerusalem around AD 30.

THE IMPACT TODAY

Because Jesus was crucified, the cross is an important symbol of Christianity today.

Shortly after his arrest, Jesus was executed. He was killed by **crucifixion** (kroo-suh-FIK-shuhn), a type of execution in which a person was nailed to a cross. In fact, the word crucifixion comes from the Latin word for "cross." After Jesus died, his followers buried him.

According to Christian beliefs, Jesus rose from the dead on the third day after he was crucified. Christians refer to Jesus's rise from the dead as the **Resurrection** (re-suh-REK-shuhn). After the Resurrection, several groups of Jesus's disciples (di-SY-puhls), or followers, claimed to see him.

Early Christians believe that the Resurrection was a sign that Jesus was the Messiah and the Son of God. Some people began to call him Jesus Christ, from the Greek word for Messiah, *Christos*. It is from this word that the words *Christian* and *Christianity* later developed.

The Teachings of Jesus

Jesus had traveled from village to village spreading his message to the Jewish people. Much of Jesus's message was rooted in older Jewish traditions. For example, he emphasized two rules that were also taught in the Torah: love God, and love other people.

Jesus expected his followers to love all people, not just friends or family. He encouraged his followers to be generous to the poor and the sick. He told people that they should even love their enemies. The way people treated others, Jesus said, showed how much they loved God.

Another important theme in Jesus's teachings was salvation, or the rescue of people from sin. Jesus taught that people who were saved from sin would enter the kingdom of God when they died. Many of Jesus's teachings dealt with how people could reach the kingdom. Jesus warned that people who loved money or goods more than they loved God would not be saved.

Over the many centuries since Jesus lived, people have interpreted his teachings in different ways. As a result, many different denominations of Christians have developed. A denomination is a group of people who hold the same religous beliefs. Still, despite their differences, Christians around

The Last Supper

1. Bartholomew
2. James, the Less
3. Andrew
4. Judas
5. Peter
6. John
7. Jesus
8. Thomas
9. James
10. Philip
11. Matthew
12. Thaddeus
13. Simon

This famous painting by Italian artist Leonardo da Vinci shows the Last Supper—the final meal that Jesus and his Apostles shared before Jesus was arrested.

LETTER
Paul's Letter to the Romans

In the late AD 50s Paul traveled to Corinth, a city in Greece. While there, he wrote a letter to the people of Rome. In this letter he told the Romans that he planned to come to their city to deliver God's message. In the meantime, he told them, they should learn to live together peacefully.

"Let love be genuine; hate what is evil, hold fast to what is good; love one another with mutual affection; outdo one another in showing honor. Do not lag in zeal, be ardent [strong] in spirit, serve the Lord. Rejoice in hope, be patient in suffering, persevere in prayer. Contribute to the needs of the saints; extend hospitality to strangers.

Bless those who persecute you; bless and do not curse them. Rejoice with those who rejoice, weep with those who weep. Live in harmony with one another; do not be haughty, but associate with the lowly; do not claim to be wiser than you are. Do not repay anyone evil for evil, but take thought for what is noble in the sight of all. If it is possible, so far as it depends on you, live peaceably with all."

—**Romans 12:9–18 NRSV**

ANALYSIS SKILL ANALYZING PRIMARY SOURCES

How did Paul's letter express Jesus's teachings?

---

the world share some basic beliefs about Jesus and his importance.

The Spread of Jesus's Teachings

The **Apostles** (uh-PAHS-uhls) were 12 disciples whom Jesus chose to receive special training. After the Resurrection, the Apostles traveled widely telling about Jesus and his teachings. Some of Jesus's disciples wrote accounts of his life and teachings. These accounts are called the Gospels. Four Gospels are found in the New Testament of the Bible. They were written by men known as Matthew, Mark, Luke, and John. Historians and religious scholars depend on the Gospels for information about Jesus's life.

Probably the most important figure in the spread of Christianity after Jesus's death was named **Paul of Tarsus**. Paul traveled throughout the Roman world spreading Christian teachings. In his letters he wrote about the Resurrection and about salvation. Paul also told Christians that they didn't have to obey all Jewish laws

and rituals. These ideas helped the Christian Church break away from Judaism.

READING CHECK Summarizing What do Christians believe happened after Jesus died?

The Growth of Christianity

The first Christians spread Jesus's teachings only among Jews. But Paul and other Christians introduced Christianity to non-Jews as well. As a result, Christianity began to spread rapidly. Within a hundred years after Jesus's death, thousands of Christians lived in the Roman Empire.

However, Christians trying to spread their beliefs faced challenges from local officials. Some officials even arrested and killed Christians who refused to worship Rome's gods. A few Roman emperors feared that Christians would cause unrest, so they banned Christianity. This began a period of persecution (puhr-si-KYOO-shuhn) against Christians. Persecution is the punishment of a group because of its beliefs.

THE IMPACT TODAY

According to Christian tradition, one of the Apostles, Peter, became the first leader of the Christian church. Some Catholics see Peter as the first pope. Today, the pope is the head of the Roman Catholic Church.

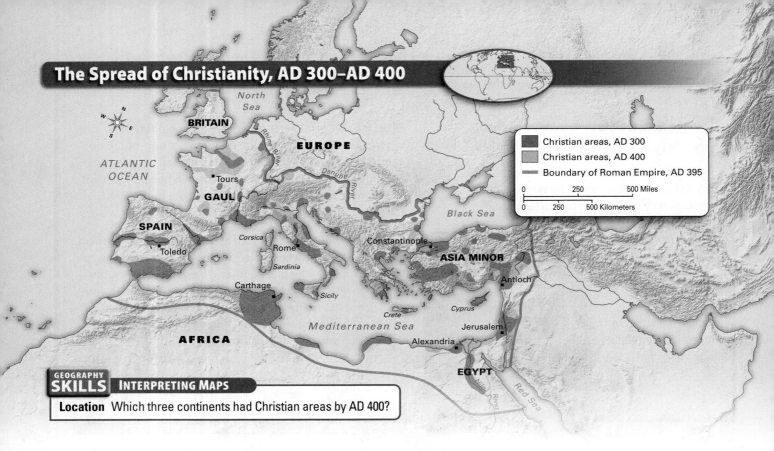

The Spread of Christianity, AD 300–AD 400

Legend:
- Christian areas, AD 300
- Christian areas, AD 400
- Boundary of Roman Empire, AD 395

0   250   500 Miles
0   250   500 Kilometers

Map labels: North Sea, BRITAIN, EUROPE, ATLANTIC OCEAN, Rhine River, Danube River, GAUL, Tours, SPAIN, Toledo, Corsica, Rome, Sardinia, Carthage, Sicily, Crete, Mediterranean Sea, AFRICA, Black Sea, Constantinople, ASIA MINOR, Antioch, Cyprus, Jerusalem, Alexandria, EGYPT, Nile River, Red Sea

GEOGRAPHY SKILLS   INTERPRETING MAPS

Location Which three continents had Christian areas by AD 400?

Christians met in secret but continued to spread their faith. In the early 300s, the emperor **Constantine** (KAHN-stuhn-teen) became a Christian. He removed the bans on the religion. Later, Emperor Theodosius made Christianity Rome's official religion.

READING CHECK **Identifying Cause and Effect** How did Paul's ideas help to spread Christianity?

SUMMARY AND PREVIEW Although usually tolerant, Roman authorities persecuted Jews and Christians in the empire. However, both Judaism and Christianity survived. In fact, Christianity eventually became the empire's official religion. Next, you will read about the fall of Rome.

Section 2 Assessment

Reviewing Ideas, Terms, and People

1. **a. Recall** Why did Roman leaders ban some religions?
   b. Explain What was one religion that Roman leaders considered a problem? Why?
2. **a. Describe** What traditions were practiced by the Jews of Judea?
   b. Explain Describe Jewish beliefs about the **Messiah**.
3. **a. Identify** From where does most of the information about **Jesus of Nazareth** come?
   b. Analyze How did the teachings of **Paul of Tarsus** change Christianity's relationship to Judaism?
4. **a. Summarize** What challenges did early Christians face in practicing and spreading their religion?
   b. Elaborate How did **Constantine** affect Christianity?

Critical Thinking

5. **Summarizing** Using your notes and a chart like the one below, identify the main teachings of Christianity. Then describe its spread and how Rome's policy toward it changed over time.

Christian Teachings	Spread	Changes in Rome's Policy

FOCUS ON WRITING

6. **Adding Details** Write down some notes and add details to your columns about what life might have been like for Jews and Christians in this period.

The End of the Empire

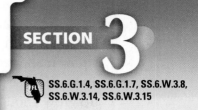
If YOU were there...

You are a former Roman soldier who has settled on lands in Gaul. In the last few months, groups of foreigners have been raiding local towns and burning farms. The commander of the local army post is an old friend, but he says he is short of loyal soldiers. Many troops have been called back to Rome. You don't know when the next raid will come.

How will you defend your lands?

BUILDING BACKGROUND Though the Roman Empire remained large and powerful, it faced serious threats from both outside and inside. Beyond the borders of the empire, many different groups of people were on the move. They threatened the peace in the provinces—and eventually attacked the heart of the empire itself.

Problems in the Empire

At its height the Roman Empire included all the land around the Mediterranean Sea. In the early AD 100s, the empire stretched from Britain south to Egypt, and from the Atlantic Ocean all the way to the Syrian Desert.

But the empire did not stay that large for long. By the end of the 200s, emperors had given up some of the land the Roman army had conquered. These emperors feared that the empire had become too large to defend or govern efficiently. As later rulers discovered, these emperors were right.

External and Internal Threats

Even as emperors were giving up territory, new threats to the empire were appearing. Tribes of fierce Germanic warriors attacked Rome's northern borders. At the same time, Persian armies invaded in the east. The Romans defended themselves from these invasions for 200 years, but only at great cost.

What You Will Learn...

Main Ideas

1. Many problems threatened the Roman Empire, leading one emperor to divide it in half.
2. Rome declined as a result of invasions and political and economic problems.
3. In the eastern empire, people created a new society and religious traditions that were very different from those in the west.

The Big Idea

Problems from both inside and outside caused the Roman Empire to split into a western half, which collapsed, and an eastern half that prospered for hundreds of years.

Key Terms and People

Diocletian, *p. 340*
Attila, *p. 341*
corruption, *p. 342*
Justinian, *p. 342*
Theodora, *p. 343*
Byzantine Empire, *p. 343*

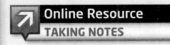 **Online Resource**
TAKING NOTES

Use the graphic organizer online to take notes on the Western Roman Empire and the Eastern Roman Empire.

SS.6.W.3.15 Explain the reasons for the gradual decline of the Western Roman Empire after the Pax Romana.

339

The Romans struggled with problems within the empire as well. The raids against Rome made people near the border nervous. In time, these people abandoned their land. To grow enough food, the Romans invited Germanic farmers to grow crops on Roman lands. These farmers often came from the same tribes that threatened Rome's borders. Over time, whole German communities had moved into the empire. They chose their own leaders and largely ignored the emperors. This caused problems for the Romans.

Other internal problems also threatened Rome's survival. Disease swept through the empire, killing many people. The government was also forced to increase taxes to pay for the defense of the empire. Desperate, the Romans looked for a strong emperor. They found one in Diocletian.

THE IMPACT TODAY

Constantinople is now called Istanbul, and is a major urban center.

Division of the Empire

Diocletian (dy-uh-KLEE-shuhn) became emperor in the late 200s. Convinced that the empire was too big for one person to rule, Diocletian ruled the eastern half and named a co-emperor to rule the west.

Not long after Diocletian left power, the emperor Constantine (KAHN-stuhn-teen) reunited the empire for a short time. He also moved the capital to the east, into what is now Turkey. He built a grand new capital city there. It was called Constantinople (kahn-stant-uhn-OH-puhl), which means "the city of Constantine." Although the empire was still called the Roman Empire, Rome was no longer the real center of power. Power had moved to the east.

READING CHECK Identifying Cause and Effect Why did Diocletian divide the Roman Empire?

Invasions of the Roman Empire, 340–500

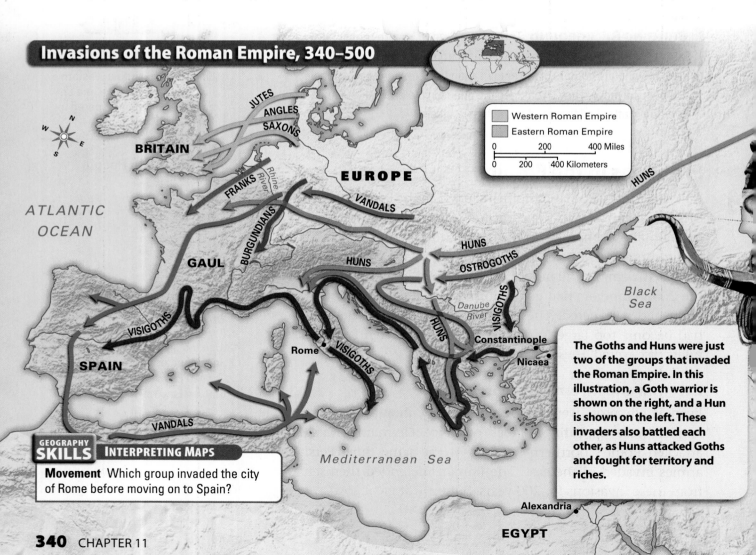

GEOGRAPHY SKILLS **INTERPRETING MAPS**

Movement Which group invaded the city of Rome before moving on to Spain?

The Goths and Huns were just two of the groups that invaded the Roman Empire. In this illustration, a Goth warrior is shown on the right, and a Hun is shown on the left. These invaders also battled each other, as Huns attacked Goths and fought for territory and riches.

The Decline of Rome

As you have read, foreign tribes had settled along the Roman Empire's northern border in the 200s. A century later, these bands of fighters began raiding deep into the heart of the empire.

Early Invasions

The source of these raids was a group of people called the Huns, fierce warriors from Central Asia. The Huns first invaded southeastern Europe and then launched raids on nearby kingdoms. Among the Huns' victims were several groups of people called the Goths, made up of the Visigoths and Ostrogoths. Unable to defeat the Huns, the Goths fled into Roman territory.

Rome's leaders feared that the Goths would destroy Roman land and property. They fought to keep the Goths out of Roman territory. The eastern armies were largely successful. They forced the Goths to move farther west. As a result, however, the western armies were defeated by the Goths. After their victory, large numbers of Goths moved into the Roman Empire.

The Romans fought desperately to keep the Goths from Rome. They even paid the Goths not to attack. In 408, however, the Romans stopped making payments. The Visigoths marched into Rome and sacked, or destroyed, the city in 410. This devastated the Romans. No one had attacked their city in nearly 800 years. Many Romans began to fear for the future of their empire.

The Fall of the Western Empire

The Gothic victory inspired other groups of foreign warriors to invade the western half of the empire. The Vandals, Angles, Saxons, Jutes, and Franks all launched attacks. Meanwhile, the Huns, under a fearsome leader named **Attila** (AT-uhl-uh), raided Roman territory in the east.

Rome needed strong leaders to survive these attacks, but the emperors were weak. Military leaders took power away from the emperors and, by the 450s, ruled Rome.

Conflict among these military leaders gave the invaders an opening. In 476 one of the foreign generals overthrew the last emperor in Rome and named himself king of Italy. Many historians consider this event the end of the Western Roman Empire.

Factors in Rome's Fall

There were several causes of Rome's decline. One was the vast size of the empire. Communication among various parts of the empire was difficult, especially during times of conflict. The Roman world simply became too big to govern effectively.

THE IMPACT TODAY

We still use the word *vandal* today to describe someone who destroys property.

BIOGRAPHY

Justinian and Theodora
483–565; c. 500–548

Justinian I was the emperor of the Byzantine Empire from AD 527 to AD 565. As emperor, Justinian reconquered parts of the fallen western empire and simplified Roman laws. He also ordered the building of many beautiful public structures and churches, including the Church of Hagia Sophia.

He married Theodora in about AD 522. Together they worked to restore the power, beauty, and strength of a vast empire. While Justinian was waging military campaigns, Theodora helped create laws to aid women and children and to end government corruption.

Evaluating Which of Justinian and Theodora's accomplishments do you find most impressive? Why?

Political crises also contributed to the decline. By the 400s **corruption**, the decay of people's values, had become widespread in Roman government. Corrupt officials used threats and bribery to achieve their goals, often ignoring the needs of Roman citizens. As a result, Rome's government was no longer **efficient**.

Many wealthy citizens fled to their country estates and created their own armies for protection. Some, however, used these armies to overthrow emperors and take power for themselves. For those people who remained in the cities, life became more difficult. Rome's population decreased, and schools closed. Taxes and prices soared, leaving more Romans poor. By the late 400s Rome was a changed city, and the empire slowly collapsed around it.

> **ACADEMIC VOCABULARY**
> **efficient**
> (i-FI-shuhnt)
> productive and not wasteful

READING CHECK Analyzing Information
Why did Rome fall to invaders in the 400s?

A New Eastern Empire

Despite the fall of Rome, the eastern empire grew in wealth and power. Its people created a new society that was different from the society in the west.

Justinian

The eastern emperors dreamed of retaking Rome. For **Justinian** (juh-STIN-ee-uhn), an emperor who ruled from 527 to 565, reuniting the old Roman Empire was a passion. His armies conquered Italy and much land around the Mediterranean.

Justinian's other passions were the law and the church. He ordered officials to remove any out-of-date or unchristian laws. He then organized all the laws into a new legal system called Justinian's Code. By simplifying Roman law, this code helped guarantee fair treatment for all.

Despite his successes, Justinian made many enemies. In 532 an uprising

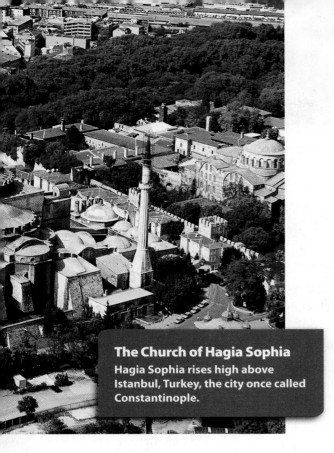

The Church of Hagia Sophia
Hagia Sophia rises high above Istanbul, Turkey, the city once called Constantinople.

The importance of Christianity in the eastern empire is reflected in the Byzantines' beautiful works of art and magnificent churches. As time passed, people began to interpret and practice Christianity differently in the east and the west. Eventually these differences led to a split within the Christian Church. In the 1000s Christians in the east formed the Orthodox Church. As a result, eastern and western Europe were divided by religion.

THE IMPACT TODAY
The Orthodox faith is still the main religion in Russia, Greece, and other parts of eastern Europe.

READING CHECK Drawing Conclusions
Why did Justinian reorganize Roman law?

SUMMARY AND PREVIEW After the fall of Rome, Roman power shifted east. The Orthodox Church became a major force in the Byzantine Empire. Next, you will learn about members of another religious group—the Muslims.

threatened to drive him from Constantinople. However, his smart and powerful wife **Theodora** (thee-uh-DOHR-uh) convinced him to stay and fight. Taking her advice, Justinian crushed the riots and ruled effectively for the rest of his reign.

After Justinian's death, the eastern empire began to decline. Invaders took over all the land Justinian had gained. The empire continued to shrink for the next several hundred years. In 1453 the Ottoman Turks captured Constantinople, bringing an end to the Eastern Roman Empire.

Byzantine Society

The society of the eastern empire was distinct from that of the west. Non-Roman influences took hold in the east. People spoke Greek rather than Latin. Historians call the society that developed in the Eastern Roman Empire the **Byzantine** (BI-zuhn-teen) **Empire**, after Byzantium, the Greek town Constantinople had replaced.

Section 3 Assessment

Reviewing Ideas, Terms, and People
1. **a. Recall** To where did Constantine move Rome's capital?
   b. Explain What effect did Roman farmers' fear of raids have on the empire?
2. **a. Identify** Who was **Attila**?
   b. Analyze Why did the Goths move into the Roman Empire?
3. **a. Summarize** What were two of **Justinian's** major accomplishments?
   b. Contrast Name two ways that the **Byzantine Empire** was different from the Western Roman Empire.

Critical Thinking
4. **Drawing Conclusions** Draw a word web like the one shown. In each of the outer circles, list a factor that helped lead to the fall of the Western Roman Empire. You may make more circles if needed.

Fall of the Western Roman Empire

FOCUS ON WRITING

5. **Adding the Final Details** Add the key events, persons, and places that were covered in this section to the list you have been making. Once your list is complete, review it to get an idea of what to include in your screenplay.

Social Studies Skills

Analysis Critical Thinking Economics Study

Interpreting Time Lines

Understand the Skill

A time line is a visual summary of important events that occurred during a period of history. It displays the events in the order in which they happened. It also shows how long after one event another event took place. In this way time lines allow you to see at a glance what happened and when. You can better see relationships between events and remember important dates when they are displayed on a timeline.

Learn the Skill

Some time lines cover huge spans of time—sometimes even many centuries. Other time lines, such as the one on this page, cover much shorter periods of time.

Time lines can be arranged either vertically or horizontally. This time line is vertical. Its dates are read from top to bottom. Horizontal time lines are read from left to right.

Follow these steps to interpret a time line.

1. Read the time line's title. Note the range of years covered and the intervals of time into which it is divided.

2. Study the order of events on the time line. Note the length of time between events.

3. Note relationships. Ask yourself how an event relates to others on the time line. Look for cause-and-effect relationships and long-term developments.

Practice and Apply the Skill

Interpret the time line to answer the following questions.

1. What is the subject of this time line? What years does it cover?

2. How long did Octavian and Antony rule after dividing Rome?

3. How long after dividing the empire did Antony ally with Cleopatra?

4. What steps did Octavian take to end his alliance with Antony and become emperor? When did he take them? How long did it take?

AUGUSTUS BECOMES EMPEROR

50 BC

45 BC Caesar becomes dictator.

44 BC Caesar is murdered.

43 BC Octavian and Antony decide to rule Rome together.

42 BC Octavian and Antony divide Rome and rule separately.

40 BC

37 BC Antony allies with Cleopatra, queen of Egypt.

31 BC Octavian defeats Antony and Cleopatra in a naval battle near Greece.

30 BC Octavian conquers Egypt. Antony and Cleopatra avoid capture by killing themselves.

30 BC

27 BC Octavian becomes emperor and is renamed Augustus.

23 BC Augustus becomes ruler for life.

Visual Summary

Use the visual summary below to help you review the main ideas of the chapter.

QUICK FACTS

An architectural wonder, the Colosseum in Rome was the site of many types of public entertainment.

The New Testament of the Bible tells the story of Jesus of Nazareth and his disciples.

The Hagia Sophia, the enormous church built during Justinian's reign, served as the spiritual center of the Byzantine Empire.

Reviewing Vocabulary, Terms, and People

1. The orator and philosopher who called on Romans to work together was

a. Constantine.   **c.** Augustus.

b. Caesar.   **d.** Cicero.

2. Latin developed into

a. Byzantium.   **c.** satire.

b. Romance languages.   **d.** Latvian.

3. Another word for God's anointed one is

a. disciple.   **c.** Messiah.

b. Judea.   **d.** Apostle.

4. The Eastern Roman Empire is also called the

a. Lost Empire.   **c.** Constantinople Empire.

b. Byzantine Empire.   **d.** Ottoman Empire.

5. Rome's 200-year period of peace was the

a. Resurrection.   **c.** crucifixion.

b. Pax Romana.   **d.** Age of Theodora.

Comprehension and Critical Thinking

SECTION 1 *(pages 322–328)*

6. a. Describe What action did Cicero recommend? How were the goals of Julius Caesar, Pompey, and Crassus different from Cicero's?

b. Analyze What were the most important events in the life of Julius Caesar? What event best qualifies as a turning point in Caesar's life? Defend your choice.

c. Elaborate How did personal relationships—between Marc Antony and Octavian, and between Marc Antony and Cleopatra—affect the history of the Roman Empire?

SECTION 2 *(pages 332–338)*

7. a. Describe How did the Romans' attitude about religion differ from that of the Jews?

b. Compare What were the crucifixion and the Resurrection? What did early Christians believe that the Resurrection showed?

c. Evaluate Why is Paul of Tarsus considered one of the most important people in the history of Christianity?

SECTION 3 *(pages 339–343)*

8. a. Identify Who were the Huns? Who were the Goths? Who were the Visigoths?

b. Compare and Contrast What did Diocletian and Constantine have in common? How did their actions differ?

c. Elaborate Who were Justinian and Theodora, and what did they accomplish?

Reviewing Themes

9. Geography How did the geography of the Roman Empire affect the spread of Christianity?

10. Science and Technology What do you feel was Rome's greatest scientific or technological advance? Why?

Using the Internet

11. Activity Go online to conduct research on what happened to Roman law when Rome changed from a republic to an empire. Then create a chart that gives examples of how Roman law influences modern issues such as the rights and responsibilities of individuals.

Reading Skills

12. Online Research Imagine you are evaluating a Web site about ancient Roman architecture. What are some important elements you might look for to determine whether the site will be helpful and accurate? Write three questions you could use to evaluate the site's value.

Social Studies Skills

13. Interpreting Time Lines Look at the time line on page 344. Then, using information you will find in the first section of this chapter, add an entry about Cicero to the time line. Be sure you put it in the correct place.

FOCUS ON WRITING

14. Creating Your Note Cards Now that you've taken notes about the people, places, and events of Rome during this time period, you're ready to prepare note cards. Choose the most interesting details from your chart to include on your cards. On each card write a one-to-two sentence description of a person, place, or event that you think should be featured in this screenplay. Then write another sentence that tells why you think the person, place, or event should be featured. Prepare six cards that you could give to a screenwriter to use to develop the script.

DIRECTIONS: Read each question and write the letter of the best response. Use the time line below to answer question 1.

1

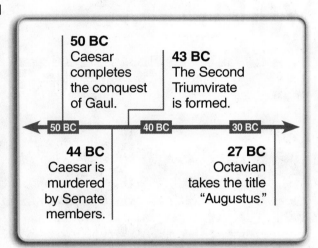

50 BC
Caesar completes the conquest of Gaul.

43 BC
The Second Triumvirate is formed.

50 BC   40 BC   30 BC

44 BC
Caesar is murdered by Senate members.

27 BC
Octavian takes the title "Augustus."

Most historians mark the end of the Roman Republic and the beginning of the Roman Empire as taking place in the year

A 50 BC.

B 44 BC.

C 43 BC.

D 27 BC.

2 **Which Roman leader seized power from the Senate and became the dictator of the entire Roman Republic?**

A Julius Caesar

B Hadrian

C Brutus

D Marc Antony

3 **Rome's contributions to the world include all of the following *except***

A techniques used to build strong bridges and other structures.

B the building of pyramids.

C the idea of civil law.

D the use of Latin, which led to the development of the Romance languages.

4 **Who was most responsible for spreading the Christian faith immediately after the death of Jesus?**

A Octavian

B Diocletian

C Paul of Tarsus

D Theodora of Constantinople

5 **In AD 410 the city of Rome was destroyed for the first time in 800 years by the army of a foreign people called the**

A Vandals.

B Visigoths.

C Huns.

D Franks.

Connecting with Past Learnings

6 **Constantine united the entire Roman Empire and introduced a new religion into the Roman government. Which leader that you learned about in an earlier chapter is known for his similar accomplishments?**

A Asoka

B Hammurabi

C Alexander

D Piankhi

7 **Earlier in this course, you learned that the Persians threatened Greek civilization for a time. All the following peoples played a similar role in Roman history *except***

A the Byzantines.

B the Goths.

C the Vandals.

D the Huns.

ROME:
ENGINEERING AN EMPIRE

The Roman Empire was one of the largest and most powerful empires in ancient history. With its strong military, the Roman Empire expanded to dominate the entire Mediterranean region, including much of western Europe and northern Africa. Keys to this expansion were the engineering and construction innovations made by Roman engineers. As the empire grew and prospered, Roman engineers made advances in city planning, road and bridge design, water and sewage systems, and many other areas.

Explore some of the incredible monuments and engineering achievements of the Roman Empire online. You can find a wealth of information, video clips, primary sources, activities, and more online.

The Glory of the Colosseum

Watch the video to go inside the Colosseum, Rome's premier entertainment venue and one of the most famous buildings of the Roman Empire.

Caesar Builds an Empire

Watch the video to learn why Julius Caesar built a bridge across the Rhine River as a demonstration of Roman power.

Growth of the Roman Empire

› Explore the map to analyze the growth of one of the largest empires of the ancient world.

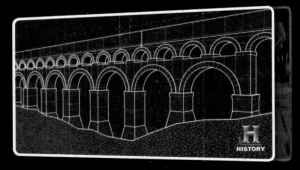

Arches, Angles, Innovations

Watch the video to learn about Roman engineering advances and the construction of aqueducts.

Historical Problem and Solution

Assignment
Write about a problem the Romans faced and what their solution was or what you think would be a better solution.

History is the story of how individuals have solved political, economic, and social problems. Learning to write an effective problem-solution paper will be useful in school and in many other situations.

1. Prewrite

Identifying a Problem
Think of a problem the Romans faced. Look at the problem closely. What caused it? What were its effects? Here is an example.
Problem: The Gauls overran Rome.
Solution A: Pay the Gauls a huge ransom to leave Rome. [caused other cities to attack in the hope of getting similar ransoms]
Solution B: Attack other cities. [caused other cities to stop attacking Rome; let Rome gain power and wealth]

Finding a Solution and Proof
Compare the Roman solution to the problem to one they didn't try. Choose either the Roman solution or your own solution to write about. Your explanation should answer these questions.
- How does the solution address the cause of the problem?
- How does the solution fix the effects of the problem?

Use historical evidence to support what you say about the problem:
- facts, examples, or quotations
- comparisons with similar problems your readers know about

2. Write
This framework can help you clearly explain the problem and its solution.

A Writer's Framework

Introduction
- Tell your reader what problem the Romans faced.
- Explain the causes and effects of the problem.
- State your purpose in presenting this problem and its solution.

Body
- Explain the solution.
- Connect the solution directly to the problem.
- Give supporting historical evidence and details that show how the solution deals with the problem.

Conclusion
- Summarize the problem and the solution.
- Discuss how well the solution deals with the problem.

3. Evaluate and Revise

Evaluating

Now you'll want to evaluate your draft to see where you can improve your paper. Try using the following questions to decide what to revise.

Evaluation Questions for a Historical Problem and Solution

- Does your introduction state the problem clearly and describe it fully?
- Does the introduction give causes and effects of the problem?
- Do you clearly explain how the solution relates to the problem?

- Do you give supporting historical evidence showing how the solution deals with the problem?
- Do you conclude by summarizing the problem and the solution?

TIP **Problem-Solution Clue Words.** It's not enough simply to tell your reader what the problem and solution are. You need to show how they are related. Here is a list of words and phrases that will help you do so.

as a result	therefore
consequently	this led to
nevertheless	thus

Revising

Revise your draft to make what you say clear and convincing. You may need to

- Add historical facts, examples, quotations and other evidence to give your readers all the information they need to understand the problem and solution
- Reorganize paragraphs to present information in a clear, logical order
- Insert words like *thus, therefore,* and *as a result* to show how causes link to effects and how the solution deals with the problem

4. Proofread and Publish

Proofreading

To improve your paper before sharing it, check the following:

- spelling of all names, places, and other historical information, especially Latin words, because they can be tricky
- punctuation around linking words such as *so, thus,* and *in addition* that you use to connect causes with effects and solutions with problems

Publishing

Choose one or more of these ideas to share your report.

- Create a poster that Roman leaders might put up to announce how they will solve the problem.
- Hold a debate between teams of classmates who have chosen similar problems but different solutions. Have the rest of the class vote on whose solutions are best.

TIP **Seeing Your Paper as Others See It.** To you, your paper makes perfect sense. To others, it may not. Whenever possible, ask someone else to read your paper. Others can see flaws and errors that you never will see. Listen closely to questions and suggestions. Do your best to see the other person's point before defending what you have written.

● Practice and Apply

Use the steps and strategies outlined in this workshop to write a problem-solution paper.

Islamic
and African
Civilizations

What You Will Learn...

In the 600s a man named Muhammad introduced the religion of Islam to the people of Southwest Asia. One hundred years later, Islam had spread throughout the region, across North Africa, and into parts of Europe. Later, Islam spread into West Africa, the home of rich and vibrant trading kingdoms.

In the next two chapters, you will learn about the rise and spread of Islam and the kingdoms of West Africa into which it spread.

Explore the Art

In this scene, a young Muslim traveler named Leo Africanus visits an official of the West African Songhai Empire. What does this scene suggest about the role of Islam in Songhai?

FLORIDA...
The Story Continues

CHAPTER 12, The Islamic World (550–1650)

PEOPLE **1528: Estevanico travels with the Pánfilo de Narváez expedition to Florida.** In 1528 an expedition led by Pánfilo de Narváez anchored off the Florida coast near Tampa. The expeditions mission was to explore the land and found a colony. Narváez came ashore with a party of some 300 men, including Estevanico, a Moroccan-born Muslim slave. Narváez ordered his ship captains to sail for a harbor up the coast. The landing party would meet them there. That proved a foolish command. The ship captains found what they thought was the right harbor, but the landing party never appeared. Unable to find the ships, Narváez and his men marched north toward the lands of the Apalachee in the Florida panhandle. The Apalachee did not welcome the party. Under attack from the Apalachee, weak from illness, and low on food, the party headed for a bay. There they constructed barges on which to make an escape. They killed their horses for food, and used their shirts to make sails. After six weeks of work, they set sail, only to capsize in a storm off the coast of Texas. In the end, only four of the landing party survived, among them Estevanico.

PLACES **1926: Opa-locka is founded in Miami-Dade County.**
Opa-locka is home to the largest collection of Moorish architecture in the United States. The town was the creation of aviation pioneer Glenn Curtiss. Curtiss became fascinated with Islamic architecture after seeing the 1924 silent film *The Thief of Baghdad*. Curtiss and architect Bernhardt Muller designed the town to look like a Muslim city—or at least how they imagined a Muslim city might look. The buildings had domes and minarets. They named the streets after characters in *One Thousand and One Nights*. A 1926 hurricane destroyed many of Opa-Locka's

buildings. Of the remaining Moorish buildings, 20 are listed on the National Register of Historic Places.

PLACES 1970s: Mosques are founded in South Florida.

Islam is one of the fastest growing religions in Florida today. Some of the oldest mosques in South Florida were founded in the 1970s. Masjid Miami—the Mosque of Miami—was founded in 1974. Masjid Al-Iman in Fort Lauderdale was also founded in the 1970s. Masjid Al-Ansar, located in the Liberty City area of Miami, began as a Nation of Islam mosque. Since the 1970s, it has followed the teachings of Muhammad and the Qur'an.

PEOPLE 1988: Khadijah Rivera founds PIEDAD.

Islamic organizations estimate that there are about 40,000 Hispanic converts to Islam in the United States. Khadijah Rivera (1950–2009) was raised a Roman Catholic in a Hispanic family. As an adult she converted to Sunni Islam. In 1988 Rivera founded PIEDAD—Propagación Islámica para la Educación e la Devoción a Alá el Divino—to educate and support Hispanic women who convert to Islam. Over the years, the organization broadened its mission to include assisting all women who convert to Islam. In addition to her work with PIEDAD, Rivera was a teacher and community organizer in Tampa.

EVENTS Present: The Appleton Museum of Art showcases Islamic art.

The Appleton Museum of Art is located in Ocala. Among the museum's permanent collections are many fine examples of Islamic art and artifacts. The museum has more than 100 pieces of Islamic pottery dating from the 700s to 1700s. The pottery collection includes many bowls, jars, and jugs. The museum's Islamic artifacts also include twelfth-century bronze pieces, silver Turkman jewelry, rugs, and weapons.

Unpacking the Florida Standards ◁···

Read the following to learn what this standard says and what it means. See FL8–FL31 to unpack all of the standards related to this chapter.

Benchmark SS.6.G.2.5   Interpret how geographic boundaries invite or limit interaction with other regions and cultures. Examples are China limits and Greece invites.

What does it mean?

Explore how the interaction between regions and cultures has been encouraged or hindered by geographic boundaries.

SPOTLIGHT ON

SS.6.E.3.2, SS.6.E.3.4 See pages FL38 and FL39 for content specifically related to these Chapter 12 standards.

CHAPTER **12** 550–1650

The Islamic World

Essential Question How were Muslim leaders able to spread Islam and create an empire?

Florida Next Generation Sunshine State Standards

LA.6.1.7.1 The student will use background knowledge of subject and related content areas, prereading strategies, graphic representations, and knowledge of text structure to make and confirm complex predictions of content, purpose, and organization of a reading selection. **SS.6.E.3.2** Categorize products that were traded among civilizations, and give examples of barriers to trade of those products. **SS.6.E.3.4** Describe the relationship among civilizations that engage in trade, including the benefits and drawbacks of voluntary trade. **SS.6.G.1.4** Utilize tools geographers use to study the world. **SS.6.G.1.6** Use a map to identify major bodies of water of the world, and explain ways they have impacted the development of civilizations. **SS.6.G.2.5** Interpret how geographic boundaries invite or limit interaction with other regions and cultures. **SS.6.G.4.1** Explain how family and ethnic relationships influenced ancient cultures. **SS.6.G.4.4** Map and analyze the impact of the spread of various belief systems in the ancient world. **SS.6.G.6.2** Compare maps of the world in ancient times with current political maps. **SS.6.W.1.1** Use timelines to identify chronological order of historical events. **SS.6.W.1.3** Interpret primary and secondary sources.

FOCUS ON WRITING

A Web Site for Children Design a Web site to tell children about the life of the prophet Muhammad, the religion of Islam, and the history and culture of the Muslim people. You'll design five pages: a home page and four links—Who Was Muhammad? What Is Islam? The Islamic Empires, and Islamic Cultural Achievements. As you read, think about what information will be interesting to your audience.

CHAPTER EVENTS

c. 550 Trade routes cross Arabia.

c. 570 Muhammad is born in Mecca.

550   600

WORLD EVENTS

618 The Tang dynasty begins in China.

This photo shows thousands of people praying in Mecca, the place where Islam began. Mecca is the most sacred place in the Islamic world.

622 Muhammad leaves Mecca.

632 Muhammad dies.

762 Baghdad becomes the capital of the Islamic Empire.

1453 The Ottomans capture Constantinople.

1501 The Safavids conquer Persia.

1631 Shah Jahan begins building the Taj Mahal.

650

700

1500

1650

657 An Indian mathematician introduces the concept of zero.

700s Viking raids begin in northern Europe.

1215 English nobles force King John to accept the Magna Carta.

1521 Cortés conquers the Aztec Empire.

1588 England defeats the Spanish Armada.

Reading Social Studies

Focus on Themes In this chapter, you will learn about the origins and **geographic** spread of one of the world's great **religions,** Islam. You will read about the founder, Muhammad, and how he united much of Arabia under Muslim rule. You will also learn about great conquests and powerful Muslim rulers. Finally, you will read about the outstanding achievements of Islamic scientists, artists, and scholars.

Questioning

Focus on Reading Asking yourself questions is a good way to be sure that you understand what you are reading. You should always ask yourself who the most important people are, when and where they lived, and what they did.

Analytical Questions Questions can also help you make sense of what happened in the past. Asking questions about how and why things happened will help you better understand historical events.

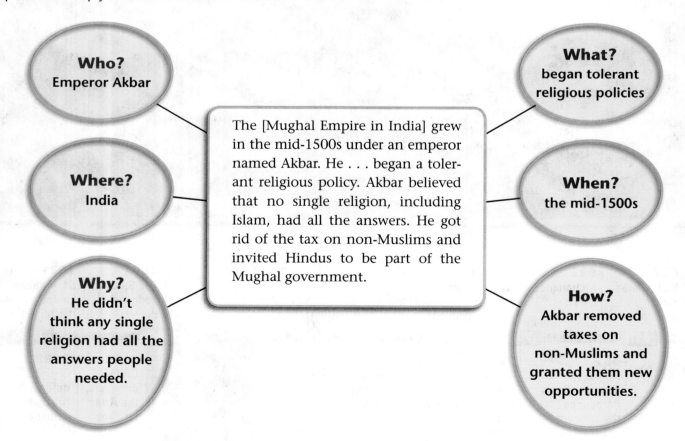

Who?
Emperor Akbar

What?
began tolerant religious policies

Where?
India

When?
the mid-1500s

Why?
He didn't think any single religion had all the answers people needed.

How?
Akbar removed taxes on non-Muslims and granted them new opportunities.

The [Mughal Empire in India] grew in the mid-1500s under an emperor named Akbar. He . . . began a tolerant religious policy. Akbar believed that no single religion, including Islam, had all the answers. He got rid of the tax on non-Muslims and invited Hindus to be part of the Mughal government.

LA.6.1.7.1 The student will use background knowledge of subject and related content areas, prereading strategies, graphic representations, and knowledge of text structure to make and confirm complex predictions of content, purpose, and organization of a reading selection.

You Try It!

Read the following passage and then answer the questions.

Geography

During the mid-1100s, a Muslim geographer named al-Idrisi collected information from Arab travelers. He was writing a geography book and wanted it to be very accurate. When al-Idrisi had a question about where a mountain, river, or coastline was, he sent trained geographers to figure out its exact location. Using the information the geographers brought back, al-Idrisi made some important discoveries. For example, he proved that land did not go all the way around the Indian Ocean as many people thought.

Answer these questions based on the passage you just read.

1. Who is this passage about?

2. What is he known for doing?

3. When did he live?

4. Why did he do what he did?

5. How did he accomplish his task?

6. How can knowing this information help you understand the past?

> **As you read Chapter 12,** ask questions to help you understand what you are reading.

Key Terms and People

Chapter 12

Section 1
oasis *(p. 354)*
caravan *(p. 355)*
Muhammad *(p. 356)*
Islam *(p. 356)*
Muslim *(p. 356)*
Qur'an *(p. 356)*
pilgrimage *(p. 356)*
mosque *(p. 357)*

Section 2
jihad *(p. 359)*
Sunnah *(p. 359)*
Five Pillars of Islam *(p. 360)*

Section 3
Abu Bakr *(p. 362)*
caliph *(p. 362)*
Janissaries *(p. 364)*
Mehmed II *(p. 364)*
Suleyman I *(p. 364)*
Shia *(p. 365)*
Sunni *(p. 365)*
tolerance *(p. 366)*

Section 4
Ibn Battutah *(p. 369)*
Sufism *(p. 369)*
Omar Khayyám *(p. 371)*
patrons *(p. 371)*
minaret *(p. 371)*
calligraphy *(p. 371)*

Academic Vocabulary

Success in school is related to knowing academic vocabulary— the words that are frequently used in school assignments and discussions. In this chapter, you will learn the following academic words:

influence *(p. 356)*
development *(p. 364)*

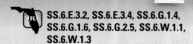

SS.6.E.3.2, SS.6.E.3.4, SS.6.G.1.4,
SS.6.G.1.6, SS.6.G.2.5, SS.6.W.1.1,
SS.6.W.1.3

The Roots of Islam

What You Will Learn...

Main Ideas

1. Arabia is mostly a desert land, where two ways of life, nomadic and sedentary, developed.
2. A new religion called Islam, founded by Muhammad, spread throughout Arabia in the 600s.

The Big Idea

In the harsh desert climate of Arabia, Muhammad, a merchant from Mecca, introduced a major world religion called Islam.

Key Terms

oasis, *p. 354*
caravan, *p. 355*
Muhammad, *p. 356*
Islam, *p. 356*
Muslim, *p. 356*
Qur'an, *p. 356*
pilgrimage, *p. 356*
mosque, *p. 357*

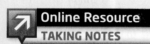

Online Resource

TAKING NOTES

Use the graphic organizer online to take notes on key places, people, and events in the origins of Islam.

If YOU were there...

You live in a town in Arabia, in a large merchant family. Your family has grown rich from selling goods brought by traders crossing the desert. Your house is larger than most others in town, and you have servants to wait on you. Although many townspeople are poor, you have always taken such differences for granted. Now you hear that some people are saying the rich should give money to the poor.

How might your family react to this idea?

BUILDING BACKGROUND For thousands of years, traders have crossed the deserts of Arabia to bring goods to market. Scorching temperatures and lack of water have made the journey difficult. But Arabia not only developed into a thriving trade center, it also became the birthplace of a new religion that challenged old ideas.

Life in a Desert Land

The Arabian Peninsula, or Arabia, is located in the southwest corner of Asia. It lies near the intersection of Africa, Europe, and Asia. For thousands of years Arabia's location, physical features, and climate have shaped life in the region.

Physical Features and Climate

Arabia lies in a region with hot and dry air. With a blazing sun and clear skies, summer temperatures in the interior reach 100°F daily. This climate has created a band of deserts across Arabia and northern Africa. Sand dunes, or hills of sand shaped by the wind, can rise to 800 feet high and stretch for hundreds of miles!

Arabia's deserts have a very limited amount of water. What water there is exists mainly in scattered oases. An **oasis** is a wet, fertile area in a desert. Oases have long been key stops along Arabia's overland trade routes.

Two Ways of Life

To live in Arabia's difficult desert environment, people developed two main ways of life. Nomads lived in tents and raised herds of sheep, goats, and camels. The animals provided milk, meat, wool, and leather. Camels carried heavy loads and provided dung, which the nomads burned to keep warm, since there were few trees in the desert. Nomads traveled with their herds in search of food and water for their animals.

Among the nomads, water and grazing land belonged to tribes. Membership in a tribe, a group of related people, offered protection from desert dangers.

Other Arabs lived a sedentary, or settled, life in oases where they could farm. These settlements, particularly the ones along trade routes, became towns. Merchants and craftspeople lived there and worked with people in the caravan trade. A **caravan** is a group of traders that travel together.

Towns became centers of trade. Many had a market or bazaar. There, nomads traded animal products for goods. Merchants sold spices, gold, leather, and other goods brought by the caravans.

READING CHECK **Categorizing** What two ways of life were common in Arabia?

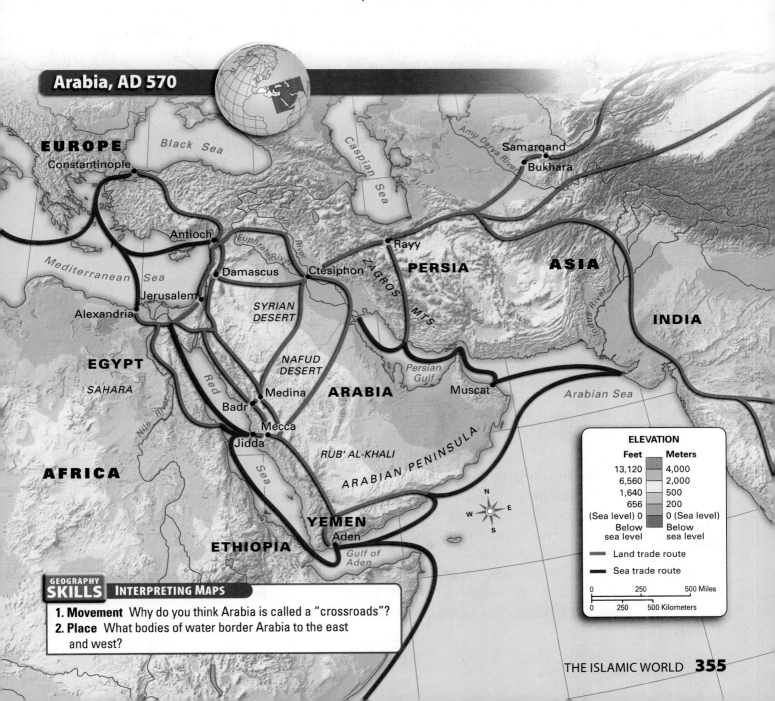

Arabia, AD 570

GEOGRAPHY SKILLS **INTERPRETING MAPS**

1. **Movement** Why do you think Arabia is called a "crossroads"?
2. **Place** What bodies of water border Arabia to the east and west?

THE ISLAMIC WORLD **355**

A New Religion

In early times, Arabs worshipped many gods. That changed, however, when a man named **Muhammad** brought a new religion to Arabia. Historians know little about Muhammad. What they do know comes from religious writings.

Muhammad, Prophet of Islam

FOCUS ON READING

Write a question you could use to analyze the text in this paragraph. Then answer it.

Muhammad was born into an important family in the city of Mecca around 570. As a child, he traveled with his uncle's caravans. Once he was grown, he managed a caravan business owned by a wealthy woman named Khadijah (ka-DEE-jah). At age 25, Muhammad married Khadijah.

The caravan trade made Mecca a rich city. But most of the wealth belonged to just a few people. Traditionally, wealthy people in Mecca had helped the poor. But as Muhammad was growing up, many rich merchants began to ignore the needy.

Concerned about these changes, Muhammad often went to the hills to pray and meditate. One day, when he was about 40 years old, he went to meditate in a cave. According to religious writings, an angel spoke to Muhammad, telling him to "Recite! Recite!" Muhammad asked what he should recite. The angel answered:

> " Recite in the name of your Lord who created, created man from clots of blood!
> Recite! Your Lord is the Most Bountiful One,
> Who by the pen taught man what he did not know."
>
> —From , translated by N. J. Dawood

Muslims believe that God had spoken to Muhammad through the angel and had made him a prophet, a person who tells of messages from God. The messages Muhammad believed he received form the basis of the religion **Islam**. In Arabic, *Islam* means "to submit to God." A follower of Islam is called a **Muslim**. Muslims

ACADEMIC VOCABULARY

influence
change, or have an effect on

believe that Muhammad continued receiving messages from God for the rest of his life. These messages were collected in the **Qur'an** (kuh-RAN), the holy book of Islam.

Muhammad's Teachings

In 613 Muhammad began to talk about his messages. He taught that there was only one God, Allah, which means "the God" in Arabic. Islam is monotheistic, a religion based on the belief in one God, like Judaism and Christianity. Although people of all three religions believe in one God, their beliefs about God are not the same.

Muhammad's teachings were new to Arabs, most of whom practiced polytheism. They had many shrines, or special places where they worshipped their gods. A very important shrine, the Kaaba (KAH-bah), was in Mecca. People traveled there every year on a **pilgrimage**, a journey to a sacred place.

Muhammad's teachings upset many Arabs. First, they didn't like being told to stop worshipping their gods. Second, Muhammad's new religion seemed like a threat to people who made money from the yearly pilgrimages to the Kaaba.

Mecca's wealthy merchants didn't like another of Muhammad's teachings: that everyone who believed in Allah would become part of a community in which rich and poor would be equal. Rich merchants also disliked Muhammad's idea that people should give money to help the poor. The merchants wanted to keep all of their money and remain more powerful than the poor.

Islam Spreads in Arabia

At first Muhammad had few followers. Slowly, more people began to listen to his ideas. As Islam began to **influence** people, Mecca's rulers became worried. They threatened Muhammad and even planned to kill him.

A group of people living north of Mecca invited Muhammad to move to their city.

Beginnings of Islam

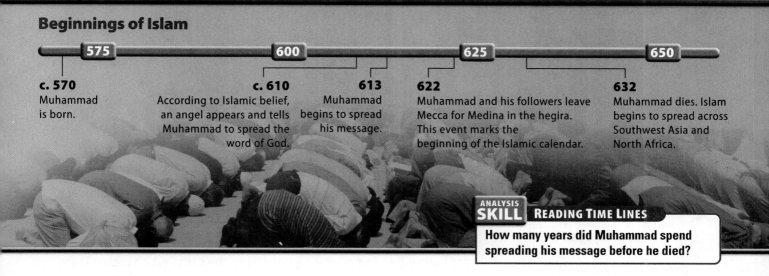

575 — **600** — **625** — **650**

c. 570
Muhammad is born.

c. 610
According to Islamic belief, an angel appears and tells Muhammad to spread the word of God.

613
Muhammad begins to spread his message.

622
Muhammad and his followers leave Mecca for Medina in the hegira. This event marks the beginning of the Islamic calendar.

632
Muhammad dies. Islam begins to spread across Southwest Asia and North Africa.

ANALYSIS SKILL **READING TIME LINES**

How many years did Muhammad spend spreading his message before he died?

So in 622 Muhammad and many followers went to Medina (muh-DEE-nuh). *Medina* means "the Prophet's city" in Arabic. Muhammad's departure from Mecca is known as the hegira (hi-JY-ruh), or journey.

Muhammad became a spiritual and political leader in Medina. His house became the first **mosque** (mahsk), or building for Muslim prayer.

As the Muslim community in Medina grew stronger, other Arab tribes began to accept Islam. But conflict with the Meccans increased. In 630, after several years of fighting, the people of Mecca gave in. They accepted Islam as their religion.

Soon most of the Arabian tribes accepted Muhammad as their spiritual and political leader and became Muslims. Muhammad died in 632, but the religion he taught would soon spread far beyond Arabia.

READING CHECK **Summarizing** How did Islam spread in Arabia?

SUMMARY AND PREVIEW The geography of Arabia encouraged trade and influenced the development of nomadic and sedentary lifestyles. In the early 600s Muhammad introduced a new religion to Arabia. Many people in Arabia became Muslims. In the next section, you will learn more about the main Islamic teachings and beliefs.

Section 1 Assessment

Reviewing Ideas, Terms, and People

1. **a. Define** What is an **oasis**?
   b. Make Generalizations Why did towns often develop near oases?
   c. Predict Do you think life would have been better for nomads or townspeople in early Arabia? Explain your answer.
2. **a. Identify** What is a key Islamic belief about God?
   b. Explain According to Islamic belief, how did **Muhammad** get the ideas that started **Islam**?
   c. Evaluate In what ways was Muhammad's time in Medina important to the growth of Islam?

Critical Thinking

3. **Sequencing** Draw a time line like the one below. Using your notes on Muhammad, identify the key dates in his life.

FOCUS ON WRITING

4. **Writing about Muhammad** Review your notes to answer the question, "Who was Muhammad?" It may help to think of Muhammad's life in three parts: "Early Life," "Muhammad Becomes a Prophet," and "Muhammad's Teachings."

Islamic Beliefs and Practices

If **YOU** were there...

Your family owns an inn in Mecca. Usually business is pretty calm, but this week your inn is packed. Travelers have come from all over the world to visit your city. One morning you leave the inn and are swept up in a huge crowd of these visitors. They speak many different languages, but everyone is wearing the same white robes. They are headed to the mosque.

What might draw so many people to your city?

BUILDING BACKGROUND One basic Islamic belief is that everyone who can must make a trip to Mecca sometime during his or her lifetime. More Islamic teachings can be found in Islam's holy books—the Qur'an and the Sunnah.

The Qur'an

During Muhammad's life, his followers memorized his messages and his words and deeds. After Muhammad's death, they collected his teachings and wrote them down to form the book known as the Qur'an. Muslims believe the Qur'an to be the exact word of God as it was told to Muhammad.

Beliefs

The central teaching in the Qur'an is that there is only one God—Allah—and that Muhammad is his prophet. The Qur'an says people must obey Allah's commands. Muslims learned of these commands from Muhammad.

Islam teaches that the world had a definite beginning and will end one day. Muhammad said that on the final day God will judge all people. Those who have obeyed his orders will be granted life in paradise. According to the Qur'an, paradise is a beautiful garden full of fine food and drink. People who have not obeyed God, however, will suffer.

Studying the Qur'an
The Qur'an plays a central role in the lives of many Muslims. Children study and memorize verses from the Qur'an at home, at Islamic schools, and in mosques. Muslims who memorize the entire book are respected as "Keepers" of the Qur'an.

Where do you think these children are studying the Qur'an?

Guidelines for Behavior

Like holy books of other religions, the Qur'an describes acts of worship, guidelines for moral behavior, and rules for social life. Muslims look to the Qur'an for guidance in their daily lives. For example, the Qur'an describes how to prepare for worship. Muslims must wash themselves before praying so they will be pure before Allah. The Qur'an also tells Muslims what they should not eat or drink. Muslims are not allowed to eat pork or drink alcohol.

In addition to guidelines for individual behavior, the Qur'an describes relations among people. Many of these ideas changed Arabian society. For example, before Muhammad's time many Arabs owned slaves. Although slavery didn't disappear among Muslims, the Qur'an encourages Muslims to free slaves. Also, women in Arabia had few rights. The Qur'an describes rights of women, including rights to own property, earn money, and get an education. However, most Muslim women still have fewer rights than men.

Another important subject in the Qur'an has to do with **jihad** (ji-HAHD), which means "to make an effort, or to struggle." Jihad refers to the inner struggle people go through in their effort to obey God and behave according to Islamic ways. Jihad can also mean the struggle to defend the Muslim community, or, historically, to convert people to Islam. The word has also been translated as "holy war."

READING CHECK **Analyzing** Why is the Qur'an important to Muslims?

The Sunnah

The Qur'an is not the only source of Islamic teachings. Muslims also study the hadith (huh-DEETH), the written record of Muhammad's words and actions. This record is the basis for the Sunnah. The **Sunnah** (SOOH-nuh) refers to the way Muhammad lived, which provides a model for the duties and the way of life expected of Muslims. The Sunnah guides Muslims' behavior.

QUICK FACTS

The Five Pillars of Islam

Saying "There is no god but God, and Muhammad is his prophet"

Praying five times a day

Giving to the poor and needy

Fasting during the holy month of Ramadan

Traveling to Mecca at least once on a hajj

ANALYSIS SKILL **ANALYZING VISUALS**

Which of the five pillars shows how Muslims are supposed to treat other people?

The Five Pillars of Islam

The first duties of a Muslim are known as the **Five Pillars of Islam**, which are five acts of worship required of all Muslims. The first pillar is a statement of faith. At least once in their lives, Muslims must state their faith by saying, "There is no god but God, and Muhammad is his prophet." Muslims say this when they accept Islam. They also say it in their daily prayers.

The second pillar of Islam is daily prayer. Muslims must pray five times a day: before sunrise, at midday, in late afternoon, right after sunset, and before going to bed. At each of these times, a call goes out from a mosque, inviting Muslims to come pray. Muslims try to pray together at a mosque. They believe prayer is proof that someone has accepted Allah.

The third pillar of Islam is a yearly donation to charity. Muslims must pay part of their wealth to a religious official. This money is used to help the poor, build mosques, or pay debts. Helping and caring for others is important in Islam.

The fourth pillar is fasting—going without food and drink. Muslims fast daily during the holy month of Ramadan (RAH-muh-dahn). The Qur'an says Allah began his revelations to Muhammad in this month. During Ramadan, most Muslims will not eat or drink anything between dawn and sunset. Muslims believe fasting is a way to show that God is more important than one's own body. Fasting also reminds Muslims of people in the world who struggle to get enough food.

The fifth pillar of Islam is the hajj (HAJ), a pilgrimage to Mecca. All Muslims must travel to Mecca at least once in their lives if they can. The Kaaba, in Mecca, is Islam's most sacred place.

The Sunnah and Daily Life

In addition to the five pillars, the Sunnah has other examples of Muhammad's actions and teachings. These form the basis for rules about how to treat others. According to Muhammad's example, people should treat guests with generosity.

In addition to describing personal relations, the Sunnah provides guidelines for relations in business and government. For example, one Sunnah rule says that it is bad to owe someone money. Another rule says that people should obey their leaders.

READING CHECK **Generalizing** What do Muslims learn from the Sunnah?

Islamic Law

The Qur'an and the Sunnah are important guides for how Muslims should live. They also form the basis of Islamic law, or Shariah (shuh-REE-uh). Shariah is a system based on Islamic sources and human reason that judges the rightness of actions an individual or community might take. These actions fall on a scale ranging from required to accepted to disapproved to forbidden. Islamic law makes no distinction between religious beliefs and daily life, so Islam affects all aspects of Muslims' lives.

Shariah sets rewards for good behavior and punishments for crimes. It also describes limits of authority. It was the basis for law in Muslim countries until modern times.

Sources of Islamic Beliefs			QUICK FACTS
Qur'an	**Sunnah**	**Shariah**	
Holy book that contains the messages Muhammad claimed to receive from God	Muhammad's example for the duties and way of life expected of Muslims	Islamic law, based on interpretations of the Qur'an and Sunnah	

Most Muslim countries today blend Islamic law with other legal systems to govern their countries.

Islamic law is not found in one book. Instead, it is a set of opinions and writings that have changed over the centuries. Different ideas about Islamic law are found in different Muslim regions.

READING CHECK **Finding Main Ideas** What is the purpose of Islamic law?

SUMMARY AND PREVIEW The Qur'an, the Sunnah, and Shariah teach Muslims how to live their lives. In the next chapter, you will learn more about Muslim culture and the spread of Islam from Arabia to other lands.

Section 2 Assessment

Reviewing Ideas, Terms, and People

1. **a. Recall** What is the central teaching of the Qur'an?
   b. Explain How does the Qur'an guide Muslims' daily lives?
2. **a. Recall** What are the **Five Pillars of Islam**?
   b. Make Generalizations Why do Muslims fast during Ramadan?
3. **a. Identify** What is Islamic law called?
   b. Make Inferences How is Islamic law different from law in the United States?
   c. Elaborate What is a possible reason that opinions and writings about Islamic law have changed over the centuries?

Critical Thinking

4. **Categorizing** Draw a chart like the one to the right. Use it to list three teachings from the Qur'an and three teachings from the Sunnah.

Qur'an	Sunnah

Focus on Writing

5. **Describing Islam** Answer the following questions to help you write a paragraph describing Islam. What is the central teaching of the Qur'an? What are Islam's Five Pillars? What is the function of the Sunnah?

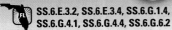
Islamic Empires

SS.6.E.3.2, SS.6.E.3.4, SS.6.G.1.4, SS.6.G.4.1, SS.6.G.4.4, SS.6.G.6.2

What You Will Learn...

Main Ideas

1. Muslim armies conquered many lands into which Islam slowly spread.
2. Trade helped Islam spread into new areas.
3. Three Muslim empires ruled large areas of Asia and Africa and parts of Europe from the 1400s to the 1800s.

The Big Idea

After the early spread of Islam, three large Islamic empires formed—the Ottoman, Safavid, and Mughal.

Key Terms and People

Abu Bakr, *p. 362*
caliph, *p. 362*
Janissaries, *p. 364*
Mehmed II, *p. 364*
Suleyman I, *p. 364*
Shia, *p. 365*
Sunni, *p. 365*
tolerance, *p. 366*

Online Resource
TAKING NOTES

Use the graphic organizer online to take notes on the spread of Islam and the three Islamic empires that were created after Muhammad's death.

If YOU were there...

You are a farmer living in a village on the coast of India. For centuries, your people have raised cotton and spun its fibers into a soft fabric. One day, a ship arrives in the harbor carrying Muslim traders from far away. They bring interesting goods you have never seen before. They also bring new ideas.

What ideas might you learn from the traders?

BUILDING BACKGROUND You know that for years traders traveled through Arabia to markets far away. Along the way, they picked up new goods and ideas, and they introduced these to the people they met. Some of the new ideas the traders spread were Islamic ideas.

Muslim Armies Conquer Many Lands

After Muhammad's death his followers quickly chose **Abu Bakr** (UH-boo BAK-uhr), one of Muhammad's first converts, to be the next leader of Islam. He was the first **caliph** (KAY-luhf), a title that Muslims use for the highest leader of Islam. In Arabic, the word *caliph* means "successor." As Muhammad's successors, the caliphs had to follow the prophet's example. This meant ruling according to the Qur'an. Unlike Muhammad, however, early caliphs were not religious leaders.

Beginnings of an Empire

Abu Bakr directed a series of battles to unite Arabia. By his death in 634, he had made Arabia into a unified Muslim state. With Arabia united, Muslim leaders turned their attention elsewhere. Their armies, strong after their battles in Arabia, won many stunning victories. They defeated the Persian and Byzantine empires, which were weak from many years of fighting.

When the Muslims conquered lands, they set certain rules for non-Muslims living there. For example, some non-Muslims could not build new places of worship or dress like Muslims. Only Christians and Jews could continue to practice their own religions. Although not forced to convert to Islam, they were second-class citizens.

Growth of the Empire

Many early caliphs came from the Umayyad (oom-EYE-yuhd) family. The Umayyads moved the capital to Damascus, in Muslim-conquered Syria, and continued to expand the empire. They took over lands in Central Asia and in northern India. The Umayyads also gained control of trade in the eastern Mediterranean and conquered parts of North Africa.

The Berbers, the native people of North Africa, resisted Muslim rule at first. After years of fighting, however, many Berbers converted to Islam.

In 711 a combined Arab and Berber army invaded Spain and quickly conquered it. Next the army moved into what is now France, but it was stopped by a Christian army near the city of Tours (TOOR). Despite this defeat, Muslims called Moors ruled parts of Spain for the next 700 years.

A new Islamic dynasty, the Abbasids (uh-BAS-idz), came to power in 749. They reorganized the government to make it easier to rule such a large region.

READING CHECK **Analyzing** What role did armies play in spreading Islam?

Trade Helps Islam Spread

Islam gradually spread through areas the Muslims conquered. Trade also helped spread Islam. Along with their goods, Arab merchants took Islamic beliefs to India, Africa, and Southeast Asia. Though Indian kingdoms remained Hindu, coastal trading cities soon had large Muslim communities. In Africa, societies often had both African and Muslim customs. Many African leaders converted to Islam. Between 1200 and 1600, Muslim traders carried Islam east to what are now Malaysia and Indonesia.

Trade also brought new products to Muslim lands. For example, Arabs learned from the Chinese how to make paper and use gunpowder. New crops such as cotton, rice, and oranges arrived from India, China, and Southeast Asia.

Many Muslim merchants traveled to African market towns too. They wanted African products such as ivory, cloves, and slaves. In return they offered fine white pottery called porcelain from China, cloth goods from India, and iron from Southwest Asia and Europe. Arab traders grew wealthy from trade between regions.

THE IMPACT TODAY

Indonesia now has the largest Muslim population in the world.

The City of Córdoba

By the early 900s, Córdoba, Spain, was one of the wealthiest cities in Europe and a center of Islamic learning. Rich examples of Islamic architecture can still be seen in the city.

A Mix of Cultures

As Islam spread through trade and warfare, Arabs came into contact with people who had different beliefs and lifestyles than they did. Muslims generally banned or controlled religious activities of the people they conquered. The Muslims did not ban all other religions in their lands. Because they shared some beliefs with Muslims, Christians and Jews in particular kept many of their rights. They did, however, have to pay a special tax. Members of both faiths were also forbidden from converting anyone to their religion.

Many people conquered by the Arabs converted to Islam. These people often adopted other parts of Arabic culture, including the Arabic language. The Arabs, in turn, adopted some customs from the people they conquered. This cultural blending changed Islam from a mostly Arab religion into a religion of many cultures. But the Arabic language and shared religion helped unify the different groups of the Islamic world.

The Growth of Cities

The growing cities of the Muslim world reflected the blending of cultures. Trade had brought people together and created wealth, which supported great cultural **development** in Muslim cities.

Baghdad, in what is now Iraq, became the capital of the Islamic Empire in 762. Trade and farming made Baghdad one of the world's richest cities. Caliphs at Baghdad supported science and the arts. The city was a center of culture and learning.

Córdoba (KAWR-doh-bah), in Spain, became another showplace of Muslim civilization. By the early 900s Córdoba was the largest and most advanced city in Europe.

READING CHECK **Finding the Main Idea** How did trade affect the spread of Islam?

ACADEMIC VOCABULARY

development
the process of growing or improving

Three Muslim Empires

The great era of Arab Muslim expansion lasted until the 1100s. Afterward, three non-Arab Muslim groups built large, powerful empires that ruled large areas in Asia and Africa and parts of Europe.

The Ottoman Empire

In the mid-1200s Muslim Turkish warriors known as Ottomans began to take territory from the Christian Byzantine Empire. They eventually ruled land from eastern Europe to North Africa and Arabia.

The key to the empire's expansion was the Ottoman army. The Ottomans trained Christian boys from conquered towns to be soldiers. These slave soldiers, called **Janissaries**, converted to Islam and became fierce warriors. The Ottomans also benefitted from their use of new gunpowder weapons.

In 1453 Ottomans led by **Mehmed II** used huge cannons to conquer Constantinople. With the city's capture, Mehmed defeated the Byzantine Empire. He became known as "the Conqueror." Mehmed made Constantinople, which the Ottomans called Istanbul, his new capital. He also turned the Byzantines' great church, Hagia Sophia, into a mosque.

A later sultan, or Ottoman ruler, continued Mehmed's conquests. He expanded the empire to the east through the rest of Anatolia, another name for Asia Minor. His armies also conquered Syria and Egypt. The holy cities of Mecca and Medina then accepted Ottoman rule.

The Ottoman Empire reached its height under **Suleyman I** (soo-lay-MAHN), "the Magnificent." During his rule from 1520 to 1566, the Ottomans took control of the eastern Mediterranean and pushed farther into Europe, areas they would control until the early 1800s.

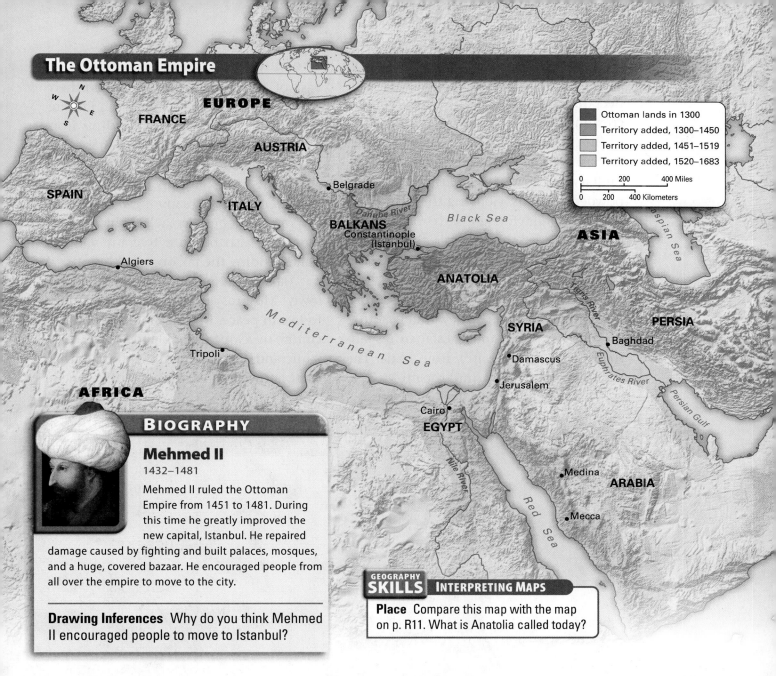

The Ottoman Empire

Map Legend:
- Ottoman lands in 1300
- Territory added, 1300–1450
- Territory added, 1451–1519
- Territory added, 1520–1683

0   200   400 Miles
0   200   400 Kilometers

EUROPE

FRANCE

AUSTRIA

SPAIN

ITALY

Belgrade

Danube River

BALKANS

Constantinople
(Istanbul)

Black Sea

ASIA

ANATOLIA

Caspian Sea

Algiers

Mediterranean Sea

SYRIA

PERSIA

Tripoli

Damascus

Baghdad

Tigris River

Euphrates River

Jerusalem

AFRICA

Cairo

EGYPT

Nile River

Red Sea

Medina

ARABIA

Mecca

Persian Gulf

BIOGRAPHY

Mehmed II
1432–1481

Mehmed II ruled the Ottoman Empire from 1451 to 1481. During this time he greatly improved the new capital, Istanbul. He repaired damage caused by fighting and built palaces, mosques, and a huge, covered bazaar. He encouraged people from all over the empire to move to the city.

Drawing Inferences Why do you think Mehmed II encouraged people to move to Istanbul?

GEOGRAPHY SKILLS **INTERPRETING MAPS**

Place Compare this map with the map on p. R11. What is Anatolia called today?

The Safavid Empire

As the Ottoman Empire reached its height, a group of Persian Muslims known as the Safavids (sah-FAH-vuhds) was gaining power to the east, in the area of present-day Iran. Before long, the Safavids came into conflict with the Ottomans and other Muslims.

The conflict arose from an old disagreement among Muslims about who should be caliph. In the mid-600s, Islam split into two groups. The two groups were the Shia (SHEE-ah) and the Sunni (SOO-nee). The **Shia** were Muslims who thought that only Muhammad's descendants could become caliphs. The **Sunni** didn't think caliphs had to be related to Muhammad. The Ottomans were Sunnis and the Safavid leaders were Shia.

The Safavid Empire began in 1501 when the Safavid leader Esma'il (is-mah-EEL) conquered Persia. He took the ancient Persian title of shah, or king.

Esma'il made Shiism—the beliefs of the Shia—the official religion of the empire. But he wanted to spread Shiism farther.

THE IMPACT TODAY

Most Muslims today belong to the Sunni branch of Islam.

He tried to gain more Muslim lands and convert more Muslims to Shiism. He battled the Uzbek people, but he suffered a crushing defeat by the Ottomans in 1514.

In 1588 the greatest Safavid leader, 'Abbas, became shah. He strengthened the military and gave his soldiers modern gunpowder weapons. Copying the Ottomans, 'Abbas trained foreign slave boys to be soldiers. Under 'Abbas's rule the Safavids defeated the Uzbeks and took back land that had been lost to the Ottomans.

The Safavids blended Persian and Muslim cultural traditions. They built beautiful mosques in their capital, Esfahan (es-fah-HAHN), and grew wealthy from trade. The Safavid Empire lasted until the mid-1700s.

The Mughal Empire

East of the Safavid Empire, in northern India, lay the Mughal (MOO-guhl) Empire. The Mughals were Turkish Muslims from Central Asia. Their empire was established in 1526 by Babur (BAH-boohr).

In the mid-1500s an emperor named Akbar conquered many new lands and worked to strengthen the Mughal government. He also began a tolerant religious policy, ending the tax on non-Muslims.

Akbar's **tolerance,** or acceptance, allowed Muslims and Hindus in the empire to live in peace. In time, a unique Mughal culture developed that blended Persian, Islamic, and Hindu elements. The Mughals became known for their monumental works of

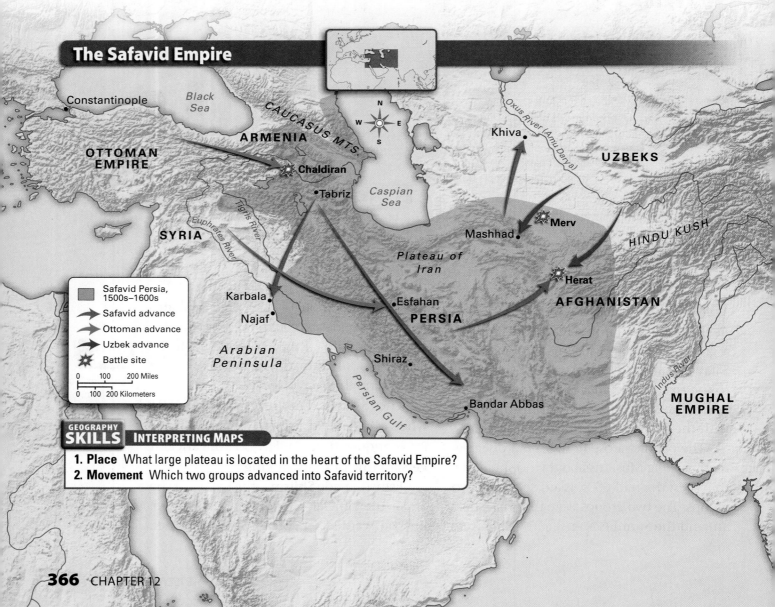

The Safavid Empire

GEOGRAPHY SKILLS INTERPRETING MAPS

1. **Place** What large plateau is located in the heart of the Safavid Empire?
2. **Movement** Which two groups advanced into Safavid territory?

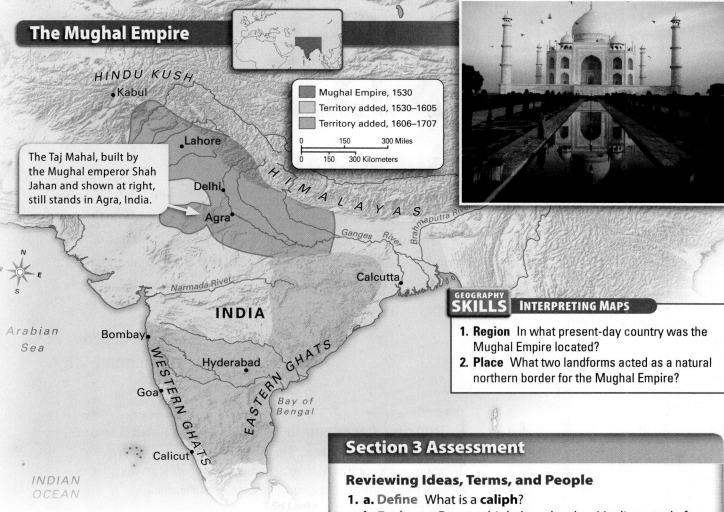

The Mughal Empire

HINDU KUSH
• Kabul

Mughal Empire, 1530
Territory added, 1530–1605
Territory added, 1606–1707

0   150   300 Miles
0 150 300 Kilometers

• Lahore

HIMALAYAS

The Taj Mahal, built by the Mughal emperor Shah Jahan and shown at right, still stands in Agra, India.

Delhi •

Agra •

Brahmaputra River

Ganges River

Narmada River

INDIA

Calcutta •

Bombay •

Hyderabad •

EASTERN GHATS

WESTERN GHATS

Goa •

Arabian Sea

Bay of Bengal

N W E S

Calicut •

INDIAN OCEAN

Sri Lanka

The Taj Mahal, built by the Mughal emperor Shah Jahan and shown at right, still stands in Agra, India.

GEOGRAPHY SKILLS **INTERPRETING MAPS**

1. **Region** In what present-day country was the Mughal Empire located?
2. **Place** What two landforms acted as a natural northern border for the Mughal Empire?

architecture—particularly the Taj Mahal, a tomb built in the 1600s by emperor Shah Jahan.

In the late 1600s, an emperor reversed Akbar's tolerant policies. He destroyed many Hindu temples, and violent revolts broke out. The Mughal Empire soon fell apart.

READING CHECK **Analyzing** How did the Ottomans gain land for their empire?

SUMMARY AND PREVIEW Islam spread beyond Arabia through warfare and trade. The Ottomans, Safavids, and Mughals built great empires and continued the spread of Islam. In Section 4, you will learn about the cultural achievements of the Islamic world.

Section 3 Assessment

Reviewing Ideas, Terms, and People

1. **a. Define** What is a **caliph**?
   b. Evaluate Do you think the rules that Muslims made for conquered non-Muslims were fair? Why or why not?
2. **a. Identify** Name three places Islam spread to through trade.
   b. Explain How did trade help spread Islam?
3. **a. Recall** Who were the **Janissaries**?
   b. Contrast How did Sunni and Shia beliefs about caliphs differ?

Critical Thinking

4. **Comparing and Contrasting** Draw a chart like the one below. Use your notes to compare and contrast characteristics of the Ottoman, Safavid, and Mughal empires.

	Ottomans	Safavids	Mughals
Leaders			
Location			
Religious policy			

FOCUS ON WRITING

5. **Writing about Islamic Empires** Review this section and write a paragraph about the three powerful Islamic empires that began to form in the 1200s.

Cultural Achievements

If YOU were there...

You are a servant in the court of a powerful Muslim ruler. Your life at court is comfortable, though not one of luxury. Now the ruler is sending your master to explore unknown lands and distant kingdoms. The dangerous journey will take him across seas and deserts. He can take only a few servants with him. He has not ordered you to come but has given you a choice.

Would you join your master's expedition or stay home? Why?

BUILDING BACKGROUND Muslim explorers traveled far and wide to learn about new places. They used what they learned to make maps. Their contributions to geography were just one way Muslim scholars made advancements in science and learning.

Science and Philosophy

The empires of the Islamic world contributed to the achievements of Islamic culture. Muslim scholars made advances in astronomy, geography, math, and science. Scholars at Baghdad and Córdoba translated many ancient writings on these subjects into Arabic. Having a common language helped scholars throughout the

Islamic Achievements

Astronomy

Muslim scientists used astrolabes like this one to figure out their location, direction, and even the time of day. Although the Greeks invented the astrolabe, Muslims scholars greatly improved it.

Islamic world share what they learned with each other.

Astronomy

Many Muslim cities had observatories where people could study the sun, moon, and stars. This study of astronomy helped scientists to better understand time and clockmaking. Muslim scientists also improved the astrolabe, which the Greeks had invented to chart the position of the stars. Arab scholars used the astrolabe to figure out their location on Earth.

Geography

Studying astronomy also helped Muslims explore the world. As people learned to use the stars to calculate time and location, merchants and explorers began to travel widely. The explorer **Ibn Battutah** traveled to Africa, India, China, and Spain in the 1320s. To help travelers, Muslim geographers made more accurate maps than were available before, and developed better ways of calculating distances.

Math

Muslim scholars also made advances in mathematics. In the 800s they combined the Indian number system, including the use of zero, with the Greek science of mathematics. A Muslim mathematician used these ideas to write two important books. One laid the foundation for modern algebra. The other explained the new number system. When his works reached Europe, Europeans called the new numbers "Arabic" numerals.

Medicine

Muslims may have made their greatest advances in medicine. They combined Greek and Indian knowledge with discoveries of their own. Muslim doctors started the first pharmacy school to teach people how to make medicine. A doctor in Baghdad discovered how to treat smallpox. Another doctor, known in the West as Avicenna (av-uh-SEN-uh), wrote a medical encyclopedia. It was used throughout Europe until the 1600s and is one of the most famous books in the history of medicine.

Philosophy

Many Muslim doctors and scientists studied the ancient Greek philosophy of rational thought. Others focused on spiritual issues, leading to a movement called **Sufism** (SOO-fi-zuhm). People who practice Sufism are Sufis (SOO-feez). Sufis believe they can find God's love by having a personal relationship with God. Sufism has attracted many followers to Islam.

READING CHECK Drawing Conclusions
How did Muslims influence the fields of science and medicine?

THE IMPACT TODAY

We still call the numerals 0, 1, 2, 3, 4, 5, 6, 7, 8, and 9 Arabic or Hindu-Arabic numerals.

Math

Muslim mathematicians combined Indian and Greek ideas with their own to dramatically increase human knowledge of mathematics. The fact that we call our numbers today "Arabic numerals" is a reminder of this contribution.

Medicine

Muslim doctors made medicines from plants and used them to treat pain and illnesses. Muslim doctors developed better ways to prevent, diagnose, and treat many diseases.

The Blue Mosque

The Blue Mosque in Istanbul was built in the early 1600s for an Ottoman sultan. It upset many people at the time it was built because they thought its six minarets—instead of the usual four—were an attempt to make it as great as the mosque in Mecca.

The mosque gets its name from its beautiful blue Iznik tiles.

Domes are a common feature of Islamic architecture. Huge columns support the center of this dome, and more than 250 windows let light into the mosque.

Tall towers called minarets are a common feature of many mosques.

The most sacred part of a mosque is the mihrab, the niche that points the way to Mecca. This man is praying facing the mihrab.

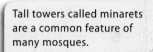

ANALYSIS SKILL **ANALYZING VISUALS**

Why do you think the decoration of the Blue Mosque is so elaborate?

Literature and the Arts

Literature, especially poetry, was popular in the Muslim world. Much poetry was influenced by Sufism. Sufi poets often wrote about their loyalty to God. One of the most famous Sufi poets was **Omar Khayyám** (OH-mahr ky-AHM).

Muslims also enjoyed reading short stories. One famous collection of short stories is *The Thousand and One Nights*. It includes tales about legendary characters such as Sinbad, Aladdin, and Ali Baba.

Architecture was one of the most important Muslim art forms. Rich Muslim rulers became great **patrons**, or sponsors, of architecture. They used their wealth to have beautiful mosques built to honor God and inspire religious followers. The main part of a mosque is a huge hall where people pray. Many mosques also have a large dome and a **minaret**, or narrow tower from where Muslims are called to prayer.

Muslim architects also built palaces, marketplaces, and libraries. Many of these buildings have complicated domes and arches, colored bricks, and decorated tiles.

You may notice, though, that most Muslim art does not show any people or animals. Muslims think only God can create humans and animals or their images. As a result, Muslim art is instead full of complex patterns. Muslim artists also turned to **calligraphy**, or decorative writing. They made sayings from the Qur'an into works of art and used them to decorate mosques and other buildings.

Muslim art and literature combined Islamic influences with the regional traditions of the places Muslims conquered. This mix of Islam with cultures from Asia, Africa, and Europe gave literature and the arts a unique style and character.

READING CHECK **Generalizing** Most mosques include which two architectural elements?

SUMMARY AND PREVIEW Islamic culture produced great achievements in science, philosophy, literature, architecture, and art. In the next chapter, you'll learn about an area that was greatly influenced by Muslim ideas—West Africa.

Section 4 Assessment

Reviewing Ideas, Terms, and People

1. **a. Identify** Who traveled to India, Africa, China, and Spain and contributed his knowledge to the study of geography?
   b. Explain How did Muslim scholars help preserve learning from the ancient world?
   c. Rank In your opinion, what was the most important Muslim scientific achievement? Why?
2. **a. Describe** What function do **minarets** serve in mosques?
   b. Explain How did Muslim artists create art without showing humans or animals?

Critical Thinking

3. **Analyzing** Using your notes, complete a chart like the one at right. For each category in the first column, list one important achievement or advance the Muslims made.

Category	Achievement or Advance
Astronomy	
Geography	
Math	
Medicine	
Philosophy	

FOCUS ON WRITING

4. **Describing Muslim Accomplishments** Review the answers you provided for the graphic organizer above and the information under the Literature and the Arts heading on this page. Then organize what you have learned into a paragraph that describes the cultural achievements of the Muslim world.

Social Studies Skills

Analysis | Critical Thinking | Economics | Study

Understanding Historical Context

Understand the Skill

A *context* is the circumstances under which something happens. *Historical context* includes values, beliefs, conditions, and practices that were common in the past. At times, some of these were quite different than what they are today. To truly understand a historical statement or event, you have to take its context into account. It is not right to judge what people in history did or said based on present-day values alone. To be fair, you must also consider the historical context of the statement or event.

Learn the Skill

To better understand something a historical figure said or wrote, use the following guidelines to understand the context of the statement.

1. Identify the speaker or writer, the date, and the topic and main idea of the statement.

2. Determine the speaker's or writer's attitude and point of view about the topic.

3. Review what you know about beliefs, conditions, or practices related to the topic that were common at the time. Find out more about those times if you need to.

4. Decide how the statement reflects the values, attitudes, and practices of people living at that time. Then determine how the statement reflects values, attitudes, and practices of today.

Applying these guidelines will give you a better understanding of a clash between Muslim and European armies in 1191. The following account of this clash was written by Baha' ad-Din, an advisor to the Muslim leader Saladin. He witnessed the battle.

> " The [king of the] Franks [the Muslim term for all Europeans] . . . ordered all the Musulman [Muslim] prisoners . . . to be brought before him. They numbered more than three thousand and were all bound with ropes. The Franks then flung themselves upon them all at once and massacred them with sword and lance in cold blood. "
>
> –Baha' ad-Din, from The Crusade of Richard I, by John Gillingham

By modern standards this event seems barbaric. But such massacres were not uncommon in those times. Plus, the description is from one side's point of view. This context should be considered when making judgments about the event.

Practice and Apply the Skill

Baha' ad-Din also described the battle itself. Read the following passage. Then answer the questions.

> " The center of the Muslim ranks was broken, drums and flags fell to the ground . . . Although there were almost 7,000 . . . killed that day God gave the Muslims victory over their enemies. He [Saladin] stood firm until . . . the Muslims were exhausted, and then he agreed to a truce at the enemy's request. "
>
> –Baha' ad-Din, from Arab Historians of the Crusades, translated by E. J. Costello

1. What happened to Saladin's army? Why do you think the writer calls the battle a Muslim victory?

2. History records this battle as a European victory. Plus, this account is part of a larger statement written in praise of Saladin. Does this additional context change your understanding and answer to the first question? Explain how or why not.

Chapter Review

Visual Summary

Use the visual summary below to help you review the main ideas of the chapter.

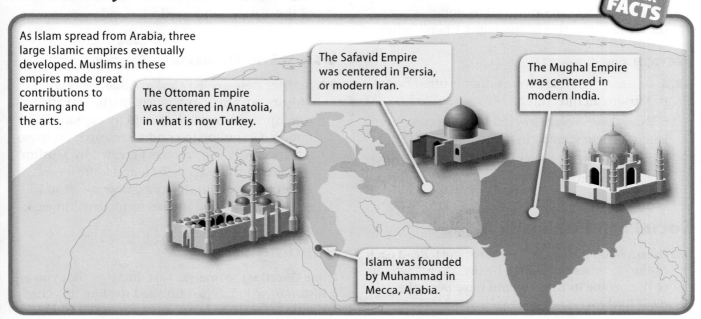

As Islam spread from Arabia, three large Islamic empires eventually developed. Muslims in these empires made great contributions to learning and the arts.

The Ottoman Empire was centered in Anatolia, in what is now Turkey.

The Safavid Empire was centered in Persia, or modern Iran.

The Mughal Empire was centered in modern India.

Islam was founded by Muhammad in Mecca, Arabia.

Reviewing Vocabulary, Terms, and People

For each statement below, write T if it is true and F if it is false. If the statement is false, write the correct term that would make the sentence a true statement.

1. Muslims gather to pray at a **jihad**.

2. Traders often traveled in **caravans** to take their goods to markets.

3. An **Islam** is a person who submits to God and follows the teachings of Muhammad.

4. According to Islamic belief, God's messages to Muhammad during his lifetime make up the **Sunnah**.

5. A **caliph** is a journey to a sacred place.

6. A **minaret** is a tower from where Muslims are called to prayer.

7. **Janissaries** converted to Islam and became fierce warriors in the Ottoman army.

8. The **Sunni** believed that only a descendant of Muhammad could become the highest leader of Islam.

Comprehension and Critical Thinking

SECTION 1 *(pages 354–357)*

9. **a. Recall** What two ways of life developed in Arabia's desert environment?

   b. Analyze Why did Muhammad have a hard time getting people in Mecca to accept his teachings?

   c. Evaluate What are some possible benefits to a nomadic lifestyle, and what are some possible benefits to a sedentary lifestyle?

SECTION 2 *(pages 358–361)*

10. **a. Define** What is the hajj?

   b. Contrast Both the Qur'an and the Sunnah guide Muslims' behavior. Apart from discussing different topics, how do these two differ?

   c. Predict Which of the Five Pillars of Islam do you think would be the most difficult to perform? Why?

SECTION 3 (pages 362–367)

11. a. Identify Who was Abu Bakr and why is he important in the history of Islam?

b. Analyze Why did the Safavids come into conflict with the Ottomans?

c. Evaluate In your opinion, was conquest or trade more effective in spreading Islam? Why?

SECTION 4 (pages 368–371)

12. a. Describe What are two elements often found in Muslim architecture?

b. Draw Conclusions How did having a common language help scholars in the Islamic world?

c. Elaborate Why might a ruler want to become a patron of a mosque?

Social Studies Skills

13. Determining the Context of Statements Read each of the statements in List A below. Decide which of the people in List B would have been the most likely writer of each statement.

List A

1. "I have conquered Constantinople."

2. "I want to build a new palace, the finest ever built in India."

3. "I want to conquer more Muslim lands and convert the people within them to Shiism."

4. "I hope my medical encyclopedia helps others to use what I have learned about treating diseases."

5. "I have decided to accept the invitation to move north to Medina."

6. "Being chosen as the first caliph is a high honor for me."

List B

a. Muhammad

b. Mehmed II

c. Avicenna

d. Esma'il

e. Abu Bakr

f. a Mughal emperor

Reviewing Themes

14. Geography How did the geography of the Arabian desert influence the lives of nomads?

15. Religion Take a position, agreeing or disagreeing with this statement: "Muslim leaders were tolerant of those they conquered." Defend your answer.

Using the Internet

16. Activity: Researching Muslim Achievements Muslim advances in science, math, and art were spread around the world by explorers and traders. Go online to conduct research on these advances. Choose an object created by Muslim scholars in the 600s or 700s and write a paragraph that explains its roots, how it spread to other cultures, and its uses in modern times.

Reading Skills

Using Questions to Analyze Text Imagine that you are a historian who has just finished reading this chapter and you want to learn more about the Islamic world. For each of the topics listed below, write one question for which you could attempt to find an answer in your research. For example, for the topic Islamic law, you might ask, "What Muslim countries today have a legal system that follows Sharia law?"

17. growth of the Ottoman Empire

18. Muslim achievements in math

19. culture and learning in Baghdad

FOCUS ON WRITING

20. Creating Your Web Site Look back over your notes from this chapter. Then, design a home page and the four links titled "Who Was Muhammad?" "What Is Islam?" "The Islamic Empires," and "Islamic Cultural Achievements." Write four or five sentences for each link on your Web site. You may design the pages either online or on a large sheet of paper.

Remember that your audience is children, so you should keep your text simple. Use plenty of vivid language and bright colors to keep your audience interested in your topic.

DIRECTIONS: Read each question and write the letter of the best response.

> "The office of Imam was set up in order to replace the office of Prophet in the defense of the faith and the government of the world. . . . One group says it derives from reason, since it is the nature of reasonable men to submit to a leader who will prevent them from injuring one another and who will settle quarrels and disputes. . . . Another group says that the obligation derives from Holy Law and not from reason, since the Imam deals with matters of Holy Law. . . ."
>
> —Abu al-Hasan al-Mawardi (972–1058)

1 **From the passage, it can be concluded that Imams in early Islam were**

 A religious leaders.

 B government leaders.

 C both religious and government leaders.

 D neither religious nor government leaders.

2 **Which of the following responsibilities of Muslims is not one of the Five Pillars of Islam?**

 A jihad

 B frequent prayer

 C hajj

 D giving to the poor

3 **The teachings of Muhammad are found mainly in the Qur'an and the**

 A Commentaries.

 B Sunnah.

 C Analects.

 D Torah.

4 **Which area of the world was least influenced by Muslim conquest and trade between the AD 600s and 1600s?**

 A North Africa

 B South America

 C Southwest Asia

 D Southeast Asia

5 **Muslim scholars are credited with developing**

 A geometry.

 B algebra.

 C calculus.

 D physics.

Connecting with Past Learnings

6 **Muslims believe that Muhammad revealed Allah's teaching to the world. Which of the following leaders that you learned about earlier did not reveal a religion's teachings to his people?**

 A Moses

 B Hammurabi

 C Buddha

 D Jesus

7 **You have learned that Muslim architects were known for their use of the dome. Which culture that you studied earlier also used many domes?**

 A the Chinese

 B the Egyptians

 C the Greeks

 D the Romans

FLORIDA...
The Story Continues

CHAPTER 13, Early African Civilizations (500 BC–AD 1600)

PLACES **500 BC–AD 1600: The land surrounding Lake Okeechobee is a vast savannah.** In 500 BC a great savannah stretched out from Lake Okeechobee. The people of the Belle Glades culture lived on the savannah and in the wetlands that surrounded the lake. The savannahs and wetlands provided the people with abundant food, including snakes, birds, turtles, and alligators. The Belle Glades people built earthen mounds and dug ditches and canals through the savannah and wetlands. Some of the ditches were circular, and some of the mounds were geometric. Archaeologists are not sure what purposes the ditches and mounds served. They may have helped drain the area to provide dry land for building and planting.

PEOPLE **c. 500 BC–AD 1600: The Native Americans of southern Florida make tools and ornaments from shells.** Stones were not plentiful in southern Florida. Shells were. People used shells to make a wide variety of tools and ornaments. The shell of the lightning whelk was particularly handy. A lightning whelk is giant sea snail. Its shell is a cone-shaped spiral with an opening on one side. The opening forms a natural handle with which to grip the shell. The people of southern Florida used whelk shells to make hammers, awls, and cups. They also carved and polished the shells to make jewelry. They even used the shells for weapons. The lightning whelk was doubly handy. People could first eat the large snails inside the shells and then use the shells to make things.

PEOPLE **c. AD 800–1600: The Calusa prosper in Southwest Florida.** The Calusa lived along the coast and inland waterways

from Estero Bay to Charlotte Harbor. The waters, mangrove forests, and seagrass meadows of the region provided a rich source of fish and other foods. Plentiful food sources meant that the Calusa could maintain a large population without turning to farming. At its height, the Calusa's population may have numbered at least 20,000 people. Some archaeologists think the population may have climbed as high as 50,000 people. The people lived in settled villages under a complex political structure headed by a chief.

PLACES **c. 800–1600: The Caloosahatchee River connects the Gulf Coast with Lake Okeechobee.** The Caloosahatchee River has its headwaters in Lake Hicpochee near Lake Okeechobee. The river flows west from Lake Hicpochee to the Gulf of Mexico. The river was a highway for Native Americans. The Calusa and the Belle Glades people used the river to travel between the coast and Lake Hicpochee. Canals between Lake Hicpochee and Lake Okeechobee allowed them to complete the journey. Today a modern canal connects the river to Lake Okeechobee.

PEOPLE **c. 800–1600: The Calusa worship three gods.** The Calusa worshipped three gods—a sky god, an earth god, and a god of war. The Calusa believed that their religious leaders had the power to call forth the wind. The leaders also controlled special objects that held religious power. Among these objects were painted carved masks. Archaeologists have found a large collection of carved masks on Marco Key. Temple mounds up to 30 feet high served as ceremonial centers. The mounds were topped with open-sided wood and thatch buildings.

Unpacking the Florida Standards ‹···

Read the following to learn what this standard says and what it means. See FL8–FL31 to unpack all of the standards related to this chapter.

Benchmark SS.6.G.2.1 Explain how major physical characteristics, natural resources, climate, and absolute and relative locations have influenced settlement, interactions, and the economies of ancient civilizations of the world.

What does it mean?

Describe how ancient civilizations were affected by geographical factors such as terrain, availability of natural resources, climate, and location. Explain how these factors affected settlement, how civilizations interacted, and whether they thrived economically.

 SPOTLIGHT ON
SS.6.E.1.3, SS.6.E.3.1, SS.6.E.3.2, SS.6.E.3.4, SS.6.G.1.2, SS.6.G.2.1 See pages FL38, FL39, FL42, and FL44 for content specifically related to these Chapter 13 standards.

Photo credits: See Chapter 1 Florida. . .The Story Continues

Early African Civilizations

Essential Question What factors shaped early African civilizations?

Florida Next Generation Sunshine State Standards

SS.6.E.1.1 Identify the factors (new resources, increased productivity, education, technology, slave economy, territorial expansion) that increase economic growth. **SS.6.E.1.3** Describe the following economic concepts as they relate to early civilization: scarcity, opportunity cost, supply and demand, barter, trade, productive resources (land, labor, capital, entrepreneurship). **SS.6.E.2.1** Evaluate how civilizations through clans, leaders, and family groups make economic decisions for that civilization providing a framework for future city-state or nation development. **SS.6.E.3.1** Identify examples of mediums of exchange (currencies) used for trade (barter) for each civilization, and explain why international trade requires a system for a medium of exchange between trading both inside and among various regions. **SS.6.E.3.2** Categorize products that were traded among civilizations, and give examples of barriers to trade of those products. **SS.6.E.3.4** Describe the relationship among civilizations that engage in trade, including the benefits and drawbacks of voluntary trade. **SS.6.G.1.2** Analyze the purposes of map projections (political, physical, special purpose) and explain the applications of various types of maps. **SS.6.G.1.3** Identify natural wonders of the ancient world. **SS.6.G.1.4** Utilize tools geographers use to study the world. **SS.6.G.2.1** Explain how major physical characteristics, natural resources, climate, and absolute and relative locations have influenced settlement, interactions, and the economies of ancient civilizations of the world. **SS.6.G.2.4** Explain how the geographical location of ancient civilizations contributed to the culture and politics of those societies. **SS.6.G.2.5** Interpret how geographic boundaries invite or limit interaction with other regions and cultures. **SS.6.G.3.2** Analyze the impact of human populations on the ancient world's ecosystems. **SS.6.G.4.1** Explain how family and ethnic relationships influenced ancient cultures. **SS.6.W.1.1** Use timelines to identify chronological order of historical events. **SS.6.W.1.3** Interpret primary and secondary sources.

FOCUS ON WRITING

A Journal Entry Many people feel that recording their lives in journals helps them to understand their own experiences. Writing a journal entry from someone else's point of view can help you to understand what that person's life is like. In this chapter, you will read about the land, people, and culture of early Africa. Then you will imagine a character and write a journal entry from his or her point of view.

CHAPTER EVENTS

WORLD EVENTS

500 BC

c. 500 BC
West Africans begin using iron and making clay sculptures.

c. 480 BC
Greece defeats Persia in the Persian Wars.

This photo shows women in front of a mosque in the city of Djenné, in present-day Mali.

c. AD 200
Camels are first used in North Africa, making Saharan trade easier.

AD 500

1281 The Mongols' attempt to conquer Japan fails.

1060s
The Empire of Ghana reaches its height.

1300

1324
Mansa Musa leaves Mali on a hajj to Mecca.

1337
The Hundred Years' War begins in France.

1580s
Moroccan invaders begin their conquest of Songhai.

1600

1521
Spanish explorers conquer the Aztec Empire.

EARLY AFRICAN CIVILIZATIONS **377**

Reading Social Studies

Focus on Themes In this chapter, you will read about West Africa—its physical **geography** and early cultures. You will see West Africa is a land of many resources and varied features. One feature, the Niger River, has been particularly important in the region's history, providing water, food, and transportation for people. In addition, salt and iron deposits can be found in the region. Such resources were the basis for a **technology** that allowed people to create strong tools and weapons.

Organization of Facts and Information

Focus on Reading How are books organized in the library? How are the groceries organized in the store? Clear organization helps us find the product we need, and it also helps us find facts and information.

Understanding Structural Patterns Writers use structural patterns to organize information in sentences or paragraphs. What's a structural pattern? It's simply a way of organizing information. Learning to recognize those patterns will make it easier for you to read and understand social studies texts.

Patterns of Organization		
Pattern	**Clue Words**	**Graphic Organizer**
Cause-effect shows how one thing leads to another	as a result, because, therefore, this led to	Cause → Effect, Effect, Effect
Chronological Order shows the sequence of events or actions.	after, before, first, then, not long after, finally	First → Next → Next → Last
Listing presents information in categories such as size, location, or importance.	also, most important, for example, in fact	Category • Fact • Fact • Fact • Fact

To use text structure to improve your understanding, follow these steps:

1. Look for the main idea of the passage you are reading.

2. Then look for clues that signal a specific pattern.

3. Look for other important ideas and think about how the ideas connect. Is there any obvious pattern?

4. Use a graphic organizer to map the relationships among the facts and details.

LA.6.1.7.1 The student will use background knowledge of subject and related content areas, prereading strategies, graphic representations, and knowledge of text structure to make and confirm complex predictions of content, purpose, and organization of a reading selection.

LA.6.1.6.1 The student will use new vocabulary that is introduced and taught directly. **LA.6.1.7.3** The student will determine the main idea or essential message in grade-level text through inferring, paraphrasing, summarizing, and identifying relevant details.

You Try It!

The following passages are from the chapter you are about to read. As you read each set of sentences, ask yourself what structural pattern the writer used to organize the information.

Recognizing Structural Patterns

A. "As the people of West Africa became more productive, villages had more than they needed to survive. West Africans began to trade the area's resources with buyers who lived thousands of miles away." (p. 383)

B. "When Sundiata was a boy, a harsh ruler conquered Mali. But as an adult, Sundiata built up an army and won back his country's independence. He then conquered nearby kingdoms, including Ghana, in the 1230s . . . After Sundiata conquered Ghana, he took over the salt and gold trades. He also worked to improve agriculture in Mali." (p. 390)

C. "Four different regions make up the area surrounding the Niger River . . . The northern band is the southern part of the Sahara . . . The next band is the Sahel (sah-HEL), a strip of land with little rainfall that divides the desert from wetter areas . . . Farther south is savannah, or open grassland . . . The fourth band, near the equator, gets heavy rain." (p. 382)

After you read the passages, answer the questions below:

1. What structural pattern did the writer use to organize the information in passage A? How can you tell?

2. What structural pattern did the writer use to organize the information in passage B? How can you tell?

3. What structural pattern did the writer use to organize the information in passage C? How can you tell?

Key Terms and People

Chapter 13

Section 1
rifts *(p. 380)*
sub-Saharan Africa *(p. 380)*
Sahel *(p. 382)*
savannah *(p. 382)*
rain forests *(p. 382)*
extended family *(p. 382)*
animism *(p. 383)*

Section 2
silent barter *(p. 386)*
Tunka Manin *(p. 388)*

Section 3
Sundiata *(p. 390)*
Mansa Musa *(p. 391)*
Sunni Ali *(p. 392)*
Askia the Great *(p. 393)*

Section 4
oral history *(p. 396)*
griots *(p. 396)*
proverbs *(p. 397)*
kente *(p. 399)*

Academic Vocabulary

Success in school is related to knowing academic vocabulary— the words that are frequently used in school assignments and discussions. In this chapter, you will learn the following academic word:

process *(p. 397)*

As you read Chapter 13, think about the organization of the ideas. Look for signal words and ask yourself why the author has arranged the text in this way.

What You Will Learn...

Main Ideas

1. Landforms, climate, and resources affected the history of West Africa.
2. The way of life of early peoples in West Africa was shaped by family ties, religion, iron technology, and trade.

The Big Idea

Geography, resources, culture, and trade influenced the growth of societies in West Africa.

Key Terms and People

rifts, *p. 380*
sub-Saharan Africa, *p. 380*
Sahel, *p. 382*
savannah, *p. 382*
rain forests, *p. 382*
extended family, *p. 382*
animism, *p. 383*

Online Resource
TAKING NOTES

Use the graphic organizer online to record information about the geography and traditional ways of life in Africa.

Geography and Early Africa

If YOU were there...

You live in a village near the great bend of the Niger River in Africa in about AD 800. The river is full of life—birds, fish, crocodiles. You use its water to grow crops and raise cattle. Traders use the river to bring wood, gold, and other products from the forests.

Why is this a good place to live?

BUILDING BACKGROUND The continent of Africa is so large that it includes many varied kinds of terrain, from barren deserts to thick rain forests. Each region has a different climate and provides different resources for the people who live there. In West Africa rivers provide water to grow crops in drier areas. The land is also a rich source of minerals, especially gold and iron. These two resources played a large role in the development of West African cultures.

Landforms, Climate, and Resources

Africa is the earth's second largest continent. An immense desert, the Sahara, stretches across most of North Africa. Along the northwestern edge of the Sahara lie the Atlas Mountains. At the opposite edge of the continent, in the southeast, the Drakensberg Mountains rise. In eastern Africa, mountains extend alongside great rifts. These **rifts** are long, deep valleys formed by the movement of the earth's crust. From all these mountains the land dips into plateaus and wide, low plains. The plains of **sub-Saharan Africa**, or Africa south of the Sahara, are crossed by mighty rivers. These rivers include the Congo, the Zambezi, and the Niger.

Regions of West Africa

As a source of water, food, and transportation, the Niger River allowed many people to live in West Africa. Along the Niger's middle section is a low-lying area of lakes and marshes. Many animals find food and shelter there. Fish are also plentiful.

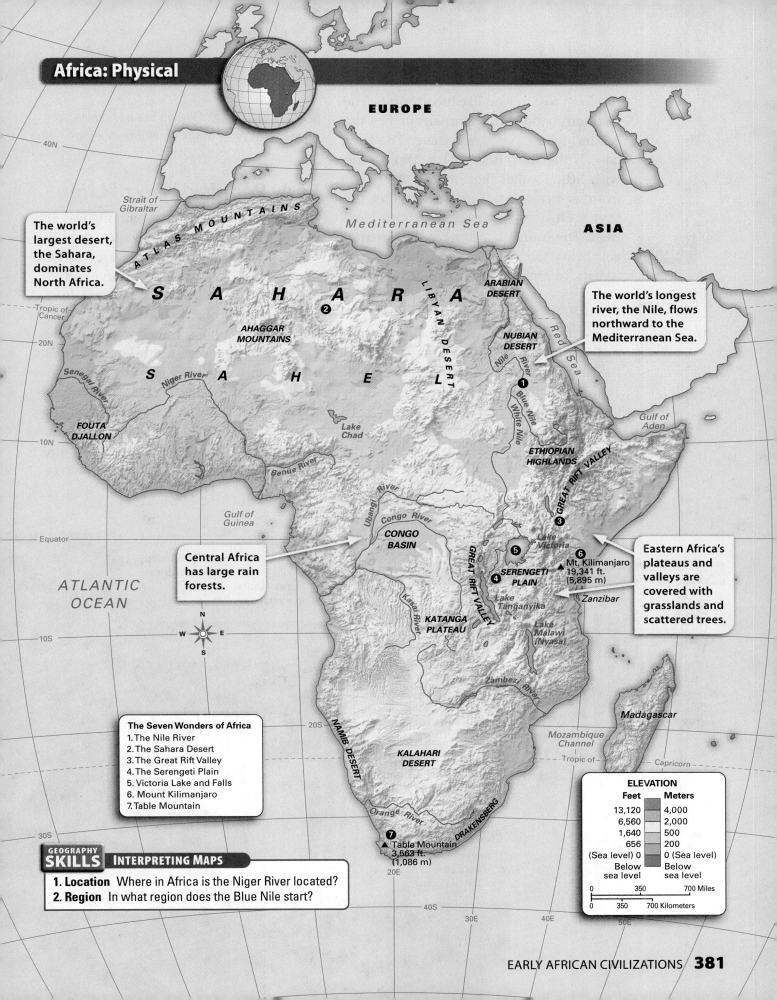

EUROPE

ASIA

Mediterranean Sea

Strait of Gibraltar

ATLAS MOUNTAINS

The world's largest desert, the Sahara, dominates North Africa.

S A H A R A

LIBYAN DESERT

ARABIAN DESERT

AHAGGAR MOUNTAINS

NUBIAN DESERT

Red Sea

The world's longest river, the Nile, flows northward to the Mediterranean Sea.

S A H E L

Senegal River

Niger River

Nile

Blue Nile

White Nile

Gulf of Aden

FOUTA DJALLON

Lake Chad

ETHIOPIAN HIGHLANDS

GREAT RIFT VALLEY

Benue River

Ubangi River

Congo River

Gulf of Guinea

CONGO BASIN

Equator

Lake Victoria

Mt. Kilimanjaro 19,341 ft. (5,895 m)

Eastern Africa's plateaus and valleys are covered with grasslands and scattered trees.

Central Africa has large rain forests.

GREAT RIFT VALLEY

SERENGETI PLAIN

Zanzibar

ATLANTIC OCEAN

Kasai River

KATANGA PLATEAU

Lake Tanganyika

Lake Malawi (Nyasa)

N
W   E
S

Zambezi River

Madagascar

Mozambique Channel

Tropic of Capricorn

The Seven Wonders of Africa
1. The Nile River
2. The Sahara Desert
3. The Great Rift Valley
4. The Serengeti Plain
5. Victoria Lake and Falls
6. Mount Kilimanjaro
7. Table Mountain

NAMIB DESERT

KALAHARI DESERT

DRAKENSBERG

Orange River

Table Mountain 3,563 ft. (1,086 m)

ELEVATION

Feet		Meters
13,120		4,000
6,560		2,000
1,640		500
656		200
(Sea level) 0		0 (Sea level)
Below sea level		Below sea level

0   350   700 Miles

0   350   700 Kilometers

GEOGRAPHY SKILLS   INTERPRETING MAPS

1. **Location** Where in Africa is the Niger River located?
2. **Region** In what region does the Blue Nile start?

Four different regions make up the area surrounding the Niger River. The regions run from east to west like broad bands. The northern band is the southern part of the Sahara. Rain is very rare there. The next band is the **Sahel** (sah-HEL), a strip of land with little rainfall that divides the desert from wetter areas. Farther south is the **savannah**, or open grassland with scattered trees. The fourth band, near the equator, gets heavy rain. This band is made of **rain forests**, or moist, densely wooded areas.

THE IMPACT TODAY

Human activities like logging and farming are rapidly destroying Africa's rain forests.

West Africa's Resources

West Africa's land is one of the region's many resources. With its many climates, the land can produce many different crops. Traditional crops grown in West Africa included dates, kola nuts, and grains.

Other resources were minerals. Gold, from the forests, was highly prized. So was salt, which came from the Sahara. Salt kept food from spoiling, and people needed it in their diet to survive Africa's hot climate.

READING CHECK **Finding Main Ideas** What are some of West Africa's major resources?

Early Peoples' Way of Life

A typical early West African family was an **extended family**. It usually included the father, mother, children, and close relatives in one household. West African society expected each person to be loyal to his or her family. In some areas people also became part of age-sets. In these groups, men born within the same two or three years formed special bonds. Women, too, sometimes formed age-sets.

Loyalty to family and age-sets helped the people of a village to work together. The men hunted, farmed, and raised livestock. Women farmed, collected firewood, ground grain, carried water, and cared for children.

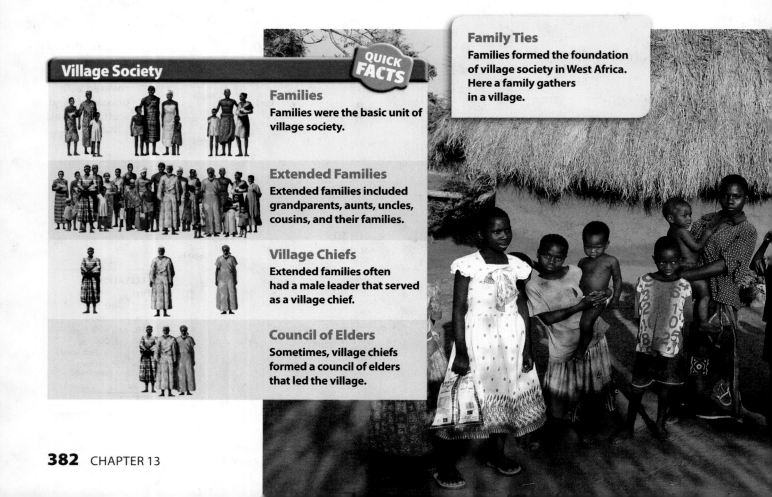

Village Society

QUICK FACTS

Families
Families were the basic unit of village society.

Extended Families
Extended families included grandparents, aunts, uncles, cousins, and their families.

Village Chiefs
Extended families often had a male leader that served as a village chief.

Council of Elders
Sometimes, village chiefs formed a council of elders that led the village.

Family Ties
Families formed the foundation of village society in West Africa. Here a family gathers in a village.

Religion was another central feature of village life. Many West Africans believed that their ancestors' spirits stayed nearby. To honor these spirits, families marked places as sacred by putting specially carved statues there. They also offered food to their ancestors. Another common West African belief was **animism**—the belief that bodies of water, animals, trees, and other natural objects have spirits.

As time passed, the people of West Africa developed advanced cultures. Changes in technology helped early communities grow. Around 500 BC West Africans found that they could heat certain kinds of rock to get a hard metal. This was iron. Stronger than other metals, iron was good for making tools and weapons. Iron tools allowed farmers to clear land faster and to grow food more easily than they could with earlier tools.

As the people of West Africa became more productive, villages had more than they needed to survive. West Africans began to trade the area's resources with buyers who lived thousands of miles away.

West Africa's gold and salt mines became a source of great wealth. Traders used camels to cross the Sahara. They took gold, salt, cloth, slaves, and other items to North Africa and the Islamic world.

READING CHECK **Analyzing** How did religion in West Africa reflect the importance of family?

SUMMARY AND PREVIEW Physical geography affected culture and trade in West Africa. When West Africans developed iron technology, communities grew. Trade, especially in gold and salt, expanded. Next, you will read about a West African empire based on this trade—Ghana.

FOCUS ON 🏴

Decision-Making
The villages of West Africa had a traditional economy. Their decisions about what goods to make, buy, and sell were based on custom. This means that economic decisions were not made by a central government. Instead, these decisions were made by the clans, or families, of the villages.

Section 1 Assessment

Reviewing Ideas, Terms, and People

1. **a. Recall** Where in Africa are the **rifts** located?
   b. Explain How were two of West Africa's valuable mineral resources related to local physical geography.
2. **a. Identify** What are two groups to which a person in early West Africa may have owed loyalty?
   b. Analyze How did the use of iron change farming?

Critical Thinking

3. **Drawing Conclusions** Draw a diagram like the one shown. Based on your notes, write a statement in the center circle of the diagram about how Africa's geography has shaped life there.

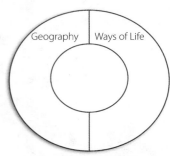

Geography | Ways of Life

FOCUS ON WRITING

4. **Reviewing Notes on Early West Africa** Review your notes on the geography and early peoples of West Africa. Consider what your character saw every day. What challenges did the environment present? What role did family, religion, and technology play in your character's way of life?

Crossing the Sahara

Crossing the Sahara has never been easy. Bigger than the entire continent of Australia, the Sahara is one of the hottest, driest, and most barren places on earth. Yet for centuries, people have crossed the Sahara's gravel-covered plains and vast seas of sand. Long ago, West Africans crossed the desert regularly to carry on a rich trade.

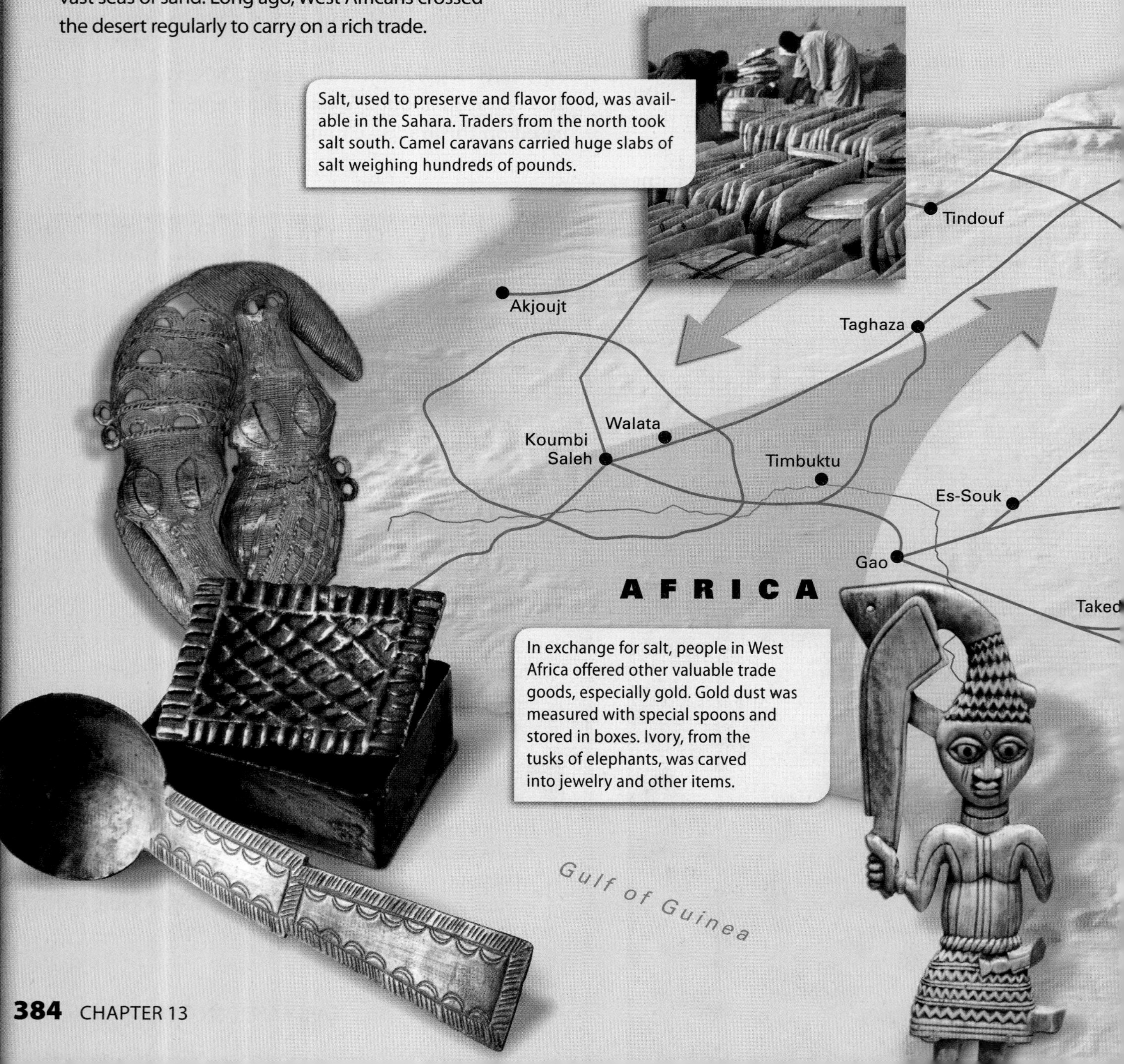

Salt, used to preserve and flavor food, was available in the Sahara. Traders from the north took salt south. Camel caravans carried huge slabs of salt weighing hundreds of pounds.

Tindouf

Akjoujt

Taghaza

Walata

Koumbi
Saleh

Timbuktu

Es-Souk

Gao

A F R I C A

Taked

In exchange for salt, people in West Africa offered other valuable trade goods, especially gold. Gold dust was measured with special spoons and stored in boxes. Ivory, from the tusks of elephants, was carved into jewelry and other items.

Gulf of Guinea

ATLANTIC OCEAN

EUROPE

Some goods that were traded across the Sahara, like silk and spices, came all the way from Asia along the Silk Road. These luxury items were traded for West African goods like gold and ivory.

MEDITERRANEAN SEA

● Ghadames

● Ghat

● Zawilah

S A H A R A

● Bilma

● Daima

A Difficult Journey

Temperature Temperatures soared to well over 100°F during the day and plunged to below freezing at night. Dying of heat or cold was a real danger.

Water Most areas of the Sahara get less than one inch of rain per year. Travelers had to bring lots of water or they could die of thirst.

Distance The Sahara is huge, and the trade routes were not well marked. Travelers could easily get lost.

Bandits Valuable trade goods were a tempting target for bandits. For protection, merchants traveled in caravans.

—— Trade route
● Settlement
Scale varies on this map.

GEOGRAPHY SKILLS **INTERPRETING MAPS**

1. **Movement** What were some goods traded across the Sahara?
2. **Human-Environment Interaction** Why was salt a valued trade good?

RED SEA

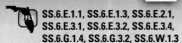
SS.6.E.1.1, SS.6.E.1.3, SS.6.E.2.1,
SS.6.E.3.1, SS.6.E.3.2, SS.6.E.3.4,
SS.6.G.1.4, SS.6.G.3.2, SS.6.W.1.3

What You Will Learn...

Main Ideas

1. Ghana controlled trade and became wealthy.
2. Through its control of trade, Ghana built an empire.
3. Ghana's decline was caused by attacking invaders, overgrazing, and the loss of trade.

The Big Idea

The rulers of Ghana built an empire by controlling the salt and gold trade.

Key Terms and People

silent barter, *p. 386*
Tunka Manin, *p. 388*

Online Resource
TAKING NOTES

Use the graphic organizer online to make a list of important events from the beginning to the end of the empire of Ghana.

The Empire of Ghana

If YOU were there...

You are a trader in a caravan heading into West Africa in about 1000. The caravan carries many goods, but the most precious is salt. Salt is so valuable that people trade gold for it! The gold traders never meet you face to face, though. You wish you could talk to them to find out where they get their gold.

Why do you think the traders are so secretive?

BUILDING BACKGROUND The various regions of Africa provided people with different resources. West Africa, for example, was rich in both fertile soils and minerals, especially gold and iron. Other regions had plentiful supplies of other resources, such as salt. Over time, trade developed between regions with different resources. This trade led to the growth of the first great empire in West Africa.

Ghana Controls Trade

Among the earliest people in West Africa were the Soninke (soh-NING-kee). They lived in small groups and farmed the land along the Niger River. After AD 300, the Soninke began to band together for protection against nomadic herders who wanted to move into the area. This banding together was the beginning of Ghana.

The people of Ghana gradually grew in strength. They learned how to work with iron and how to use iron tools for farming. They also herded cattle for meat and milk. Because Ghana's farmers and herders could produce plenty of food, their population increased. Towns and villages sprang up.

Ghana lay between the vast Sahara to the north and deep forests that spread out to the south. In this location, people were in a good position to trade in the region's two main resources—gold and salt. The exchange of gold and salt sometimes followed a specific process called silent barter. **Silent barter** is a process in which people exchange goods with-

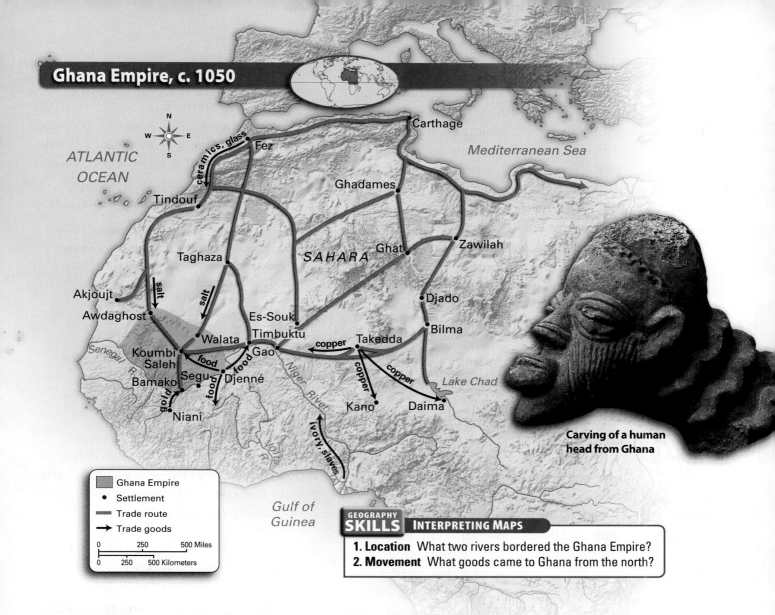

Ghana Empire, c. 1050

ATLANTIC OCEAN

ceramics, glass

Fez

Carthage

Mediterranean Sea

Ghadames

Tindouf

SAHARA

Ghat

Zawilah

Taghaza

salt

salt

Akjoujt

Awdaghost

Djado

Es-Souk

Bilma

Walata

Timbuktu

copper

Takedda

Koumbi Saleh

food

Gao

food

Senegal R.

Segu

Djenné

copper

copper

Bamako

food

Niger River

Kano

Daima

Lake Chad

gold

Niani

Volta R.

ivory, slaves

Gulf of Guinea

Carving of a human head from Ghana

Ghana Empire
• Settlement
— Trade route
→ Trade goods

0   250   500 Miles
0 250 500 Kilometers

GEOGRAPHY SKILLS | **INTERPRETING MAPS**

1. **Location** What two rivers bordered the Ghana Empire?
2. **Movement** What goods came to Ghana from the north?

out contacting each other directly. In Ghana salt traders left slabs of salt on a riverbank. In exchange, gold miners left what they thought was a fair amount of gold. The method made sure that trade was done peacefully. It also kept the location of the gold mines secret.

As trade in gold and salt increased, Ghana's rulers gained power. They built armies equipped with iron weapons that were superior to the weapons of nearby peoples. Over time, Ghana took over control of trade from the North African merchants. Then, additional goods were added to the mix of items traded. Wheat came from the north. Sheep, cattle, and honey

came from the south. Local products, such as leather and cloth, were also traded. Before long, this extensive trade made Ghana very prosperous indeed.

READING CHECK **Generalizing** How did trade help Ghana develop?

Ghana Builds an Empire

By 800 Ghana was firmly in control of West Africa's trade routes. Nearly all trade between northern and southern Africa passed through Ghana. Ghana's army kept the trade routes safe. Trade increased, and so did Ghana's wealth.

Taxes and Gold

With so many traders passing through their lands, Ghana's rulers looked for ways to profit from their dealings. One way was to force every trader who entered Ghana to pay a special tax on the goods he carried. Then each trader had to pay another tax on the goods he took with him when he left. The people of Ghana also had to pay taxes. In addition, Ghana forced small neighboring tribes to pay tribute.

Ghana's gold mines brought even more income into the royal treasury. Some gold was carried by traders to lands as far away as England. But not all of Ghana's gold was traded. Ghana's kings also kept huge stores of the precious metal for themselves.

The rulers of Ghana banned everyone else in Ghana from owning gold nuggets. Common people could only own gold dust, which they used as money. This ensured that the king was richer than his subjects.

Expansion of the Empire

Part of Ghana's wealth went to support its powerful army. Ghana's kings used this army to conquer many neighboring areas. To keep order in their large empire, Ghana's kings allowed conquered rulers to retain much of their power. These local rulers acted as governors of their territories, answering only to the king.

The empire of Ghana reached its peak under **Tunka Manin** (TOOHN-kah MAH-nin). This king had a lavish court where he displayed the wealth of the empire. A Spanish writer noted the court's splendor.

> "The king adorns himself . . . round his neck and his forearms, and he puts on a high cap decorated with gold and wrapped in a turban of fine cotton. Behind the king stand ten pages [servants] holding shields and swords decorated with gold."
>
> –al-Bakri, from *The Book of Routes and Kingdoms*

READING CHECK Summarizing How did the rulers of Ghana control trade?

Ghana's Decline

In the mid-1000s, Ghana was rich and powerful, but by the early 1200s, the empire had collapsed. Three major factors contributed to its end.

Invasion

The first factor that hurt Ghana was invasion. A group of North African Muslims called the Almoravids (al-moh-RAH-vidz) attacked Ghana in the 1060s. After 14 years of fighting, the Almoravids defeated the people of Ghana. The Almoravids didn't control Ghana for long, but they weakened the empire. They cut off many trade routes. Without this trade, Ghana could not support its empire.

Overgrazing

A second factor in Ghana's decline also involved the Almoravids. These invaders brought herds of animals with them. These animals ate all the grass in many pastures. This overgrazing combined with a long drought left the soil exposed to hot desert winds. These

FOCUS ON READING

In the section titled "Ghana's Decline," what type of structural pattern is used? How do you know?

BIOGRAPHY

Tunka Manin
Ruled around 1068

All we know about Tunka Manin comes from the writings of a Muslim geographer who wrote about Ghana. From his writings, we know that Tunka Manin was the nephew of the previous king, a man named Basi. Kingship and property in Ghana did not pass from father to son, but from uncle to nephew. Only the king's sister's son could inherit the throne. Once he did become king, Tunka Manin surrounded himself with finery and many luxuries.

Contrasting How was inheritance in Ghana different from inheritance in other societies you have studied?

Overgrazing

Too many animals grazing in one area can lead to problems, such as the loss of farmland that occurred in West Africa.

1 Animals are allowed to graze in areas with lots of grass.

2 With too many animals grazing, however, the grass disappears, leaving the soil below exposed to the wind.

3 Desertification occurs. The wind blows the soil away, turning what was once grassland into desert.

winds blew away the soil, leaving it worthless for farming or herding. Many farmers had to leave in search of new homes.

Internal Rebellion

A third factor also helped bring about the decline of Ghana's empire. In about 1200 the people of a country that Ghana had conquered rose up in rebellion. Within a few years these rebels had taken over the entire empire of Ghana.

Once in control, however, the rebels found that they could not keep order.

Weakened, Ghana was attacked and defeated by one of its neighbors. The empire fell apart.

READING CHECK **Identifying Cause and Effect** Why did Ghana decline in the AD 1000s?

SUMMARY AND PREVIEW The empire of Ghana in West Africa grew rich and powerful through its control of trade routes and its gold production. The empire lasted from about 800 to 1200. In the next section, you will learn about two empires that arose after Ghana—Mali and Songhai.

Section 2 Assessment

Reviewing Ideas, Terms, and People

1. **a. Identify** What were the two major resources traded in Ghana?
   b. Explain How did the **silent barter** system work?
2. **a. Identify** Who was **Tunka Manin**?
   b. Generalize What did Ghana's kings do with the money they raised from taxes and gold mining?
   c. Elaborate Why did the rulers of Ghana not want everyone to have gold?
3. **a. Recall** What group invaded Ghana in the late 1000s?
   b. Analyze How did overgrazing help cause the fall of Ghana?

Critical Thinking

4. **Categorizing** Look through the events you listed in your notes. Decide which contributed to Ghana's rise and which led to its fall. Organize the events in a diagram like this one.

The Empire of Ghana

Rise   Fall

FOCUS ON WRITING

5. **Reviewing Notes on Ghana** Review this section and your notes on the rise and fall of Ghana's trading empire. Keep in mind how your character's life may have been impacted by Ghana's history.

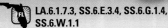
Later Empires

What You Will Learn...

Main Ideas

1. The empire of Mali reached its height under the ruler Mansa Musa, but the empire fell to invaders in the 1400s.
2. The Songhai built a new Islamic empire in West Africa, conquering many of the lands that were once part of Mali.
3. Great Zimbabwe was a powerful state that developed in southern Africa.

The Big Idea

Between 1000 and 1500, three great kingdoms—Mali, Songhai, and Great Zimbabwe—developed in Africa.

Key People

Sundiata, *p. 390*
Mansa Musa, *p. 391*
Sunni Ali, *p. 392*
Askia the Great, *p. 393*

Online Resource
TAKING NOTES

Use the graphic organizer online to take notes about life in the cultures that developed in West Africa—Mali and Songhai—and the one that developed in southern Africa—Great Zimbabwe.

If YOU were there...

You are a servant of the great Mansa Musa, ruler of Mali. You've been chosen as one of the servants who will travel with him on a pilgrimage to Mecca. The king has given you all fine new clothes of silk for the trip. He will carry much gold with him. You've never left your home before. But now you will see the great city of Cairo, Egypt, and many other new places.

How do you feel about going on this journey?

BUILDING BACKGROUND Mansa Musa was one of Africa's greatest rulers, and his empire, Mali, was one of the largest in African history. Rising from the ruins of Ghana, Mali took over the trade routes of West Africa and grew into a powerful state.

Mali

Like Ghana, Mali (MAH-lee) lay along the upper Niger River. This area's fertile soil helped Mali grow. Mali's location on the Niger also allowed its people to control trade on the river. As a result, the empire grew rich and powerful. According to legend, Mali's rise to power began under a ruler named **Sundiata** (soohn-JAHT-ah).

Sundiata Makes Mali an Empire

When Sundiata was a boy, a harsh ruler conquered Mali. But as an adult, Sundiata built up an army and won back his country's independence. He then conquered nearby kingdoms, including Ghana, in the 1230s.

After Sundiata conquered Ghana, he took over the salt and gold trades. He also worked to improve agriculture in Mali. Sundiata had new farmlands cleared for beans, onions, rice, and other crops. Sundiata even introduced a new crop—cotton. From the cotton fibers people made clothing that was comfortable in the warm climate. They also sold cotton to other people.

To keep order in his prosperous kingdom, Sundiata took power away from local leaders. Each of these local leaders had the title *mansa* (MAHN-sah), a title Sundiata now took

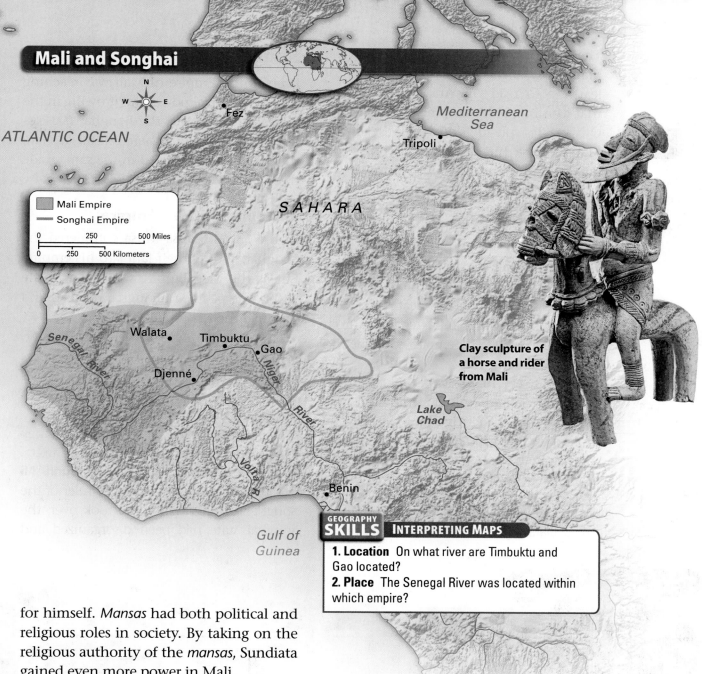

Mali and Songhai

ATLANTIC OCEAN

Fez

Mediterranean Sea

Tripoli

SAHARA

Mali Empire
Songhai Empire

0   250   500 Miles
0   250   500 Kilometers

Walata
Senegal River
Timbuktu
Gao
Djenné
Niger River
Volta R.
Benin
Lake Chad

Gulf of Guinea

Clay sculpture of a horse and rider from Mali

GEOGRAPHY SKILLS | **INTERPRETING MAPS**

1. Location On what river are Timbuktu and Gao located?
2. Place The Senegal River was located within which empire?

for himself. *Mansas* had both political and religious roles in society. By taking on the religious authority of the *mansas*, Sundiata gained even more power in Mali.

Sundiata died in 1255. Later rulers of Mali took the title of *mansa*. Unlike Sundiata, most of these rulers were Muslims.

Mansa Musa

Mali's most famous ruler was a Muslim named **Mansa Musa** (MAHN-sah moo-SAH). Under his skillful leadership, Mali reached the height of its wealth, power, and fame in the 1300s. Because of Mansa Musa's influence, Islam spread through a large part of West Africa, gaining many new believers.

Mansa Musa ruled Mali for about 25 years, from 1312 to 1337. During that time, Mali added many important trade cities to its empire, including Timbuktu (tim-buhk-TOO).

Religion was very important to Mansa Musa. In 1324 he left Mali on a pilgrimage to Mecca. Through his journey, Mansa Musa introduced his empire to the Islamic world. He spread Mali's fame far and wide.

Mansa Musa also supported education. He sent many scholars to study in Morocco.

These scholars later set up schools in Mali. Mansa Musa stressed the importance of learning to read the Arabic language so that Muslims in his empire could read the Qur'an. To spread Islam in West Africa, Mansa Musa hired Muslim architects to build mosques throughout his empire.

The Fall of Mali

When Mansa Musa died, his son Maghan (MAH-gan) took the throne. Maghan was a weak ruler. When raiders from the southeast poured into Mali, he couldn't stop them. The raiders set fire to Timbuktu's great schools and mosques. Mali never fully recovered from this terrible blow. The empire continued to weaken and decline.

In 1431 the Tuareg (TWAH-reg), nomads from the Sahara, seized Timbuktu. The people living at the edges of Mali's empire broke away. By 1500 nearly all of the lands the empire had once ruled were lost. Only a small area of Mali remained.

READING CHECK **Sequencing** What steps did Sundiata take to turn Mali into an empire?

Songhai

Even as the Empire of Mali was reaching its height, a rival power was growing in the area. That rival was the Songhai (SAHNG-hy) kingdom. From their capital at Gao, the Songhai participated in the same trade that had made Ghana and Mali so rich.

The Building of an Empire

In the 1300s Mansa Musa conquered the Songhai, adding their lands to his empire. But as the Mali Empire weakened in the 1400s, the people of Songhai rebelled and regained their freedom.

The Songhai leaders were Muslims. So too were many of the North African Berbers who traded in West Africa. Because of this shared religion, the Berbers were willing to trade with the Songhai, who grew richer.

As the Songhai gained in wealth, they expanded their territory and built an empire. Songhai's expansion was led by **Sunni Ali** (SOOH-nee ah-LEE), who became ruler of the Songhai in 1464. Before he took over, the Songhai state had been disorganized and

The people of Songhai depended on the Niger River for many things. It was an important transportation route and provided fertile lands and a source of water for farming.

poorly run. As ruler, Sunni Ali worked to unify, strengthen, and enlarge his empire. Much of the land that he added to Songhai had been part of Mali.

As king, Sunni Ali encouraged everyone in his empire to work together. To build religious harmony, he participated in both Muslim and local religions. As a result, he brought stability to Songhai.

Askia the Great

Sunni Ali died in 1492. He was followed as king by his son Sunni Baru, who was not a Muslim. The Songhai people feared that if Sunni Baru didn't support Islam, they would lose their trade with Muslim lands. They rebelled against the king.

The leader of that rebellion was a general named Muhammad Ture (moo-HAH-muhd too-RAY). After overthrowing Sunni Baru, Muhammad Ture chose the title *askia,* a title of high military rank. Eventually, he became known as **Askia the Great**.

Askia supported education and learning. Under his rule, Timbuktu flourished, drawing thousands to its universities, schools, libraries, and mosques. The city was especially known for the University of Sankore (san-KOH-rah). People arrived there from North Africa and other places to study math, science, medicine, grammar, and law. Djenné was another city that became a center of learning.

Most of Songhai's traders were Muslim, and as they gained influence in the empire so did Islam. Askia, himself a devout Muslim, encouraged the growth of Islamic influence. He made many laws similar to those in other Muslim nations.

To help maintain order, Askia set up five provinces within Songhai. He removed local leaders and appointed new governors who were loyal to him. Askia also created a professional army and specialized departments to oversee specific tasks.

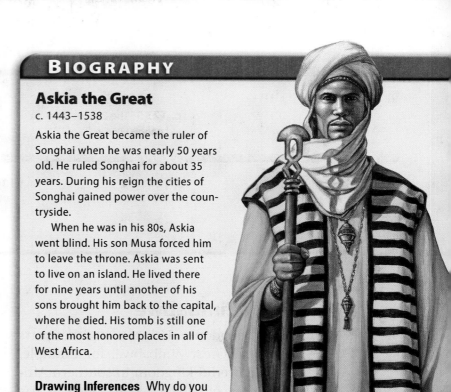

BIOGRAPHY

Askia the Great
c. 1443–1538

Askia the Great became the ruler of Songhai when he was nearly 50 years old. He ruled Songhai for about 35 years. During his reign the cities of Songhai gained power over the countryside.

When he was in his 80s, Askia went blind. His son Musa forced him to leave the throne. Askia was sent to live on an island. He lived there for nine years until another of his sons brought him back to the capital, where he died. His tomb is still one of the most honored places in all of West Africa.

Drawing Inferences Why do you think Askia the Great's tomb is still considered an honored place?

Songhai Falls to Morocco

A northern rival of Songhai, Morocco, wanted to gain control of Songhai's salt mines. So the Moroccan army set out for the heart of Songhai in 1591. Moroccan soldiers carried advanced weapons, including the terrible arquebus (AHR-kwih-buhs). The arquebus was an early form of a gun.

The swords, spears, and bows used by Songhai's warriors were no match for the Moroccans' guns and cannons. The invaders destroyed Timbuktu and Gao.

Changes in trade patterns completed Songhai's fall. Overland trade declined as port cities on the Atlantic coast became more important. Africans south of Songhai and European merchants both preferred trading at Atlantic ports to dealing with Muslim traders. Slowly, the period of great West African empires came to an end.

READING CHECK **Evaluating** What do you think was Askia's greatest accomplishment?

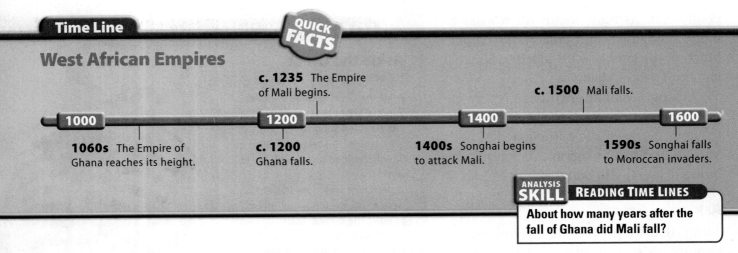

c. 1235 The Empire of Mali begins.

c. 1500 Mali falls.

| 1000 | 1200 | 1400 | 1600 |

1060s The Empire of Ghana reaches its height.

c. 1200 Ghana falls.

1400s Songhai begins to attack Mali.

1590s Songhai falls to Moroccan invaders.

ANALYSIS SKILL **READING TIME LINES**

About how many years after the fall of Ghana did Mali fall?

Great Zimbabwe

Strong kingdoms also arose in other parts of Africa. Great Zimbabwe, for example, was a powerful kingdom in southern Africa. Great Zimbabwe was founded in the late 1000s as a small trading and herding center. Gold mining increased in the area in the 1100s. Farming expanded and the kingdom's population grew. In time, Great Zimbabwe became the center of a large trading network.

THE IMPACT TODAY

The stone fortress remains a major cultural monument in the modern nation of Zimbabwe.

Trade made Great Zimbabwe's rulers wealthy and powerful. They built a huge stone-walled fortress to protect their capital. In the 1400s the gold trade declined.

Deprived of its main source of wealth, Great Zimbabwe weakened. By 1500 it was no longer a political and trading center.

READING CHECK **Comparing** How was Great Zimbabwe similar to the empires of West Africa?

SUMMARY AND PREVIEW Sundiata and Mansa Musa helped Mali become a large empire famous for its wealth and centers of learning. Songhai similarly thrived under leaders such as Askia the Great. In the next section, you will read more about the major West African cultures.

Section 3 Assessment

Reviewing Ideas, Terms, and People

1. **a. Identify** Who was **Sundiata**?
   b. Explain What major river was important to the people of Mali? Why?
   c. Elaborate What effects did the rule of **Mansa Musa** have on Mali and West Africa?

2. **a. Identify** Who led the expansion of Songhai in the 1400s?
   b. Explain How did **Askia the Great's** support of education affect Timbuktu?

3. **a. Recall** What made Great Zimbabwe's rulers wealthy and powerful?
   b. Analyze What led to the decline of Great Zimbabwe?

Critical Thinking

4. **Finding Main Ideas** Use your notes to help you list three major accomplishments of Sundiata and Askia.

Sundiata	Askia

FOCUS ON WRITING

5. **Comparing and Contrasting** Review this section and your notes on African cultures. Consider how your character's life may have been shaped by the culture in which he or she lived. What were the differences between the cultures? How were they the same? How did specific leaders affect the development of the lands they ruled?

Mansa Musa

How could one man's travels become a major historic event?

When did he live? the late 1200s and early 1300s

Where did he live? Mali

What did he do? Mansa Musa, the ruler of Mali, was one of the Muslim kings of West Africa. He became a major figure in African and world history largely because of a pilgrimage he made to the city of Mecca.

Why is he important? Mansa Musa's spectacular journey attracted the attention of the Muslim world and of Europe. For the first time, other people's eyes turned to West Africa. During his travels, Mansa Musa gave out huge amounts of gold. His spending made people eager to find the source of such wealth. Within 200 years, European explorers would arrive on the shores of western Africa.

Identifying Points of View How do you think Mansa Musa changed people's views of West Africa?

KEY FACTS

According to chroniclers of the time, Mansa Musa was accompanied on his journey to Mecca by some 60,000 people. Of those people

12,000 were servants to attend to the king.

500 were servants to attend to his wife.

14,000 more were slaves wearing rich fabrics such as silk.

500 carried staffs heavily decorated with gold. Historians have estimated that the gold Mansa Musa gave away on his trip would be worth more than $100 million today.

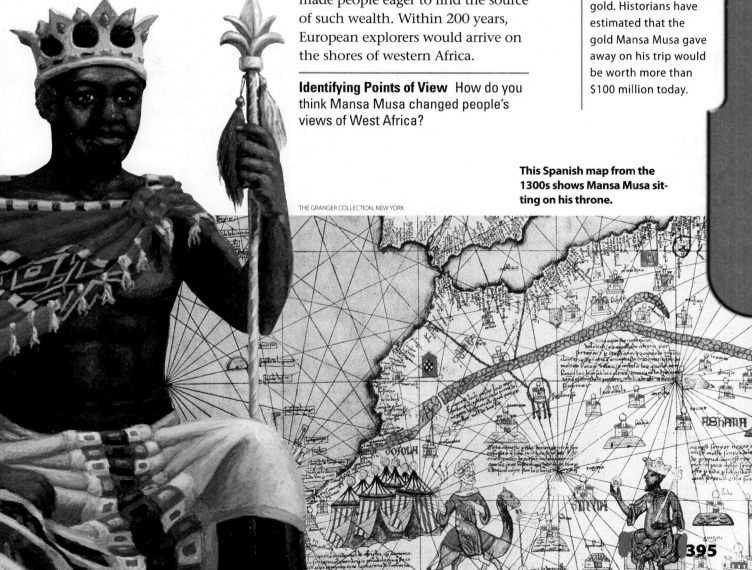

THE GRANGER COLLECTION, NEW YORK

This Spanish map from the 1300s shows Mansa Musa sitting on his throne.

Historical and Artistic Traditions

What You Will Learn...

Main Ideas

1. The history of West Africa has been preserved through storytelling and written accounts.
2. Through art, music, and dance, West Africans have expressed their creativity and kept alive their cultural traditions.

The Big Idea

Although the people of West Africa did not have a written language, their culture has been passed down through oral history, writings by other people, and the arts.

Key Terms

oral history, *p. 396*
griots, *p. 396*
proverbs, *p. 397*
kente, *p. 399*

Online Resource
TAKING NOTES

Use the graphic organizer online to take notes on West African historical and artistic traditions.

If **YOU** were there...

You are the youngest and smallest in your family. People often tease you about not being very strong. In the evenings, when work is done, your village gathers to listen to storytellers. One of your favorite stories is about the hero Sundiata. As a boy he was small and weak, but he grew to be a great warrior and hero.

How does the story of Sundiata make you feel?

BUILDING BACKGROUND Although trading empires rose and fell in West Africa, many traditions continued through the centuries. In every town and village, storytellers passed on the people's histories, legends, and wise sayings. These were at the heart of West Africa's arts and cultural traditions.

Preserving History

Writing was never very common in West Africa. In fact, none of the major early civilizations of West Africa developed a written language. Arabic was the only written language they used. The lack of a native written language does not mean that the people of West Africa didn't know their history, though. They passed along information through oral histories. An **oral history** is a spoken record of past events. The task of remembering and telling West Africa's history was entrusted to storytellers.

The Griots

The storytellers of early West Africa were called **griots** (GREE-ohz). They were highly respected in their communities because the people of West Africa were very interested in the deeds of their ancestors. Griots helped keep this history alive for each new generation.

The griots' stories were both entertaining and informative. They told of important past events and of the accomplishments of distant ancestors. For example, some stories explained the rise and fall of the West African empires. Other stories described the actions of powerful kings and warriors. Some griots made their stories more lively by acting out the events like scenes in a play.

In addition to stories, the griots recited **proverbs**, or short sayings of wisdom or truth. They used proverbs to teach lessons to the people. For example, one West African proverb warns, "Talking doesn't fill the basket in the farm." This proverb reminds people that they must work to accomplish things. It is not enough for people just to talk about what they want to do.

In order to tell their stories and proverbs, the griots memorized hundreds of names and events. Through this memorization **process** the griots passed on West African history from generation to generation. However, some griots confused names and events in their heads. When this happened, the facts of some historical events became distorted. Still, the griots' stories tell us a great deal about life in the West African empires.

West African Epics

Some of the griot poems are epics—long poems about kingdoms and heroes. Many of these epic poems are collected in the *Dausi* (DAW-zee) and the *Sundiata*.

The *Dausi* tells the history of Ghana. Intertwined with historical events, though, are myths and legends. One story is about a seven-headed snake god named Bida. This god promised that Ghana would prosper if the people sacrificed a young woman to him every year. One year a mighty warrior killed Bida. As the god died, he cursed Ghana. The griots say that this curse caused the empire of Ghana to fall.

The *Sundiata* is about Mali's great ruler. According to the epic, when Sundiata was still a boy, a conqueror captured Mali and killed Sundiata's father and 11 brothers.

ACADEMIC VOCABULARY

process a series of steps by which a task is accomplished

Oral Traditions

West African storytellers called griots had the job of remembering and passing on their people's history. Here, people gather to perform traditional dances and to listen to the stories of a griot.

Music from Mali to Memphis

Did you know that the music you listen to today may have begun with the griots? From the 1600s to the 1800s, many people from West Africa were brought to America as slaves. In America, these slaves continued to sing the way they had in Africa. They also continued to play traditional instruments such as the *kora* played by Senegalese musician Soriba Kouyaté (right), the son of a griot. Over time, this music developed into a style called the blues, made popular by such artists as B.B. King (left). In turn, the blues shaped other styles of music, including jazz and rock. So, the next time you hear a Memphis blues track or a cool jazz tune, listen for its ancient African roots!

ANALYSIS SKILL **ANALYZING INFORMATION**

How did West African music affect modern American music?

He didn't kill Sundiata, however, because the boy was sick and didn't seem like a threat. But Sundiata grew up to be an expert warrior. Eventually he overthrew the conqueror and became king.

Visitors' Written Accounts

In addition to the oral histories told about West Africa, visitors wrote about the region. In fact, much of what we know about early West Africa comes from the writings of travelers and scholars from Muslim lands such as Spain and Arabia.

Ibn Battutah was the most famous Muslim visitor to write about West Africa. From 1353 to 1354 he traveled through the region. Ibn Battutah's account of this journey describes the political and cultural lives of West Africans in great detail.

READING CHECK **Drawing Conclusions** Why were oral traditions important in West Africa?

Art, Music, and Dance

Like most peoples, West Africans valued the arts. They expressed themselves creatively through sculpture, mask-making, cloth-making, music, and dance.

Sculpture

Of all the visual art forms, the sculpture of West Africa is probably the best known. West Africans made ornate statues and carvings out of wood, brass, clay, ivory, stone, and other materials.

Most statues from West Africa are of people—often the sculptor's ancestors. Usually these statues were made for religious rituals, to ask for the ancestors' blessings. Sculptors made other statues as gifts for the gods. These sculptures were kept in holy places. They were never meant to be seen by people.

Because their statues were used in religious rituals, many African artists were deeply respected. People thought artists had been blessed by the gods.

Long after the decline of Ghana, Mali, and Songhai, West African art is still admired. Museums around the world display African art. In addition, African sculpture inspired some European artists of the 1900s, including Henri Matisse and Pablo Picasso.

Masks and Clothing

In addition to statues, the artists of West Africa carved elaborate masks. Made of wood, these masks bore the faces of animals such as hyenas, lions, monkeys, and antelopes. Artists often painted the masks after carving them. People wore the masks during rituals as they danced around fires. The way firelight reflected off the masks made them look fierce and lifelike.

Many African societies were famous for the cloth they wove. The most famous of these cloths is called kente (ken-TAY). **Kente** is a hand-woven, brightly colored fabric. The cloth was woven in narrow strips that were then sewn together. Kings and queens in West Africa wore garments made of kente for special occasions.

Music and Dance

In many West African societies, music and dance were as important as the visual arts. Singing, drumming, and dancing were great entertainment, but they also helped people honor their history and mark special occasions. For example, music was played when a ruler entered a room.

Dance has long been a central part of African society. Many West African cultures used dance to celebrate specific events or ceremonies. For example, they may have performed one dance for weddings and another for funerals. In some parts of West Africa, people still perform dances similar to those performed hundreds of years ago.

READING CHECK **Summarizing** Summarize how traditions were preserved in West Africa.

SUMMARY AND PREVIEW The societies of West Africa did not have written languages, but they preserved their histories and cultures through storytelling and the arts. You will next read about another place where traditions are important—China.

Section 4 Assessment

Reviewing Ideas, Terms, and People

1. **a. Define** What is **oral history**?
   b. Make Generalizations Why were **griots** and their stories important in West African society?
   c. Evaluate Why may an oral history provide different information than a written account of the same event?
2. **a. Identify** What were two forms of visual art popular in West Africa?
   b. Make Inferences Why do you think that the sculptures made as gifts for the gods were not meant to be seen by people?
   c. Elaborate What role did music and dance play in West African society?

Critical Thinking

3. **Summarizing** Use a chart like this one and your notes to summarize the importance of each tradition in West Africa.

Tradition	Importance
Storytelling	
Epics	
Sculpture	

FOCUS ON WRITING

4. **Reviewing West African Traditions** Review this section and your notes on the oral and written history of Western Africa and the art, music, and dance of the region. Think about how the griots, visitors from distant lands, or the arts may have affected your character.

Social Studies Skills

Analysis | Critical Thinking | Economics | Study

Interpreting Political Maps

Understand the Skill

Many types of maps are useful in the study of history. *Physical maps* show natural features on Earth's surface. *Political maps* show human cultural features such as cities, states, and countries. Modern political maps show the present-day borders of states and countries. Historical political maps show what cultural features were in the past.

Some historical political maps show how boundaries and features changed over time. Being able to interpret such maps makes the growth and disintegration of countries and empires easier to visualize and understand.

Learn the Skill

Use these guidelines to interpret maps that show political change.

1. Read the title to find out what the map is about.

2. Read the legend. The map's title may state the time period covered by the map. However, in this type of map, information about dates is often found in the legend.

3. Study the legend carefully to be sure you understand what each color or symbol means. Pay special attention to colors or symbols that might indicate changes in borders, signs of the growth or loss of a country's territory.

4. Study the map itself. Compare the colors and symbols in the legend to those on the map. Note any labels, especially those that may show political change. Look for other indications of political changes on the map.

Practice and Apply the Skill

Interpret the map below to answer the following questions about the Mali and Songhai Empires.

1. Which empire was older? Which empire expanded the most?

2. Was Songhai ever part of the Mali Empire? Explain how the map provides this information.

3. Who likely controlled the city of Gao in the year 1100? in 1325? in 1515?

4. By what date do you know for sure that the Mali Empire had disintegrated? How do you know?

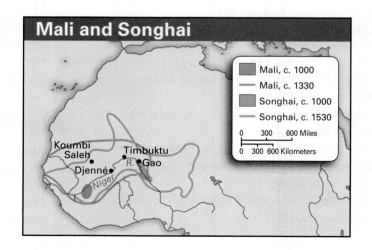

Mali and Songhai

Mali, c. 1000
Mali, c. 1330
Songhai, c. 1000
Songhai, c. 1530

0   300   600 Miles
0   300 600 Kilometers

Koumbi Saleh
Timbuktu
R. Gao
Djenné
Niger

Chapter Review

Visual Summary

Use the visual summary below to help you review the main ideas of the chapter.

The Ghana Empire developed in West Africa and controlled the trade of salt and gold.

Mali's kings built an empire and spread Islam in West Africa.

The Songhai Empire continued to spread Islam.

The history of West Africa has been preserved through story telling, visitors' accounts, art, music, and dance.

Reviewing Vocabulary, Terms, and People

Choose the letter of the answer that best completes each statement below.

1. An area near the equator that has many trees and heavy rainfall may be called a
   - **a.** tropical area.
   - **b.** rain forest.
   - **c.** savannah.
   - **d.** woodland.

2. The belief that natural objects have spirits is called
   - **a.** animism.
   - **b.** vegetism.
   - **c.** animalism.
   - **d.** naturalism.

3. Between the Sahara and the savannah lies the
   - **a.** rain forest.
   - **b.** inland delta.
   - **c.** Zambezi.
   - **d.** Sahel.

4. Mali's rise to power began under a ruler named
   - **a.** Tunka Manin.
   - **b.** Sunni Ali.
   - **c.** Ibn Battutah.
   - **d.** Sundiata.

5. A spoken record of the past is
   - **a.** a Soninke.
   - **b.** an oral history.
   - **c.** a Gao.
   - **d.** an age-set proverb.

6. A West African storyteller is
   - **a.** an Almoravid.
   - **b.** a griot.
   - **c.** an arquebus.
   - **d.** a rift.

7. The Muslim leader of Mali who supported education, spread Islam, and made a famous pilgrimage to Mecca was
   - **a.** Sunni Baru.
   - **b.** Askia the Great.
   - **c.** Mansa Musa.
   - **d.** Muhammad Ture.

8. A brightly colored fabric woven in many African societies is a
   - **a.** kente.
   - **b.** mansa.
   - **c.** Timbuktu.
   - **d.** Tuareg.

Comprehension and Critical Thinking

SECTION 1 *(pages 380–383)*

9. a. Identify Along what river did great civilizations develop in early West Africa?

b. Draw Conclusions Today salt is not nearly as valuable as gold. Why do you think salt was so important in West Africa?

c. Predict How might West Africans have benefited from living in extended families?

SECTION 2 *(pages 386–389)*

10. a. Identify What were the two major trade goods that made Ghana rich? Where did each come from?

b. Make Inferences Why did merchants in Ghana not want other traders to know where their gold came from?

c. Evaluate Who do you think was more responsible for the collapse of Ghana, the people of Ghana or outsiders? Why?

SECTION 3 *(pages 390–394)*

11. a. Describe How did Islam influence society in Mali?

b. Compare and Contrast How were Sundiata and Mansa Musa similar? How were they different?

c. Evaluate Which group do you think played a more important role in Songhai society, warriors or traders?

SECTION 4 *(pages 396–399)*

12. a. Recall What different types of information did griots pass on to their listeners?

b. Analyze Why are the writings of visitors to West Africa so important to our understanding of the region?

c. Evaluate Which of the various arts of West Africa do you think is most important? Why?

Reviewing Themes

13. Geography In which of the four regions were West Africa's two main resources found?

14. Technology How did the development of iron technology affect life in West Africa?

Reading Skills

15. Organization of Facts and Information *Read the paragraph below. What form of organization does the paragraph use? How can you tell?*

> In order to tell their stories and proverbs, the griots memorized hundreds of names and events. Through this memorization process the griots passed on West African history from generation to generation. However, some griots confused names and events in their heads. When this happened, the facts of some historical events became distorted. Still, the griots' stories tell us a great deal about life in the West African empires. *(p. 397)*

Using the Internet

16. Activity: Writing a Proverb Does the early bird get the worm? If you go outside at sunrise to check, you missed the fact that this is a proverb that means "The one that gets there first can earn something good." Griots created many proverbs that expressed wisdom or truth. Go online to research the great West African empires. Write three proverbs that might have been said by griots during this time. Make sure your proverbs are written from the point of view of a West African person living during those centuries.

Social Studies Skills

Interpreting Maps *Look at the map on page 400. Then answer the following question.*

17. Which empire extended farther eastward?

FOCUS ON WRITING

18. Writing Your Journal Entry Review your notes and choose an imaginary character. You might choose, for example, a Berber caravan leader, someone who trades goods with a nearby village, or a griot. Then match that person with a place. Finally, write 5–6 sentences as your journal entry. Include details on what the character sees, feels, and does on a typical day.

DIRECTIONS: Read each question and write the letter of the best response.

> Well placed for the caravan trade, it was badly situated to defend itself from the Tuareg raiders of the Sahara. These restless nomads were repeatedly hammering at the gates of Timbuktu, and often enough they burst them open with disastrous results for the inhabitants. Life here was never quite safe enough to recommend it as the centre [center] of a big state.
>
> —Basil Davidson, from *A History of West Africa*

1 In this quote, the author is discussing why Timbuktu was

A a good place for universities.

B not a good place for a capital city.

C a good location for trade.

D not a good location for the center of the Tuareg state.

2 In the second sentence of the passage above, what does the phrase *hammering at the gates of Timbuktu* mean?

A driving nails into Timbuktu's gates

B knocking on the door to get into the city

C trying to get into and conquer the city

D making noise to anger the inhabitants

3 The region in Africa of open grasslands and scattered trees is the

A griot.

B Sahara.

C savannah.

D Sahel.

4 How were social groups defined in traditional West African cultures?

A by family and age-set

B by religion and family

C by age-set, family, and religion

D by extended family only

5 The two rulers who were most responsible for spreading Islam in West Africa were

A Sunni Ali and Mansa Musa.

B Sundiata and Sunni Ali.

C Ibn Battutah and Tunka Manin.

D Mansa Musa and Askia the Great.

Connecting with Past Learnings

6 You learned earlier about civilizations that developed along the Tigris and Euphrates rivers in what is now Iraq, and along the Huang He in ancient China. Such developments can be compared to changes along which river in West Africa?

A the Niger

B the Congo

C the Nile

D the Zambezi

7 Like Ghana, which East African kingdom that you learned about earlier grew rich from trade but eventually collapsed due to factors that included overgrazing and invasion?

A Sumer

B Kush

C Babylon

D Mohenjo Daro

A Summary of a History Lesson

After you read something, do you have trouble recalling what it was about? Many people do. Writing a summary briefly restating the main ideas and details of something you have read can help you remember it.

Assignment
Write a summary of one section in a chapter you read in Unit 6, "Islamic and African Civilizations."

TIP **How Long Is a Summary?**
Here are some guidelines you can use to plan how much to write in a summary. If you are summarizing

- only a few paragraphs, your summary should be about one third as long as the original.

- longer selections such as an article or textbook chapter, write one sentence for each paragraph or heading in the original.

1. Prewrite

Reading to Understand
The first thing you need to do is to read the section at least twice.
- **Read** it straight through the first time to see what it is about.
- **Reread** it as many times as necessary to be sure you understand the main topic of the whole section.

Identifying the Main Idea
Next, identify the main idea in each paragraph or for each heading in the chapter. Look back at the facts, examples, quotations, and other information in each of them. Ask yourself, *What is the main idea that they all support, or refer to?* State this idea in your own words.

Noting Details
Note the information that directly and best supports each main idea. Often, several details and examples are given to support a single idea. Choose only those that are most important and provide the strongest support.

2. Write
As you write your summary, refer to the framework below to help you keep on track.

A Writer's Framework

Introduction
- Give the section number and title.
- State the main topic of the section.
- Introduce the first main heading in the section and begin your summary by identifying the main idea and supporting information under it.

Body
- Give the main idea, along with its most significant supporting details, for each heading in the section.
- Use words and phrases that show connections between ideas.
- Use your own words as much as you can, and limit quotations in number and length.

Conclusion
- Restate the main idea of the section.
- Comment on maps, charts, other visual content, or other features that were especially important or useful.

3. Evaluate and Revise

Now you need to evaluate your summary to make sure that it is complete and accurate. The following questions can help you decide what to change.

Evaluation Questions for a Summary

- Does your introduction identify the number and title of the section and its main topic?
- Do you identify the main idea of the section?
- Do you include supporting details for each heading or paragraph in the section?
- Do you connect ideas and information by using words that show how they are related?

- Have you written the summary in your own words and limited the number and length of your quotations?
- Does your conclusion state the underlying meaning, or main idea, of the section?

TIP **Finding Main Ideas in a History Chapter** Boldfaced headings in textbooks usually tell what subject is discussed under those headings. The first and last sentences of paragraphs under headings can also be a quick guide to what is said about a subject.

4. Proofread and Publish

Proofreading

Be sure to enclose all quotations in quotation marks and to place other marks of punctuation correctly before or after closing quotation marks.

- **Commas** and **periods** go **inside** closing quotation marks.
- **Semicolons** and **dashes** go **outside** closing quotation marks.
- **Question marks** and **exclamation points** go **inside** closing quotation marks **when they are part of the quotation** and **outside when they are not**.

Publishing

Team up with classmates who have written summaries on different sections of the same chapter you have. Review each other's summaries. Make sure the summaries include all the main ideas and most significant details in each section.

Collect all the summaries to create a chapter study guide for your team. If possible, make copies for everyone on the team. You may also want to make extra copies so that you can trade study guides with teams who worked on other chapters.

TIP **Using Special Historical Features** Don't forget to look at maps, charts, timelines, pictures, historical documents, and even study questions and assignments. They often contain important ideas and information.

● Practice and Apply

Use the steps and strategies outlined in this workshop to write a summary of one section of a chapter in this unit.

UNIT **7** 500–1868

Empires of Asia and the Americas

The Asian civilizations of China and Japan were great centers of learning and culture. In China, a series of dynasties ruled a large and unified empire. China made many advances during this time, including the invention of paper money and gunpowder.

To the east, Japan reached a golden age of art and literature during the Heian Period. Later, the country developed a government run by generals called shoguns and warriors known as samurai.

Across the world, people began to build cities and empires in the Americas. Religion and an interest in astronomy guided the lives of these people.

In the next three chapters, you will learn about the history and culture of the people of China, Japan, and the early Americas.

Explore the Art

In this scene, a young Japanese girl is shown writing in her journal. What does the scene suggest about Japanese society?

FLORIDA...
The Story Continues

CHAPTER 14, China (589–1644)

PLACES **c. 800–1644: The peoples of Southwest Florida build canals.**   Like the Chinese, the Calusa built canals to link the settlements in their lands. They also built canals to connect their settlements to rivers and streams. They even built canals within settlements. Small canals enabled the Calusa to pull their canoes next to their houses. Larger canals served as shortcuts. On Pine Island, the Calusa built a canal that was 18-to-23 feet wide and 3-to-5 feet deep. The canal stretched the entire width of the island. All of the water was not at sea level. This meant that the Calusa had to find a way to span the different water levels. The Calusa solved the problem by building the canal in segments. Workers dammed each segment on both ends to keep the water inside. Travelers lifted their canoes over each dam as they made their way across the different elevations of the island.

PEOPLE **c. 800–1644: Canoes allow the Calusa to travel far.**   Like other coastal people's of Florida, the Calusa built several kinds of boats for transportation. They built sturdy sea-going canoes and small cargo canoes. They also built barges by connecting a platform across two parallel canoes. The Calusa used the boats for fishing and trade and to travel between their coastal settlements. The king used the royal barge to travel by canal and river throughout the lands he controlled. The Calusa's sea-going canoes enabled them to travel as far away as Cuba and other Caribbean islands to trade goods. The Caloosahatchee River was their main waterway in Florida. Caloosahatchee means "River of the Calusa."

PEOPLE **c. 1000–1250: Symbols reflect the power of Fort Walton chiefs.**

The chiefs of the Fort Walton people of Northwest Florida were very powerful. The people believed that the power of the ruling class was tied to the supernatural. The chiefs used their supernatural powers to protect the villages and farms and the crops the people planted. The ruling class's power and importance were reflected in the symbols used to decorate their clothes and ceremonial objects. Eagles, hawks, and falcons held special meaning. Chiefs wore bird costumes for important ceremonies.

PEOPLE **c. 1000–1250: The Fort Walton people are a farming society.**

The people of the Fort Walton culture farmed the Florida panhandle. It was farming that provided the chiefs with wealth and power. Chiefs that controlled the best farmland held the most power. The ruling class—the chief and other officials—lived in a central town. Small individual farms and groups of farms occupied the land around the central town. The farmers paid tribute to the ruling class.

PEOPLE **c. 1000: Bureaucracies help Fort Walton and Calusa societies.**

The Fort Walton people needed to grow a lot of food to feed their large population. The Calusa needed to catch a great deal of fish and other food and maintain the canals and canoes essential for their survival. Both cultures developed a bureaucracy to efficiently carry out these tasks. In the Fort Walton bureaucracy the main chief, his family, and religious leaders were at the top. Below the top layer were the lesser chiefs who served the main chief and the regional chiefs who controlled smaller towns and farmlands. The farmers who worked the land were at the bottom of the Fort Walton bureaucracy.

Unpacking the Florida Standards ◄···

Read the following to learn what this standard says and what it means. See FL8–FL31 to unpack all of the standards related to this chapter.

Benchmark SS.6.W.4.8   Describe the contributions of classical and post classical China. Examples are Great Wall, Silk Road, bronze casting, silk-making, movable type, gunpowder, paper-making, magnetic compass, horse collar, stirrup, civil service system, The Analects.

What does it mean?

Identify the leading achievements of classical and post classical China.

 SPOTLIGHT ON
SS.6.E.1.2, SS.6.E.1.3, SS.6.E.3.1, SS.6.E.3.2, SS.6.E.3.4 See pages FL37–FL39 for content specifically related to these Chapter 14 standards.

14

589–1644

China

> **Essential Question** How did China change after the fall of the Han dynasty?

Florida Next Generation Sunshine State Standards

SS.6.E.1.1 Identify the factors (new resources, increased productivity, education, technology, slave economy, territorial expansion) that increase economic growth. **SS.6.E.1.2** Describe and identify traditional and command economies as they appear in different civilizations. **SS.6.E.1.3** Describe the following economic concepts as they relate to early civilization: scarcity, opportunity cost, supply and demand, barter, trade, productive resources (land, labor, capital, entrepreneurship). **SS.6.E.2.1** Evaluate how civilizations through clans, leaders, and family groups make economic decisions for that civilization providing a framework for future city-state or nation development. **SS.6.E.3.1** Identify examples of mediums of exchange (currencies) used for trade (barter) for each civilization, and explain why international trade requires a system for a medium of exchange between trading both inside and among various regions. **SS.6.E.3.2** Categorize products that were traded among civilizations, and give examples of barriers to trade of those products. **SS.6.E.3.4** Describe the relationship among civilizations that engage in trade, including the benefits and drawbacks of voluntary trade. **SS.6.G.1.4** Utilize tools geographers use to study the world. **SS.6.G.1.6** Use a map to identify major bodies of water of the world, and explain ways they have impacted the development of civilizations. **SS.6.G.3.2** Analyze the impact of human populations on the ancient world's ecosystems. **SS.6.G.4.1** Explain how family and ethnic relationships influenced ancient cultures. **SS.6.W.1.1** Use timelines to identify chronological order of historical events. **SS.6.W.1.2** Identify terms (decade, century, epoch, era, millennium, BC/BCE, AD/CE) and designations of time periods. **SS.6.W.1.3** Interpret primary and secondary sources. **SS.6.W.4.4** Explain the teachings of Buddha, the importance of Asoka, and how Buddhism spread in India, Ceylon, and other parts of Asia. **SS.6.W.4.6** Describe the concept of the Mandate of Heaven and its connection to the Zhou and later dynasties. **SS.6.W.4.7** Explain the basic teachings of Laozi, Confucius, and Han Fei Zi. **SS.6.W.4.8** Describe the contributions of classical and post classical China. **SS.6.W.4.9** Identify key figures from classical and post classical China. **SS.6.W.4.11** Explain the rise and expansion of the Mongol empire and its effects on peoples of Asia and Europe including the achievements of Ghengis and Kublai Khan. **SS.6.W.4.12** Identify the causes and effects of Chinese isolation and the decision to limit foreign trade in the 15th century.

FOCUS ON WRITING

A Magazine Article In this chapter you will read about a great period in the history of China. You will learn about many important accomplishments made during this period, and then you will write a magazine article about them. The purpose of the article will be to explain Chinese contributions to world society.

CHAPTER EVENTS

589 China is reunified under the Sui dynasty.

600

WORLD EVENTS

613 Muhammad begins teaching the basic beliefs of Islam.

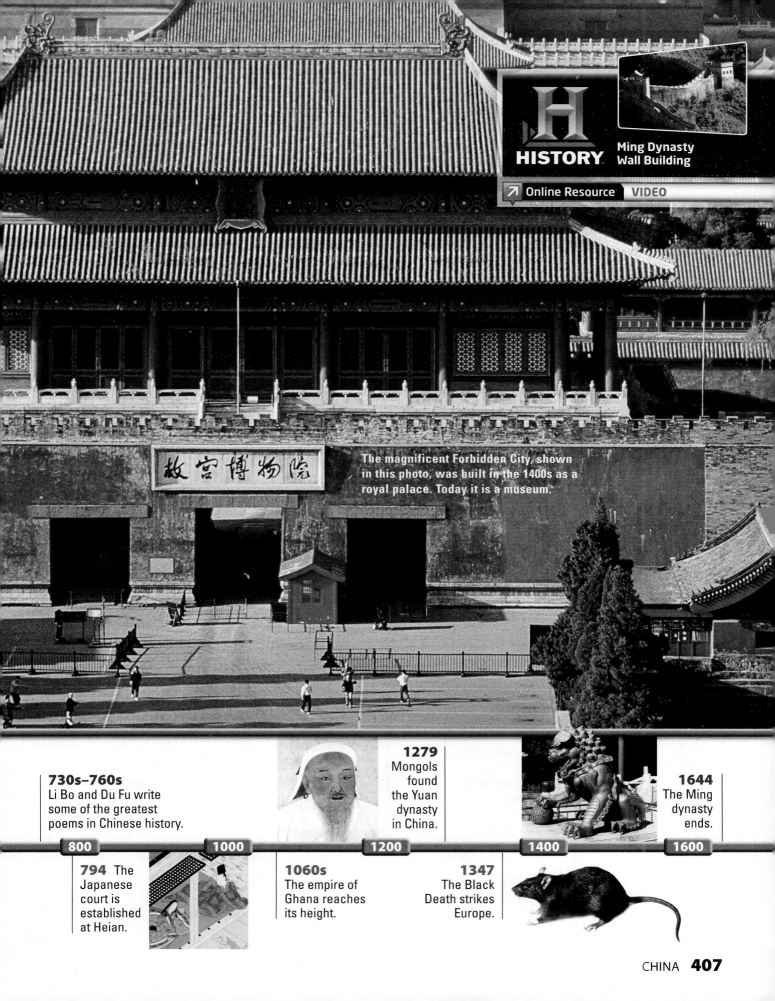

The magnificent Forbidden City, shown in this photo, was built in the 1400s as a royal palace. Today it is a museum.

730s–760s
Li Bo and Du Fu write some of the greatest poems in Chinese history.

1279
Mongols found the Yuan dynasty in China.

1644
The Ming dynasty ends.

800   1000   1200   1400   1600

794 The Japanese court is established at Heian.

1060s
The empire of Ghana reaches its height.

1347
The Black Death strikes Europe.

Reading Social Studies

Economics	Geography	Politics	Religion	Society and Culture	Science and Technology

Focus on Themes This chapter will explore the history of China from the late 500s until the 1600s. As you read, you will discover that many different dynasties ruled the country during that period, leading to great political changes. Some of those dynasties supported trade, leading to great **economic** growth and stability. Others favored isolation, limiting Chinese contact with the rest of the world. You will also learn that this period saw huge leaps forward in **science and technology**.

Drawing Conclusions about the Past

Focus on Reading You have no doubt heard the phrase, "Put two and two together." When people say that, they don't mean "two + two = four." They mean, "Put the information together."

Using Background Knowledge to Draw Conclusions A **conclusion** is a judgment you make by combining information. You put information from what you are reading together with what you already know, your background knowledge.

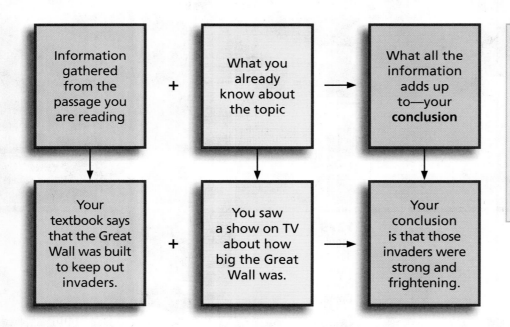

Information gathered from the passage you are reading + What you already know about the topic → What all the information adds up to—your **conclusion**

Your textbook says that the Great Wall was built to keep out invaders. + You saw a show on TV about how big the Great Wall was. → Your conclusion is that those invaders were strong and frightening.

Steps for Drawing Conclusions

1. Read the passage, looking for information the author gives you about the topic.

2. Think about what you already know about the topic. Consider things you've studied, books you've read, or movies you've seen.

3. Put your background knowledge together with what the passage says.

LA.6.1.6.2 The student will listen to, read, and discuss familiar and conceptually challenging text. **LA.6.1.7.3** The student will determine the main idea or essential message in grade-level text through inferring, paraphrasing, summarizing, and identifying relevant details.

Key Terms and People

You Try It!

The following passage is from the chapter you are getting ready to read. As you read the passage, look for facts about China.

Advances in Agriculture

From Chapter 14, p. 414

Chinese civilization had always been based on agriculture. Over thousands of years, the Chinese had become expert farmers. In the north farmers grew wheat, barley, and other grains. In the warmer and wetter south they grew rice.

During the Song dynasty, though, Chinese farming reached new heights. The improvement was largely due to new irrigation techniques. For example, some farmers dug underground wells. A new irrigation device, the dragon backbone pump, allowed one person to do the work of several. With this light and portable pump, a farmer could scoop up water and pour it into an irrigation canal. Using these new techniques, farmers created elaborate irrigation systems.

After you have finished the passage, answer the questions below, drawing conclusions about what you have read.

1. Think back on what you've learned about irrigation systems in other societies. What do you think irrigation was like in China before the Song dynasty?

2. What effect do you think this improved irrigation had on Chinese society? Why do you think this?

3. Based on this passage, what kinds of conditions do you think rice needs to grow? How does this compare to the conditions wheat needs?

4. Which crop was most likely grown near the Great Wall—wheat or rice? Why do you think so?

As you read Chapter 14, think about what you already know about China and draw conclusions to fill gaps in what you are reading.

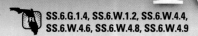
SS.6.G.1.4, SS.6.W.1.2, SS.6.W.4.4, SS.6.W.4.6, SS.6.W.4.8, SS.6.W.4.9

China Reunifies

What You Will Learn...

Main Ideas

1. The Period of Disunion was a time of war and disorder that followed the end of the Han dynasty.
2. China was reunified under the Sui, Tang, and Song dynasties.
3. The Age of Buddhism saw major religious changes in China.

The Big Idea

The Period of Disunion was followed by reunification by rulers of the Sui, Tang, and Song dynasties.

Key Terms and People

Period of Disunion, *p. 410*
Grand Canal, *p. 411*
Empress Wu, *p. 412*

Online Resource
TAKING NOTES

Use the graphic organizer online to take notes about important dates and events in China during the dynasties following the Period of Disunion.

If YOU were there...

You are a peasant in China in the year 264. Your grandfather often speaks of a time when all of China was united, but all you have known is warfare among rulers. A man passing through your village speaks of even more conflict in other areas.

Why might you want China to have just one ruler?

BUILDING BACKGROUND Most of China's history is divided into dynasties. The first dynasties ruled China for centuries. But when the Han dynasty collapsed in 220, China plunged into disorder.

The Period of Disunion

When the Han dynasty collapsed, China split into several rival kingdoms, each ruled by military leaders. Historians sometimes call the time of disorder that followed the collapse of the Han the **Period of Disunion**. It lasted from 220 to 589.

War during the Period of Disunion was frequent and bloody. For the first time, heavily armored warriors with lances could charge into battle, due to the invention of the stirrup. These mounted warriors could easily overpower several opposing soldiers on foot. During this period, nomadic peoples settled in northern China. Some Chinese people adopted the nomads' culture, while the invaders adopted some Chinese practices. Thus, the culture of the invaders and traditional Chinese mixed.

A similar cultural blending took place in southern China. Many northern Chinese, unwilling to live under the rule of the nomadic invaders, fled to southern China. There, northern Chinese culture mixed with the more southern cultures.

As a result of this mixing, Chinese culture changed. New types of art and music developed. New foods and clothing styles became popular. The new culture spread over a wider geographic area than ever before, and more people became Chinese.

READING CHECK **Finding Main Ideas** How did Chinese culture change during the Period of Disunion?

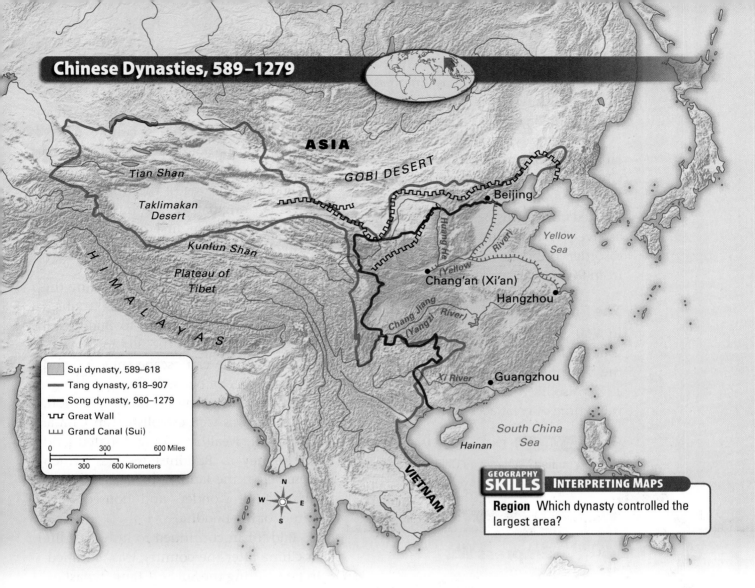

Chinese Dynasties, 589–1279

ASIA

Tian Shan

Taklimakan Desert

GOBI DESERT

Beijing

Kunlun Shan

Yellow Sea

Plateau of Tibet

H I M A L A Y A S

Huang He (Yellow River)

Chang'an (Xi'an)

Hangzhou

Chang Jiang (Yangzi River)

Xi River

Guangzhou

Hainan

South China Sea

VIETNAM

Legend:
- Sui dynasty, 589–618
- Tang dynasty, 618–907
- Song dynasty, 960–1279
- Great Wall
- Grand Canal (Sui)

0   300   600 Miles
0   300   600 Kilometers

N W E S

GEOGRAPHY SKILLS | **INTERPRETING MAPS**

Region Which dynasty controlled the largest area?

The Sui, Tang, and Song

Finally, after centuries of political confusion and cultural change, China was reunified. For about 700 years, it remained unified under a series of powerful dynasties.

The Sui Dynasty

The man who finally ended the Period of Disunion was a northern ruler named Yang Jian (YANG jee-EN). In 589, he conquered the south, unified China, and created the Sui (SWAY) dynasty.

The Sui dynasty didn't last long, only from 589 to 618. During that time, though, its leaders restored order to China and began the **Grand Canal,** a canal linking northern and southern China.

The Tang Dynasty

A new dynasty arose in China in 618 when a former Sui official overthrew the old government. This dynasty, the Tang, would rule for nearly 300 years. As you can see on the map, China grew under the Tang dynasty to include much of eastern Asia, as well as large parts of Central Asia.

Historians view the Tang dynasty as a golden age of Chinese civilization. One of its greatest rulers was Taizong (TY-tzoong). He conquered many lands, reformed the military, and created law codes. Another brilliant Tang ruler was Xuanzong (SHOO-AN-tzoong). During his reign, culture flourished. Many of China's finest poets wrote while Xuanzong ruled.

FOCUS ON

Post-Classical China The Sui dynasty marks the beginning of post-classical China. Historians describe the post-classical age of China as the period of the Sui, Tang, and Song dynasties.

SS.6.W.4.9 Identify key figures from classical and post classical China.

The Tang dynasty also included the only woman to rule China—**Empress Wu**. Her methods were sometimes vicious, but she was intelligent and talented.

The Tang dynasty fell partly due to a large rebellion mainly incited by famine. China entered another period of chaos with separate kingdoms. China was so divided during this period that it is known as Five Dynasties and Ten Kingdoms. The disorder only lasted 53 years, though, from 907 to 960.

The Song Dynasty

In 960, China was again reunified, this time by the Song dynasty. Like the Tang, the Song ruled for about 300 years, until 1279. Also like the Tang, the Song dynasty was a time of great accomplishments.

READING CHECK **Sequencing** When was China reunified? When was China not unified?

BIOGRAPHY

Empress Wu
625–705

Married to a sickly emperor, Empress Wu became the virtual ruler of China in 655. After her husband died, Wu decided her sons were not worthy of ruling. She kept power for herself, and ruled with an iron fist. Those who threatened her power risked death. Unlike many earlier rulers, she chose advisors based on their abilities rather than their ranks. Although she was not well liked, Wu was respected for bringing stability and prosperity to China.

Drawing Conclusions Why do you think Empress Wu was never very popular?

The Age of Buddhism

While China was experiencing changes in its government, another major change was taking place in Chinese culture. A new religion was spreading quickly throughout the vast land.

Buddhism is one of the world's major religions, originating in India around 500 BC. Buddhism first came to China during the Han dynasty. But for some time, there were few Buddhists in China.

Buddhism's status changed during the Period of Disunion. During this troubled time, many people turned to Buddhism. They took comfort in the Buddhist teaching that people can escape suffering and achieve a state of peace.

By the end of the Period of Disunion, Buddhism was well established in China. As a result, wealthy people donated land and money to Buddhist temples, which arose across the land. Some temples were architectural wonders and housed huge statues of the Buddha.

Buddhism continued to influence life in China after the country was reunified. In fact, during the Sui and Tang dynasties, Buddhism continued to grow and spread. Chinese missionaries, people who travel to spread their religion, introduced Buddhism to Japan, Korea, and other Asian lands.

Buddhism influenced many aspects of Chinese culture, including art, literature, and architecture. In fact, so important was Buddhism in China that the period from about 400 to about 845 can be called the Age of Buddhism.

This golden age of Buddhism came to an end when a Tang emperor launched a campaign against the religion. He burned many Buddhist texts, took lands from Buddhist temples, destroyed many temples, and turned others into schools.

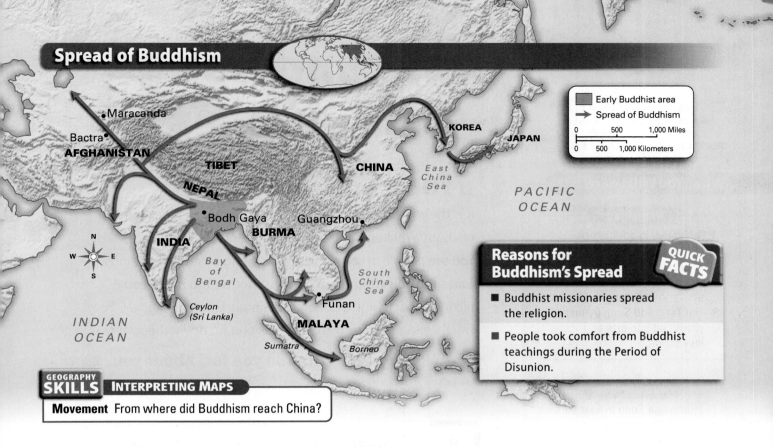

Spread of Buddhism

Maracanda
Bactra
AFGHANISTAN
TIBET
NEPAL
Bodh Gaya
INDIA
BURMA
Guangzhou
CHINA
KOREA
JAPAN
East China Sea
PACIFIC OCEAN
Bay of Bengal
South China Sea
Ceylon (Sri Lanka)
Funan
MALAYA
INDIAN OCEAN
Sumatra
Borneo

Early Buddhist area
→ Spread of Buddhism
0   500   1,000 Miles
0   500   1,000 Kilometers

Reasons for Buddhism's Spread
QUICK FACTS

- Buddhist missionaries spread the religion.
- People took comfort from Buddhist teachings during the Period of Disunion.

GEOGRAPHY SKILLS **INTERPRETING MAPS**

Movement From where did Buddhism reach China?

The emperor's actions weakened the influence of Buddhism in China, but they did not destroy it completely. Buddhism continued to play a key role in Chinese society for centuries. As it had during the early Tang period, it continued to shape Chinese art and literature. But even as it influenced life in China, Buddhism changed. People began to blend elements of Buddhism with elements of other philosophies, especially Confucianism and Daoism, to create a new way of thinking.

READING CHECK **Identifying Cause and Effect** Why did Buddhism spread more easily during the Period of Disunion?

SUMMARY AND PREVIEW From the disorder that followed the fall of the Han dynasty, new dynasties arose to restore order in China. You will read about their many advances in the next section.

Section 1 Assessment

Reviewing Ideas, Terms, and People
1. **a. Define** What was the **Period of Disunion**?
   b. Explain How did Chinese culture change during the Period of Disunion?
2. **a. Identify** Who was **Empress Wu**? What did she do?
   b. Evaluate How do you think the reunification of China affected the common people?
3. **a. Identify** When was the Age of Buddhism in China?
   b. Explain Why did people turn to Buddhism during the Period of Disunion?
   c. Elaborate How did Buddhism influence Chinese culture?

Critical Thinking
4. **Sequencing** Draw a time line like this one. Using your notes on important events, place the main events and their dates on the time line.

200   1300

FOCUS ON WRITING

5. **Getting an Overview** In this section you read an overview of three major dynasties and the contributions of Buddhism. Make a note of any ideas or contributions that you might want to include in your article.

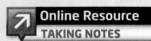
What You Will Learn...

Main Ideas

1. Advances in agriculture led to increased trade and population growth.
2. Cities and trade grew during the Tang and Song dynasties.
3. The Tang and Song dynasties produced fine arts and inventions.

The Big Idea

The Tang and Song dynasties were periods of economic, cultural, and technological accomplishments.

Key Terms

porcelain, *p. 417*
woodblock printing, *p. 418*
gunpowder, *p. 418*
compass, *p. 418*

Online Resource
TAKING NOTES

Use the graphic organizer online to take notes about accomplishments of the Tang and Song dynasties.

SS.6.W.4.8 Describe the contributions of classical and post classical China.

Tang and Song Achievements

If YOU were there...

It is the year 1270. You are a rich merchant in a Chinese city of about a million people. The city around you fills your senses. You see people in colorful clothes among beautiful buildings. Glittering objects lure you into busy shops. You hear people talking—discussing business, gossiping, laughing at jokes. You smell delicious food cooking at a restaurant down the street.

How do you feel about your city?

BUILDING BACKGROUND The Tang and Song dynasties were periods of great wealth and progress. Changes in farming formed the basis for other advances in Chinese civilization.

Advances in Agriculture

Chinese civilization had always been based on agriculture. Over thousands of years, the Chinese had become expert farmers. In the north farmers grew wheat, barley, and other grains. In the warmer and wetter south they grew rice.

During the Song dynasty, though, Chinese farming reached new heights. The improvement was largely due to new irrigation techniques. For example, some farmers dug underground wells. A new irrigation device, the dragon backbone pump, allowed one person to do the work of several. With this light and portable pump, a farmer could scoop up water and pour it into an irrigation canal. Using these new techniques, farmers created elaborate irrigation systems.

414

Under the Song, the amount of land under cultivation increased. Lands along the Chang Jiang that had been wild now became farmland. Farms also became more productive, thanks to the discovery of a new type of fast-ripening rice. Because it grew and ripened quickly, this rice enabled farmers to grow two or even three crops in the time it used to take to grow just one.

Chinese farmers also learned to grow new crops, such as cotton, efficiently. Workers processed cotton fiber to make clothes and other goods. The production of tea, which had been grown in China for centuries, also increased.

Agricultural surpluses helped pay taxes to the government. Merchants also traded food crops. As a result, food was abundant not just in the countryside but also in the cities. Because food was plentiful, China's population grew quickly. During the Tang dynasty, the population had been about 60 million. During the Song dynasty, the farmers of China fed a country of nearly 100 million people. At the time, China was the largest country in the world.

READING CHECK **Identifying Cause and Effect** How did agricultural advances affect population growth?

THE IMPACT TODAY

China is still the world's most populous country. More than 1.3 billion people live there today.

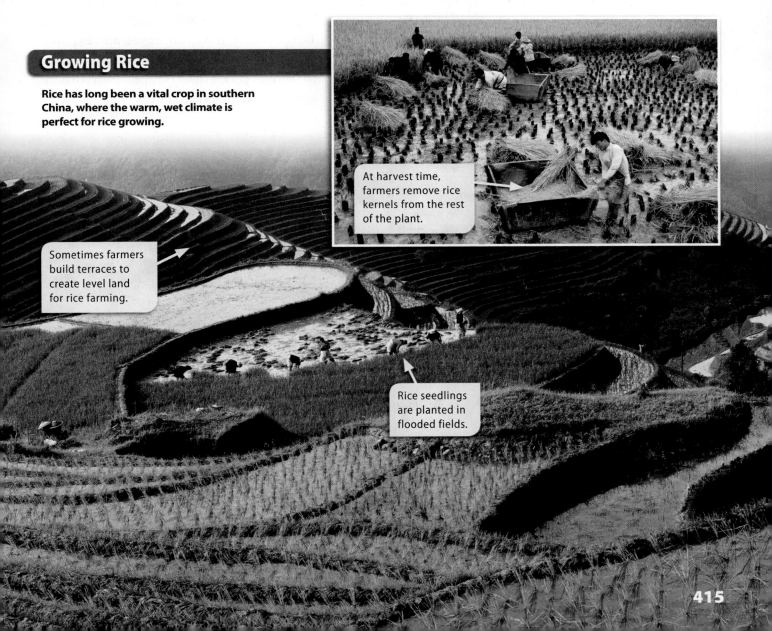

Growing Rice

Rice has long been a vital crop in southern China, where the warm, wet climate is perfect for rice growing.

At harvest time, farmers remove rice kernels from the rest of the plant.

Sometimes farmers build terraces to create level land for rice farming.

Rice seedlings are planted in flooded fields.

415

Cities and Trade

Throughout the Tang and Song dynasties, much of the food grown on China's farms flowed into the growing cities and towns. China's cities were crowded, busy places. Shopkeepers, government officials, doctors, artisans, entertainers, religious leaders, and artists made them lively places as well.

City Life

FOCUS ON READING

What can you conclude about the link between the Grand Canal and the growth of cities?

China's capital and largest city of the Tang dynasty was Chang'an (chahng-AHN), a huge, bustling trade center. With a population of more than a million, it was by far the largest city in the world at the time.

Chang'an, like other trading cities, had a mix of people from many cultures—China, Korea, Persia, Arabia, and Europe. It was also known as a religious and philosophical center, not just for Buddhists and Daoists but for Asian Christians as well.

Cities continued to grow under the Song. Several cities, including the Song capital, Kaifeng (KY-fuhng), had about a million people. A dozen more cities had populations of close to half a million.

Trade in China and Beyond

Trade grew along with Chinese cities. This trade, combined with China's agricultural base, made China richer than ever before.

Much trade took place within China itself. Traders used the country's rivers to ship goods on barges and ships.

The Grand Canal, a series of waterways that linked major cities, carried a huge amount of trade goods, especially farm products. Construction on the canal had begun during the Sui dynasty. During the Tang dynasty, it was improved and expanded. The Grand Canal allowed the Chinese to move goods and crops from distant agricultural areas into cities.

The Grand Canal

Beijing

Huang He (Yellow River)

Yellow Sea

Zhenjiang

Chang'an

Chang Jiang (Yangzi River)

Hangzhou

East China Sea

Grand Canal (Sui)

The Chinese also carried on trade with other lands and peoples. During the Tang dynasty, most foreign trade was over land routes leading west to India and Southwest Asia, though Chinese traders also went to Korea and Japan in the east. The Chinese exported many goods, including tea, rice, spices, and jade. However, one export was especially important—silk. So valuable was silk that the Chinese tried to keep the method of making it secret. In exchange for their exports, the Chinese imported different foods and plants, wool, glass, gold, and silver.

During the Song dynasty, maritime trade, or sea trade, became more important. China opened its Pacific ports to foreign traders. The sea-trade routes connected China to many other countries. During this time, the Chinese also developed another valuable product—a thin, beautiful type of pottery called **porcelain**.

China's Grand Canal is the world's longest human-made waterway. It was built largely to transport rice and other foods from the south to feed China's cities and armies in the north. Barges like the ones at left crowd the Grand Canal, which is still an important transportation link in China. Some people even live on the canal in small houseboats like the one above.

All of this trade helped create a strong economy. As a result, merchants became important members of Chinese society during the Song dynasty. Also as a result of the growth of trade and wealth, the Song invented the world's first system of paper money in the 900s.

READING CHECK **Summarizing** How far did China's trade routes extend?

Arts and Inventions

While China grew rich economically, its cultural riches also increased. In literature, art, and science, China made huge advances.

Artists and Poets

The artists and writers of the Tang dynasty were some of China's greatest. Wu Daozi (DOW-tzee) painted murals that celebrated Buddhism and nature. Li Bo and Du Fu wrote poems that readers still enjoy for their beauty. This poem by Li Bo expresses the homesickness that one feels late at night:

> " Before my bed
> there is bright moonlight
> So that it seems
> like frost on the ground:
> Lifting my head
> I watch the bright moon,
> Lowering my head
> I dream that I'm home. "
> –Li Bo, *Quiet Night Thoughts*

Also noted for its literature, the Song period produced Li Qingzhao (ching-ZHOW), perhaps China's greatest female poet. She once said that the purpose of her poetry was to capture a single moment in time.

Artists of both the Tang and Song dynasties made exquisite objects in clay. Tang figurines of horses clearly show the animals' strength. Song artists made porcelain items covered in a pale green glaze called celadon (SEL-uh-duhn).

THE IMPACT TODAY

Porcelain became so popular in the West that it became known as chinaware, or just china.

Chinese Inventions

Paper
Invented during the Han dynasty around 105, paper was one of the greatest of all Chinese inventions. It gave the Chinese a cheap and easy way of keeping records and made printing possible.

Porcelain
Porcelain was first made during the Tang dynasty, but it wasn't perfected for many centuries. Chinese artists were famous for their work with this fragile material.

Woodblock printing
The Chinese invented printing during the Tang dynasty, centuries before it was known in Europe. Printers could copy drawings or texts quickly, much faster than they could be copied by hand.

Gunpowder
Invented during the late Tang or early Song dynasty, gunpowder was used to make fireworks and signals. The Chinese did not generally use it as a weapon.

Movable type
Inventors of the Song dynasty created movable type, which made printing much faster. Carved letters could be rearranged and reused to print many different messages.

Magnetic compass
Invented no later than the Han period, the compass was greatly improved by the Tang. The new compass allowed sailors and merchants to travel vast distances.

Paper money
The world's first paper money was invented by the Song. Lighter and easier to handle than coins, paper money helped the Chinese manage their growing wealth.

Important Inventions

The Tang and Song dynasties produced some of the most remarkable—and most important—inventions in human history. Some of these inventions influenced events around the world.

According to legend, a man named Cai Lun invented paper in the year 105 during the Han dynasty. A later Tang invention built on Cai Lun's achievement—**woodblock printing,** a form of printing in which an entire page is carved into a block of wood. The printer applies ink to the block and presses paper against the block to create a printed page. The world's first known printed book was printed in this way in China in 868.

Another invention of the Tang dynasty was gunpowder. **Gunpowder** is a mixture of powders used in guns and explosives. It was originally used only in fireworks, but it was later used to make small bombs and rockets. Eventually, gunpowder was used to make explosives, firearms, and cannons. Gunpowder dramatically altered how wars were fought and, in doing so, changed the course of human history.

One of the most useful achievements of Tang China was the perfection of the magnetic **compass**. This instrument, which uses the earth's magnetic field to show direction, revolutionized travel. A compass made it possible to find direction more accurately than ever before. The perfection of the compass had far-reaching effects. Explorers the world over used the compass to travel vast distances. The navigators of trading ships and warships also came to rely on the compass. Thus, the compass has been a key factor in some of the most important sailing voyages in history.

The Song dynasty also produced many important inventions. Under the Song, the Chinese invented movable type. Movable type is a set of letters or characters that are

The Paper Trail

The dollar bill in your pocket may be crisp and new, but paper money has been around a long time. Paper money was printed for the first time in China in the AD 900s and was in use for about 700 years, through the Ming dynasty, when the bill shown here was printed. However, so much money was printed that it lost value. The Chinese stopped using paper money for centuries. Its use caught on in Europe, though, and eventually became common. Most countries now issue paper money.

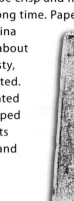

ANALYSIS SKILL **ANALYZING INFORMATION**

What are some advantages of paper money?

used to print books. Unlike the blocks used in block printing, movable type can be rearranged and reused to create new lines of text and different pages.

The Song dynasty also introduced the concept of paper money. People were used to buying goods and services with bulky coins made of metals such as bronze, gold, and silver. Paper money was far lighter and easier to use. As trade increased and many people in China grew rich, paper money became more popular.

READING CHECK **Finding Main Ideas** What were some important inventions of the Tang and Song dynasties?

SUMMARY AND PREVIEW The Tang and Song dynasties were periods of great advancement. Many great artists and writers lived during these periods. Tang and Song inventions also had dramatic effects on world history. In the next section you will learn about the government of the Song dynasty.

Section 2 Assessment

Reviewing Ideas, Terms, and People

1. **a. Recall** What advances in farming occurred during the Song dynasty?
   b. Explain How did agricultural advancements affect China's population?
2. **a. Describe** What were the capital cities of Tang and Song China like?
   b. Draw Conclusions How did **geography** affect trade in China?
3. **a. Identify** Who was Li Bo?
   b. Draw Conclusions How may the inventions of paper money and **woodblock printing** have been linked?
   c. Rank Which Tang or Song invention do you think was most important? Defend your answer.

Critical Thinking

4. **Categorizing** Copy the chart at right. Use it to organize your notes on the Tang and Song into categories.

	Tang dynasty	Song dynasty
Agriculture		
Cities		
Trade		
Art		
Inventions		

FOCUS ON WRITING

5. **Identifying Achievements** You have just read about the achievements of the Tang and Song dynasties. Make a list of those you might include in your article.

Confucianism and Government

What You Will Learn...

Main Ideas

1. Confucianism underwent changes and influenced Chinese government.
2. Scholar-officials ran China's government during the Song dynasty.

The Big Idea

Confucian thought influenced the Song government.

Key Terms

bureaucracy, *p. 422*
civil service, *p. 422*
scholar-official, *p. 422*

Online Resource
TAKING NOTES

Use the graphic organizer online to take notes on Confucianism and the Song government.

If YOU were there...

You are a student in China in 1184. Night has fallen, but you cannot sleep. Tomorrow you have a test. You know it will be the most important test of your entire life. You have studied for it, not for days or weeks or even months—but for *years*. As you toss and turn, you think about how your entire life will be determined by how well you do on this one test.

How could a single test be so important?

BUILDING BACKGROUND The Song dynasty ruled China from 960 to 1279. This was a time of improvements in agriculture, growing cities, extensive trade, and the development of art and inventions. It was also a time of major changes in Chinese government.

Confucianism

The dominant philosophy in China, Confucianism is based on the teachings of Confucius. He lived more than 1,500 years before the Song dynasty. His ideas, though, had a dramatic effect on the Song system of government.

Confucian Ideas

Confucius's teachings focused on ethics, or proper behavior, for individuals and governments. He said that people should conduct their lives according to two basic principles. These principles were *ren*, or concern for others, and *li*, or appropriate behavior. Confucius argued that society would **function** best if everyone followed *ren* and *li*.

Confucius thought that everyone had a proper role to play in society. Order was maintained when people knew their place and behaved appropriately. For example, Confucius said that young people should obey their elders and that subjects should obey their rulers.

The Influence of Confucianism

After his death, Confucius's ideas were spread by his followers, but they were not widely accepted. In fact, the Qin dynasty officially suppressed Confucian ideas and teachings. By the time of the Han dynasty, Confucianism had again come into favor, and Confucianism became the official state philosophy.

During the Period of Disunion, which followed the Han dynasty, Confucianism was overshadowed by Buddhism as the major tradition in China. As you recall, many Chinese people turned to Buddhism for comfort during these troubled times. In doing so, they largely turned away from Confucian ideas and outlooks.

Later, during the Sui and early Tang dynasties, Buddhism was very influential. Unlike Confucianism, which stressed ethical behavior, Buddhism stressed a more spiritual outlook that promised escape from suffering. As Buddhism became more popular in China, Confucianism lost some of its influence.

ACADEMIC VOCABULARY

function work or perform

PHOTOGRAPH © 2012 MUSEUM OF FINE ARTS, BOSTON

In addition to ethics, Confucianism stressed the importance of education. This painting, created during the Song period, shows earlier Confucian scholars during the Period of Disunion sorting scrolls containing classic Confucian texts.

Civil Service Exams

This painting from the 1600s shows civil servants writing essays for China's emperor. Difficult exams were designed to make sure that government officials were chosen by ability—not by wealth or family connections.

Difficult Exams

- Students had to memorize entire Confucian texts.

- To pass the most difficult tests, students might study for more than 20 years!

- Some exams lasted up to 72 hours, and students were locked in private rooms while taking them.

- Some dishonest students cheated by copying Confucius's works on the inside of their clothes, paying bribes to the test graders, or paying someone else to take the test for them.

- To prevent cheating, exam halls were often locked and guarded.

Neo-Confucianism

Late in the Tang dynasty, many Chinese historians and scholars again became interested in the teachings of Confucius. Their interest was sparked by their desire to improve Chinese government and society.

During and after the Song dynasty, a new philosophy called Neo-Confucianism developed. The term *neo* means "new." Based on Confucianism, Neo-Confucianism was similar to the older philosophy in that it taught proper behavior. However, it also emphasized spiritual matters. For example, Neo-Confucian scholars discussed such issues as what made human beings do bad things even if their basic nature was good.

Neo-Confucianism became much more influential under the Song. Later its influence grew even more. In fact, the ideas of Neo-Confucianism became official government teachings after the Song dynasty.

ACADEMIC VOCABULARY

incentive something that leads people to follow a certain course of action

READING CHECK **Contrasting** How did Neo-Confucianism differ from Confucianism?

Scholar-Officials

The Song dynasty took another major step that affected China for centuries. They improved the system by which people went to work for the government. These workers formed a large **bureaucracy,** or a body of unelected government officials. They joined the bureaucracy by passing civil service examinations. **Civil service** means service as a government official.

To become a civil servant, a person had to pass a series of written examinations. The examinations tested students' grasp of Confucianism and related ideas.

Because the tests were so difficult, students spent years preparing for them. Only a very small fraction of the people who took the tests would reach the top level and be appointed to a position in the government. However, candidates for the civil service examinations had a strong **incentive** for studying hard. Passing the tests meant life as a **scholar-official**—an educated member of the government.

Scholar-Officials

First rising to prominence under the Song, scholar-officials remained important in China for centuries. These scholar-officials, for example, lived during the Qing dynasty, which ruled from the mid-1600s to the early 1900s. Their typical responsibilities might include running government offices; maintaining roads, irrigation systems, and other public works; updating and maintaining official records; or collecting taxes.

Scholar-officials were elite members of society. They performed many important jobs in the government and were widely admired for their knowledge and ethics. Their benefits included considerable respect and reduced penalties for breaking the law. Many also became wealthy from gifts given by people seeking their aid.

The civil service examination system helped ensure that talented, intelligent people became scholar-officials. The civil service system was a major factor in the stability of the Song government.

READING CHECK **Analyzing** How did the Song dynasty change China's government?

SUMMARY AND PREVIEW During the Song period, Confucian ideas helped shape China's government. In the next section, you will read about the two dynasties that followed the Song—the Yuan and the Ming.

Section 3 Assessment

Reviewing Ideas, Terms, and People

1. **a. Identify** What two principles did Confucius believe people should follow?
   b. Explain What was Neo-Confucianism?
   c. Elaborate Why do you think Neo-Confucianism appealed to many people?
2. **a. Define** What was a **scholar-official**?
   b. Explain Why would people want to become scholar-officials?
   c. Evaluate Do you think **civil service** examinations were a good way to choose government officials? Why or why not?

Critical Thinking

3. **Sequencing** Review your notes to see how Confucianism led to Neo-Confucianism and Neo-Confucianism led to government bureaucracy. Use a graphic organizer like the one here.

Confucianism → Neo-Confucianism → Government bureaucracy

FOCUS ON WRITING

4. **Gathering Ideas about Confucianism and Government** In this section you read about Confucianism and new ideas about government. What did you learn that you could add to your list of achievements?

SS.6.E.3.2, SS.6.E.3.4, SS.6.G.1.4, SS.6.G.4.1, SS.6.W.1.2, SS.6.W.1.3, SS.6.W.4.8, SS.6.W.4.9, SS.6.W.4.11, SS.6.W.4.12

What You Will Learn...

Main Ideas

1. The Mongol Empire included China, and the Mongols ruled China as the Yuan dynasty.
2. The Ming dynasty was a time of stability and prosperity.
3. China under the Ming saw great changes in its government and relations with other countries.

The Big Idea

The Chinese were ruled by foreigners during the Yuan dynasty, but they threw off Mongol rule and prospered during the Ming dynasty.

Key Terms and People

Genghis Khan, *p. 424*
Kublai Khan, *p. 425*
Zheng He, *p. 427*
isolationism, *p. 430*

Online Resource
TAKING NOTES

Use the graphic organizer online to take notes about the Yuan and Ming dynasties.

SS.6.W.4.11 Explain the rise and expansion of the Mongol empire and its effects on peoples of Asia and Europe including the achievements of Ghengis and Kublai Khan.

The Yuan and Ming Dynasties

If YOU were there...

You are a farmer in northern China in 1212. As you pull weeds from a wheat field, you hear a sound like thunder. Looking toward the sound, you see hundreds—no, *thousands*—of armed horsemen on the horizon, riding straight toward you. You are frozen with fear. Only one thought fills your mind—the dreaded Mongols are coming.

What can you do to save yourself?

BUILDING BACKGROUND Throughout its history, northern China had been attacked over and over by nomadic peoples. During the Song dynasty these attacks became more frequent and threatening.

The Mongol Empire

Among the nomadic peoples who attacked the Chinese were the Mongols. For centuries, the Mongols had lived as separate tribes in the vast plains north of China. Then in 1206, a powerful leader, or khan, united them. His name was Temüjin. When he became leader, though, he was given a new title: "Universal Ruler," or **Genghis Khan** (JENG-guhs KAHN).

The Mongol Conquest

Genghis Khan organized the Mongols into a powerful army and led them on bloody expeditions of conquest. The brutality of the Mongol attacks terrorized people throughout much of Asia and Eastern Europe. Genghis Khan and his army killed all of the men, women, and children in countless cities and villages. Within 20 years, he ruled a large part of Asia.

Genghis Khan then turned his attention to China. He first led his armies into northern China in 1211. They fought their way south, wrecking whole towns and ruining farmland. By the time of Genghis Khan's death in 1227, all of northern China was under Mongol control.

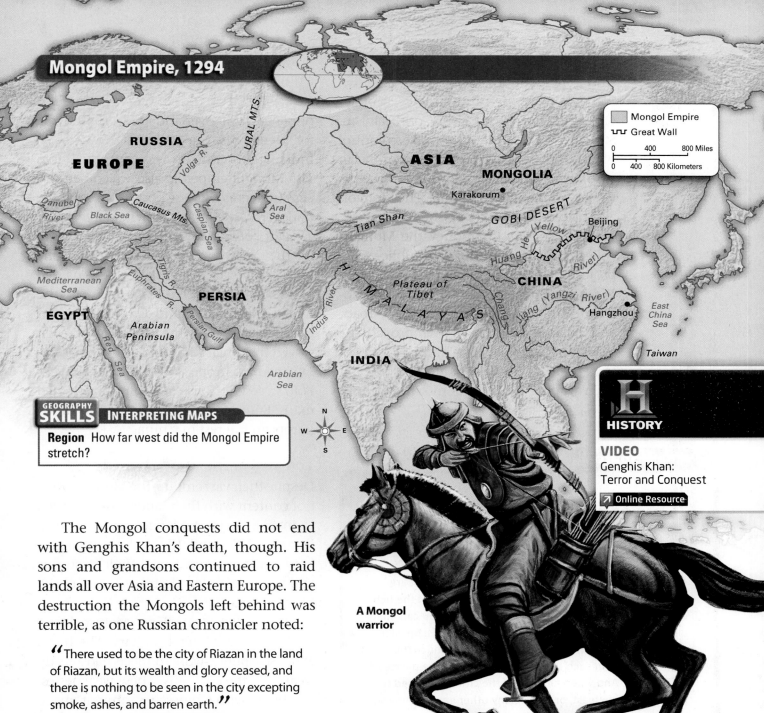

Mongol Empire, 1294

Legend:
- Mongol Empire
- Great Wall

0 400 800 Miles
0 400 800 Kilometers

RUSSIA

EUROPE

URAL MTS.

Volga R.

Danube River

Black Sea

Caucasus Mts.

Caspian Sea

Mediterranean Sea

Tigris R.

Euphrates R.

Aral Sea

ASIA

MONGOLIA

Karakorum

Tian Shan

GOBI DESERT

Huang He (Yellow River)

Beijing

EGYPT

Arabian Peninsula

Persian Gulf

Red Sea

PERSIA

Indus River

HIMALAYAS

Plateau of Tibet

CHINA

Chang Jiang (Yangzi River)

Hangzhou

East China Sea

Taiwan

INDIA

Arabian Sea

N W E S

GEOGRAPHY SKILLS **INTERPRETING MAPS**

Region How far west did the Mongol Empire stretch?

HISTORY

VIDEO
Genghis Khan:
Terror and Conquest
↗ Online Resource

A Mongol warrior

The Mongol conquests did not end with Genghis Khan's death, though. His sons and grandsons continued to raid lands all over Asia and Eastern Europe. The destruction the Mongols left behind was terrible, as one Russian chronicler noted:

❝There used to be the city of Riazan in the land of Riazan, but its wealth and glory ceased, and there is nothing to be seen in the city excepting smoke, ashes, and barren earth.❞
–from "The Tale of the Destruction of Riazan," in *Medieval Russia's Epics, Chronicles, and Tales*, edited by Serge Zenkovsky

In 1260 Genghis Khan's grandson **Kublai Khan** (KOO-bluh KAHN) became ruler of the Mongol Empire. He completed the conquest of China and in 1279 declared himself emperor of China. This began the Yuan dynasty, a period that some people also call the Mongol Ascendancy. For the first time in its long history, foreigners ruled all of China.

Life in Yuan China

Kublai Khan and the Mongol rulers he led belonged to a different ethnic group than the Chinese did. They spoke a different language, worshipped different gods, wore different clothing, and had different customs. The Chinese resented being ruled by these foreigners, whom they saw as rude and uncivilized.

However, Kublai Khan did not force the Chinese to accept Mongol ways of life. Some Mongols even adopted aspects of the Chinese culture, such as Confucianism. Still, the Mongols made sure to keep control of the Chinese. They prohibited Confucian scholars from gaining too much power in the government, for example. The Mongols also placed heavy taxes on the Chinese.

Much of the tax money the Mongols collected went to pay for vast public-works projects. These projects required the labor of many Chinese people. The Yuan extended the Grand Canal and built new roads and palaces. Workers also improved the roads that were part of China's postal system. In addition, the Yuan emperors built a new capital, Dadu, near modern Beijing.

Mongol soldiers were sent throughout China to keep the peace as well as to keep a close watch on the Chinese. The soldiers' presence kept overland trade routes safe for merchants. Sea trade between China, India, and Southeast Asia continued, too. The Mongol emperors also welcomed foreign traders at Chinese ports. Some of these traders received special privileges.

Part of what we know about life in the Yuan dynasty comes from one such trader, an Italian merchant named Marco Polo. Between 1271 and 1295 he traveled in and around China. Polo was highly respected by the Mongols and even served in Kublai Khan's court. When Polo returned to Europe, he wrote of his travels. Polo's descriptions of China fascinated many Europeans. His book sparked much European interest in China.

The End of the Yuan Dynasty

Despite their vast empire, the Mongols were not content with their lands. They decided to invade Japan. A Mongol army sailed to Japan in 1274 and 1281. The campaigns, however, were disastrous. Violent storms and fierce defenders destroyed most of the Mongol force.

The failed campaigns against Japan weakened the Mongol military. The huge, expensive public-works projects had already weakened the economy. These weaknesses, combined with Chinese resentment, made China ripe for rebellion.

In the 1300s many Chinese groups rebelled against the Yuan dynasty. In 1368 a former monk named Zhu Yuanzhang (JOO yoo-ahn-JAHNG) took charge of a rebel army. He led this army in a final victory over the Mongols. China was once again ruled by the Chinese.

READING CHECK Finding Main Ideas How did the Mongols come to rule China?

Primary Source

BOOK

A Chinese City

In this passage Marco Polo describes his visit to Hangzhou (HAHNG-JOH), a city in southeastern China.

"Inside the city there is a Lake . . . and all round it are erected [built] beautiful palaces and mansions, of the richest and most exquisite [finest] structure that you can imagine . . . In the middle of the Lake are two Islands, on each of which stands a rich, beautiful and spacious edifice [building], furnished in such style as to seem fit for the palace of an Emperor. And when any one of the citizens desired to hold a marriage feast, or to give any other entertainment, it used to be done at one of these palaces. And everything would be found there ready to order, such as silver plate, trenchers [platters], and dishes, napkins and table-cloths, and whatever else was needful. The King made this provision for the gratification [enjoyment] of his people, and the place was open to every one who desired to give an entertainment."

–Marco Polo, from *Description of the World*

ANALYSIS SKILL ANALYZING PRIMARY SOURCES

From this description, what impression might Europeans have of Hangzhou?

The Voyages of Zheng He

Zheng He's ocean voyages were remarkable. Some of his ships, like the one shown here, were among the largest in the world at the time.

This large ship was more than 300 feet long and carried about 500 people.

Sailors grew vegetables and herbs in special containers and brought livestock for food on the long voyages.

Zheng He brought back exotic animals like these giraffes from Africa.

The Ming Dynasty

After his army defeated the Mongols, Zhu Yuanzhang became emperor of China. The Ming dynasty that he founded ruled China from 1368 to 1644—nearly 300 years. Ming China proved to be one of the most stable and prosperous times in Chinese history. The Ming expanded China's fame overseas and sponsored incredible building projects across China.

Great Sea Voyages

During the Ming dynasty, the Chinese improved their ships and their sailing skills. The greatest sailor of the period was **Zheng He** (juhng HUH), also spelled as Chengho. Between 1405 and 1433, he led seven grand voyages to places around Asia. Zheng He's fleets were huge. One included more than 60 ships and 25,000 sailors. Some of the ships were gigantic too, perhaps more than 300 feet long.

In the course of his voyages Zheng He sailed his fleet throughout the Indian Ocean. He sailed as far west as the Persian Gulf and the easternmost coast of Africa.

Everywhere his ships landed, Zheng He presented leaders with beautiful gifts from China. He boasted about his country and encouraged foreign leaders to send gifts to China's emperor. From one voyage, Zheng He returned to China with representatives of some 30 nations, sent by their leaders to honor the emperor. He also brought goods and stories back to China.

Zheng He's voyages rank among the most impressive in the history of seafaring. Although they did not lead to the creation of new trade routes or the exploration of new lands, they served as a clear sign of China's power.

Great Building Projects

The Ming were also known for their grand building projects. Many of these projects were designed to impress both the Chinese people and their enemies to the north.

In Beijing, for example, Ming emperors built the Forbidden City. This amazing palace complex included hundreds of imperial residences, temples, and other government buildings. Within the buildings were some 9,000 rooms. The name "Forbidden City" came from the fact that the common people were not even allowed to enter the complex. For centuries, this city within a city was a symbol of China's glory.

The Forbidden City

The Forbidden City is not actually a city. It's a huge complex of almost 1,000 buildings in the heart of China's capital. The Forbidden City was built for the emperor, his family, his court, and his servants, and ordinary people were forbidden from entering.

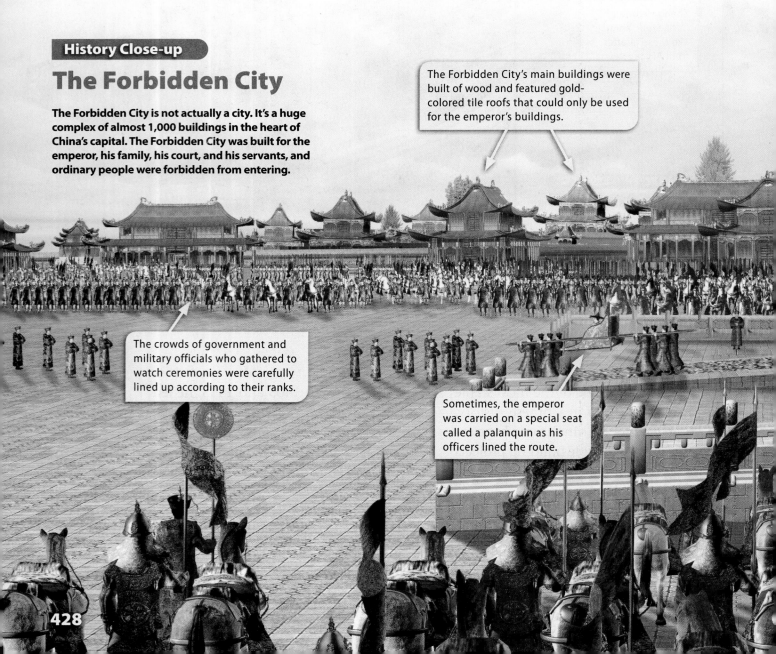

The Forbidden City's main buildings were built of wood and featured gold-colored tile roofs that could only be used for the emperor's buildings.

The crowds of government and military officials who gathered to watch ceremonies were carefully lined up according to their ranks.

Sometimes, the emperor was carried on a special seat called a palanquin as his officers lined the route.

Ming rulers also directed the restoration of the famous Great Wall of China. Large numbers of soldiers and peasants worked to rebuild collapsed portions of walls, connect existing walls, and build new ones. The result was a construction feat unmatched in history. The wall was more than 2,000 miles long. It would reach from San Diego to New York! The wall was about 25 feet high and, at the top, 12 feet wide. Protected by the wall—and the soldiers who stood guard along it—the Chinese people felt safe from invasions by the northern tribes.

READING CHECK **Generalizing** In what ways did the Ming dynasty strengthen China?

China Under the Ming

During the Ming dynasty, Chinese society began to change. This change was largely due to the efforts of the Ming emperors. Having expelled the Mongols, the Ming emperors worked to eliminate all foreign influences from Chinese society. As a result, China's government and relations with other countries changed dramatically.

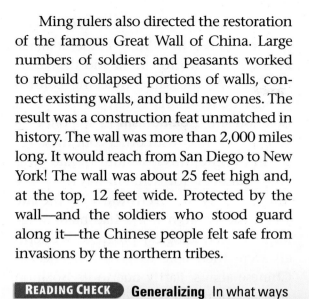

The Hall of Supreme Harmony is the largest building in the Forbidden City. Grand celebrations for important holidays, like the emperor's birthday and the New Year, were held there.

ANALYSIS SKILL **ANALYZING VISUALS**

How did the Forbidden City show the power and importance of the emperor?

429

SS.6.W.4.12 Identify the causes and effects of Chinese isolation and the decision to limit foreign trade in the 15th century.

Government

When the Ming took over China, they adopted many government programs that had been created by the Tang and the Song. However, the Ming emperors were much more powerful than the Tang and Song emperors had been. They abolished the offices of some powerful officials and took a larger role in running the government themselves. These emperors fiercely protected their power, and they punished anyone whom they saw as challenging their authority.

Despite their personal power, though, the Ming did not disband the civil service system. Because he personally oversaw the entire government, the emperor needed officials to keep his affairs organized.

The Ming also used examinations to appoint censors. These officials were sent throughout China to investigate the behavior of local leaders and to judge the quality of schools and other institutions. Censors had existed for many years in China, but under the Ming emperors their power and influence grew.

ACADEMIC VOCABULARY

consequences effects of a particular event or events

Relations with Other Countries

In the 1430s a new Ming emperor made Zheng He return to China and dismantle his fleet. At the same time, he banned foreign trade. China entered a period of isolationism. **Isolationism** is a policy of avoiding contact with other countries.

In the end, this isolationism had great **consequences** for China. In 1644 the Ming dynasty was overthrown. By the late 1800s the Western world had made huge leaps in technological progress. Westerners were then able to gain influence in Chinese affairs. Partly due to its isolation and lack of progress, China was too weak to stop them.

READING CHECK **Identifying Cause and Effect** How did isolationism affect China?

SUMMARY AND PREVIEW Under the Yuan and Ming dynasties, Chinese society changed. Eventually, the Ming began a policy of isolationism. In the next chapter you will read about Japan, another country that was isolated at times.

Section 4 Assessment

Reviewing Ideas, Terms, and People

1. **a. Identify** Who was **Genghis Khan**?
   b. Explain How did the Mongols gain control of China?
   c. Evaluate Judge this statement: "The Mongols should never have tried to invade Japan."
2. **a. Identify** Who was **Zheng He**, and what did he do?
   b. Analyze What impression do you think the Forbidden City had on the residents of Beijing?
   c. Develop How may the Great Wall have both helped and hurt China?
3. **a. Define** What is **isolationism**?
   b. Explain How did the Ming change China?
   c. Develop How might a policy of isolationism have both advantages and disadvantages?

Critical Thinking

4. **Comparing and Contrasting** Draw a diagram like this one. Use your notes to see how the Yuan and Ming dynasties were alike and different.

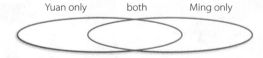

Yuan only   both   Ming only

FOCUS ON WRITING

5. **Identifying Achievements of the Later Dynasties** Make a list of the achievements of the Yuan and Ming dynasties. Then look back over all your notes and rate the achievements or inventions. Which three do you think are the most important?

Kublai Khan

How did a Mongol nomad settle down to rule a vast empire?

When did he live? 1215–1294

Where did he live? Kublai came from Mongolia but spent much of his life in China. His capital, Dadu, was near the modern city of Beijing.

What did he do? Kublai Khan completed the conquest of China that Genghis Khan had begun. He ruled China as the emperor of the Yuan dynasty.

Why is he important? The lands Kublai Khan ruled made up one of the largest empires in world history. It stretched from the Pacific Ocean to Eastern Europe. As China's ruler, Kublai Khan welcomed foreign visitors, including the Italian merchant Marco Polo and the Arab historian Ibn Battutah. The stories these two men told helped create interest in China and its products among Westerners.

Generalizing How did Kublai Khan's actions help change people's views of China?

KEY FACTS

- Unified all of China under his rule

- Established peace, during which China's population grew

- Extended the Grand Canal so that food could be shipped from the Huang He (Yellow River) to his capital near modern Beijing

- Linked China to India and Persia with better roads

- Increased contact with the West

This painting from the 1200s shows Kublai Khan hunting on horseback.

Social Studies Skills

Understanding Chance, Error, and Oversight

Define the Skill

History is nothing more than what people thought and did in the past, and the people of the past were just as human as people today. Like us, they occasionally forgot or overlooked things. They made mistakes in their decisions or judgments. Unexpected things happened that they couldn't control. Sometimes, these oversights, errors, and just plain luck shaped history.

Learn the Skill

There are several examples of the role of chance, error, and oversight in Chinese history.

1. **Chance** Ancient Chinese alchemists were searching for a potion to create everlasting life for the emperor. Although they did not discover the secret of everlasting life, they did discover that mixing certain ingredients together produced an explosion. By chance, they had discovered gunpowder.

2. **Oversight** As the Mongols were about to attack Western Europe, their khan died. The Mongols had focused so much on their military strength that they had neglected to develop a plan for the continuation of their government. Their law required them to go in person back to their land to elect a new khan. As a result, the Mongols never attacked Western Europe. Instead, they focused on China.

3. **Error** In the early 1100s, a new empire was gaining strength near Song China. Between the Song and the new empire lay an old enemy of China's. The Song emperor decided to ally himself with the new empire against the old enemy. This proved to be a disastrous decision. The Chinese defeated their old enemy, but China lost its buffer against the new strong empire. The alliance soon fell apart, and the new empire attacked the Song, taking one third of its land.

Practice the Skill

As you read in the chapter, China's silk industry was very successful. But what if chance, error, or oversight had played a role in the silk trade? For each fictional event below, determine whether it would have been a chance, an error, or oversight and describe how it might have affected Chinese history if it had happened.

1. The Chinese taught visitors how to make silk.

2. The Chinese decided that their silk was so valuable that they didn't want to export any of it.

3. The Chinese did not discover how to make silk.

Visual Summary

Use the visual summary below to help you review the main ideas of the chapter.

QUICK FACTS

China was reunified, and Buddhism spread during the Sui and Tang dynasties.

Farming and trade grew under the Tang and Song dynasties.

Confucian thought influenced Chinese government and education.

The powerful Yuan and Ming dynasties strengthened China, and expanded trade, but then China became isolated.

Reviewing Vocabulary, Terms, and People

Match the words or names with their definitions or descriptions.

a. Kublai Khan   g. compass

b. movable type   h. porcelain

c. scholar-official   i. Genghis Khan

d. Empress Wu   j. isolationism

e. bureaucracy   k. incentive

f. Zheng He   l. gunpowder

1. ruthless but effective Tang dynasty ruler
2. a set of letters or characters that can be moved to create different lines of text
3. leader who united the Mongols and began invasion of China
4. body of unelected government officials
5. thin, beautiful pottery
6. a device that indicates direction
7. policy of avoiding contact with other countries
8. founder of the Yuan dynasty
9. a mixture of powders used in explosives
10. commanded huge fleets of ships
11. educated government worker
12. something that leads people to follow a certain course of action

Comprehension and Critical Thinking

SECTION 1 *(Pages 410–413)*

13. **a. Identify** What period did China enter after the Han dynasty collapsed? What dynasty brought an end to this period?

    b. Analyze Why is the Tang dynasty considered a golden age of Chinese civilization?

    c. Predict How might Chinese culture have been different in the Tang and Song dynasties if Buddhism had not been introduced to China?

SECTION 2 (Pages 414–419)

14. a. Describe What did Wu Daozi, Li Bo, Du Fu, and Li Qingzhao contribute to Chinese culture?

b. Analyze What led to the growth of cities in China? What were China's cities like during the Tang and Song dynasties?

c. Evaluate Which Chinese invention has had a greater effect on world history—the magnetic compass or gunpowder? Why do you think so?

SECTION 3 (Pages 420–423)

15. a. Define What is Confucianism? How did it change during and after the Song dynasty?

b. Make Inferences Why do you think the civil service examination system was created?

c. Elaborate Why were China's civil service examinations so difficult?

SECTION 4 (Pages 424–430)

16. a. Describe How did the Mongols create their huge empire? What areas were included in it?

b. Draw Conclusions How did Marco Polo and Zheng He help shape ideas about China?

c. Elaborate Why do you think the Ming emperors spent so much time and money rebuilding and enlarging the Great Wall?

Using the Internet

17. Activity: Creating a Mural The Tang and Song periods saw many agricultural, technological, and commercial developments. New irrigation techniques, movable type, and gunpowder were a few of them. Go online to research such developments. Imagine that a city official has hired you to create a mural showing all of the great things the Chinese developed during the Tang and Song dynasties. Create a large mural that depicts as many advances as possible.

Reviewing Themes

18. Science and Technology How did Chinese inventions alter the course of world history?

19. Economics How did the strong agricultural and trading economy of Tang and Song China affect the country?

Reading Skills

20. Drawing Conclusions about the Past Read the statements about the Ming dynasty below. For each conclusion that follows, decide whether the statements provide sufficent evidence to justify the conclusion.

> The Ming ruled China from 1368 to 1644.
>
> Zhu Yuanzhang was a Ming emperor.
>
> The Great Wall was rebuilt by the Ming.

a. The Great Wall is located in China.

b. Zhu Yuanzhang was a good emperor.

c. Zhu Yuanzhang ruled some time between 1368 and 1644.

d. Zhu Yuanzhang rebuilt the Great Wall.

Social Studies Skills

Chance, Error, and Oversight in History You read in this chapter about how the Mongol rulers of China decided to invade Japan. Three sentences from the text have been revised below. Read each sentence carefully. Then state whether it is an example of oversight, error, or chance.

21. Violent storms destroyed most of the Mongol force.

22. Despite their vast empire, the Mongols were not content with their lands and decided to invade Japan.

FOCUS ON WRITING

23. Writing a Magazine Article Now that you have identified three achievements or inventions you want to write about, begin your article. Open with a sentence that states your main idea. Include three or four sentences about each achievement or invention you have chosen. These sentences should describe the achievement or invention and explain why it was so important. End your article with a sentence or two summarizing China's importance to the world.

DIRECTIONS: Read each question, and write the letter of the best response.

1

This object displays Chinese expertise at working with

A woodblocks.

B gunpowder.

C cotton fibers.

D porcelain.

2 **Trade and other contact with peoples far from China stopped under which dynasty?**

A Ming

B Yuan

C Song

D Sui

3 **Which of the following was *not* a way that Confucianism influenced China?**

A emphasis on family and family values

B expansion of manufacturing and trade

C emphasis on service to society

D well-educated government officials

4 **What was a major cause for the spread of Buddhism to China and other parts of Asia?**

A the teachings of Kublai Khan

B the writings of Confucius

C the travels of Buddhist missionaries

D the support of Empress Wu

5 **All of the following flourished during *both* the Tang and the Song dynasties, *except***

A art and culture.

B sea voyages of exploration.

C science and technology.

D trade.

Connecting with Past Learnings

6 **Earlier you learned about the deeds of emperor Shi Huangdi. He had laborers work on a structure that Ming rulers improved. What was that structure?**

A the Great Wall

B the Great Tomb

C the Forbidden City

D the Temple of Buddha

7 **Earlier you learned that the ancient Egyptians increased food production by digging irrigation canals to water their fields. Under which dynasty did the Chinese develop new irrigation techniques to increase their production of food?**

A Han

B Ming

C Song

D Sui

FLORIDA...
The Story Continues

CHAPTER 15, Japan (550–1868)

PEOPLE **c. 800–1700s: The Calusa of Florida's southwestern coast are master fishers.** Most hunter-gatherer societies remain fairly small. It usually requires farming for a population to grow to sizeable numbers. This was not true for the Calusa. Their population grew through fishing. The Calusa were master fishers. They used nets, fish weirs (a fence-like structure that traps fish), traps, and holding pens to catch large quantities of fish. The Calusa made different kinds of nets to catch different size fish. The knots they used to make their nets are still used to make nets today. Based on the number and type of shells and fish bones found at Calusa sites, archaeologists know that the people fished on a large scale. Evidence indicates that they ate more than 50 kinds of fish and 20 kinds of mollusks and crustaceans. Some Calusa shell middens are made almost entirely of whelk shells. A whelk is an adult snail. Some whelks can weigh nearly two pounds! The millions of whelk shells indicate that the Calusa had plentiful amounts of food.

PEOPLE **c. 800–1700s: The Calusa create detailed works of art.** Because the Calusa lived in a land of plentiful food, they did not need to spend most of their time looking for food. This gave the Calusa time to create detailed works of art. Archaeologists have found many carved and painted wooden masks and finely sculpted wooden figures of people and animals. The Calusa painted their masks in red, white, blue, and black. Archaeologists do not know how the Calusa applied the paint or whether the colors had special meanings.

PEOPLE **c. 800–1700s: The Calusa create a class-based society.** Like Japanese samurai society, Calusa society was class based. At the top were the chief and his family—the Calusa nobility. Members of the chief's family served as the religious and civil leaders. An elite military force made up another segment of society. A large group of commoners supported the nobility and the elite military force. Enslaved captives were at the bottom of society.

EVENTS **c. 1500s: The Spanish weaken Native American societies.**
The Mongol invasion of Japan in the late 1200s led to the breakdown of social order in samurai society. Similarly, the arrival of the Spanish forces in the 1500s weakened Native American society. Over time, warfare, European diseases, enslavement, and other pressures lead to the collapse of many societies. By the end of the 1700s, the Calusa and many other groups were gone.

PLACES **1904–: The Japanese farming colony of Yamato is established.**
In 1903 Jo Sakai visited Florida. Originally from Miyazu, Japan, he wanted to establish a colony of Japanese farmers near present-day Boca Raton to grow pineapples. He called his colony Yamato, an ancient name for Japan. Sakai signed an agreement with the Florida East Coast Railway to establish a station in Yamato to ship the pineapples. The first settlers arrived in 1904–1905. A few years of successful pineapple crops made Sakai optimistic. However, a disease struck the pineapples in 1908. Most of the crop was lost. The operation never fully recovered. Over time, most of the settlers returned to Japan.

Unpacking the Florida Standards ‹···

Read the following to learn what this standard says and what it means. See FL8–FL31 to unpack all of the standards related to this chapter.

Benchmark SS.6.G.3.1 Explain how the physical landscape has affected the development of agriculture and industry in the ancient world. Examples are terracing, seasonal crop rotations, resource development.

What does it mean?
Analyze how farming and industry in ancient civilizations were affected by physical geography.

 SPOTLIGHT ON
SS.6.G.2.1 See page FL44 for content specifically related to this Chapter 15 standard.

Japan

Essential Question   How did the Japanese blend borrowed customs and native traditions into a unique culture?

Florida Next Generation Sunshine State Standards

LA.6.1.6.2 The student will listen to, read, and discuss familiar and conceptually challenging text. **LA.6.1.7.1** The student will use background knowledge of subject and related content areas, prereading strategies, graphic representations, and knowledge of text structure to make and confirm complex predictions of content, purpose, and organization of a reading selection. **LA.6.1.7.3** The student will determine the main idea or essential message in grade-level text through inferring, paraphrasing, summarizing, and identifying relevant details. **SS.6.G.1.4** Utilize tools geographers use to study the world. **SS.6.G.2.1** Explain how major physical characteristics, natural resources, climate, and absolute and relative locations have influenced settlement, interactions, and the economies of ancient civilizations of the world. **SS.6.G.3.1** Explain how the physical landscape has affected the development of agriculture and industry in the ancient world. **SS.6.G.4.1** Explain how family and ethnic relationships influenced ancient cultures. **SS.6.W.1.1** Use timelines to identify chronological order of historical events. **SS.6.W.1.3** Interpret primary and secondary sources.

FOCUS ON WRITING

A Travel Brochure You've been hired to create a travel brochure called "Japan's Rich History." Your brochure will describe tourist attractions in Japan that show the country's fascinating past. As you read this chapter, think about how you might encourage people to visit Japan.

CHAPTER EVENTS

c. 550 Buddhism is introduced into Japan from China.

550

WORLD EVENTS

632–651 Arab armies conquer Southwest Asia.

This photo shows Mount Fuji, a snow-covered volcano that has long been a symbol of Japan.

HISTORY Rise of the Samurai Class

↗ Online Resource | VIDEO

c. 1000
Lady Murasaki Shikibu writes *The Tale of Genji*.

1192
The first shogun rules Japan.

1603–1868
The Tokugawa shoguns rule Japan.

825 | 1100 | 1375 | 1650

768–814
Charlemagne rules much of western Europe.

1279
The Mongols take over China.

1588
England defeats the Spanish Armada.

Reading Social Studies

Economics | Geography | **Politics** | Religion | **Society and Culture** | Science and Technology

Focus on Themes As you read this chapter, you will step into the world of early Japan. You will learn about the first Japanese people and their religion, Shinto, and about how the people of China and Korea began to influence the development of Japanese culture. As you read about the history of Japan, you will learn about the **political** systems the Japanese used to govern their nation and their attitudes toward **society and culture**. Finally, you will learn how social elements of medieval Japanese culture continue to affect life in Japan to this day.

Main Ideas and Their Support

Focus on Reading You know that if you take the legs out from under a table it will fall flat on the floor. In just the same way, a main idea will fall flat without details to support it.

Understanding a Writer's Support for Ideas A writer can support main ideas with several kinds of details. These details might be facts, statistics, eyewitness accounts, brief stories, examples, definitions, or comments from experts on the subject.

Notice the types of details the writer uses to support the main idea in the passage below.

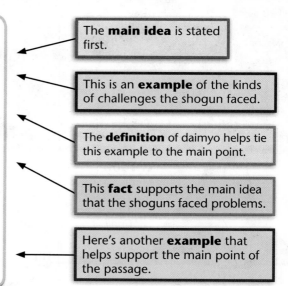

After the Mongol invasion, new problems arose for the shogun. The emperor, tired of having no say in the government, began to fight the shogun for control of the country. At the same time daimyo, the nobles who owned much of Japan's land, fought to break free of the shogun's control. During these struggles for power, small wars broke out all over Japan.

By the 1400s, the shoguns had lost most of their authority. The emperor was still largely powerless, and daimyo ruled much of Japan. Each daimyo controlled his own territory. Within that territory, he made laws and collected taxes. There was no powerful central authority of any sort to impose order in Japan.

The **main idea** is stated first.

This is an **example** of the kinds of challenges the shogun faced.

The **definition** of daimyo helps tie this example to the main point.

This **fact** supports the main idea that the shoguns faced problems.

Here's another **example** that helps support the main point of the passage.

LA.6.1.7.1 The student will use background knowledge of subject and related content areas, prereading strategies, graphic representations, and knowledge of text structure to make and confirm complex predictions of content, purpose, and organization of a reading selection.

You Try It!

The following passage is from the chapter you are about to read. As you read it, look for the writer's main idea and supporting details.

Samurai

The word *samurai* comes from the Japanese word for servant. Every samurai, from the weakest soldier to the most powerful warrior, was supposed to serve his lord. Because all lords in Japan were supposed to serve the emperor, all samurai were required to be loyal to him.

From Chapter 15, p. 455

An army of samurai was expensive to support. Few lords could afford to buy armor and weapons for their warriors. As a result, lords paid their samurai with land and food.

After you read the passage, answer the following questions.

1. Which sentence best states the main idea of the passage?
   a. Samurai, which comes from the word servant, were supposed to serve their lords.
   b. Samurai were paid with land and food.
   c. Few lords could afford to buy armor and weapons for their warriors.

2. Which of the following is not a detail that supports the main idea of the passage?
   a. An army of samurai was expensive to support.
   b. Every samurai was supposed to serve his lord.
   c. In Japan at this time, there were more than 10,000 samurai.

3. Which of the following methods of supporting a main idea does the author use in this passage?
   a. statistics
   b. eyewitness account
   c. facts

Key Terms and People

Chapter 15

Section 1
clans *(p. 440)*
Shinto *(p. 440)*
Prince Shotoku *(p. 442)*
regent *(p. 442)*

Section 2
court *(p. 444)*
Lady Murasaki Shikibu *(p. 445)*
Zen *(p. 448)*

Section 3
daimyo *(p. 454)*
samurai *(p. 454)*
figurehead *(p. 455)*
shogun *(p. 455)*

Academic Vocabulary

Success in school is related to knowing academic vocabulary—the words that are frequently used in school assignments and discussions. In this chapter, you will learn the following academic words:

structure *(p. 439)*
values *(p. 457)*

As you read Chapter 15, look for the types of details that the writer uses to support the main ideas.

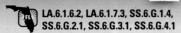

What You Will Learn...

Main Ideas

1. Geography shaped life in Japan.
2. Early Japanese society was organized in clans, which came to be ruled by an emperor.
3. Japan learned about language, society, and government from China and Korea.

The Big Idea

Japan's early societies were both isolated from and influenced by China and Korea.

Key Terms and People

clans, *p. 442*
Shinto, *p. 442*
Prince Shotoku, *p. 444*
regent, *p. 444*

 **Online Resource**
TAKING NOTES

Use the graphic organizer online to take notes on how geography, early peoples, and neighboring countries affected the Japanese people's way of life, government, and religion.

Geography and Early Japan

If YOU were there...

You live in a small farming village on one of the islands of Japan. You're very happy with your life. The sea is nearby and food is plentiful. You have a large, extended family to protect and take care of you. Your grandmother says that life in your village has not changed for hundreds of years, and that is good. But now you have heard that some people from across the sea are coming to your village. They are bringing new ideas and new ways of doing things.

How do you feel about these changes?

BUILDING BACKGROUND Japan is a large group of islands located east of the Asian mainland. Life in Japan has always been influenced by many factors. The islands' geography and location shaped how people lived there, and as you read above, visitors from other lands also affected Japanese society.

Geography Shapes Life in Japan

The islands of Japan are really just the tops of undersea mountains and volcanoes, sticking up out of the ocean. Those mountains, as you can see on the map, cover nearly all of Japan. Only about 20 percent of the land is flat. Because it is difficult to live and farm on mountain slopes, most Japanese people have always lived in those flat areas, the coastal plains.

In addition to the mountains and the lack of flat land, the nearness of the sea shaped the lives of Japanese people. Their homes were never far from the sea. Naturally, they turned to the sea for food. They learned to prepare all kinds of seafood, from eel to shark to octopus to seaweed. As a result, seafood has been a key part of the Japanese diet for thousands of years.

The islands' location affected the Japanese people in another way as well. Because they lived on islands, the Japanese were separated from the other people of Asia. This separation allowed

440

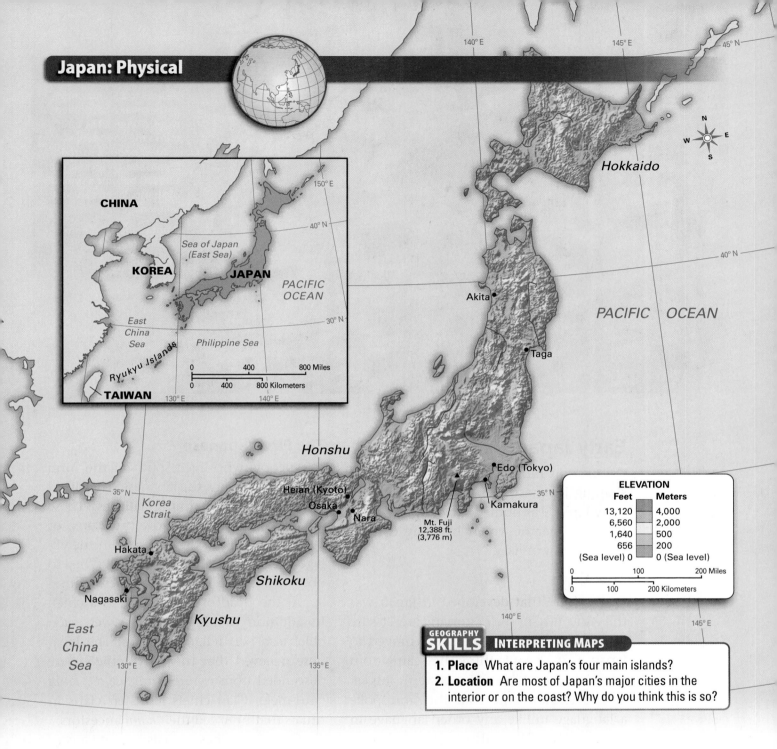

CHINA

Sea of Japan
(East Sea)

KOREA   JAPAN   PACIFIC
OCEAN

East
China
Sea

Philippine Sea

Ryukyu Islands

TAIWAN

150° E

40° N

30° N

0   400   800 Miles

0   400   800 Kilometers

130° E   140° E

Hokkaido

Akita

Taga

PACIFIC   OCEAN

45° N

40° N

Honshu

Heian (Kyoto)
Osaka   Nara   Mt. Fuji
12,388 ft.
(3,776 m)

Edo (Tokyo)

Kamakura

35° N

35° N

ELEVATION

Feet		Meters
13,120		4,000
6,560		2,000
1,640		500
656		200
(Sea level) 0		0 (Sea level)

0   100   200 Miles

0   100   200 Kilometers

Korea
Strait

Hakata

Nagasaki

Shikoku

Kyushu

East
China
Sea

130° E   135° E

140° E

145° E

GEOGRAPHY SKILLS INTERPRETING MAPS

1. **Place** What are Japan's four main islands?
2. **Location** Are most of Japan's major cities in the interior or on the coast? Why do you think this is so?

the Japanese to develop their own culture. For example, they created a religion and a social **structure** very different from those in other parts of Asia. This separation has always been an important part of Japanese society.

Japan isn't totally isolated, however. Look at the inset map above to find Korea and China. As you can see, neither country is very far from the Japanese islands. Korea is only about 100 miles away from Japan. China is about 400 miles away. Those short distances allowed the older Korean and Chinese cultures to influence the new culture of Japan.

READING CHECK   **Summarizing** What is Japan's geography like?

ACADEMIC VOCABULARY

structure the way something is set up or organized

A Shinto Shrine
Visitors to a Shinto shrine gather near a gate called a torii (TOR-ee). The torii marks the boundary of a shrine or other sacred Shinto site. Over time, the torii has become a symbol of Shinto, Japan's ancient religion.

What elements of nature can you see in this painting?

Early Japanese Society

Korea and China did play a major part in shaping Japanese society, but not at first. Early Japan was home to two different cultures, neither of which had any contact with the rest of Asia.

The Ainu

One culture that developed in Japan was the Ainu (EYE-noo). Historians aren't sure exactly when or how the Ainu moved to Japan. Some people think they came from what is now Siberia in eastern Russia. Wherever they came from, the Ainu spoke a language unlike any other language in eastern Asia. They also looked different from the other people of Japan.

Over time, the Ainu began to fight with other people for land. They lost most of these fights, and so they lost their land as well. Eventually the Ainu were driven back onto a single island, Hokkaido. Over time the Ainu culture almost disappeared. Many people gave up the Ainu language and adopted new customs.

THE IMPACT TODAY

Few Ainu remain in Japan today, and most of them live on Hokkaido.

The First Japanese

The people who lived south of the Ainu eventually became the Japanese. They lived mostly in small farming villages. These villages were ruled by powerful **clans**, or extended families. Other people in the village, including farmers and workers, had to obey and respect members of these clans.

At the head of each clan was a chief. In addition to his political power, each chief also had religious duties. The Japanese believed that their clan chiefs were descended from nature spirits called *kami* (KAH-mee). Clan chiefs led their clans in rituals that honored their *kami* ancestors.

Over time, these rituals became a central part of the traditional religion of Japan, **Shinto**. According to Shinto teachings, everything in nature—the sun, the moon, trees, waterfalls, and animals—has *kami*. Shintoists believe that some *kami* help people live and keep them from harm. They build shrines to *kami* and perform ceremonies in which they ask the *kami* to bless them.

The First Emperors

The clans of early Japan weren't all equal. Some clans were larger and more powerful than others. In time a few of these powerful clans built up armies and set out to conquer their neighbors.

One clan that gained power in this way lived in the Yamato region, the western part of Japan's largest island, Honshu. In addition to military might, the Yamato rulers claimed to have a glorious family history. They believed they were descended from the most powerful of all *kami*, the goddess of the sun.

By the 500s the Yamato rulers had extended their control over much of Honshu. Although they didn't control the whole country, the leaders of the Yamato clan began to call themselves the emperors of all Japan.

READING CHECK **Sequencing** How did emperors take power in Japan?

Japan Learns from China and Korea

Early Japanese society received very little influence from cultures on the Asian mainland. Occasionally, officials from China, Korea, or other parts of Asia visited Japan. For the most part, however, these visits didn't have a great impact on the Japanese way of life.

By the mid-500s, though, some Japanese leaders thought that Japan could learn a great deal from other cultures. In particular, they wanted to learn more about the cultures of China and Korea.

To learn what they wanted to know, the rulers of Japan decided to send representatives to China and Korea to gather information about their cultures. They also invited people from China and Korea to move to Japan. The emperors hoped that these people could teach the Japanese new ways of working and thinking.

Influences from China and Korea

QUICK FACTS

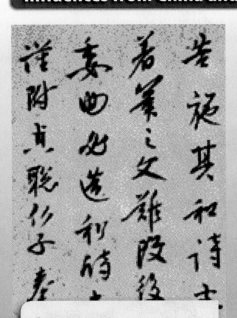

Language
The earliest Japanese writing used Chinese characters.

THE GRANGER COLLECTION, NEW YORK

Philosophy
The ideas of the Chinese philosopher Confucius helped shape Japanese culture and family life.

Religion
Buddhism came to Japan from Korea.

Changes in Language

One of the first things the Japanese learned from China and Korea was language. The early Japanese didn't have a written language. Therefore, many learned to write in Chinese. They continued to speak in Japanese, however, which is very different from Chinese. It wasn't until about 200 years later that people devised a way of writing in Japanese. They used Chinese characters to represent the sounds used in Japanese.

As Japan's contact with China increased, some Japanese people—especially rich and well-educated people—began to write in the Chinese language. Japanese writers used Chinese for their poems and stories. One of the first histories of Japan, written in the 700s, is in Chinese. For many years Chinese was even the official language of Japan's government.

Changes in Religion and Philosophy

One of the people most influential in bringing Chinese ideas to Japan was **Prince Shotoku** (shoh-toh-koo). He served from 593 to 621 as regent (REE-juhnt) for his aunt, the empress. A **regent** is a person who rules a country for someone who is unable to rule alone.

All his life, Prince Shotoku admired Chinese culture. As regent, Shotoku saw a chance for Japan to adopt more Chinese ideas. He sent scholars to China to learn all they could about Chinese society.

The ideas these scholars brought back changed Japanese society. For example, they taught the Japanese about Confucianism.

BIOGRAPHY

Prince Shotoku
573–621

Prince Shotoku was one of Japan's greatest leaders. He helped rule Japan when he was only 20 years old. For many centuries, people have admired him. Legends have developed about his wisdom. According to one early biography, Shotoku was able to talk as soon as he was born and never made a wrong decision.

Prince Shotoku's Japan

Under Prince Shotoku, Buddhism spread across Japan. Shotoku ordered beautiful Buddhist temples to be built, such as the one below in Nara, Japan. The spread of Buddhism changed many areas of Japanese culture during Prince Shotoku's time.

Horyuji Temple in Nara, Japan

Among other things, Confucianism outlined how families should behave. Confucius taught that fathers should rule their families. He believed that wives should obey their husbands, children should obey their parents, and younger brothers should obey older brothers. Families in China lived according to these rules. As Confucian ideas spread through Japan, the Japanese began to live by them as well.

More important than these social changes, though, were the vast religious changes Shotoku made in Japan. He was a Buddhist, and he wanted to spread Buddhism throughout his country. Buddhism wasn't new to Japan. Korean visitors had introduced the religion to Japan about 50 years earlier. But it was not very popular. Most people preferred to keep their traditional religion, Shinto.

Shotoku worked to change people's minds about Buddhism. He built a grand Buddhist temple that still stands today. He also wrote commentaries on Buddhist teachings. Largely because of his efforts, Buddhism became very popular, especially among Japanese nobles.

Statue of the Buddha in Horyuji

Changes in Government

Shotoku also wanted to change Japan's government to be more like China's. He especially wanted Japan's emperors to have more power, like China's emperors did.

Afraid that they would lose power to the emperor, many clan leaders opposed Shotoku's government plans. As a result, Japan's emperors gained little power.

READING CHECK **Categorizing** What aspects of Chinese society did Shotoku bring to Japan?

SUMMARY AND PREVIEW In this section, you learned how early Japan grew and developed. Next you'll see how Japan's emperors encouraged nobles to create great works of art and literature.

Section 1 Assessment

Reviewing Ideas, Terms, and People

1. **a. Recall** What types of landforms cover most of Japan?
   b. Explain How did Japan's location both separate it from and tie it to China and Korea?
2. **a. Define** What is **Shinto**?
   b. Sequence How did the Yamato rulers gain power?
3. **a. Explain** How did **Prince Shotoku** help spread Buddhism in Japan?
   b. Rate What do you think was the most important idea the Japanese borrowed from China or Korea? Why?

Critical Thinking

4. **Categorizing** Draw a diagram like this one. Using your notes on Japan's culture, list ideas that developed within Japan in the circle and ideas that the Japanese borrowed from other people in the arrow.

FOCUS ON WRITING

5. **Taking Notes on Early Japan** Think about the section you have just read. Which details from this section might be appealing to tourists? Write down some thoughts in your notebook. Plan to include them in a section of your travel brochure called "Fun Facts."

Art and Culture in Heian

What You Will Learn...

Main Ideas

1. Japanese nobles created great art in their court at Heian.
2. Buddhism changed in Japan during the Heian period.

The Big Idea

Japanese culture experienced a golden age during the Heian period of the 800s to the 1100s.

Key Terms and People

court, *p. 446*
Lady Murasaki Shikibu, *p. 447*
Zen, *p. 450*

Online Resource
TAKING NOTES

Use the graphic organizer online to take notes on the changes in Japanese art and religion in the golden age of the Heian period.

If YOU were there...

You are a noble, serving the empress of Japan and living in the capital city. While walking in the garden one day, she gives you a small book with blank pages. When you ask her why, she says the book is a diary for you to write in. She tells you that nobles, both men and women, keep diaries to record their lives.

What will you write in your new diary?

BUILDING BACKGROUND In 794 the emperor and empress of Japan moved to Heian (HAY-ahn), a city now called Kyoto. Many nobles, like the one you just read about, followed their rulers to the new city. These nobles loved art and beauty, and they tried to make their new home a beautiful place.

Japanese Nobles Create Great Art

The nobles who followed Japan's emperor to Heian wanted to win his favor by living close to him. In Heian, these nobles created an imperial **court**, a group of nobles who live near and serve or advise a ruler.

Members of the noble court had little to do with the common people of Heian. They lived apart from poorer citizens and seldom left the city. These nobles enjoyed their lives of ease and privilege. In fact, their lives were so easy and so removed from the rest of Japan that many nobles called themselves "dwellers among the clouds."

The nobles of this court loved beauty and elegance. Because of this love, many nobles were great supporters of the arts. As a result, the court at Heian became a great center of culture and learning. In fact, the period between 794 and 1185 was a golden age of the arts in Japan.

Heian (Kyoto)

446

JOURNAL ENTRY
The Pillow Book

Sei Shonagon (SAY shoh-nah-gohn), author of The Pillow Book, *served Japan's empress from 991 to 1000. The Pillow Book was her journal. In it she wrote poems and thoughts about nature as well as descriptions of daily events. Here she describes the first time she met the empress.*

An actress playing Sei Shonagon in the 1800s

"When I first entered her Majesty's service I felt indescribably shy, and was indeed constantly on the verge of tears. When I came on duty the first evening, the Empress was sitting with only a three-foot screen in front of her, and so nervous was I that when she passed me some picture or book to look at, I was hardly capable of putting out my hand to take it. While she was talking about what she wanted me to see—telling me what it was or who had made it—I was all the time wondering whether my hair was in order.**"**

—Sei Shonagon, from *The Pillow Book*

ANALYSIS SKILL **ANALYZING PRIMARY SOURCES**

How did Sei Shonagon feel when she met the empress?

Fashion

The nobles' love of beauty began with their own appearances. They had magnificent wardrobes full of silk robes and gold jewelry. Nobles loved elaborate outfits. For example, women wore long gowns made of 12 layers of colored silk cleverly cut and folded to show off many layers at once.

To complete their outfits, nobles often carried delicate decorative fans. These fans were painted with flowers, trees, and birds. Many nobles also attached flowers and long silk cords to their fans.

Literature

In addition to how they looked, Japanese nobles took great care with how they spoke and wrote. Writing was very popular among the nobles, especially among the women. Many women wrote diaries and journals about their lives at court. In their diaries, these women carefully chose their words to make their writing beautiful.

Unlike men, who usually wrote in Chinese, noble women wrote in the Japanese language. As a result, many of the greatest works of early Japanese literature were written by women.

One of the greatest writers in early Japanese history was **Lady Murasaki Shikibu** (moohr-ah-sahk-ee shee-kee-boo). Around 1000, she wrote *The Tale of Genji*. Many historians consider this book to be the world's first full-length novel. Many readers also consider it one of the best.

The Tale of Genji is the story of a prince named Genji and his long quest for love. During his search he meets women from many different social classes.

Many people consider *The Tale of Genji* one of Japan's greatest novels. The characters it describes are very colorful and seem real. In addition, Lady Murasaki's writing is clear and simple but graceful at the same time. She describes court life in Japan with great detail.

Most early Japanese prose was written by women, but both men and women wrote poetry. Nobles loved to read and write poems. Some nobles held parties at which they took turns writing poetry and reading their poems aloud to each other.

Poems from this time usually had only five lines. They followed a specific structure that outlined how many syllables each line could include. Most were about love or nature, but some described everyday events. Here is an example of a nature poem about the end of winter:

"The breezes of spring
Are blowing the ripples astray
Along the water—
Today they will surely melt
The sheet of ice on the pond."

–Kino Tomonori, from the *Gosenshu*

Visual Art

Besides literature, Japan's nobles also loved the visual arts. The most popular art forms of the period were paintings, calligraphy, and architecture.

In their paintings, the nobles of Heian liked bright, bold colors. They also liked paintings that illustrated stories. In fact, many of the greatest paintings from this period illustrate scenes from literature, such as *The Tale of Genji*. Other paintings show scenes from nature or from court life. Many artists painted on doors and furniture rather than on paper.

Another popular form of art in Heian was calligraphy, or decorative writing. Calligraphers spent hours carefully copying poems. They wanted the poems to look as beautiful as they sounded.

The Arts in Heian

Heian was Japan's capital for many centuries. The wealthy nobles who lived there were great supporters of the arts. With their support, literature, painting, calligraphy, and other arts flourished in Heian.

A favorite theme in Japanese painting was *The Tale of Genji*. In this illustration of a scene from the novel, Genji's son is reading a letter as his wife approaches.

Architecture

The nobles of Heian worked to make their city beautiful. They greatly admired Chinese architecture and modeled Heian after the Chinese capital, Chang'an. They copied Chinese building styles, especially in the many temples they built. These styles featured buildings with wooden frames that curved slightly upward at the ends. The wooden frames were often left unpainted to look more natural. Thatched roofs also added to the natural feel.

For other buildings, the nobles liked simple, airy designs. Most buildings were made of wood with tiled roofs and large, open spaces inside. To add to the beauty of these buildings, the nobles surrounded them with elegant gardens and ponds. Similar gardens are still popular in Japan.

Performing Arts

The performing arts were also popular in Japan during the Heian period. The roots of later Japanese drama can be traced back to this time. People often gathered to watch performances by musicians, jugglers, and acrobats. These performances were wild and fun. Especially popular were the plays in which actors skillfully mimicked other people.

In later centuries, these types of performances developed into a more serious form of drama called Noh. Created in the 1300s, Noh plays combine music, speaking, and dance. These plays often tell about great heroes or figures from Japan's past.

THE IMPACT TODAY

Noh plays are still popular in Japan today.

READING CHECK Categorizing What forms of art were popular in the Heian period?

The Buddha was a popular subject for statues in the Heian period.

Japanese writing could be an art form in itself. This album made in the shape of a fan is covered in text and pictures.

ANALYSIS SKILL **ANALYZING VISUALS**

How does art from this period reflect the culture of Heian?

Many Zen gardens like this one include raked gravel shaped to look like water and small boulders arranged like mountains.

Buddhism Changes

Religion became something of an art form in Heian. The nobles' religion reflected their love of elaborate rituals. Most of the common people in Japan, though equally religious, didn't have the time or money for these ceremonies. As a result, different forms of Buddhism developed in Japan.

One new form of Buddhism was very popular with Japan's common people. It was called Pure Land Buddhism and didn't require any special rituals. Instead, Pure Land Buddhists chanted the Buddha's name over and over to achieve an enlightened state.

In the 1100s another popular new form of Buddhism called **Zen** arrived from China. Zen Buddhists believed that neither faith nor good behavior led to wisdom. Instead, people seeking wisdom should practice self-discipline and meditation, or quiet thinking. These ideas appealed to many Japanese, especially warriors. As these warriors gained more influence in Japan, so did Zen Buddhism.

READING CHECK Finding Main Ideas How did Buddhism change in Japan?

SUMMARY AND PREVIEW At Heian, Japan's emperors presided over an elegant court. In the next section, you'll learn what happened when emperors and the court lost power and prestige.

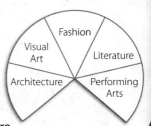

Section 2 Assessment

Reviewing Ideas, Terms, and People

1. **a. Recall** Where did Japan's **court** move in the late 700s?
   b. Make Generalizations Why are the 800s to the 1100s considered a golden age for Japanese literature and art?
   c. Evaluate Do you think women in Heian had more rights and freedoms than women in other societies? Why or why not?

2. **a. Identify** What new form of Buddhism developed in Japan?
   b. Compare and Contrast How was religion among Japan's nobles different from religion among the common people?
   c. Elaborate Why do you think Pure Land Buddhism was popular with common people?

Critical Thinking

3. **Categorizing** Draw a Japanese fan like the one shown here. Use your notes about the arts to list two contributions that the Japanese made in each category shown here.

Fashion
Visual Art
Literature
Architecture
Performing Arts

Focus on Writing

4. **Writing about Japanese Art** Japan's nobles left a legacy of beautiful art that today's visitors can still enjoy. Choose two art forms described in this section and take notes for your brochure. What kinds of pictures could you use to illustrate your text?

Lady Murasaki Shikibu

How would you describe the people you observe in life every day?

When did she live? around 1000

Where did she live? Heian

What did she do? Lady Murasaki was a noble and a servant to the Empress Akiko. While in the empress's service, she wrote lively observations of court life in her diaries. She also wrote the novel *The Tale of Genji.*

Why is she important? *The Tale of Genji* is one of the world's oldest novels, and—some would argue—one of the best. Besides entertaining readers for hundreds of years, *The Tale of Genji* describes the daily lives, customs, and attitudes of Japanese nobles of the time.

Drawing Conclusions What qualified Lady Murasaki to comment on upper-class life in Japan?

This painting from the 1600s is an illustration of court life from *The Tale of Genji.*

KEY IDEAS

Observations of Lady Murasaki Shikibu

- "Lady Dainagon is very small and refined . . . Her hair is three inches longer than her height."

- "Lady Senji is also a little person, and haughty . . . She puts us to shame, her carriage is so noble."

- "Lady Koshosho, all noble and charming. She is like a weeping-willow tree at budding time. Her style is very elegant and we all envy her her manners."

–from The Diary of Lady Murasaki Shikibu, in *Anthology of Japanese Literature,* edited by Donald Keene

from
The Tale of Genji

by Lady Murasaki Shikibu
translated by Edward G. Seidensticker

About the Reading The Tale of Genji *was written by Lady Murasaki Shikibu at the height of Japan's golden age. This thousand-page novel traces the life and adventures—especially in love—of a noble known as "the shining Genji." Although Genji is the favorite son of the emperor, his mother is only a commoner, so Genji cannot inherit the throne. Instead, it passes first to his half-brother Suzaku (soo-zah-koo) and then to Genji's own son. Here, Genji's son and his half-brother Suzaku visit Genji's mansion in Rokujo (roh-koo-joh), a district of Heian.*

AS YOU READ Look for details that describe the lives of Japanese nobles.

The emperor paid a state visit to Rokujo late in the Tenth Month. ❶ Since the colors were at their best and it promised to be a grand occasion, the Suzaku emperor accepted the invitation of his brother, the present emperor, to join him. It was a most extraordinary event, the talk of the whole court. The preparations, which occupied the full attention of everyone at Rokujo, were unprecedented in their complexity and in the attention to brilliant detail.

Arriving late in the morning, the royal party went first to the equestrian grounds, where the inner guards were mustered for mounted review in the finery usually reserved for the iris festival. There were brocades spread along the galleries and arched bridges and awnings over the open places when, in early afternoon, the party moved to the southeast quarter. The royal cormorants had been turned out with the Rokujo cormorants on the east lake, where there was a handsome take of small fish. Genji hoped that he was not being a fussy and overzealous host, but he did not want a single moment of the royal progress to be dull. ❷ The autumn leaves were splendid, especially in Akikonomu's southwest garden. Walls had been taken down and gates opened, and not so much as an autumn mist was permitted to obstruct the royal view. Genji showed his guests to seats on a higher level than his own. The emperor ordered this mark of inferiority dispensed with, and thought again what a satisfaction it would be to honor Genji as his father.

GUIDED READING

WORD HELP

unprecedented having no equal

equestrian related to horses

mustered gathered together

brocades rich cloths with designs woven into them

cormorants large diving birds

inferiority lower rank

❶ *What kind of modern-day American event might be compared to the emperor's visit?*

❷ *What do Genji's thoughts and actions tell you about his attitude toward his guests?*

The lieutenants of the inner guards advanced from the east and knelt to the left and right of the stairs before the royal seats, one presenting the take from the pond and the other a brace of fowl taken by the royal falcons in the northern hills. To no Chujo received the royal command to prepare and serve these delicacies. ❸ An equally interesting repast had been laid out for the princes and high courtiers. The court musicians took their places in late afternoon . . . The concert was quiet and unpretentious and there were court pages to dance for the royal guests. It was as always the excursion to the Suzaku Palace so many years before that people

A portrait of Lady Murasaki Shikibu, author of *The Tale of Genji*

GUIDED READING

WORD HELP

brace pair

repast meal

unpretentious simple; modest

coronets small crowns

❸ To no Chujo is Genji's best friend. During the Heian period, food preparation was considered an art, and chefs were highly honored for their skill.

❹ A koto is a stringed instrument sometimes called a Japanese harp.

remembered. One of To no Chujo's sons, a boy of ten or so, danced "Our Gracious Monarch" most elegantly. The emperor took off a robe and laid it over his shoulders, and To no Chujo himself descended into the garden for ritual thanks . . .

The evening breeze had scattered leaves of various tints to make the ground a brocade as rich and delicate as the brocades along the galleries. The dancers were young boys from the best families, prettily dressed in coronets and the usual grayblues and roses, with crimsons and lavenders showing at their sleeves. They danced very briefly and withdrew under the autumn trees, and the guests regretted the approach of sunset. The formal concert, brief and unassuming, was followed by impromptu music in the halls above, instruments having been brought from the palace collection. As it grew livelier a koto was brought for each of the emperors and a third for Genji. ❹ . . . It was cause for general rejoicing that the two houses should be so close.

CONNECTING LITERATURE TO HISTORY

1. **Summarizing** The nobles of the court at Heian loved beauty and elegance. Because of this love, many nobles were great supporters of the arts. Based on this passage, what specific arts did Japanese nobles enjoy?

2. **Generalizing** The nobles enjoyed their lives of ease and privilege. What details suggest that Japanese nobles lived lives of luxury?

3. **Evaluating** After reading this passage, what is your overall impression of Japanese court life?

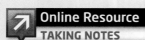
Growth of a Military Society

If YOU were there...

You are a Japanese warrior, proud of your fighting skills. For many years you've been honored by most of society, but you face an awful dilemma. When you became a warrior, you swore to protect and fight for both your lord and your emperor. Now your lord has gone to war against the emperor, and both sides have called for you to join them.

How will you decide whom to fight for?

BUILDING BACKGROUND Wars between lords and emperors were not uncommon in Japan after 1100. Closed off from society at Heian, emperors had lost touch with the rest of Japan. As a result, order broke down throughout the islands.

Samurai and Shoguns Take Over Japan

By the late 1100s, Heian was the great center of Japanese art and literature. But in the rest of Japan, life was very different. Powerful nobles fought each other over land. Rebels fought against imperial officials. This fighting destroyed land, which made it difficult for peasants to grow food. Some poor people became bandits or thieves. Meanwhile, Japan's rulers were so focused on courtly life, they didn't notice the many problems growing in their country.

The Rise of the Samurai

With the emperor distracted by life in his court, Japan's large landowners, or **daimyo** (DY-mee-oh), decided that they needed to protect their own lands. They hired **samurai** (SA-muh-ry), or trained professional warriors, to defend them and their property. The samurai wore light armor and fought with swords and bows. Most samurai came from noble families and inherited their positions from their fathers.

The word *samurai* comes from the Japanese word for servant. Every samurai, from the weakest soldier to the most powerful warrior, was supposed to serve his lord. Because all lords in Japan were supposed to serve the emperor, all samurai were required to be loyal to him.

An army of samurai was expensive to support. Few lords could afford to buy armor and weapons for their warriors. As a result, lords paid their samurai with land or food.

Only the most powerful samurai got land for their service. Most of these powerful samurai didn't live on the land they received, but they did profit from it. Every year, the peasant farmers who worked on the land gave the samurai money or food. Samurai who received no land were given food—usually rice—as payment.

Shoguns Rule Japan

Many of the nobles outside Heian were unhappy with the way Japan's government was being run. Frustrated, these nobles wanted a change of leadership. Eventually a few very strong noble clans decided to try to take power for themselves.

Two of these powerful clans went to war with each other in the 1150s. For almost 30 years, the two clans fought. Their fighting was terrible, destroying land and property and tearing families apart.

In the end, the Minamoto clan won. Because he had a very powerful army, and because the emperor was still busy in Heian, the leader of the Minamoto clan was the most powerful man in Japan. He decided to take over ruling the country.

He didn't, however, want to get rid of the emperor. He kept the emperor as a **figurehead**, a person who appears to rule even though real power rests with someone else. As a samurai, the Minamoto leader was supposed to be loyal to the emperor, but he decided to rule in the emperor's place. In 1192 he took the title **shogun**, a general who ruled Japan in the emperor's name. When he died, he passed his title and power on to one of his children. For about the next 700 years, one shogun would rule in Japan.

READING CHECK **Sequencing** How did the shogun rise to power in Japan?

QUICK FACTS

Samurai Society

Emperor
The emperor was a figurehead for the powerful shogun.

Shogun
A powerful military leader, the shogun ruled in the emperor's name.

Daimyo and Samurai
Daimyo were powerful lords who often led armies of samurai. Samurai warriors served the shogun and daimyo.

Peasants
Most Japanese were poor peasants who had no power.

ANALYSIS SKILL **ANALYZING VISUALS**
Who was the most powerful person in Japan's samurai society?

Samurai Live Honorably

FOCUS ON READING

As you read this section, notice the facts and examples that support the main idea.

Under the shogun, who were military rulers, samurai warriors became more central to Japanese society. As a result, samurai enjoyed many social privileges. Common people had to treat the samurai with respect. Anyone who disrespected a samurai could be killed.

At the same time, tradition placed restrictions on samurai. For example, they couldn't attend certain types of entertainment, such as theater, which were considered beneath them. They also couldn't take part in trade or commerce.

Bushido

More importantly, all samurai had to follow a strict code of rules that taught them how to behave. The samurai code of rules was known as **Bushido** (BOOH-shi-doh). This name means "the way of the warrior." Both men and women from samurai families had to follow Bushido rules.

Bushido required samurai to be brave and honorable fighters. Both men and women of samurai families learned how to fight, though only men went to war. Women learned to fight so they could protect their homes from robbers.

Japan's Samurai

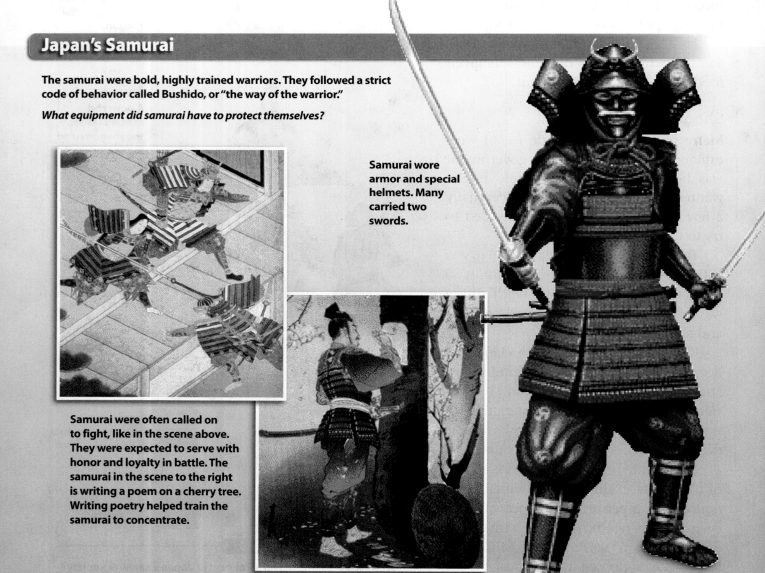

The samurai were bold, highly trained warriors. They followed a strict code of behavior called Bushido, or "the way of the warrior."

What equipment did samurai have to protect themselves?

Samurai wore armor and special helmets. Many carried two swords.

Samurai were often called on to fight, like in the scene above. They were expected to serve with honor and loyalty in battle. The samurai in the scene to the right is writing a poem on a cherry tree. Writing poetry helped train the samurai to concentrate.

Samurai were expected to live simple, disciplined lives. They believed that self-discipline made them better warriors. To improve their discipline, many samurai participated in peaceful rituals that required great concentration. Some created intricate flower arrangements or grew miniature bonsai trees. Others held elaborate tea ceremonies. Many samurai also adopted Zen Buddhism, which stressed self-discipline and meditation.

More than anything else, Bushido required a samurai to be loyal to his lord. Each samurai had to obey his master's orders without hesitation, even if it caused the samurai or his family to suffer. One samurai expressed his duties in this way:

" If one were to say in a word what the condition of being a samurai is, its basis lies first in seriously devoting one's body and soul to his master. "

–Yamamoto Tsunetomo, from Hagakure

Obeying his lord was important to the samurai's sense of honor. Honor was the most important thing in a samurai's life. If he did anything to lose honor, a samurai was expected to commit suicide rather than live with his shame. Such shame might be caused by disobeying an order, losing a fight, or failing to protect his lord.

Bushido and Modern Japan

Although it was created as a code for warriors, Bushido influenced much of Japanese society. Even today, many Japanese feel a connection to the samurai. For example, the samurai's dedication and discipline are still greatly admired in Japan. **Values** such as loyalty and honor, the central ideas of the samurai code, remain very important in modern Japan.

ACADEMIC VOCABULARY

values ideas that people hold dear and try to live by

READING CHECK   **Finding Main Ideas** What customs did samurai follow?

LINKING TO TODAY

Modern Samurai

Although the samurai class disappeared from Japan at the end of the 1800s, samurai images and values live on. Fierce samurai appear on posters, in advertisements and movies, and in video games, challenging foes with their sharp swords and deadly skills. Many people study the same martial arts, such as sword fighting, that the samurai practiced. In addition, the loyalty that samurai felt toward their lords is still a key part of Japanese society. Many Japanese feel that same loyalty toward other groups—their families, companies, or favorite sports teams. Samurai values such as hard work, honor, and sacrifice have also become deeply rooted in Japanese society.

HISTORY

VIDEO
Samurai in the Modern World
↗ Online Resource

ANALYSIS SKILL   ANALYZING INFORMATION
How are Japan's samurai values still alive today?

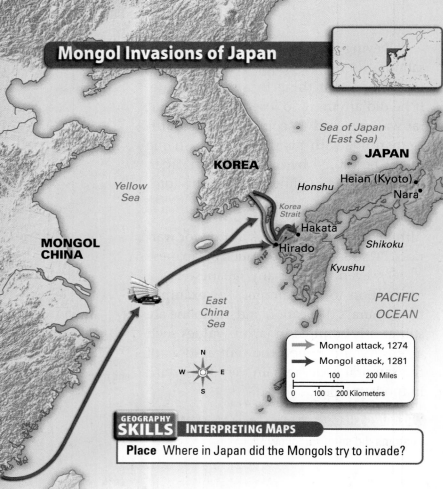

Mongol Invasions of Japan

Sea of Japan (East Sea)

JAPAN

KOREA

Yellow Sea

Honshu

Heian (Kyoto)

Nara

MONGOL CHINA

Korea Strait

Hakata

Hirado

Shikoku

East China Sea

Kyushu

PACIFIC OCEAN

→ Mongol attack, 1274
→ Mongol attack, 1281

0   100   200 Miles
0   100   200 Kilometers

GEOGRAPHY SKILLS INTERPRETING MAPS

Place Where in Japan did the Mongols try to invade?

Order Breaks Down

For about a century, the shoguns kept order in Japan. Supported by the samurai, the shoguns were able to put down challenges to their authority. Eventually, however, more serious challenges arose that brought this order to an end.

Foreign Invasion

One of the greatest challenges to the shoguns was an invasion by the Mongols from China. China's emperor, Kublai Khan, sent an army to conquer the islands in 1274. Faced with invasion, the shogun sent troops to fight the Mongols. In addition, Japan's warring nobles put aside their differences to fight the enemy. The Japanese warriors were aided by a great storm. The storm sank many Mongol ships and forced the Mongols to flee.

In 1281 the Mongols invaded again. This time they sent two huge armies and threatened to overwhelm the Japanese warriors. For weeks, the two armies were locked in deadly combat.

Once again, though, the weather helped the Japanese. A huge storm swept over Japan, sinking most of the Mongol fleet. Many Mongol soldiers drowned, and many more returned to China. The grateful Japanese called the storm that had saved them the kamikaze (kah-mi-KAH-zee), or "divine wind." They believed the gods had sent the storm to save Japan.

But many nobles were left unhappy by the war. They didn't think the shogun gave them enough credit for their part in the fighting. Many came to resent the shogun's power over them.

Internal Rebellion

After the Mongol invasion, new problems arose for the shogun. The emperor, tired of having no say in the government, began to fight the shogun for control of the country. At the same time daimyo, the nobles who owned much of Japan's land, fought to break free of the shogun's control. During these struggles for power, small wars broke out all over Japan.

By the 1400s the shoguns had lost most of their authority. The emperor was still largely powerless, and daimyo ruled much of Japan. Each daimyo controlled his own territory. Within that territory, he made laws and collected taxes. There was no powerful central authority of any sort to impose order in Japan.

READING CHECK **Summarizing** What challenges appeared to the shogun's authority?

Strong Leaders Take Over

Soon new leaders rose to power. They began as local rulers, but these men wanted more power. In the 1500s, each fought to unify all of Japan under his control.

Unification

The first such leader was Oda Nobunaga (ohd-ah noh-booh-nah-gah). Oda gave his soldiers guns that had been brought to Japan by Portuguese traders. This was the first time guns had been used in Japan. With these new weapons, Oda easily defeated his opponents.

After Oda died, other leaders continued his efforts to unify Japan. By 1600, one of them, Tokugawa Ieyasu (toh-koohg-ah-wuh ee-e-yahs-ooh), had conquered his enemies. In 1603 Japan's emperor made Tokugawa shogun. From his capital at Edo (AY-doh)—now Tokyo—Tokugawa ruled all of Japan.

Tokugawa's rise to power began the Tokugawa shogunate (SHOH-guhn-uht), or rule by shoguns of the Tokugawa family. Early in this period, which lasted until 1868, Japan traded with other countries and let Christian missionaries live in Japan.

Isolation

Not all of the shoguns who followed Tokugawa liked this contact with the world, though. Some feared that Japan would become too much like Europe, and the shoguns would lose their power. To prevent such a thing from happening, in the 1630s the ruling shogun closed Japan off from the rest of the world.

Japan's rulers also banned guns. They feared that peasants with guns could defeat their samurai armies. The combination of isolation from the world and limited technology helped extend the samurai period in Japan until the 1800s, far longer than it might have otherwise lasted.

READING CHECK **Drawing Conclusions** How did Japan change in the Tokugawa shogunate?

SUMMARY AND PREVIEW By the 1100s, the growing power of shoguns, daimyo, and samurai had turned Japan into a military society. Next you will read about societies that developed on the other side of the world—in the Americas.

Section 3 Assessment

Reviewing Ideas, Terms, and People

1. **a. Recall** What was the relationship between **samurai** and **daimyo**?
   b. Elaborate Why do you think the first **shogun** wanted to keep the emperor as a **figurehead**?
2. **a. Define** What was **Bushido**?
   b. Explain Why did samurai take up pursuits like flower arranging?
3. **a. Identify** Who invaded Japan in the 1270s and 1280s?
   b. Summarize How did the daimyo help weaken the shoguns?
4. **Identify** What strong leaders worked to unify Japan in the late 1500s?

Critical Thinking

5. **Analyzing** Draw a word web. In the center, write a sentence that describes the samurai. Using your notes about life in a military society, write one of the samurai's jobs, duties, or privileges in each outer circle.

FOCUS ON WRITING

6. **Describing the Samurai** A Japanese history museum will offer a special exhibit on the samurai warrior. Add notes about the samurai to encourage tourists to visit the exhibit. Tell who they were, what they did, and how they lived.

Social Studies Skills

Solving Problems

Understand the Skill

Problem solving is a process for finding good solutions to difficult situations. It involves asking questions, identifying and evaluating information, comparing and contrasting, and making judgments. It is useful in studying history because it helps you better understand problems a person or group faced in the past and how they dealt with those issues.

The ability to understand and evaluate how people solved problems in the past also can help in solving similar problems today. The skill can be applied to many other kinds of difficulties besides historical ones. It is a method for thinking through almost any situation.

Learn the Skill

Using the following steps will help you to better understand and solve problems.

1 **Identify the problem.** Ask questions of yourself and others. This first step helps you to be sure you know exactly what the situation is. It also helps you understand why it is a problem.

2 **Gather information.** Ask other questions and do research to learn more about the problem. For example, what is its history? What caused the problem? What contributes to it?

3 **List options.** Based on the information you have gathered, identify possible options for solving the problem. It will be easier to find a good solution if you have several options.

4 **Evaluate the options.** Weigh each option you are considering. Think of the advantages it has as a solution. Then think of its potential disadvantages. It may help you to compare your options if you make a list of advantages and disadvantages for each possible solution.

5 **Choose and apply a solution.** After comparing the advantages and disadvantages of each possible solution, choose the one that seems best and apply it.

6 **Evaluate the solution.** Once the solution has been tried, evaluate how effective it is in solving the problem. This step will tell you if the solution was a good one, or if you should try another of the options instead. It will also help you know what to do in the future if you happen to face the same problem again.

Practice and Apply the Skill

Read again the "If you were there" in Section 3. Imagine that you are the warrior with this problem. You can apply the steps for solving problems to help you decide what to do. Review the information in the section about the samurai and this time period in Japan's history. Then, in the role of the samurai warrior, answer the questions below.

1. What is the specific problem that you face? Why is it a problem?

2. What events led to your problem? What circumstances and conditions have contributed to it?

3. What options can you think of to solve your problem? List the advantages and disadvantages of each.

4. Which of your options seems to be the best solution for your problem? Explain why. How will you know if it is a good solution?

Chapter Review

Visual Summary

Use the visual summary below to help you review the main ideas of the chapter.

Japan's early culture was influenced by China and Korea.

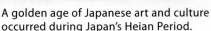

A golden age of Japanese art and culture occurred during Japan's Heian Period.

After the Heian Period, the Japanese created a military society.

Reviewing Vocabulary, Terms, and People

Unscramble each group of letters below to spell a term that matches the given definition.

1. **etrgne**—a person who rules in someone else's name
2. **misaaru**—a Japanese warrior
3. **aclsn**—large, extended families
4. **elauvs**—ideas that people hold dear
5. **uctro**—a group of nobles who surround a ruler
6. **nguosh**—a great Japanese general who ruled instead of the emperor
7. **enz**—a form of Japanese Buddhism
8. **osnith**—a nature religion that began in Japan
9. **odmiya**—Japanese lords who gave land to samurai
10. **kosouth**—prince who introduced many Chinese ideas to Japan
11. **rctusrteu**—the way something is set up

Comprehension and Critical Thinking

SECTION 1 *(Pages 438–443)*

12. **a. Identify** Who was Prince Shotoku, and what did he do?

    b. Compare and Contrast Why was Japan isolated from China and Korea? How did China and Korea still affect Japan?

    c. Predict How would Japan's physical geography affect the development of Japanese government and society?

SECTION 2 *(Pages 444–448)*

13. **a. Recall** Why is Murasaki Shikibu a major figure in the history of Japanese culture?

    b. Analyze What made the period between the 800s and the 1100s a golden age of the arts in Japan?

    c. Evaluate Would you like to have been a member of the imperial court at Heian? Why or why not?

14. a. Define What was the Tokugawa shogunate?

b. Analyze How did Japan develop into a military society? What groups made up that society?

c. Elaborate What was daily life like for the samurai?

Reviewing Themes

15. Politics How did Prince Shototku try to change the political system in Japan?

16. Science and Technology What new technological advance did Japan's rulers ban, starting in the 1630s? Why?

17. Society and Culture How did Bushido affect modern Japanese culture?

Reading Skills

Main Ideas and Their Support *The passage below is taken from this textbook. Read the passage and then answer the questions that follow.*

> "One of the people most influential in bringing Chinese ideas to Japan was Prince Shotoku. He served from 593 to 621 as regent for his aunt, the empress. A regent is a person who rules a country for someone who is unable to rule alone.
>
> All his life, Prince Shotoku admired Chinese culture. As regent, Shotoku saw a chance for Japan to adopt more Chinese ideas. He sent scholars to China to learn more about Chinese society."

18. Explain in your own words the main idea of this passage.

19. Which other method might the author have used to make the explanation more informative and interesting? What would this method have contributed to the passage's meaning?

20. What is a definition the author gives in this passage? How does it help support the main idea?

Using the Internet

21. Activity: Drawing a Comic Strip A strong military influence affected the governing structure of Japan. Eventually, warriors and generals gained power in Japan as emperors lost some of it. Go online to conduct research on who held power in Japan from the 1100s to the 1600s. Create a comic strip about them, similar in style to Japanese anime.

Social Studies Skills

22. Solving Problems Imagine that you are a samurai warrior who has been called upon to help fight the Mongol invasion. You are stationed in a small village that is directly in the path of the Mongol army. Some people in the village want to stay and fight the Mongols, but you know they will be killed if they try to fight. The town's leaders want your opinion about what they should do. Write down one or two ideas you might suggest for how to save the people of the village. For each idea, make notes about what consequences your proposed action may have.

FOCUS ON WRITING

23. Creating Your Travel Brochure Look back over your notes from this chapter, and then create a travel brochure that describes Japan's historic attractions. Keep your writing brief—remember that you have to get your audience's attention with just a few words. To help get their attention, draw or find pictures to illustrate your travel brochure.

CHAPTER 7

Florida Standardized Test Practice

DIRECTIONS: Read each question, and write the letter of the best response.

1

> I was brought up in a distant province which lies farther than the farthest end of the Eastern Road. I am ashamed to think that inhabitants of the Royal City will think me an uncultured girl.
> Somehow I came to know that there are such things as romances in the world and wished to read them. When there was nothing to do by day or at night, one tale or another was told me by my elder sister or stepmother, and I heard several chapters about the shining Prince Genji.

From the content of this passage, it can be concluded that its author was a

A samurai warrior.

B noble woman from Heian.

C farmer from northern Japan.

D daimyo.

2 The importance of loyalty, honor, and discipline in Japanese society today are *mainly* the result of what influence in Japan's history?

A the code of the samurai

B the teachings of Shinto

C the reforms of Prince Shotoku

D the spread of Chinese Buddhism

3 Most great works of early Japanese literature were written by

A Buddhist scholars.

B samurai warriors.

C Shinto priests.

D noble women.

4 The influence of China and Korea on Japan's history, culture, and development is found in all of the following *except*

A Japan's first writing system.

B the traditional Japanese diet.

C early rules for family behavior.

D the practice of Buddhism.

5 The main function of samurai in Japanese society was to

A write poetry.

B manage farmland.

C defend lords.

D conquer China.

Connecting with Past Learnings

6 Early Japanese society under the clans was not a single unified country but many small states. This type of government *most* resembled that of

A the early city-states of ancient Greece.

B the Roman Empire during the Pax Romana.

C the Old Kingdom of ancient Egypt.

D the New Kingdom of ancient Egypt.

7 The nobles of Heian placed great emphasis on art and learning, just like the people of which ancient Greek city-state that you learned about earlier?

A Sparta

B Athens

C Macedonia

D Troy

Japan and the Samurai Warrior

For over a thousand years, the samurai—an elite warrior class—were a powerful force in Japanese society. The way of life of the samurai lords and warriors was, in many ways, like those of the medieval lords and knights of Europe. The great samurai warlords ruled large territories and relied on the fighting skills of their fierce samurai warriors to battle their enemies. But samurai warriors were more than just soldiers. Samurai were expected to embrace beauty and culture, and many were skilled artists. They also had a strict personal code that valued personal honor above all things—even life itself.

Explore the fascinating world of the samurai warrior online. You can find a wealth of information, video clips, primary sources, activities, and more online.

Rise of the Samurai Class

Watch the video to learn how the samurai developed from armed tax collectors into warlords and armies that ruled Japan.

A New Way of Life in Japan

Watch the video to learn how peace and isolation took hold in Japan and changed the role of the samurai in society.

> " I have no eyes;
>   I make the Flash of Lightning my Eyes.
> I have no ears; I make Sensibility my Ears.
> I have no limbs;
>   I make Promptitude my Limbs.
> I have no laws;
>   I make Self-Protection my Laws. "

A Code for Samurai Living

Read the document to learn about the strict but lyrical code of the samurai warrior.

Death of the Samurai Class

Watch the video to see how the end of Japan's isolation from the outside world signaled the beginning of the end of the samurai class.

FLORIDA...
The Story Continues

CHAPTER 16, The Early Americas (500 BC–AD 1537)

PEOPLE **AD 750–1500: Northern Florida groups grow maize.**
By around AD 750, several cultures living in northern Florida were growing maize. The most successful farmers were the people of the Fort Walton culture in the eastern panhandle. The Fort Walton villages were located between the Aucilla and Apalachicola rivers. The villagers cleared large areas of land to grow corn and other crops. These crops made up a large part of the people's diet. A better diet helped the population grow. The Fort Walton people developed a complex political and social structure to support farming and their growing population.

EVENTS **1513: Juan Ponce de León lands in Florida.** Ponce de León and his party set sail from Puerto Rico on March 3, 1513, in three ships. After nearly a month at sea, they sighted what they thought was an island. They came ashore sometime on or slightly after April 2. Taken by its beauty and the fact that it was the Easter season, Ponce de León named the land La Florida—the flowery land. The land, of course, was not an island. Ponce de León had landed on the peninsula of Florida. Some historians believe that Ponce de León first came ashore below Cape Canaveral near what is now Melbourne Beach.

EVENTS **Early 1500s: Florida's Native Americans encounter the Spanish.** Estimates vary on how many Native Americans lived in Florida when the Spanish first arrived. Some historians set the number at about 100,000. Others believe that there may have been as many as 350,000 people scattered throughout the state. Whatever the number, the arrival of the Spanish and other Europeans changed the future for Florida's native people. Disease, slave-raiding parties, and warfare would destroy most of Florida's native cultures over the next 300 years.

EVENTS **c. 1513 and 1521: The Calusa drive away the Spanish caravels of Ponce de León.**   When the first Europeans came to Southwest Florida, they found a land controlled by the Calusa. From his base in Charlotte Harbor near present-day Fort Myers, the Calusa chief Carlos ruled as many as 20,000 people occupying more than 50 villages. His political influence extended across most of southern Florida. Twice the Calusa were able to drive away Ponce de León. In 1513, Ponce de León and his men came ashore on Calusa lands. While the Spanish looked for food and water, the Calusa untied the ships' anchors and cables and attempted to board the

vessels. The Spanish fled. In 1521, Ponce de León returned with ships carrying 200 settlers, 50 horses, and other livestock. Again, the Calusa drove the Spanish away, killing many in the process.

EVENTS **1539–1540: Hernando de Soto explores Florida.**   In 1537, the Spanish crown gave Hernando de Soto the right to explore Florida. De Soto raised an army and set sail for Cuba, where he spent half a year planning his Florida campaign. He finally sailed into a bay near Tampa in 1539, eager to find gold. De Soto did not find gold. What he did find were forests, rivers, bogs, and sand hills. He also found hostile Native Americans. De Soto was equipped to fight a traditional war on horseback, but not the guerrilla tactics the Native Americans used. In March 1540 the Spanish expedition left Florida and entered Georgia. De Soto would never see Florida again. He died along the Mississippi River in 1542.

Unpacking the Florida Standards ‹···

Read the following to learn what this standard says and what it means. See FL8–FL31 to unpack all of the standards related to this chapter.

Benchmark SS.6.W.2.10   Compare the emergence of advanced civilizations in Meso and South America with the four early river valley civilizations. Examples are Olmec, Zapotec, Chavin.

What does it mean?
Explain how the civilizations of Meso and South America were similar to and different from the four early river valley civilizations.

    SPOTLIGHT ON
SS.6.G.1.5, SS.6.G.2.1 See pages FL43 and FL44 for content specifically related to these Chapter 16 standards.

The Early Americas

Essential Question   What led to the development of complex societies in the Americas?

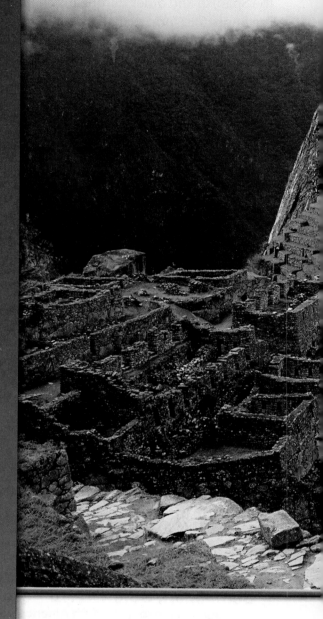

Florida Next Generation Sunshine State Standards

LA.6.1.6.1 The student will use new vocabulary that is introduced and taught directly. **LA.6.1.6.2** The student will listen to, read, and discuss familiar and conceptually challenging text. **SS.6.E.1.1** Identify the factors (new resources, increased productivity, education, technology, slave economy, territorial expansion) that increase economic growth. **SS.6.G.1.4** Utilize tools geographers use to study the world. **SS.6.G.1.5** Use scale, cardinal, and intermediate directions, and estimation of distances between places on current and ancient maps of the world. **SS.6.G.1.7** Use maps to identify characteristics and boundaries of ancient civilizations that have shaped the world today. **SS.6.G.2.1** Explain how major physical characteristics, natural resources, climate, and absolute and relative locations have influenced settlement, interactions, and the economies of ancient civilizations of the world. **SS.6.G.3.1** Explain how the physical landscape has affected the development of agriculture and industry in the ancient world. **SS.6.G.3.2** Analyze the impact of human populations on the ancient world's ecosystems. **SS.6.G.5.1** Identify the methods used to compensate for the scarcity of resources in the ancient world. **SS.6.G.5.2** Use geographic terms and tools to explain why ancient civilizations developed networks of highways, waterways, and other transportation linkages. **SS.6.G.5.3** Use geographic tools and terms to analyze how famine, drought, and natural disasters plagued many ancient civilizations. **SS.6.W.1.1** Use timelines to identify chronological order of historical events. **SS.6.W.1.3** Interpret primary and secondary sources. **SS.6.W.2.10** Compare the emergence of advanced civilizations in Meso and South America with the four early river valley civilizations.

FOCUS ON WRITING

A Newspaper Article You are a writer for a European newspaper who is traveling with some explorers to the Americas. Your newspaper wants you to write an article to share what you have seen with readers back home in Europe. As you read this chapter, you will decide what to write about—the land, the people, or the events that occurred after the explorers arrived.

REGION EVENTS

c. AD 200 The Maya begin building large cities in the Americas.

c. 900 The Maya Classic Age ends.

500 BC

WORLD EVENTS

c. 500 BC Athens develops the world's first democracy.

HISTORY Machu Picchu

↗ Online Resource VIDEO

The ruins of the Inca city Machu Picchu, shown here, lie high in the Andes Mountains.

c.1325
The Aztecs set up their capital at Tenochtitlán.

c. 1440
Pachacuti begins to expand the Inca Empire.

1519
Cortés arrives in Mexico.

1537
Pizarro conquers the Inca Empire.

| 1350 | 1450 | 1550 |

1337
The Hundred Years' War between France and England begins.

1433
China's emperor ends ocean exploration of Asia and Africa.

1453
The Ottomans conquer Constantinople.

1517
Martin Luther posts his Ninety-five Theses.

Reading Social Studies

Economics   Geography   Politics   Religion   Society and Culture   Science and Technology

Focus on Themes In this chapter, you will read about the development of civilizations in the Americas—in Mesoamerica, which is in the southern part of North America, and in the Andes, which is in South America. As you read about the Maya in Mesoamerica, the Aztecs in central Mexico, and the Incas in South America, you will see how the **geography** of the areas affected their way of life. You will learn that these ancient civilizations made interesting advancements in **science**.

Analyzing Historical Information

Focus on Reading History books are full of information. As you read, you are confronted with names, dates, places, terms, and descriptions on every page. Because you're faced with so much information, you don't want to have to deal with unimportant or untrue material in a history book.

Identifying Relevant and Essential Information Information in a history book should be relevant, or related to the topic you're studying. It should also be essential, or necessary, to understanding that topic. Anything that is not relevant or essential distracts from the important material you are studying.

The passage below comes from an encyclopedia, but some irrelevant and nonessential information has been added so that you can learn to identify it.

The Maya

The first sentence of the paragraph expresses the main idea. Anything that doesn't support this idea is nonessential.

Who They Were Maya were an American Indian people who developed a magnificent civilization in Mesoamerica, which is the southern part of North America. They built their largest cities between AD 250 and 900. Today, many people travel to Central America to see Maya ruins.

The last sentence does not support the main idea and is nonessential.

This paragraph discusses Maya communication. Any other topics are irrelevant.

Communication The Maya developed an advanced form of writing that used many symbols. Our writing system uses 26 letters. They recorded information on large stone monuments. Some early civilizations drew pictures on cave walls. The Maya also made books of paper made from the fig tree bark. Fig trees need a lot of light.

The needs of fig trees have nothing to do with Maya communication. This sentence is irrelevant.

Portions of this text and the one on the next page were taken from the 2004 World Book Online Reference Center.

You Try It!

The following passage has some sentences that aren't important, necessary, or relevant. Read the passage and identify those sentences.

The Maya Way of Life

Religion The Maya believed in many gods and goddesses. More than 160 gods and goddesses are named in a single Maya manuscript. Among the gods they worshipped were a corn god, a rain god, a sun god, and a moon goddess. The early Greeks also worshipped many gods and goddesses.

Family and Social Structure Whole families of Maya—including parents, children, and grandparents—lived together. Not many houses today could hold all those people. Each family member had tasks to do. Men and boys, for example, worked in the fields. Very few people are farmers today. Women and older girls made clothes and meals for the rest of the family. Now most people buy their clothes.

After you read the passage, answer the following questions.

1. Which sentence in the first paragraph is irrelevant to the topic? How can you tell?

2. Which three sentences in the second paragraph are not essential to learning about the Maya? Do those sentences belong in this passage?

Key Terms and People

Chapter 16

Section 1
maize *(p. 468)*
observatories *(p. 472)*

Section 2
causeways *(p. 474)*
conquistadors *(p. 477)*
Hernán Cortés *(p. 478)*
Moctezuma II *(p. 478)*

Section 3
Pachacuti *(p. 479)*
Quechua *(p. 480)*
masonry *(p. 481)*
Atahualpa *(p. 482)*
Francisco Pizarro *(p. 482)*

Academic Vocabulary

Success in school is related to knowing academic vocabulary—the words that are frequently used in school assignments and discussions. In this chapter, you will learn the following academic words:

aspect *(p. 471)*
rebel *(p. 472)*
motive *(p. 478)*
distribute *(p. 480)*

As you read Chapter 16, practice detemining what is relevant information for each section.

The Maya

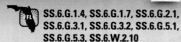 SS.6.G.1.4, SS.6.G.1.7, SS.6.G.2.1, SS.6.G.3.1, SS.6.G.3.2, SS.6.G.5.1, SS.6.G.5.3, SS.6.W.2.10

What You Will Learn...

Main Ideas

1. Geography helped shape the lives of the early Maya in Mesoamerica.
2. During the Classic Age, the Maya built great cities linked by trade.
3. Maya culture was influenced by social structure, religion, and achievements in science and the arts.
4. The decline of Maya civilization began in the 900s, for reasons that are still unclear.

The Big Idea

The Maya developed an advanced civilization that thrived in Mesoamerica from about 250 until the 900s.

Key Terms and People

maize, p. 468
Pacal, p. 469
observatories, p. 472

Online Resource
TAKING NOTES

Use the graphic organizer online to take notes on different aspects of Maya civilization.

SS.6.W.2.10 Compare the emergence of advanced civilizations in Meso and South America with the four early river valley civilizations.

If YOU were there...

You are a Maya farmer, growing corn in fields outside a city. Often you enter the city to join in religious ceremonies. You watch the king and his priests standing at the top of a tall pyramid. They wear capes of brightly colored feathers and gold ornaments that glitter in the sun. Far below them, thousands of worshippers crowd into the plaza with you to honor the gods.

How do these ceremonies make you feel?

BUILDING BACKGROUND Religion was very important to the Maya, one of the early peoples in the Americas. The Maya believed the gods controlled everything in the world around them.

Geography and the Early Maya

The region known as Mesoamerica stretches from the central area of Mexico south to the northern part of Central America. It was in this region that a people called the Maya (MY-uh) developed a remarkable civilization.

Around 1000 BC the Maya began settling in the lowlands of what is now northern Guatemala. Thick tropical forests covered most of the land, but the people cleared areas to farm. They grew a variety of crops, including beans, squash, avocados, and **maize**, or corn. The forests provided valuable resources, too. Forest animals such as deer, rabbits, and monkeys were sources of food. In addition, trees and other plants made good building materials. For example, some Maya used wooden poles and vines, along with mud, to build their houses.

The early Maya lived in small, isolated villages. Eventually, though, these villages started trading with one another and with other groups in Mesoamerica. As trade increased, the villages grew. By about AD 200, the Maya had begun to build large cities in Mesoamerica.

READING CHECK Finding Main Ideas How did the early Maya make use of their physical environment?

The Classic Age

The Maya civilization reached its height between about AD 250 and 900. This time in Maya history is known as the Classic Age. During this time, Maya territory grew to include more than 40 large cities.

Maya cities were really city-states. Each had its own government and its own king. No single ruler ever united the many cities into one empire. However, trade helped hold Maya civilization together. People exchanged goods for products that were not available locally. For example, Maya in the lowlands exported forest goods, cotton, and cacao (kuh-KOW) beans, which are used in making chocolate. In return, they received obsidian (a glasslike volcanic rock), jade, and colorful bird feathers.

Through trade, the Maya got supplies for construction. Maya cities had grand buildings, such as palaces decorated with carvings and paintings. The Maya also built stone pyramids topped with temples. Some temples honored local kings. For example, in the city of Palenque (pah-LENG-kay), the king **Pacal** (puh-KAHL) built a temple to record his achievements.

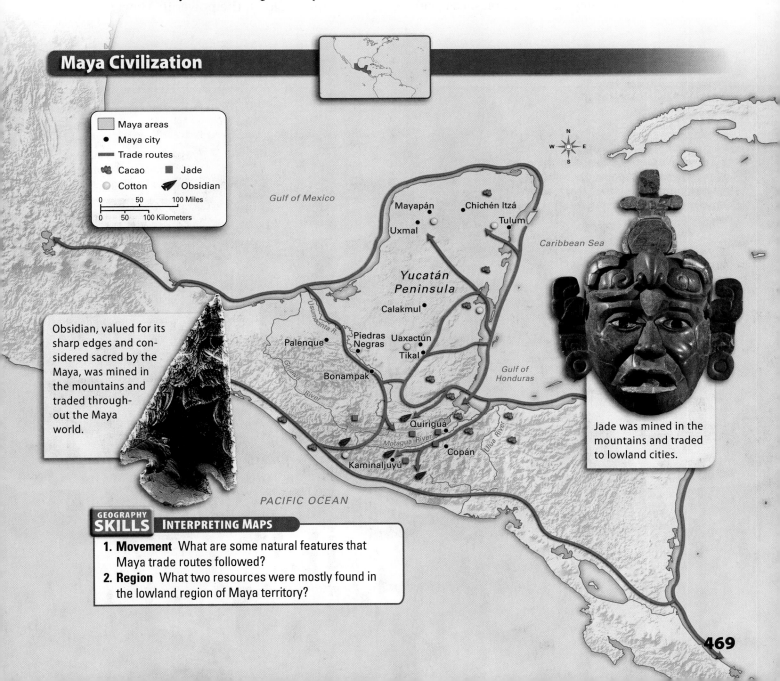

Maya Civilization

Legend:
- Maya areas
- Maya city
- Trade routes
- Cacao
- Cotton
- Jade
- Obsidian

0   50   100 Miles
0   50   100 Kilometers

Gulf of Mexico

Mayapán
Chichén Itzá
Tulum
Uxmal

Caribbean Sea

Yucatán Peninsula

Calakmul

Piedras Negras
Uaxactún
Palenque
Tikal

Bonampak

Gulf of Honduras

Usumacinta R.
Grijalva River
Motagua River
Ulúa River

Quiriguá
Copán
Kaminaljuyú

PACIFIC OCEAN

Obsidian, valued for its sharp edges and considered sacred by the Maya, was mined in the mountains and traded throughout the Maya world.

Jade was mined in the mountains and traded to lowland cities.

GEOGRAPHY SKILLS INTERPRETING MAPS

1. **Movement** What are some natural features that Maya trade routes followed?
2. **Region** What two resources were mostly found in the lowland region of Maya territory?

In addition to palaces and temples, the Maya built canals and paved large plazas, or open squares, for public gatherings. Farmers used stone walls to shape hillsides into flat terraces so they could grow crops on them. Almost every Maya city also had a stone court for playing a special ball game. Using only their heads, shoulders, or hips, players tried to bounce a heavy, hard rubber ball through stone rings attached high on the court walls. The winners of these games received jewels and clothing.

READING CHECK **Analyzing** Why is Maya civilization not considered an empire?

Maya Culture

In Maya society, people's everyday lives were heavily influenced by two main forces. One was the social structure, and the other was religion.

Social Structure

The king held the highest position in Maya society. Because he was believed to be related to the gods, the king had religious as well as political authority. Priests, merchants, and noble warriors were also part of the upper class. Together with the king, they held all the power in Maya society.

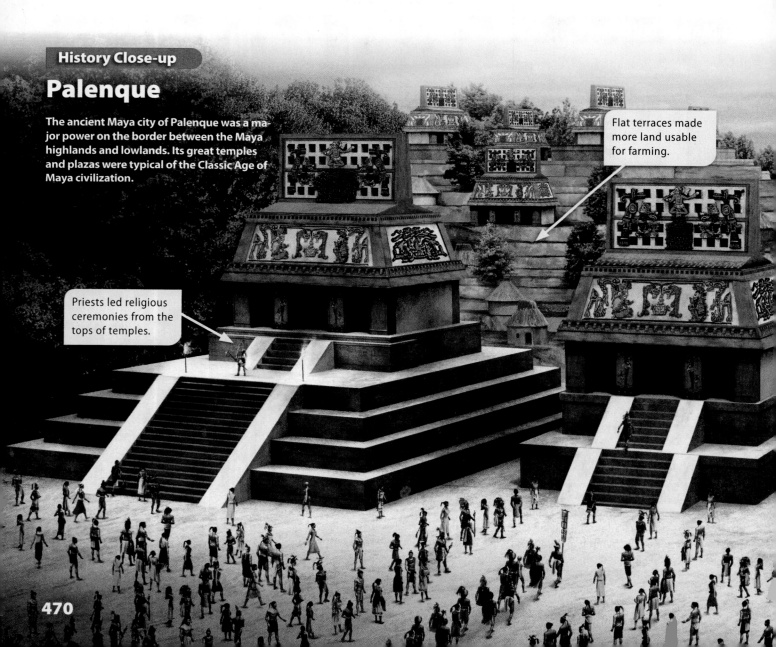

History Close-up

Palenque

The ancient Maya city of Palenque was a major power on the border between the Maya highlands and lowlands. Its great temples and plazas were typical of the Classic Age of Maya civilization.

Flat terraces made more land usable for farming.

Priests led religious ceremonies from the tops of temples.

Most Maya, though, belonged to the lower class. This group was made up of farming families who lived outside the cities. The women cared for the children, cooked, made yarn, and wove cloth. The men farmed, hunted, and crafted tools.

Lower-class Maya had to "pay" their rulers by giving the rulers part of their crops and goods such as cloth and salt. They also had to help construct temples and other public buildings. If their city went to war, Maya men had to serve in the army, and if captured in battle, they usually became slaves. Slaves carried goods along trade routes or worked as servants or farmers for upper-class Maya.

Religion

The Maya worshipped many gods, including a creator, a sun god, a moon goddess, and a maize god. Each god was believed to control a different **aspect** of daily life.

According to Maya beliefs, the gods could be helpful or harmful, so people tried to please the gods to get their help. The Maya believed their gods needed blood to prevent disasters or the end of the world. Every person offered blood to the gods by piercing their tongue or skin. On special occasions, the Maya also made human sacrifices. They usually used prisoners captured in battle, offering their hearts to stone carvings of the gods.

ACADEMIC VOCABULARY

aspect a part of something

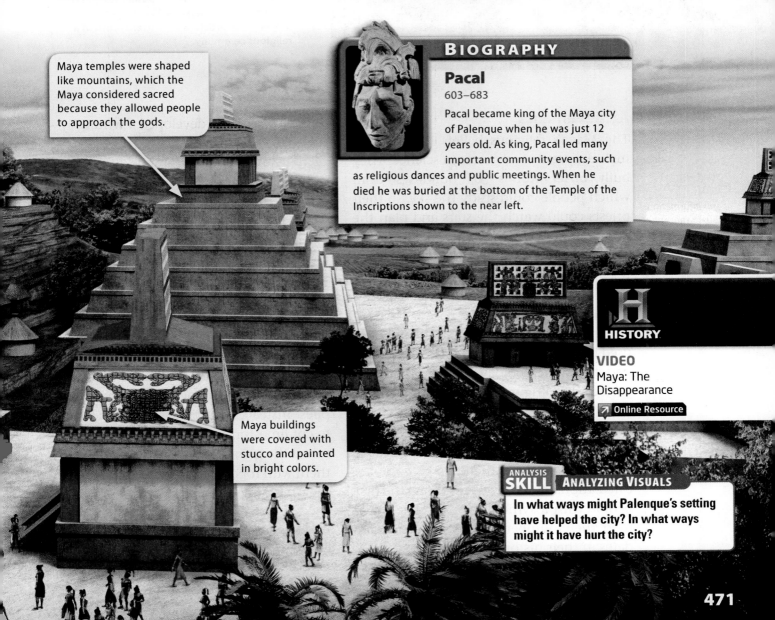

Maya temples were shaped like mountains, which the Maya considered sacred because they allowed people to approach the gods.

Maya buildings were covered with stucco and painted in bright colors.

BIOGRAPHY

Pacal
603–683

Pacal became king of the Maya city of Palenque when he was just 12 years old. As king, Pacal led many important community events, such as religious dances and public meetings. When he died he was buried at the bottom of the Temple of the Inscriptions shown to the near left.

HISTORY

VIDEO
Maya: The Disappearance
↗ Online Resource

ANALYSIS SKILL ANALYZING VISUALS

In what ways might Palenque's setting have helped the city? In what ways might it have hurt the city?

October 28, AD 709

She is letting blood.

Lady Xoc

Lord of Yaxchilán

This photo (left) shows the observatory at the Maya city of Chichén Itzá. The stone carving (above) is an artistic and written record of a religious ceremony.

Achievements

FOCUS ON READING
Is any information in this paragraph irrelevant?

The Maya's religious beliefs led them to make impressive advances in science. They built **observatories**, or buildings from which people could study the sky, so their priests could watch the stars and plan the best times for religious festivals. With the knowledge they gained about astronomy, the Maya developed two calendars. One, with 365 days, guided planting, harvesting, and other farming activities. This calendar was more accurate than the calendar used in Europe at that time. The Maya also had a separate 260-day calendar that they used for keeping track of religious events.

The Maya could measure time accurately partly because they were skilled mathematicians. They created a number system that helped them make complex calculations, and they were among the first people with a symbol for zero. The Maya used their number system to record key dates in their history.

The Maya also developed a writing system. In a way, it was similar to Egyptian hieroglyphics, because symbols represented both objects and sounds. The Maya carved series of these symbols into large stone tablets to record their history and the achievements of their kings. They also wrote in bark paper books and passed down stories and poems orally.

The Maya created amazing art and architecture as well. Maya jade and gold jewelry was exceptional. Also, their huge temple-pyramids were masterfully built. The Maya had neither metal tools for cutting nor wheeled vehicles for carrying supplies. Instead, workers used obsidian tools to cut limestone into blocks. Then workers rolled the giant blocks over logs and lifted them with ropes. The Maya often decorated their buildings with paintings.

READING CHECK **Categorizing** What groups made up the different classes in Maya society?

Decline of Maya Civilization

Maya civilization began to collapse in the AD 900s. People stopped building temples and other structures. They left the cities and moved back to the countryside. What caused this collapse? Historians aren't sure, but they think a combination of factors was probably responsible.

One factor could have been the burden on the common people. Maya kings forced their subjects to farm for them or work on building projects. Perhaps people didn't want to work for the kings. They might have decided to **rebel** against their rulers' demands and abandon their cities.

Increased warfare between cities could also have caused the decline. Maya cities had always fought for power. But if battles became more widespread or destructive, they would have cost many lives and disrupted trade. People might have fled the cities for their safety.

A related theory is that perhaps the Maya could not produce enough to feed everyone. Growing the same crops year after year could have weakened the soil. In addition, as the population grew, the demand for food would have increased. To meet this demand, cities might have begun competing fiercely for new farmland. But the resulting battles would have ruined more crops, damaged more land, and created even greater food shortages.

Climate change could have played a role, too. Scientists know that Mesoamerica suffered from droughts during the period when the Maya were leaving their cities. Droughts would have made it hard to grow enough food for city dwellers.

Whatever the reasons, the collapse of Maya civilization happened gradually. The Maya scattered after 900, but they did not disappear entirely. In fact, the Maya civilization later revived in the Yucatán Peninsula. But by the time Spanish conquerors reached the Americas in the 1500s, Maya power had faded.

READING CHECK **Summarizing** What factors may have caused the end of Maya civilization?

SUMMARY AND PREVIEW The Maya built a civilization that peaked between about 250 and 900 but later collapsed for reasons still unknown. In Section 2, you will learn about another people of Mesoamerica, the Aztecs.

ACADEMIC
VOCABULARY
rebel
to fight against
authority

Section 1 Assessment

Reviewing Ideas, Terms, and People

1. **a. Recall** What resources did the Maya get from the forest?
   b. Elaborate How do you think Maya villages grew into large cities?
2. **a. Describe** What features did Maya cities include?
   b. Make Inferences How did trade strengthen the Maya civilization?
3. **a. Identify** Who belonged to the upper class in Maya society?
   b. Explain How did the Maya try to please their gods?
   c. Rank What do you think was the most impressive cultural achievement of the Maya? Why?
4. **a. Describe** What happened to the Maya after 900?
   b. Evaluate What would you consider to be the key factor in the collapse of Maya civilization? Explain.

Critical Thinking

5. **Evaluating** Draw a diagram like the one to the right. Use your notes to rank Maya achievements, with the most important at the top.

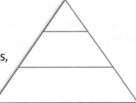

FOCUS ON WRITING

6. **Gathering Information about the Maya** Part of your article would likely be devoted to the Maya. Use the map and pictures in this section to help you decide which places to write about. How would you describe the land and the Maya cities? What would you add about the history and culture of the Maya?

SS.6.E.1.1, SS.6.G.1.4, SS.6.G.1.7, SS.6.G.2.1, SS.6.G.3.1, SS.6.G.5.2, SS.6.W.1.3, SS.6.W.2.10

What You Will Learn...

Main Ideas

1. The Aztecs built a rich and powerful empire in central Mexico.
2. Life in the empire was shaped by social structure, religion, and warfare.
3. Hernán Cortés conquered the Aztec Empire in 1521.

The Big Idea

The strong Aztec Empire, founded in central Mexico in 1325, lasted until the Spanish conquest in 1521.

Key Terms and People

causeways, *p. 474*
conquistadors, *p. 478*
Hernán Cortés, *p. 478*
Moctezuma II, *p. 478*

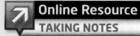

Online Resource
TAKING NOTES

Use the graphic organizer online to take notes on the founding of the Aztec Empire, life in the empire at its height, and the fall of the Aztec Empire.

The Aztecs

If YOU were there...

You live in a village in southeast Mexico that is ruled by the powerful Aztec Empire. Each year your village must send the emperor many baskets of corn. You have to dig gold for him, too. One day some pale, bearded strangers arrive by sea. They want to overthrow the emperor, and they ask for your help.

Should you help the strangers? Why or why not?

BUILDING BACKGROUND The Aztecs ruled a large empire in Mesoamerica. Each village they conquered had to contribute heavily to the Aztec economy. This system helped create a mighty state, but one that did not inspire loyalty.

The Aztecs Build an Empire

The first Aztecs were farmers who migrated from the north to central Mexico. Finding the good farmland already occupied, they settled on a swampy island in the middle of Lake Texcoco (tays-KOH-koh). There, in 1325, they began building their capital and conquering nearby towns.

War was a key factor in the Aztecs' rise to power. The Aztecs fought fiercely and demanded tribute payments from the people they conquered. The cotton, gold, and food that poured in as a result became vital to their economy. The Aztecs also controlled a huge trade network. Merchants carried goods to and from all parts of the empire. Many merchants doubled as spies, keeping the rulers informed about what was happening in their lands.

War, tribute, and trade made the Aztec Empire strong and rich. By the early 1400s the Aztecs ruled the most powerful state in Mesoamerica. Nowhere was the empire's greatness more visible than in its capital, Tenochtitlán (tay-NAWCH-teet-LAHN).

To build this amazing island city, the Aztecs first had to overcome many geographic challenges. One problem was difficulty getting to and from the city. The Aztecs addressed this challenge by building three wide **causeways**—raised roads across water or wet ground—to connect the island to the lake shore.

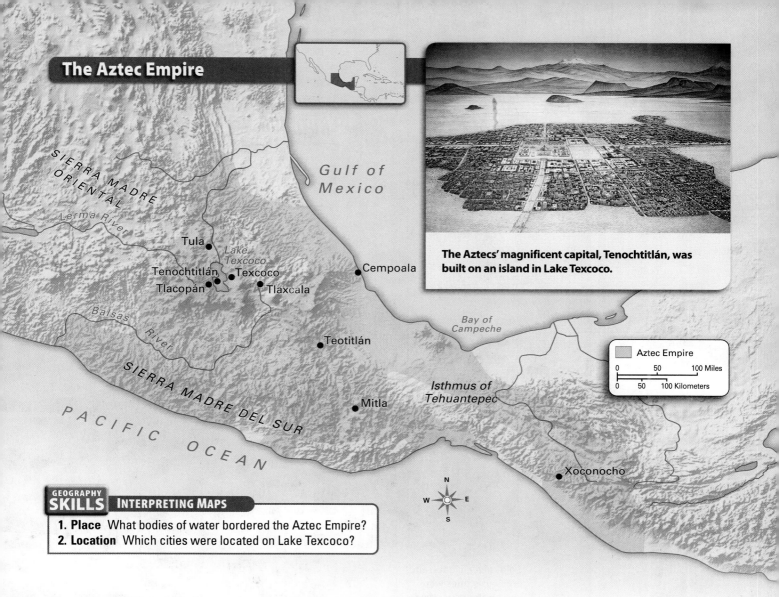

The Aztec Empire

Gulf of Mexico

SIERRA MADRE ORIENTAL

Lerma River

Tula

Lake Texcoco

Tenochtitlán • Texcoco

Tlacopán

Tlaxcala

Cempoala

Balsas River

SIERRA MADRE DEL SUR

PACIFIC OCEAN

Teotitlán

Bay of Campeche

Mitla

Isthmus of Tehuantepec

Xoconocho

The Aztecs' magnificent capital, Tenochtitlán, was built on an island in Lake Texcoco.

Aztec Empire

0   50   100 Miles
0   50   100 Kilometers

GEOGRAPHY SKILLS — INTERPRETING MAPS

1. **Place** What bodies of water bordered the Aztec Empire?
2. **Location** Which cities were located on Lake Texcoco?

They also built canals that crisscrossed the city. The causeways and canals made travel and trade much easier.

Tenochtitlán's island location also limited the amount of land available for farming. To solve this problem, the Aztecs created floating gardens called *chinampas* (chee-NAHM-pahs). They piled soil on top of large rafts, which they anchored to trees that stood in the water.

The Aztecs made Tenochtitlán a truly magnificent city. Home to some 200,000 people at its height, it had huge temples, a busy market, and a grand palace.

READING CHECK **Finding Main Ideas** How did the Aztecs rise to power?

Life in the Empire

The Aztecs' way of life was as distinctive as their capital city. They had a complex social structure, a demanding religion, and a rich culture.

Aztec Society

The Aztec emperor, like the Maya king, was the most important person in society. From his great palace, he attended to law, trade, tribute, and warfare. Trusted nobles helped him as tax collectors, judges, and other government officials. Noble positions were passed down from fathers to sons, and young nobles went to school to learn their responsibilities.

THE IMPACT TODAY

Mexico's capital, Mexico City, is located where Tenochtitlán once stood.

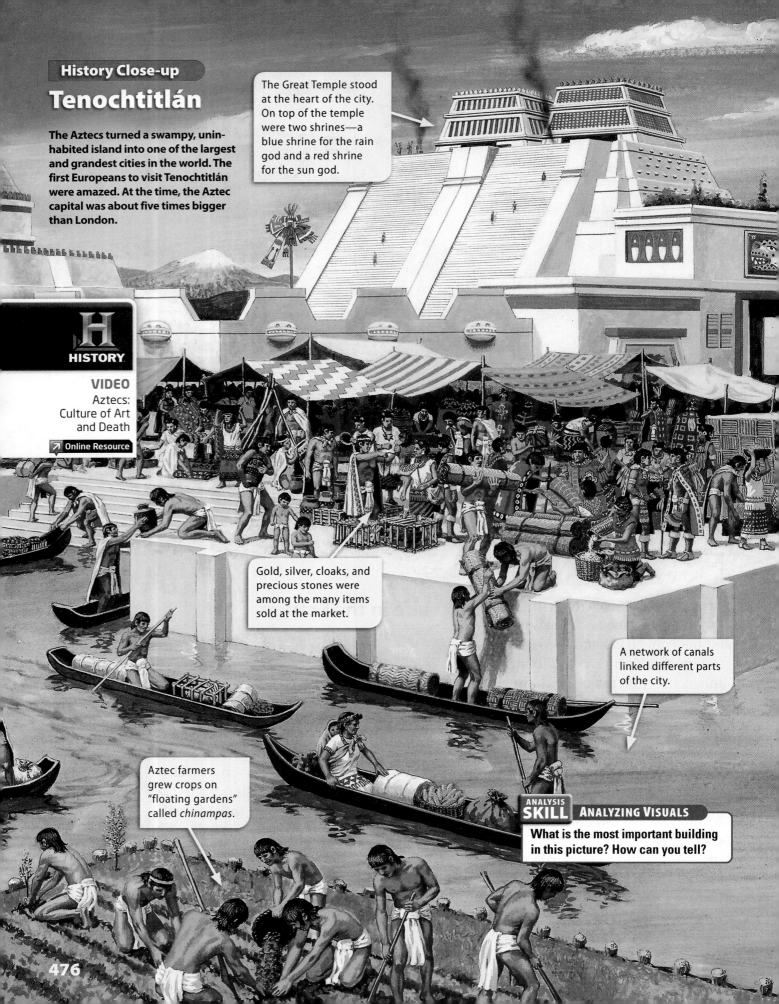

Tenochtitlán

The Aztecs turned a swampy, unin-
habited island into one of the largest
and grandest cities in the world. The
first Europeans to visit Tenochtitlán
were amazed. At the time, the Aztec
capital was about five times bigger
than London.

The Great Temple stood
at the heart of the city.
On top of the temple
were two shrines—a
blue shrine for the rain
god and a red shrine
for the sun god.

HISTORY

VIDEO
Aztecs:
Culture of Art
and Death

➚ Online Resource

Gold, silver, cloaks, and
precious stones were
among the many items
sold at the market.

A network of canals
linked different parts
of the city.

Aztec farmers
grew crops on
"floating gardens"
called *chinampas*.

ANALYSIS SKILL **ANALYZING VISUALS**

**What is the most important building
in this picture? How can you tell?**

Aztec Arts: Ceremonial Jewelry

Aztec artists were very skilled. They created detailed and brightly colored items. This double-headed serpent was probably worn during religious ceremonies. The man on the right is wearing it on his chest.

What are some features of Aztec art that you can see in these pictures?

Just below the emperor and his nobles was a class of warriors and priests. Warriors were highly respected and had many privileges, but priests were more influential. They led religious ceremonies, passed down history, and, as keepers of the calendars, decided when to plant and harvest.

The next level of Aztec society included merchants and artisans. Below them, in the lower class, were farmers and laborers, who made up the majority of the population. Many didn't own their land, and they paid so much in tribute that they often found it tough to survive. Only slaves, at the very bottom of society, struggled more.

Religion and Warfare

Like the Maya, the Aztecs worshipped many gods who were believed to control both nature and human activities. To please the gods, Aztec priests regularly made human sacrifices. Most victims were battle captives or slaves. In ritual ceremonies, priests would slash open their victims' chests to "feed" human hearts and blood to the gods. The Aztec sacrificed as many as 10,000 people a year. To supply enough victims, Aztec warriors waged frequent battles with neighboring peoples.

Cultural Achievements

As warlike as the Aztecs were, they also appreciated art and beauty. Architects and sculptors created fine stone pyramids and statues. Artisans used gold, gems, and bright feathers to make jewelry and masks. Women embroidered colorful designs on the cloth they wove.

The Aztecs valued learning as well. They studied astronomy and devised a calendar much like the Maya one. They took pride in their history and kept detailed written records. They also had a strong oral tradition. Stories about ancestors and the gods were passed from one generation to the next. The Aztecs also enjoyed fine speeches and riddles such as these:

> **"**What is a little blue-green jar filled with popcorn? Someone is sure to guess our riddle: it is the sky.
>
> What is a mountainside that has a spring of water in it? Our nose.**"**
>
> –Bernardino de Sahagún, from *Florentine Codex*

Knowing the answers to riddles showed that one had paid attention in school.

READING CHECK **Identifying Cause and Effect** How did their religious practices influence Aztec warfare?

Cortés Conquers the Aztecs

In the late 1400s the Spanish arrived in the Americas, seeking adventure, riches, and converts to Catholicism. One group of **conquistadors** (kahn-kees-tuh-DOHRZ), or Spanish conquerors, reached Mexico in 1519. Led by **Hernán Cortés** (er-NAHN kawr-TAYS), their <u>motives</u> were to find gold, claim land, and convert native peoples.

ACADEMIC VOCABULARY

motive
reason for doing something

The Aztec emperor, **Moctezuma II** (MAWK-tay-SOO-mah), cautiously welcomed the strangers. He believed Cortés to be the god Quetzalcoatl (ket-suhl-kuh-WAH-tuhl), whom the Aztecs believed had left Mexico long ago. According to legend, the god had promised to return in 1519.

Moctezuma gave the Spaniards gold and other gifts, but Cortés wanted more. He took the emperor prisoner, enraging the Aztecs, who attacked the Spanish. They managed to drive out the conquistadors, but Moctezuma was killed in the fighting.

Within a year, Cortés and his men came back. This time they had help from other Indians in the region who resented the Aztecs' harsh rule. In addition, the Spanish had better weapons, including armor, cannons, and swords. Furthermore, the Aztecs were terrified of the enemy's big horses—animals they had never seen before. The Spanish had also unknowingly brought deadly diseases such as smallpox to the Americas. These diseases weakened or killed thousands of native people. In 1521 the Aztecs surrendered. Their once mighty empire came to a swift end.

READING CHECK **Summarizing** What factors helped the Spanish defeat the Aztecs?

SUMMARY AND PREVIEW The Aztec Empire, made strong by warfare and tribute, fell to the Spanish in 1521. Next you will learn about another empire in the Americas, that of the Incas.

Section 2 Assessment

Reviewing Ideas, Terms, and People

1. **a. Recall** Where and when did Aztec civilization develop?
   b. Explain How did the Aztecs in Tenochtitlán adapt to their island location?
   c. Elaborate How might Tenochtitlán's location have been both a benefit and a hindrance to the Aztecs?

2. **a. Recall** What did the Aztecs feed their gods?
   b. Rate Consider the roles of the emperor, warriors, priests, and others in Aztec society. Who do you think had the hardest role? Explain.

3. **a. Identify** Who was **Moctezuma II**?
   b. Make Generalizations Why did allies help **Cortés** defeat the Aztecs?
   c. Predict The Aztecs vastly outnumbered the **conquistadors**. If the Aztecs had first viewed Cortés as a threat rather than a god, how might history have changed?

Critical Thinking

4. **Evaluating** Draw a diagram like the one shown. Use your notes to identify three factors that contributed to the Aztecs' power. Put the factor you consider most important first, and put the least important last. Explain your choices.

1.	2.	3.

FOCUS ON WRITING

5. **Describing the Aztec Empire** Tenochtitlán would certainly be described in your article. Make notes about how you would describe Tenochtitlán. Be sure to explain the causeways, *chinampas*, and other features. What activities went on in the city? Your article should also describe the events that occurred when the Spanish discovered the Aztec capital. Make notes on the fall of the Aztec Empire.

The Incas

If YOU were there...

You live in the Andes Mountains, where you raise llamas. You weave their wool into warm cloth. Last year, soldiers from the powerful Inca Empire took over your village. They brought in new leaders, who say you must all learn a new language and send much of your woven cloth to the Inca ruler. They also promise that the government will provide for you in times of trouble.

How do you feel about living in the Inca Empire?

> **BUILDING BACKGROUND** The Incas built their huge empire by taking over village after village in South America. They brought many changes to the people they conquered before they were themselves conquered by the Spanish.

The Incas Create an Empire

While the Aztecs were ruling Mexico, the Inca Empire arose in South America. The Incas began as a small tribe in the Andes. Their capital was Cuzco (KOO-skoh) in what is now Peru.

In the mid-1400s a ruler named **Pachacuti** (pah-chah-KOO-tee) began to expand Inca territory. Later leaders followed his example, and by the early 1500s the Inca Empire was huge. It stretched from modern Ecuador to central Chile and included coastal deserts, snowy mountains, fertile valleys, and thick forests. About 12 million people lived in the empire. To rule effectively, the Incas formed a strong central government.

What You Will Learn...

Main Ideas

1. The Incas created an empire with a strong central government in South America.
2. Life in the Inca Empire was influenced by social structure, religion, and the Incas' cultural achievements.
3. Francisco Pizarro conquered the Incas and took control of the region in 1537.

The Big Idea

The Incas controlled a huge empire in South America, but it was conquered by the Spanish.

Key Terms and People

Pachacuti, *p. 479*
Quechua, *p. 480*
masonry, *p. 481*
Atahualpa, *p. 482*
Francisco Pizarro, *p. 482*

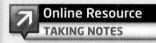

Online Resource
TAKING NOTES

Use the graphic organizer online to take notes about the **geography**, government, society, religion, achievements, and conquest of the Inca Empire.

The Incas lived in a region of high plains and mountains.

Central Rule

Pachacuti did not want the people he conquered to have too much power. He began a policy of removing local leaders and replacing them with new officials he trusted. He also made the children of conquered leaders travel to Cuzco to learn about Inca government and religion. When the children were grown, they were sent back to govern their villages, where they taught people the Inca way of life.

As another means of unifying the empire, the Incas used an official Inca language, **Quechua** (KE-chuh-wuh). Although people spoke many other languages, all official business had to be done in Quechua. Even today, many people in Peru speak Quechua.

A Well-Organized Economy

The Inca government strictly controlled the economy and told each household what work to do. Most Incas had to spend time working for the government as well as themselves. Farmers tended government land in addition to their own. Villagers made cloth and other goods for the army. Some Incas served as soldiers, worked in mines, or built roads and bridges. In this way, the people paid taxes in the form of labor rather than money. This labor tax system was called the *mita* (MEE-tah).

Another feature of the Inca economy was that there were no merchants or markets. Instead, government officials would **distribute** goods collected through the *mita*. Leftover goods were stored in the capital for emergencies. If a natural disaster struck, or if people simply could not care for themselves, the government provided supplies to help them.

ACADEMIC VOCABULARY
distribute to divide among a group of people

READING CHECK **Summarizing** How did the Incas control their empire?

The Inca Empire

Quito
Chan Chan
Sausa
Machu Picchu
Cuzco
Nasca
Lake Titicaca
Chuquiapo
Arequipa
Lake Poopo
Catarpe
Tilcara
Copiapo
Talca
Maule River
ANDES
SOUTH AMERICA
PACIFIC OCEAN
ATLANTIC OCEAN

Inca Empire
Inca roads
⊛ Capital

0   150   300 Miles
0   150   300 Kilometers

N S E W

GEOGRAPHY SKILLS **INTERPRETING MAPS**

1. **Place** About how many miles did the Inca Empire stretch from north to south?
2. **Location** Why was Cuzco a better location for the Inca capital than Quito?

Most Incas were farmers. The Incas in this drawing from the mid-1500s are harvesting potatoes.

Life in the Inca Empire

Because the rulers controlled Inca society so closely, the common people had little personal freedom. At the same time, the government protected the general welfare of all in the empire. But that did not mean everyone was treated equally.

Social Divisions

Inca society had two main social classes. The emperor, priests, and government officials made up the upper class. Members of this class lived in stone houses in Cuzco and wore the best clothes. They didn't have to pay the labor tax, and they enjoyed many other privileges. Inca rulers, for example, could relax in luxury at Machu Picchu (MAH-choo PEEK-choo). This royal retreat lay nestled high in the Andes. Palaces and gardens could be found behind its gated wall.

The lower class in Inca society included farmers, artisans, and servants. There were no slaves, however, because the Incas did not practice slavery. Most Incas were farmers. In the warmer valleys, they grew crops like maize and peanuts. In the cooler mountains, they carved terraces into the hillsides and grew potatoes. High in the Andes, people raised llamas—South American animals related to camels—for meat and wool.

Lower-class Incas dressed in plain clothes and lived simply. By law, they couldn't own more goods than what they needed to survive. Most of what they produced went to the *mita* and the upper class.

Religion

The Inca social structure was partly related to religion. For example, the Incas thought that their rulers were related to the sun god and never really died. As a result, priests brought mummies of former kings to many ceremonies. People gave these royal mummies food and gifts.

Inca ceremonies often included sacrifices. But unlike the Maya and the Aztecs, the Incas rarely sacrificed humans. Instead they sacrificed llamas, cloth, or food.

In addition to practicing the official religion, people outside Cuzco worshipped other gods at local sacred places. The Incas believed certain mountaintops, rocks, and springs had magical powers. Many Incas performed sacrifices at these places as well as at the temple in Cuzco.

Achievements

Inca temples were grand buildings. The Incas were master builders, known for their expert **masonry**, or stonework. They cut stone blocks so precisely that they didn't need cement to hold them together. The Incas also built a network of roads. Two major highways ran the length of the empire and linked to many other roads.

The Incas produced works of art as well. Artisans made pottery and gold and silver jewelry. They even created a life-sized cornfield of gold and silver, crafting each cob, leaf, and stalk individually. Inca weavers also made some of the finest textiles in the Americas.

THE IMPACT TODAY

The ruins of Machu Picchu draw thousands of tourists to Peru every year.

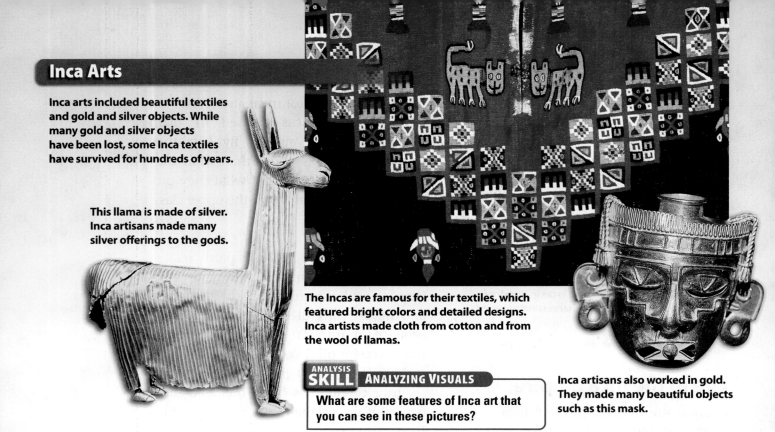

Inca Arts

Inca arts included beautiful textiles and gold and silver objects. While many gold and silver objects have been lost, some Inca textiles have survived for hundreds of years.

This llama is made of silver. Inca artisans made many silver offerings to the gods.

The Incas are famous for their textiles, which featured bright colors and detailed designs. Inca artists made cloth from cotton and from the wool of llamas.

ANALYSIS SKILL **ANALYZING VISUALS**

What are some features of Inca art that you can see in these pictures?

Inca artisans also worked in gold. They made many beautiful objects such as this mask.

While such artifacts tell us much about the Incas, nothing was written about their empire until the Spanish arrived. Indeed, the Incas had no writing system. Instead, they kept records with knotted cords called *quipus* (KEE-pooz). Knots in the cords represented numbers. Different colors stood for information about crops, land, and other important topics.

The Incas also passed down their history orally. People sang songs and told stories about daily life and military victories. Official "memorizers" learned long poems about Inca legends and history. Eventually, after the conquistadors came, records were written in Spanish and Quechua. We know about the Incas from these records and from the stories that survive in the songs, dances, and religious practices of the people in the region today.

READING CHECK **Contrasting** How did daily life differ for upper- and lower-class Incas?

Pizarro Conquers the Incas

The arrival of conquistadors changed more than how the Incas recorded history. In the late 1520s, a civil war began in the Inca Empire after the death of the ruler. Two of the ruler's sons, **Atahualpa** (ah-tah-WAHL-pah) and Huáscar (WAHS-kahr), fought to claim the throne. Atahualpa won the war in 1532, but fierce fighting had weakened the Inca army.

On his way to be crowned as king, Atahualpa got news that a band of about 180 Spanish soldiers had arrived in the Inca Empire. They were conquistadors led by **Francisco Pizarro**. When Atahualpa came to meet the group, the Spanish attacked. They were greatly outnumbered, but they caught the unarmed Incas by surprise. They quickly captured Atahualpa and killed thousands of Inca soldiers.

To win his freedom, Atahualpa asked his people to fill a room with gold and silver for Pizarro. Incas brought jewelry, states, and other valuable items from all parts of the empire. Melted down, the precious metals may have totaled 24 tons. They would have been worth millions of dollars today. Despite this huge payment, the Spaniards killed Atahualpa. They knew that if they let the Inca ruler live, he might rally his people and overpower their forces.

Some Incas fought back after the emperor's death. In 1537, though, Pizarro defeated the last of the Incas. Spain took control over the entire Inca Empire and ruled the region for the next 300 years.

READING CHECK **Identifying Cause and Effect** What events ended the Inca Empire?

SUMMARY AND PREVIEW The Incas built a huge empire with a strong central government, but they could not withstand the Spanish conquest in 1537. In the next chapter, you will turn to Europe in an earlier age—an age before the Spanish even learned of the Americas.

BIOGRAPHY

Atahualpa
1520–1533

Atahualpa was the last Inca emperor. He was brave and popular with the Inca army, but he didn't rule long. At his first meeting with Pizarro, he was offered a religious book to convince him to accept Christianity. Atahualpa held the book to his ear and listened. When the book didn't speak, Atahualpa threw it on the ground. The Spanish considered this an insult and a reason to attack.

Identifying Bias How do you think the Spanish viewed non-Christians?

BIOGRAPHY

Francisco Pizarro
1475–1541

Francisco Pizarro organized expeditions to explore the west coast of South America. His first two trips were mostly uneventful. But on his third trip, Pizarro met the Inca. With only about 180 men, he conquered the Inca Empire, which had been weakened by disease and civil war. In 1535 Pizarro founded Lima, the capital of modern Peru.

Predicting If Pizarro had not found the Inca Empire, what do you think might have happened?

Section 3 Assessment

Reviewing Ideas, Terms, and People

1. **a. Identify** Where was the Inca Empire located? What kinds of terrain did it include?
   b. Explain How did the Incas control their economy?
   c. Evaluate Do you think the *mita* system was a good government policy? Why or why not?
2. **a. Describe** What social classes existed in Inca society?
   b. Make Inferences How might the Inca road system have helped strengthen the empire?
3. **a. Recall** When did the Spanish gain full control over Inca lands?
   b. Analyze Why do you think **Pizarro** was able to defeat the much larger forces of the Incas?
   c. Elaborate What effect do you think the civil war with his brother had on **Atahualpa**'s kingship? How might history have been different if the Spanish had not arrived until a few years later?

Critical Thinking

4. **Analyzing** Draw a diagram like the one below. Using your notes, write a sentence in each box about how that topic influenced the topic its arrow points to.

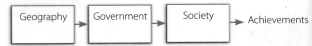

FOCUS ON WRITING

5. **Adding Information about the Inca Empire** Your article would also describe the lands where the Incas lived. How would you highlight the diversity of the geography? What specific sites would you describe? Include some comments about how the Incas' building activities related to their environment. You will also want to include information on what happened when the Spanish arrived.

Inca Roads

Inca roads were more than just roads—they were engineering marvels. The Incas built roads across almost every kind of terrain imaginable: **coasts, deserts, forests, grasslands, plains,** and **mountains.** In doing so, they overcame the **geography** of their rugged empire.

Although the Incas had no wheeled vehicles, they relied on their roads for transportation, communication, and government administration. The roads symbolized the power of the Inca government.

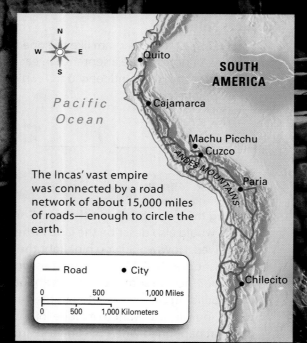

The Incas' vast empire was connected by a road network of about 15,000 miles of roads—enough to circle the earth.

Road • City

0   500   1,000 Miles
0 500 1,000 Kilometers

Many roads were just three to six feet wide, but that was wide enough for people on foot and for llamas, which the Incas used as pack animals.

Inca engineers built rope bridges to cross the valleys of the Andes Mountains. Rope bridges could stretch more than 200 feet across high gorges.

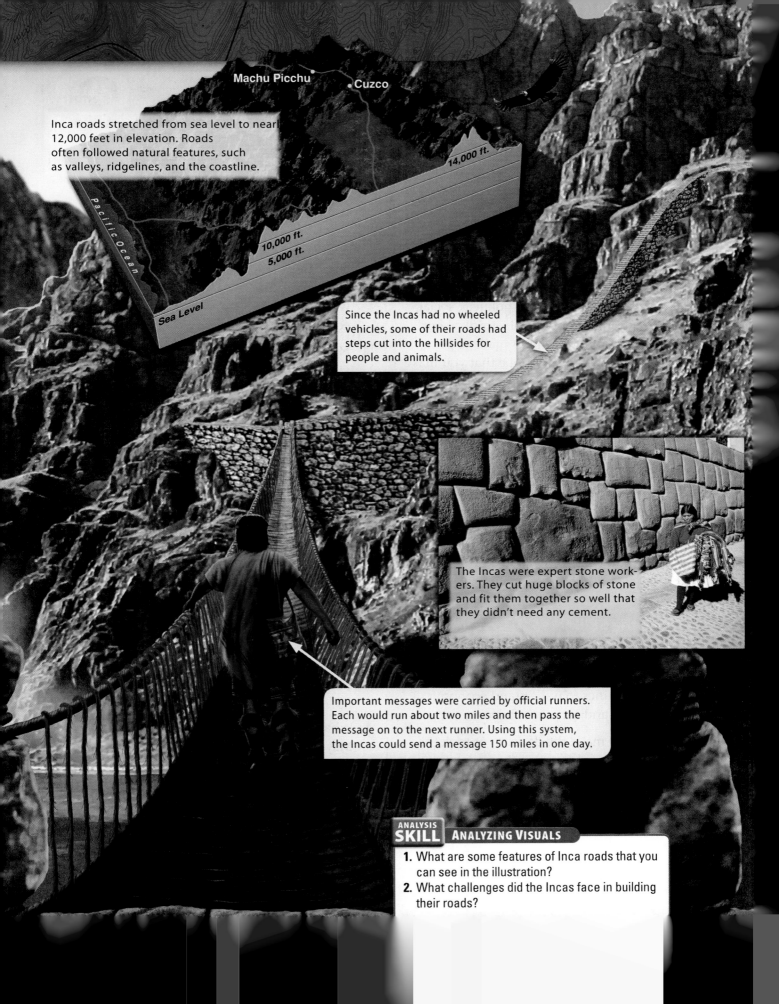

Inca roads stretched from sea level to near 12,000 feet in elevation. Roads often followed natural features, such as valleys, ridgelines, and the coastline.

Machu Picchu

Cuzco

Pacific Ocean

14,000 ft.

10,000 ft.

5,000 ft.

Sea Level

Since the Incas had no wheeled vehicles, some of their roads had steps cut into the hillsides for people and animals.

The Incas were expert stone workers. They cut huge blocks of stone and fit them together so well that they didn't need any cement.

Important messages were carried by official runners. Each would run about two miles and then pass the message on to the next runner. Using this system, the Incas could send a message 150 miles in one day.

ANALYSIS SKILL **ANALYZING VISUALS**

1. What are some features of Inca roads that you can see in the illustration?
2. What challenges did the Incas face in building their roads?

Social Studies Skills

Analyzing Economic Effects

Understand the Skill

Most decisions people make or actions they take have several effects. Effects can be political, social, personal, or economic. For example, think about the effects of a decision you might make to get a summer job. A social effect might be that you make new friends at your job. A personal effect might be that you have less time for other activities that you enjoy. An economic effect would be that you have more money to spend.

Throughout history, many decisions have had economic effects—either intended or unintended. Even a decision made for a political, social, or environmental reason can have economic effects. Since economic circumstances have often been a factor in the rise and fall of civilizations, learning to analyze economic effects can be useful in your study of history.

Learn the Skill

Analyzing economic effects can help you to better understand and evaluate historical events. Follow these guidelines to understand economic effects of decisions and actions in history.

1. Determine who made the decision or took the action and decide what the goal was.

2. Consider whether the goal was to improve or change economic circumstances.

3. Sometimes an economic effect is not the main effect of a decision. Think about any unintended consequences of the decision or action. Consider whether any social or political effects are also economic effects.

4. Note that sometimes economic effects can be viewed either positively or negatively depending on whom they affect.

Practice and Apply the Skill

Review the information in the chapter about the Maya. Use that information to help you answer the following questions.

1. What was an economic effect of the Maya in lowland cities exporting forest goods and cotton? Was that effect expected or unexpected?

2. What might have been a positive economic effect of the Maya king's making lower-class Maya farm and work for him? What might have been a negative effect?

3. Do you think the development of the Maya calendar had any economic effects? Why or why not?

4. What economic effects did warfare have on Maya civilization? Were these effects expected or unexpected?

Chapter Review

Visual Summary

Use the visual summary below to help you review the main ideas of the chapter.

QUICK FACTS

The Aztecs
Aztec warriors played an extremely important role in the powerful Aztec civilization.

The Maya
Maya cities were known for their impressive structures, including pyramids that were many stories tall.

The Incas
The huge Inca Empire was linked together by an elaborate system of roads and rope bridges.

Reviewing Vocabulary, Terms and People

For each statement below, write T if it is true and F if it is false. If the statement is false, replace the underlined term with one that would make the sentence a true statement.

1. The main crops of the Maya included **maize** and beans.

2. The **Quechua** came to the Americas to find land, gold, and converts to Catholicism.

3. The Aztecs mistook **Hernán Cortés** for the god Quetzalcoatl.

4. Maya priests studied the sun, moon, and stars from stone **observatories**.

5. **Francisco Pizarro** led a party of Spanish soldiers to Mexico in 1519.

6. **Atahualpa** tried to buy his freedom by having his people deliver great riches to the Spanish.

7. The official language of the Inca Empire was **Pachacuti**.

8. The Aztecs built raised roads called **masonry** to cross from Tenochtitlán to the mainland.

9. **Moctezuma II** was the Inca leader at the time of the Spanish conquest.

10. Many people in Mesoamerica died at the hands of the **conquistadors**.

Comprehension and Critical Thinking

SECTION 1 *(Pages 468–473)*

11. **a. Recall** Where did the Maya live, and when was their Classic Age?

b. Analyze What was the connection between Maya religion and astronomy?

c. Elaborate Why did Maya cities trade with each other? Why did they fight?

SECTION 2 *(Pages 474–478)*

12. a. Describe What was Tenochtitlán like? Where was it located?

b. Make Inferences Why do you think warriors were such respected members of Aztec society?

c. Evaluate What factor do you think played the biggest role in the Aztecs' defeat? Defend your answer.

SECTION 3 *(Pages 479–483)*

13. a. Identify Name two Inca leaders and explain their roles in Inca history.

b. Draw Conclusions What geographic and cultural problems did the Incas overcome to rule their empire?

c. Predict Do you think most people in the Inca Empire appreciated or resented the *mita* system? Explain your answer.

Social Studies Skills

14. Analyzing Economic Effects Organize your class into groups. Choose one member of your group to represent the ruler of a Maya city. The rest of the group will be his or her advisers. As a group, decide on some policies for your city. For example, will you go to war, or will you trade? Will you build a new palace, or will you construct terraces for farming? Once you have determined policies for your city, share your ideas with representatives of other cities. As a class, discuss the economic effects of each policy you have chosen.

Using the Internet

15. Making Diagrams In this chapter you learned about the rise and fall of Maya civilization and of the Aztec and Inca empires. What you may not know is that the rise and fall of empires is a pattern that occurs again and again throughout history. Go online to research more about this topic. Then create a diagram that shows factors that cause empires to form and factors that cause empires to fall apart.

Reading Skills

Analyzing Historical Information *In each numbered passage below, the first sentence expresses the main idea. One of the following sentences is irrelevant or nonessential to the main idea. Identify the irrelevant or nonessential sentence in each passage.*

16. Cacao beans had great value to the Maya. Cacao trees are evergreens. They were the source of chocolate, known as a favorite food of rulers and the gods. The Maya also used cacao beans as money.

17. Tenochtitlán was surrounded by water, but the water was undrinkable. As a result, the Aztecs built a stone aqueduct, or channel, to bring fresh water to the city. In many parts of the world, access to clean water is still a problem.

18. Most Inca children did not attend school. Does that idea appeal to you? Inca children learned skills by watching and helping their parents.

Reviewing Themes

19. Geography How did the geography of Meso and South America differ from the geography of the ancient civilizations of Egypt, Sumer, and India?

20. Science and Technology Compare the buildings of the Maya, Aztec, and Inca civilizations with the buildings of the ancient river civilizations, such as Egypt and Sumer.

FOCUS ON WRITING

21. Writing Your Article Your newspaper article will include information about your journey through the Americas. Choose at least one place of interest from the Maya civilization, the Aztec Empire, and the Inca Empire. For each site, use your notes to write several sentences to describe its location and how it looked at its height. Try to include details that would help a European reader imagine what life was like for the people who lived there. You will also want to explain to your readers what happened to these civilizations when the Spanish arrived.

DIRECTIONS: Read each question, and write the letter of the best response. Use the map below to answer question 1.

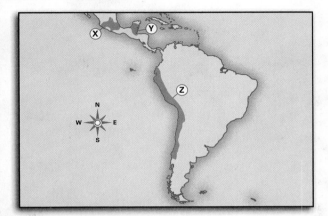

1 The Aztec and Inca empires are indicated on this map by

A X for the Inca and Y for the Aztec.

B Y for the Aztec and Z for the Inca.

C Y for the Inca and Z for the Aztec.

D X for the Aztec and Z for the Inca.

2 Maya, Aztec, and Inca societies were similar in many ways. Which of the following practices were common to all three civilizations?

A producing works of art and keeping written records

B engaging in trade and demanding tribute payments

C offering sacrifices to the gods and building stone temples

D practicing slavery and worshipping many gods

3 Farming was important to the Maya, the Aztecs, and the Incas. Which of the following is *not* a true statement?

A The Maya grew crops on *chinampas*.

B Farmers in all three civilizations grew maize, but only the Incas raised llamas.

C Maya farmers might not have been able to produce enough food for the entire population.

D Maya and Aztec priests decided the best times to plant and harvest.

4 The following factors all helped the Spanish to conquer the Aztecs and the Incas *except*

A European diseases.

B a greater number of soldiers.

C superior weapons.

D existing problems within the empires.

5 Which statement *best* describes the social structure in Maya, Aztec, and Inca civilizations?

A The ruler held the highest position in society, and slaves held the lowest.

B The Aztecs had a simpler class structure than the Maya or the Incas.

C Social divisions were very important to the Maya and the Aztecs, but power and wealth were equally distributed in the Inca Empire.

D Social class helped shape daily life, with the upper class enjoying special privileges made possible by the labor of the common people.

Connecting with Past Learnings

6 In this chapter you read that Maya civilization during the Classic Age included independent city-states. What other civilization that you have studied was organized into city-states?

A ancient Greece

B ancient Persia

C Han China

D the Roman Empire

7 The Maya and the Incas both believed their rulers were related to the gods. Which ancient people believed the same thing?

A Jews

B Indians

C Phoenicians

D Egyptians

THE
Maya

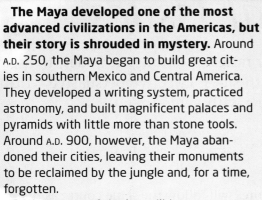

The Maya developed one of the most advanced civilizations in the Americas, but their story is shrouded in mystery. Around A.D. 250, the Maya began to build great cities in southern Mexico and Central America. They developed a writing system, practiced astronomy, and built magnificent palaces and pyramids with little more than stone tools. Around A.D. 900, however, the Maya abandoned their cities, leaving their monuments to be reclaimed by the jungle and, for a time, forgotten.

Explore some of the incredible monuments and cultural achievements of the ancient Maya online. You can find a wealth of information, video clips, primary sources, and more online.

"Thus let it be done! Let the emptiness be filled! Let the water recede and make a void, let the earth appear and become solid; let it be done . . . "Earth!" they said, and instantly it was made."

The Popol Vuh

Read the document to learn how the Maya believed the world was created.

Destroying the Maya's Past

Watch the video to learn how the actions of one Spanish missionary nearly destroyed the written record of the Maya world.

Finding the City of Palenque

Watch the video to learn about the great Maya city of Palenque and the European discovery of the site in the eighteenth century.

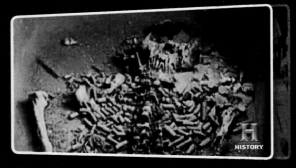

Pakal's Tomb

Watch the video to explore how the discovery of the tomb of a great king helped archaeologists piece together the Maya past.

Persuasion and Historical Issues

The study of history raises questions, or issues, that can be argued from both sides. Effective persuasive writing supports a point of view with evidence.

1. Prewrite

Taking a Position

Do you think all great empires will follow the same course as the Maya and Aztecs, or could an empire take a different course? Write a sentence that states your position, or opinion about, this topic or another topic.

Supporting Your Position

To convince your audience to agree with your position, you will need reasons and evidence. **Reasons** tell *why* a writer has a particular point of view. **Evidence** backs up, or helps prove, the reasons. Evidence includes facts, examples, and opinions of experts, like historians. You can find this evidence in this textbook or other books recommended by your teacher.

Organizing Reasons and Evidence

Try to present your reasons and evidence in order of importance, so that you can end with your most convincing points. Use transitions such as *mainly*, *last*, and *most important* to emphasize ideas.

2. Write

This framework can help you state your position clearly and present convincing reasons and evidence.

Assignment

Write an essay stating your opinion on this topic or another historical topic of your choice: All great empires are likely to end in the same way the Maya and Aztec empires did.

TIP **Fact vs. Opinion** A fact is a statement that can be proved true. Facts include

- measurements
- dates
- locations
- definitions

An opinion is a statement of a personal belief. Opinions often include judgmental words and phrases such as *better, should,* and *think.*

A Writer's Framework

Introduction

- Introduce the topic by using a surprising fact, quotation, or comparison to get your reader's attention.
- Identify at least two differing positions on this topic.
- State your own position on the topic.

Body

- Present at least two reasons to support your position.
- Support each reason with evidence (facts, examples, expert opinions).
- Organize your reasons and evidence in order of importance with your most convincing reason last.

Conclusion

- Restate your position.
- Summarize your supporting reasons and evidence.
- Project your position into history by using it to predict the course of current and future events.

3. Evaluate and Revise

Evaluating

Use the following questions to evaluate your draft and find ways to make your paper more convincing.

Evaluation Questions for a Persuasive Essay

- Does your introduction include an opinion statement that clearly states your position?
- Have you given at least two reasons to support your position?
- Do you provide convincing evidence to back up your reasons?

- Are your reasons and evidence organized by order of importance, ending with the most important?
- Does your conclusion restate your position and summarize your reasons and evidence? Do you apply your opinion to future history?

Revising

Strengthen your argument with loaded words. Loaded words are words with strong positive or negative connotations.

- Positive—leader
- Negative—tyrant, despot
- Neutral—ruler, emperor

Loaded words can add powerful emotional appeals to your reader's feelings and help convince them to agree with your opinion.

4. Proofread and Publish

Proofreading

Keep the following guidelines in mind as you reread your paper.

- Wherever you have added, deleted, or changed anything, make sure your revision fits in smoothly and does not introduce any errors.
- Double-check names, dates, and other factual information.

Publishing

Team up with one of your classmates who has taken the same position you have. Combine your evidence to create the most powerful argument you can. Challenge a team that has taken an opposing view to a debate. Ask the rest of the class for feedback: Which argument was more convincing? What were the strengths and weaknesses of each position?

Practice and Apply

Use the steps and strategies outlined in this workshop to write a persuasive composition.

TIP Using a Computer to Check Spelling in History Papers Whenever you can, use a spell-checker program to help you catch careless errors. However, keep in mind that it will not solve all your spelling problems.

- It will not catch misspellings that correctly spell other words, such as *their, they're,* and *there,* or *an* instead of *and.*
- It will highlight but not give the preferred spelling for many proper names.
- It cannot be relied upon for correct capitalization.

Reference Section

↗ **Online Resources**

• Reading Like a Historian
• Geography and Map Skills Handbook
• Economics Handbook

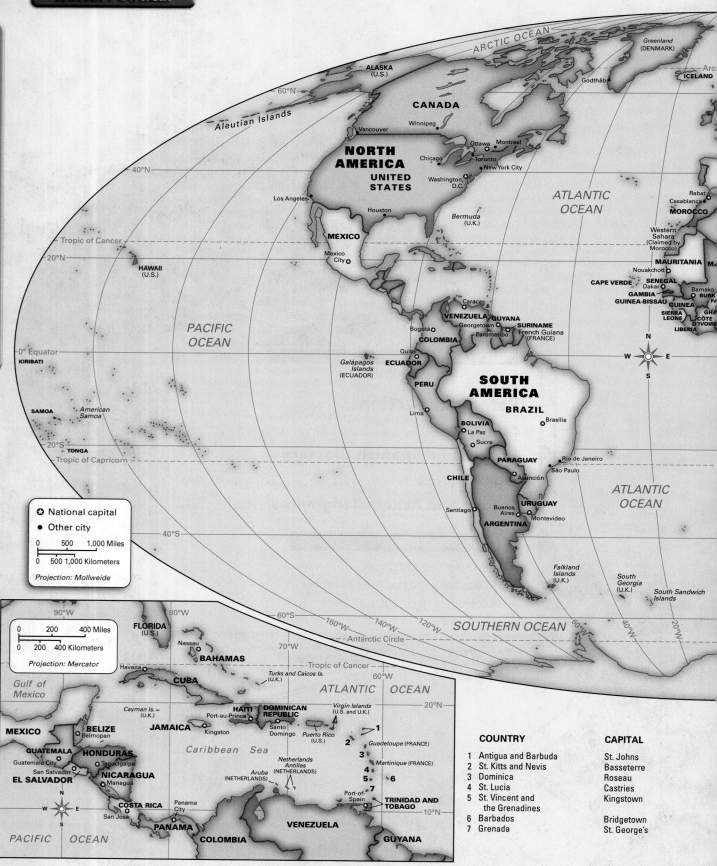

World: Political

ATLAS

ARCTIC OCEAN

Greenland (DENMARK)

ALASKA (U.S.)

ICELAND

Arc

Aleutian Islands

CANADA

Winnipeg

Godthåb

Vancouver

NORTH AMERICA

Ottawa · Montreal

Chicago · Toronto

Washington, D.C.

New York City

Rabat

Casablanca

MOROCCO

UNITED STATES

ATLANTIC OCEAN

Los Angeles

Houston

Bermuda (U.K.)

Western Sahara (Claimed by Morocco)

Tropic of Cancer

MEXICO

Mexico City

Nouakchott

MAURITANIA

MA

20°N

HAWAII (U.S.)

CAPE VERDE

SENEGAL

Dakar

Bamako

BURK

GAMBIA

GUINEA-BISSAU

GUINEA

FA

Caracas

VENEZUELA

GUYANA

Georgetown

SURINAME

Paramaribo

French Guiana (FRANCE)

SIERRA LEONE

CÔTE D'IVOIRE

GHA

LIBERIA

PACIFIC OCEAN

Bogotá

COLOMBIA

0° Equator

KIRIBATI

Quito

Galápagos Islands (ECUADOR)

ECUADOR

PERU

SOUTH AMERICA

BRAZIL

Brasília

N

W   E

S

SAMOA

American Samoa

Lima

BOLIVIA

La Paz

Sucre

20°S

TONGA

PARAGUAY

Rio de Janeiro

Tropic of Capricorn

CHILE

Asunción

São Paulo

ATLANTIC OCEAN

Santiago

Buenos Aires

URUGUAY

40°S

ARGENTINA

Montevideo

⊕ National capital
● Other city

0   500   1,000 Miles
0   500 1,000 Kilometers

Projection: Mollweide

Falkland Islands (U.K.)

South Georgia (U.K.)

South Sandwich Islands

60°S

160°W

140°W

120°W

SOUTHERN OCEAN

Antarctic Circle

90°W   80°W

FLORIDA (U.S.)

0   200   400 Miles
0   200   400 Kilometers

Projection: Mercator

Nassau

BAHAMAS

70°W

Tropic of Cancer

60°W

ATLANTIC   OCEAN

Gulf of Mexico

Havana

CUBA

Turks and Caicos Is. (U.K.)

Virgin Islands (U.S. and U.K.)

20°N

Cayman Is. (U.K.)

HAITI

DOMINICAN REPUBLIC

1

MEXICO

BELIZE

Belmopan

JAMAICA

Port-au-Prince

Kingston

Santo Domingo

Puerto Rico (U.S.)

2

Guadeloupe (FRANCE)

GUATEMALA

HONDURAS

Caribbean Sea

3

Martinique (FRANCE)

Guatemala City

Tegucigalpa

Netherlands Antilles (NETHERLANDS)

4

EL SALVADOR

NICARAGUA

San Salvador

Managua

Aruba (NETHERLANDS)

5

6

N

W   E

S

7

COSTA RICA

Panama City

Port-of-Spain

TRINIDAD AND TOBAGO

San José

10°N

PACIFIC OCEAN

PANAMA

VENEZUELA

COLOMBIA

GUYANA

COUNTRY	CAPITAL
1 Antigua and Barbuda	St. Johns
2 St. Kitts and Nevis	Basseterre
3 Dominica	Roseau
4 St. Lucia	Castries
5 St. Vincent and the Grenadines	Kingstown
6 Barbados	Bridgetown
7 Grenada	St. George's

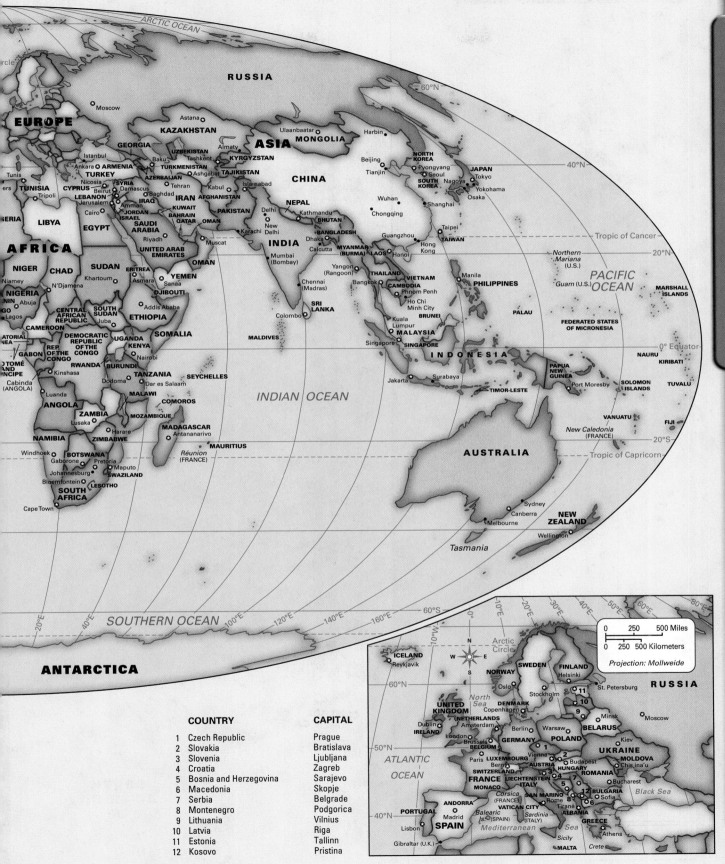

ARCTIC OCEAN

RUSSIA

EUROPE
Moscow

KAZAKHSTAN
Astana
Ulaanbaatar
Harbin
60°N

GEORGIA
Almaty
ASIA
MONGOLIA
NORTH
KOREA
JAPAN

Istanbul
UZBEKISTAN
Tashkent
KYRGYZSTAN
Beijing
Pyongyang
Seoul
Nagoya
Tokyo
40°N

Ankara
ARMENIA
TURKMENISTAN
TAJIKISTAN
CHINA
Tianjin
SOUTH
KOREA
Yokohama

Baku
AZERBAIJAN
Ashgabat
Osaka

Tunis
TUNISIA
CYPRUS
SYRIA
Nicosia
Damascus
Tehran
Kabul
Islamabad
NEPAL
Wuhan
Shanghai

ers
Tripoli
LEBANON
Beirut
IRAQ
Baghdad
IRAN
AFGHANISTAN
Kathmandu
Chongqing

Jerusalem
Amman
ISRAEL
JORDAN
KUWAIT
BAHRAIN
QATAR
PAKISTAN
Delhi
BHUTAN
BANGLADESH
Taipei
TAIWAN

Cairo
SAUDI
ARABIA
OMAN
Karachi
New
Delhi
Dhaka
Guangzhou
Hong
Kong
Tropic of Cancer

ERIA
EGYPT
Riyadh
Muscat
INDIA
Calcutta
MYANMAR
(BURMA)
LAOS
Hanoi
Northern
Mariana
(U.S.)
20°N

AFRICA
UNITED ARAB
EMIRATES
OMAN
Mumbai
(Bombay)
Yangon
(Rangoon)
THAILAND
VIETNAM
Manila
PHILIPPINES
Guam (U.S.)
PACIFIC
OCEAN
MARSHALL
ISLANDS

NIGER
CHAD
SUDAN
ERITREA
YEMEN
Chennai
(Madras)
Bangkok
CAMBODIA
Phnom Penh
PALAU
FEDERATED STATES
OF MICRONESIA

Niamey
N'Djamena
Khartoum
Asmara
Sanaa
SRI
LANKA
Ho Chi
Minh City
BRUNEI

NIGERIA
DJIBOUTI
Colombo
Kuala
Lumpur
MALAYSIA
NAURU
KIRIBATI

NIN
GO
Abuja
CENTRAL
AFRICAN
REPUBLIC
SOUTH
SUDAN
Addis Ababa
MALDIVES
Singapore
SINGAPORE
0° Equator

Lagos
CAMEROON
Juba
ETHIOPIA
SOMALIA
UGANDA
KENYA
INDONESIA

ATORIAL
NEA
GABON
DEMOCRATIC
REPUBLIC
OF THE
CONGO
RWANDA
BURUNDI
Nairobi
PAPUA
NEW
GUINEA
TUVALU

O TOMÉ
AND
NCIPE
REP.
OF THE
CONGO
Kinshasa
TANZANIA
Dodoma
SEYCHELLES
Jakarta
Surabaya
Port Moresby
SOLOMON
ISLANDS

Cabinda
(ANGOLA)
Luanda
Dar es Salaam
TIMOR-LESTE
VANUATU
FIJI

ANGOLA
ZAMBIA
MALAWI
MOZAMBIQUE
COMOROS
INDIAN OCEAN
New Caledonia
(FRANCE)
20°S

NAMIBIA
Lusaka
Harare
MADAGASCAR
Antananarivo
MAURITIUS
AUSTRALIA
Tropic of Capricorn

Windhoek
BOTSWANA
ZIMBABWE
Réunion
(FRANCE)

Gaborone
Pretoria
Maputo
SWAZILAND

Johannesburg
Bloemfontein
LESOTHO
Sydney
NEW
ZEALAND

SOUTH
AFRICA
Canberra
Melbourne

Cape Town
Wellington

SOUTHERN OCEAN
20°E
40°E
60°E
100°E
120°E
140°E
160°E
60°S
Tasmania
0°

ANTARCTICA

	COUNTRY	CAPITAL
1	Czech Republic	Prague
2	Slovakia	Bratislava
3	Slovenia	Ljubljana
4	Croatia	Zagreb
5	Bosnia and Herzegovina	Sarajevo
6	Macedonia	Skopje
7	Serbia	Belgrade
8	Montenegro	Podgorica
9	Lithuania	Vilnius
10	Latvia	Riga
11	Estonia	Tallinn
12	Kosovo	Pristina

ICELAND
Reykjavik
NORWAY
SWEDEN
FINLAND
Helsinki
Arctic
Circle
10°E
20°E
30°E
40°E
50°E
60°E
80°E

0   250   500 Miles
0   250   500 Kilometers
Projection: Mollweide

60°N
Oslo
Stockholm
St. Petersburg
RUSSIA

North
Sea
DENMARK
Copenhagen
11
10
Minsk
Moscow

UNITED
KINGDOM
NETHERLANDS
Amsterdam
Berlin
Warsaw
9
BELARUS
Kiev

Dublin
IRELAND
London
Brussels
BELGIUM
GERMANY
POLAND
UKRAINE
MOLDOVA

50°N
LUXEMBOURG
Paris
Vienna
1
2
Budapest
Chisinau

ATLANTIC
OCEAN
Bern
SWITZERLAND
AUSTRIA
HUNGARY
ROMANIA
Bucharest

FRANCE
LIECHTENSTEIN
3
4
12
BULGARIA
Black Sea

MONACO
Corsica
(FRANCE)
SAN MARINO
ITALY
Rome
5
8
7
Sofia

ANDORRA
VATICAN CITY
Sardinia
(ITALY)
6
ALBANIA
Tirane

PORTUGAL
Balearic
Is. (SPAIN)
GREECE

40°N
Madrid
Athens

Lisbon
SPAIN
Mediterranean   Sea
Sicily

Gibraltar (U.K.)
MALTA
Crete

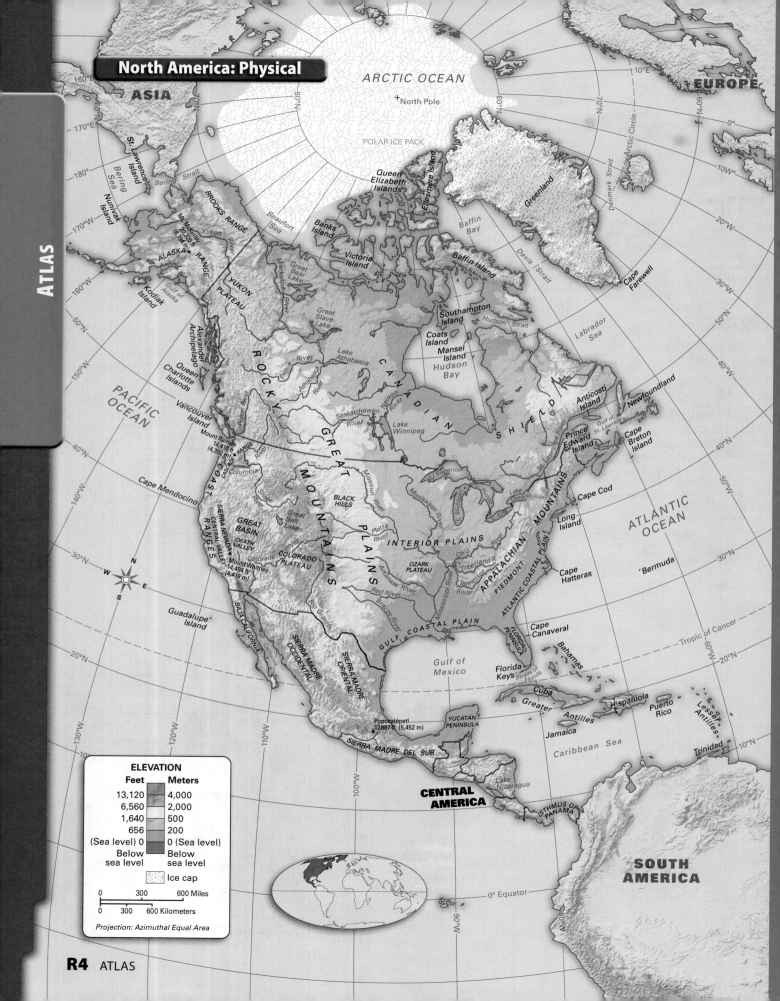

North America: Physical

ASIA

EUROPE

ARCTIC OCEAN

+ North Pole

POLAR ICE PACK

St. Lawrence Island

Bering Sea

Bering Strait

Nunivak Island

BROOKS RANGE

Mt. McKinley 20,320 ft (6,194 m)

ALASKA RANGE

Yukon River

Beaufort Sea

Queen Elizabeth Islands

Ellesmere Island

Greenland

Banks Island

Baffin Bay

Denmark Strait

Cape Farewell

Gulf of Alaska

Kodiak Island

YUKON PLATEAU

Great Bear Lake

Victoria Island

Mackenzie River

Baffin Island

Davis Strait

Alexander Archipelago

Queen Charlotte Islands

Peace River

Great Slave Lake

Southampton Island

Hudson Strait

Labrador Sea

PACIFIC OCEAN

Vancouver Island

Cape Mendocino

Fraser River

Athabasca River

Lake Athabasca

Coats Island

Mansel Island

Hudson Bay

R O C K Y

Saskatchewan River

Nelson River

Lake Winnipeg

C A N A D I A N   S H I E L D

Anticosti Island

Newfoundland

Mount Rainier 14,410 ft (4,392 m)

CASCADE RANGE

COAST RANGES

Columbia River

Snake River

G R E A T

M O U N T A I N S

Missouri River

Superior

St. Lawrence River

Gulf of St. Lawrence

Prince Edward Island

Cape Breton Island

SIERRA NEVADA

GREAT BASIN

Great Salt Lake

BLACK HILLS

L. Michigan

Lake Huron

Lake Ontario

APPALACHIAN MOUNTAINS

Cape Cod

Long Island

ATLANTIC OCEAN

CENTRAL VALLEY

DEATH VALLEY

Mount Whitney 14,494 ft (4,419 m)

Colorado River

COLORADO PLATEAU

P L A I N S

Platte River

Lake Erie

I N T E R I O R   P L A I N S

Mississippi River

Ohio R.

Cumberland R.

Tennessee River

PIEDMONT

ATLANTIC COASTAL PLAIN

Cape Hatteras

Bermuda

BAJA CALIFORNIA

Gulf of California

SIERRA MADRE OCCIDENTAL

Rio Grande

OZARK PLATEAU

Arkansas River

Red River

Brazos River

Mississippi River

GULF COASTAL PLAIN

FLORIDA PENINSULA

Cape Canaveral

SIERRA MADRE ORIENTAL

Gulf of Mexico

Florida Keys

Straits of Florida

Bahamas

Tropic of Cancer

Guadalupe Island

Cuba

Greater Antilles

Hispaniola

Puerto Rico

Lesser Antilles

Popocatépetl 17,887 ft (5,452 m)

YUCATÁN PENINSULA

Jamaica

Trinidad

SIERRA MADRE DEL SUR

Caribbean Sea

CENTRAL AMERICA

Lake Nicaragua

ISTHMUS OF PANAMA

SOUTH AMERICA

0° Equator

ATLAS

ELEVATION

Feet	Meters
13,120	4,000
6,560	2,000
1,640	500
656	200
(Sea level) 0	0 (Sea level)
Below sea level	Below sea level

Ice cap

0   300   600 Miles

0   300   600 Kilometers

Projection: Azimuthal Equal Area

North America: Political

ARCTIC OCEAN

EUROPE

ASIA

North Pole

ATLAS

ICELAND

ASIA

Bering Strait

St. Lawrence Island
Bering Sea
Nunivak Island

Point Barrow
Beaufort Sea

Queen Elizabeth Islands
Ellesmere Island

Greenland (DENMARK)

Arctic Circle

Denmark Strait

ALASKA (U.S.)

Banks Island
Victoria Island

Baffin Bay

Davis Strait

Cape Farewell

Anchorage

Great Bear Lake

Baffin Island

Kodiak Island
Gulf of Alaska

Great Slave Lake

Labrador Sea

PACIFIC OCEAN

Alexander Archipelago
Juneau

Southampton Island
Coats Island
Mansel Island

Hudson Strait

Queen Charlotte Islands

Hudson Bay

Anticosti Island
Newfoundland

Edmonton

CANADA

Vancouver Island

Calgary

Lake Winnipeg

Prince Edward Island
Gulf of St. Lawrence
Cape Breton Island
St. Pierre and Miquelon (FRANCE)

Vancouver

Seattle
Portland

Winnipeg

Lake Superior

Quebec
Montreal

Ottawa
Toronto

Lake Huron
Lake Michigan
Lake Ontario
Lake Erie

Boston
Cape Cod

San Francisco
San Jose

Minneapolis

Milwaukee
Chicago
Detroit
Cleveland
Columbus

New York City
Philadelphia
Baltimore
Washington, D.C.

ATLANTIC OCEAN

Great Salt Lake
Salt Lake City

Denver

Kansas City

Indianapolis
St. Louis

Norfolk

Los Angeles
San Diego
Tijuana

UNITED STATES

Memphis

Atlanta
Birmingham

Bermuda (U.K.)

Phoenix

Dallas

Jacksonville

Tropic of Cancer

Austin
San Antonio

Houston

New Orleans

Miami
Florida Keys

BAHAMAS

Turks and Caicos Islands (U.K.)

Nassau

DOMINICAN REPUBLIC

Puerto Rico (U.S.)

San Juan

ST. KITTS & NEVIS
ANTIGUA & BARBUDA

Monterrey

Gulf of Mexico

Havana

Straits of Florida

CUBA

HAITI

Santo Domingo

Virgin Is. (U.S. & U.K.)

Guadeloupe (FRANCE)
DOMINICA
BARBADOS

MEXICO

Guadalajara
Mexico City
Puebla

Mérida

Cayman Is. (U.K.)

Kingston

JAMAICA

Port-au-Prince

Martinique (FRANCE)

ST. LUCIA
ST. VINCENT AND THE GRENADINES

GRENADA

Belmopan
BELIZE

Caribbean Sea

Netherlands Antilles (NETHERLANDS)

○ National capital
• Other city

GUATEMALA
Guatemala City
San Salvador
EL SALVADOR

HONDURAS
Tegucigalpa
NICARAGUA
Managua

Aruba (NETHERLANDS)
Panama Canal

TRINIDAD AND TOBAGO

0   300   600 Miles

0   300   600 Kilometers

San José

Panama City

Projection: Azimuthal Equal-Area

COSTA RICA

PANAMA

SOUTH AMERICA

Equator

South America: Physical

CENTRAL AMERICA

Caribbean Sea

Panama Canal

Gulf of Panama

Malpelo Island

Galápagos Islands

Gulf of Guayaquil

PACIFIC OCEAN

Margarita Island
Tobago
Trinidad
Orinoco River Delta

Lake Maracaibo

Cauca River
Magdalena River

Mount Tolima 18,425 ft (5,616 m)

LLANOS

Meta River

Orinoco River

Angel Falls

GUIANA HIGHLANDS

Devil's Island
Cape Orange

Amazon River Delta

ATLANTIC OCEAN

Orinoco River

Caqueta River

Mount Chimborazo 20,561 ft (6,267 m)

Japurá River
Rio Negro

AMAZON BASIN

Amazon River

0° Equator

ANDES

Marañón River

Amazon River
Juruá River

Purus River

Madeira River

Tapajós River

Xingu River

Araguaia River

Tocantins River

Parnaíb River

BRAZILIAN HIGHLANDS

Mount Huascarán 22,205 ft (6,768 m)

Ucayali River

Beni River

Mamore River

MATO GROSSO PLATEAU

São Francisco River

Lake Titicaca

Ancohuma Peak 20,958 ft (6,388 m)

ATACAMA DESERT

Lake Poopo

San Ambrosio Island
San Félix Island

Pilcomayo River

CHACO

Paraguay River

BRAZILIAN PLATEAU

Tropic of Capricorn

Salado River

ANDES

Juan Fernández Islands

Mount Aconcagua 22,834 ft (6,960 m)

Salado River

PAMPAS

Paraná River

Uruguay River

Rio de la Plata

ATLANTIC OCEAN

Colorado River

Gulf of San Matías

ELEVATION

Feet		Meters
13,120		4,000
6,560		2,000
1,640		500
656		200
(Sea level) 0		0 (Sea level)
Below sea level		Below sea level

0   250   500 Miles
0   250   500 Kilometers

Projection: Azimuthal Equal Area

Chiloé Island

Chonos Archipelago

PATAGONIA

Gulf of San Jorge

Cape Tres Puntas

Bahía Grande

Strait of Magellan

Tierra del Fuego

Falkland Islands

South Georgia Islands

Cape Horn

South America: Political

Caribbean Sea

CENTRAL AMERICA

Barranquilla
Cartagena
Caracas

Lake Maracaibo

VENEZUELA

Georgetown
Paramaribo

ATLANTIC OCEAN

Medellín

Bogotá

GUYANA
SURINAME
Cayenne
French Guiana (FRANCE)

COLOMBIA

Cali

Malpelo Island (COLOMBIA)

Quito

ECUADOR

Guayaquil

0° Equator

Galápagos Islands (ECUADOR)

0° Equator

Belém

PERU

BRAZIL

Recife

Trujillo

Callao Lima

PACIFIC OCEAN

10°S

Arequipa

Lake Titicaca

La Paz
Lake Poopó

BOLIVIA

Sucre

Brasília

Salvador

Belo Horizonte

PARAGUAY

Campinas
São Paulo

Rio de Janeiro

Tropic of Capricorn

Asunción

Curitiba

San Ambrosio Island (CHILE)

San Félix Island (CHILE)

CHILE

Pôrto Alegre

Juan Fernández Islands (CHILE)

Córdoba

Valparaíso
Santiago

Rosario

URUGUAY
Montevideo

ATLANTIC OCEAN

Buenos Aires

ARGENTINA

⊛ National capital
• Other city

0   250   500 Miles
0   250   500 Kilometers

Projection: Azimuthal Equal-Area

Strait of Magellan

Falkland Islands (U.K.)

Tierra del Fuego

South Georgia Island (U.K.)

Europe: Physical

ASIA

SOUTHWEST ASIA

URAL MOUNTAINS

NORTHERN EUROPEAN PLAIN

Pechora River

Kama River

Ural River

Volga

Don River

Dnipro River

Dniester River

Nistru River

Caspian Sea

Mt. Elbrus (5,642 m) 18,510 ft

CAUCASUS MTS.

Sea of Azov

CRIMEAN PENINSULA

Black Sea

KOLA PENINSULA

White Sea

Barents Sea

North Cape

Lake Onega

Lake Ladoga

Rybinsk Reservoir

Northern Dvina River

Daugava R.

Gulf of Finland

BALTIC PLAINS

Baltic Sea

Vistula River

Oder River

Elbe River

CARPATHIAN

TRANSYLVANIAN ALPS

Danube River

Sea of Marmara

Aegean Sea

Rhodes

Crete

BALKAN PENINSULA

DINARIC ALPS

Adriatic Sea

APENNINES

Tiber River

Tyrrhenian Sea

Sicily

Malta

ARCTIC OCEAN

KJÖLEN MOUNTAINS

Gulf of Bothnia

Lake Vänern

Lake Vättern

Skagerrak

Kattegat

Arctic Circle

North Sea

Norwegian Sea

Shetland Islands

Orkney Islands

Faeroe Islands

Hebrides

British Isles

Irish Sea

PENNINES

Thames River

English Channel

Seine River

Loire River

Garonne River

Rhine River

ALPS

Lake Geneva

Mont Blanc 15,781 ft (4,810 m)

Rhône River

Po River

Corsica

Sardinia

Mediterranean Sea

Balearic Islands

Bay of Biscay

Cape Finisterre

PYRENEES

Ebro River

Duero River

Tagus River

Guadiana River

Guadalquivir River

IBERIAN PENINSULA

Strait of Gibraltar

ATLANTIC OCEAN

Iceland

AFRICA

Mediterranean Sea

30°E

20°E

10°E

0°

10°W

20°W

20°N

30°N

40°N

50°N

60°N

70°N

20°W

30°W

40°W

10°W

N E S W

ELEVATION

Feet	Meters
13,120	4,000
6,560	2,000
1,640	500
656	200
0 (Sea level)	0 (Sea level)

Below sea level — Below sea level

Ice cap

300 Miles
0   150   300
0   150   300 Kilometers

Projection: Azimuthal Equal Area

ATLAS

Europe: Political

ASIA

URAL MOUNTAINS

RUSSIA

Nizhny Novgorod

Moscow

St. Petersburg

SOUTHWEST ASIA

Caspian Sea

Black Sea

Barents Sea

White Sea

North Cape

FINLAND

Helsinki

Gulf of Bothnia

Gulf of Finland

Tallinn

ESTONIA

LATVIA

Riga

LITHUANIA

Vilnius

RUSSIA

Minsk

BELARUS

Warsaw

POLAND

Krakow

Kiev

UKRAINE

Chişinău

MOLDOVA

ROMANIA

Bucharest

BULGARIA

Sofia

Belgrade

SERBIA

MACEDONIA

Skopje

KOSOVO

Priština

MONTENEGRO

Podgorica

Tirana

ALBANIA

GREECE

Athens

Aegean Sea

Rhodes

Crete

SWEDEN

Stockholm

Göteborg

Baltic Sea

NORWAY

Oslo

Bergen

DENMARK

Copenhagen

Hamburg

North Sea

GERMANY

Berlin

Dresden

Prague

CZECH REPUBLIC

Vienna

AUSTRIA

Bratislava

SLOVAKIA

Budapest

HUNGARY

Zagreb

CROATIA

SLOVENIA

Ljubljana

BOSNIA AND HERZEGOVINA

Sarajevo

SAN MARINO

San Marino

ITALY

Rome

VATICAN CITY

Naples

Adriatic Sea

MONACO

Monaco

Corsica (FRANCE)

Sardinia (ITALY)

Sicily

MALTA

Valletta

Mediterranean Sea

Cologne

Bonn

Amsterdam

THE NETHERLANDS

Brussels

BELGIUM

LUXEMBOURG

Luxembourg

Paris

FRANCE

SWITZERLAND

Bern

LIECHTENSTEIN

Vaduz

Munich

Milan

Lake Geneva

Lyon

Marseille

PYRENEES

ANDORRA

Andorra la Vella

Barcelona

Balearic Islands (SPAIN)

SPAIN

Madrid

Valencia

Seville

Gibraltar (U.K.)

Strait of Gibraltar

PORTUGAL

Lisbon

AFRICA

Bay of Biscay

SCOTLAND

Edinburgh

UNITED KINGDOM

ENGLAND

London

Liverpool

WALES

NORTHERN IRELAND

Belfast

IRELAND

Dublin

British Isles

English Channel

Channel Islands (U.K.)

Faeroe Islands (DENMARK)

Shetland Islands

ICELAND

Reykjavík

ARCTIC OCEAN

Arctic Circle

ATLANTIC OCEAN

National capital
Other city

300 Miles
150
0
300 Kilometers
150
0

Projection: Azimuthal Equal-Area

70°N

60°N

50°N

40°N

30°W

20°W

10°W

0°

10°E

20°E

30°E

40°E

50°E

ATLAS **R9**

Asia: Physical

ELEVATION

Feet	Meters
13,120	4,000
6,560	2,000
1,640	500
656	200
(Sea level) 0	0 (Sea level)
Below sea level	Below sea level

Ice cap

0   250   500   750 Kilometers
0   250   500   750 Miles

Projection: Two-Point Equidistant

PACIFIC OCEAN

AUSTRALIA

EUROPE

AFRICA

INDIAN OCEAN

Arctic Circle

North Pole

North Land

Franz Josef Land

Novaya Zemlya

New Siberian Islands

Wrangel Island

Aleutian Islands

KAMCHATKA PENINSULA

Bering Sea

Sea of Okhotsk

Sakhalin Island

Kuril Islands

Hokkaido

Honshu

Shikoku

Kyushu

Okinawa

Ryukyu Islands

Taiwan

Luzon

Mindanao

Philippines

Borneo

Celebes Sea

Celebes

Banda Sea

Molucca Sea

Arafura Sea

New Guinea

MAOKE MOUNTAINS

Java Sea

Java

Bangka

Sumatra

Mentawai Islands

MALAY PENINSULA

INDOCHINA PENINSULA

Gulf of Thailand

South China Sea

Hainan

Gulf of Tonkin

Chao Phraya River

Mekong River

Irrawaddy River

Andaman Sea

Andaman Islands

Nicobar Islands

Bay of Bengal

Sri Lanka

Maldives

Lakshadweep Islands

Arabian Sea

Socotra Island

Gulf of Aden

Red Sea

Gulf of Oman

Persian Gulf

ZAGROS MTS.

RUB' AL-KHALI

AN-NAFUD

SYRIAN DESERT

SINAI PENINSULA

Cyprus

Mediterranean Sea

ANATOLIAN PLATEAU

Mount Ararat 16,945 ft (5,165 m)

CAUCASUS MTS.

Black Sea

Bosporus

Tigris River

Euphrates River

Caspian Sea

USTYURT PLATEAU

Aral Sea

Ural River

KARA KUM

KYZYL KUM

TURAN LOWLAND

Amu Darya

Syr Darya

GREAT SALT DESERT

HINDU KUSH

KAZAKH UPLANDS

Balqash Lake

TIAN SHAN

TAKLIMAKAN DESERT

TARIM BASIN

KUNLUN MOUNTAINS

PLATEAU OF TIBET

HIMALAYAS

Mount Everest 29,035 ft (8,850 m)

Brahmaputra River

Ganges River

INDO-GANGETIC PLAIN

Sutlej River

Indus River

THAR DESERT

DECCAN PLATEAU

Godavari River

WESTERN GHATS

EASTERN GHATS

URAL MOUNTAINS

WEST SIBERIAN PLAIN

Ob River

Irtysh River

Ishim River

Tobol River

CENTRAL SIBERIAN PLATEAU

Yenisey River

Lower Tunguska River

Angara River

Lake Baikal

SAYAN MOUNTAINS

ALTAY MOUNTAINS

MONGOLIAN PLATEAU

GOBI

GREATER KHINGAN RANGE

YABLONOY RANGE

STANOVOY MOUNTAINS

Shilka River

Amur River

Lena River

Aldan River

VERKHOYANSKY RANGE

CHERSKY RANGE

KOLYMA MTS.

CENTRAL RANGE

TAYMYR PENINSULA

Kara Sea

Barents Sea

Laptev Sea

S I B E R I A

QIN LING

Huang He (Yellow River)

NORTH CHINA PLAIN

BOHAI HILLS

Yellow Sea

East China Sea

Sea of Japan (East Sea)

Korea Strait

Chang Jiang (Yangzi River)

Xi River

Tropic of Cancer

Equator

150°E

140°E

130°E

120°E

110°E

100°E

90°E

80°E

70°E

60°E

50°E

40°E

30°E

20°E

170°W

180°

170°E

160°E

150°E

140°E

130°E

120°E

110°E

100°E

90°N

80°N

70°N

60°N

50°N

40°N

30°N

20°N

10°N

0°

10°S

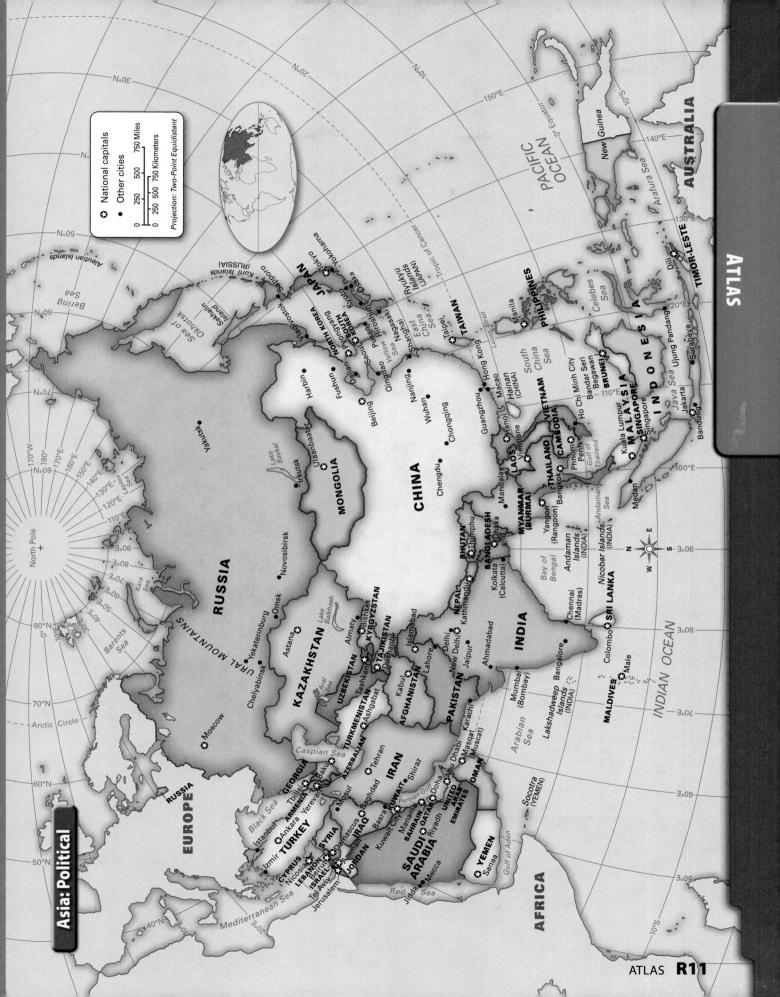

Asia: Political

National capitals
Other cities

0 250 500 750 Miles
0 250 500 750 Kilometers
Projection: Two-Point Equidistant

EUROPE

RUSSIA

Moscow

Arctic Circle

North Pole

Aleutian Islands

Bering Sea

Sea of Okhotsk

Sakhalin Island

Kuril Islands (RUSSIA)

Yakutsk

Irkutsk

Lake Baykal

Ulaanbaatar

MONGOLIA

Novosibirsk

Omsk

URAL MOUNTAINS

Yekaterinburg

Chelyabinsk

Astana

KAZAKHSTAN

Aral Sea

Lake Balkhash

Almaty

Bishkek

KYRGYZSTAN

Tashkent

UZBEKISTAN

TAJIKISTAN

Dushanbe

TURKMENISTAN

Ashgabat

Kabul

AFGHANISTAN

Barents Sea

Kara Sea

Laptev Sea

Caspian Sea

Black Sea

GEORGIA

Tbilisi

ARMENIA

Yerevan

AZERBAIJAN

Baku

Istanbul

Ankara

TURKEY

Izmir

CYPRUS

Nicosia

LEBANON

Beirut

ISRAEL

Tel Aviv

Jerusalem

Damascus

SYRIA

Amman

JORDAN

Mosul

Baghdad

IRAQ

Basra

KUWAIT

Kuwait City

Mediterranean Sea

AFRICA

Red Sea

Jidda

Mecca

SAUDI ARABIA

Riyadh

Manama

BAHRAIN

QATAR

Doha

Abu Dhabi

UNITED ARAB EMIRATES

Masqat (Muscat)

OMAN

YEMEN

Sanaa

Gulf of Aden

Socotra (YEMEN)

Arabian Sea

IRAN

Tehran

Shiraz

Persian Gulf

PAKISTAN

Islamabad

Lahore

Karachi

INDIA

New Delhi

Delhi

Jaipur

Ahmadabad

Mumbai (Bombay)

Bangalore

Chennai (Madras)

Lakshadweep Islands (INDIA)

MALDIVES

Male

Colombo

SRI LANKA

INDIAN OCEAN

NEPAL

Kathmandu

BHUTAN

Thimphu

BANGLADESH

Dhaka

Kolkata (Calcutta)

CHINA

Chengdu

Chongqing

Wuhan

Nanjing

Beijing

Harbin

Fushun

Dalian

Qingdao

Shanghai

Guangzhou

Hong Kong

Macao

Hainan (CHINA)

MYANMAR (BURMA)

Mandalay

Yangon (Rangoon)

Bay of Bengal

Andaman Islands (INDIA)

Nicobar Islands (INDIA)

Andaman Sea

LAOS

Vientiane

THAILAND

Bangkok

Gulf of Thailand

CAMBODIA

Phnom Penh

VIETNAM

Hanoi

Ho Chi Minh City

MALAYSIA

Kuala Lumpur

SINGAPORE

Singapore

Medan

BRUNEI

Bandar Seri Begawan

INDONESIA

Ujung Pandang

Jakarta

Bandung

Surabaya

Java Sea

Celebes Sea

South China Sea

PHILIPPINES

Manila

Luzon Strait

TAIWAN

Taipei

East China Sea

Yellow Sea

Shanghai

NORTH KOREA

Pyongyang

SOUTH KOREA

Seoul

Pusan

JAPAN

Tokyo

Yokohama

Osaka

Kyoto

Hiroshima

Nagasaki

Sapporo

Vladivostok

RUSSIA

Ryukyu Islands (JAPAN)

Tropic of Cancer

PACIFIC OCEAN

New Guinea

Arafura Sea

AUSTRALIA

TIMOR-LESTE

Dili

Equator

RUSSIA

Africa: Physical

EUROPE

SOUTHWEST ASIA

Azores

Madeira Islands

Strait of Gibraltar

Mediterranean Sea

Gulf of Sidra

Suez Canal

Persian Gulf

Canary Islands

ATLAS MOUNTAINS

Tropic of Cancer

Cape Blanc

S A H A R A

AHAGGAR MOUNTAINS

EL DJOUF

AIR MTS.

TIBESTI MOUNTAINS

LIBYAN DESERT

QATTARA DEPRESSION

Lake Nasser

Nile River

NUBIAN DESERT

Red Sea

Cape Verde Islands

S A H E L

Niger River

Cape Verde

Senegal R.

White Volta R.

S U D A N

Black Volta R.

CHAD BASIN

Lake Chad

Lake Tana

Blue Nile

White Nile

Gulf of Aden

FOUTA DJALLON

Benue River

SUDAN BASIN

ETHIOPIAN HIGHLANDS

HORN OF AFRICA

SOMALI PENINSULA

Cape Palmas

Lake Volta

ADAMAWA MTS.

Gulf of Guinea

Ubangi River

RIFT VALLEY

Cape Lopez

Congo River

CONGO BASIN

Lake Albert

Lake Edward

Lake Victoria

Lake Turkana

Mount Kenya 17,058 ft (5,199 m)

0° Equator

Kasai River

Lake Kivu

SERENGETI PLAIN

Mount Kilimanjaro 19,340 ft (5,895 m)

INDIAN OCEAN

MITUMBA MOUNTAINS

WESTERN RIFT VALLEY

Lake Tanganyika

MASAI STEPPE

Zanzibar

Seychelles

EASTERN RIFT VALLEY

Cuanza River

Lake Mweru

Lake Rukwa

ATLANTIC OCEAN

Ascension

Lake Malawi (Nyasa)

Cape Delgado

Comoro Islands

10°S

Lake Kariba

Zambezi River

Mozambique Channel

Madagascar

Mauritius

Réunion

Okavango Delta

Victoria Falls

KALAHARI BASIN

Impopo River

NAMIB DESERT

KALAHARI DESERT

Tropic of Capricorn

Orange River

Vaal River

DRAKENSBERG MOUNTAINS

GREAT KARROO

Cape of Good Hope

ELEVATION

Feet		Meters
13,120		4,000
6,560		2,000
1,640		500
656		200
(Sea level) 0		0 (Sea level)
Below sea level		Below sea level

0   250   500 Miles

0   250   500 Kilometers

Projection: Azimuthal Equal-Area

Africa: Political

EUROPE

SOUTHWEST ASIA

Mediterranean Sea

Strait of Gibraltar

Azores
(PORTUGAL)

Madeira
(PORTUGAL)

Canary Islands
(SPAIN)

El Aaiún

WESTERN
SAHARA
(Claimed by
Morocco)

Casablanca ● Rabat ✪

Algiers ✪   Tunis ✪

TUNISIA

Tripoli ✪

MOROCCO

ALGERIA

LIBYA

EGYPT

Alexandria ●
Giza ● Cairo ✪

Red Sea

Tropic of Cancer

CAPE
VERDE

● Praia ✪

MAURITANIA

✪ Nouakchott

MALI

NIGER

CHAD

SUDAN

Khartoum ✪

ERITREA
✪ Asmara

Gulf of Aden

DJIBOUTI
● Djibouti

SENEGAL
Dakar ✪
Banjul ✪
GAMBIA
Bissau ✪
GUINEA
BISSAU
Conakry ✪
Freetown ✪
SIERRA LEONE
Monrovia ●

Bamako ●

BURKINA
FASO
Niamey ●

Ouagadougou ●

GUINEA

CÔTE
D'IVOIRE

GHANA
Yamoussoukro ●
Abidjan ● Accra ✪

LIBERIA

BENIN
TOGO
Lomé ●

NIGERIA
Abuja ✪
Lagos ●
Porto-
Novo ✪

N'Djamena ✪

*Lake
Chad*

CENTRAL AFRICAN
REPUBLIC

Bangui ✪

SOUTH
SUDAN

Juba ✪

ETHIOPIA

Addis Ababa ●

SOMALIA

● Mogadishu

CAMEROON

Yaoundé ●

EQUATORIAL GUINEA

SÃO TOMÉ AND PRÍNCIPE
São Tomé ●

Malabo ●

*Gulf of
Guinea*

REPUBLIC
OF THE
CONGO

GABON

Libreville ●

Kisangani ●

UGANDA
Kampala ●

RWANDA
Kigali ✪
Bujumbura ● BURUNDI

KENYA
Nairobi ●

*Lake
Victoria*

SEYCHELLES
Victoria ●

*INDIAN
OCEAN*

Equator

ATLANTIC
OCEAN

Brazzaville ✪

CABINDA
(ANGOLA)

Kinshasa ✪

DEMOCRATIC
REPUBLIC
OF THE CONGO

TANZANIA
Dodoma ✪
*Lake
Tanganyika*

Mombasa ●
Pemba
Zanzibar ●
Dar es Salaam ●

St. Helena
● (U.K.)

Luanda ✪

ANGOLA

ZAMBIA
Lusaka ✪

Lubumbashi ●

*Lake Malawi
(Nyasa)*

MALAWI
Lilongwe ✪

COMOROS
● Moroni

Antananarivo ✪
MAURITIUS
Port Louis ✪

NAMIBIA

Windhoek ✪

BOTSWANA

Gaborone ✪

Harare ✪
ZIMBABWE
Bulawayo ●

MOZAMBIQUE

Pretoria ✪
Johannesburg ●
Bloemfontein ●

Maputo ✪
Mbabane ✪
SWAZILAND
Maseru ✪
LESOTHO

MADAGASCAR

Réunion
(FRANCE)

Tropic of Capricorn

SOUTH AFRICA

Cape Town ✪

Legend

✪ National capital
● Other city

0   250   500 Miles
0   250   500 Kilometers

Projection: Azimuthal Equal-Area

English and Spanish Glossary

MARK	AS IN	RESPELLING	EXAMPLE
a	alphabet	a	*AL-fuh-bet
ā	Asia	ay	AY-zhuh
ä	cart, top	ah	KAHRT, TAHP
e	let, ten	e	LET, TEN
ē	even, leaf	ee	EE-vuhn, LEEF
i	it, tip, British	i	IT, TIP, BRIT-ish
ī	site, buy, Ohio	y	SYT, BY, oh-HY-oh
	iris	eye	EYE-ris
k	card	k	KAHRD
kw	quest	kw	KWEST
ō	over, rainbow	oh	OH-vuhr, RAYN-boh
ů	book, wood	ooh	BOOHK, WOOHD
ò	all, orchid	aw	AWL, AWR-kid
òi	foil, coin	oy	FOYL, KOYN
aů	out	ow	OWT
ə	cup, butter	uh	KUHP, BUHT-uhr
ü	rule, food	oo	ROOL, FOOD
yü	few	yoo	FYOO
zh	vision	zh	VIZH-uhn

*A syllable printed in small capital letters receives heavier emphasis than the other syllable(s) in a word.

Phonetic Respelling and Pronunciation Guide

Many of the key terms in this textbook have been respelled to help you pronounce them. The letter combinations used in the respelling throughout the narrative are explained in the following phonetic respelling and pronunciation guide. The guide is adapted from *Merriam-Webster's Collegiate Dictionary, Eleventh Edition; Merriam-Webster's Biographical Dictionary;* and *Merriam-Webster's Geographical Dictionary.*

A

acropolis (uh-KRAH-puh-luhs) a high hill upon which a Greek fortress was built (p. 232)
acrópolis colina elevada sobre la que se construyó una fortaleza griega (pág. 232)

acupuncture (AK-yoo-punk-cher) the Chinese practice of inserting fine needles through the skin at specific points to cure disease or relieve pain (p. 183)
acupuntura práctica china que consiste en insertar pequeñas agujas en la piel en puntos específicos para curar enfermedades o aliviar el dolor (pág. 183)

afterlife life after death, much of Egyptain religion focused on the afterlife (p. 92)
la otra vida vida después de la muerte (pág. 92)

agriculture farming (p. 42)
agricultura cultivo de la tierra (pág. 42)

alliance an agreement to work together (p. 270)
alianza acuerdo de colaboración (pág. 270)

alloy a mixture of two or more metals (p. 150)
aleación mezcla de dos o más metales (pág. 150)

alphabet a set of letters that can be combined to form words (p. 77)
alfabeto conjunto de letras que pueden combinarse para formar palabras (pág. 77)

ancestor a relative who lived in the past (p. 28)
antepasado pariente que vivió hace muchos años (pág. 28)

animism the belief that bodies of water, animals, trees, and other natural objects have spirits (p. 383)
animismo creencia de que las masas de agua, los animales, los árboles y otros elementos naturales tienen espíritu (pág. 383)

Apostles (uh-PAHS-uhls) the 12 chosen disciples of Jesus who spread his teachings (p. 337)
  apóstoles los 12 discípulos elegidos por Jesucristo que difundieron sus enseñanzas (pág. 337)

aqueduct (A-kwuh-duhkt) a human-made raised channel that carries water from distant places (p. 327)
  acueducto canal hecho por el ser humano que transporta agua desde lugares alejados (pág. 327)

archaeology (ar-kee-AH-luh-jee) the study of the past based on what people left behind (p. 7)
  arqueología estudio del pasado a través de los objetos que dejaron las personas tras desaparecer (pág. 7)

architecture the science of building (p. 68)
  arquitectura ciencia de la construcción (pág. 68)

aristocrat (uh-RIS-tuh-krat) a rich landowner or noble (p. 237)
  aristócrata propietario de tierras o noble rico (pág. 237)

artifact an object created and used by humans (p. 10)
  artefacto objeto creado y usado por los humanos (pág. 10)

astronomy the study of stars and planets (p. 151)
  astronomía estudio de las estrellas y los planetas (pág. 151)

B

Buddhism a religion based on the teachings of the Buddha that developed in India in the 500s BC (p. 138)
  budismo religión basada en las enseñanzas de Buda, originada en la India en el siglo VI a. C. (pág. 138)

bureaucracy a body of unelected government officials (p. 422)
  burocracia cuerpo de empleados no electos del gobierno (pág. 422)

Bushido (BOOH-shi-doh) the code of honor followed by the samurai in Japan (p. 456)
  Bushido código de honor por el que se regían los samuráis en Japón (pág. 456)

Byzantine Empire the society that developed in the eastern Roman Empire after the fall of the western Roman Empire (p. 343)
  Imperio bizantino sociedad que surgió en el Imperio romano de oriente tras la caída del Imperio rhomano de occidente (pág. 343)

C

caliph (KAY-luhf) a title that Muslims use for the highest leader of Islam (p. 362)
  califa título que los musulmanes le dan al líder supremo del Islam (pág. 362)

calligraphy decorative writing (p. 371)
  caligrafía escritura decorativa (pág. 371)

canal a human-made waterway (p. 56)
  canal vía de agua hecha por el ser humano (pág. 56)

caravan a group of traders that travel together (p. 355)
  caravana grupo de comerciantes que viajan juntos (pág. 355)

caste system the division of Indian society into groups based on rank, wealth, or occupation (p. 131)
  sistema de castas división de la sociedad india en grupos basados en la clase social, el nivel económico o la profesión (pág. 131)

cataracts rapids along a river, such as those along the Nile in Egypt (p. 87)
  rápidos fuertes corrientes a lo largo de un río, como las del Nilo en Egipto (pág. 87)

causeway a raised road across water or wet ground (p. 474)
  carretera elevada carretera construida sobre agua o terreno pantanoso (pág. 474)

cavalry a unit of soldiers who ride horses (p. 262)
  caballería grupo de soldados a caballo (pág. 262)

ENGLISH AND SPANISH GLOSSARY

chariot a wheeled, horse-drawn cart used in battle (p. 74)

cuadriga carro tirado por caballos usado en las batallas (pág. 74)

checks and balances a system that balances the distribution of power in a government (p. 305)

pesos y contrapesos sistema creado para equilibrar la distribución del poder en un gobierno (pág. 305)

Christianity a religion based on the teachings of Jesus of Nazareth that developed in Judea at the beginning of the first century AD (p. 334)

cristianismo religión basada en las enseñanzas de Jesús de Nazaret que se desarrolló en Judea a comienzos del siglo I d. C. (pág. 334)

citizen a person who has the right to participate in government (p. 237)

ciudadano persona que tiene el derecho de participar en el gobierno (pág. 237)

city-state a political unit consisting of a city and its surrounding countryside (p. 60)

ciudad estado unidad política formada por una ciudad y los campos que la rodean (pág. 60)

civil law a legal system based on a written code of laws (p. 328)

derecho civil sistema jurídico basado en un código de leyes escritas (pág. 328)

civil service service as a government official (p. 422)

administración pública servicio como empleado del gobierno (pág. 422)

clan an extended family (p. 442)

clan familia extensa (pág. 442)

classical an age marked by great achievements (p. 232)

clásica época marcada por grandes logros (pág. 232)

climate the average weather conditions in a certain area over a long period of time (p. 12)

clima condiciones del tiempo medias de una zona específica durante un largo período de tiempo (pág. 12)

compass an instrument that uses the earth's magnetic field to indicate direction (p. 418)

brújula instrumento que utiliza el campo magnético de la Tierra para indicar la dirección (pág. 418)

Confucianism a philosophy based on the ideas of Confucius that focuses on morality, family order, social harmony, and government (p. 169)

confucianismo filosofía basada en las ideas de Confucio que se basa en la moralidad, el orden familiar, la armonía social y el gobierno (pág. 169)

conquistadors (kahn-kees-tuh-DOHRS) Spanish soldiers (p. 478)

conquistadores soldados españoles (pág. 478)

consuls (KAHN-suhlz) the two most powerful officials in Rome (p. 303)

cónsules los dos funcionarios más poderosos en Roma (pág. 303)

corruption the decay of people's values (p. 342)

corrupción decadencia de los valores de las personas (pág. 342)

court a group of nobles who live near and serve or advise a ruler (p. 448)

corte grupo de nobles que viven cerca de un gobernante y lo sirven o aconsejan (pág. 448)

crucifixion (kroo-suh-FIK-shuhn) a type of execution in which a person was nailed to a cross (p. 336)

crucifixión tipo de ejecución en la que se clavaba a una persona en una cruz (pág. 336)

culture the knowledge, beliefs, customs, and values of a group of people (p. 7)

cultura el conocimiento, las creencias, las costumbres y los valores de un grupo de personas (pág. 7)

cuneiform (kyoo-NEE-uh-fohrm) the world's first system of writing; developed in Sumer (p. 65)

cuneiforme primer sistema de escritura del mundo; desarrollado en Sumeria (pág. 65)

currency money (p. 326)

moneda dinero (pág. 326)

D

daimyo (DY-mee-oh) large landowners of feudal Japan (p. 454)
daimyo grandes propietarios de tierras del Japón feudal (pág. 454)

Daoism (DOW-ih-zum) a philosophy that developed in China and stressed the belief that one should live in harmony with the Dao, the guiding force of all reality (p. 170)
taoismo filosofía que se desarrolló en China y que enfatizaba la creencia de que se debe vivir en armonía con el Tao, la fuerza que guía toda la realidad (pág. 170)

Dead Sea Scrolls writings about Jewish beliefs created about 2,000 years ago (p. 212)
manuscritos del mar Muerto escritos sobre las creencias judías, redactados hace unos 2,000 años (pág. 212)

delta a triangle-shaped area of land made from soil deposited by a river (p. 87)
delta zona de tierra de forma triangular creada a partir de los sedimentos que deposita un río (pág. 87)

democracy a type of government in which people rule themselves (p. 236)
democracia tipo de gobierno en el que el pueblo se gobierna a sí mismo (pág. 236)

Diaspora (dy-AS-pruh) the dispersal of the Jews outside of Judah after the Babylonian Captivity (p. 206)
diáspora la dispersión de los judíos desde Judá tras el cautiverio en Babilonia (pág. 206)

dictator a ruler who has almost absolute power (p. 298)
dictador gobernante que tiene poder casi absoluto (pág. 298)

diffusion the spread of ideas from one culture to another (p. 189)
difusión traspaso de ideas de una cultura a otra (pág. 189)

division of labor an arrangement in which each worker specializes in a particular task or job (p. 56)

división del trabajo organización mediante la que cada trabajador se especializa en un trabajo o tarea en particular (pág. 56)

domestication the process of changing plants or animals to make them more useful to humans (p. 41)
domesticación proceso en el que se modifican los animales o las plantas para que sean más útiles para los humanos (pág. 41)

dynasty a series of rulers from the same family (p. 89)
dinastía serie de gobernantes pertenecientes a la misma familia (pág. 89)

E

elite (AY-leet) people of wealth and power (p. 93)
élite personas ricas y poderosas (pág. 93)

empire land with different territories and peoples under a single rule (p. 61)
imperio zona que reúne varios territorios y pueblos bajo un mismo gobierno (pág. 61)

engineering the application of scientific knowledge for practical purposes (p. 94)
ingeniería aplicación del conocimiento científico para fines prácticos (pág. 94)

environment all the living and nonliving things that affect life in an area (p. 13)
medio ambiente todos los seres vivos y elementos inertes que afectan la vida de un área (pág. 13)

epics long poems that tell the stories of heroes (p. 66)
poemas épicos poemas largos que narran hazañas de héroes (pág. 66)

ethics moral values (p. 169)
ética valores morales (pág. 169)

Exodus the journey of the Israelites, led by Moses, from Egypt to Canaan after they were freed from slavery (p. 203)
Éxodo viaje de los Israelita, guiados por Moisés, desde Egipto hasta Canaán después de su liberación de la esclavitud (pág. 203)

exports items sent to other regions for trade (p. 111)

    exportaciones productos enviados a otras regiones para el intercambio commercial (pág. 111)

extended family a family group that includes the father, mother, children, and close relatives (p. 382)

    familia extensa grupo familiar que incluye al padre, la madre, los hijos y los parientes cercanos (pág. 382)

fable a short story that teaches a lesson about life or gives advice on how to live (p. 247)

    fábula relato breve que presenta una enseñanza u ofrece algún consejo sobre la vida (pág. 247)

fasting going without food for a period of time (p. 137)

    ayunar dejar de comer durante un período de tiempo (pág. 137)

Fertile Crescent an area of rich farmland in Southwest Asia where the first civilizations began (p. 55)

    Media Luna de las tierras fértiles zona de ricas tierras de cultivo situada en el sudoeste de Asia, en la que comenzaron las primeras civilizaciones (pág. 55)

figurehead a person who appears to rule even though real power rests with someone else (p. 455)

    títere persona que aparentemente gobierna aunque el poder real lo ostenta otra persona (pág. 455)

Five Pillars of Islam five acts of worship required of all Muslims (p. 360)

    los cinco pilares del Islam cinco prácticas religiosas que los musulmanes tienen que observar (pág. 360)

Forum a Roman public meeting place (p. 305)

    foro lugar público de reuniones en Roma (pág. 305)

fossil a part or imprint of something that was once alive (p. 10)

    fósil parte o huella de un ser vivo ya desaparecido (pág. 10)

geography the study of Earth's physical and cultural features (p. 12)

    geografía estudio de las características físicas y culturales de la Tierra (pág. 12)

Grand Canal a canal linking northern and southern China (p. 411)

    canal grande un canal que conecta el norte con el sur de China (pág. 411)

Great Wall a barrier made of walls across China's northern frontier (p. 175)

    Gran Muralla barrera formada por muros situada a lo largo de la frontera norte de China (pág. 175)

griot a West African storyteller (p. 396)

    griot narrador de relatos de África occidental (pág. 396)

gunpowder a mixture of powders used in guns and explosives (p. 418)

    pólvora mezcla de polvos utilizada en armas de fuego y explosivos (pág. 418)

Hammurabi's Code a set of 282 laws governing daily life in Babylon; the earliest known collection of written laws (p. 73)

    Código de Hammurabi conjunto de 282 leyes que regían la vida cotidiana en Babilonia; la primera colección de leyes escritas conocida (pág. 73)

Hellenistic Greek-like; heavily influenced by Greek ideas (p. 275)

    helenístico al estilo griego; muy influido por las ideas de la Grecia clásica (pág. 275)

hieroglyphics (hy-ruh-GLIH-fiks) the ancient Egyptian writing system that used picture symbols (p. 102)

jeroglíficos sistema de escritura del antiguo Egipto, en el cual se usaban símbolos ilustrados (pág. 102)

High Holy Days the two most sacred of all Jewish holidays—Rosh Hashanah and Yom Kippur (p. 219)

Supremos Días Santos los dos días más sagrados de las festividades judías, Rosh Hashanah y Yom Kippur (pág. 219)

Hindu-Arabic numerals the number system we use today; it was created by Indian scholars during the Gupta dynasty (p. 150)

numerales indoarábigos sistema numérico que usamos hoy en día; fue creado por estudiosos de la India durante la dinastía Gupta (pág. 150)

Hinduism the main religion of India; it teaches that everything is part of a universal spirit called Brahman (p. 133)

hinduismo religión principal de la India; sus enseñanzas dicen que todo forma parte de un espíritu universal llamado Brahman (pág. 133)

history the study of the past (p. 6)

historia el estudio del pasado (pág. 6)

hominid an early ancestor of humans (p. 28)

homínido antepasado primitivo de los humanos (pág. 28)

hunter-gatherers people who hunt animals and gather wild plants, seeds, fruits, and nuts to survive (p. 33)

cazadores y recolectores personas que cazan animales y recolectan plantas, semillas, frutas y nueces para sobrevivir (pág. 33)

ice ages long periods of freezing weather (p. 36)

eras glaciales largos períodos de clima helado (pág. 36)

imports goods brought in from other regions (p. 111)

importaciones bienes que se introducen en un país procedentes de otras regiones (pág. 111)

inoculation (i-nah-kyuh-LAY-shuhn) injecting a person with a small dose of a virus to help build up defenses to a disease (p. 150)

inoculación acto de inyectar una pequeña dosis de un virus a una persona para ayudarla a crear defensas contra una enfermedad (pág. 150)

irrigation a way of supplying water to an area of land (p. 56)

irrigación método para suministrar agua a un terreno (pág. 56)

Islam a religion based on the messages Muhammad is believed to have received from God (p. 356)

Islam religión basada en los mensajes que se cree que Mahoma recibió de Dios (pág. 356)

isolationism a policy of avoiding contact with other countries (p. 430)

aislacionismo política de evitar el contacto con otros países (pág. 430)

jade a hard gemstone often used in jewelry (p. 163)

jade piedra preciosa de gran dureza que se suele utilizar en joyería (pág. 163)

Jainism an Indian religion based on the teachings of Mahavira that teaches all life is sacred (p. 134)

jainismo religión de la India basada en las enseñanzas de Mahavira, que proclama que toda forma de vida es sagrada (pág. 134)

Janissary an Ottoman slave soldier (p. 364)

jenízaro soldado esclavo otomano (pág. 364)

jihad (ji-HAHD) to make an effort or to struggle; has also been interpreted to mean holy war (p. 359)

yihad esforzarse o luchar; se ha interpretado también con el significado de guerra santa (pág. 359)

ENGLISH AND SPANISH GLOSSARY

Judaism (JOO-dee-i-zuhm) the religion of the Hebrews and Israelites (practiced by Jews today); the oldest monotheistic religion (p. 202)
judaísmo religión de los hebreos y los Israelitas (practicada por los judíos hoy en día); es la religión monoteísta más antigua (pág. 202)

K

karma in Buddhism and Hinduism, the effects of good or bad actions on a soul (p. 134)
karma en el budismo y el hinduismo, los efectos que las buenas o malas acciones producen en el alma (pág. 134)

kente a hand-woven, brightly colored West African fabric (p. 399)
kente tela muy colorida, tejida a mano, característica de África occidental (pág. 399)

L

land bridge a strip of land connecting two continents (p. 36)
puente de tierra franja de tierra que conecta dos continentes (pág. 36)

landforms the natural features of the land's surface (p. 12)
accidentes geográficos características naturales de la superficie terrestre (pág. 12)

Latin the language of the Romans (p. 304)
latín idioma de los romanos (pág. 304)

Legalism the Chinese belief that people were bad by nature and needed to be controlled (p. 170)
legalismo creencia china de que las personas eran malas por naturaleza y debían ser controladas (pág. 170)

legion (LEE-juhn) a group of up to 6,000 Roman soldiers (p. 309)
legión grupo que podía incluir hasta 6,000 soldados romanos (pág. 309)

lord a person of high rank who owned land but owed loyalty to his king (p. 167)
señor feudal persona de alto nivel social que poseía tierras y debía lealtad al rey (pág. 167)

M

magistrate (MA-juh-strayt) an elected official in Rome (p. 303)
magistrado funcionario electo en Roma (pág. 303)

maize (MAYZ) corn (p. 468)
maíz cereal también conocido como elote o choclo (pág. 468)

masonry stonework (p. 481)
mampostería obra de piedra (pág. 481)

meditation deep thought that focuses the mind on spiritual ideas (p. 137)
meditación reflexión profunda, durante la cual la persona se concentra en ideas espirituales (pág. 137)

megalith a huge stone monument (p. 42)
megalito enorme monumento de piedra (pág. 42)

merchant a trader (p. 111)
mercader comerciante (pág. 111)

Mesolithic Era the middle part of the Stone Age; marked by the creation of smaller and more complex tools (p. 38)
Mesolítico período central de la Edad de Piedra, caracterizado por la creación de herramientas más pequeñas y complejas (pág. 38)

Messiah (muh-SY-uh) in Judaism, a new leader that would restore the greatness of ancient Israel; in Christianity, Jesus, a leader sent by God to bring salvation to the world (p. 334)
Mesías en el judaísmo, nuevo líder que restablecería la grandeza del antiguo Israel; en christianismo, Jesús, un líder enviado por Dios para traer salvación al mundo (pág. 334)

metallurgy (MET-uhl-uhr-jee) the science of working with metals (p. 150)
metalurgia ciencia de trabajar los metales (pág. 150)

Middle Kingdom the period of Egyptian history from about 2050 to 1750 BC and marked by order and stability (p. 96)

 Reino Medio período de la historia de Egipto que abarca aproximadamente del 2050 al 1750 a. C. y que se caracterizó por el orden y la estabilidad (pág. 96)

migrate to move to a new place (p. 36)

 migrar desplazarse a otro lugar (pág. 36)

minaret a narrow tower from which Muslims are called to prayer (p. 371)

 minarete torre fina desde la que se llama a la oración a los musulmanes (pág. 371)

missionary someone who works to spread religious beliefs (p. 140)

 misionero alguien que trabaja para difundir sus creencias religiosas (pág. 140)

monarch (MAH-nark) a ruler of a kingdom or empire (p. 72)

 monarca gobernante de un reino o imperio (pág. 72)

monotheism the belief in only one God (p. 208)

 monoteísmo creencia en un solo Dios (pág. 208)

monsoon a seasonal wind pattern that causes wet and dry seasons (p. 125)

 monzón viento estacional cíclico que causa estaciones húmedas y secas (pág. 125)

mosque (MAHSK) a building for Muslim prayer (p. 357)

 mezquita edificio musulmán para la oración (pág. 357)

mummy a specially treated body wrapped in cloth for preservation (p. 93)

 momia cadáver especialmente tratado y envuelto en tela para su conservación (pág. 93)

Muslim a follower of Islam (p. 356)

 musulmán seguidor del Islam (pág. 356)

mythology stories about gods and heroes that try to explain how the world works (p. 243)

 mitología relatos sobre dioses y héroes que tratan de explicar cómo funciona el mundo (pág. 243)

N

Neolithic Era the New Stone Age; when people learned to make fire and tools such as saws and drills (p. 41)

 Neolítico Nueva Edad de Piedra; el ser humano aprendió a producir fuego y a fabricar herramientas como sierras y taladros manuales (pág. 41)

New Kingdom the period from about 1550 to 1050 BC in Egyptian history when Egypt reached the height of its power and glory (p. 97)

 Reino Nuevo período de la historia egipcia que abarca aproximadamente desde el 1550 hasta el 1050 a. C., en el que Egipto alcanzó la cima de su poder y su gloria (pág. 97)

nirvana in Buddhism, a state of perfect peace (p. 138)

 nirvana en el budismo, estado de paz perfecta (pág. 138)

noble a rich and powerful person (p. 91)

 noble persona rica y poderosa (pág. 91)

nonviolence the avoidance of violent actions (p. 135)

 no violencia rechazo de las acciones violentas (pág. 135)

O

oasis a wet, fertile area within a desert (p. 354)

 oasis zona húmeda y fértil en un desierto (pág. 354)

obelisk (AH-buh-lisk) a tall, pointed, four-sided pillar in ancient Egypt (p. 104)

 obelisco pilar alto, de cuatro caras y acabado en punta, propio del antiguo Egipto (pág. 104)

observatories buildings used to study astronomy; Mayan priests watched the stars from these buildings (p. 472)

 observatorios edificios que sirven para estudiar la astronomía; los sacerdotes mayas observaban las estrellas desde estos edificios (pág. 472)

Old Kingdom the period from about 2700 to 2200 BC in Egyptian history that began shortly after Egypt was unified (p. 90)
  Reino Antiguo período de la historia egipcia que abarca aproximadamente del 2700 hasta el 2200 a. C. y comenzó poco después de la unificación de Egipto (pág. 90)

oligarchy (AH-luh-gar-kee) a government in which only a few people have power (p. 237)
  oligarquía gobierno en el que sólo unas pocas personas tienen el poder (pág. 237)

oracle a prediction by a wise person, or a person who makes a prediction (p. 164)
  oráculo predicción de un sabio o de alguien que hace profecías (pág. 164)

oral history a spoken record of past events (p. 396)
  historia oral registro hablado de hechos ocurridos en el pasado (pág. 396)

P

Paleolithic Era (pay-lee-uh-LI-thik) the first part of the Stone Age; when people first used stone tools (p. 31)
  Paleolítico primera parte de la Edad de Piedra; cuando el ser humano usó herramientas de piedra por primera vez (pág. 31)

papyrus (puh-PY-ruhs) a long-lasting, paper-like material made from reeds that the ancient Egyptians used to write on (p. 102)
  papiro material duradero hecho de juncos, similar al papel, que los antiguos egipcios utilizaban para escribir (pág. 102)

Passover a holiday in which Jews remember the Exodus (p. 219)
  Pascua judía festividad en la que los judíos recuerdan el Éxodo (pág. 219)

patricians (puh-TRI-shunz) the nobility in Roman society (p. 299)
  patricios nobles de la sociedad romana (pág. 299)

patron a sponsor (p. 371)
  mecenas patrocinador (pág. 371)

Pax Romana Roman Peace; a period of general peace and prosperity in the Roman Empire that lasted from 27 BC to AD 180 (p. 326)
  Pax Romana Paz Romana; período de paz y prosperidad generales en el Imperio romano que duró del 27 a. C. al 180 d. C. (pág. 326)

peasant a farmer with a small farm (p. 167)
  campesino agricultor dueño de una pequeña granja (pág. 167)

Peloponnesian War a war between Athens and Sparta in the 400s BC (p. 270)
  guerra del Peloponeso guerra entre Atenas y Esparta en el siglo V a. C. (pág. 270)

Period of Disunion the time of disorder following the collapse of the Han Dynasty (p. 410)
  período de desunión la época de desorden que siguió el derrumbe de la dinastía Han (pág. 410)

Persian Wars a series of wars between Persia and Greece in the 400s BC (p. 263)
  guerras persas serie de guerras entre Persia y Grecia en el siglo V a. C. (pág. 263)

phalanx (FAY-langks) a group of Greek warriors who stood close together in a square formation (p. 273)
  falange grupo de guerreros griegos que se mantenían unidos en formación compacta y cuadrada (pág. 273)

pharaoh (FEHR-oh) the title used by the rulers of Egypt (p. 89)
  faraón título usado por los gobernantes de Egipto (pág. 89)

pictograph a picture symbol (p. 66)
  pictograma símbolo ilustrado (pág. 66)

pilgrimage a journey to a sacred place (p. 356)
  peregrinación viaje a un lugar sagrado (pág. 356)

plebeians (pli-BEE-uhnz) the common people of ancient Rome (p. 299)
  plebeyos gente común de la antigua Roma (pág. 299)

polis (PAH-luhs) the Greek word for a city-state (p. 232)
  polis palabra griega para designar una ciudad estado (pág. 232)

polytheism the worship of many gods (p. 62)
  politeísmo culto a varios dioses (pág. 62)

porcelain a thin, beautiful pottery invented in China (p. 417)
  porcelana cerámica bella y delicada creada en China (pág. 417)

prehistory the time before there was writing (p. 28)
  prehistoria período anterior a la existencia de la escritura (pág. 28)

priest a person who performs religious ceremonies (p. 63)
  sacerdote persona que lleva a cabo ceremonias religiosas (pág. 63)

primary source an account of an event by someone who took part in or witnessed the event (p. 10)
  fuente primaria relato de un hecho por parte de alguien que participó o presenció el hecho (pág. 10)

prophet someone who is said to receive messages from God to be taught to others (p. 211)
  profeta alguien del que se cree que recibe mensajes de Dios para transmitírselos a los demás (pág. 211)

proverb a short saying of wisdom or truth (p. 397)
  proverbio refrán breve que expresa sabiduría o una verdad (pág. 397)

Punic Wars a series of wars between Rome and Carthage in the 200s and 100s BC (p. 309)
  guerras púnicas sucesión de guerras entre Roma y Cartago en los siglos III y II a. C. (pág. 309)

pyramid a huge triangular tomb built by the Egyptians and other peoples (p. 94)
  pirámide tumba triangular y gigantesca construida por los egipcios y otros pueblos (pág. 94)

Q

Quechua (KE-chuh-wuh) the language of the Inca (p. 480)
  quechua idioma de los incas (pág. 480)

Qur'an (kuh-RAN) the holy book of Islam (p. 356)
  Corán libro sagrado del Islam (pág. 356)

R

rabbi (RAB-eye) a Jewish religious leader and teacher (p. 216)
  rabino líder y maestro religioso judío (pág. 216)

rain forest a moist, densely wooded area that contains many different plants and animals (p. 382)
  selva tropical zona húmeda y con muchos árboles que contiene muchas variedades de plantas y animales (pág. 382)

reason clear and ordered thinking (p. 281)
  razón pensamiento claro y ordenado (pág. 281)

regent a person who rules a country for someone who is unable to rule alone (p. 444)
  regente persona que gobierna un país en lugar de alguien que no puede hacerlo por su cuenta (pág. 444)

region an area with one or more features that make it different from surrounding areas (p. 15)
  región zona con una o varias características que la diferencian de las zonas que la rodean (pág. 15)

reincarnation a Hindu and Buddhist belief that souls are born and reborn many times, each time into a new body (p. 133)
  reencarnación creencia hindú y budista de que las almas nacen y renacen muchas veces, siempre en un cuerpo nuevo (pág. 133)

republic a political system in which people elect leaders to govern them (p. 298)
  república sistema político en el que el pueblo elige a los líderes que lo gobernarán (pág. 298)

resources the materials found on Earth that people need and value (p. 16)
  recursos materiales de la Tierra que las personas necesitan y valoran (pág. 16)

ENGLISH AND SPANISH GLOSSARY

Resurrection in Christianity, Jesus's rise from the dead (p. 336)

Resurrección en el cristianismo, la vuelta a la vida de Jesús (pág. 336)

rift a long, deep valley formed by the movement of the earth's crust (p. 380)

fisura valle largo y profundo formado por el movimiento de la corteza terrestre (pág. 380)

Roman Senate a council of wealthy and powerful citizens who advised Rome's leaders (p. 303)

Senado romano consejo de ciudadanos ricos y poderosos que aconsejaba a los gobernantes de Roma (pág. 303)

Romance languages languages that developed from Latin, such as Italian, French, Spanish, Portuguese, and Romanian (p. 328)

lenguas romances lenguas que surgieron del latín, como el italiano, el francés, el español, el portugués y el rumano (pág. 328)

Rosetta Stone a huge stone slab inscribed with hieroglyphics, Greek, and a later form of Egyptian that allowed historians to understand Egyptian writing (p. 103)

piedra Roseta gran losa de piedra en la que aparecen inscripciones en jeroglíficos, en griego y en una forma tardía del idioma egipcio que permitió a los historiadores descifrar la escritura egipcia (pág. 103)

rural a countryside area (p. 60)

rural zona del campo (pág. 60)

Sahel (sah-HEL) a semiarid region in Africa just south of the Sahara that separates the desert from wetter areas (p. 382)

Sahel región semiárida de África, situada al sur del Sahara, que separa el desierto de otras zonas más húmedas (pág. 382)

samurai (SA-muh-rye) a trained professional warrior in feudal Japan (p. 454)

samurai guerrero profesional del Japón feudal (pág. 454)

Sanskrit the most important language of ancient India (p. 129)

sánscrito el idioma más importante de la antigua India (pág. 129)

savannah an open grassland with scattered trees (p. 382)

sabana pradera abierta con árboles dispersos (pág. 382)

scholar-official an educated member of the government (p. 422)

funcionario erudito miembro culto del gobierno (pág. 422)

scribe a writer (p. 66)

escriba escritor (pág. 66)

secondary source information gathered by someone who did not take part in or witness an event (p. 10)

fuente secundaria información recopilada por alguien que no participó ni presenció un hecho (pág. 10)

seismograph a device that measures the strength of an earthquake (p. 182)

sismógrafo aparato que mide la fuerza de un terremoto (pág. 182)

Shia (SHEE-ah) a member of the second-largest branch of Islam (p. 365)

shia miembro de la segunda rama más importante del Islam (pág. 365)

Shinto the traditional religion of Japan (p. 442)

sintoísmo religión tradicional de Japón (pág. 442)

shogun a general who ruled Japan in the emperor's name (p. 455)

shogun general que gobernaba Japón en nombre del emperador (pág. 455)

Sikhism a monotheistic religion that developed in India in the 1400s (p. 135)

sijismo una religion monoteísta que se desarrolló en la India en el siglo XV (pág. 135)

silent barter a process in which people exchange goods without contacting each other directly (p. 386)

trueque silencioso proceso mediante el que las personas intercambian bienes sin entrar en contacto directo (pág. 386)

silk a soft, light, and highly valued fabric developed in China (p. 187)

seda tejido suave, ligero y muy apreciado que se originó en China (pág. 187)

Silk Road a network of trade routes that stretched across Asia from China to the Mediterranean Sea (p. 187)

Ruta de la Seda red de rutas comerciales que se extendían a lo largo de Asia desde China hasta el mar Mediterráneo (pág. 187)

silt a mixture of fertile soil and tiny rocks that can make land ideal for farming (p. 55)

cieno mezcla de tierra fértil y piedrecitas que pueden crear un terreno ideal para el cultivo (pág. 55)

social hierarchy the division of society by rank or class (p. 63)

jerarquía social división de la sociedad en clases o niveles (pág. 63)

society a community of people who share a common culture (p. 33)

sociedad comunidad de personas que comparten la misma cultura (pág. 33)

sphinx (sfinks) an imaginary creature with a human head and the body of a lion that was often shown on Egyptian statues (p. 104)

esfinge criatura imaginaria con cabeza humana y cuerpo de león que aparecía re-presentada a menudo en las estatuas egipcias (pág. 104)

subcontinent a large landmass that is smaller than a continent, such as India (p. 124)

subcontinente gran masa de tierra menor que un continente, como la India (pág. 124)

sub-Saharan Africa Africa south of the Sahara (p. 380)

África subsahariana parte de África que queda al sur del Sahara (pág. 380)

Sufism (soo-fi-zuhm) a movement in Islam that taught people they can find God's love by having a personal relationship with God (p. 369)

sufismo movimiento perteneciente al Islam que enseñaba a las personas que pueden hallar el amor de Dios si establecen una relación personal con Él (pág. 369)

sundial a device that uses the position of shadows cast by the sun to tell the time of day (p. 182)

reloj de sol dispositivo que utiliza la posición de las sombras que proyecta el sol para indicar las horas del día (pág. 182)

Sunnah (SOOH-nuh) a collection of writings about the way Muhammad lived that provides a model for Muslims to follow (p. 359)

Sunna conjunto de escritos sobre la vida de Mahoma que proporciona un modelo de comportamiento para los musulmanes (pág. 359)

Sunni a member of the largest branch of Islam (p. 365)

suní miembro de la rama más importante del Islam (pág. 365)

surplus more of something than is needed (p. 56)

excedente cantidad que supera lo que se necesita (pág. 56)

synagogue (SI-nuh-gawg) a Jewish house of worship (p. 210)

sinagoga lugar de culto judío (pág. 210)

T

Talmud (TAHL-moohd) a set of commentaries and lessons for everyday life in Judaism (p. 212)

Talmud Conjunto de comentarios y lecciones para la vida diaria en el judaísmo (pág. 212)

Ten Commandments in the Bible, a code of moral laws given to Moses by God (p. 204)

los Diez Mandamientos en la Biblia, código de leyes morales que Dios le entregó a Moisés (pág. 204)

tolerance acceptance (p. 366)

tolerancia aceptación (pág. 366)

ENGLISH AND SPANISH GLOSSARY

tool an object that has been modified to help a person accomplish a task (p. 30)
herramienta objeto que ha sido modificado para ayudar a una persona a realizar una tarea (pág. 30)

Torah the first five books of the Hebrew Bible and the most sacred text of Judaism (p. 210)
Torá los primeros cinco libros de la biblia hebrea y el texto más sagrado (pág. 210)

trade network a system of people in different lands who trade goods back and forth (p. 111)
red comercial sistema de personas en diferentes lugares que comercian productos entre sí (pág. 111)

trade route a path followed by traders (p. 97)
ruta comercial itinerario seguido por los comerciantes (pág. 97)

tyrant an ancient Greek leader who held power through the use of force (p. 237)
tirano gobernante de la antigua Grecia que mantenía el poder mediante el uso de la fuerza (pág. 237)

urban a city area (p. 60)
urbano zona de ciudad (pág. 60)

veto (VEE-toh) to reject or prohibit actions and laws of other government officials (p. 304)
vetar rechazar o prohibir acciones y leyes de otros funcionarios del gobierno (pág. 304)

woodblock printing a form of printing in which an entire page is carved into a block of wood, covered with ink, and pressed to a piece of paper to create a printed page (p. 418)
xilografía forma de impresión en la que una página completa se talla en una plancha de madera, se cubre de tinta y se presiona sobre un papel para crear la página impresa (pág. 418)

X, Y, Z

Zealots (ZE-luhts) radical Jews who supported rebellion against the Romans (p. 214)
zelotes judíos radicales que apoyaron la rebelión contra los romanos (pág. 214)

Zen a form of Buddhism that emphasizes meditation (p. 452)
zen forma del budismo que se basa en la meditación (pág. 452)

ziggurat a pyramid-shaped temple in Sumer (p. 68)
zigurat templo sumerio en forma de pirámide (pág. 68)

Index

INDEX

Credits and Acknowledgments

HISTORY Unless otherwise indicated below, all video reference screens are © 2010 A&E Television Networks, LLC. All rights reserved.

Grateful acknowledgment is made to the following sources for permission to reproduce copyrighted material:

Cesar E. Chavez Foundation: Quote from "Core Values of Cesar E. Chavez' from *Cesar E. Chavez Foundation* Web site; accessed September 24, 2004, at http://www.cesar-chavezfoundation.org. Copyright © by Cesar E. Chavez Foundation.

Columbia University Press: From *Records of the Grand Historian of China, Vol. II: The Age of Emperor Wu* by Burton Watson. Copyright © 1961 by Columbia University Press. From "Heinrich Von Treitschke" from *Introduction to Contemporary Civilization in the West* by the staff of Columbia College. Copyright © 1946, 1954, 1960 by Columbia University Press.

Doubleday, a division of Random House, Inc., www. randomhouse.com: From "A Personal Account: The Diary of Anne Frank" from *The Diary of a Young Girl: The Definitive Edition* by Anne Frank, edited by Otto H. Frank & Mirjam Pressler, translated by Susan Massotty. Copyright © 1995 by Doubleday, a division of Random House, Inc.

Benedict Fitzgerald for the Estate of Robert Fitzgerald: From *The Iliad* by Homer, translated by Robert Fitzgerald. Copyright © 1974 by Robert Fitzgerald. From *The Odyssey* by Homer, translated by Robert Fitzgerald. Copyright © 1961, 1963, by Robert Fitzgerald; copyright renewed © 1989 by Benedict R. C. Fitzgerald, on behalf of the Fitzgerald Children.

Penelope Fitzgerald for the Estate of Robert Fitzgerald: From *The Aeneid* by Virgil, translated by Robert Fitzgerald. Translation copyright © 1980, 1982, 1983 by Robert Fitzgerald.

Grove Press, Inc.: From "Poetry from the Six Collections" by Ki no Tomonori from *Anthology of Japanese Literature: From the earliest era to the mid-nineteenth century,* compiled and edited by Donald Keene. Copyright © 1955 by Grove Press.

Harcourt Education: From *Things Fall Apart* by Chinua Achebe. Copyright © 1959 by Chinua Achebe.

The Jewish Publication Society: From Exodus 20:2–14, Psalms 23:1–3, Genesis 7:1–12, and Genesis 11:1–9 from *Tanakh: A New Translation of the Holy Scriptures According to the Traditional Hebrew Text.* Copyright © 1985 by The Jewish Publication Society. Reproduced by permission of the copyright holder.

Kendall/Hunt Publishing Company: From *Kings, Saints, and Parliaments: A Sourcebook for Western Civilization, 1050–1700,* edited by Sears McGee, et al. Copyright © 1994 by Kendall/Hunt Publishing Company.

Alfred A. Knopf, a division of Random House, Inc., www. randomhouse.com: From *The Tale of Genji* by Lady Murasaki Shikibu, translated by Edward G. Seidensticker. Copyright © 1976 by Edward G. Seidensticker.

Caroline Miley: From "Proclamation at La Coruña 1808 before the Napoleonic Invasion of Spain," translated by Caroline Miley, from the *Napoleon Series* Web site, accessed February 2, 2005, at http://www.napoleon-series.org/research/miscellaneous/c_lacoruna.html. Originally printed in Spanish on the Spanish language Web site, *The Royal Green Jackets.* Copyright © by Caroline Miley.

Penguin Books Ltd.: "Quiet Night Thoughts" by Li Po from *Li Po and Tu Fu: Poems,* translated by Arthur Cooper. Copyright © 1973 by Arthur Cooper. From *The Epic of Gilgamesh: an English version with an Introduction* by N. K. Sandars. Copyright © 1960, 1964, 1972 by N. K. Sandars.

Plume, a division of Penguin Group (USA) Inc: From *Girl with a Pearl Earring* by Tracy Chevalier. Copyright © 1999 by Tracy Chevalier. Originally published by Dutton.

John Porter: From *Polybius 6.11–18: The Constitution of the Roman Republic,* translated by John Porter. Copyright © 1995 by John Porter, University of Saskatchewan.

Royal Green Jackets: From "Proclamation at La Coruña 1808 before the Napoleonic Invasion of Spain," translated by Caroline Miley. Originally printed in Spanish on the Spanish language Web site, *The Royal Green Jackets.* Copyright © by Royal Green Jackets.

Simon & Schuster Adult Publishing Group: From *Popol Vuh: The Definitive Edition of the Mayan Book of the Dawn of Life and the Glories of Gods and Kings* by Dennis Tedlock. Copyright © 1985, 1996 by Dennis Tedlock.

The University of Chicago Press: From *The Panchatantra,* translated from the Sanskrit by Arthur William Ryder. Copyright 1925 by the University of Chicago Press.

The Arthur Waley Estate: From *The Pillow Book of Sei Shonagon,* translated by Arthur Waley. Copyright 1928, 1929, 1949, 1957 by The Arthur Waley Estate.

Weidenfeld & Nicolson, Ltd.: Excerpt (Retitled "A Knight Speaks") by Rutebeuf from *The Medieval World: Europe 1100–1350* by Friedrich Heer, translated from the German by Janet Sondheimer. Copyright © 1961 by George Weidenfeld and Nicolson Ltd. English translation copyright © 1962 by George Weidenfeld and Nicolson Ltd.

Sources Cited:

From "Richard the Lionheart Massacres the Saracens, 1191" from the *Eyewitness to History* Web site, accessed November 1, 2004, at www.eyewitnesstohistory.com.

From "Saladin and the Third Crusade" from *Arab Historians of the Crusades—Selected and Translated from the Arabic Sources* by Francesco Gabrieli, translated and edited by E. J. Costello. Published by University of California Press, 1969.

Illustrations and Photo Credits

Cover: ©Time Life Pictures/Getty Images

Front Matter: ii (t), Seth Joel/Getty Images/HMH Photo; ii (b), Clay McClachlan/Getty Images/HMH Photo.

Table of Contents: vi, Ronald Sheridan/Ancient Art & Architecture Collection Ltd.; vii, Robert Harding Picture Library; viii, © Christopher Arnesen/Stone/Getty Images; ix, © Peter Guttman/Corbis; x, © Anders Blomqvist/Lonely Planet Images; xi, © Christopher Groenhout/Lonely Planet Images; xii, Richard T. Nowitz/National Geographic Image Collection; xiii, Private Collection/Photo © Heini Schneebeli/The Bridgeman Art Library; xiv, Snark/Art Resource, NY; xv, © Angelo Cavalli/SuperStock.

Chapter 1: 2-3 (t), O. Louis Mazzatenta/National Geographic Image Collection; 6-7, Rohan/Stone/Getty Images; 8 (b), Garry Gay/Alamy Images; 10-11 (t), ©STR/Reuters/Corbis; 11 (tc), Instituto Nacional de Antropología y Historia, Mexico (Detail)/All Rights Reserved, Image Archives, Denver Museum of Nature & Science; 11 (tr), ©Bojan Brecelj/Corbis; 11 (tl), Instituto Nacional de Antropología y Historia, Mexico (Detail)/All Rights Reserved, Image Archives, Denver Museum of Nature & Science; 13 (tl), Anne Rippy/Image Bank/Getty Images; 13 (tr), ©Royalty-Free/CORBIS; 16-17 (t), Gavin Hellier/Robert Harding World Imagery/Getty Images; 19 (tr), ©Kevin Schafer/CORBIS; 23, ©Egyptian National Museum, Cairo, Egypt/ET Archive, London/SuperStock.

Chapter 2: 24-25 (t), ©Pierre Vauthey/Sygma/CORBIS; 24 (b), ©Michael Holford Photographs; 24 (bc), Kenneth Garrett/National Geographic Image Collection; 25 (bl), Pascal Goetgheluck/Photo Researchers, Inc.; 25 (c), Réunion des Musées Nationaux/Art Resource, NY; 25 (br), Photodisc/Getty Images; 29 (b), Robert I.M. Campbell/National Geographic Image Collection; 29 (t), ©Ferorelli 2005; 30 (l), Pascal Goetgheluck/Photo Researchers, Inc.; 30 (tr), Pascal Goetgheluck/Photo Researchers, Inc.; 30 (br), ©Michael Holford Photographs; 31 (tr), Pascal Goetgheluck/Photo Researchers, Inc.; 31 (tl), Pascal Goetgheluck/Photo Researchers, Inc.; 31 (br), Erich Lessing/Art Resource, NY; 31 (bl), John Reader/Photo Researchers, Inc.; 33 (r), Taxi/Getty Images; 33 (l), ©David R. Frazier Photolibrary, Inc./Alamy; 34, Robert Harding Picture Library Ltd/Alamy Images; 35 (tl), South Tyrol Museum of Archaeology, Bolzano, Italy/Wolfgang Neeb/The Bridgeman Art Library; 35 (br), ©Vienna Report Agency/Sygma/Corbis; 38 (r), ©Photo courtesy of Dr. James Dixon/Photograph by Eric Parrish; 38 (l), Sisse Brimberg/National Geographic Image Collection.